Developing and Securing the Cloud

OTHER BOOKS BY BHAVANI THURAISINGHAM
FROM AUERBACH PUBLICATIONS

Building Trustworthy Semantic Webs
ISBN: 978-0-8493-5080-1

Database and Applications Security: Integrating Information Security and Data Management
ISBN: 978-0-8493-2224-2

Data Management Systems: Evolution and Interoperation
ISBN: 978-0-8493-9493-5

Data Mining: Technologies, Techniques, Tools, and Trends
ISBN: 978-0-8493-1815-3

Data Mining Tools for Malware Detection
with Mehedy Masud and Latifur Khan
ISBN: 978-1-4398-5454-9

Design and Implementation of Data Mining Tools
with Lei Wang, Latifur Khan, and M. Awad
ISBN: 978-1-4200-4590-1

Developing and Securing the Cloud
ISBN: 978-1-4398-6291-9

Managing and Mining Multimedia Databases
ISBN: 978-0-8493-0037-0

Secure Semantic Service-Oriented Systems
ISBN: 978-1-4200-7331-7

Web Data Mining and Applications in Business Intelligence and Counter-Terrorism
ISBN: 978-0-8493-1460-5

XML Databases and the Semantic Web
ISBN: 978-1-4200-7331-7

AUERBACH PUBLICATIONS
www.auerbach-publications.com
To Order Call: 1-800-272-7737 • Fax: 1-800-374-3401
E-mail: orders@crcpress.com

Developing and Securing the Cloud

Bhavani Thuraisingham

CRC Press
Taylor & Francis Group
Boca Raton London New York

CRC Press is an imprint of the
Taylor & Francis Group, an **informa** business

AN AUERBACH BOOK

CRC Press
Taylor & Francis Group
6000 Broken Sound Parkway NW, Suite 300
Boca Raton, FL 33487-2742

First issued in paperback 2019

© 2013 by Taylor & Francis Group, LLC
CRC Press is an imprint of Taylor & Francis Group, an Informa business

No claim to original U.S. Government works

ISBN-13: 978-1-4398-6291-9 (hbk)
ISBN-13: 978-1-138-37453-9 (pbk)

Library of Congress Cataloging-in-Publication Data

Thuraisingham, Bhavani M.
   Developing and securing the cloud / Bhavani Thuraisingham.
      pages cm
   Includes bibliographical references and index.
      ISBN 978-1-4398-6291-9 (hbk. : alk. paper) 1. Cloud computing. 2. Cloud computing--Security measures. I. Title.

   QA76.585.T48 2013
   004.67'82--dc23   2013034921

Visit the Taylor & Francis Web site at
http://www.taylorandfrancis.com

and the CRC Press Web site at
http://www.crcpress.com

To My Colleague and Friend
The late Dr. James R. Johnson (aka Dr. Bob)
April 9, 1951–February 15, 2013
Thank you for the fruitful collaboration we have had on
Text Mining, Security Analytics, and Cloud Computing.

Contents

PART IV EXPERIMENTAL CLOUD COMPUTING SYSTEMS

PART IX BUILDING AN INFRASTRUCTURE, AN EDUCATION INITIATIVE, AND A RESEARCH PROGRAM FOR A SECURE CLOUD

Preface

Background

Recent developments in information systems technologies have resulted in computerizing many applications in various business areas. Data have become a critical resource in many organizations, and therefore, efficient access to data, sharing the data, extracting information from the data, and making use of the information have become urgent needs. As a result, there have been many efforts on not only integrating the various data sources scattered across several sites, but extracting information from these databases in the form of patterns and trends has also become important. These data sources may be databases managed by database management systems, or they could be data warehoused in a repository from multiple data sources.

The advent of the World Wide Web (WWW) in the mid-1990s has resulted in even greater demand for managing data, information and knowledge effectively. During this period, the consumer service provider concept has been digitized and enforced via the web. This way, we now have web-supported services where a consumer may request a service via the web site of a service provider and the service provider provides the requested service. This service could be making an airline reservation or purchasing a book from the service provider. Such web-supported services have come to be known as web services. Note that services do not necessarily have to be provided through the web. A consumer could send an email message to the service provider and request the service. Such services are computer-supported services. However, much of the work on computer-supported services has focused on web services.

The services paradigm has evolved into providing computing infrastructures, software, databases, and applications as services. For example, just as we obtain electricity as a service from the power company, we can obtain computing as a service from service providers. Such capabilities have resulted in the notion of cloud computing. As defined by the National Institute of Standards and Technology (http://csrc.nist.gov/publications/nistpubs/800-145/SP800-145.pdf),

> Cloud computing is a model for enabling ubiquitous, convenient, on-demand network access to a shared pool of configurable computing

resources (e.g., networks, servers, storage, applications, and services) that can be rapidly provisioned and released with minimal management effort or service provider interaction.

Over the past five years developments in cloud computing have exploded and we now have several companies providing infrastructure software, applications, and computing platforms as services.

As the demand for data and information management increases, there is also a critical need for maintaining the security of the databases, applications, and information systems. Data and information have to be protected from unauthorized access as well as from malicious corruption. With the advent of the cloud it is even more important to protect the data and information as the cloud is usually managed by third parties. Therefore, we need effective mechanisms to secure the cloud.

This book will review the developments in cloud computing and discuss concepts, issues, and challenges in secure cloud computing. We will also discuss several experimental systems, infrastructures, and education programs that we have developed at the University of Texas at Dallas (UTD) on cloud computing and secure cloud computing.

We have written two series of books for CRC Press on data management/data mining and data security. The first series consists of 10 books. Book #1 (*Data Management Systems Evolution and Interoperation*, 1997) focused on the general aspects of data management and also addressed interoperability and migration. Book #2 (*Data Mining: Technologies, Techniques, Tools and Trends*, 1998) discussed data mining. It essentially elaborated on Chapter 9 of book #1. Book #3 (*Web Data Management and E-Commerce*, 2000) discussed web database technologies and discussed e-commerce as an application area. It essentially elaborated on Chapter 10 of book #1. Book #4 (*Managing and Mining Multimedia Databases*, 2001) addressed both multimedia database management and multimedia data mining. It elaborated on both Chapter 6 of book #1 (for multimedia database management) and Chapter 11 of book #2 (for multimedia data mining). Book #5 (*XML, Databases and the Semantic Web*, 2002) described XML technologies related to data management. It elaborated on Chapter 11 of book #3. Book #6 (*Web Data Mining Technologies and Their Applications in Business Intelligence and Counter-terrorism*, 2003) elaborated on Chapter 9 of book #3.

Book #7 (*Database and Applications Security*, 2005) examines security for technologies discussed in each of our previous books. It focuses on the technological developments in database and applications security. It is essentially the integration of Information Security and Database Technologies. Book #8 (*Building Trustworthy Semantic Webs*, 2008) applies security to semantic web technologies and elaborates on Chapter 25 of book #7. Book #9 (*Secure Semantic Service Oriented Systems*, 2011) is an elaboration of Chapter 16 of book #8. Book #10, our current book (*Developing and Securing the Cloud*) is an elaboration of Chapters 5 and 25 of book #9.

Currently, our second series of books consist of two books. Book #1 is on the *Design and Implementation of Data Mining Tools*, 2009. Book #2 is on the *Design and Implementation of Data Mining Tools for Malware Detection*, 2011. For this series, we are converting some of the practical aspects of our work with students into books. The relationships between our texts will be illustrated in Appendix A.

Organization of This Book

This book is divided into nine parts, each describing some aspect of technology that is relevant to building and securing the cloud. A major focus of this book will be on cloud query processing and the surrounding security issues. Security applications that utilize cloud computing such as malware detection, assured information sharing, and insider threat detection will also be discussed.

Part I consisting of three chapters describes supporting technologies for the cloud. These include the evolution of computing systems discussed in Chapter 2, security technologies discussed in Chapter 3, and data, information and knowledge management technologies discussed in Chapter 4. Part II consisting of three chapters discusses concepts in services and secure services technologies. Chapter 5 discusses SOA and web services, service-oriented analysis and design as well as secure services. Semantic web services and related security issues will be discussed in Chapter 6. Specialized web services such as services for information and knowledge management will be discussed in Chapter 7.

Part III consisting of five chapters will discuss the core topics in cloud computing. In Chapter 8, we will discuss the basic cloud computing concepts and our implementation of a cloud computing framework. Cloud computing functions including virtualization, storage management, and data management will be discussed in Chapter 9. We will devote the entire Chapter 10 to cloud data management as many of the prototypes we have developed focus on cloud data management. Applications are discussed in Chapter 11. Chapter 12 discusses the various cloud products and secure providers.

Part IV consists of three chapters and discusses the prototypes we have developed on experimental cloud computing systems. The first is a cloud query processing system prototype and will be discussed in Chapter 13. Chapter 14 discusses social networking in the cloud. Chapter 15 discusses ontology management in the cloud.

Part V consists of six chapters and discusses secure cloud computing. Chapter 16 discusses security for cloud computing. Secure cloud computing functions such as secure virtualization, storage, and data management as well as cloud forensics will be discussed in Chapter 17. Since much of our work is focused on secure cloud data management, we devote the entire Chapter 18 to this topic. Secure cloud computing guidelines will be discussed in Chapter 19. Various standards and products for secure cloud computing will be discussed in Chapter 20. Finally, the notion of security as a service will be discussed in Chapter 21.

Part VI consists of three chapters and discusses the systems we have developed for secure cloud computing. Secure cloud query processing system with relational data is the subject of Chapter 22. Secure query processing with semantic web data will be discussed in Chapter 23. Security for Amazon web services and information integration will be discussed in Chapter 24.

Part VII consists of four chapters that describe the use of cloud computing for security applications. Chapter 25 describes the use of cloud for malware detection. Cloud-based insider threat detection will be discussed in Chapter 26. Chapter 27 discusses assured cloud-based information sharing. Chapter 28 discusses assured semantic cloud-based information sharing. We have defined a semantic cloud to be a cloud that utilizes semantic web technologies.

Part VIII consists of three chapters and describes our ideas on developing trustworthy clouds. In Chapter 29, we discuss trust management for cloud services. In Chapter 30, we discuss privacy issues for cloud services. In Chapter 31, we discuss integrity and data quality for cloud services.

Part IX consists of three chapters and discusses the infrastructure, education initiative, and research program we are developing for a secure cloud. Our secure cloud computing infrastructure is discussed in Chapter 32. Our education initiative on this topic is discussed in Chapter 33. Finally our collaborative research program that has influenced much of the discussion in this book is discussed in Chapter 34.

Each part begins with an introduction and ends with a conclusion. Furthermore, each of Chapters 2 through 34 starts with an introduction and ends with a summary and directions for further work. In addition, references are also provided at the end of each chapter. Chapter 35 summarizes the book and discusses future directions for secure cloud computing. We have included four appendices for background information. Appendix A provides an overview of data management and discusses the relationship between the texts we have written. This has been the standard practice with all of our books. In Appendix B, we discuss data mining techniques as we have used such techniques for cloud data management and for cloud-based malware detection. Appendix C discusses secure data management that has influenced our work on secure cloud data management. Finally, Appendix D discusses our work on assured information sharing that has influenced our work on cloud-based assured information sharing. This book ends with an index.

I have tried my best to obtain references from books, journals, magazines, and conference and workshop proceedings. Although I tried not to give uniform resources locators (URLs) as references, I found that it was almost impossible to write a text today, especially about the cloud and the web without giving some URLs as references. Many URLs contain excellent reference material, but some of them may not be available by the time the book is published. Therefore, I urge the reader to check the web from time to time for the most up-to-date information about the cloud and secure cloud.

Data, Information and Knowledge

In general, data management includes managing the databases, interoperability, migration, warehousing, and mining. For example, the data on the web has to be managed and mined to extract information and patterns and trends. Data could be in files, relational databases, or other types of databases such as multimedia databases. Data may be structured or unstructured. We repeatedly use the terms data, data management, database systems, and database management systems in this book. We elaborate on these terms in the appendix. We define data management systems to be systems that manage the data, extract meaningful information from the data, and make use of the information extracted. Therefore, data management systems include database systems, data warehouses, and data mining systems. Data could be structured data such as those found in relational databases, or it could be unstructured such as text, voice, imagery, and video.

There have been numerous discussions in the past to distinguish between data, information and knowledge. In some of our previous books on data management and mining, we did not attempt to clarify these terms. We simply stated that, data could be just bits and bytes or it could convey some meaningful information to the user. However, with the web and also with increasing interest in data, information and knowledge management as separate areas, in this book we take a different approach to data, information and knowledge by differentiating between these terms as much as possible. For us data are usually some value like numbers, integers, and strings. Information is obtained when some meaning or semantics is associated with the data, such as, John's salary is $20 K. Knowledge is something that you acquire through reading and learning, and as a result understand the data and information and take actions. That is, data and information can be transferred into knowledge when uncertainty about the data and information is removed from someone's mind. It should be noted that it is rather difficult to give strict definitions of data, information and knowledge. Sometimes we will use these terms interchangeably also. Our framework for data management discussed in the appendix helps clarify some of the differences. To be consistent with the terminology in our previous books, we will also distinguish between database systems and database management systems. A database management system is that component which manages the database containing persistent data. A database system consists of both the database and the database management system.

Final Thoughts

The goal of this book is to explore security issues for cloud computing and discuss their applications. We also discuss concepts in cloud computing. We discuss secure web services as they are at the center of cloud computing. In addition to concepts and technologies we also present several of the experimental systems in cloud computing and secure cloud computing that we have designed and developed at the UTD. We have used the material in this book together with the numerous references listed in each chapter for a graduate level course at the UTD on secure web services and cloud computing. We have also provided several experimental systems developed by our graduate students.

It should be noted that the field is expanding very rapidly with the emerging standards. Therefore, it is important for the reader to keep up with the developments of the prototypes, products, tools, and standards for cloud computing and secure cloud computing. Security cannot be an afterthought. Therefore, while the technologies for cloud computing are being developed, it is important to include security at the onset.

Acknowledgments

I would like to thank the administration at the Erik Jonsson School of Engineering and Computer Science at the UTD for giving me the opportunity to direct the Cyber Security Research and Education Center. I thank my colleagues and students for giving me many insights. I would especially like to thank my colleagues Dr. Latifur Khan and Dr. Murat Kantarcioglu and my PhD student Vaibhav Khadilkar at the UTD for their research on secure cloud and for our discussions which gave me many insights to write this book. I thank Ms. Rhonda Walls, our project coordinator, for proofreading and editing the chapters.

I would also like to thank many people who have supported me in secure cloud computing.

- Dr. Robert Herklotz from the Air Force Office of Scientific Research for funding our research on secure cloud computing. Without this support I would never have been able to gain the knowledge to write this book.
- Dr. Victor Piotrowski from the National Science Foundation for funding our capacity building work on assured cloud computing.
- My colleagues Dr. Kevin Hamlen, Dr. Zhiqiang Lin, Dr. Kamil Sarac, and Dr. I-Ling Yen at the UTD for discussions on secure cloud computing.
- Our collaborators at King's College, University of London and the University of Insubria, Italy for our work on cloud-based assured information sharing. In particular, I would like to thank the late Dr. Steve Barker of King's College and Dr. Elena Ferrari and Dr. Barbara Carminati of the University of Insubria, Italy.
- Our collaborators on secure cloud computing, especially the late Dr. James R. Johnson (Dr. Bob) and Ms. Anita Miller at ADB Consulting and Dr. Elisa Bertino at Purdue University.
- Professor C. V. Ramamoorthy at the University of California Berkeley for his encouragement.
- My former student, Dr. Tyrone Cadenhead, for his comments.
- My students for their technical contributions to the book: Mr. Vaibhav Khadilkar (Chapters 14, 15, 22, 24, 27, 28, 32), Mr. Satyen Abrol (Chapter 14),

Ms. Jyothsna Rachapalli (Chapter 29), Mr. Pranav Parikh (Chapter 24), Mr. Arindam Khaled (Chapter 23), Mr. Anduleep Ifthekar (Chapter 33), Dr. Tyrone Cadenhead (Chapters 27, 28), Dr. Mehedy Masud (Chapter 25), Dr. Farhan Husain (Chapters 13, 23, 26), and Dr. Neda Alipanah (Chapter 15).
■ My husband Thevendra for his continued support for my work and my son Breman for being such a wonderful person and for motivating me.

Author

Dr. Bhavani Thuraisingham is the Louis A. Beecherl, Jr. Distinguished Professor in the Erik Jonsson School of Engineering and Computer Science at the University of Texas at Dallas (UTD) and the executive director of UTD's Cyber Security Research and Education Institute. Her current research is on integrating cyber security, cloud computing, and big data analytics. Prior to joining UTD in October 2004, she worked at the MITRE Corporation for 16 years, which included a three-year stint as a program director at the National Science Foundation (NSF). At MITRE, she led team efforts on developing secure data management systems and data mining tools. She initiated the Data and Applications Security program at NSF and was part of the Cyber Trust theme. Prior to MITRE, she worked for the commercial industry for six years, conducting research in data security, data management, and distributed systems.

Dr. Thuraisingham is the recipient of numerous awards, including the IEEE Computer Society's 1997 Technical Achievement Award, the ACM SIGSAC 2010 Outstanding Contributions Award, the IEEE SMC and Transportation Systems Societies' 2010 joint award on Research Leadership in Intelligence and Security Informatics, the Society for Design and Process Science (SDPS) 2012 Transformative Achievement Gold Medal for interdisciplinary research on integrating computer sciences, with social sciences, and a 2013 IBM Faculty Award. She is a fellow of IEEE, AAAS and the British Computer Society. She has published over 100 journal articles, over 200 conference papers, and 12 books, and has delivered over 100 keynote and invited addresses. She has five patents (two pending) and is the founder of Knowledge and Security Analytics, LLC. Dr. Thuraisingham received her PhD from the University of Wales, Swansea in theory of computation and her earned higher doctorate (Doctor of Engineering) from the University of Bristol, England for her published work in data security.

Copyright Permissions

Chapter 13: Experimental Cloud Query Processing System
Heuristics-Based Query Processing for Large RDF Graphs Using Cloud Computin, Reprinted, with permission, from IEEE Transactions on Knowledge and Data Engineering, Volume 23, Number 9, p. 1312-1327 (2011) (co-authors: Mohammad Farhan Husain, James P. McGlothlin, Mohammad M. Masud, Latifur R. Khan. © 2011 IEEE.

Chapter 14: Social Networking on the Cloud
Design and implementation of SNODSOC: Novel class detection for social network analysis, Reprinted, with permission, from the Proceedings of the 2012 International Conference on Intelligence and Security Informatics, p. 215 -220, 2012 (co-authors: Satyen Abrol, Latifur Khan, Vaibhav Khadilkar, Tyrone Cadenhead. © 2012 IEEE.

Chapter 15: Experimental Semantic Web-based Cloud Computing Systems
StormRider: harnessing "storm" for social networks, Reprinted with permission of the authors from the Proceedings of World Wide Web 2012 (Companion Volume), p. 543–544, 2012 (co-authors: Vaibhav Khadilkar, Murat Kantarcioglu).

Jena-HBase: A Distributed, Scalable and Efficient RDF Triple Store, Reprinted with permission of the authors from the Proceedings of the International Semantic Web Conference (Posters & Demos) 2012 (co-authors: Vaibhav Khadilkar, Murat Kantarcioglu).

Ontology-Driven Query Expansion Using Map/Reduce Framework to Facilitate Federated Queries, Reprinted with permission from the authors from the Proceedings of the International Conference on Web Services, p. 712–713, 2011 (co-authors: Neda Alipanah, Pallabi Parveen, Latifur Khan) © 2011, IEEE.

Chapter 22: Secure Cloud Query Processing with Relational Data
Secure data storage and retrieval in the cloud, This paper appears in the Proceedings of CollaborateCom 2010, pg. 1 –8, 2010 (co-authors: Vaibhav Khadilkar, Anuj Gupta, Murat Kantarcioglu, Latifur Khan).

Chaper 23: Secure Cloud Query Processing with Semantic Web Data
A Token-Based Access Control Systemfor RDF Data in the Clouds, Reprinted, with permission, from the Proceedings of the 2010 IEEE Second International Conference on Cloud Computing Technology and Science (CloudCom), p. 104–111, 2010 (co-authors: Arindam Khaled, Mohammad Farhan Husain, Latifur Khan, Kevin W. Hamlen) © 2010 IEEE.

Chapter 24: Secure Cloud-based Information Integration
Secure information integration with a semantic web-based framework, Reprinted, with permission, from the Proceedings of the IEEE 13th International Conference on Information Reuse & Integration, (IRI 2012), p. 649–663, 2012 (co-authors: Pranav Parikh, Murat Kantarcioglu, Vaibhav Khadilkar, Latifur Khan) © 2012 IEEE.

Chapter 25: Cloud-Based Malware Detection for Evolving Data Streams
Cloud-based malware detection for evolving data streams, Reprinted by permission. "Cloud-based Malware Detection for Evolving Data Streams", ACM Transactions on Management Information Systems, Volume 2, Number 3, Article No. 16. http://doi.acm.org/lO.1145/2019618.2019622 (co-authors: Mohammad M. Masud, Tahseen AI-Khateeb, Kevin W. Hamlen, Jing Gao, Latifur Khan, Jiawei Han) © 2011 ACM, Inc.

Chapter 27 Cloud Centric Assured Information Sharing
Cloud-Centric Assured Information Sharing, Reprinted with kind permission of Springer Science+Business Media from Lecture Notes in Computer Science 7299, 2012, p. 1–26 (Proceedings of Intelligence and Security Informatics-Pacific Asia Workshop, PAISI 2012, Kuala Lumpur, Malaysia, May 29, 2012) (co-authors: Vaibhav Khadilkar, Jyothsna Rachapalli, Tyrone Cadenhead, Murat Kantarcioglu, Kevin W. Hamlen, Latifur Khan, Mohammad Farhan Husain) ISBN 978-3-642-30427-9. © Springer.

Chapter 28 Design and Implementation of a Semantic Cloud-based Assured Information Sharing System
Design and Implementation of a Cloud-Based Assured Information Sharing System, Reprinted with kind permission of Springer+Business Media from Lecture Notes in Computer Science 7531,2012, p. 36–50 (Proceedings of Computer Network Security - 6th International Conference on Mathematical Methods, Models and Architectures for Computer Network Security, MMM-ACNS 2012, St. Petersburg, Russia, October 17-19,2012) (co-authors: Tyrone Cadenhead, Murat Kantarcioglu, Vaibhav Khadilkar). © Springer

Chapter 32: An Infrastructure for a Secure Cloud
Security Issues for Cloud Computing, This paper appears in the International Journal of Information Security and Privacy (Volume 4, Number 2, 2010, p. 36-48) edited by Hamid Namati, (co-authors: Kevin W. Hamlen, Murat Kantarcioglu, Latifur Khan) © 2010, IGI Global, www.igi-global.com. Posted by permission of the publisher.

Appendix D: Assured Information Sharing Life Cycle
This paper appeared in the IEEE International Conference on Intelligence and Security Informatics 2009, p. 307–309, 2009 (co-authors: T. Finin, A, Joshi, H. Kargupta, Y. Yesha, J. Sachs, E. Bertino, L. Ninghui, C. Clifton, G. Spafford, M. Kantarcioglu, A. Bensoussan, N. Berg, L. Khan, J. Han, Z. Cheng Xiang, R. Sandhu, X. Shouhuai, J. Massaro, L. Adamic) © 2009 IEEE.

Chapter 1

Introduction

1.1 About This Book

In the nineteenth century, we had the mechanical computing machines invented by Charles Babbage. Then, in the 1930s, Turing proved that the famous halting problem was unsolvable and subsequently, the von Neumann machine was developed in the 1940s that has resulted in the modern electronic computing machines. This was followed by the mainframes of the 1950s and 1960s, minicomputers of the 1970s, personal computers of the 1980s, mobile/wireless computing of the 1990s, and cloud computing of the 2000s. At the same time, computing paradigms have also evolved from single processor to multiprocessors to distributed and parallel processing. Now, we also have multicore architectures with multiple processors on a single chip.

During the past 10 years, with the advent of the World Wide Web (WWW), the consumer service provider concept has been digitized and enforced via the web. This way, we now have web-supported services where a consumer may request a service via the website of a service provider and the service provider provides the requested service. This service could be making an airline reservation or purchasing a book from the service provider. Such web-supported services have come to be known as web services. An information system that supports service implementation is a service-oriented information system. An architecture that provides support for the implementation of services has come to be known as a service-oriented architecture (SOA).

With the integration of cloud computing and service-oriented computing, the services are now provided through a cloud. These services are not only domain services such as booking travel or hotel, but they also include carrying out the entire computations via the cloud and providing them as services to the customers.

So what then is a cloud? As defined by the National Institute of Standards and Technology,

> Cloud computing is a model for enabling ubiquitous, convenient, on-demand network access to a shared pool of configurable computing resources (e.g., networks, servers, storage, applications, and services) that can be rapidly provisioned and released with minimal management effort or service provider interaction. [NIST]

This chapter details the organization of this book. The organization of this chapter is as follows. Supporting technologies for building and securing the cloud will be discussed in Section 1.2. Secure services technologies, which are at the heart of secure cloud computing, will be discussed in Section 1.3. The concepts in cloud computing will be discussed in Section 1.4. The experimental cloud systems that we have developed will be discussed in Section 1.5. Secure cloud technologies will be discussed in Section 1.6. Experimental secure cloud systems that we have developed will be discussed in Section 1.7. Experimental systems that use the cloud for security applications will be discussed in Section 1.8. Some of the directions toward building a trustworthy cloud that incorporate confidentiality, trust, privacy, and integrity will be discussed in Section 1.9. Finally, our efforts on building a secure cloud infrastructure, an education program, as well as our collaborative activities on the secure cloud are discussed in Section 1.10. The organization of this book will be given in Section 1.11. We conclude this chapter with useful resources in Section 1.12. It should be noted that the contents of Sections 1.2 through 1.10 will be elaborated in Parts I through IX of this book. Figure 1.1 illustrates the contents covered in this chapter.

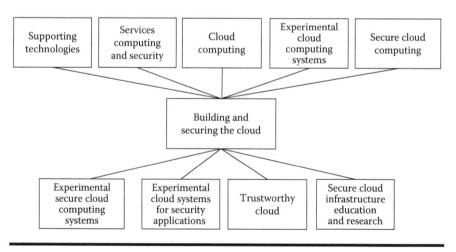

Figure 1.1   Building and securing the cloud.

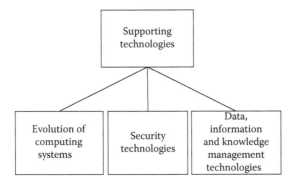

Figure 1.2 Supporting technologies.

1.2 Supporting Technologies

We will discuss three sets of supporting technologies for the cloud. First, we will discuss the evolution of computing systems. Then, we will discuss security technologies. Finally, we will discuss the data, information and knowledge management technologies. More details of the supporting technologies will be discussed in Part II of this book. Figure 1.2 illustrates the supporting technologies.

1.2.1 From Mainframe to the Cloud

As stated in Section 1.1, computing systems have evolved over the past 70 years. The unsolvability results of the 1930s and the von Neumann machines of the 1940s paved the way for modern computers. We saw the rapid development of the mainframes in the 1950s and 1960s, minicomputers of the 1970s, and the personal computers of the 1980s. Networking also developed in the 1970s and 1980s resulting in distributed systems.

The next wave in computing began in the 1990s with the advent of the WWW. This resulted in the semantic web and service-computing technologies. Then the 2000s saw the emergence of social computing, mobile computing, and cloud computing. We expect these three computing technologies to be integrated in the future with the capability to process massive amounts of data, known as "big data." That is, the future of computing will be to process massive amounts of data rapidly and to provide the useful nuggets to the user through his/her phone. The chapters in this book will focus on some of the developments in data management, information management, and social networking offered as services through the cloud. More details on the evolution of computing will be given in Chapter 2.

1.2.2 Security Technologies

Secure cloud computing systems essentially integrate cloud computing technologies with security technologies. Security technologies will be lumped into trustworthy information systems. These systems consist of many aspects, including trustworthy systems, secure data and information systems, and the aspect of confidentiality, privacy, and trust management that will be addressed throughout this book.

Trustworthy systems are systems that are secure and dependable. By dependable systems, we mean systems that have high integrity, are fault-tolerant, and meet real-time constraints. Trustworthy systems may include data management systems, information management systems, and secure networks. For a system to be trustworthy, it must be secure, fault-tolerant, meet timing deadlines, and manage high-quality data. However, integrating these features into a system means that the system has to meet conflicting requirements. For example, if the system makes all the access control checks, then it may miss some of its deadlines. The challenge in designing trustworthy systems is to design systems that are flexible. For example, in some situations, it may be important to meet all the timing constraints whereas in some other situations, it may be critical to satisfy all the security constraints.

Trustworthy systems have sometimes been referred to as dependable systems, whereas in some other cases, dependability is considered to be a part of trustworthiness. For example, in some papers, dependability mainly includes fault-tolerant systems and when one integrates fault-tolerance with security, then one gets trustworthy systems. Regardless of what the definitions are, for systems to be deployed in operational environments, especially for command and control and other critical applications, we need end-to-end dependability as well as security. For some applications, not only do we need security and confidentiality, we also need to ensure that the privacy of the individuals is maintained. Therefore, privacy is also another feature of trustworthiness.

For a system to be dependable/trustworthy, we need end-to-end dependability/trustworthiness. Note that the components that comprise a system include the network, operating systems, middleware and infrastructure, data manager, and applications. We need all the components to be dependable/trustworthy. However, more recently, the goal of secure systems is to build trustworthy systems from untrustworthy components. It is assumed that the components may come from multiple vendors and even from multiple countries and therefore, it is not feasible to trust all the components. Therefore, the challenge is to develop trustworthy systems from untrustworthy components and ensure the execution of the mission.

Security technologies for secure services include services for secure data, information and knowledge management. Secure data and information systems include secure database systems such as secure relational database systems and secure information systems such as secure multimedia information systems and digital libraries.

Underlying the focus of trustworthy information systems is the notion of confidentiality, privacy, and trust. Confidentiality is about websites or servers releasing only the data to authorized individuals. Privacy is about an individual determining what information should be released about him/her. Trust is about how much value one can place on the various individuals (e.g., parties, organizations) and the information they produce. We will discuss security technologies in Chapter 3.

1.2.3 Data, Information, and Knowledge Management

Since cloud data management is the major emphasis in this book, due to our expertise in this field, we consider data, information, and knowledge management to be a key supporting technology for the cloud. It should be noted that several computing technologies, including operating systems, networking, and middleware are also supporting technologies. Describing every cloud component in detail is beyond the scope of this book.

The data management technologies we will focus on in this book include query processing, transaction management, storage management, as well as information management technologies such as data mining and semantic web. In addition, we will focus on hosting applications such as social networking in the cloud. Knowledge management is also a technology that can be provided through the cloud. We will discuss the various aspects of data, information, and knowledge management in Chapter 4.

1.3 Secure Services Technologies

Services are at the heart of cloud computing. This is because clouds provide a collection of services (including the platform as a service, software as a service, data as a service, and infrastructure as a service) to their clients. Therefore, we will devote Part II to services and secure services technologies. The various types of services we will discuss are illustrated in Figure 1.3.

1.3.1 Secure Services Technologies

The basic service technologies consist of multiple thrusts including service-oriented concepts, SOA and web services, semantic web services, and service-oriented analysis and design (SOAD). Service-oriented computing has evolved from object-oriented computing. In object-oriented computing, the world is viewed as a collection of objects and these objects communicate with each other through messages.

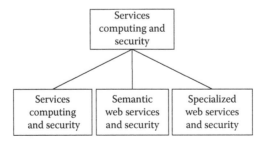

Figure 1.3   Types of services.

Similarly, in service-oriented computing, the world is viewed as a collection of services. Therefore, services could communicate with each other through messages as well as communicate with the consumers through messages. While there are numerous object-oriented programming (OOP) languages that have been developed, including Smalltalk, Java, and C++, there is no computing language for service-oriented computing. However, one can implement services through packages and objects.

SOA is the architecture that is the foundation of service-oriented computing. This architecture specifies the services and the communication between the services. Web services are services that are involved via the web. Currently, web services are the most popular representation of service-oriented computing although it should be noted that web services are only a subset of service-oriented computing.

SOAD follows the OOAD (object-oriented analysis and design) paradigm. Note that OOAD such as UML (unified modeling language) has evolved over several years of research and experimentation. The idea here is to develop a methodology to model applications, data, and activities surrounding the notion of objects. Similarly, in SOAD, the idea is to model, analyze, and reason about the services and the interactions between the services. Often, OOAD has been taught as a prerequisite for SOA. While OOAD is essential for OOP, we need SOAD for SOAP (simple object access protocol). In Part II of this book, we will elaborate on all the basic services.

For many applications, the services provided by cloud computing has to be secure. That is, not only should the data be securely stored and managed, but the processing also has to be secure. Therefore, secure web services are essential for secure cloud computing. Now, SOA-based web services consist of three concepts: the consumer, the service provider, and the directory. The directory is called UDDI (universal description, discovery, and integration). The service provider will publish its services on the UDDI. The consumer will query the UDDI for the services. The UDDI will give the consumer the address of the service provider. The consumer then invokes the service. Communication is carried out through SOAP (used to be called the synchronized object access protocol) messaging that is based on XML (eXtensible markup language). From a security point of view, we need to incorporate security into this communication. Web services 1.0 provides support for secure services. More recently with Web Services 2.0, there are more advanced concepts for SOA.

Before we design secure applications based on services, we need to apply the SOAD methodology. However, SOAD as it has been defined is not adequate for secure applications. In this book, we will discuss our work on extending SOAD for secure applications. We will base this on the work we carried out in the 1990s on extending object-modeling technologies for secure applications.

Various standards have been developed for services and secure services mainly based on web services. For example, the World Wide Web consortium (W3C) has developed standards for XML and XML security that are an essential part of the web services framework. In addition, standards such as WSDL (web services description language) have been developed for specifying the services and SOAP for message communication. XML security standards include XML encryption and XML key management for confidentiality and integrity.

More advanced standards for specifying security policies include those proposed by OASIS (formerly known as the Organization for the Advancement of Structured Information Standards) as well as the W3C. For example, SAML (security assertions markup language) specifies a language for security assertions. XACML (eXtensible access control markup language) specifies a language for policy specification. In addition, there are standards for federated identity management such as the consortium work of Liberty Alliance and standards for advanced web services security including WS and WS* security. Some of our research on secure web services includes models for delegation.

1.3.2 Secure Semantic Services

Semantic services are services that integrate services technologies with semantic web technologies. Semantic web was invented by Tim Berners Lee to support the idea of machine-understandable web pages. Today, the semantic web is viewed as a very large linked graph with semantics associated with nodes and links. The semantic web is a collection of technologies including XML and the resource description framework (RDF). Web services that utilize these semantic web technologies are semantic web services.

Secure semantic information systems essentially integrate semantic web, services, and security technologies. Semantic web technologies provide machine-understandable web services. Web services that utilize semantic web technologies can handle semantic heterogeneity and other interoperability problems. Secure web services need to utilize secure semantic web technologies. That is the XML and RDF documents that are utilized by web services have to be secure documents. Some of the key aspects of secure semantic web services include the relationship between XML security and web services, RDF security and web services, secure ontologies and web services, and finally secure rules and web services. We define a cloud that utilizes semantic services to be a semantic cloud. Many of our experimental systems utilize semantic clouds.

1.3.3 Specialized Secure Services

Specialized web services include services for secure data, information, knowledge and activity management, as well as domain web services. Data management services include those for secure transactions, secure storage, and secure query processing. Complex data management services include secure multimedia and geospatial web services. Information management services include secure information retrieval and secure information visualization. Knowledge management services include secure intellectual property management. Activity management services include secure e-business and assured information sharing (AIS).

We will elaborate on some of the points. Knowledge management is about reusing the knowledge and expertise of an organization to improve profits and other benefits. In Parts I and II, we will examine in more detail security issues for data, information, and knowledge management and then discuss how semantic web technologies may be applied for managing data, information, and knowledge. The interoperability of heterogeneous data sources is the key for many applications. The challenge is how do the different secure systems interoperate with each other? How do you integrate the heterogeneous security policies? E-business (also referred to as e-commerce) is about organizations conducting transactions on the web. Various models, architectures, and technologies are being developed for e-business. Since we are dealing with critical data such as funds and accounts, carrying out e-business, confidentiality, and privacy of information are crucial. We also have to ensure that the data are not maliciously corrupted. AIS is about organizations sharing information but at the same time enforcing policies and procedures so that the data are integrated and mined to extract nuggets and at the same time to maintain security. For all the above applications, web services play a major role.

Web services are being deployed for many applications, including medical, financial, command and control, and telecommunications. They are also applied to many other technologies such as e-business, knowledge management, and AIS. Other emerging web services include web services for grids (more recently corporations such as Oracle are developing grid-based web services). Furthermore, Amazon web services are also based on the grid paradigm.

Other types of web services include data as a service and software as a service. For example, data centers manage data for customers. Customers can invoke such data services through web services. Customers can also invoke various software (such as compilers and operating systems) as web services. In Parts III and V, we will discuss the use of web services and secure web services for cloud data, information, knowledge, and activity management.

1.4 Cloud Computing Concepts

Cloud computing is an emerging paradigm in the information technology and data-processing communities. Enterprises utilize cloud computing services to outsource data maintenance, which can result in significant financial benefits. Businesses store and access data at remote locations in the "cloud." The emerging cloud computing model attempts to address the growth of web-connected devices and handle massive amounts of data. Google has now introduced the MapReduce framework for processing large amounts of data on commodity hardware. Apache's Hadoop distributed file system (HDFS) is emerging as a superior

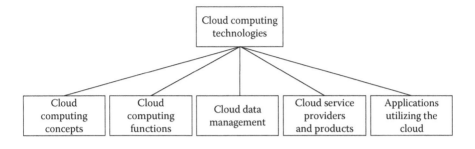

Figure 1.4   Cloud computing concepts.

software component for cloud computing combined with integrated parts such as MapReduce.

The need to augment human reasoning, interpreting, and decision-making abilities has resulted in the emergence of the semantic web, which is an initiative that attempts to transform the web from its current, merely human-readable form, to a machine-processable form. This in turn has resulted in numerous social-networking sites with massive amounts of data to be shared and managed. Therefore, we need technologies that can scale to handle a large number of sites and process massive amounts of data.

Cloud computing technologies will be discussed in Part III of this book. The topics to be discussed include (i) cloud computing functions such as virtualization and storage management, (ii) cloud, data management functions such as cloud query processing and transaction management, (iii) cloud computing applications, and (iv) cloud computing products and tools. Our framework for cloud computing will also be discussed. Figure 1.4 illustrates the cloud computing technologies.

Note that the cloud essentially offers a collection of services to its customers. These include infrastructure services, platform services and application services, as well as data, information knowledge, and activity management services. Clouds could also offer semantic services. We call such clouds semantic clouds.

1.5 Experimental Cloud Computing Systems

As the popularity of cloud computing grows, service providers face ever-increasing challenges. They have to maintain large quantities of heterogeneous data while providing efficient information retrieval. Thus, a key emphasis for cloud computing solutions is scalability and query efficiency. Therefore, we have designed and developed various experimental cloud query processing systems. These include query processing with semantic web data as well as with relational data in the cloud. We have also hosted applications such as ontology management and social networking in the cloud.

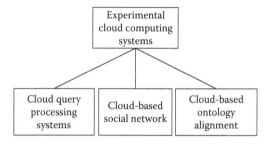

Figure 1.5   Experimental cloud computing systems.

Part IV will discuss the experimental systems that we have developed based on cloud computing technologies. We will discuss the cloud query processing system that we have developed utilizing the Hadoop/MapReduce framework. Our system processes massive amounts of semantic web data. In particular, we have designed and developed a query optimizer for the SPARQL protocol and RDF query language (SPARQL) query processor that functions in the cloud. We have developed cloud systems that host social networking and ontology management applications. Figure 1.5 illustrates some of the experimental cloud systems that we have developed.

1.6 Secure Cloud Computing

The current cloud computing technologies such as those utilizing HDFS and MapReduce are not sufficient due to the fact that they do not provide adequate security mechanisms to protect sensitive data. Therefore, with funding from the Air Force Office of Scientific Research (AFOSR), we have utilized state-of-the-art hardware, software, and data components and are developing a secure cloud computing platform that will handle the inadequacies of the current cloud computing systems. In particular, our goal is to (i) use modern hardware parts (e.g., secure coprocessors) to improve the performance due to incorporating additional security functionalities, (ii) integrate open-source software parts as well as custom-developed software parts to support query operations on complex data, (iii) support fine-grained access control and reference monitor support to provide security for complex data, and (iv) provide strong authentication mechanisms for cloud computing.

We will describe security for cloud computing systems in Part V. In particular, we will discuss (i) our framework for secure cloud computing, (ii) secure cloud computing functions such as secure virtualization, (iii) secure cloud query processing, and (iv) secure cloud computing products. Secure cloud computing technologies are illustrated in Figure 1.6.

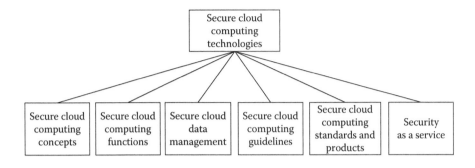

Figure 1.6 Secure cloud computing technologies.

1.7 Experimental Secure Cloud Computing Systems

With funding from the AFOSR to explore security for cloud computing as well as from the National Science Foundation to build infrastructure as well as an education program in assured cloud computing, we have developed a number of secure cloud computing experimental systems both for research and education purposes. We discuss some of our systems in detail in Part VI. In this section, we will list these systems.

The first system carried out cloud-based secure query processing system for relational data. The second system carried out cloud-based secure query processing for semantic web data. We have essentially utilized the system that we discuss in Part IV and incorporated security for this system. This will be followed by a secure cloud computing system that we have developed utilizing Amazon secure cloud services. Figure 1.7 illustrates the experimental systems.

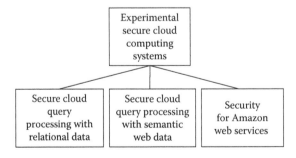

Figure 1.7 Experimental secure cloud computing systems.

1.8 Experimental Cloud Computing for Security Applications

While the previous sections discussed cloud technologies, secure cloud technologies as well as some of the experimental systems that we have developed, in this section, we will discuss how various security applications can benefit from using the cloud. Some of these applications will be elaborated in Part VII of this book.

Our first application is malware detection. Massive amounts of data have to be mined to detect whether the system has been compromised due to malware. Often, the malware may change its patterns to avoid being detected. We have developed a cloud-based malware detection solution. The second application we have developed is cloud-based insider threat detection. Owing to terrorism as well as intense competition between corporations, insider threat is becoming an increasingly dangerous problem. We are developing data mining tools for insider threat detection. We will discuss one such tool that uses cloud computing technologies. The third application is AIS. Organizations (e.g., law enforcement, health care, and government coalitions) have to work together and share information to solve a problem. The appropriate security policies have to be enforced so that only authorized information is shared. Such AIS applications can benefit a great deal by using a cloud. This way, the organizations can store the data and policies in the cloud and information is shared based on the policies. The fourth application is AIS in a semantic cloud.

Other security applications that could be hosted on the cloud include identity and access management as well as e-mail spam filtering. The security applications that we have discussed in this section are illustrated in Figure 1.8. Note that for such applications, the cloud provides security as a service.

1.9 Toward Trustworthy Clouds

In our definition, trustworthiness consists of aspects such as confidentiality, privacy, trust, integrity, high assurance, fault-tolerance, and meeting real-time constraints.

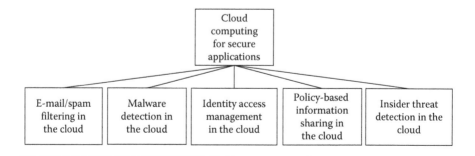

Figure 1.8   Cloud computing for secure applications.

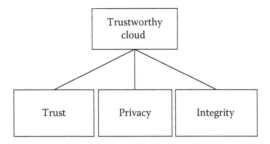

Figure 1.9 Trustworthy clouds.

Much of the focus in this book is on secure clouds and the main topic addressed is confidentiality. Our ultimate objective is to build dependable clouds. Such a cloud has to maintain privacy, ensure trust, have high integrity, and ensure data quality among others. Note that this is not a standard definition. That is, some papers and books have used the terms trustworthiness and dependability interchangeably. Furthermore, some papers have also implied that security includes confidentiality, integrity, and privacy.

Figure 1.9 illustrates the aspects of trustworthy clouds. The challenge is to ensure that the cloud provides all the features such as privacy, trust, confidentiality, and integrity. Essentially, the cloud has to be flexible. Part VIII will focus on such trustworthy clouds.

1.10 Building an Infrastructure, Education Program, and a Research Program for a Secure Cloud

While technological developments are being made on secure cloud computing, it is also important to build secure infrastructures, education programs, and research programs on secure cloud computing. Figure 1.10 illustrates our efforts in these areas.

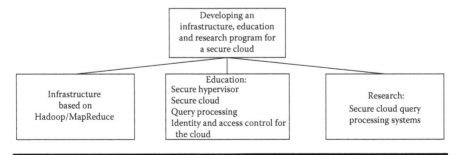

Figure 1.10 Infrastructure, education, and research programs for a secure cloud.

There is a critical need to securely store, manage, share, and analyze massive amounts of complex (e.g., semistructured and unstructured) data to determine patterns and trends to improve the quality of health care, better safeguard the nation, and explore alternative energy. However, to the best of our knowledge, there is no off-the-shelf infrastructure that addresses the above need. Therefore, we at the University of Texas at Dallas (UTD) are developing an infrastructure for a secure cloud with funding from the AFOSR and the National Science Foundation. Using this infrastructure, users can query massive amounts of complex (e.g., semantic web and geospatial) data while ensuring the confidentiality of this data and the privacy of individuals.

To build effective secure cloud computing systems, we also need to build a strong education program on this topic so that we get students to work on the projects. Therefore, we are also establishing a strong education program with several courses in assured cloud computing with funding from the National Science Foundation. These courses form a comprehensive set that will provide an example for secure cloud computing capacity building and education in other institutions.

While cloud computing has received a great deal of attention, there is a lot of work to be done on securing the cloud. Therefore, we started a multiorganizational collaborative research project funded by the AFOSR between 2008 and 2014 that includes an investigation of security issues for the cloud such as secure cloud storage, secure cloud data and information management, information as well as security models for the cloud.

1.11 Organization of This Book

This book is divided into nine parts, each describing some aspect of technology that is relevant to building and securing the cloud. A major focus of this book will be on cloud query processing and the surrounding security issues. Security applications that utilize cloud computing such as malware detection, AIS, and insider threat detection will also be discussed.

Part I, consisting of three chapters, will describe supporting technologies for the cloud. These include the evolution of computing systems discussed in Chapter 2, security technologies discussed in Chapter 3, and data, information, and knowledge management technologies discussed in Chapter 4. These supporting technologies provide the background information for cloud data management and secure cloud computing.

Part II, consisting of three chapters, will discuss concepts in services and secure services technologies. Web services are at the heart of cloud computing and therefore, understanding the security issues for web services is important for secure cloud computing. This is because a cloud provides services to its customer including infrastructure services, platform services, and application services. Chapter 5 discusses SOA and web services, SOAD, as well as secure services. Semantic web services and related security issues will be discussed in Chapter 6. Specialized web services such as services for information and knowledge management will be discussed in Chapter 7.

Part III, consisting of five chapters, will discuss the core topics in cloud computing. In Chapter 8, we will discuss the basic cloud computing concepts and our implementation of a cloud computing framework. Cloud computing functions including virtualization, storage management, and data management will be discussed in Chapter 9. We will devote the entire Chapter 10 to cloud data management as many of the prototypes we have developed focus on cloud data management. The applications are discussed in Chapter 11. Chapter 12 discusses the various cloud products and service providers.

Part IV, consisting of three chapters, will discuss the prototypes we have developed on experimental cloud computing systems. The first is a cloud query processing system prototype and will be discussed in Chapter 13. Chapter 14 discusses social networking in the cloud. Chapter 15 discusses multiple cloud computing systems we have developed including cloud-based social networking, cloud-based semantic web data management, and ontology-based query processing in the cloud.

Part V, consisting of six chapters, will discuss secure cloud computing. Chapter 16 discusses security for cloud computing. Secure cloud computing functions such as secure virtualization, storage and data management, as well as cloud forensics will be discussed in Chapter 17. Since much of our work is focused on secure cloud data management, we devote the entire Chapter 18 to this topic. Secure cloud computing guidelines will be discussed in Chapter 19. The notion of security as a service will be discussed in Chapter 20. Finally, products for secure cloud computing will be discussed in Chapter 21.

Part VI, consisting of three chapters, will discuss the experimental systems we have developed for secure cloud data management. Secure cloud query processing with relational data is the subject of Chapter 22. Secure query processing with semantic web data will be discussed in Chapter 23. Security for Amazon web services and information integration will be discussed in Chapter 24.

Part VII, consisting of four chapters, will describe the use of cloud computing for security applications. Chapter 25 describes the use of cloud for malware detection. Cloud-based insider threat detection will be discussed in Chapter 26. Chapter 27 discusses assured cloud-based information sharing. Chapter 28 discusses semantic cloud-based AIS.

While the security issues discussed in Parts II through VII mainly focus on confidentiality aspects of security, in Part VIII, consisting of three chapters, we will discuss some of our ideas on building trustworthy clouds. Such clouds not only have to ensure that sensitive data are protected, they also have to ensure trust, privacy, and integrity. In Chapter 29, we discuss trust management for cloud services. In Chapter 30, we discuss privacy issues for cloud services. In Chapter 31, we discuss integrity and data quality for cloud services.

Finally Part IX, consisting of three chapters, discusses our efforts on developing an infrastructure, education program, and research collaboration for a secure cloud.

Chapter 32 describes an infrastructure for a secure cloud that consists of a hardware infrastructure, software infrastructure, and a data infrastructure. Chapter 33 describes the education program that we are developing on secure cloud computing. It consists of a capstone course in secure cloud computing as well as enhancements to our current security courses such as data and application security with units on relevant secure cloud computing topics (e.g., secure cloud data management). In Chapter 34, we describe the research collaboration we have established for a secure cloud. We have defined a framework for secure cloud and have identified several research problems and are developing solutions to several of the problems.

Each part begins with an overview of the chapter and ends with a summary and directions. Furthermore, Chapters 2 through 34 each start with an overview and ends with a summary and references. Chapter 35 summarizes the book and discusses directions. We have included four appendices to supplement the concepts discussed in this book. Appendix A provides an overview of data management and discusses the relationship among the chapters we have written. This has been the standard practice with all of our books. In Appendix B, we discuss data mining techniques. This is because much of our work on cloud computing focusses on cloud data management as well as applying data mining techniques for malware detection and insider threat detection in the cloud. Cloud data mining, which is also sometimes referred to as "Big Data Analytics" has numerous applications not only for malware detection, but also for health care management, financial analysis, and scientific data management. Appendix C describes some of the important concepts of data security such as access control and query modification (also called query rewriting). We apply many of these concepts throughout the book for secure cloud data management. Since we have devoted several chapters to cloud-based AIS, we discuss our project on AIS in Appendix D.

We have essentially developed a nine-layer framework to explain the concepts better in this book. This framework is illustrated in Figure 1.11. Layer 1 is the supporting technologies layer and covers Part I of this book. Layer 2 is the secure services layer and covers Part II. Layer 3 is the cloud technologies layer and covers Part III. Layer 4 is the experimental systems layer and covers Part IV. Layer 5 is the secure cloud technologies layer and covers Part V. Layer 6 is the secure experimental cloud systems layer and covers Part VI. Layer 7 is the cloud applications layer and covers Part VII. Layer 8 is the trustworthy cloud layer and covers Part VIII. Layer 9 is the cloud infrastructure, education, and research layer and covers Part IX. The relationships between the chapters of the book and the components of the framework are given in Figure 1.12.

1.12 Next Steps

This chapter has provided an introduction to the book. We first provided a brief overview of the supporting technologies for secure cloud technologies that include security and data management. Next, we discussed secure web services

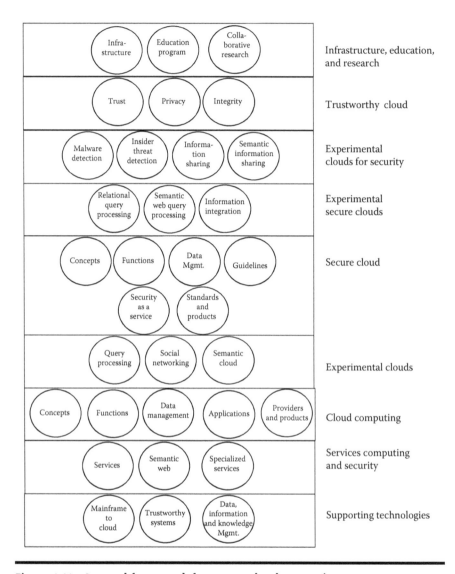

Figure 1.11   Layered framework for secure cloud computing.

and semantic web services. This was followed by a discussion of cloud technologies and secure cloud technologies. Next, the security applications that utilize the cloud were discussed. This was followed by a discussion on trustworthy clouds. Finally, our approach toward building an infrastructure, an education program, and research collaboration for a secure cloud were discussed.

This book provides the information for a reader to get familiar with cloud computes and secure cloud computing. We discuss some topics such as secure cloud query processing in depth as we have carried out much research on this topic.

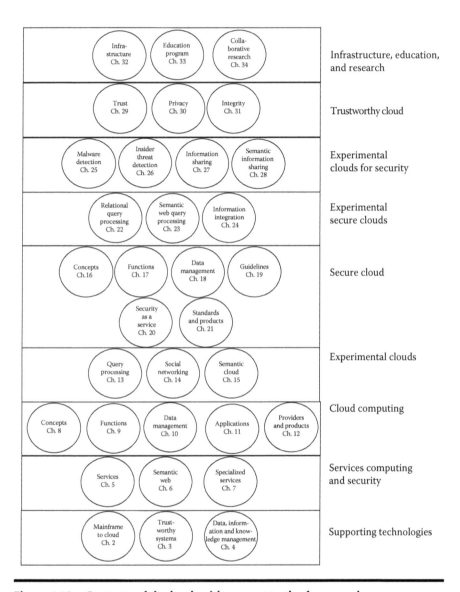

Figure 1.12 Contents of the book with respect to the framework.

Some other topics are only briefly discussed such as secure virtualization and cloud forensics. However, we have provided references for these topics. However, it should be noted that many of the topics we have discussed are still in the research stages.

One of the main contributions of this book is raising the awareness of the importance of security for cloud computing. That is, to be consistent with our previous books, our purpose is to explain, especially to technical managers, what secure cloud computing is all about. However, because of our fairly extensive research in secure cloud computing, we have also tried to include technical details as well as descriptions of experimental systems that would help the technologists and researchers. We have given references throughout the book.

Several new cloud computing conferences have emerged in recent years. These include the IEEE (Institute of Electrical and Electronic Engineers) Computer Society's Cloud Computing Conference held in conjunction with Services Computing Conference as well as CloudCom. The ACM (Association of Computing Machinery) has recently started its own cloud computing conference. We believe that as progress is made on secure cloud computing technologies, conferences and journals entirely devoted to secure cloud computing will emerge. We encourage the reader to keep up with the developments of this very rapidly growing field. We strongly believe that the future of computing is with cloud computing. Services and components will be developed by multiple vendors from all over the world. The challenge is to put these services and components together and to build secure cloud computing systems and applications. Furthermore, even if parts of the cloud may be corrupted, the challenge is to ensure that the cloud is operational and provides secure services to its client.

References

[NIST] The NIST definition of Cloud Computing, http://csrc.nist.gov/publications/nistpubs/800-145/SP800-145.pdf

SUPPORTING TECHNOLOGIES

Introduction to Part I

For secure cloud computing to be successful we need to ensure that several supporting technologies have to work together. These include computing technologies, security technologies, and data/information/knowledge management technologies. We will discuss these supporting technologies in Part I.

Part I consists of three chapters: 2, 3, and 4. In Chapter 2, we will provide an overview of computing technologies. In particular, the evolution of computing from mainframe to cloud computing will be discussed. In Chapter 3, we will discuss security technologies. In particular, aspects of designing secure systems will be discussed. In Chapter 4, we will discuss data, information, and knowledge management technologies. Note that many of our experimental systems in cloud computing are based on data, information, and knowledge management technologies.

Chapter 2

From Mainframe to the Cloud

2.1 Overview

While early computing systems were based on the mechanical systems of Charles Babbage, the modern electronic computing system dawned in the 1940s with the work of von Neumann. This resulted from the research carried out by the famous mathematicians and logicians such as Kurt Gödel, Alan Turing, and Alonzo Church, among others in the 1930s. These mathematicians and logicians focused on the notion of computability. That is, can one determine ahead of time whether a program would halt or not? This was the famous halting problem of Alan Turing.

Since the 1940s, with the advent of the electronic computing machine, computers have progressed a great deal with the mainframes of the 1950s to the cloud of the 2000s. This chapter provides an overview of the evolution of computing systems. In Section 2.2, we discuss mainframe computing, mini-computers, and the personal computers. In Section 2.3, we discuss distributed computing including distributed object management. In Section 2.4, we discuss the emergence of the web and in Section 2.5, we discuss the emergence of the cloud. This chapter is summarized in Section 2.6. Figure 2.1 illustrates this evolution.

2.2 Early Computing Systems

Mainframe computing took off in the 1950s and gained much prominence throughout the 1960s. Corporations such as IBM (International Business Machines), Univac,

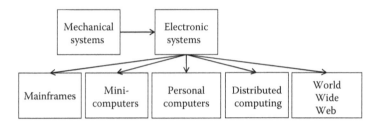

Figure 2.1 Evolution of computing.

DEC (Digital Equipment Corporation), and Control Data Corporation started developing powerful mainframe systems. These mainframe systems mainly carried out number-crunching for scientists and engineers. The main programming language used was Fortran. Then in the 1960s, the notion of database systems was conceived and corporations developed database systems based on the network and hierarchical data models. The database applications at that time were written mainly in COBOL.

In the 1970s, corporations such as DEC created the notion of mini-computers. An example is DEC's VAX machine. These machines were much smaller than the mainframe systems. Around that time, terminals were developed. This way, programmers did not have to go to computing centers and use punch cards for their computations. They could use their terminals and submit the jobs to the computing machines. This was a huge step forward. It was also during this time that languages such as C and operating systems such as UNIX were developed.

A significant development in the late 1970s was the emergence of the personal computer. This resulted in Apple Computers. Soon after, IBM developed its own personal computers. Microsoft developed the DOS operating system for these IBM machines. Powerful workstations were developed in the early 1980s by corporations such as Sun Microsystems, Apollo, and HP (Hewlett Packard). Database systems based on the relational data model were developed by corporations such as IBM and Oracle. By the mid-1980s, computers were poised to take over the world. Figure 2.2 illustrates early computing.

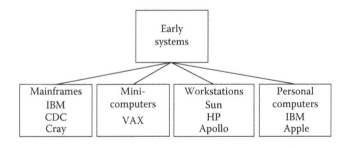

Figure 2.2 Early systems.

2.3 Distributed Computing

With the invention of the Internet by DARPA (Defense Advanced Research Projects Agency), networked systems gained momentum in the 1970s and the early products came out in the 1980s. Computers were networked together and were communicating with each other and exchanging messages through what is now known as email. Several applications were developed for these distributed systems. The idea was to utilize the resources and carry out a computation in multiple machines. The late 1980s also saw the emergence of parallel computing.

A computing paradigm that exploded in the early 1990s was the distributed object paradigm. Here, computers were encapsulated as objects. This way objects communicated with each other by exchanging messages. This work resulted in consortia such as the Object Management Group (OMG) to be formed. It was at this time that object-oriented languages such as Smalltalk and C++ rose to prominence. Figure 2.3 illustrates distributed object computing.

2.4 World Wide Web

In the early 1990s, one of the major innovations of the twentieth century was initiated and that was the World Wide Web (WWW). Tim Berners Lee, the inventor of the WWW was a programmer at CERN in Geneva, Switzerland. He started a project to support physicists sharing data. This project resulted in the WWW. Around the same time, programmers at the University of Illinois National Computing Center developed the MOSAIC browser. These two innovations resulted in ordinary people using the WWW to query and search for information. The late 1990s saw the emergence of several search engines such as Alta Vista and Lycos. Then two researchers from Stanford University started a company called Google that is now the largest web search company in the world. Java became one of the popular programming languages.

The late 1990s also saw what is now called the dot-com boom. Several companies that provided services were formed and this resulted in electronic commerce. However, the infrastructure technologies were not mature at that time and, as a

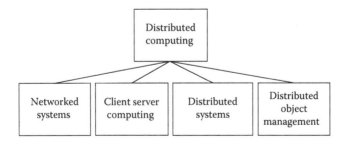

Figure 2.3 Distributed computing.

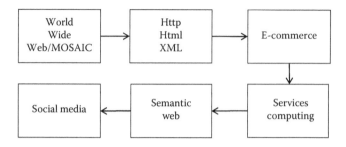

Figure 2.4 Evolution of the WWW.

result, many of these companies did not survive. In the late 1990s and early 2000s, the notion of web services based on the service paradigm was created. With the service technologies, better infrastructures were built for e-commerce. Corporations were providing services to the consumer based on the service paradigm.

The late 1990s and early 2000s also saw the emergence of semantic web technologies. Tim Berners Lee's vision was to create a more intelligent web that would understand web pages. He created mark-up languages such as XML and RDF. Ontologies were also created so that different communities could understand each other. The development of services computing and the semantic web resulted in the birth of social media. Corporations such as Facebook were formed in the mid-2000s that enabled ordinary people not only to search for information on the web, but also to communicate with each other and share information through the web. Figure 2.4 illustrates the evolution of the World Wide Web.

2.5 Cloud Computing

Developments in services computing, distributed computing, and the WWW have resulted in cloud computing. The idea was to provide computing as a service just like we use electricity as a service. That is, a cloud service provider would provide different levels of service to the consumer. The service could be to use the cloud for computing, for database management, or for application support such as organizing one's finances.

Parts III, IV, V, and VI of this book will focus on cloud computing concepts, experimental systems, and security for the cloud. Since services computing is a key aspect of cloud computing, we devote Part II to services computing. In particular, we discuss web services and security for web services. Figure 2.5 illustrates the notion of cloud computing.

2.6 Summary and Directions

In this chapter, we have provided a brief overview of the evolution of computing. We started with the works of the mathematical logicians followed by the von Neumann

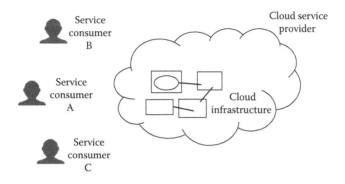

Figure 2.5 Cloud computing.

machines. Then, we discussed the evolution of computers from the mainframe to the personal computers. Finally, we provided an overview of distributed computing, services computing, the WWW, and cloud computing.

The discussion in this chapter will lay the foundations for the topics addressed in this book. First, we will provide some background discussions on secure systems as well as data, information and knowledge management systems. This will be followed by discussions on secure web services and trustworthy semantic web. Then, we will focus on the main topics of cloud computing and secure cloud computing. In particular, we will discuss technologies, products as well as the experimental systems we have developed for both cloud computing and secure cloud computing.

We believe that computing will continue to advance and the challenge is to handle massive amounts of data. This challenge is called the "big data" problem. Therefore, developing scalable solutions utilizing cloud computing for solving the big data problem will be a major focus area for the future.

References

[BABB] The Babbage engine, http://www.computerhistory.org/babbage/
[HEIJ67] J. Van Heijenoort, *From Frege to Gödel: A Source Book in Mathematical Logic, 1879–1931*, Harvard University Press, Cambridge, MA, 1967.
[HIST] Computer history, http://www.computerhope.com/history/
[NEUM] von Neumann machine, http://www.britannica.com/EBchecked/topic/1252440/von-Neumann-machine
[OMG] Object Management Group, http://www.omg.org
[TURI] Barker-Plummer, David, Turing machines, http://plato.stanford.edu/entries/turing-machine/
[W3C] World Wide Web Consortium, http://www.w3c.org

Chapter 3

Trustworthy Systems

3.1 Overview

As we have stated in Chapter 1, secure cloud computing integrates cloud computing technologies with security technologies. We will discuss cloud computing technologies in Part III of this book. In this chapter, we will discuss security technologies. In particular, we will provide an overview of trustworthy information systems that include security, privacy, integrity, dependability, and real-time processing. Trustworthy systems are systems that are secure and dependable. By dependable systems, we mean systems that have high integrity, are fault-tolerant and meet real-time constraints. In other words, for a system to be trustworthy it must be secure, fault-tolerant, meet timing deadlines, and manage high-quality data.

This chapter provides an overview of the various developments in trustworthy systems with special emphasis on secure systems including secure data systems. We focus on secure data systems as several of our experimental cloud systems focus on secure query processing in the cloud. The organization of this chapter is as follows. In Section 3.2, we discuss secure systems in some detail. Section 3.3 provides an overview of dependable systems which includes trust, privacy, integrity, data quality, high assurance systems, real-time processing, and fault-tolerance. In Section 3.4, we discuss some of the security threats and the solutions that are being proposed. In Section 3.5, we discuss end-to-end security versus building secure systems from untrusted components. This chapter is summarized in Section 3.6. Figure 3.1 illustrates the concepts discussed in this chapter.

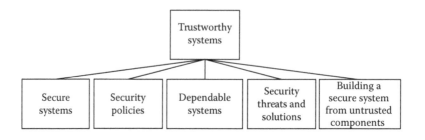

Figure 3.1   Trustworthy systems.

3.2 Secure Systems

3.2.1 Overview

Secure systems include secure operating systems, secure data management systems, secure networks, and other types of systems such as web-based secure systems and secure digital libraries among others. This section provides an overview of the various developments in information security.

In Section 3.2.2, we discuss basic concepts such as access control for information systems. Section 3.2.3 provides an overview of the various types of secure systems. Secure operating systems will be discussed in Section 3.2.4. Secure database systems will be discussed in Section 3.2.5. Network security will be discussed in Section 3.2.6. Emerging trends is the subject of Section 3.2.7. Impact of the web is given in Section 3.2.8. An overview of the steps to building secure systems will be provided in Section 3.2.9. Figure 3.2 illustrates the various concepts addressed in this section.

3.2.2 Access Control and Other Security Concepts

Access control models include those for discretionary security and mandatory security. In this section, we discuss both aspects of access control and also consider other issues. In discretionary access control models, users or groups of users are granted access to data objects. These data objects could be files, relations, objects, or even data items. Access control policies include rules such as User U has read access

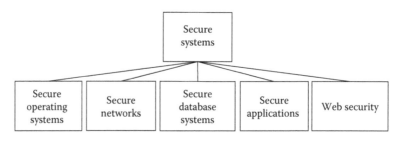

Figure 3.2   Secure systems.

to Relation R1 and write access to Relation R3. Access control could also include negative access control where User U does not have read access to Relation R.

In mandatory access control, subjects that act on behalf of users are granted access to objects based on some policy. A well-known policy is the Bell and LaPadula policy [BELL73] where subjects are granted clearance levels and objects have sensitivity levels. The set of security levels form a partially ordered lattice where Unclassified < Confidential < Secret < TopSecret. The policy has two properties and is the following. A subject has read access to an object if its clearance level dominates that of the object. A subject has write access to an object if its level is dominated by that of the object. Other types of access control include role-based access control. Here, access is granted to users depending on their roles and the functions they perform. For example, personnel managers have access to salary data while project managers have access to project data.

While the early access control policies were formulated for operating systems, these policies have been extended to include other systems such as database systems, networks, and distributed systems. For example, a policy for networks includes policies for not only reading and writing but also for sending and receiving messages. Other security policies include administration policies. These policies include those for ownership of the data as well as how to manage and distribute the data. Database administrators as well as system security officers are involved in formulating the administration policies.

Security policies also include policies for identification and authentication. Each user or subject acting on behalf of a user has to be identified and authenticated possibly using some password mechanisms. Identification and authentication become more complex for distributed systems. For example, how can a user be authenticated at a global level?

The steps to developing secure systems include developing a security policy, developing a model of the system, designing the system, and verifying and validating the system [ANDE01]. The methods used for verification depend on the level of assurance that is expected. Testing and risk analysis are also a part of the process. These activities will determine the vulnerabilities as well as assess the risks involved. Figure 3.3 illustrates various types of security policies.

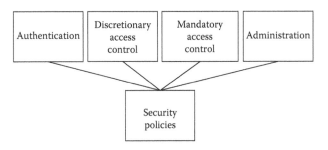

Figure 3.3   Security policies.

3.2.3 Types of Secure Systems

In the previous section we discussed various policies for building secure systems. In this section, we elaborate on various types of secure systems. Much of the early research in the 1960s and 1970s was on securing operating systems. Early security policies such as the Bell and LaPadula policy were formulated for operating systems. Subsequently, secure operating systems such as Honeywell's SCOMP and MULTICS were developed (see [IEEE83]). Other policies such as those based on noninterference also emerged in the early 1980s.

While early research on secure database systems was reported in the 1970s, it was not until the early 1980s that active research began in this area. Much of the focus was on multilevel secure database systems. The security policy for operating systems was modified slightly. For example, the write policy for secure database systems was modified to state that a subject has write access to an object if the subject's level is that of the object. Since database systems enforced relationships between data and focused on semantics, there were additional security concerns. For example, data could be classified based on content, context, and time. The problem of posing multiple queries and inferring sensitive information from the legitimate responses became a concern. This problem is now known as the inference problem. Also, research was carried out not only on securing relational systems but also on object systems as well as distributed systems, among others.

Research on computer networks began in the late 1970s and continued throughout the 1980s and beyond. The networking protocols were extended to incorporate security features. The result was secure network protocols. The policies include those for reading, writing, sending, and receiving messages. Research on encryption and cryptography has received much prominence due to networks and the web. Security for stand-alone systems was extended to include distributed systems. These systems included distributed databases and distributed operating systems. Much of the research on distributed systems now focuses on securing the web, known as web security, as well as securing systems such as distributed object management systems.

As new systems emerge, such as data warehouses, collaborative computing systems, multimedia systems, and agent systems, security for such systems has to be investigated. With the advent of the WWW, security is being given serious consideration by not only the government organizations but also by commercial organizations. With e-commerce, it is important to protect the company's intellectual property. Figure 3.4 illustrates various types of secure systems.

3.2.4 Secure Operating Systems

Work on security for operating systems was carried out extensively in the 1960s and 1970s. The research still continues as new kinds of operating systems such as Windows, Linux, and other products emerge. The early ideas included access

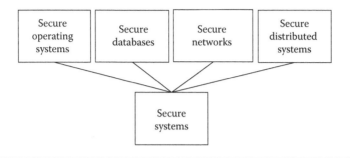

Figure 3.4   Types of secure systems.

control lists and capability-based systems. Access control lists specify the types of access that processes, which are called subjects, have on files, which are objects. The access is usually read or write access. Capability lists are capabilities that a process must possess to access certain resources in the system. For example, a process with a particular capability can write into certain parts of the memory.

Work on mandatory security for operating systems started with the Bell and LaPadula security model, which has two properties.

- ■ The simple security property states that a subject has read access to an object if the subject's security level dominates the level of the object.
- ■ The *-property (pronounced star property) states that a subject has write access to an object if the subject's security level is dominated by that of the object.

Since then, variations of this model as well as a popular model called the noninterference model (see [GOGU82]) have been proposed. The noninterference model is essentially about higher-level processes not interfering with lower-level processes.

Corporations such as Microsoft are putting in many resources to ensure that their products are secure. Often we hear of vulnerabilities in various operating systems and about hackers trying to break into the operating systems, especially with those with networking capabilities. Therefore, this is an area that will continue to receive much attention for the next several years. This is because many of the applications including database systems are usually hosted on the operating system. Therefore, if the operating system is corrupted then it will likely impact the entire computing system. Figure 3.5 illustrates some key aspects of operating systems security.

3.2.5 Secure Database Systems

Work on discretionary security for databases began in the 1970s when security aspects were investigated for System R at IBM Almaden Research Center.

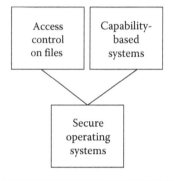

Figure 3.5 Secure operating systems.

Essentially the security properties specified the read and write access that a user may have to relations, attributes, and data elements. Techniques such as query modification were proposed for access control in relational systems [GRIF76]. In the 1980s and 1990s, security issues were investigated for object systems. Here, the security properties specified the access that users had to objects, instance variables, and classes. In addition to read and write access, method execution access was also specified [FERN81].

Since the early 1980s, much focus was on multilevel secure database management systems [AFSB83]. These systems essentially enforce the mandatory policy discussed in Section 3.2.2 with the modification described in Section 3.3 (i.e., read at or below your level and write at your level policy). Since the 1980s, various designs, prototypes, and commercial products of multilevel database systems have been developed. Ferrari and Thuraisingham give a detailed survey of some of the developments [FERR00]. Example efforts include the SeaView effort by SRI International and the LOCK Data Views effort by Honeywell. These efforts extended relational models with security properties. One challenge was to design a model where a user sees different values at different security levels. For example, at the Unclassified level an employee's salary may be 20 K and at the secret level it may be 50 K. In the standard relational model, such ambiguous values cannot be represented due to integrity properties.

Note that several other significant developments have been made on multilevel security for other types of database systems. These include security for object database systems [THUR89]. In this effort, security properties specify read, write, and method execution policies. Much work was also carried out on secure concurrency control and recovery. The idea here is to enforce security properties and still meet consistency without having covert channels. Research was also carried out on multilevel security for distributed, heterogeneous, and federated database systems. Another area that received a lot of attention was the inference problem. For details on the inference problem, we refer the reader to [THUR93]. For secure concurrency control, we refer to the numerous algorithms by Atluri, Bertino, Jajodia et al.

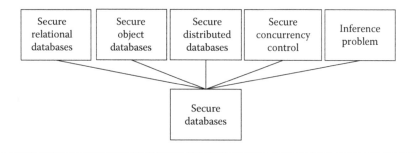

Figure 3.6   Secure database systems.

(see, e.g., [ATLU97]). For information on secure distributed and heterogeneous databases as well as secure federated databases, we refer to [THUR91] and [THUR94].

As database systems become more sophisticated, securing these systems will become more and more difficult. Some of the current work focuses on securing data warehouses, multimedia databases, and web databases (see, e.g., *Proceedings of the IFIP Database Security Conference Series*). Figure 3.6 illustrates various types of secure database systems. Since many of the experimental cloud systems that we have developed carry out secure data management, we will describe the concepts and technologies for secure data management in Appendix C.

3.2.6 Secure Networks

With the advent of the web and the interconnection of different systems and applications, networks have proliferated over the past decade. There are public networks, private networks, classified networks, and unclassified networks. We continually hear about networks being infected with viruses and worms. Furthermore, networks are being intruded by malicious code and unauthorized individuals. Therefore, network security is emerging as one of the major areas in information security.

Various techniques have been proposed for network security. Encryption and cryptography are still dominating much of the research. For a discussion on various encryption techniques we refer to [HASS00]. Data mining techniques are being applied for intrusion detection extensively (see [NING04]). There has also been a lot of work on network protocol security where security is incorporated into the various layers of the protocol stack such as the network layer, transport layer, and session layer (see [TANN90]). Verification and validation techniques are also being investigated for securing networks. Various books on the topic have also been published (see [KAUF02]). Figure 3.7 illustrates network security techniques.

3.2.7 Emerging Trends

In the mid-1990s, research in secure systems expanded to include emerging systems. These included secure collaborative computing systems, multimedia computing,

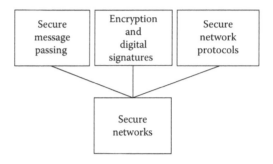

Figure 3.7   Secure networks.

and data warehouses. Data mining has resulted in new security concerns. Since users now have access to various data mining tools and they could make sensitive associations, it could exacerbate the inference problem. On the other hand, data mining could also help with security problems such as intrusion detection and auditing.

The advent of the web resulted in extensive investigations of security for digital libraries and electronic commerce. In addition to developing sophisticated encryption techniques, security research also focused on securing the web clients as well as servers. Programming languages such as Java were designed with security in mind. Much research was also carried out on securing agents.

Secure distributed system research focused on security for distributed object management systems. Organizations such as the OMG started working groups to investigate security properties [OMG]. As a result, we now have secure distributed object management systems commercially available. Figure 3.8 illustrates the various emerging secure systems and concepts.

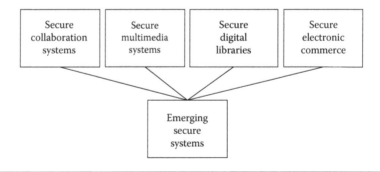

Figure 3.8   Emerging trends.

3.2.8 Impact of the Web

The advent of the web has greatly impacted security. Security is now a part of mainstream computing. Government organizations as well as commercial organizations are concerned about security. For example, in a financial transaction, millions of dollars could be lost if security is not maintained. With the web, all sorts of information are available about individuals and therefore privacy may be compromised.

Various security solutions are being proposed to secure the web. In addition to encryption, focus is on securing clients as well as servers. That is, end-to-end security has to be maintained. Web security also has an impact on electronic commerce. That is, when one carries out transactions on the web, it is critical that security is maintained. Information such as credit card numbers and social security numbers must be protected.

All the security issues discussed in the previous sections have to be considered for the web. For example, appropriate security policies have to be formulated. This is a challenge as no one person owns the web. The various secure systems including secure operating systems, secure database systems, secure networks, and secure distributed systems may be integrated in a web environment. Therefore, this integrated system has to be secure. Problems such as the inference and privacy problems may be exacerbated due to the various data mining tools. In certain cases, trade-offs need to be made between security and other features. That is, quality of service is an important consideration. In addition to technological solutions, legal aspects have to be examined. That is, lawyers and engineers have to work together. While much progress has been made on web security, there is still a lot to be done as progress is made on web technologies. Figure 3.9 illustrates aspects of web security. For a discussion on web security we refer to [GHOS98].

3.2.9 Steps to Building Secure Systems

In this section we outline the steps to building secure systems. Note that our discussion is general and applicable to any secure system. However, we may need to adapt

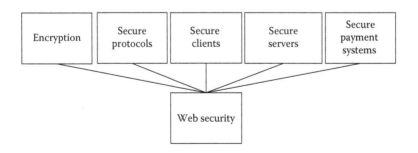

Figure 3.9   Web security.

the steps for individual systems. For example, to build secure distributed database systems, we need secure database systems as well as secure networks. Therefore, multiple systems have to be composed.

The first step to building a secure system is developing a security policy. The policy can be stated in an informal language and then formalized. The policy essentially specifies the rules that the system must satisfy. Then the security architecture has to be developed. The architecture will include the security critical components. These are the components that enforce the security policy and therefore should be trusted. The next step is to design the system. For example, if the system is a database system, the query processor, transaction manager, storage manager, and metadata manager modules are designed. The design of the system has to be analyzed for vulnerabilities. The next phase is the development phase. Once the system is implemented, it has to undergo security testing. This will include designing test cases and making sure that the security policy is not violated. Furthermore, depending on the level of assurance expected of the system, formal verification techniques may be used to verify and validate the system. Finally, the system will be ready for evaluation. Note that initially systems were being evaluated using the Trusted Computer Systems Evaluation Criteria [TCSE85]. There are interpretations of these criteria for networks [TNI87] and for databases [TDI91]. There are also several companion documents for various concepts such as auditing and inference control. Note that more recently some other criteria have been developed including the Federal Criteria in the 1990s and the Common Criteria in the 2000s.

Note that before the system is installed in an operational environment, one needs to develop a concept of operation of the environment. Risk assessment has to be carried out. Once the system is installed, it has to be monitored so that security violations including unauthorized intrusions are detected. Figure 3.10 illustrates the steps. An overview of building secure systems can be found in [GASS88].

3.3 Dependable Systems

3.3.1 Overview

As we discussed in Section 1.2.2, by dependability we mean features such as trust, privacy, integrity, data quality and provenance, and rights management among others. We have separated confidentiality and included it as part of security. Therefore, trustworthy systems include both secure systems and dependable systems, essentially (note that this is not a standard definition).

Whether we are discussing security, integrity, privacy, trust, or rights management, there is always a cost involved. That is, at what cost do we enforce security, privacy, and trust? Is it feasible to implement some of the complex privacy policies and trust management policies (e.g., the privacy policies for the Health Information

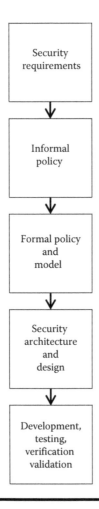

Figure 3.10   Steps to building secure systems.

Portability and Accountability Act)? In addition to bringing lawyers and policy makers together with the technologists, we also need to bring economists into the picture. We need to carry out economic trade-offs for enforcing security, privacy, and trust and rights management. Essentially what we need are flexible policies for security, privacy, and trust and rights management. For a discussion on the economic impact on security, we refer to [NSF03].

In this section, we will discuss various aspects of dependability. Trust issues will be discussed in Section 3.3.3. Digital rights management is discussed in Section 3.3.3. Privacy is discussed in Section 3.3.4. Integrity issues, data quality, and data provenance are discussed in Section 3.3.5. Figure 3.11 illustrates the dependability aspects.

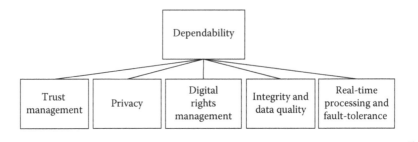

Figure 3.11 Aspects of dependability.

3.3.2 Trust Management

Trust management is all about managing the trust that one individual or group has of another. That is, even if a user has the access to the data, do I trust the user so that I can release the data? The user may have the clearance or possess the credentials; but he may not be trustworthy. Trust is formed by the user's behavior. The user may have betrayed one's confidence or carried out some act that is inappropriate in nature. Therefore, I may not trust that user. Now, even if I do not trust say John, Jane may trust John and she may share her data with John. That is, John may not be trustworthy to Jim, but he may be trustworthy to Jane.

The question is how do we implement trust? Can we trust someone partially? Can we trust John 50% of the time and Jane 70% of the time? If we trust someone partially then can we share some of the information? How do we trust the data that we have received from Bill? That is, if we do not trust Bill, then can we trust the data he gives us? There have been many efforts on trusted management systems as well as trust negotiation systems. Winslett et al. have carried out extensive work and developed specification languages for trust as well as designed trust negotiation systems (see [YU03]). The question is how do two parties negotiate trust? A may share data D with B if B shares data C with A. A may share data D with B only if B does not share this data with F. There are many such rules that one can enforce and the challenge is to develop a system that consistently enforces the trust rules or policies.

3.3.3 Digital Rights Management

Closely related to trust management is managing digital rights. This area has come to be called DRM (Digital Rights Management). This is especially critical for entertainment applications. Who owns the copyright to a video or an audio recording? How can rights be propagated? What happens if the rights are violated? That is, can I distribute copyrighted films and music on the web?

We have heard a lot about the controversy surrounding Napster and similar organizations. Is DRM a technical issue or is it a legal issue? How can we bring technologists, lawyers, and policy makers together so that rights can be managed properly? There have been numerous articles, discussions, and debates about DRM. A useful source is [DRM].

3.3.4 Privacy

Privacy is about protecting information about individuals. Furthermore, an individual can specify to a web service provider the information that can be released about him or her. Privacy has been discussed a great deal in the past, especially when it relates to protecting medical information about patients. Social scientists as well as technologists have been working on privacy issues.

Privacy has received enormous attention during recent years. This is mainly because of the advent of the web, the semantic web, counter-terrorism, and national security. For example, to extract information about various individuals and perhaps prevent and/or detect potential terrorist attacks, data mining tools are being examined. We have heard much about national security vs. privacy in the media. This is mainly due to the fact that people are now realizing that to handle terrorism, the government may need to collect data about individuals and mine the data to extract information. Data may be in relational databases or it may be text, video, and images. This is causing a major concern with various civil liberties unions (see [THUR03]). Therefore, technologists, policy makers, social scientists, and lawyers are working together to provide solutions to handle privacy violations.

3.3.5 Integrity, Data Quality, and High Assurance

Integrity is about maintaining the accuracy of the data as well about the processes. Accuracy of the data is discussed as a part of data quality. The process integrity is about ensuring that the processes are not corrupted. For example, we need to ensure that the processes are not malicious processes. Malicious processes may corrupt the data due to unauthorized modifications. To ensure integrity, the software has to be tested as well as verified in order to develop high assurance systems.

The database community has ensured integrity by enforcing integrity constraints (e.g., the salary value has to be positive) as well as by ensuring the correctness of the data when multiple processes access the data. To achieve correctness, techniques such as concurrency control are enforced. The idea is to enforce appropriate locks so that multiple processes do not access the data at the same time and corrupt the data.

Data quality is about ensuring the accuracy of the data. The accuracy of the data may depend on who touched the data. For example, if the source of the data is not trustworthy, then the data quality value may be low. Essentially some quality value is assigned to each piece of data. When data are composed, quality values are assigned to the data in such a way that the resulting value is a function of the quality values of the original data.

Data provenance techniques also determine the quality of the data. Note that data provenance is about maintaining the history of the data. This will include information such as who accesses the data for read/write purposes. Then based on this history, one could then assign quality values to the data as well as to determine when the data are misused.

Other closely related topics include real-time processing and fault-tolerance. Real-time processing is about the processes meeting the timing constraints. For example, if we are to get stock quotes to purchase stocks, we need to get the information in real time. It does not help if the information arrives after the trading desk is closed for business for the day. Similarly, real-time processing techniques also have to ensure that the data are current. Getting yesterday's stock quotes is not sufficient to make intelligent decisions. Fault-tolerance is about ensuring that the processes recover from faults. Faults could be accidental or malicious. In the case of faults, the actions of the processes have to be redone in case the processes aborted.

Note that in order to build high assurance systems, we need the systems to handle faults, be secure, and also handle real-time constraints. Real-time processing and security are conflicting goals as we have discussed in [THUR05a]. For example, a malicious process could ensure that critical timing constraints are missed. Furthermore, to enforce all the access control checks, some processes may miss the deadlines. Therefore, what we need are flexible policies that will determine which aspects are critical for a particular situation.

3.4 Security Threats and Solutions

In recent years, we have heard a lot about viruses and Trojan horses that disrupt activities on the web. These security threats and violations are costing several millions of dollars to businesses. Identity thefts are quite rampant these days. Furthermore, unauthorized intrusions, the inference problem, and privacy violations are also occurring. In this section, we provide an overview of some of these threats. A very good overview of these threats has also been provided in [GHOS98]. In this chapter, we discuss some of the security threats and the solutions that are being proposed. Figure 3.12 illustrates these threats.

Authentication Violations: Passwords could get stolen and this could result in authentication violations. One may need to have multiple passwords and additional information about the user to solve this problem. Biometrics and other techniques are being examined to handle authentication violations.

Nonrepudiation: The sender of a message could very well deny that he has sent the message. Nonrepudiation techniques will ensure that one can track the message to the sender. Today it is not difficult to track the owner of the message. However, it is not easy to track the person who has accessed the web page. That is, while progress has been made to analyze web logs, it is still difficult to determine the exact location of the user who has accessed a web page.

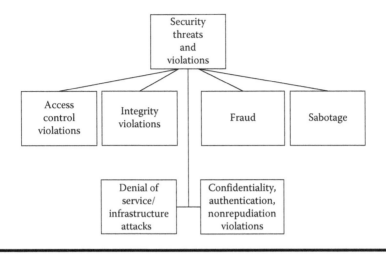

Figure 3.12 Security threats.

Trojan Horses and Viruses: Trojan horses and viruses are malicious programs that can cause all sorts of attacks. In fact, many of the threats discussed in this section could be caused by Trojan horses and viruses. Viruses can spread from machine to machine and could erase files in various computers. Trojan horses could leak information from a higher level to a lower level. Various virus protection packages have been developed and are now commercially available.

Sabotage: We hear of hackers breaking into systems and posting inappropriate messages. For example, some information on the sabotage of various government web pages is reported in [GHOS98]. One only needs to corrupt one server, client, or network for the problem to cascade to several machines.

Fraud: With so much of business and commerce being carried out on the web without proper controls, Internet fraud could cause businesses to lose millions of dollars. Intruders could obtain the identity of legitimate users and through masquerading may empty bank accounts.

Denial of Service and Infrastructure Attacks: We hear about infrastructures being brought down by hackers. Infrastructures could be the telecommunication system, power system, or the heating system. These systems are being controlled by computers and often through the web. Such attacks would cause denial of service.

Natural Disasters: In addition to terrorism, computers and networks are also vulnerable to natural disasters such as hurricanes, earthquakes, fire, and other similar disasters. The data have to be protected and databases have to be recovered from disasters. In some cases, the solutions to natural disasters are similar to those for threats due to terrorist attacks. For example, fault-tolerant processing techniques are used to recover the databases from damages. Risk analysis techniques may contain the damage.

Access Control Violations: The traditional access control violations could be extended to the web. Users may access unauthorized data across the web. Note that with the web, there is so much data all over the place that controlling access to this data will be quite a challenge.

Integrity Violations: Data on the web may be subject to unauthorized modifications. Also, data could originate from anywhere and the producers of the data may not be trustworthy. This makes it easier to corrupt the data. Incorrect data could cause serious damages such as incorrect bank accounts, which could result in incorrect transactions.

Confidentiality Violations: Security includes confidentiality as well as integrity. That is, confidential data has to be protected from those who are not cleared. Statistical database techniques have also been developed to prevent confidentiality violations.

Authenticity Violations: This is a form of data integrity violation. For example, consider the case of a publisher, subscriber, and the owner. The subscriber will subscribe to various magazines and the owner creates the magazines (in electronic form) and the publisher who is the third party will publish the magazines. If the publisher is not trusted, he could alter the contents of the magazine. This violates the authenticity of the document. Various solutions have been examined to determine the authenticity of documents (see, e.g., [BERT04]). These include cryptography and digital signatures.

Privacy Violations: With the web one can obtain all kinds of information collected about individuals. Also, with data mining tools and other analysis tools, one can make all kinds of unauthorized associations about individuals.

Inference Problem: Inference is the process of posing queries and deducing unauthorized information from the legitimate responses. In fact, we consider the privacy problem to be a form of inference problem. Various solutions have been proposed to handle the inference problem including constraint processing and the use of conceptual structures. We discuss some of them in the next section.

Identity Theft: We are hearing a lot about identity theft these days. The thief gets hold of one's social security number and from there can wipe out the bank account of an individual. Here, the thief is posing legitimately as the owner and he now has much of the critical information about the owner. This is a threat that is very difficult to handle and manage. Viable solutions are yet to be developed. Data mining offers some hope, but may not be sufficient.

Insider Threats: Insider threats are considered to be quite common and quite dangerous. In this case one never knows who the terrorists are. They could be the database administrators or any person who may be considered to be trusted by the corporation. Background checks alone may not be sufficient to detect insider threats. Role-based access controls as well as data mining techniques are being proposed.

All the threats/attacks discussed here plus various other cyber security threats/attacks collectively have come to be known as cyber terrorism. Essentially cyber

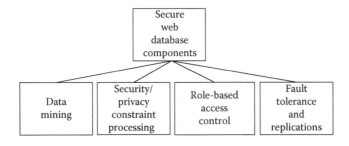

Figure 3.13   Security solutions.

terrorism is about corrupting the web and all its components so that the enemy or adversary's system collapses. There is currently a lot of funds being invested by the various governments in the United States and Europe to conduct research on protecting the web and preventing cyber terrorism. Note that terrorism includes cyber terrorism, bioterrorism, and violations to physical security, including bombing buildings and poisoning food and water supplies.

Various solutions are being proposed to handle the threats, including firewalls, data mining, cryptography, and access control. Figure 3.13 illustrates the solutions. Details of the solutions are given in [THUR05], [MASU11], [THUR93], [DENN82], and [HASS00].

3.5 Building Secure Systems from Untrusted Components

In Section 3.2 when we discussed the steps to building a secure system, we promoted end-to-end security. That is, our thesis was that to have a truly secure system, we need all the components (e.g., operating systems, database systems, networks, and applications) to be secure. This was the view of the security researchers and practitioners until recently. This is because one could envisage that all the components that comprise a secure system would be built by a single organization. However, due to globalization, this assumption is no longer feasible. That is, the operating system could be developed in China, the database system in India, and the applications in the United States. This means there is a greater probability of the components to be insecure. Therefore, the challenge is for the designer to build a secure system from untrusted components.

In a recent effort together with several other universities, we carried out an initial investigation of building a secure system from untrusted components. Our challenge was to design secure applications even though the operating system may be corrupted. Our results are presented in [UTD10]. This work is also applicable

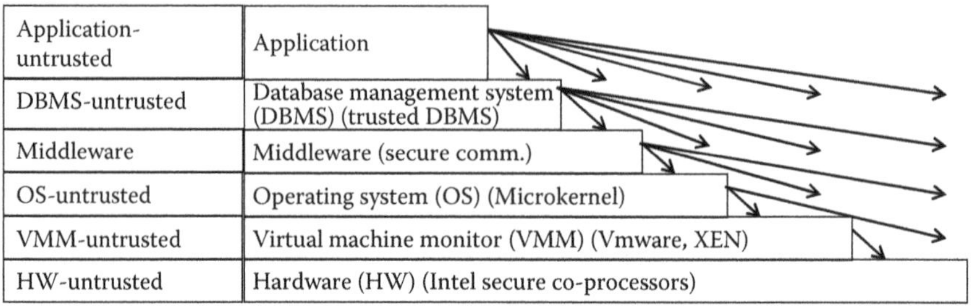

Application-untrusted	Application
DBMS-untrusted	Database management system (DBMS) (trusted DBMS)
Middleware	Middleware (secure comm.)
OS-untrusted	Operating system (OS) (Microkernel)
VMM-untrusted	Virtual machine monitor (VMM) (Vmware, XEN)
HW-untrusted	Hardware (HW) (Intel secure co-processors)

Figure 3.14 Building a secure system from untrusted components.

to what the Department of Defense calls Mission Assurance. Their challenge is to carry on with the mission as long as possible even though the system may be attacked. With the advent of outsourcing, this is a topic that will continue to expand and evolve in future years. Figure 3.14 illustrates aspects of building secure systems from untrusted components.

3.6 Summary and Directions

This chapter has provided a brief overview of the developments in trustworthy systems. We first discussed secure systems including basic concepts in access control as well as discretionary and mandatory policies, types of secure systems such as secure operating systems, secure databases, secure networks, and emerging technologies, the impact of the web and the steps to building secure systems. Next, we discussed dependable systems including aspects on trust, rights, privacy, integrity, quality, and real-time processing. Then we focused in more detail on aspects of security threats and solutions. Finally, we provide an overview of securing systems with untrusted components.

While much progress has been made on trustworthy systems, there is still a lot to be done. We need to investigate security for emerging systems such as semantic web technologies and services technologies. In addition, security for knowledge management systems as well as geospatial systems is critical. In this book, we will focus on one such aspect and that is on secure services. As discussed in Chapter 1, secure cloud computing integrates security technologies with cloud computing technologies. Since secure web service is a building block to secure cloud computing, we discuss secure web services in Part II. We will describe cloud computing technologies in Parts III and IV. Secure cloud computing technologies and systems will be discussed in Parts V and VI. The applications of the cloud for security such as malware detection are discussed in Part VII. Finally trust, privacy, and integrity for the cloud will be discussed in Part VIII.

References

[AFSB83] *Air Force Studies Board, Committee on Multilevel Data Management Security, Multilevel Data Management Security*, National Academy Press, Washington, DC, 1983.

[ANDE01] Anderson, R., *Security Engineering: A Guide to Building Dependable Distributed Systems*, Wiley, New York, 2001.

[ATLU97] Atluri, V. and S. Jajodia, E. Bertino, Transaction processing in multilevel secure databases with kernelized architectures: Challenges and solutions. *IEEE Transactions on Knowledge and Data Engineering*, 9(5): 693–708, 1997.

[BELL73] Bell, D. and L. LaPadula, *Secure Computer Systems: Mathematical Foundations and Model, M74-244*, The MITRE Corporation, Bedford, MA, 1973.

[BERT04] Bertino, E. et al. Secure selective third party publication of XML data. *IEEE Transactions on Knowledge and Data Engineering*, 16(10): 1263–1278, October 2004.

[DENN82] Denning, D., *Cryptography and Data Security*, Addison-Wesley, MA, 1983.

[DRM] Digital Rights Management Architectures, http://www.dlib.org/dlib/june01/iannella/06iannella.html

[FERN81] Fernandez, E. et al. *Database Security and Integrity*, Addison-Wesley, MA, 1981.

[FERR00] Ferrari, E. and B. Thuraisingham, Secure database systems, In: *Advances in Database Management* (Editors: M. Piatini and O. Diaz), Artech House, UK, 2000.

[GASS88] Gasser, M., *Building a Secure Computer System*, Van Nostrand Reinhold, New York, 1988.

[GHOS98] Ghosh, A., *E-commerce Security, Weak Links and Strong Defenses*, John Wiley, New York, 1998.

[GOGU82] Goguen, J. and J. Meseguer, Security policies and security models, *Proceedings of the IEEE Symposium on Security and Privacy*, Oakland, CA, April 1983.

[GRIF76] Griffiths, P.P. and B.W. Wade, An authorization mechanism for a relational database system. *ACM Transactions on Database Systems* 1(3): 242–255, 1976.

[HASS00] Hassler, V., *Security Fundamentals for E-Commerce*, Artech House , UK, 2000.

[IEEE83] *IEEE Computer Magazine, Special Issue on Computer Security Technology*, 16(7): 26–46, July 1983.

[KAUF02] Kaufmann, C. et al. *Network Security: Private Communication in a Public World*, Prentice Hall, PT, 2002, Upper Saddle River, NJ.

[MASU11] Masud, M., L. Khan, and B. Thuraisingham, *Data Mining for Malware Detection*, CRC Press, Boca Raton, FL, 2011.

[NING04] Ning, P. et al. Techniques and tools for analyzing intrusion alerts. *ACM Transactions on Information and Systems Security*, 7(2): 274–318, 2004.

[NSF03] Proceedings of NSF cyber trust principal investigator meeting, Baltimore, MD, August 2003.

[OMG] The Object Management Group, http://www.omg.org.

[TANN90] Tannenbaum, A., *Computer Networks*, Prentice-Hall, NJ, 1990.

[TCSE85] *Trusted Computer Systems Evaluation Criteria*, National Computer Security Center, MD, 1983.

[TDI91] *Trusted Database Interpretation*, National Computer Security Center, MD, 1991.

[THUR89] Thuraisingham, B., Mandatory security for object-oriented database systems, *Proceedings of the ACM OOPOSLA Conference*, New Orleans, LA, October 1989.

[THUR91] Thuraisingham, B., Multilevel security for distributed database systems. *Computers and Security*, 10, 727–747, 1991.

[THUR93] Thuraisingham, B., W. Ford, and M. Collins, Design and implementation of a database inference controller, *Data and Knowledge Engineering Journal*, 11(3): 271–297, 1993.

[THUR94] Thuraisingham, B., Multilevel security for federated database systems. *Computers and Security*, 13, 509–525, 1994.

[THUR98] Thuraisingham, B., *Data Mining: Technologies, Techniques, Tools and Trends*, CRC Press, Boca Raton, FL, December 1998.

[THUR03] Thuraisingham, B., *Web Data Mining Technologies and Their Applications in Business Intelligence and Counter-Terrorism*, CRC Press, Boca Raton, FL, 2003.

[THUR05a] Thuraisingham, B., *Database and Applications Security: Integrating Data Management and Information Security*, CRC Press, Boca Raton, FL, 2003.

[THUR05b] Thuraisingham, B, Privacy constraint processing in a privacy enhanced database management systems. *Data and Knowledge Engineering Journal*, November, 2003.

[TNI87] *Trusted Network Interpretation*, National Computer Security Center, MD, 1983.

[UTD10] Securing the Execution Environment Applications and Data from Multi-Trusted Components, University of Texas at Dallas, Technical Report, UTDCS-03-10, 2010.

[YU03] Yu, T. and M. Winslett, A unified scheme for resource protection in automated trust negotiation, *IEEE Symposium on Security and Privacy*, Oakland, CA, May 2003.

Chapter 4

Data, Information, and Knowledge Management

4.1 Overview

While Chapter 2 discussed the evolution of computer systems and Chapter 3 discussed trustworthy systems, this chapter will discuss some of the basic concepts in data, information and knowledge management. This is because much of the discussion of our work on experimental cloud systems is based on secure data, information and knowledge management.

Various definitions of data, information, and knowledge have been proposed. We adopt the following. By data we mean the data that is managed by databases. Information is the data extracted from the data in the databases. Knowledge is the information that is understood. Therefore, one needs to have knowledge to carry out activities. For example, AA126 is data. When we say American Airlines Flight 126, we extract information from the data. When we say AA126 goes from Boston to Dallas daily at 9 a.m., we know what to do with this information such as book a flight.

The organization of this chapter is as follows. In Section 4.2, we will discuss data management. Information and knowledge management will be discussed in Sections 4.3 and 4.4, respectively. Activity management such as e-commerce and information sharing will be discussed in Section 4.5. This chapter concludes with Section 4.6. It should be noted that the concepts discussed in this chapter are the foundation for the emerging topic of big data. Therefore, we also briefly discuss big data in Section 4.6. Figure 4.1 illustrates the various concepts discussed in this chapter.

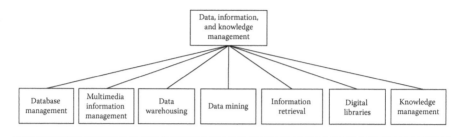

Figure 4.1 Data, information, knowledge, and activity management.

4.2 Data Management

In Section 4.2.1, we discuss database management which includes both a discussion of data models and database functions, distributed data management, and web data management. In Section 4.2.2, we discuss complex data management that includes a discussion of multimedia and geospatial data management.

4.2.1 Data Management

4.2.1.1 Data Model

The purpose of a data model is to capture the universe that it is representing as accurately, completely, and naturally as possible [TSIC82]. Data models include hierarchical models, network models, relational models, entity relationship models, object models, and logic-based models. Relational data model is the most popular data model for database systems. With the relational model [CODD70], the database is viewed as a collection of relations. Each relation has attributes and rows. Various languages to manipulate the relations have been proposed. Notable among these languages is the ANSI Standard SQL (Structured Query Language). This language is used to access and manipulate data in relational databases [SQL3]. A detailed discussion of the relational data model is given in [DATE90] and [ULLM88].

4.2.1.2 Functions

The function of a DBMS (database management system) is to carry out its operations. A DBMS essentially manages a database, and it provides support to the user by enabling him to query and update the database. Therefore, the basic functions of a DBMS are query processing and update processing. In some applications such as banking, queries and updates are issued as part of the transactions. Therefore, transaction management is also another function of a DBMS. To carry out these functions, information about the data in the database has to be maintained. This information is called the metadata. The function that is associated with managing

Figure 4.2   Architecture for an DBMS.

the metadata is metadata management. Special techniques are needed to manage the data stores that actually store the data. The function that is associated with managing these techniques is storage management. To ensure that the above functions are carried out properly and that the user gets accurate data, there are some additional functions. These include security management, integrity management, and fault management (i.e., fault-tolerance). The functional architecture of a DBMS is illustrated in Figure 4.2 (see also [ULLM88]).

4.2.1.3 Data Distribution

As stated by [CERI84], a distributed database system includes a distributed database management system (DDBMS), a distributed database, and a network for interconnection. The DDBMS manages the distributed database. A distributed database is data that is distributed across multiple databases. The nodes are connected via a communication subsystem and local applications are handled by the local DBMS. In addition, each node is also involved in at least one global application, so there is no centralized control in this architecture. The DBMS are connected through a component called the Distributed Processor. Distributed database system functions include distributed query processing, distributed transaction management, distributed metadata management, and enforcing security and integrity across the multiple nodes [THUR97]. It has been stated that the semantic web can be considered to be a large distributed database.

4.2.1.4 Web Data Management

A major challenge for web data management researchers and practitioners is coming up with an appropriate data representation scheme. The question is: is there a need for a standard data model for web database systems? Is it at all possible to develop such a standard? If so, what are the relationships between the standard model and the individual models used by the databases on the web?

Database management functions for the web include those such as query processing, metadata management, security, and integrity. In [THUR00] we have examined various DBMS functions and discussed the impact of web database access on these functions. Some of the issues are discussed here. Figure 4.3 illustrates the functions. Querying and browsing are two of the key functions. First of all, an appropriate query language is needed. Since SQL is a popular language, appropriate extensions to SQL may be desired. XML-QL and XQuery which have evolved from XML and SQL, are moving in this direction. Query processing involves developing a cost model. Are there special cost models for Internet database management? With respect to browsing operation, the query processing techniques have to be integrated with techniques for following links. That is, hypermedia technology has to be integrated with database management technology.

Transaction management is essential for many applications. There may be new kinds of transactions on the web. For example, various items may be sold through the Internet. In this case, the item should not be locked immediately when a potential buyer makes a bid. It has to be left open until several bids are received and the item is sold. That is, special transaction models are needed. Appropriate concurrency control and recovery techniques have to be developed for the transaction models.

Metadata management is a major concern for web data management. The question is: what is metadata? Metadata describes all of the information pertaining to the library. This could include the various web sites, the types of users, access control issues, and policies enforced. Where should the metadata be located? Should each participating site maintain its own metadata? Should the metadata be replicated or should there be a centralized metadata repository? Metadata in such an environment could be very dynamic especially since the users and the web sites may be changing continuously.

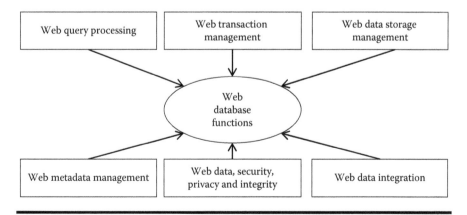

Figure 4.3 Web database functions.

Storage management for web database access is a complex function. Appropriate index strategies and access methods for handling web data are needed. In addition, due to the large volumes of data, techniques for integrating database management technology with mass storage technology are also needed. Other data management functions include integrating heterogeneous databases, managing multimedia data, and mining. We discuss them in [THUR02a].

4.2.2 Complex Data Management

4.2.2.1 Multimedia Data Systems

A multimedia data manager (MM-DM) provides support for storing, manipulating, and retrieving multimedia data from a multimedia database. In a sense, a multimedia database system is a type of heterogeneous database system, as it manages heterogeneous data types. Heterogeneity is due to the multiple media of the data such as text, video, and audio. Because multimedia data also conveys information such as speeches, music, and video, we have grouped this under information management. One important aspect of multimedia data management is data representation. Both extended relational models and object models have been proposed.

An MM-DM must provide support for typical DBMS functions. These include query processing, update processing, transaction management, storage management, metadata management, security, and integrity. In addition, in many cases, the various types of data such as voice and video have to be synchronized for display, and therefore, real-time processing is also a major issue in an MM-DM.

Various architectures are being examined to design and develop an MM-DM. In one approach, the data manager is used just to manage the metadata, and a multimedia file manager is used to manage the multimedia data. There is a module for integrating the data manager and the multimedia file manager. In this case, the MM-DM consists of the three modules: the data manager managing the metadata, the multimedia file manager, and the module for integrating the two. The second architecture is the tight coupling approach. In this architecture, the data manager manages both the multimedia data as well as the metadata. The tight coupling architecture has an advantage because all of the data management functions could be applied on the multimedia database. This includes query processing, transaction management, metadata management, storage management, and security and integrity management. Note that with the loose coupling approach, unless the file manager performs the DBMS functions, the DBMS only manages the metadata for the multimedia data.

There are also other aspects to architectures as discussed in [THUR97]. For example, a multimedia database system could use a commercial database system such as an object-oriented database system to manage multimedia objects. However, relationships between objects and the representation of temporal relationships may

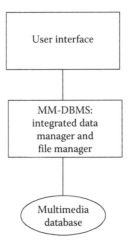

Figure 4.4   Multimedia information management system.

involve extensions to the DBMS. That is, a DBMS together with an extension layer provide complete support to manage multimedia data. In the alternative case, both the extensions and the database management functions are integrated so that there is one DBMS to manage multimedia objects as well as the relationships between the objects. Further details of these architectures as well as managing multimedia databases are discussed in [THUR01]. Figure 4.4 illustrates a multimedia information management system.

4.2.2.2 Geospatial Data Management

A geospatial data manager, also often referred to as Geographical Information System (GIS) is any system that captures, stores, analyzes, manages, and presents data that is linked to location. As stated in [GIS], a GIS is a system that includes mapping software with applications to remote sensing, land surveying, aerial photography, mathematics, photogrammetry, and geography. GIS can be regarded to be the integrating of cartography and database technology. Therefore, the challenges include representing spatial data (e.g., maps) as well as storing and querying such data.

Geospatial data management has gained prominence mainly due to the activities of OGC (Open Geospatial Consortium). In addition to developing GML (Geospatial Markup Language) which is essentially XML for geospatial data, OGC is also involved with specifying standards for representing, storing, and managing geospatial data. Many of the challenges we have described for multimedia data systems (which manage a combination of text, voice, video, and audio data) are applicable to geospatial systems. Other complex data include sensor data. Technologies such as SensorML are being developed for representing sensor data.

4.3 Information Management

We include data warehouse and data mining as part of information management as these systems extract some nuggets from the raw data possibly stored in databases. We also discuss information retrieval and digital libraries under information management.

4.3.1 Data Warehousing and Data Mining

Data warehousing is one of the key data management technologies to support data mining and data analysis. As stated by Inman [INMO93], data warehouses are subject-oriented. Their design depends to a great extent on the application utilizing them. They integrate diverse and possibly heterogeneous data sources. They are persistent. That is, the warehouses are very much like databases. They vary with time. This is because as the data sources from which the warehouse is built get updated, the changes have to be reflected in the warehouse. Essentially, data warehouses provide support for decision support functions of an enterprise or an organization. For example, while the data sources may have the raw data, the data warehouse may have correlated data, summary reports, and aggregate functions applied to the raw data.

Figure 4.5 illustrates a data warehouse. The data sources are managed by database systems A, B, and C. The information in these databases is merged and put into a warehouse. With a data warehouse, data may often be viewed differently by different applications. That is, the data are multidimensional. For example, the payroll department may want data to be in a certain format while the project department may want data to be in a different format. The warehouse must provide support for such multidimensional data.

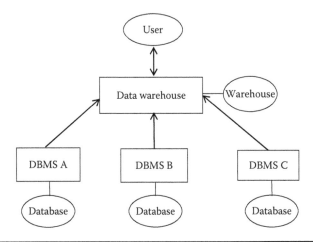

Figure 4.5   Data warehouse.

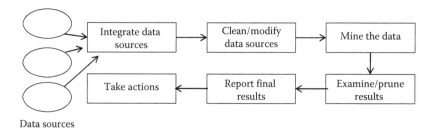

Figure 4.6 Steps to data mining.

Data mining is the process of posing various queries and extracting useful information, patterns, and trends often previously unknown from large quantities of data possibly stored in databases. Essentially for many organizations, the goals of data mining include improving marketing capabilities, detecting abnormal patterns, and predicting the future based on past experiences and current trends.

Some of the data mining techniques include those based on statistical reasoning techniques, inductive logic programming, machine learning, fuzzy sets, and neural networks, among others. The data mining outcomes include classification (finding rules to partition data into groups), association (finding rules to make associations between data), and sequencing (finding rules to order data). Essentially one arrives at some hypothesis, which is the information extracted, from examples and patterns observed. These patterns are observed from posing a series of queries; each query may depend on the responses obtained to the previous queries posed. There have been several developments in data mining. A discussion of the various tools is given in [KDN]. A good discussion of the outcomes and techniques are given in [BERR97]. Figure 4.6 illustrates the data mining process. Since we have used data mining techniques for many of our cloud applications such as malware detection and insider threat detection, we will provide an overview of data mining in Appendix B.

4.3.2 Information Retrieval

Information retrieval systems essentially provide support for managing documents. The functions include document retrieval, document update, and document storage management among others. These systems are essentially DBMSs for managing documents. There are various types of information retrieval systems and they include text retrieval systems, image retrieval systems, and audio and video retrieval systems. Figure 4.7 illustrates a general purpose information retrieval system that may be utilized for text retrieval, image retrieval, audio retrieval, and video retrieval. Such architecture can also be utilized for a multimedia data management system. Special features of each type of information retrieval system are discussed in [THUR01].

Figure 4.7   Information retrieval system.

Information retrieval systems include Text Retrieval, Image Retrieval, Video Retrieval, and Audio Retrieval [IEEE03]. For example, text retrieval system is essentially a DBMS for handling text data. Text data could be documents such as books, journals, magazines, and so on. One needs a good data model for document representation. A considerable amount of work has gone into developing semantic data models and object models for document management. For example, a document could have paragraphs and a paragraph could have sections, etc. Querying documents could be based on many factors. One could specify keywords and request the documents with the keywords to be retrieved. One could also retrieve documents that have some relationships with one another. Recent research on information retrieval is focusing on querying documents based on semantics. For example, "retrieve documents that describe scenic views" or "retrieve documents that are useful to children under ten years" are types of such queries.

Examples of information retrieval systems are digital libraries. Digital libraries gained prominence with the initial effort by the National Science Foundation (NSF), Defense Advanced Research Projects Agency (DARPA), and National Aeronautical and Space Administration (NASA). NSF continued to fund special projects in this area and as a result, the field has grown very rapidly. The idea behind digital libraries is to digitize all types of documents and provide efficient access to these digitized documents.

Several technologies have to work together to make digital libraries a reality. These include web data management, markup languages, search engines, and question answering systems. In addition, multimedia information management as well as information retrieval systems play an important role. This section will review the various developments in some of the digital libraries technologies. Figure 4.8 illustrates an example of a digital library system.

4.3.3 Search Engines

Since the early 1990s, numerous search engines have been developed. They have origins in the information retrieval systems developed in the 1960s and beyond.

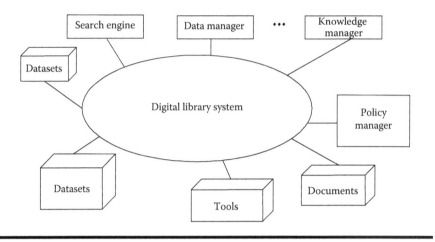

Figure 4.8 Digital library system.

Typically when we invoke a browser such as Netscape or Microsoft's Internet Explorer, we have access to several search engines. Some of the early search engines were AltaVista, Yahoo, Info seek, and Lycos. These systems were around in 1995 and were fairly effective for their times. They are much improved now. Since around 1999, one of the popular search engines has been Google. It started off as a Stanford University research project funded by organizations like the NSF and the Central Intelligence Agency as well as the industry, and was later commercialized. Systems such as Google as well as some of the other search engines provide intelligent searches. However, they still have a long way to go before users can get exact answers to their queries.

Search engines are accessed via browsers. When you click on the search engines, you will get a window requesting what you want to search for. Then you list the keywords for the information you are looking. The search engine will then list the links to the web pages. The question is how does a search engine find the web pages? It essentially uses information retrieval on the web.

The rating of a search engine is determined by the speed in which it produces results, and more importantly the accuracy in which it produces the results. That is, does the search engine list the relevant web pages for the query? For example, when you type a query called "lung cancer," does it provide the relevant information you are looking for with respect to lung cancer? It can, for example, list resources about lung cancer or list information about who has had lung cancer. Usually people want to get resources about lung cancer. If they want to find out who has lung cancer, then they could type in "people with lung cancer."

The problem with many searches, although extremely useful, is that they often provide a lot of irrelevant information. To get accurate results, they have to build sophisticated indexing techniques. They also may cache information from web servers for frequently posed queries. The search engines have a directory about the various web servers they have to search. This directory is updated as new servers enter. Then the search engines build indices for the various keywords. When a user poses a query, the search engine will consult its knowledge base, which consists of information about the web servers and various indices; it also examines the caches if it has any, and will then search the web servers for the information. All this has to be carried out in real-time.

Web mining enables one to mine the user log and build profiles for the various users so that search can be made more efficient. Note that there are millions of users and building profiles is not straightforward. We need to mine the web logs and find out what the preferences of the users are. Then we list those web pages for the user. Furthermore, if a user is searching for some information, from time to time the search engines can list web pages that could be relevant to the user's request. That is, search engines will have to dynamically carry out searches depending on what the user wants.

4.4 Knowledge Management

Knowledge management is the process of using knowledge as a resource to manage an organization. It could mean sharing expertise, developing a learning organization, teaching the staff, learning from experiences, as well as collaboration. Essentially knowledge management will include data management and information management. However, this is not a view shared by everyone. Various definitions of knowledge management have been proposed. Knowledge management is a discipline invented mainly by business schools. The concepts have been around for a long time. But the word knowledge management was coined as a result of information technology (IT) and the web.

In the collection of papers on knowledge management by Morey et al. [MORE01], knowledge management is divided into three areas. These are strategies such as building a knowledge company and making the staff knowledge workers, processes (such as techniques) for knowledge management including developing a method to share documents and tools, and metrics that measure the effectiveness of knowledge management. In the *Harvard Business Review* on knowledge management, there is an excellent collection of articles describing a knowledge-creating company, building a learning organization, and teaching people how to learn [HARV96]. Organizational behavior and team dynamics play major roles in knowledge management.

Knowledge management technologies consist of several information management technologies including knowledge representation and knowledge base management systems. Other knowledge management technologies include collaboration tools, tools for organizing information on the web as well as tools for measuring the effectiveness of the knowledge gained such as collecting various metrics. Knowledge management technologies essentially include data management and information management technologies as well as decision support technologies.

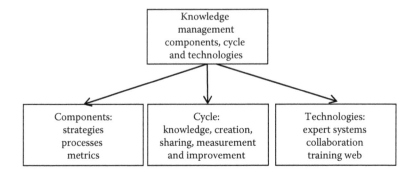

Figure 4.9 Knowledge management components and technologies.

Figure 4.9 illustrates some of the knowledge management components and technologies. It also lists the aspects of knowledge management cycle. Web technologies play a major role in knowledge management. Knowledge management and the web are closely related. While knowledge management practices have existed for many years, it is the web that has promoted knowledge management.

Many corporations now have Intranets which are the single most powerful knowledge management tool. Thousands of employees are connected through the web in an organization. Large corporations have sites all over the world and the employees are becoming well-connected with one another. Email can be regarded to be one of the early knowledge management tools. Now there are many tools such as search engines and e-commerce tools.

With the proliferation of web data management and e-commerce tools, knowledge management will become an essential part of the web and e-commerce. A collection of papers on knowledge management experiences including strategies, processes, and metrics is given in [MORE01]. Collaborative knowledge management is discussed in [THUR02b].

4.5 Activity Management

Activities include e-business, information integration, and information sharing, and supply chain management. We discuss these activities in this section. In Part II, we will describe how web services may be invoked to carry out these activities. In Parts III and IV, we will discuss how cloud services may be invoked to carry out these activities.

4.5.1 E-Business and E-Commerce

Various models, architectures, and technologies are being developed. Business-to-business e-commerce is all about two businesses conducting transactions on the web. We give some examples. Suppose corporation A is an automobile manufacturer and needs microprocessors to be installed in its automobiles. It will then purchase the microprocessors from corporation B who manufactures the microprocessors. Another example is when an individual purchases some goods such as toys from a toy manufacturer. This manufacturer then contacts a packaging company via the web to deliver the toys to the individual. The transaction between the manufacturer and the packaging company is a business-to-business transaction. Business-to-business e-commerce also involves one business purchasing a unit of another business or two businesses merging. The main point is that such transactions have to be carried out on the web. Business-to-consumer e-commerce is when a consumer such as a member of the mass population makes purchases on the web. In the toy manufacturer example, the purchase between the individual and the toy manufacturer is a business-to-consumer transaction.

The modules of the e-commerce server may include modules for managing the data and web pages, mining customer information, security enforcement, as well as transaction management. E-commerce client functions may include presentation management, user interface as well as caching data and hosting browsers. There could also be a middle tier, which may implement the business objects to carry out the business functions of e-commerce. These business functions may include brokering, mediation, negotiations, purchasing, sales, marketing, and other e-commerce functions. The e-commerce server functions are impacted by the information management technologies for the web. In addition to the data management functions and the business functions, the e-commerce functions also include those for managing distribution, heterogeneity, and federations.

E-commerce also includes nontechnological aspects such as policies, laws, social impacts, and psychological impacts. We are now doing business in an entirely different way and therefore we need a paradigm shift. We cannot carry out successful e-commerce if we still want the traditional way of buying and selling products. We have to be more efficient and rely on the emerging technologies such as web

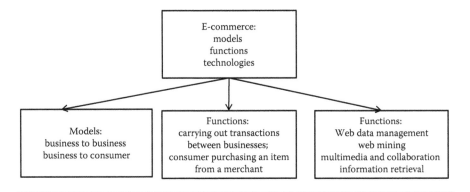

Figure 4.10   E-business components.

services and cloud computing to gain a competitive edge. This is because with cloud computing one can obtain scalable solutions for e-commerce. Some key-points for e-commerce are illustrated in Figure 4.10.

4.5.2 Collaboration and Workflow

Although the notion of computer-supported cooperative work (CSCW) was first proposed in the early 1980s, it was only in the 1990s that much interest was shown on this topic. Collaborative computing enables people, groups of individuals, and organizations to work together with one another to accomplish a task or a collection of tasks. These tasks could vary from participating in conferences, solving a specific problem, or working on the design of a system (see [ACM91]).

One aspect of collaborative computing of particular interest to the database community is workflow computing. Workflow is defined as the automation of a series of functions that comprise a business process such as data entry, data review, and monitoring performed by one or more people. An example of a process that is well-suited for workflow automation is the purchasing process. Some early commercial workflow system products targeted for office environments were based on a messaging architecture. This architecture supports the distributed nature of current work teams. However, the messaging architecture is usually file-based and lacks many of the features supported by DBMSs such as data representation, consistency management, tracking, and monitoring. The emerging workflow systems utilize data management capabilities.

Figure 4.11 illustrates an example where teams A and B are working on a geographical problem such as analyzing and predicting the weather in North America. The two teams must have a global picture of the map as well as any notes that go with it. Any changes made by one team should be instantly visible to the other team and both teams communicate as if they were in the same room.

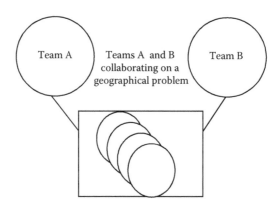

Figure 4.11 Collaborative computing system.

To enable such transparent communication, data management support is needed. One could utilize a DBMS to manage the data or some type of data manager that provides some of the essential features such as data integrity, concurrent access, and retrieval capabilities. In the above example, the database may consist of information describing the problem the teams are working on, the data that is involved, history data, as well as the metadata information. The data manager must provide appropriate concurrency control features so that when both teams simultaneously access the common picture and make changes, these changes are coordinated.

The web has increased the need for collaboration even further. Users now share documents on the web and work on papers and designs on the web. Corporate information infrastructures promote collaboration and sharing of information and documents. Therefore, the collaborative tools have to work effectively on the web [IEEE99]. As stated in Chapter 5, various web services standards have emerged for collaboration and workflow. Such services are now being offered by the cloud.

4.5.3 Information Integration

Figure 4.12 illustrates an example of interoperability between heterogeneous database systems or information sources. The goal is to provide transparent access, both for users and application programs, for querying and executing transactions (see, e.g., [WIED92]). Note that in a heterogeneous environment, the local DBMSs may be heterogeneous. Furthermore, the modules of the distributed processor (discussed

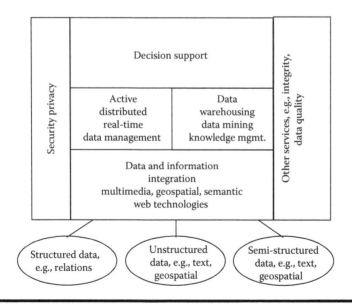

Figure 4.12   Information integration.

in Section 4.2.2) have both local DBMS specific processing as well as local DBMS independent processing. We call such a distributed processor a heterogeneous distributed processor (HDP). There are several technical issues that need to be resolved for the successful interoperation between these diverse database systems. Note that heterogeneity could exist with respect to different data models, schemas, query processing techniques, query languages, transaction management techniques, semantics, integrity, and security.

Some of the nodes in a heterogeneous database environment may form a federation. Such an environment is classified as federated data mainsheet environment. As stated by Sheth and Larson [SHET90], a federated database system is a collection of cooperating but autonomous database systems belonging to a federation. That is, the goal is for the DBMSs, which belong to a federation, to cooperate with one another and yet maintain some degree of autonomy. Web services for information integration will be discussed in Chapter 7. We will discuss an experimental secure cloud-based information integration system in Part VI.

4.5.4 Information Sharing

The 9/11 commission report has encouraged organizations to move from a need to know to a need to share paradigm. Information sharing is important not only for the defense and intelligence organizations but also for healthcare organizations. For example, in an emergency situation (e.g., accident), patient data may have to be released so that the most appropriate care can be provided to the patient. During normal operations, the patient data may have to be relayed only if the patient has authorized to do so.

Information sharing adds complexity with respect to security and privacy. Organizations have to enforce appropriate security and privacy policies so that only appropriate data are shared. Furthermore, organizations should also enforce policies to determine the actions to be taken in emergency situations. Another important aspect of information sharing is managing trust. For example, do organizations in a coalition trust one another? Should an organization share information with another organization that it does not trust? Are there different levels of trust?

Perhaps the most important aspect of information sharing is providing incentives for sharing. Even if there are policies conducive to information sharing, why should organizations share information when it has no incentives? Furthermore, what are the incentives? Should they be monetary or should they be recognition awards, or provide the tools for an organization to effectively carry out its functions?

We are conducting extensive research on information sharing under a MURI (Multi-Disciplinary University Research Initiative) project funded by AFOSR (Air Force Office of Scientific Research). For more details we refer to [FINI09]. Figure 4.13 illustrates a scenario for information sharing. Our main focus is on applying policies for information sharing as well as determining the incentives for sharing. The requests for information between the coalition organizations may be

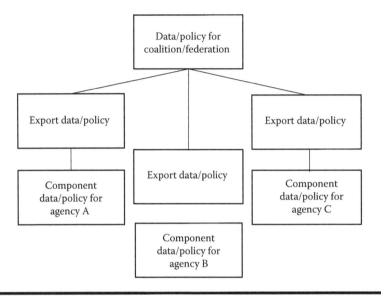

Figure 4.13   Information sharing.

implemented as web service client requests while the servers that respond to the requests may be implemented as web services. Furthermore, semantic web technologies may also be utilized as the data may be represented as XML or RDF and ontologies may be utilized for understanding the various concepts for information sharing. We will discuss cloud-based assured information-sharing prototype systems that we have developed in Part VII. We also provide an overview of assured information sharing in Appendix D.

4.5.5 Social Networking

An activity that is receiving much attention is social networking. The idea is to study how networks are formed. These networks may be friendship networks, terror networks, transportation networks, communication networks, and human networks. These networks are often referred to by the name social networks. The technologies that are utilized to develop and manage the social networks are graph theory-based techniques, data mining techniques to extract social networks from the behavior of the individuals as well as to mine the existing networks to determine patterns, and visualization techniques to visualize the activities of the members of a network.

Social networks are formed by analyzing/mining the data on the web or otherwise and determining the links between the data. Essentially this amounts to forming nodes and links. Once the network is constructed, it continually evolves as new members enter the world. Furthermore, these networks are also analyzed/mined to extract nuggets that will feed into the network. Figure 4.14 illustrates this process. Cloud-based experimental social network systems are discussed in Part IV.

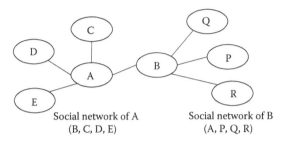

Social network of A   Social network of B
(B, C, D, E)   (A, P, Q, R)

Figure 4.14   Social networking.

4.5.6 Supply Chain Management

The final activity that we will consider in our discussion is supply chain management. Organizations cannot function by themselves. They need other organizations from which they can purchase parts or supply parts to. For example, consider a company that makes automobiles. Such a company would need to get supplies from other companies, including electronic devices, engines, and other parts that are needed to manufacture an automobile. Its supplier could get its parts from other suppliers. Suppose a supplier provides a GPS (Global Positioning System) system for the automobile. This supplier will get its parts (e.g., chips, processors) from other companies. The challenge is for the organizations to form partnerships so that the benefits can be maximized. One does not want redundant parts. The parts have to arrive at the right time to the right place.

ITs play a major role in supply chain management. Database systems are used to keep track of all the parts and where they came from. Data mining techniques may be used to analyze the data and determine the suppliers to select. Information-sharing techniques are needed for the partners in a supply chain to share information and maximize their benefits. Information integration techniques are used for disparate databases from multiple supplies to be integrated so

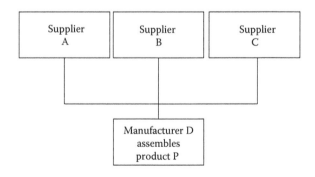

Figure 4.15   Supply chain management.

that a common picture is presented to the customer. Figure 4.15 illustrates supply chain management. Web services for supply chain management will be discussed in Chapter 7.

4.6 Summary and Directions

In this chapter, we discussed aspects of data, information and knowledge management. First, we discussed data management and complex data management. Then we discussed information management and knowledge management. In particular, we discussed data models, database systems, multimedia and geospatial data management, data warehousing, data mining, information retrieval, e-commerce, and information sharing. Cloud computing and secure cloud computing concepts that are based on the technologies we have discussed in this chapter are given in Parts III and V. In Parts IV, VI, and VII, we will discuss some of the experimental cloud computing and secure cloud computing systems that we have developed for data, information, and knowledge and activity management.

One of the major challenges in data, information and knowledge management is Big Data Management and Analytics. While 20 years ago big data was considered to be petabytes of data, today it is exabytes of data and beyond. That is, big data are data that cannot be handled with current technologies. We need techniques for modeling big data, querying big data, analyzing big data, and visualizing big data. Owing to the fact that there are large amounts of data such as massive graph structures representing social networks that have to be represented, analyzed, and visualized, we need technologies for managing such big data. Cloud computing is an essential tool for managing big data. Therefore, much of the discussion in the ensuing entire book is relevant to big data management and analytics.

References

[ACM91] *Communications of the ACM, Special Issue in Computer Supported Cooperative Work (CSCW)*, 34(12), December 1991.

[BERR97], Berry, M. and G. Linoff, *Data Mining Techniques*, Wiley, Hoboken, NJ, 1997.

[CERI84] Ceri, S. and G. Pelagatti, *Distributed Databases, Principles and Systems*, McGraw-Hill, New York, 1984.

[CODD70] Codd, E. F., A relational model of data for large shared data banks, *Communications of the ACM*, 13, 6, 1970.

[DATE90] Date, C., *An Introduction to Database Systems*, Addison-Wesley, Reading, MA 1990.

[FINI09] Finin, T. et al., Assured information sharing lifecyle, *Proceedings Intelligence and Security Informatics Conference*, Dallas, TX, June 2009.

[GIS] Geospatial Information Systems, http://en.wikipedia.org/wiki/Geographic_information_system

[HARV96] Knowledge management. *Harvard Business Review*, 1996.

[IEEE99] *IEEE Computer, Special Issue in Collaborative Computing Systems*, September 1999.

[IEEE03] Special Issue. *IEEE Compute*, 36(2), January 2003.

[INMO93] Inmon, W., *Building a Data Warehouse*, Wiley, Hoboken, NJ, 1993.

[KDN] KDnuggets, http://www.kdnuggets.com

[MORE01] Morey, D., M. Maybury and B. Thuraisingham (Eds), *Knowledge Management*, MIT Press, Cambridge, MA, 2001.

[SHET90] Sheth, A. and J. Larson, Federated database systems for managing distributed, heterogeneous, and autonomous databases. *ACM Computing Surveys*, 22(3), 183–236, 1990.

[SQL3] SQL3, American National Standards Institute, Draft, 1992.

[THUR97] Thuraisingham, B., *Data Management Systems Evolution and Interoperation*, CRC Press, Boca Raton, FL, 1997.

[THUR00] Thuraisingham, B., *Web Data Management and Electronic Commerce*, CRC Press, Boca Raton, FL, 2000.

[THUR01] Thuraisingham, B., *Managing and Mining Multimedia Databases for the Electronic Enterprise*, CRC Press, Boca Raton, FL, 2001.

[THUR02a] Thuraisingham, B., *XML, Databases and the Semantic Web*, CRC Press, Boca Raton, FL, 2001.

[THUR02b] Thuraisingham, B. et al., Collaborative commerce and knowledge management. *Knowledge and Process Management*, 9(1), 43–53, 2002.

[ULLM88] Ullman, J., *Principles of Database and Knowledge Base Systems*, Computer Science Press, New York, NY.

[WIED92] Wiederhold, G., Mediators in the architecture of future information systems. *IEEE Computer*, 25(3), 38–49, 1992.

Conclusion to Part I

Part I provided an overview of the supporting technologies for the cloud. In particular, we discussed the evolution of computing, security technologies, and data, information and knowledge management. We selected these technologies as they are relevant to the concepts, technologies, products, and experimental systems discussed in this book.

Chapter 2 provided a brief overview of the evolution of computing. We discussed the work of the mathematical logicians, the von Neumann machines, and the evolution of computers from the mainframe to the personal computers. Finally, we provided an overview of distributed computing, services computing WWW, and cloud computing.

Chapter 3 provided a brief overview of the developments in trustworthy systems. We first discussed secure systems including basic concepts in access control as well as discretionary and mandatory policies, types of secure systems such as secure operating systems, secure databases, secure networks, and emerging technologies, the impact of the web and the steps to building secure systems. Next, we discussed dependable systems including aspects of trust, privacy, integrity, quality, and real-time processing. Then, we focused more in detail on aspects of security threats and solutions. Finally, we provided an overview of securing systems with untrusted components.

Chapter 4 discussed aspects of data, information and knowledge management. First, we discussed data management and complex data management. Then, we discussed information management and knowledge management. In particular, we discussed data models, database systems, multimedia and geospatial data management, data warehousing, data mining, information retrieval, e-commerce, and information sharing.

SECURE SERVICES TECHNOLOGIES

Introduction to Part II

Web services are at the heart of cloud computing. This is because a cloud offers various services such as infrastructure services, platform services, and application services to the consumer. We will therefore discuss both service technologies as well as security issues for services in Part II.

Part II consists of three chapters: 5, 6, and 7. Chapter 5 discusses web services and secure web services. In particular, we first discuss what is meant by services. Next, we discuss high-level concepts in service-oriented computing. Realizing service-oriented information systems through SOA and web services is discussed next. We also discuss security issues for services. Chapter 6 discusses semantic web services since several of our prototypes for the cloud utilize semantic web technologies. Specialized secure web services such as data management services are the subject of Chapter 7.

Chapter 5

Service-Oriented Computing and Security

5.1 Overview

As stated in Chapter 1, computing paradigms have evolved over the last six decades. In the beginning, computers were used for numerical processing. Later they were used to store and manage data in databases where the world was viewed as a collection of tables. Then the migration was to object-oriented computing where the world was viewed as a collection of objects. Not only were the databases viewed as a collection of objects, objects were also the main unit of computation. More recently, the world has evolved into a collection of services. Essentially a consumer requests a service from a service provider. The service provider and the consumer draw up a contract, the service is provided and the consumer pays for the service. Services could be healthcare services, financial services, or telecommunication services. This has resulted in what has come to be known as service-oriented computing or as services computing (see also [ZHAN07] and [ERL05]). In other words, service-oriented computing views the world as a collection of services. These services are produced by the service provider and utilized by the service consumer. Furthermore, services have become the heart and soul of cloud computing since cloud computing provides a collection of services to the clients.

Security for service-oriented computing has become a critical issue. For example, consider the process of ordering a book from an agency. We go to the catalog published by the agency. The agency has to ensure that we are authorized to read the information about the books (i.e., the metadata). We place the order. The agency will then determine which part of the book we can read, if any. The appropriate parts of the book are then released to us (the consumer). Now, this secure service can be implemented in software as follows. The customer checks the website of the agency and finds the book and places the order. The website will only display the books the customer is authorized to see. The secure order management service implemented by the agency takes the order, sends a message to the warehouse service and requests the book. The warehouse service then finds that the book is in its inventory and sends a message to the order management service. The warehouse is where they would invoke the security service and then send the appropriate parts of the book to the shipping service. The shipping service then ships the book to the customer. If the book has to be displayed electronically, then appropriate parts of the book may be displayed through the order management service. So there is a composition of secure services starting from the order management service, the warehouse service, and the shipping service. These three services provide the customer with what he wants. All these services have to enforce appropriate security controls. In implementing the secure services, we need to enforce activation, access control, trust management, and privacy control. In addition, the documents that the customer gets must be authentic which means integrity has to be maintained.

Services computing is fundamental to cloud computing where the infrastructure, platform, and software are provided as services by the cloud. Therefore, in this chapter we discuss services-oriented computing and the surrounding security issues since they are essential for secure cloud computing. In Section 5.2, we will provide an overview of service-oriented computing. The key aspects of services computing are SOAs, web services (WS), and SOAD. In Section 5.3, we will discuss security issues for services computing. The security issues to be discussed include access control and identity management and some of the emerging WS security standards as well as security models. Figure 5.1 illustrates the concepts in this chapter. The concepts, technologies, standards, and protocols discussed in this chapter are being utilized to provide cloud services and secure cloud services. Such cloud services will be discussed in Parts IV and VI of this book.

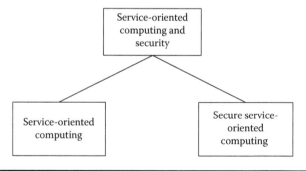

Figure 5.1 Service-oriented computing and security.

5.2 Service-Oriented Computing

5.2.1 Services Paradigm

To best illustrate the notion of a service, we will use the example of telecommunication. We wish to use a telephone service. We then sign up with a service provider which could be AT&T or Sprint or some other service provider. We know about them through the yellow pages or some advertisement in the newspaper. We can discuss with them and negotiate for the best service. Once we decide on the service provider, then a contract is produced by the service provider. Once we sign the contract, we can then use the service provider's telephone lines for telephone communication with our friends, relatives, and business associates. Similarly for an email service, the service provider will publish its services, in this case either in the yellow pages or on the web. We contact the service provider, sign a contract, and then use the email service provided by the service provider. In both cases, the service provider will publish its services in some language that we understand. We contact the service provider, draw up a contract, and then utilize the service.

We are using numerous services in a typical day which include not only the telephone service and the email service but also the healthcare service and the financial service. With the healthcare service provider, we get consultation about our health; our financial service provider manages our money for us and even our pastor provides us with a service such as religious service. One can also provide data and software as services. In the case of data, the various data centers store lots of data and allow consumers to use the data for various purposes. In the case of software, some software companies develop software for customer relationship management and healthcare management and allow consumers to use their software as a service.

Service-oriented computing is essential to implementing the services as software. Another example is purchasing an airline ticket. The customer will call the airline reservation system, talk to the agent, and the agent books the seat and sends the ticket to the customer. With service-oriented computing, the customer will book the reservation online; the reservation service will then find a seat and assign the seat to the customer. This service can ask the customer if he wants a hotel reservation and automatically sends a message to the hotel reservation service and books a hotel room for the customer. Then the service sends a message to the car rental service for a booking and finally sends a message to the customer. Here again the airline reservation service, the hotel reservation service and the rental car booking services are comprised into a single service. That is, multiple services are composed into a single service. Figure 5.2 illustrates the example of a travel service.

Note that while the unit of computation in object-oriented computing is that of an object, one could regard the unit of computing for service-oriented computing

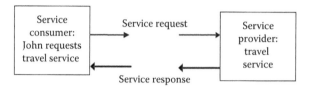

Figure 5.2 Service-oriented computing example.

to be a service. However, the actual implementation of services could be carried out using packages or even objects. We believe that service-oriented computing is still in its infancy and at the conceptual stage. As we make more progress in this field, an appropriate programming language for service-oriented computing may be developed. Note that at present, most of the applications in service-oriented computing are web-based applications especially relating to e-business.

5.2.1.1 SOAs and Web Services

SOA is the architecture of the system that implements the services with software technology. In this architecture, there are three major components: the service consumer, the service provider, and the service directory. The service publisher publishes its service in a standard language with the service directory. The service consumer requests the directory to find the service. The directory gives the name and/or address of the service provider to the service consumer. The service consumer then contacts the service provider. Much of the software on services is implemented with web technology. Therefore, the service technology that implements SOA is called WS. The service provider published its service (i.e., the web service) on a web-based directory. The service consumer queries this directory which then guides the consumer to the service provider. The web-based directory is called UDDI (Universal Description, Discovery, and Integration). The language used to publish the service is called WSDL (Web Services Description Language). The messages exchanged between the three components use a protocol called SOAP. These messages are communicated in XML. Figure 5.3 illustrates the implementation of SOA with WS.

5.2.1.2 SOA and Design

Note that with object-oriented information systems, one needs to first identify the objects, the object classes, the methods, and the relationship between the objects. In addition, the activities are also analyzed and incorporated into the design of the system. Such an approach has come to be known as object-oriented analysis and design (OOAD) and UML is now the standard OOAD approach. Once the system is designed, then an appropriate object language may be selected for the implementation. Similarly, before we design a service-oriented information system, we need

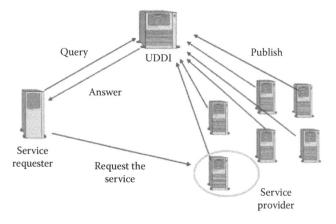

Figure 5.3 SOA and web services.

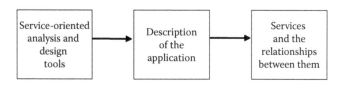

Figure 5.4 Service-oriented analysis and design.

to determine the services, how they are composed, how they are involved as well as the relationship between services. Such an approach has come to be known as service-oriented analysis and design (SOAD).

While OOAD is mature, SOAD is in its infancy. Before we design an information system to implement airline reservations, we need to determine what the services are. The services may include reserve-airline-seat, reserve-hotel-room, and reserve-rental car. Next, the relationships between the services are analyzed. Here one could invoke reserve-hotel-room from reserve-airline-seat and invoke reserve-rental-car, or also reserve-airline-seat. The two services may be invoked in parallel or sequentially. Once the services and the relationships are designed, then service descriptions are specified. Figure 5.4 illustrates the application of SOAD to service-oriented information systems design.

Realizing services through WS and SOAs is discussed in Section 5.2.2. SOAD is discussed in Section 5.2.3.

5.2.2 SOA and Web Services

In Section 5.2.1, we introduced the notion of services computing (also known as service-oriented computing) and discussed the various aspects of services computing. In this section, we will describe service computing through SOA and WS. SOA is the architecture that implements service-oriented computing. WS is one way to realize service-oriented computing through the WWW. The most popular implementation of service-oriented computing is through SOA and WS. WS is defined by the various standards that are emerging from organizations such as W3C (World Wide Web Consortium) and OASIS.

In this section, we will survey the Standards organizations that are defining WS and then describe the SOA paradigm, the protocol stack for WS and an alternative way to implement WS which is Restful WS. Next, a popular web service technology that resulted in more or less the first cloud implementation, the Amazon web service [AMAZON], is discussed. Finally the various specialized services that are key to cloud computing will be discussed. We give several references throughout this section. These references are essentially various URLs (Universal Resource Locator) that describe the standards that are evolving. As we stress throughout this book, WS technology is evolving very rapidly. Therefore, the discussions in this book could soon be outdated. We urge the reader to keep up with the developments of standards organization such as OASIS and W3C. This is one of the main reasons we have not delved into the details of the standards. Our goal is to introduce the various concepts at a higher level.

Two major standards organizations for SOA and WS are W3C and OASIS. W3C has developed standards for XML as well as secure XML, including XML encryption and XML signature. In addition, W3C has also developed standards for semantic web, RDF, OWL, SWRL, and many others. OASIS has developed standards for authentication and authorization for WS including SAML (Security Assertions Markup Language) and XACML (eXtensible Access Control Markup Language). In addition, WS-Security as well as WS-* Security Framework are major security standards developed by OASIS [OASIS].

Another key standards organization is WS-I (web services interoperability). Although WS-I does not specify standards, they oversee the standards that are being developed. Another consortium relevant to secure WS is Liberty Alliance. This consortium has proposed standards for identity management. Organizations such as the Object Management Group as well as Open Geospatial Consortium have also developed web service-related standards. Figure 5.5 illustrates the various standards relevant to SOA and WS.

W3C: World Wide Web Consortium
OGC: Open Geospatial Consortium
OASIS: Organization for the Advancement
     of Structured Information Standards

Figure 5.5 Standards organizations for services.

As stated in [OASIS], WS refers, to the technologies that allow for making connections. Services are what you connect together using WS. Examples of WS are query service and directory service. A service is the endpoint of a connection. Also, a service has some type of underlying computer system that supports the connection offered. The combination of services, internal and external to an organization, makes up an SOA.

An SOA supports a collection of services [ERL05]. These services communicate with each other. The communication can involve either simple data passing or it could involve two or more services coordinating some activity such as planning travel. Some means of connecting services to each other is needed. SOAs are not new. The first SOA can be considered to be DCOM (distributed component object model) and Object Request Brokers (ORBs) based on the CORBA (common object request architecture) specification [OMG]. If an SOA is to be effective, we need a clear understanding of the term service. A service is a function that is well-defined and self-contained, and does not depend on the context or state of other services.

SOA has three major components: a service provider, a service consumer, and a directory. The service provider publishes its service on the directory. The service consumer requests the directory for a service. The directory sends back the name and address of the service. The consumer then sends the request to the service provider and obtains the service. Now, WS are the most popular way to date which implements the SOA paradigm. Next, we will discuss the specific technologies and specifications for SOA with WS.

5.2.2.1 WS Model

The early web models were based on the client–server paradigm where the web client accesses a web server through the HTTP (Hypertext Transfer Protocol). The web server would typically store web pages that the client would request for retrieval. This model, while sufficient for displaying web pages, is not sufficient for conducting e-business activities on the web. With e-business, multiple corporations have to work together to carry out a common goal. In such an environment there may be asynchronous communication between the multiple organizations and each organization may provide a service to another organization. We need a more powerful mechanism to conduct e-business activities.

In the late 1990s and early 2000, we saw both of the second generation of web technologies that went beyond the display of web pages and consumers purchasing items on the web. Around the same time, the notion of service-oriented computing was born and the technologies for e-business and service-oriented computing merged. This resulted in the invention of WS.

The technology of WS is the most likely connection technology of SOAs. WS essentially use XML technology to create a robust connection. A service consumer sends a service request message to a service provider. The service provider returns a response message to the service consumer. The request and subsequent response connections are defined in some way that is understandable to both the service consumer and service provider. A service provider can also be a service consumer. The WSDL forms the basis for WS. WSDL uses XML to define messages. The steps involved in providing and consuming a service are

- A service provider describes its service using WSDL. This definition is published to a directory of services. The directory could use UDDI. Other forms of directories can also be used.
- A service consumer issues one or more queries to the directory to locate a service and determines how to communicate with that service.
- Part of the WSDL provided by the service provider is passed to the service consumer. This tells the service consumer what the requests and responses are for the service provider.
- The service consumer uses the WSDL to send a request to the service provider.
- The service provider provides the expected response to the service consumer.

The UDDI registry is intended to eventually serve as a means of "discovering" WS described using WSDL. The idea is that the UDDI registry can be searched in various ways to obtain contact information and the WS available for various organizations. UDDI registry is a way to keep up-to-date on the WS your organization currently uses. Alternative to UDDI is ebXML Directory. All the messages are sent using SOAP. (SOAP at one time stood for Simple Object Access Protocol; now, the letters in the acronym have no particular meaning.) SOAP essentially provides the envelope for sending the WS messages. SOAP generally uses HTTP, but other means of connection may be used. Security and authorization are important topics with WS.

5.2.2.2 Composition of WS

WS can be composed of multiple WS. For example, a customer may request a trip from a travel service. The travel service will then invoke three services: flight service, hotel service, and car rental service. WSDL will specify these services and register them with UDDI. However, we need a language to specify the flow of the services. The language that has been developed for this purpose is Business Process Execution Language (BPEL). The specific BPEL that is commonly used is the one proposed by IBM and Microsoft and is called BPEL4WS (BPEL for WS).

Now to book the flight, hotel, and car, the order is not important. Therefore, BPEL statements will be specified in XML and will issue requests to make flight reservations, hotel reservations, and car rental reservations. The WSDL for each of these services will then specify the actions of carrying out the services. Now, if the order of booking the flight is most important, then BPEL has constructs to specify the order of the invocation of the services. For more details of BPEL, we refer the reader to [SRIV]. Figure 5.6 illustrates the composition of WS.

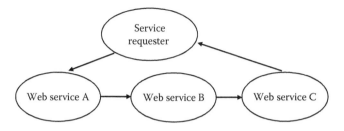

Figure 5.6 Composition of web services.

5.2.2.3 WS Protocols

WS are defined through a protocol stack. This stack includes specifications for Metadata, Messaging, Transactions and Business Processes, Portal and Presentation, Security, Management, and Business Domains. We will focus on some of the layers of the protocol stack. They are: Metadata, Messaging and Transactions, and Business Processes. Figure 5.7 illustrates the protocol stack.

The Metadata protocols include those for Metadata Retrieval (WS-Metadata Exchange), Data Service, and Message Description [WSDL], Policy (WS-Policy, WS-Policy Assertions) and Publication and Discovery [UDDI], [WSIL]. In Section 5.2.2.1, we discussed WSDL and UDDI. WS-Metadata Exchange essentially specifies the metadata that other endpoints need to know to access the web service. As stated in [META], "To bootstrap communication with web services this specification defines how metadata can be treated as resources for retrieval purposes, how metadata can be embedded in web service endpoint references, and how web service endpoints can optionally support a request-response interaction for the retrieval of metadata." WS-Policy provides a policy framework for specifying various policies and policy alternatives. As stated in [POLICY], "WS-Policy provides a flexible and extensible grammar for expressing the capabilities, requirements, and general characteristics of entities in an XML web services-based system. WS-Policy defines a framework and a model for the expression of these properties as policies." WS-Policy Assertions specifies a language by which policies can be stated [PA].

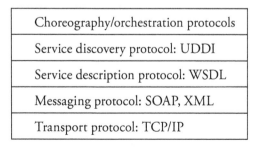

Figure 5.7 Web services protocol stack.

As stated in [WSIL], the WS-Inspection Language (WSIL) specification provides an XML format for assisting in the inspection of a site for available services and a set of rules for how inspection-related information should be made available for consumption.

The Messaging protocols include the following: Message Packing [SOAP], [MTOM], Reliable Messaging (WS-ReliableMessaging, WS-Reliability), Routing/Addressing (WS-Addressing, WS-MessageDelivery), Multiple Message Sessions (WS-Enumeration, WS-Transfer), and Events and Notification (WS-Events, WS-Notification). In Section 5.2.2.1, we discussed SOAP. MTOM (Message Transmission and Optimization) provides an optimized mechanism for exchanging messaging between WS and may be used with SOAP. WS-Reliable Messaging is an OASIS specification that allows for messages to be exchanged reliably between nodes [RELIABILITY]. As stated in [RELIABILITY], WS-Reliability is a generic and open model for ensuring reliable message delivery for WS. Essentially WS-Reliability and WS-Reliable Messaging are competing specifications with much commonality. It is also stated in [RELIABILITY] that WS-Reliable Messaging will oust WS-Reliability. WS-Addressing is a transport neutral mechanism to address WS and to identify the endpoints of WS [ADDRESS]. Another routing protocol is WS-Message Delivery that presents a "mechanism to deliver and correlate messages in the context of message exchange patterns (MEPs), found in the service description." An MEP "describes the pattern of messages required by a communications protocol to establish or use a communication channel" [MEP]. There are two major message exchange patterns—a *request-response* pattern, and a *one-way* pattern. For example, the TCP (Transmission Control Protocol) has a *request-response* pattern protocol, and the UDP (User Datagram Protocol) has a *one-way* pattern. WS-Enumeration is a specification that "describes how to enable an application to ask for items from a list of data that is held by a web service. In this way, WS-Enumeration is useful for reading event logs, message queues, or other data collections" [ENUM]. WS-Transfer is a specification defining the transfer of an XML-representation of a WS-addressable resource, as well as creating and deleting such resources [ADDRESS]. WS-Eventing is used for a WS (subscriber) to register with another web service (subscriptor) to notify it when certain events occur [EVENT]. WS-Notification is a collection of specifications that enable multiple WS to be notified of the occurrence of various events [NOTIFY].

Protocols for Transactions and Business Processing include the following: Orchestration (BPEL4WS, WS-CDL), Transaction (WS-Transaction, WS-Coordination, WS-CAF) and Asynchronous Services (ASAP). In Section 5.2.2.2, we discussed BPEL4WS. WS-CDL is the Web Services Choreography Description Language. It is stated in [BPEL] that "While BPEL is a programming language to specify the behavior of a participant in choreography, it is concerned with describing the message interchanges between participants. Participants of choreography are peers, there is no center of control." Essentially WS-CDL is an XML-based language that describes peer-to-peer collaboration between multiple parties/agents [CHORE]. WS-Transaction specifications define mechanisms for transactional interoperability between WS domains [TRANS]. WS-Coordination describes an extensible framework for providing protocols that coordinate the actions of distributed applications [COORD]. WS-CAF which stands for Web Services Composite Application Framework (WS-CAF) is an open framework developed by OASIS so that applications that contain multiple services are used in combination. Such applications are called composite applications [CAF]. ASAP (Asynchronous Service Access Protocol) is an OASIS standard which creates an extension of SOAP that supports generic asynchronous WS or long-running web services [ASAP].

5.2.2.4 Rest

We have discussed the basic components of WS which include HTTP, SOAP, and WSDL. However, there is an alternative to designing software systems that is not based on HTTP and the WWW. This approach is called REST (Representational Transfer Interface). REST is described in its wiki entry as follows [REST]: An important concept in REST is the existence of resources (sources of specific information), each of which is referenced with a global identifier (e.g., a URI in HTTP). To manipulate these resources, components of the network (user agents and origin servers) communicate via a standardized interface (e.g., HTTP) and exchange representations of these resources (the actual documents conveying the information).

It is also stated in [REST-SOAP], any number of connectors (e.g., clients, servers, caches, tunnels) can mediate the request, but each does so without "seeing past" its own request (referred to as "layering," another constraint of REST and a common principle in many other parts of information and networking architecture). Thus, an application can interact with a resource by knowing two things: the identifier of the resource, and the action required—it does not need to know whether there are caches, proxies, gateways, firewalls, tunnels, or anything else between it and the server actually holding the information. The application does, however, need to understand the format of the information (representation) returned (e.g., HTML, XML document).

5.2.3 Service-Oriented Analysis and Design

Analysis and design approaches are crucial for good software development. In the beginning we had software analysis and design approaches for better software engineering. Then with the explosion of object-oriented software development including languages such as Smalltalk, C++, and Java, there came several object-oriented analysis and design approaches, also called OOAD. Eventually after much debate, UML became the unified approach for OOAD. Today service-oriented computing is exploding. Unlike object-oriented programming, service-oriented programming does not have its own language. We are using languages such as C, C++, and Java for service-oriented computing. However, the main question is how do we model and analyze these services? Is there a unified SOAD methodology? For now, at least several approaches are being proposed. We believe that eventually it is very likely that there will be a unified approach.

There have been several efforts on defining software lifecycle as well as defining the lifecycle of objects. For example, in the case of software, the first step is to gather requirements, then determine the inputs/outputs, next design the algorithms, then develop the software, test the software, integrate the software into the system, conduct system testing, and finally deploy the software. This is not the end of the process. The software has to be maintained, the bugs fixed, and support provided to the customer. This is also the top-down approach to developing software. In the bottom-up approach, software modules are developed as needed. Similarly, with object software development, in the top-down approach one has to analyze the application, determine the objects, the relationships between the objects, develop the objects, test the objects, and integrate the objects. The system also has to be maintained. In the bottom-up approach, objects are developed as needed.

Similarly, services also have lifecycles. In his book on SOA, Thomas Erl has explained the service lifecycle [ERL05]. He has stated three ways to develop services: one is the top-down approach, the second is the bottom-up approach, and the third is what he called the agile approach. In the top-down approach, one has to conduct analysis, then design the services, develop the services, test the services, integrate the services, and then maintain the services. In the bottom-up approach, services are designed and developed as needed. In the agile approach, an integrated approach is used. That is, the application is analyzed and the services are identified. However, one does not have to wait until all the services are identified. One then develops some of the critical services, then conducts more of the analysis and design and then develops some other services. The process continues and is adaptable to changes in the applications. Figure 5.8 describes the service lifecycle.

Often, object-oriented analysis methods and UML are taught in SOA classes. While one can learn some of the principles behind OOAD, SOAD is not the same as OOAD. SOAD is about designing services. Note that objects may be used to implement the services. However, the concept of service is not the same as the

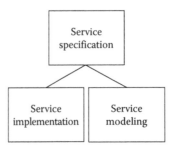

Figure 5.8 Service-oriented lifecycle.

concept of objects. Therefore, it is important to introduce the concept of SOAD if one has to design good service-based systems.

The first step is to analyze the application and determine the services that describe the applications. The logic encapsulated by each service, the reuse of the logic encapsulated by the service, and the interfaces to the service have to be identified. It is also desirable for a service to be autonomous. The next step that needs to be identified is the relationship between the services including the composition of services. In a top-down strategy, one has to identify all the services and the relationships before conducting the detailed design and development of the services. For large application design, this may not be feasible. In the case of bottom-up design, one has to identify services and start developing them. In the agile design, both strategies are integrated. In an airline reservation application, the services are reserve-airline, reserve-hotel, and reserve-rental car. They can be implemented as three independent services, or the reserve-hotel and reserve-rental car services can be invoked by the reserve-airline service.

Erl, in his book, [ERL05] makes a strong case for business services. That is, the business logic is modeled as services. He further states that such an approach sets the stage for orchestration-based SOAs. Orchestration essentially implements workflow logic that enables different applications to interoperate with each other. It should be noted that orchestrations themselves may be implemented as services. Therefore, the orchestration service may be invoked for different applications also implemented as services to interoperate with each other. Business services also promote reuse. For example, an accounts payable service may be reused by different applications.

The main question is how do you define a service? At the highest level, an entire application such as order management can be one service. However, this is not desirable. At the other extreme, a business process can be broken into several steps and each step can be a service. In the case of order management, the steps include (i) search the web for a book store that has the book you want, (ii) compare the price of the book at different book stores, (iii) examine the shipping rules and return policies, (iv) check whether the book stores will accept the credit card you have, (v) select a book store, (vi) search for the book, (vi) place the book in the shopping cart, (vii) purchase the book by filling out all details, and (viii) wait for confirmation, and (ix) check out. Now each step could be a service. But this would mean for a medium-sized application, there could be hundreds of services. Therefore, the challenge is to group steps that carry out some specific task into a service. As Erl states, there are two major design principles in a good service design [ERL05]. One is reusability and the other is autonomy. Services can also be defined based on the operations that are performed. Initially one does not define the explicit service or the operations. The services and operations are called candidate services and candidate operations.

Next, examine the service candidates and determine the relationships between them. One service may call other services. Two services may be composed to obtain a composite service. This would mean identifying the boundaries and the interface and make the composition and separations as clean as possible. Dependencies may result

SOMA: Service oriented modeling architecture
SOMF: Service oriented modeling framework
UML for services

Figure 5.9 SOAD approaches.

in complex service designs. The service operations could be simple operations such as performing calculations or complex operations such as invoking multiple services.

Once the candidate services and the service operations are indemnified, the next step is to refine the candidates and state the design of the services and the service operations. Note that this also depends on whether one follows the top-down, bottom-up, or agile strategies. This would result in whether all the services have to be defined before the development or one can define some of the services and then start the development while other services are still being defined. Details of the various methods for SOAD as well as relating to the service-oriented enterprise and enterprise modeling are given in [ERL05]. We discuss some of the approaches being investigated in the next section.

In the late 1980s and early 1990s, several object-oriented edit methodologies were competing. These included Rumbaugh's OMT and Booch's and Ivar Jacobson's Use Cases. Then with UML, the various approaches were unified and there is now a standard OOAD. However, we do not yet have standards for SOAD. There are multiple approaches and as we get a better understanding of SOAD, we expect that these various approaches would be unified. Some of the current approaches include IBM's SOAD, called SOMA as well as Services UML, among others. We discuss some of these approaches in this section and Figure 5.9 illustrates them. A good discussion of service-oriented modeling is discussed in [MODEL], [SURVEY], and [SOAD]. Below we will discuss some of the well-known SOAD approaches. More details can be found in [THUR10].

5.2.3.1 IBM Service-Oriented Analysis and Design

IBM first coined the term SOAD and then refined it with SOMA. As stated in the survey paper by Ramollari et al. on SOAD approaches, IBM's SOAD proposes elements that should be part of a SOAD methodology; hence, it is an abstract framework rather than a holistic methodology [IBM]. SOAD builds upon existing, proven techniques, such as OOAD. It also introduces SOA-specific techniques, such as service conceptualization, service categorization, and aggregation.

IBM SOMA: IBM's SOMA (service-oriented modeling architecture) can be considered to be an implementation of IBM's SOAD. As stated in [SOMA], SOMA implements SOAD through the identification, specification, and realization of services, components that realize the service components and flows that can be used to compose services. IBM's approach extends object-oriented component-based analysis and design approaches for SOA. It is also stated that SOMA identifies services, component boundaries, flows, compositions, and information through complementary techniques which include domain decomposition, goal-service modeling, and existing asset analysis.

5.2.3.2 Service-Oriented Modeling Framework

Another SOAD approach is SOMF (the Service-Oriented Modeling Framework). As stated in [SOAD], SOMF is a service-oriented development lifecycle methodology and offers a number of modeling practices and disciplines that contribute to a successful service-oriented lifecycle management and modeling. There are four sections of the modeling: practices, environments, disciplines, and artifacts.

5.2.3.3 UML for Services

Those who have worked with UML are strongly promoting UML for SOAD. IBM's Rational Rose product has UML-to-SOA Transformation tool as part of it. As stated by IBM [IBM], the UML-to-SOA transformation typically accepts the UML model as its source and creates domain-specific SOA output.

Much of the work on SOAD has been influenced by OOAD which also includes UML-based modeling. SOAD is still in its infancy. Therefore, we believe that just like UML won the battle with OOAD, there will very likely be a uniform SOAD methodology. Details of UML can be found in [UML].

5.3 Secure Service-Oriented Computing

5.3.1 Secure Services Paradigm

Secure services essentially incorporate security into services technologies. For example, what credentials should an agent have to invoke a web service? What credentials should a web service have to invoke another web service? Should all web service descriptions be visible to every agent? How can access control be enforced on web service descriptions? How can security be incorporated into the SOAs? What are the security standards being proposed by W3C and OASIS? We explore answers to these questions. For more details on secure services we refer to [BERT06]. More recently, an edited book with a collection of papers in secure WS was published and this book gives an excellent overview of the emerging standards and research directions in the field [GUTI10].

To best illustrate the notion of a secure service we will use the example of a credit application. Suppose we want to get our credit report. We will contact a service provider that gets credit reports. First, we should have the access to read the existence of such a service provider. Once we know about this service provider, we invoke this service provider. The service provider should ensure that we have the access to this particular service. Furthermore, it should ensure that the information about the credit it retrieves can be read by us. To do this, we also have to send some identification information to the service provider. If the service is not secure, then anyone can obtain anyone's credit reports. Similarly, to obtain healthcare reports, the secure service provider should ensure that the person requesting the service has the appropriate credentials to read the healthcare records. Furthermore, the owner of the healthcare records may enforce various privacy policies, in which case the service provider should only release appropriate information to the consumer. In some cases, the consumer may use the service provider to purchase information. The service provider can state its privacy policies and if the consumer agrees with the policies, private information can be released about him/her.

This simple example shows several aspects. One is that the user of the service has to be attested by the service provider. The service provider has to be trusted in the sense that one does not want to get service from an unreliable provider. The service provider has to ensure that the user/consumer has the proper credentials to obtain the service and that any information released is something the consumer is authorized to read. The service provider also has to ensure that private information about a person is not released to the consumer. Essentially, we need confidentiality, privacy, trust, and integrity features to be enforced by the WS.

Our focus on SOA implementation will be through WS. Therefore, our realization of secure SOA will be through secure WS. The basic SOA is essentially about a consumer requesting a service from the UDDI. The UDDI sends the name/address of the service. The consumer then gets this service from the service provider. With secure SOA, we have to ensure that the communication between the consumer, the UDDI, and the service provider is secure. Furthermore, only authorized consumers can get the required services. Furthermore, the SOAP messages that are encoded in XML have to be secure. XML encryption standard provides confidentiality while XML signature standard provides integrity. Both XML encryption and XML signature are standards provided by W3C.

Security and authorization specifications for WS are based on XML and can be found in [OASIS], [XACML], and [SAML]. Various types of controls have been proposed including access control, rights, assertions, and protection. We describe some of them in the next section. The list of specifications includes the following:

- eXtensible Access Control Markup Language (XACML)
- eXtensible Rights Markup Language (XRML)
- Security Assertion Markup Language (SAML)
- Service Protection Markup Language (SPML)
- Web Services Security (WSS)
- XML Common Biometric Format (XCBF)
- XML Key Management Specification (XKMS)

OASIS is a key standards organization promoting security standards for WS. It is a not-for-profit, global consortium that drives the development, convergence, and adoption of e-business standards. Two prominent standards provided by OASIS are XACML and SAML. XACML provides fine-grained control of authorized activities, the effect of characteristics of the access requestor, the protocol over which the request is made, authorization based on classes of activities, and content introspection. SAML is an XML framework for exchanging authentication and authorization information. We will discuss details of secure WS in the ensuing sections.

We were the first to examine secure OOAD based on the OMT model. We developed a secure object model, secure dynamic model, and secure functional model. Since then, several researchers have developed secure OOAD methodologies based on objects. With the SOAD approach, the goal is to identify the services and the relationships between the services for an application. For example, the services for the book order application will include order monument service, warehouse service, and shipping service. These services have associated with them various security policies. The challenge is to capture the services and the policies in an appropriate modeling language.

There is little work on secure service-oriented design and analyses (S-SOAD). Later in this chapter, we will make an attempt based on the developments with secure OOAD. In particular, we will examine the SOAD principles and examine security for SOAD. It should be noted as security for WS as well as SOAD methodologies mature, we will see better approaches for S-SOAD.

Identity management, usually also referred to as federated identity management, is closely inter-twined with WS. Users as well as WS have to be authenticated before accessing resources. Single sign-on (SSO) is the popular solution where one time sign-on gives a user or a service access to the various resources. Furthermore, SAML currently provides authentication facilities for WS. However, with regulatory requirements for e-business, one needs a stronger mechanism for authentication and this mechanism has come to be known as identity management.

As discussed in [FED], Federated Identity "describes the technologies, standards and use cases which serve to enable the portability of identity information across otherwise autonomous security domains." The goal is to ensure that users of one domain take advantage of all the technologies offered by another domain in a seamless manner. Note that federation is about organizations working together to carry out a task (such as B2B operations) or solve a particular problem. While the ideas have been around for many years, it is only recently with the emerging standards for WS that we can now develop realistic federations. In such federations, access to the resources by users has to be managed without burdening the user.

Security standards for services have essentially been developed by W3C and Security SIS. Standards for Web Services 1.0 essentially consisted of a service consumer requesting a service from the service provider who then provides the service. The XML messages that are exchanged in the SOAP protocols are encrypted and signed to provide confidentiality and integrity. The goal is to encrypt the message

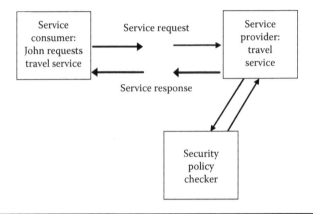

Figure 5.10 Secure service-oriented computing example.

to provide confidentiality and sign the message to ensure that the message is not tampered with. XML Key Management and XML Encryption have played a major role in providing confidentiality and integrity of the messages.

Web Services 2.0 has resulted in several additional standards including secure messaging, reliability, and identity management. In addition, standards for policy management such as WS-Policy, standards for access control such as XACML, and standards for security assertions such as SAML have also been developed. We will discuss these standards later in this chapter.

For many applications, the access control models are not sufficient. For example, in the case of composite WS, one web service, S1, may invoke another web service, S2. In such an invocation, S1's privileges will be enforced and not those of the user U who invoked S1. This means that the information that is returned to U may be something the user is not authorized to know. To avoid such security compromises, a user U may have to delegate its privileges to S1 so that U's privileges are used when S1 invokes S2. Such an invocation is governed by the delegation models that are utilized [SHE08].

Another security concern for composite WS is information flow. That is, when WS are composed, it is critical that there is no information flow from a high level to a low level. Our research focuses on various aspects of WS security including the delegation models and information flows for web service composition. We illustrate the notion of secure service-oriented computing in Figure 5.10.

5.3.2 Secure SOA and WS

Our approach is to implement SOA through WS; therefore, SOA security essentially is about WS security. There are specifications to provide security for Web Services 1.0. These specifications are WS-Security, XML-Signature, and XML-Encryption. WS-* security is the second generation of technologies for SOA security. SSO is a form

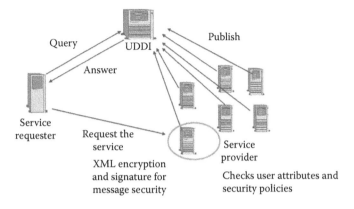

Figure 5.11 Secure SOA and web services.

of centralized security mechanism that complements the WS-Security extensions. Related specifications for SOA security include the following: WS-Security, WS-SecurityPolicy, WS-Trust, WS-SecureConversation, WS-Federation, XACML, Extensible Rights Markup Language, XML Key Management, XML, Signature, SAML, .NET Passport, Secure Socket Layer, and WS-I Basic Security Profile. Figure 5.11 illustrates the notion of secure WS architecture.

Next, we will provide an overview of both WS and WS-* Security. For details on secure SOA, we refer to [BERT06] and [WSS].

5.3.2.1 WS-Security

Before we get into the details of WS-security, we will discuss some of the security properties that are needed for WS. They include the following:

Identification: For a service requestor to access a secure service provider, it must first provide information that expresses its origin or owner. This is referred to as making a claim.

Authentication: A message being delivered to a recipient must prove that the message is in fact from the sender that it claims.

Authorization: Once authenticated, the recipient of a message may need to determine what the requestor is allowed to do.

Single sign-on: User must sign-on one time and have access to all the resources. It is supported by SAML, .NET Passport and XACML.

Confidentiality and Integrity: Confidentiality is concerned with protecting the privacy of the message content; integrity ensures that the message has not been altered.

Transport Level and Message Level Security: Transport level security is provided by SSL (securing HTTP); message level confidentiality and integrity are provided by XML-Encryption and XML-Signature.

Securing WS mainly requires providing facilities for securing the integrity and confidentiality of the messages and ensuring that the service acts only on requests in messages that express the claims required by policies. The role of standards includes providing a Web Services Security Framework that is an integral part of the Web Services Architecture. This framework is a layered and composable set of standard specifications. Next, we will briefly describe the various components of WS-Security.

XML Encryption: XML Encryption Syntax and Processing is a W3C standard and was recommended in 2002. Its goal is to provide confidentiality for applications that exchange structured data by representing in a standard way digitally encrypted resources, separating encryption information from encrypted data, and supporting reference mechanisms for addressing encryption information from encrypted data sections and vice versa, providing a mechanism for conveying encryption key information to a recipient and providing for the encryption of a part or totality of an XML document.

XML Signature: This is a W3C standard and recommended in 2002. XML Signature is a building block for many WS security standards (e.g., XKMS and WS-Security). Its goal is to represent a digital signature as an XML element and process rules for creating this XML element. The signed data items can be of different types and granularity (XML documents, XML Elements, files containing any type of digital data).

Securing SOAP messages is crucial for WS-Security. SOAP Message Security 1.0 became an approved OASIS Standard Specification in 2006. Its goal is to provide *single* SOAP message integrity and confidentiality by using *existing* digital signature, encryption, and security token mechanisms, provide mechanisms for associating security tokens with message content (header and body blocks) and support extensibility (i.e., support multiple security token format). Security Token is a representation of security-related information (e.g., 9.509 certificates, Kerberos tickets and authenticators, mobile device security tokens from SIM cards, username, etc.). Signed Security Token is a security token that contains a set of related claims (assertions) cryptographically endorsed by an issuer (Examples: 9.509 certificates and Kerberos tickets).

So now we come back to WS-Security. What is it? WS-Security enhances SOAP messaging to provide *quality of protection* through: message integrity, message confidentiality, and single message authentication. These mechanisms can be used to accommodate a wide variety of security models and encryption technologies. WS-Security also provides a general purpose, extensible mechanism for associating security tokens with messages. WS-Security describes how to encode binary security tokens (9.509 certificates and Kerberos tickets). Figure 5.12 illustrates WS Security.

WS-security: Mechanisms for signing SOAP messages, encrypting SOAP messages, and attaching security tokens
SOAP foundation
XML security: XML signature, XML encryption
Transport level security: SSL/TLS
Network level Security: IPSec

Figure 5.12 WS-security.

5.3.2.2 WS-* Security

WS-* security standard specifications address interoperability aspects. Each standard specification provides a specific section describing security threats that are not addressed by that specification. The framework for WS-* security makes use of WS-Security. Implementation of this framework has been carried out by Microsoft .NET Framework 2.0 (WSE3.0), SUN Web Services Interoperability Technology (WSIT), IBM WebSphere, and Open Software [APAC]. In theory, the framework mandates a layered approach where every upper layer standard could/should reuse and extend the specification of lower layer standards. In practice, specifications released by different organizations are not always compatible. However, they adhere to profiles and improve interoperability. It should be noted that the implementations of different vendors are not always interoperable. Three major components that provide security are: WS-Policy, WS-Trust, and WS-Addressing. WS-Addressing is a specification of transport-neutral mechanisms that allow web services to communicate address information. Below we will discuss WS-Policy and WS-Trust. Figure 5.13 illustrates WS*-Security. It should be noted that this stack is continually evolving. Some of the standards have been adopted while some others are in the experimental stages. Still some others are only in the specification stages. Therefore, the stage of a particular protocol could change with time.

WS-Policy: Web Services Policy 1.2—Framework (WS-Policy) is a W3C submission. A Policy is a potentially empty collection of policy alternatives. Alternatives are not ordered. A Policy Alternative is a potentially empty collection of policy assertions. An alternative with zero assertions indicates no behaviors. Alternatives are mutually exclusive (exclusive OR). A Policy Assertion identifies a requirement (or capability) of a policy subject. Assertions indicate domain-specific (e.g., security, transactions) semantics and are expected to be defined in separate, domain-specific specifications.

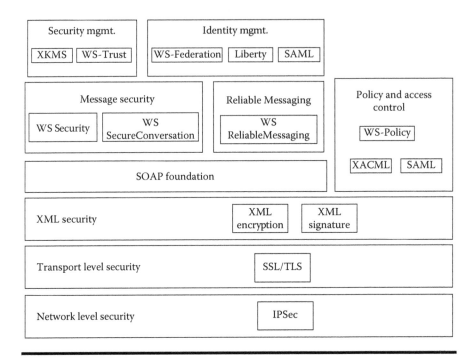

Figure 5.13 WS*-security.

WS-Policy can be considered to be an extensible model for expressing all types of domain-specific policy models: transport-level security, resource usage policy, even end-to-end business-process level policy. It defines a basic policy, policy statement, and policy assertion models. WS-Policy is also able to incorporate other policy models such as SAML and XACML. WS-Policy Assertion defines a few generic policy assertions. WS-Policy Attachment defines how to associate a policy with a service, either by directly embedding it in the WSDL definition or by indirectly associating it through UDDI. WS-SecurityPolicy defines security policy assertions corresponding to the security claims defined by WS-Security: message integrity assertion, message confidentiality assertion, and message security token assertion.

The goal of WS-Policy and WS-PolicyAttachment are to offer mechanisms to represent the capabilities and requirements of WS as Policies. The Policy view in WS-Policy is as follows: A policy is used to convey conditions on an interaction between two web service endpoints. The provider of a web service exposes a policy to convey conditions under which it provides the service. A requester might use this policy to decide whether or not to use the service.

WS-Trust: As stated in [TRUST], WS-Trust is a WS-* specification and OASIS standard that provides extensions to WS-Security. It deals with the issuing, renewing, and validating of security tokens. It also brokers trust relationships between participants in a secure message exchange carried out via Secure Conversation.

Security (confidentiality and integrity) is achieved through encryption, digital signatures, and certificates. Ultimately, security depends on the *secure management* of cryptographic keys and security tokens: Key/security token issuance, Key/security token transmission, Key/security token storage, and Key/security token exchange. More formally, Web Services Trust Language (WS-Trust) was released in 2005 and its goal is to enable the issuance and dissemination of credentials among different trust domains. WS-Trust defines extensions to WS-Security that provide: *methods for issuing, renewing, and validating security tokens and ways to establish, assess the presence of, and broker trust relationships.* The recipient of a WS-Security-protected SOAP message has three potential issues with the security token contained within the Security header: Format: the format or syntax of the token is not known to the recipient; Trust: the recipient may be unable to build a chain-of-trust from its own trust anchors (e.g., its X.509 Certificate Authority, a local Kerberos KDC (Key Distribution Center), or a SAML Authority to the issuer or signer of the token; Namespace: the recipient may be unable to directly comprehend the set of claims within the token because of syntactical differences.

Message reliability is provided by WS-ReliableMessaging standard. Message security is provided by WS-Security and SecureConversation standards. As stated in [CONV], WS-SecureConversation is a Web Services specification, created by IBM and others, that works in conjunction with WS-Security, WS-Trust, and WS-Policy to allow the creation and sharing of security contexts. The goal of WS-SecureConversation is to establish security contexts for multiple SOAP message exchanges. This in turn reduces the overhead of key establishment. Conversations focus on the public processes in which the participants of a web service engage. WSCL is the Web Services Conversation Language. More formally, WS-Conversation provides secure communication across one or more messages and extends WS-Security mechanisms. It slows the authentication of a *series* of SOAP messages (conversation) by establishing and sharing between two endpoints of a *security context* for a message conversation using a series of derived keys to increase security. The security context is defined as a new token type that is obtained using a binding of WS-Trust. Security Context is an abstract concept that refers to an established authentication state and negotiated key(s) that may have additional security-related properties. A *security context token (SCT)* is a representation of that security context abstract concept, which allows a context to be named by a URI and used with WS-Security.

Policy and access control are provided by WS-Policy, XACML, and SAML. SAML was developed by the OASIS XML-based Security Services Technical Committee (SSTC) and its main goal is to provide *authentication* and *authorization*. It promotes interoperability between disparate authentication and authorization systems. It achieves this by defining an XML-based framework for communicating security and identity information (e.g., authentication, entitlements, and attribute) between computing entities using different security infrastructures available (e.g., Punlic Key Infrastructure (PKI), Kerberos, LDAP, etc.). XACML Version 2.0 is an OASIS standard. It is a general-purpose access control policy language for managing access to resources. It describes both a policy language and an access control decision request/response language. It also provides fine-grained access control where access control is based on subject and object attributes. It is consistent with and building upon SAML.

Security Management is essentially provided by SAML and XKMS. As stated by W3C, the XML Key Management Specification (XKMS) comprises of two parts: the XML Key Information Service Specification (XKISS) and the XML Key Registration Service Specification (XKRSS). As stated in the W3C specification, XKISS allows a client to delegate part or all of the tasks required to process XML Signature elements to an XKMS service. Essentially XKISS minimizes the complexity of applications using XML Signature by becoming a client of the XKMS service. This way, W3C stated that the application is relieved of the complexity and syntax of the underlying PKI used to establish trust relationships. W3C also stated that XKRSS describes a protocol for registration and subsequent management of public key information. The final component we will discuss is identity management. The standards for this service are SAML, WS-Federation, and Liberty Alliance.

As stated in [FED], WS-Federation is an Identity Federation specification, developed by BEA Systems (now Oracle), IBM, Microsoft, and others. It defines mechanisms for allowing disparate security entities to broker information on identities, identity attributes, and authentication. The Liberty Alliance was formed in September 2001 by approximately 30 organizations to establish open standards, guidelines, and best practices for identity management.

5.3.3 Secure SOAD

As services technologies explode, we need a way to effectively model applications based on services. SOAD approaches were developed for this purpose and IBM is one of the leaders in this field. In [THUR10] we discussed service-oriented lifecycle and approach for SOAD including SOMA and SOMF. While SOAD works for services modeling, we need secure SOAD for modeling secure services. In this section, we discuss some preliminary ideas toward developing secure SOAD.

Secure service modeling has benefited a lot from OOAD. OOAD approaches were developed in the 1980s and 1990s and evolved from the entity relationship modeling. These approaches include Rumbaugh's OMT and Booch's class diagrams. We have incorporated security into OMT in [SELL93]. For example, we developed an approach for modeling the relationships between objects from both dynamic and functional points of view. We also applied the methodology for healthcare applications as well as real-time applications [THUR94a], [THUR94b].

As we mentioned in [THUR10], the various OOAD approaches were unified in the mid-1990s. Subsequently, UML was developed. UML was applied to secure applications by several researchers including the work of Indrakshi Ray [RAY04]. Some of the developments were also applied to aspect-oriented modeling and analysis. However, with the emergence of services technologies, UML is now being applied to model services and we expect that this approach will be applied to secure services. However, we have to be careful not to artificially model services as objects. Therefore, we need a bottom-up approach to model both services and secure services.

Security has been incorporated into the software engineering lifecycle and more recently in the object-oriented lifecycle. For example, security engineering deals with defining security policies, incorporating security into the design of the system, security testing, and maintenance. In the case of object-oriented system lifecycle, security considerations will include defining the security policies on objects and the activities as well as incorporating security into the design of the object system and security testing and maintenance. Similarly, in the case of secure service-oriented lifecycle, we need to determine the security policies, the security levels of the services and the interactions between the services including the composition of the services, incorporating security into the design and development of the services and subsequently testing the secure services.

As we have discussed [THUR10], in his book on SOA, Thomas Erl explained the service lifecycle. He stated three ways to develop services: one is the top-down approach, the second is the bottom-up approach, and the third is what he called the agile approach. Security cannot be an afterthought in the design of service. One has to consider security in the top-down, bottom-up, and the agile approaches. In the top-down approach, one has to conduct analysis, then design the services, develop the services, test the services, integrate the services, and then maintain the services. Here, security policies have to guide throughout the process. For example, when two services are composed, what is the resulting policy on the composed service? In the bottom-up approach, services are designed and developed as needed. Therefore, as services are designed, security has to be considered. For example, when a new service is designed, it should not violate the security policies specified for the prior services. In the agile approach, an integrated approach is used. That is, the application is analyzed and the services are identified. However, one does not have to wait until all the services are identified. Security impact on this agile approach is yet to be investigated.

Another aspect when considering security is dynamic policies. That is, security policies enforced on the services and service compositions may change with time. The challenge is to ensure that there is no security violation when accommodating changing policies and security levels. This is also a major challenge in designing secure service-oriented systems.

We will consider the SOAD approach that we discussed in Section 5.2 and examine the security impact. The first step is to analyze the application and determine the services that describe the applications. The logic encapsulated by each service, the reuse of the logic encapsulated by the service, and the interfaces to the service have to be identified. From a security point of view, in defining the services we have to consider the security policies. What is the security level of the service? What are the policies enforced on the service? Who can have access to the service? When do we decompose the service into smaller services so that security is not violated? For example, service A may not have access to service B. However, service B may be decomposed into services C and D wherein A has access to C and not to D. Now, if A has access both to C and D then the policy that A does not have access to B may be violated.

The next step is for the relationship between the services including the composition of services to be identified. In a top-down strategy, one has to identify all the services and the relationships before conducting the detailed design and development of the services. For large application design, this may not be feasible. In the case of bottom-up design, one has to identify services and start developing them. In the agile design, both strategies are integrated. From a security point of view, there may be policies that define the relationship between the services. The example we gave earlier regarding services A, B, C, and D shows that while A may have access to C, A may not have access to D if we are to enforce the policy that A does not have access to B. Here access means invoking a particular service.

In [THUR10], we discussed that the business logic could be modeled as services. Furthermore, such an approach sets the stage for orchestration-based SOAs. Orchestration essentially implements workflow logic that enables different applications to interoperate with each other. Also we have stated orchestrations themselves may be implemented as services. Therefore, the orchestration service may be invoked for different applications also implemented as services to interoperate with each other. Business services also promote reuse. From a security point of view, we have yet to determine who can invoke the business logic and orchestration services. A lot of work has gone into security for workflow systems including the BFA (Bertino–Ferrari–Atluri) model [BERT99]. Therefore, we need to examine the principles in this work for business logic and orchestration services. When a service is reused, what happens if there are conflicting policies on reuse? Also we have to make sure that there is no security violation through reuse.

Next, we will consider the key points in service modeling discussed in [THUR10] and examine the security impact. The main question is how do you define a service? At the highest level, an entire application such as order management can be one service. However, this is not desirable. At the other extreme, a business process can be broken into several steps and each step can be a service. The challenge is to group steps that carry out some specific task into a service. However, when security is given consideration, then not only do we have to group steps that carry out some specific task into service, but we also have to group steps that can be meaningfully executed. If security is based on multilevel security, then we may want to assign a security level for each service. In this way, the service can be executed by someone cleared at an appropriate level. Therefore, the challenge is to group steps not only meaningful from a task point of view but also from a security point of view.

Next, we must examine the service candidates and determine the relationships between them. One service may call other services. Two services may be composed to create a composite service. This would mean identifying the boundaries

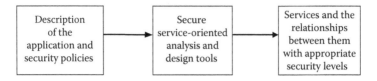

Figure 5.14 Secure SOAD.

and the interface and making the composition and separations as clear as possible. Dependencies may result in complex service designs. The service operations could be simple operations such as performing calculations or complex operations such as invoking multiple services. Here again, security may impact the relationships between the services. If two services have some relationships between them, then both services should be accessible to a group of users or users cleared at a particular level. For example, if services A and B are tightly integrated, it may not make sense for a service C to have access to A and not to B. If A is about making a hotel reservation and B is about making a rental car reservation, then an airline reservation service C should be able to invoke both services A and B.

Once the candidate services and the service operations are identified, the next step is to define the candidates and state the design of the services and the service operations. Therefore, from a security point of view, we have to define the services and service operations that are not only meaningful but also secure. Mapping of the candidate service to the actual service has to be carried out according to the policies. A high-level view of secure SOAD is illustrated in Figure 5.14.

As we have discussed in Section 5.2, there are multiple SOAD methods. Next, we will examine the security impact of the various methods. We believe that we make progress toward a uniform SOAD mythology like, for instance, UML; we will have a better idea on security for such a methodology.

5.3.3.1 Secure SOMA

As stated in [SOMA], SOMA implements SOAD through the identification, specification, and realization of services, components that realize the service components and flows that can be used to compose services. With secure SOMA, we need to identify the policies enforced on the services and the various components. For multilevel secure WS, we also need to assign security levels of services. In addition, the execution level of services should also be defined.

5.3.3.2 Secure SOMF

As stated in [THUR10], SOMF is a service-oriented development lifecycle methodology and offers a number of modeling practices and disciplines that contribute to successful service-oriented lifecycle management and modeling. The security impact on this framework needs to be examined.

5.3.3.3 Secure UML for Services

Secure UML for services essentially developed secure UML for service-oriented analysis and modeling. Several efforts on applying UML and other OOAD approaches for secure applications have been proposed. We need to extend these approaches to secure SOAD. We also need to examine the security impact on service-oriented discovery and analysis modeling, service-oriented business integration modeling, service-oriented logical design modeling, service-oriented conceptual architecture modeling, and service-oriented logical architecture modeling.

5.3.4 Access Control for WS

Much of our work on WS is based on access control. Access control policies specify rules that must be satisfied for subjects to access objects. Several access control policies have been developed for information systems, including discretionary access control policies, mandatory access control policies, and more recently, the role-based access control policies and usage control policies. One type of access control that is being adopted by many applications including the Department of Defense is attribute-based access control (ABAC) as such a model is more amenable to open systems such as the web environment. Furthermore, the models that are being developed by standards organizations such as OASIS are also based on some form of attribute-based access control. In this section, we will focus on various standards for access control and then discuss attribute-based access control. In addition, some other features such as establishing trust in a web environment as well as approaches for inference control based on access control are also discussed. Some of the emerging standards for access control for WS are SAML and XACML, respectively.

5.3.4.1 Security Assertions Markup Language

[SAML] provides a single point of authorization. It aims to "solve the web single sign-on" problem. One identity provider in a group allows access. It has Public/Private Key Foundations. Those who are providing SAML in their products are: Microsoft Passport, OpenID (VeriSign), and Global Login System (Open Source). As stated in SAML specifications, its three main components are:

Assertions: SAML has three kinds of assertions. Authentication assertions are those in which the user has proven his identity ("John Smith authenticated with a password at 9:00am").

Attribute assertions contain specific information about the user, such as his spending limits ("John Smith is an account manager with a $1000 spending limit per one-day travel"). Authorization decision assertions identify what the user can do, for example, whether he can buy an item ("John Smith is permitted to buy a specified item").

SAML authority: a system entity that makes SAML assertions (also called Identity Provider—IdP—and Asserting Party).

Service provider: a system entity making use of SAML assertions.

Relying party: a system entity that uses received assertions (named also SAML requester).

Protocol: defines the way that SAML asks for and assertions, for example, using SOAP over HTTP for now, although using other methods in the future.

Binding: details exactly how SAML message exchanges are mapped into SOAP exchanges.

SAML addresses one key aspect of identity management and that is how identity information can be communicated from one domain to another. SAML 2.0 will be the basis on which Liberty Alliance builds additional federated identity applications (such as web service-enabled permissions-based attribute sharing).

SAML profile is another important concept. It defines constraints and/or extensions of the core protocols and assertions in support of the usage of SAML for a particular application. It activates interoperability and stipulates how particular statements are communicated using appropriate protocol messages over specified bindings. (E.g., Web Browser SSO Profile specifies how SAML authentication assertions are communicated using the Authentication Query and Response messages over a number of different bindings in order to enable SSO for a browser user.) By agreeing to support a particular SAML profile (as opposed to the complete specification set), parties who wish to exchange SAML messages have a much simpler job of achieving interoperability.

Outstanding issues for SAML include performance, federations, and handling legacy applications. With respect to performance, there is no support for caching and also it has to be implemented over HTTP protocols using SOAP. Furthermore, it does not specify encryption and as a result the policies may be compromised. With respect to federations, SAML does not specify authentication protocols. Furthermore, multiple domains cannot be handled. Therefore, OASIS is examining federated identity management. SAML does not work with legacy applications as it is expensive to retrofit.

5.3.4.2 *eXtensible Access Control Markup Language*

[XACML] is a general-purpose authorization policy model and XML-based specification language. It is independent of SAML specification and has triple-based policy syntax: <Object, Subject, Action>. It supports negative authorization. Input/output to the XACML policy processor is clearly defined as XACML context data structure. Input data are referred by XACML-specific attribute designator as well as XPath expression.

A policy consists of multiple rules and a set of policies is combined by a higher level policy (PolicySet element). XACML combines multiple rules into a single policy. It permits multiple users to have different roles. It provides separation between policy writing and application environment. The goal is to standardize access control languages. A policy has four main components: a target, a rule-combining algorithm identifier, a set of rules, and obligations. The rule is the elementary unit of a policy. The main components of a rule are: a target, an effect; permit or deny; and a condition. A policy target specifies a set of Resources, Subjects, Actions, and the Environment to which it applies.

Some elements of XACML are the following. The users interact with resources. Every resource is protected by an entity known as a Policy Enforcement Point (PEP). This is where the language is actually used and does not actually determine access. PEP sends its request to a Policy Decision Point (PDP). Policies may or may not be actually stored here, but have the final say on access. Decision is relayed to PEP, which then grants or denies access. In the architecture for XACML, when a client makes a resource request upon a server, the PEP is charged with enforcing the access control polices. However, in order to enforce the policies, the PEP will formalize the attributes describing the requester at the Policy Information Point (PIP) and delegate the authorization decision to the PDP. Applicable policies are located in a policy store, managed by the PAP (Policy Administration Point), and evaluated at the PDP, which then returns the authorization decision. Using this information, the PEP can deliver the appropriate response to the client. As stated in Section 5.3.4.2, XACML Request is triple-based (Subject, Object, and Action). XACML Response is one of the following: Permit, Permit with Obligations, Deny, Not Applicable (the PDP cannot locate a policy whose target matches the required resource), Indeterminate (an error occurred or some required value was missing).

In summary, the XACML protocol works as follows. The *Policy Administration Point* (PAP) creates security policies and stores these policies in the appropriate repository. The *Policy Enforcement Point* (PEP) performs access control by making decision requests and enforcing authorization decisions. The *Policy Information Point* (PIP) serves as the source of attribute values, or the data required for policy evaluation. The *Policy Decision Point* (PDP) evaluates the applicable policy and renders an authorization decision. Note that the PEP and PDP might be contained within the same application, or might be distributed across different servers.

Outstanding issues of XACML include distributed responsibility and policy cross-referencing. With respect to distributed responsibility, what happens when the PEP is responsible for multiple objects? What happens when we can compromise the PDP or spoof its communication? How do we guarantee that we reference the right object? While the system is distributed, a policy is still in only one

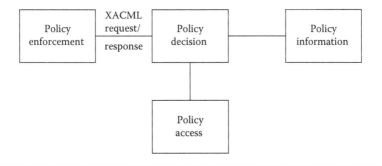

Figure 5.15 XACML access control model.

location. With respect to policy cross-referencing, one policy may access another. Typical issues arise as with inheritance and unions/intersections of related work. The challenge is to deal with conflicts. Figure 5.15 illustrates the XACML access control model for WS.

Attribute-based access control: XACML essentially implements attribute-based access control [ABAC]. While password-based access control works well in a closed environment, in an open environment such as the web, it is difficult to implement such mechanisms. Therefore, the concept of attribute-based access control was developed in early 2000. With this approach the user will present his credentials. These credentials will be issued by some credential authority. The system (or server) will validate the user's credentials with multiple credential authorities if needed. Once the credentials are verified, the system will then check the policies for the credentials and determine the access that the user has to the resources.

ABAC has been implemented in many systems including DoD's network centric enterprise services and the global information grid. ABAC can also be utilized to implement RBAC (role-based access control). In this case, a user has credentials depending on his or her roles and based on the credentials, the user is granted access. The credentials are essentially the user's attributes. More recently the UCON (Usage Control) model has been developed and this model is about controlling the usage of a resource as well as controlling access to the resource. For example, in the case of a phone card, as one uses the phone card, its value is dominated and access is dependent on the value of the phone card which is essentially the amount of minutes remaining for usage. What would be desirable is to integrate ABAC with UCON so that one has a model which controls access based on attributes of the subject/user and the usage of the resource [PARK04].

5.3.5 Digital Identity Management

Identity management, also referred to as federated identity management or digital identity management, is closely intertwined with WS. Users as well as WS have to be authenticated before accessing resources. Single sign-on is the popular solution where one time sign-on gives a user of services access to the various resources. Furthermore, SAML currently provides authentication facilities for WS. However, with regulatory requirements for e-business, one needs a stronger mechanism for authentication and this mechanism has come to be known as identity management.

Two concepts that are at the foundations of digital identity management are (i) SSO and (ii) federated identity management. We discuss these concepts as well as the technologies and standards developed for SSO and federated identity management. These include the work of Liberty Alliance, the Identity Metasystem and its Information Card implementation, Open-ID project, and Shibboleth.

As stated in [SSO], SSO is a property where a user logs in once and gains access to all systems possibly in a federation. This way the user has to log in once and has access to the resources in the federation or coalition or organization, without being prompted to log in again at each of them. Two types of SSO mechanisms are Kerberos based and smart card based. With the Kerberos mechanism, Kerberos ticket-granting ticket TGT is used to grant credentials. In the smart card-based sign-on, the user uses the smart card for sign-on. Enterprise single sign-on (ESSO), provides the support for minimizing the number of passwords and user IDs when accessing multiple applications.

As stated in [FED], "federated identity," or the "federation" of identity, describes the technologies, standards, and use cases which serve to enable the portability of identity information across otherwise autonomous security domains. The use cases include typical use cases such as cross-domain, web-based SSO. The various web sites are now implementing federated identity management through Open-ID. The goal is to ensure that users of one domain take advantage of all the technologies offered by another domain in a seamless manner. Note that federation is about organizations working together to carry out a task (such as B2B operations) or solving a particular problem. While the idea has been around for many years, it is only recently with the emerging standards for WS that we can now have secure federations. In such federations, access to the resources by users has to be managed without burdening the user.

With appropriate federated identity management, users should be able to share data across domains, support SSO as well as enable cross domain user attribute management. Cross domain SSO is one of the popular techniques for federated identity management. However, more recently there are many new techniques that are being developed. One of the prominent consortiums for deepening standards for federated identity management is the Liberty Alliance. Other efforts include the Open ID project as well as Information Card. This section will provide an overview of the various developments with identity management.

As stated in [INFO], Identity Metasystem is an "interoperable architecture for digital identity that enables people to have and employ a collection of digital identities based on multiple underlying technologies, implementations, and providers." Essentially with this approach, users can continue to maintain their identities and choose the identity system that will work for them so that the system will manage their identities when migrating to different technologies. The roles of the Identity Metasystem are identity provider, relying parties, and subjects. Identity providers issue digital identities. Relying parties are the ones who require identities such as various services. Subjects include the end users and organizations.

Identities are represented using claims which are essentially security tokens. With these claims, the identity providers, relying parties, and subjects can carry out the operations such as negotiation. WS-Trust and WS-Federation are used to obtain claims. The negotiation between the parties is carried out with WS-Security Policy and WS-MetadataExchange. The seamless operation expatriated by the user is provided by what is called an IdentitySelector client software which may access technologies such as Information Cards.

Information Card is an implementation of the Identity Metasystem. As stated in [INFO], information cards are personal digital identities that people can use online. The information cards are card-shaped pictures and people can use these cards to manage their identities. Since it implements the Identity Metasystems, the parties involved in the Information Card implementation are the identity providers, relying parties, and the subject. Identity selectors such as Windows CardSpace are used to store and manage the user identities. Information cards support SSO as users can sign in at one place and have access to the various resources on the web.

There are two types of information cards. The personal information cards enable a user to issue the claims (e.g., name, phone, etc.) and inform the various sites. The other type is managed information cards where the identity providers make claims about the user.

5.3.5.1 OpenID

As stated in [OPEN], OpenID is an open, decentralized user identification standard, allowing users to log on to many services with the same digital identity. OpenID is essentially a URL and the user is authenticated by their OpenID provider. Many corporations such as Symantec and Microsoft support OpenID. For example, Microsoft provides interoperability between OpenID and its Windows CardSpace. OpenID extends the entities of the Identity Metasystem and consists of the following:

- *End-user:* The person who wants to assert his or her identity to a site.
- *Identifier:* The URL chosen by the end-user as their OpenID identifier.
- *Identity provider or OpenID provider:* This entity provides the service of registering OpenID URLs and provides OpenID authentication.
- *Relying party:* The site that wants to verify the end-user's identifier (this is essentially the service provider).
- *Server or server-agent:* The server that verifies the end-user's identifier.
- *User-agent:* The users access the identity provider or a relying party through the user agent (e.g., the browser).

The use of OpenID is as follows. A user visits a relying party's (e.g., service provider) website to request a service. This relying party has an OpenID form which is the login for the user. The user would then give his identity which is provided by an identity prior to the logic process. From this information the relying party will discover the identity provider website. As stated in [OPEN], the relying party and the identity provider may have a shared secret which is referenced by an association handle and stored by the relying party. The relying party then directs the user's browser to the identity provider so that the user can authenticate with the identity provider, which the relying party then stores. The relying party redirects the user's web browser to the identity provider so that the user can authenticate with the provider. Usually the identity provider requests a password from the user and then requests the user whether he/she wants to trust the relying party. If the user rejects this request, then access to the services are denied. If not, the user browser is directed to the relying party with the user's credential. The browser is redirected to the designated return page on the relying party website along with the user's credentials. The relying party has to verify that the credential indeed came from the identity provider.

5.3.5.2 Shibboleth

Shibboleth is a distributed web resource access control system that allows federations to cooperate together to share web-based resources [SHIB]. It defines a protocol for carrying authentication information and user attributes from a home to a resource site. The resource site can then use the attributes to make access control decisions about the user. This web-based middleware layer uses SAML. Access control is carried out in stages. In stage one, the resource site redirects the user to their home site and obtains a handle for the user that is authenticated by the home site. In stage two, the resource site returns the handle to the attribute authority of the home site and it returns a set of attributes of the user, upon which to make an access control decision.

There are some issues with SSO with Shibboleth. How does the resource site know the home site of the user? How does it trust the handle returned? The answer is, it is handled by the system trust model. Authentication procedure is as follows. When the resource site asks for home site from the user, he selects it from the list of trusted sites which are already authenticated by Certificates. Handles are validated by the SAML signature along with the message. The user selects the home site from the list. The home site authenticates the user if he is already registered. After the home server authentication, it returns a message with SAML sign to the Target Resource Site. The Resource site (if sign matches) then provides a pseudonym (handle) for the user and sends an assertion message to the home page to find out if the necessary attributes are available with the user. To ensure privacy, the system provides a different pseudonym for the user's identity each time. It needs the release attribute policy from the user attributes each time to provide control over the authority attributes in the target site. Agreement attribute release policy is between the user and the administrator.

Trust is the heart of Shibboleth. It completely trusts the Target Resource Site and the Origin Home Site registered in the federation. The disadvantage of the existing Trust Model is that there is no differentiation between authentication authorities and attribute authorities. There is a scope of allowing more sophisticated distribution of trust, such as static or dynamic delegation of authority. Another disadvantage in the existing trust model is it provides only basic access control capabilities. It lacks the flexibility and sophistication that many applications have to provide access control decisions based on role hierarchies or various constraints such as the time of day or separation of duties.

In the basic Shibboleth, target site trusts the origin site to authenticate its users and manage their attributes correctly while the original site trusts the target site to provide services to its users. Trust is conveyed with digitally signed SAML messages using target and origin server key pairs. Each site has only one key pair per Shibboleth system. Thus, there is only a single point of trust per Shibboleth system. Therefore, there is a need for a finer-grained distributed trust model and to be able to use multiple origin authorities to issue and sign the authentication and attribute assertions. Multiple authorities should be able to issue attributes to users and the target site should be able to verify issuer/user bindings. The target should be able to state in its policy which of the attribute authorities it trusts to issue and which attributes to which groups of users. The target site should be able to decide independently of the issuing site which attributes and authorities to trust when making its access control decisions. Not all attribute-issuing authorities need be part of the origin site. A target site should be able to allow a user to gain access to its resources if it has attributes issued by multiple authorities. The trust infrastructure should support dynamic delegation of authority, so that a holder of a privilege attribute may delegate (a subset of) this to another person without having to reconfigure anything in the system. The target site should be able to decide if it really does trust the origin's attribute repository, and if not, be able to demand a stronger proof-of-attribute entitlement than that conferred by a SAML signature from the sending Web server.

Shibboleth defines various trust models. These models have been implemented using X.509. We can look at trust from two different aspects:

- Distribution of trust in attribute-issuing authorities.
- Trustworthiness of an origin site's attribute repository.

Further details of the trust models and their implementations as well as authorization and privacy issues are discussed in [TRUST].

5.3.5.3 Liberty Alliance

The Liberty Alliance was formed to promote standards for identity management. It now consists of over a 100 members which include technology developers and vendors, as well as consumers. Two major efforts released by this consort are the

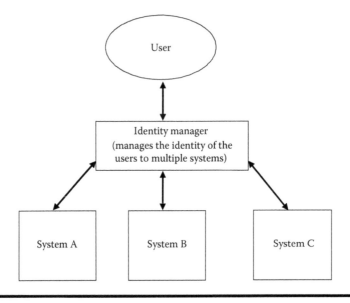

Figure 5.16 Identity management.

Liberty Identity Federation (also called identity federation) and Liberty Identity Web Services (also called identity WS).

Liberty Identity Federation enables the web users (e.g., e-commerce users) to authenticate and sign-on a domain and from there have access to multiple services. This is the basis of SAML 2.0. As stated in [LIB], the identity WS standard is an open framework for deploying and managing identity-based WS. These WS applications include Geo-location, Contact Book, Calendar, Mobile Messaging, and Liberty People Service. With these services, one can manage bookmarks, blogs, photo sharing, and related social services on the web in a privacy-preserving manner. Privacy and policy management are key aspects of the work of Liberty Alliance. It is also stated in [LIB] that more than a billion Liberty-enabled devices have been tracked globally. More recent efforts include the Identity Governance Framework and the Identity Assurance Framework. The Identity Governance Framework is a collection of Standards that supports the storage and management of the identity. It uses LDAP (Lightweight Directory Access Protocol), SAML, and WS-Trust standards. The identity assurance framework supports four identity assurance levels and these levels have been determined by the National Institute of Standards and Technology. Figure 5.16 illustrates the various identity management technologies.

5.3.6 Security Models for WS

Much of the work on secure WS has focused on access control models. That is, access control policies will determine the access that a user has to the resources

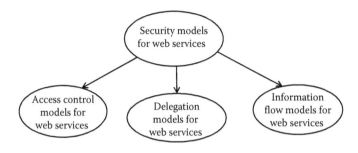

Figure 5.17 Security models for web services.

provided by WS. Several standards such as XACML have been developed based on the access control models. However, for many applications, the access control models are not sufficient. For example, in the case of composite WS, one web service, S1, may invoke another web service, S2. In such an invocation, S1's privileges will be enforced and not those of the user U who invoked S1. This means that the information that is returned to U may be something the user is not authorized to know. To avoid such security compromises, a user U may have to delegate its privileges to S1 so that U's privileges are used when S1 invokes S2. Such an invocation is governed by the delegation models that are utilized.

Another security concern for composite WS is information flow. That is, when WS are composed, it is critical that there is no information flow from a high level to a low level. Our research has focused on various aspects of WS security including the delegation models and information flows for web service composition. Therefore in this section, we will provide an overview of our research in WS security. In particular, we summarize the work we have reported in our recent papers [SHE07], [SHE08], and [SHE09]. In this section, we will present our delegation model for WS as well as our information flow in service composition. Multilevel security for WS is also discussed. Figure 5.17 illustrates the security models for WS.

5.3.6.1 Delegation Model

Access control models specify the access that subjects have on objects. It does not specify policies for invoking WS. We need appropriate policies for invoking WS. For example, suppose service S1 invokes service S2. Furthermore, suppose S1 does not have access to a resource X while S2 has access to resource X. If S2 has to access X and returns X to S1, then there is a security violation. This means when S2 accesses X on behalf of S1, then S1's privileges must be passed to S2. In the above example, such a policy will work as S2 has additional credentials that do not belong to S1. The question is what happens if S2 does not have access to X while S1 has access to X. If S1's credentials are passed to S2, then S2 will have access to X.

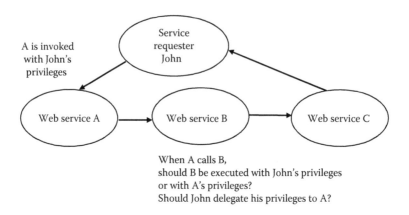

Figure 5.18 Delegation model.

However, S2 should not have access to X. As a result, we need to pass the credentials that are both common to S1 and S2. In this case, when S1 involves S2, S2 will get the credentials that are common to both S1 and S2. This also means that S2 will be operating with limited credentials.

We have conducted extensive research on delegation models for WS [SHE07] and [SHE08]. We believe that delegations models have to be flexible. In some cases, S2 will operate with a limited set of credentials in which case no access control policies will be violated. That is, if S1 invokes S2, then S2 will not access any resources that are not accessible to S1. However, in some cases S2 may need to operate using its full credential. Then S2 has to decide what information is to be passed on to S1.

Delegation models get more complicated if there are no overlapping credentials. That is, if S1 and S2 do not have any credentials in common, then S1 cannot invoke S2. For example, if S1 operates with credentials of a professor and S2 operates with the credentials of a secretary and if professor and secretary do not have any common credentials then a professor cannot request a secretary to carry out some functions. In such a case, the system has to determine how to delegate. Separation of duty is an important condition in security models. The challenge is how to bring the separation of duty concepts into security models for WS. Combining access control models with delegation models for composition of WS as well as chain-based WS needs substantial research. Note that a chain-based web service is of the form S1 invoking S2, S2 invoking S3 and S3 invoking S4. Figure 5.18 illustrates the delegation model.

5.3.6.2 Information Flow Model

To understand the information flow models, we need to examine the historical models. Back in 1973, the Bell and LaPadula model was developed for access control. While this model prevented a low-level subject from getting high-level data directly, it did not prevent illegal information flow. For example, by manipulating the locks in a file, data could be covertly passed from a high-level subject to a low-level subject. To prevent this type of flow, Goguen and Meseguer developed the noninterference model around 1982. With this model, it was not possible for data to flow from a high-level subject to a low-level subject. Essentially, the actions of a high-level subject did not interfere with those of a low-level subject. Our research applied a similar principle for WS.

There have been many efforts on preventing illegal information flow for WS. However, the prior work focused on the following aspects. Each web service satisfied security properties. The composition of the WS also satisfied security properties. However, the information flow between the intermediate services was not considered. For example, if web service S1 is composed of WS S2, S3, and S4, while the end result was secure, there could still be illegal information flow from S3 to S1. Figure 5.19 illustrates the information flow model.

Our approach prevents such information flows. Another assumption made by previous models is that the composition of WS was carried out by a trusted process. This is not realistic when in the web environment there are multiple security domains; therefore, we cannot make such an assumption. Our work does not make such an assumption.

Our work on information flow models for WS is detailed in [SHE09]. In particular, we specify transformation factors which measure how likely it is to infer the inputs and logical data of a service from its outputs. This in turn is used to determine whether information is flowing illegally from a higher-level service to a lower-level service. We also develop protocols so that the composition processes are not trusted. We then develop algorithms for collaboratively carrying out security validation in a web environment.

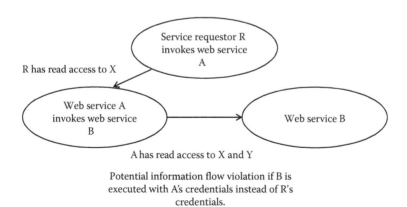

Figure 5.19 Information flow model.

5.3.6.3 Multilevel Secure WS

Much of the security research for WS is based on discretionary security. In particular, attribute-based access control is enforced in many of the models for WS. Our research is focusing on delegation models and information flow models which have been influenced by the Goguen and Meseguer model for noninterference.

There is not much work reported on multilevel security for WS. Nevertheless, we believe that it is an important aspect. We need to ensure that not only are the Bell and LaPadula model's simple security and the star properties satisfied, but the Gouge and Meseguer's noninterference property is also satisfied. In the Bell and LaPadula model, a subject can read from an object if the subject's security level dominates that of the object. A subject writes into an object if the subject's security level is dominated by that of the object. In addition, for WS we also need policies for invocation. That is, a service S1 invoked another service S2 if the S1 security level of the service description of S1 dominates the security level of the service description of S2. However, when S1 invokes S2, S2 will operate at the operating level of S1. This way S2 will have all the credentials of S1. Therefore, if the service description of S2 dominates that of S1, then S1 cannot invoke S2. For example, if service description of S2 is Secret and service description of S1 is Unclassified and S1 operates at the Unclassified level then S1 cannot invoke S2. If for example, S1 is allowed to invoke S2, then S2 must operate at the unclassified level and this is a problem since the description of S2 is Secret. Suppose now the service descriptions of S1 and S2 satisfied the policies. If, however, S1 operates at Unclassified and S2 is allowed to operate at the Secret level, then S2 cannot send any results back to S1 as it will violate the star property.

5.4 Summary and Directions

This chapter has provided an overview of the service-oriented computing paradigm and security issues for services. As we have stated, services are at the heart and soul of cloud computing. This is because cloud computing capabilities are provided as services to the customers. First, we discussed the notion of services, SOA and WS, the emerging X as a service paradigm and SOAD. Then, we discussed security for SOA and WS. In particular, we discussed access control for WS, standards such as SAML and XACML and some emerging security models such as models for delegation, information flow, and multilevel security. We also discussed identity management for WS.

There are several areas for future research and development. While there are numerous developments on WS, the application of semantic web technologies and securing the WS are major challenges. Furthermore, major initiatives such as the global information grid and network centric enterprise services are based on WS and SOA. Therefore, securing these technologies as well as making WS more intelligent by using the semantic web will be critical for the next-generation web.

With respect to SOAD, there is no standard way to model and analyze services as well as secure services. We also need an appropriate security model for services. ABAC is one such model. We need to examine how ABAC can be integrated with UCON. We also need to examine the inference problem in more detail for services. Finally, we need to develop standards similar to SAML and XACML to include more sophisticated forms of fine-grained access control. As WS explode and we carry out more and more transactions on the web and we get involved in social networks, it is critical that we protect the identity of individuals as well as ensure authorized access. Furthermore, a user may be involved in multiple social networks and multiple transactions. The user may have different identities in different systems. Therefore, we need an effective mechanism to manage the numerous identities of possibly billions of users. Research on identity management is just beginning. We need a lot more work in this area to include developing appropriate standards. Finally, with respect to security models, while much of the work has focused on access control models for WS, we have carried out some work on delegation models and information flow models. With the delegation models, the idea is for services to delegate its credentials to another service that it invokes for execution. With the information flow models, the goal is to ensure that information is not passed from a high level to a low level during service composition. While access control models for WS are fairly advanced, research in delegation models and information flow models is still in its infancy. Our work has explored only some initial ideas. We need to formally specify security properties and prove that the services are secure with respect to the delegation models and information flow models. We also need to examine the integration of access control, delegation, and information flow models.

We have given URLs as references for the various web serviced and secure WS technologies, standards, and protocols. It should be noted that these URLs could change and therefore we urge the reader to check the W3C and OASIS web pages as well as the web pages of corporations developing standards such as Microsoft and IBM to keep up with the developments. As stated in Section 5.1, cloud computing is usually provided as a collection of services to the consumer. Therefore, the topics discussed in this chapter form the essence of cloud computing and secure cloud computing.

References

[ABAC] Information System Security Operation: Attribute-Based Access Control, http://www.docstoc.com/docs/44587189/Information-System-Security-Operation-Attribute-Based-Access-Control

[ADDRESS] Web Services Addressing, http://www.w3.org/Submission/ws-addressing/

[AMAZON] Amazon.com, http://aws.amazon.com/

[APAC] The Apache Software Foundation Web Services Project, http://ws.apache.org/

[ASAP] OASIS Asynchronous Service Access Protocol, http://www.oasis-open.org/committees/tc_home.php?wg_abbrev=asap

[BERT99] Bertino, E., E. Ferrari, and V. Atluri. The specification and enforcement of authorization constraints in workflow management systems. *ACM Transactions on Information Systems Security (TISSEC)*, 2(1): 65–104, 1999.

[BERT06] Bertino, E. and L. Martino. Security in SOA and web services. *IEEE International Conference on Services Computing (SCC 2006)*. Chicago, IL, USA.

[BPEL] http://en.wikipedia.org/wiki/Business_Process_Execution_Language

[CAF] Web Services Composite Application Framework, http://en.wikipedia.org/wiki/WS-CAF

[CONV] WS-Secure conversation, http://docs.oasis-open.org/ws-sx/ws-secureconversation/200512/ws-secureconversation-1.3-os.html

[COORD] Web services transactions specifications, http://www.ibm.com/developerworks/library/specification/ws-tx/#coor

[ENUM] WS-Enumeration, http://www.w3.org/Submission/2006/02/

[ERL05] Erl, T. *Service-Oriented Architecture (SOA): Concepts, Technology, and Design*, Prentice-Hall, New Jersey, 2005.

[EVENT] WS-Eventing, http://www.w3.org/Submission/WS-Eventing/

[FED] Federated Identity, http://en.wikipedia.org/wiki/Federated_identity_management

[GUTI10] Gutierrez, C., E. Fernandez-Medina, and M. Piattini (Editors), *Web Services Security Development and Architecture*, Information Science Reference, Hershey, PA, 2010.

[IBM] Transformation to SOA, http://www.ibm.com/developerworks/rational/library/08/0115_gorelik/

[INFO] Information card, http://en.wikipedia.org/wiki/Information_Card

[LIB] Liberty Alliance, http://en.wikipedia.org/wiki/Liberty_Alliance

[MEP] Message Exchange Pattern, http://en.wikipedia.org/wiki/Message_Exchange_Pattern

[META] Web Services Metadata Exchange, http://www.ibm.com/developerworks/library/specification/ws-mex/

[MODEL] Analysis and design techniques for service-oriented development and integration, http://www.perspectivesonwebservices.de/download/INF05.ServiceModelingv11.pdf

[NOTIFY] WS-Notification, http://www.ibm.com/developerworks/library/specification/ws-notification/

[OASIS] OASIS Standards, http://www.oasis-open.org/specs/

[OMG] Object Management Group, http://www.omg.org

[OPEN] OpenID, http://en.wikipedia.org/wiki/OpenID

[PA] WS-Policy assertions, http://xml.coverpages.org/ws-policyassertionsV11.pdf

[PARK04] Park, J. and R. S. Sandhu, The $UCON_{ABC}$ usage control model. *ACM Transactions on Information Systems Security*, 7(1): 128–174, 2004.

[POLICY] WS-Policy, http://www.w3.org/Submission/2006/SUBM-WS-Policy-20060425/

[RAY04] Ray, I., R. B. France, and N. GeriGeorg, An aspect-based approach to modeling access control concerns. *Information & Software Technology*, 46(9): 575–587, 2004.

[RELIABILITY] WS-Reliability, http://www.service-architecture.com/web-services/articles/web_services_reliability_ws-reliability.html

[REST] Representational State Transfer, http://en.wikipedia.org/wiki/Representational_state_transfer

[REST-SOAP] REST vs. SOAP at Amazon, http://www.oreillynet.com/pub/wlg/3005

[SAML] Security Assertion Markup Language, http://en.wikipedia.org/wiki/Security_Assertion_Markup_Language.

[SELL93] Sell, P. J. and B. M. Thuraisingham, Applying OMT for designing multilevel database applications. *Database Security, VII: Status and Prospects, Proceedings of the IFIP*

WG11.3 Working Conference on Database Security, Lake Guntersville, Alabama, USA, 12–15 September, 1993, pp. 41–64.

[SHE07] She, W., B. M. Thuraisingham, and I.-L. Yen, Delegation-based security model for web services. *IEEE International Symposium on High Assurance Systems Engineering (HASE 2007)*, November 2007, Dallas, TX, USA, pp. 85–91.

[SHE08] She, W., I-L. Yen, and B.M. Thuraisingham, Enhancing security modeling for web services using delegation and pass-on. *2008 IEEE International Conference on Web Services (ICWS 2008)*, September 2008, Beijing, China, pp. 545–552.

[SHE09] She, W., I-L. Yen, B. M. Thuraisingham, and E. Bertino, The SCIFC model for information flow control in web service composition. *IEEE International Conference on Web Services, ICWS 2009*, Los Angeles, CA, USA, July 2009, pp. 1–8.

[SHIB] Shibboleth Internet 2 http://en.wikipedia.org/wiki/Shibboleth_%28Internet2%29

[SOAD] Service Oriented Analysis and Modeling, http://en.wikipedia.org/wiki/Service-oriented_modeling

[SOMA] Sevice Oriented Modeling and Analysis, http://www.ibm.com/developerworks/library/ws-soa-design1/

[SRIV] Srivastava, B. and J. Koehler, *Web Service Composition—Current Solutions and Open Problems*, http://www.zurich.ibm.com/pdf/ebizz/icaps-ws.pdf

[SSO] Single Sign On http://en.wikipedia.org/wiki/Single_sign-on

[SURVEY] A Survey of Service Oriented Development Methodologies, http://www.dcs.shef.ac.uk/~ajhs/research/papers/soasurvey.pdf

[THUR94a] Thuraisingham, B. and A. Schafer, Applying OMT for real-time applications, *Proceedings of the IEEE Real-time Applications Workshop*, Bethesda, MD, July 1994.

[THUR94b] Thuraisingham, B. Applying OMT for healthcare applications, *Proceedings IEEE Dual Use Technology Conference*, Rome, NY, May 1994.

[THUR10] Thuraisingham, B. *Secure Semantic Service Oriented Systems*, CRC Press, Boca Raton, FL, 2010.

[TRANS] Web Services Transactions Specifications, http://www.ibm.com/developerworks/library/specification/ws-tx/

[TRUST] WS-Trust, http://en.wikipedia.org/wiki/WS-Trust

[UML] Unified Modeling Language, http://en.wikipedia.org/wiki/Unified_Modeling_Language

[WSIL] Web Services Inspection Language, http://www.ibm.com/developerworks/library/specification/ws-wsilspec/

[WSS] WS-Security, http://en.wikipedia.org/wiki/WS-Security

[XACML] XACML, http://en.wikipedia.org/wiki/XACML

[ZHAN07] Zhang, L.-J., J. Zhang, and H. Cai, *Services Computing*, Springer, Heidelberg, 2007.

Chapter 6

Semantic Web Services and Security

6.1 Overview

In the previous chapter, we discussed services computing and secure services computing. While services are becoming an essential aspect of cloud computing, at present the services are not semantically enabled. Furthermore, while the current web technologies facilitate the integration of information from a syntactic point of view, there is still a lot to be done to handle the different semantics of various systems and applications. That is, current web technologies depend a lot on the "human-in-the-loop" for information management and integration. In this chapter, we will discuss semantic web technologies and how WS could exploit these technologies so that they are semantically enabled. Note that we define a cloud that utilizes semantic web technologies to be a semantic cloud. Later on in this book we discuss several experimental systems that are based on the semantic cloud.

Tim Berners Lee, the father of WWW, realized the inadequacies of current web technologies and subsequently strived to make the web more intelligent. His goal was to have a web that would essentially alleviate humans from the burden of having to integrate disparate information sources as well as to carry out extensive searches. He then came to the conclusion that one needs machine-understandable web pages and the use of ontologies for information integration. This resulted in the notion of the semantic web [LEE01]. The WS that take advantage of semantic web technologies are semantic web services.

A semantic web can be thought of as a web that is highly intelligent and sophisticated so that one needs little or no human intervention to carry out tasks such as scheduling appointments, coordinating activities, searching for complex documents, as well as integrating disparate databases and information systems. While much progress has been made toward developing such an intelligent web, there is still a lot to be done. For example, technologies such as ontology matching, intelligent agents, and markup languages are contributing a lot toward developing the semantic web. Nevertheless, one still needs the human to make decisions and take actions.

There have been many recent developments on the semantic web. The W3C is specifying standards for the semantic web [W3C]. These standards include specifications for XML, RDF, and Interoperability. However, it is also very important that the semantic web be secure. That is, the components that constitute the semantic web have to be secure. The components include XML, RDF, and Ontologies. In addition, we need secure information integration. We also need to examine trust issues for the semantic web. It is therefore important that we need standards for securing the semantic web including specifications for secure XML, secure RDF, and secure interoperability (see [THUR05]). In this chapter, we will discuss the various components of the semantic web and discuss semantic web services.

While agents are crucial to manage the data and the activities on the semantic web, usually agents are not treated as part of semantic web technologies by some while others consider agents as part of the semantic web. Because the subject of agents is vast and there are numerous efforts on developing agents as well as secure agents, we do not discuss agents as part of this book. However, we mention agents throughout the book as it is these agents that use XML and RDF and make sense of the data and understand web pages. Agents act on behalf of the users. Agents communicate with each other using well-defined protocols. Various types of agents have been developed depending on the tasks they carry out. These include mobile agents, intelligent agents, search agents, and knowledge management agents. Agents invoke WS to carry out the operations. For details of agents we refer to [HEND01].

As the demand for data and information management increases, there is also a critical need for maintaining the security of the databases, applications, and information systems. Data and information have to be protected from unauthorized access as well as from malicious corruption. With the advent of the web, it is even more important to protect the data and information as numerous individuals now have access to these data and information. Therefore, we need effective mechanisms to secure the semantic web technologies. In particular, we need to secure XML and RDF documents as well as other components such as secure ontologies and secure web rules.

The organization of this chapter is as follows. In Section 6.2, we will provide an overview of semantic web technologies. In particular, we will discuss the layered architecture for the semantic web as specified by Tim Berners Lee, the components such as XML, RDF, ontologies, and web rules and semantic web services. Security for semantic web technologies is discussed in Section 6.3. This chapter is summarized in Section 6.4. Figure 6.1 illustrates the concepts

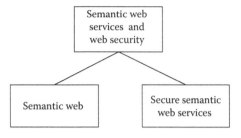

Figure 6.1   Semantic web services and security.

discussed in this chapter. Much of the discussion of the semantic web is summarized from the book by Antoniou and van Harmelen [ANTO08]. For an up-to-date specification, see [W3C].

6.2 Semantic Web

6.2.1 Layered Technology Stack

Figure 6.2 illustrates the layered technology stack for the semantic web. This is the architecture that was developed by Tim Berners Lee. Essentially the semantic web consists of layers where each layer takes advantage of the technologies of the previous layer. The lowest layer is the protocol layer and this is usually not included in the discussion of the semantic technologies. The next layer is the XML layer. XML is a document representation language and will be discussed in Section 6.2.2. While XML is sufficient to specify syntax, semantics such as "the creator of document D is John" is hard to specify in XML. Therefore, the W3C developed RDF which uses XML syntax. We describe RDF in Section 6.2.3.

The semantic web community then went further and came up with a specification of ontologies in languages such as OWL. Note that OWL addresses the inadequacies of RDF. We discuss OWL in Section 6.2.4. To reason about various policies,

Logic, proof, and trust
Rules/query
RDF, ontologies
XML, XML schemas
URI, UNICODE

Figure 6.2   Technology stack for the semantic web.

the semantic web community has come up with a web rules language such as SWRL (Semantic Web Rules Language) and Rules ML (Rules Markup Language). Rules are discussed in Section 6.2.5. Semantic web services are discussed in Section 6.2.6.

6.2.2 eXtensible Markup Language

XML is needed due to the limitations of HTML and complexities of SGML (Standard Generalized Markup Language). It is an extensible markup language specified by the W3C and designed to make the interchange of structured documents over the Internet easier. An important aspect of XML used to be Document Type Definitions (DTDs) which define the role of each element of the text in a formal model. XML schemas have now become critical to specify the structure. XML schemas are also XML documents. This section will discuss various components of XML including: statements, elements, attributes, and schemas. The components of XML are illustrated in Figure 6.3.

6.2.2.1 XML Statement and Elements

The following is an example of an XML statement that describes the fact that "John Smith is a Professor in Texas." The elements are name and state. The XML statement is as follows:

```
<Professor>
       <name> John Smith </name>
       <state> Texas </state>
</Professor>
```

6.2.2.2 XML Attributes

Suppose we want to specify that there is a professor called John Smith who makes $60 K. Then we can use either elements or attributes to specify this. The example below shows the use of attributes Name and Salary.

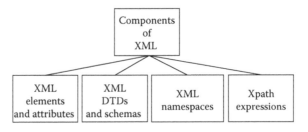

Figure 6.3   Components of XML.

```
<Professor
      Name = "John Smith", Access = All, Read
      Salary = "60K"
      </Professor>
```

6.2.2.3 XML DTDs

DTDs essentially specify the structure of XML documents. Consider the following DTD for Professor with elements Name and State. This will be specified as:

```
<!ELEMENT Professor Officer (Name, State)>
<!ELEMENT name (#PCDATA)>
<!ELEMENT state (#PCDATA)>
<!ELEMENT access (#PCDATA).>
```

6.2.2.4 XML Schemas

While DTDs were the early attempts to specify structure for XML documents, XML schemas are far more elegant to specify structures. Unlike DTDs, XML schemas essentially use the XML syntax for specification. Consider the following example:

```
<ComplexType = name = "ProfessorType">
      <Sequence>
      <element name = "name" type = "string"/>
      <element name = "state" type = "string"/>
      <Sequence>
</ComplexType>
```

6.2.2.5 XML Namespaces

Namespaces are used for DISAMBIGUATION. An example is given below.

```
<CountryX: Academic-Institution
      Xmlns: CountryX = http://www.CountryX.edu/Institution DTD"
      Xmlns: USA = "http://www.USA.edu/Institution DTD"
      Xmlns: UK = "http://www.UK.edu/Institution DTD"
<USA: Title = College
      USA: Name = "University of Texas at Dallas"
      USA: State = "Texas"
<UK: Title = University
      UK: Name = "Cambridge University"
      UK: State = Cambs
</CountryX: Academic-Institution>
```

6.2.2.6 XML Federations/Distribution

XML data may be distributed and the databases may form federations. This is illustrated in the segment below.

Site 1 document:

```
<Professor-name>
      <ID> 111 </ID>
      <Name> John Smith </name>
      <State> Texas </state>
</Professor-name>
```

Site 2 document:

```
<Professor-salary>
      <ID> 111 </ID>
      <salary> 60K </salary>
</Professor-salary>
```

6.2.2.7 XML-QL, XQuery, XPath, XSLT

XML-QL and XQuery are query languages that have been proposed for XML. XPath is used to specify the queries. Essentially, Xpath expressions may be used to reach a particular element in the XML statement. In our research, we have specified policy rules as Xpath expressions (see [BERT04]). XSLT is used to present XML documents. Details are given in [W3C] as well as in [ANTO08]. Another useful reference is [LAUR00].

6.2.3 Resource Description Framework

While XML is ideal to specify the syntax of various statements, it is difficult to specify the semantics of a statement with XML. For example, with XML, it is difficult to specify statements such as:

- Engineer is a subclass of Employee
- Engineer inherits all properties of Employee

Note that the above statement specifies the class/subclass and inheritance relationships. RDF was developed by Tim Berners Lee and his team so that the inadequacies of XML could be handled. RDF uses XML syntax. Additional constructs are needed for RDF and we discuss some of them. Details can be found in [ANTO08].

RDF is the essence of the semantic web. It provides semantics with the use of ontologies to various statements and uses XML syntax. RDF concepts include the basic model which consists of resources, properties, and statements, and the container model which consists of bag, sequence, and alternative. We discuss some of the essential concepts. The components of RDF are illustrated in Figure 6.4.

```
                    ┌──────────┐
                    │Components│
                    │    of    │
                    │   RDF    │
                    └──────────┘
        ┌────────┬──────┴──────┬────────┐
   ┌────────┐ ┌────────┐ ┌──────────┐ ┌────────┐
   │  RDF   │ │  RDF   │ │   RDF    │ │  RDF   │
   │statements│ │ basic │ │container │ │schemas │
   │        │ │ model  │ │  model   │ │        │
   └────────┘ └────────┘ └──────────┘ └────────┘
```

Figure 6.4   Components of RDF.

6.2.3.1 RDF Basics

The RDF basic model consists of resource, property, and statement. In RDF everything is a resource such as person, vehicle, and animal. Properties describe relationships between resources such as "bought," "invented," and "ate." Statement is a triple of the form: (object, property, value). Examples of statements are:

- Berners Lee invented the semantic web
- Tom ate the apple
- Mary brought a dress

Figure 6.5 illustrates a statement in RDF. Here, Berners Lee is the object, semantic web is the value, and invented is the property.

6.2.3.2 RDF Container Model

RDF container model consists of bag, sequence, and alternative. As described in [ANTO08], these constructs are specified in RDF as follows:

Bag: Unordered container, may contain multiple occurrences
  • Rdf: Bag
Seq: Ordered container, may contain multiple occurrences
  • Rdf: Seq
Alt: a set of alternatives
  • Rdf: Alt

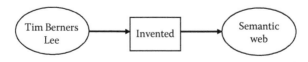

Figure 6.5   RDF statement.

6.2.3.3 RDF Specification

As stated in [ANTO08], RDF specifications have been given for Attributes, Types, Nesting, Containers, and so on. An example is the following: "Berners Lee is the Author of the book Semantic Web."

The above statement is specified as follows (see also [ANTO08]):

```
<rdf: RDF
  xmlns: rdf = "http://w3c.org/1999/02-22-rdf-syntax-ns#"
  xmlns: xsd = "http://- - -
  xmlns: uni = "http://- - - -
<rdf: Description: rdf: about = "949352"
  <uni: name = Berners Lee </uni:name>
  <uni: title> Professor <uni:title>
</rdf: Description>
<rdf: Description rdf: about: "ZZZ"
  <uni: bookname> semantic web <uni:bookname>
  <uni: authoredby:Berners Lee <uni:authoredby>
</rdf: Description>
</rdf: RDF>
```

6.2.3.4 RDF Schemas

While XML schemas specify the structure of the XML document and can be considered to be metadata, RDF schema specifies relationships such as the class/subclass relationships. For example, we need RDF Schema to specify statements such as engineer is a subclass of employee. The following is the RDF specification for this statement.

```
<rdfs: Class rdf: ID = "engineer"
<rdfs: comment>
The class of Engineers
All engineers are employees
<rdfs: comment>
<rdfs: subClassof rdf: resource = "employee" />
<rdfs: Class>
```

6.2.3.5 RDF Axiomatic Semantics

First-order logic is used to specify formulas and inferencing. The following constructs are needed:

Built-in functions (first) and predicates (type)
Modus Ponens: From A and If A then B, deduce B

The following example is taken from [ANTO08]:

EXAMPLE

All Containers are Resources; that is if X is a container, then X is a resource.

Type(?c, Container) → Type(?c, Resource)
If we have Type (A, Container) then we can infer Type (A, Resource)

6.2.3.6 RDF Inferencing

Unlike XML, RDF has inferencing capabilities. While first-order logic provides a proof system, it will be computationally infeasible to develop such a system using first-order logic. As a result, horn clause logic was developed for logic programming [LLOY87]; this is still computationally expensive. Semantic web is based on a restricted logic called Descriptive Logic and details can be found in [ANTO08]. RDF uses If then Rules as follows:

IF E contains the triples (?u, rdfs: subClassof, ?v)
and (?v, rdfs: subClassof ?w)
THEN
E also contains the triple (?u, rdfs: subClassOf, ?w)
That is, if u is a subclass of v, and v is a subclass of w, then u is a subclass of w.

6.2.3.7 RDF Query

Like XML Query languages such as X-Query and XML-QL, query languages are also being developed for RDF. One can query RDF using XML, but this will be very difficult as RDF is much richer than XML. Therefore, RQL has been developed. RQL is an SQL-like language which has been developed for RDF. It is of the form:

Select from "RDF document" where some "condition."

6.2.3.8 SPARQL Protocol and RDF Query Language

The RDF Data group at W3C has developed a query language for RDF called SPARQL which is becoming the standard now for querying RDF documents. We are developing SPARQL query processing algorithms for clouds. We have also developed query optimizer for SPARQL queries.

6.2.4 Ontologies

Ontologies are common definitions for any entity, person, or thing. Ontologies are needed to clarify various terms and therefore they are crucial for machine-understandable web pages. Several ontologies have been defined and available for use. Defining a common ontology for an entity is a challenge as different groups may come up with different definitions. Therefore, we need mappings for multiple ontologies. That is, these mappings map one ontology to another. Specific languages have been developed for ontologies. Note that RDF was developed as XML and is not sufficient to specify semantics such as class/subclass relationship. RDF is also limited as one cannot express several other properties such as Union and Intersection. Therefore, we need a richer language. Ontology languages were developed by the semantic web community for this purpose.

OWL (Web Ontology Language) is a popular ontology specification language. It is a language for ontologies and relies on RDF. DARPA (Defense Advanced Research Projects Agency) developed the early language DAML (DARPA Agent Markup Language). The Europeans developed OIL (Ontology Interface Language). DAML + OIL combine both and were the starting point for OWL. OWL was developed by W3C. OWL is based on a subset of first-order logic and that is descriptive logic.

OWL features include: subclass relationship, class membership, equivalence of classes, classification and consistency (e.g., x is an instance of A, A is a subclass of B, x is not an instance of B).

There are three types of OWL: OWL-Full, OWL-DL, OWL-Lite. Automated tools for managing ontologies are called ontology engineering.

Below is an example OWL specification:

Textbooks and Coursebooks are the same
EnglishBook is not a FrenchBook
EnglishBook is not a GermanBook

```
<owl: Class rdf: about = "#EnglishBook">
 <owl: disjointWith rdf: resource "#FrenchBook" />
 <owl: disjointWith rdf: resource = #GermanBook" />
</owl:Class>
<owl: Class rdf: ID = "TextBook">
 <owl: equivalentClass rdf: resource = "CourseBook" />
</owl: Class>
```

Below is an OWL specification for Property

Englishbooks are read by Students

```
<owl: ObjectProperty rdf: about = "#readBy">
 <rdfs domain rdf: resource = "#EnglishBook" />
 <rdfs: range rdf: resource = "#student" />
<rdfs: subPropertyOf rdf: resource = #involves" />
</owl: ObjectProperty>
```

Below is an OWL spec for property restriction.

All Frenchbooks are read only by Frenchstudents

```
<owl: Class rdf: about = "#"FrenchBook">
<rdfs: subClassOf>
 <owl: Restriction>
<owl: onProperty rdf: resource = "#readBy">
<owl: allValuesFrom rdf: resource = #FrenchStudent"/>
</rdfs: subClassOf>
</owl: Class>
```

6.2.5 Web Rules and SWRL

6.2.5.1 Web Rules

RDF is built on XML and OWL is built on RDF. We can express subclass relationships in RDF and additional relationships can be expressed in OWL. However, reasoning power is still limited in OWL. Therefore, we need to specify rules and subsequently a markup language for rules so that machines can understand and make inferences.

Below are some examples as given in [ANTO08].

Studies(X,Y), Lives(X,Z), Loc(Y,U), Loc(Z,U) → DomesticStudent(X)

That is, if John Studies at UTD and John lives on Campbell Road and the location of Campbell Road and UTD are Richardson then John is a Domestic student.

Note that Person (X) → Man(X) or Woman(X) is not a rule in predicate logic.

That is if X is a person then X is either a man or a woman cannot be expressed in first-order predicate logic. Therefore, in predicate logic we express the above as if X is a person and X is not a man then X is a woman and similarly if X is a person and X is not a woman then X is a man. That is, in predicate logic, we can have a rule of the form

Person(X) and Not Man(X) → Woman(X)
However, in OWL we can specify the rule if X is a person then X is a man or X
   is a woman.
Rules can be monotonic or nonmonotonic.
Below is an example of a monotonic rule:
→ Mother(X,Y)
Mother(X,Y) → Parent(X,Y)
If Mary is the mother of John, then Mary is the parent of John
Rule is of the form:
B1, B2, …, Bn → A
That is, if B1, B2, …, Bn hold then A holds

In the case of nonmonotonic reasoning, if we have X and NOT X, we do not treat them as inconsistent as in the case of monotonic reasoning. For example, as discussed in [ANTO08], consider the example of an apartment that is acceptable to John. That is, in general John is prepared to rent an apartment unless the apartment has less than two bedrooms and does not allow pets. This can be expressed as follows:

- → Acceptable(X)
- Bedroom(X,Y), Y < 2 → NOT Acceptable(X)
- NOT Pets(X) → NOT Acceptable(X)

The first rule states that an apartment is in general acceptable to John. The second rule states that if the apartment has less than two bedrooms, it is not acceptable to John. The third rule states that if pets are not allowed, then the apartment is not acceptable to John. Note that there could be a contradiction. But with nonmonotonic reasoning this is allowed, while it is not allowed in monotonic reasoning.

We need rule markup languages for the machine to understand the rules. The various components of logic are expressed in the Rule Markup Language called RuleML developed for the semantic web. Both monotonic and nonmonotonic rules can be represented in RuleML.

An example representation of Fact Parent(A) that is A is a parent is expressed as follows:

```
<fact>
      <atom>
   <predicate>Parent</predicate>
     <term>
       <const>A</const>
     </term>
   </atom>
</fact>
```

6.2.5.2 Semantic Web Rules Language

W3C has come up with a new rules language that integrates both OWL and Web Rules and this is SWRL. The authors of SWRL state that SWRL extends the set of OWL axioms to include Horn-like rules. This way, Horn-like rules can be combined with an OWL knowledge base. Such a language will have the representational power of OWL and the reasoning power of logic programming. We illustrate SWRL components in Figure 6.6.

The authors of SWRL (Horrocks et al.) also state that the proposed rules are in the form of an implication between an antecedent (body) and consequent (head). The intended meaning can be read as: whenever the conditions specified in the antecedent hold, then the conditions specified in the consequent must also hold. An XML syntax is also given for these rules based on RuleML and the OWL XML presentation syntax. Furthermore, an RDF concrete syntax based on the OWL

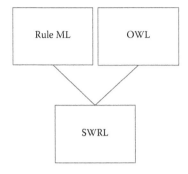

Figure 6.6 SWRL components.

RDF/XML exchange syntax is presented. The rule syntaxes are illustrated with several running examples. Finally, we give usage suggestions and cautions.

The following is an SWRL example that we have taken from the W3C specification of SWRL [SWRL]. It states that if x1 is the child of x2 and x3 is the brother of x2, then x3 is the uncle of x1. For more details of SWRL, we refer the reader to the W3C specification [SWRL]. The example uses XML syntax.

```
<ruleml:imp>
  <ruleml:_rlab ruleml:href = "#example1"/>
  <ruleml:_body>
    <swrlx:individualPropertyAtom swrlx:property="hasParent">
      <ruleml:var>x1</ruleml:var>
      <ruleml:var>x2</ruleml:var>
    </swrlx:individualPropertyAtom>
    <swrlx:individualPropertyAtom swrlx:property="hasBrother">
      <ruleml:var>x2</ruleml:var>
      <ruleml:var>x3</ruleml:var>
    </swrlx:individualPropertyAtom>
  </ruleml:_body>
  <ruleml:_head>
    <swrlx:individualPropertyAtom swrlx:property="hasUncle">
      <ruleml:var>x1</ruleml:var>
      <ruleml:var>x3</ruleml:var>
    </swrlx:individualPropertyAtom>
  </ruleml:_head>
</ruleml:imp>
```

6.2.6 Semantic Web Services

Semantic web services utilize semantic web technologies. As we have stated in Chapter 5, WS utilize WSDL and SOAP messages which are based on XML. With semantic web technologies, one could utilize RDF to express semantics in the messages as well as with WS description languages. Ontologies could be utilized for

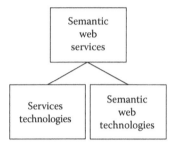

Figure 6.7   Semantic web services.

handling heterogeneity. For example, if the words in the messages or service descriptions are ambiguous, then ontologies could resolve these ambiguities. Finally, rule languages such as SWRL could be used for reasoning power for the messages as well as the service descriptions.

As stated in [SWS], the mainstream XML standards for interoperation of WS specify only syntactic interoperability, not the semantic meaning of messages. For example, WSDL can specify the operations available through a web service and the structure of data sent and received but cannot specify semantic meaning of the data or semantic constraints on the data. This requires programmers to reach specific agreements on the interaction of WS and makes automatic web service composition difficult.

Semantic web services are built around semantic web standards for the interchange of semantic data, which makes it easy for programmers to combine data from different sources and services without losing meaning. WS can be activated "behind the scenes" when a web browser makes a request to a web server, which then uses various WS to construct a more sophisticated reply than it would have been able to do on its own. Semantic web services can also be used by automatic programs that run without any connection to a web browser.

Later on in this book we will discuss how semantic web, security, and WS could be integrated for semantic web services. Figure 6.7 illustrates various components of semantic web services.

6.3 Secure Semantic Web Services

6.3.1 Security for the Semantic Web

We first provide an overview of security issues for the semantic web and then discuss some details on XML security, RDF security, and secure information integration, which are components of the secure semantic web. As more progress is made on investigating these various issues, we hope that appropriate standards would be developed for securing the semantic web. Security cannot be considered in isolation. That is, there is no one layer that should focus on security. Security cuts across all layers and this is a challenge. That is, we need security for each of the layers as illustrated in Figure 6.8.

For example, consider the lowest layer. One needs secure TCP/IP, secure sockets, and secure HTTP. There are now security protocols for these various lower layer protocols. One needs end-to-end security. That is, one cannot just have secure TCP/IP built on untrusted communication layers; we need network security. The next layer is XML and XML schemas. One needs secure XML. That is, access must be controlled to various portions of the document for reading, browsing, and modifications. There is research on securing XML and XML schemas. The next step is securing RDF. Now with RDF not only do we need secure XML, we also need security for the interpretations and semantics. For example, under certain contexts, portions of the document may be Unclassified while under certain other contexts the document may be Classified.

Once XML and RDF have been secured, the next step is to examine security for ontologies and interoperation. That is, ontologies may have security levels attached to them. Certain parts of the ontologies could be Secret while certain other parts may be Unclassified. The challenge is how does one use these ontologies for secure information integration? Researchers have done some work on the secure interoperability of databases. We need to revisit this research and then determine what else needs to be done so that the information on the web can be managed, integrated, and exchanged securely. Logic, proof, and trust are at the highest layers of the semantic web. That is, how can we trust the information that the web gives us?

We also need to examine the inference problem for the semantic web. Inference is the process of posing queries and deducing new information. It becomes a problem when the deduced information is something the user is unauthorized to know. With the semantic web, and especially with data mining tools, one can make all kinds of inferences. Recently there has been some research on controlling unauthorized inferences on the semantic web. We need to continue with such research (see, e.g., [FARK03], [THUR06]).

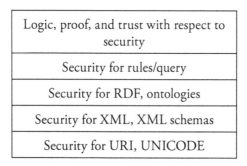

| Logic, proof, and trust with respect to security |
| Security for rules/query |
| Security for RDF, ontologies |
| Security for XML, XML schemas |
| Security for URI, UNICODE |

Figure 6.8 Layers for the secure semantic web.

Security should not be an afterthought. We have often heard that one needs to insert security into the system right from the beginning. Similarly, security cannot be an afterthought for the semantic web. However, we cannot also make the system inefficient if we must guarantee 100% security at all times. What is needed is a flexible security policy. During some situations we may need 100% security, while during some other situations say 30% security may be sufficient.

6.3.2 XML Security

Various research efforts have been reported on XML security (see, e.g., [BERT02]). We briefly discuss some of the key points. The main challenge is whether to give access to the entire XML documents or parts of the documents. Bertino et al. have developed authorization models for XML. They have focused on access control policies as well as on dissemination policies. They also considered push and pull architectures. They specified the policies in XML. The policy specification contains information about which users can access which portions of the documents. In [BERT02], algorithms for access control as well as computing views of the results are presented. In addition, architectures for securing XML documents are also discussed. In [BERT04], the authors go further and describe how XML documents may be published on the web. The idea is for owners to publish documents, subjects to request access to the documents, and untrusted publishers to give the subjects the views of the documents they are authorized to see.

W3C is specifying standards for XML security. The XML security project (see [XML1]) is focusing on providing the implementation of security standards for XML. The focus is on XML-Signature Syntax and Processing, XML-Encryption Syntax and Processing and XML Key Management. W3C also has a number of working groups including XML Signature working group (see [XML2]) and XML encryption working group (see [XML3]). While the standards are focusing on what can be implemented in the near-term, much research is needed on securing XML documents.

6.3.3 RDF Security

RDF is the foundation of the semantic web. While XML is limited in providing machine-understandable documents, RDF handles this limitation. As a result, RDF provides better support for interoperability as well as searching and cataloging. It also describes contents of documents as well as relationships between various entities in the document. While XML provides syntax and notations, RDF supplements this by providing semantic information in a standardized way.

The basic RDF model has three components: they are resources, properties, and statements. Resource is anything described by RDF expressions. It could be a web page or a collection of pages. Property is a specific attribute used to describe a resource. RDF statements are resources together with a named property plus the value of the property. Statement components are subject, predicate, and object. So for example, if we have a sentence of the form "John is the creator of xxx," then xxx is the subject or resource, property, or predicate is "creator" and object or literal is "John." There are RDF diagrams very much like say ER diagrams or object diagrams to represent statements. It is important that the intended interpretation be used for RDF sentences. This is accomplished by RDF schemas. Schema is sort of a dictionary and has interpretations of various terms used in sentences.

More advanced concepts in RDF include the container model and statements about statements. The container model has three types of container objects and they are Bag, Sequence, and Alternative. A bag is an unordered list of resources or literals. It is used to mean that a property has multiple values but the order is not important. A sequence is a list of ordered resources. Here, the order is important. Alternative is a list of resources that represent alternatives for the value of a property. Various tutorials in RDF describe the syntax of containers in more detail.

RDF also provides support for making statements about other statements. For example, with this facility one can make statements of the form "The statement A is false" where A is the statement "John is the creator of X." Again one can use object-like diagrams to represent containers and statements about statements. RDF also has a formal model associated with it. This formal model has a formal grammar. For further information on RDF we refer to the excellent discussion in the book by Antoniou and van Harmelen [ANTO08].

Now to make the semantic web secure, we need to ensure that RDF documents are secure. This would involve securing XML from a syntactic point of view. However, with RDF, we also need to ensure that security is preserved at the semantic level. The issues include the security implications of the concepts resource, properties, and statements. That is, how is access control ensured? How can statements and properties about statements be protected? How can one provide access control at a finer grain of granularity? What are the security properties of the container model? How can bags, lists, and alternatives be protected? Can we specify security policies in RDF? How can we resolve semantic inconsistencies for the policies? How can we express security constraints in RDF? What are the security implications of statements about statements? How can we protect RDF schemas? These are difficult questions and we need to start research to provide answers. XML security is just the beginning. Securing RDF is much more challenging (see also [CARM04]).

6.3.4 Security and Ontologies

Ontologies are essentially representations of various concepts in order to avoid ambiguity. Numerous ontologies have been developed. These ontologies have been used by agents to understand the web pages and conduct operations such as the integration of databases. Furthermore, ontologies can be represented in languages such as RDF or special languages such as OWL.

Now, ontologies have to be secure. That is, access to the ontologies has to be controlled. This means that different users may have access to different parts of the ontology. On the other hand, ontologies may be used to specify security policies just as XML and RDF have been used to specify the policies. That is, we will describe how ontologies may be secured as well as how ontologies may be used to specify the various policies.

6.3.5 Secure Query and Rules Processing

The layer above the Secure RDF layer is the Secure Query and Rules processing layer. While RDF can be used to specify security policies (see, e.g., [CARM04]), the web rules language being developed by W3C is more powerful to specify complex policies. Furthermore, inference engines are being developed to process and reason about the rules (e.g., the Pellet engine developed at the University of Maryland). One could integrate ideas from the database inference controller that we have developed (see [THUR93]) with web rules processing to develop an inference or privacy controller for the semantic web.

The query-processing module is responsible for accessing the heterogeneous data and information sources on the semantic web. Researchers are examining ways to integrate techniques from web query processing with semantic web technologies to locate, query, and integrate the heterogeneous data and information sources. We need to examine the security impact of query processing.

6.3.6 Privacy and Trust for the Semantic Web

Privacy is about protecting information about individuals. Furthermore, an individual can specify say to a web service provider the information that can be released about him or her. Privacy has been discussed a great deal in the past especially when it relates to protecting medical information about patients. Social scientists as well as technologists have been working on privacy issues. However, privacy has received enormous attention during the past year. This is mainly because of the advent of the web, the semantic web, counter-terrorism, and national security. For example, in order to extract information about various individuals and perhaps prevent and/or detect potential terrorist attacks, data mining tools are being examined. We have heard much about national security versus privacy in the media. This is mainly due to the fact that people are now realizing that to handle terrorism, the government may need to collect data about individuals and mine the data to extract information. Data may be in relational databases or it may be text, video, and images. This is causing a major concern with various civil liberties unions (see [THUR02]). Closely related to privacy is anonymity. Some argue that it is more important to maintain anonymity.

With the web and the semantic web, there is now an abundance of data about individuals that one can obtain within seconds. The data could be structured data or could be multimedia data such as text, images, video, and audio. Information could be obtained through mining or just from information retrieval. Data mining is an important tool in making the web more intelligent. That is, data mining may be used to mine the data on the web so that the web can evolve into the semantic web. However, this also means that there may be threats to privacy. Therefore, one needs to enforce privacy controls on databases and data mining tools on the semantic web. This is a very difficult problem. In summary, one needs to develop techniques to prevent users from mining and extracting information from data whether they are on the web or on networked servers. Note that data mining is a technology that is critical for analysts so that they can extract patterns previously unknown. However, we do not want the information to be used in an incorrect manner. For example, based on information about a person, an insurance company could deny insurance or a loan agency could deny loans. In many cases, these denials may not be legitimate. Therefore, information providers have to be very careful in what they release. Also, data mining researchers have to ensure that privacy aspects are addressed.

While little work has been reported on privacy issues for the semantic web, we are moving in the right direction. As research initiatives are started in this area, we can expect some progress to be made. Note that there are also social and political aspects to consider. That is, technologists, sociologists, policy experts, counter-terrorism experts, and legal experts have to work together to develop appropriate data mining techniques as well as to ensure privacy. Privacy policies and standards are also urgently needed. That is, while the technologists develop privacy solutions, we need the policy makers to work with standards organizations so that appropriate privacy standards are developed. W3C has made a good start with P3P (the platform for privacy preferences).

The challenge is to provide solutions to enhance national security but at the same time ensure privacy. There is now research at various laboratories on privacy enhanced/sensitive/preserving data mining (e.g., Agrawal at IBM Almaden, Gehrke at Cornell University and Clifton at Purdue University, see for example [AGRA00], [CLIF02], [GEHR02]). The idea here is to continue with mining but at the same time ensure privacy as much as possible. For example, Clifton has proposed the use of the multi-party security policy approach for carrying out privacy sensitive data mining. While there is some progress, we still have a long way to go. Some useful references are provided in [CLIF02] (see also [EVFI02]).

We give some more details on our approach. Note that one mines the data and extracts patterns and trends. The privacy constraints determine which patterns are private and to what extent. For example, suppose one could extract the names and healthcare records. If we have a privacy constraint that states that names and healthcare records are private, then this information is not released to the general public. If the information is semi-private, then it is released to those who have a need to know. Essentially, the inference controller approach we have discussed is one solution to achieving some level of privacy. It could be regarded to be a type of privacy-sensitive data mining. In our research study we have found many challenges to the inference controller approach that we have developed (see [THUR93]). These challenges will have to be addressed when handling privacy constraints (see also [THUR04]). Figure 6.9 illustrates privacy controllers for the semantic web. As illustrated, there are data mining tools on the web that mine the web databases. The privacy controller should ensure privacy-preserving data mining. Ontologies may be used by the privacy controllers. For example, there may be ontology specification for privacy constructs. Furthermore, XML may be extended to include privacy constraints. RDF may incorporate privacy semantics. We need to carry out more research on the role of ontologies for privacy control.

Much of the work on privacy-preserving data mining focuses on relational data. We need to carry out research on privacy-preserving semantic web data mining. We need to combine techniques for privacy-preserving data mining with techniques for semantic web data mining to obtain solutions for privacy-preserving semantic web data mining.

Recently there has been much work on trust and the semantic web (see the research by Finin et al. [DENK03], [KAGA03]). The challenges include how do you trust the information on the web? How do you trust the sources? How do you negotiate between different parties and develop contracts? How do you incorporate constructs for trust management and negotiation into XML and RDF? What are the semantics for trust management?

Researchers are working on protocols for trust management. Languages for specifying trust management constructs are also being developed. Also there is research on the foundations of trust management. For example, if A trusts B and B trusts C, then can A trust C? How do you share the data and information on the semantic web and still maintain autonomy. How do you propagate trust? For example, if A trusts B at say 50% of the time and B trusts C 30% of the time, then what value do you assign for A trusting C? How do you incorporate trust into semantic

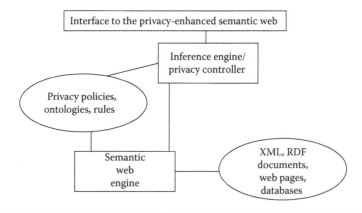

Figure 6.9   Privacy controller for the semantic web.

interoperability? What is the quality of service primitives for trust and negotiation? That is, for certain situations one may need 100% trust while for certain other situations, 50% trust may suffice (see also [YU03]).

Another topic that is being investigated is trust propagation and propagating privileges. For example, if you grant privileges to A, what privileges can A transfer to B? How can you compose privileges? Is there an algebra and calculus for the composition of privileges? Much research still needs to be done here. One of the layers of the semantic web is Logic, Proof, and Trust. Essentially this layer deals with trust management and negotiation between different agents and examining the foundations and developing logics for trust management.

6.3.7 Secure Semantic Web and WS

Integration of WS and the semantic web results in semantic web services. That is, WS to the WWW are semantic web services to the semantic web. Tim Finin and his team have discussed an architecture for semantic web services [BURS05]. They have described the inadequacies of WS and discussed the need for semantic web services. They state that current technologies allow the usage of WS. In particular, current WS support syntactic information descriptions as well as syntactic support for service discovery, composition, and execution. They argue that we need semantically marked-up content and services and therefore we need to develop semantic web services. They then define an architecture called the semantic web service architecture which consists of a set of architectural and protocol abstractions that serves as a foundation for semantic web service technologies. These technologies support the following:

- Dynamic service discovery
- Service engagement
- Service process enactment, community support services
- Quality of service

Service discovery is the process of identifying candidate services by clients. Matchmakers connect the service requesters to the providers. Ontologies may be needed to specify the services. Service engagement specified the agreements between the requester and the provider. Therefore, contract negotiation is carried out during this phase. Once the service is ready to be initiated, the service enactment phase begins. As stated in [SHIB], during this phase the requester determines the information necessary to request performance of service and appropriate reaction to service success or failure. This will also include interpreting the responses and carrying out transitions, Community management services support authentication and security management. Quality of service provides support for negotiation as well as tradeoffs between security and timely delivery of the data.

Security cuts across all these services. Note that while the community management service specially calls for authentication and security management, security

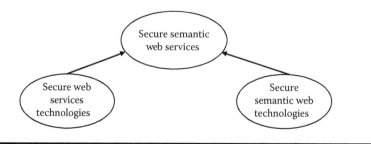

Figure 6.10   Secure semantic web services.

services are needed for service discovery, engine segment, and enactment. For example, not all services can be discovered. This will depend on the sensitivity of the service and the security credentials possessed by the requester. Therefore, security specifications for XML, RDF, and OWL have to be examined for semantic web service descriptions. Figure 6.10 illustrates secure semantic web services.

6.4 Summary and Directions

This chapter first provided an overview of semantic web technologies and the notion of semantic web services. In particular, we discussed Tim Berners Lee's technology stack. Then we discussed XML, RDF, and ontologies as well as WS for the semantic web. Finally, we discussed semantic WS and how they can make use of semantic web technologies. Note that just like WS are at the heart of the cloud, semantic web services are at the heart of the semantic cloud. As stated earlier, a semantic cloud is a cloud that utilizes semantic web technologies. That is, they provide a collection of semantic services.

Next, we provided an overview of the semantic web and discussed security standards. We first discussed security issues for the semantic web. We argued that security must cut across all the layers. Next, we provided some more details on XML security, RDF security, secure information integration, and trust. If the semantic web is to be secure, we need all of its components to be secure. We also described some of our research on access control and dissemination of XML documents. Next, we discussed privacy for the semantic web.

There is still a lot of work to be carried out on semantic web services. Much of the development of WS has focused on XML technologies. We need to develop standards for using RDF for WS. For example, we need to develop RDF-like languages for WS descriptions. Research on semantic web services is just beginning. Secure semantic web services essentially integrate semantic web services technologies and security technologies.

Much research also needs to be done with respect to securing the semantic web. We need to continue with the research on XML security. We must start examining security for RDF. This is more difficult as RDF incorporates semantics. We need to examine the work on security constraint processing and context-dependent security constraints and see if we can apply some of the ideas for RDF security. Finally, we need to examine the role of ontologies for secure information integration. We have to address some hard questions such as how do we integrate security policies on the semantic web? How can we incorporate policies into ontologies? We also cannot forget about privacy and trust for the semantic web. That is, we need to protect the privacy of individuals and at the same time ensure that the individuals have the information they need to carry out their functions. Finally, we need to formalize the notions of trust and examine ways to negotiate trust on the semantic web. We have a good start and are well on our way to building the semantic web. Security must be considered at the beginning and not as an afterthought.

Standards play an important role in the development of the semantic web. W3C has been very effective in specifying standards for XML and RDF. We need to continue with the developments and try as much as possible to transfer the research to the standards efforts. We also need to transfer the research and standards to commercial products. The next step for the semantic web standards efforts is to examine security, privacy, quality of service, integrity, and other features such as secure query services. As we have stressed, security and privacy are critical and must be investigated while the standards are being developed.

We have provided an overview of semantic web and secure semantic web services as cloud services need to utilize semantic web services if they want to provide machine-understandable services. Furthermore, several of the experimental systems that we have designed for the cloud and secure cloud have utilized semantic web technologies. We call such cloud services to be semantic cloud services. These experimental systems will be discussed in Parts IV, VI, and VII.

References

[AGRA00] Agrawal, R. and R. Srikant. Privacy-preserving data mining, *Proceedings of the ACM SIGMOD Conference*, Dallas, TX, May 2000.

[ANTO08] Antoniou, G. and F. van Harmelen. *A Semantic Web Primer*, MIT Press, Cambridge, MA, 2008 (2nd Edition).

[BERT02] Bertino, E. et al. Access control for XML documents. *Data and Knowledge Engineering*, 43(): 19–34, 2002.

[BERT04] Bertino, E., B. Carminati, E. Ferrari, B. Thuraisingham, and A. Gupta. Selective and authentic third party distribution of XML documents. *IEEE Transactions on Knowledge and Data Engineering*, 161(10): 1263–1278, October 2004.

[BURS05] Burstein, M. H., C. Bussler, M. Zaremba, T. W. Finin, M. N. Huhns, M. Paolucci, A. P. Sheth, and S. K. Williams. A semantic web services architecture. *IEEE Internet Computing*, 9(5): 72–81, 2005.

[CARM04] Carminati, B., E. Ferrari, and B. Thuraisingham, Using RDF for policy specification and enforcement, *Proceedings of the DEXA Conference Workshop on Web Semantics*, Zaragoza, Spain, 2004, pp. 163–167.

[CLIF02] Clifton, C., M. Kantarcioglu, and J. Vaidya. *Data Mining: Next Generation Challenges and Future Directions*, H. Kargupta, A. Joshi, K. Sivakumar, and Y. Yesha (eds), Defining Privacy for Data Mining, AAAI/MIT Press 2004, pp. 255–272.

[DENK03] Denker, G., L. Kagal, T. Finin, and M. Paolucci, Security for DAML web services: Annotation and matchmaking, *International Semantic Web Conference*, Sanibel Island, FL, USA, 2003.

[EVFI02] Evfimievski, A., R. Srikant, R. Agrawal, and J. Gehrke, Privacy preserving mining of association rules, *Proceedings of the Eighth ACM SIGKDD International Conference on Knowledge Discovery and Data Mining*. Edmonton, Alberta, Canada, July 2002.

[FARK03] Farkas, C. et al., Inference Problem for the Semantic Web, *Proceedings of the IFIP Conference on Data and Applications Security*, Colorado, August 2003 (formal proceedings published by Kluwer, 2004).

[GEHR02] Gehrke, J., Research problems in data stream processing and privacy-preserving data mining, *Proceedings of the Next Generation Data Mining Workshop*, Baltimore, MD, November 2002.

[HEND01] Hendler, J., Agents and the semantic web, *IEEE Intelligent Systems Journal*, Match 2001.

[KAGA03] Kagal, L., T. W. Finin, and A. Joshi, A policy based approach to security for the semantic web. *International Semantic Web Conference* 2003, Sanibel Island, FL, USA, pp. 402–418.

[LAUR00] St. Laurent, S., *XML: A Primer*, Power Books Publishing, UK, 2000.

[LEE01] Lee, T. B. and J. Hendler, The semantic web, *Scientific American*, May 2001.

[LLOY87] Lloyd, J. *Logic Programming*, Springer, Germany. 1987.

[SHIB] Shibboleth Internet 2, http://en.wikipedia.org/wiki/Shibboleth_%28Internet2%29

[SWS] Semantic web services, http://en.wikipedia.org/wiki/Semantic_Web_Services

[SWRL] World Wide Web Consortium, http://www.w3.org/Submission/SWRL/#1

[THUR93] Thuraisingham, B. et al. Design and implementation of a database inference controller. *Data and Knowledge Engineering Journal*, 11(3), 271–297, 1993.

[THUR02] Thuraisingham, B. M. Data mining, national security, privacy and civil liberties. *SIGKDD Explorations*, 4(2), 1–5, 2002.

[THUR04] Thuraisingham, B. Privacy constraint processing in a privacy enhanced database system. *Data and Knowledge Engineering Journal*, 55(2), 159–188, 2005.

[THUR05] Thuraisingham, B. *Database and Applications Security: Integrating Data Management and Information Security*, CRC Press, Boca Raton, FL, 2006.

[THUR06] Thuraisingham, B. et al. Administering the semantic web, confidentiality, privacy and trust. *Journal of Information Security and Privacy*, 2006.

[W3C] The World Wide Web Consortium, www.w3c.org

[XML1] The Apache Foundation, http://xml.apache.org/security/

[XML2] The World Wide Web Consortium, http://www.w3.org/Signature/

[XML3] The World Wide Web Consortium, http://www.w3.org/Encryption/2001/

[YU03] Yu, T. and M. Winslett, A unified scheme for resource protection in automated trust negotiation, *IEEE Symposium on Security and Privacy*, Oakland, CA, May 2003, pp. 110–122.

Chapter 7

Specialized Web Services and Security

7.1 Overview

While Chapter 4 discussed some of the basic concepts in data, information, and knowledge management, Chapter 5 discussed security for WS, and Chapter 6 discussed semantic WS and security, in this chapter, we discuss specialized WS and associated security issues. Specialized WS include services for data and information as well as knowledge management, WS for activity management such as information interoperability and e-commerce, and WS for domain industries such as healthcare and finance.

We first discuss some details of specialized WS such as WS for data management, information management, knowledge management, and activity management. We also discuss domain WS and the notions of software and data as a service. Then, we discuss security for each of these topics. For example, we discuss the security impact on WS for data, information, and knowledge, and activity management as well as secure domain WS and security for software and data as a service. We also integrate the semantic web technologies discussed in Chapter 6 for specialized WS.

The organization of this chapter is as follows. In Section 7.2, we will discuss specialized WS such as WS for data, information, and knowledge, and activity management. Security for specialized WS will be discussed in Section 7.3. This chapter concludes with Section 7.4. Figure 7.1 illustrates the concepts discussed in this chapter. As we have discussed earlier, WS are at the heart of cloud computing. Therefore, WS for data, information, knowledge, and activity management are the essence of cloud data, information, knowledge, and activity management. For example, the

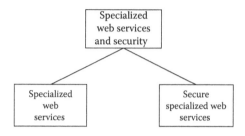

Figure 7.1 Specialized web services and security.

cloud data management services (e.g., query services) will utilize the data management services that we discuss in this chapter. Parts III and V will discuss WS for cloud data, information, knowledge, and activity management. Experimental systems related to such cloud-based WS are discussed in Parts IV, V, and VII.

7.2 Specialized Web Services

7.2.1 Overview

In Section 7.2, we will discuss various types of specialized WS. These include WS for data, information, and knowledge management as well as domain WS. These WS use the standards discussed in Chapter 5 such as SOAP, XML, UDDI, and WSDL.

The organization of this section is as follows. WS for data management will be discussed in Section 7.2.2. WS for complex data management such as geospatial data management will be discussed in Section 7.2.3. WS for information management will be discussed in Section 7.2.4. WS for knowledge management will be discussed in Section 7.2.5. WS for activity management such as e-commerce and information sharing will be discussed in Section 7.2.6. Domain WS will be discussed in Section 7.2.7. Some emerging WS will be discussed in Section 7.2.8.

7.2.2 Web Services for Data Management

The various data management functions may be invoked as WS. For example, the query WS will include the composition of multiple WS such as the query modification services and the query optimization service. The query service will invoke the storage service to retrieve the data from the storage. The transaction service will execute the transaction.

Semantic web technologies may also be utilized by the WS to produce semantic WS. First of all, policies (e.g., administrative and integrity) may be expressed in languages such as XML and RDF. This is one of the significant contributions of the

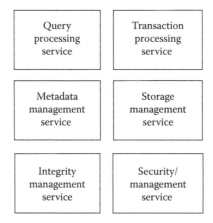

Figure 7.2 Web services for data management.

semantic web. Now, databases may also consist of XML and RDF documents. For example, products such as those by Oracle Corporation now have the capability of managing XML and RDF documents. Therefore, we need to apply data management techniques for managing XML and RDF documents.

Semantic web technologies have applications in heterogeneous database integration. For example, ontologies are needed for handling semantic heterogeneity. XML is now being used as the common data representation language. With respect to data warehousing, XML and RDF may be used to specify the policies. Furthermore, ontologies may be used for data transformation to bring the data into the warehouse. Ontologies have applications in data mining as they clarify various concepts to facilitate data mining. On the other hand, the vast quantities of data on the web will have to be mined to extract information to guide the agents to understand the web pages. In summary, in every aspect of data management, WS and semantic web technologies have applications. Figure 7.2 illustrates the WS for data management.

7.2.3 Web Services for Complex Data Management

Multimedia and geospatial data management operations such as querying can be invoked as WS. Furthermore, XML is being extended for multimedia and geospatial data. For example, SMIL (Synchronized Multimedia Integration Language) is a markup language for video while Voice is a markup language for audio data. The access control policies specified in XML and RDF or more descriptive languages such as REI can be enforced on video data represented in SMIL. Organizations such as OGC have specified GML. OGC specifies geospatial standards that rely on GML as the data layer encoding. OWL-S provides a semantic-rich application-level platform to encode the web service metadata using descriptive logic. OGC is monitoring innovative ways to integrate these two methods as part of their geospatial semantic web interoperability experiment. Figure 7.3 illustrates the WS for complex data management (e.g., geospatial data management). Here, service providers publish the services in GML or GRDF (geospatial RDF, which is a language that we have designed) and the client will obtain the location of the service from the directory and subsequently obtain the service from the service provider.

We have extended the RDF to develop GRDF for geospatial data. We are using ontologism specified in GRDF for handling semantic heterogeneity. This ontologism is then used for semantic interoperability. Our details of GRDF can be found in [ALAM06]. On top of GRDF we have developed geospatial ontologies. These ontologies are described in [THUR07]. Our team (Thuraisingham, Ashraful, Subbiah, and Khan) have developed a system called DAGIS that reasons with the ontologies and answers queries. This system is described in [THUR07]. It is a framework that provides a methodology to realize the semantic interoperability, both at the geospatial data encoding level and for the service framework. DAGIS is an integrated platform that provides the mechanism and architecture for building geospatial data exchange interfaces using the OWL-S service ontology. Coupled with the geospatial domain-specific ontology for automatic discovery, dynamic composition, and invocation of services, DAGIS is a one-stop platform to fetch and integrate geospatial data. The data encoding is in GRDF and provides the ability to reason out the payload data by the DAGIS or client agents to provide intelligent inferences. DAGIS at the service level and GRDF at the data encoding layer provide a complete unified model for realizing the vision of geospatial semantic web. The architecture also enhances the query response for the client queries posed to the DAGIS interface. Figure 7.4 illustrates the DAGIS architecture.

Other efforts on WS for geospatial data include GeoRSS, an application of geospatial semantic web technologies, which we will discuss in this section. As stated in [OGC], GeoRSS is simple proposal for geo-enabling, or tagging, "really simple

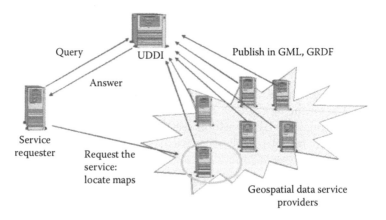

Figure 7.3   Web services for complex data management.

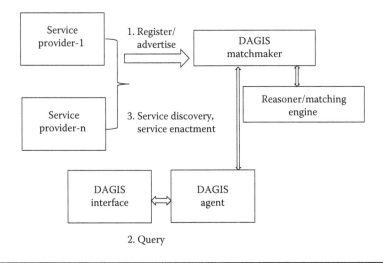

Figure 7.4 DAGIS architecture.

syndication" (RSS) feeds with location information. GeoRSS proposes a standard-ized way in which the location is encoded with enough simplicity and descriptive power to satisfy most needs to describe the location of the web content. GeoRSS is also intended to be a lightweight way to express geography in other XML-based formats—including XHTML.

7.2.4 Web Services for Information Management

WS may be invoked for the various information management applications. For example, data mining and data warehousing operations may be implemented as WS. Similarly, the information retrieval operation as well as the digital library management operation may also be invoked as WS. As in the case of data manage-ment, semantic web technologies such as XML, RDF, and OWL can be used to represent various administrative and integrity policies.

Semantic web technologies have also been applied for information management, especially for digital library management. A significant direction in applying seman-tic web for digital libraries has been provided by Studer and his team [STUD]. They state that "Typical usage scenarios for Semantic Technologies in Digital Libraries include among others user interfaces and human–computer interaction (displaying information, allowing for visualization and navigation of large information collec-tions), user profiling (taking into account the overall information space), personal-ization (balancing between individual and community-based personalization), user interaction." They describe their SEKT project that attempts to solve many of the challenges. They further state that while there will be several digital libraries, with the use of ontologies and semantic web technologies, it will be possible to provide a

Figure 7.5 Web services for information management.

consistent view of the digital libraries. We will summarize some of the prominent semantic web technologies they have discussed in their paper that are useful for digital libraries. They are ontologies, ontology editors, annotation tools, and inference engines. More details with example can be found in [THUE10]. Figure 7.5 illustrates the WS for information management.

7.2.5 Web Services for Knowledge Management

Various knowledge management operations such as creating and managing intellectual property, storing and managing the expertise in a corporation, and maintaining the corporate website may be invoked as WS. These WS may utilize semantic web technologies.

Semantic web technologies have many applications in knowledge management. For example, we need ontologies to capture and represent knowledge and reason about the knowledge. In his article on the semantic web and knowledge management, Paul Warren gives an example on how "a political scientist, Sally, who wants to research the extent to which British Prime Minister Tony Blair's stance on Zimbabwe has changed over a year and what factors might have caused that change." He further states that "in the world of the Semantic Web, Sally could search for everything written by Blair on this topic over a specific time period. She could also search for transcripts of his speeches. Information markup wouldn't stop at the article or report level but would also exist at the article section level. So, Sally could also locate articles written by political commentators that contain transcripts of Blair's speeches" [WARR06].

Now, knowledge management also has applications for building the semantic web. For example, prior knowledge captured as a result of knowledge management can be used by agents to better understand the web pages. Figure 7.6 illustrates the WS for knowledge management.

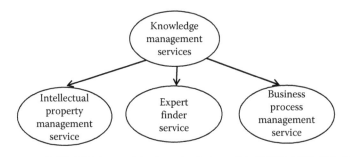

Figure 7.6   Web services for knowledge management.

7.2.6 Web Services for Activity Management

In Chapter 4, we discussed activity management, including e-commerce, information sharing, and information interoperability. In this section, we discuss WS for activity management. Figure 7.7 illustrates the relationship between WS and activity management. We will discuss the details for each activity.

7.2.6.1 E-Business

WS and semantic web have been applied to e-business in multiple directions. One is developing specialized markup languages such as Electronic Business using eXtensible Markup Language (ebXML) for e-business applications, another is semantic e-business where e-business processes make use of semantic web technologies, and the third is applying WS to invoke e-business applications.

As stated in [EBXM], ebXML "is a family of XML-based standards sponsored by OASIS and UN/CEFACT (between the United Nations Centre for Trade

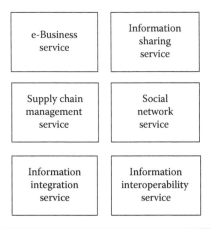

Figure 7.7   Web services for activity management.

Facilitation and Electronic Business) whose mission is to provide an open, XML-based infrastructure that enables the global use of electronic business information in an interoperable, secure, and consistent manner by all trading partners." The initial goal of this project was to specify XML standards for business processes. These standards include collaboration protocol agreements, core data components, messaging, registries, and repositories.

Ontologies have also been developed for e-commerce applications specified in languages such as RDF, RDF-S, OWL, and OWL-S. For example, in the Obelix project, a very good description of e-business and ontologies is provided. The authors state that a problem with e-commerce is the vague ideas that lack precise description. They then discuss their approach based on requirements engineering and they define ontologies for e-commerce.

More details of this project are given in [OBEL]. It is stated that "OBELIX is the first ontology-based e-business system of its kind in the world to provide smart, scalable integration and interoperability capabilities." They also state that this project "incorporates ontology management and configuration, an e-business application server and ontology-based e-application tools as well as an e-business library." OBELIX is a European Commission project and the goal is to automate e-business services in a semantic web environment that has come to be called semantic e-business.

Some interesting efforts on semantic e-business are being carried out by the group at the University of North Carolina Greensboro. They have stated that semantic e-business is about organizations collaboratively designing business processes that utilize knowledge of the corporation [SING06]. It essentially integrates semantic web technologies with business process management and knowledge management. The business processes utilize knowledge management to improve their efficiency and utility and uses semantic web technologies such as ontologies for better understanding.

Semantic commerce that is more or less semantic e-business is being also investigated. For example, researchers at HP Labs in Bristol present a lifecycle of a business-to-business e-commerce interaction, and show how the semantic web can support a service description language that can be used throughout this lifecycle. They show that by using DAML + OIL, they were able to develop a service description language that is useful not only to represent advertisements but also to implement matchmaking queries, negotiation proposals, and agreements [TRAS].

7.2.6.2 Collaboration and Workflow

Semantic web technologies can also be applied for workflow and collaborative applications. For example, the Workflow Management Coalition has developed two languages. The first being Wf-XML (Workflow XML) and as stated in [WFMC], "Wf-XML extends the ASAP (Asynchronous Service Access Protocol by OASIS) model to include BPM (Business Process Management) and workflow interchange capabilities." This coalition has also developed XPDL (XML Process Definition Language). As stated in [WFMC], "XPDL provides a framework for implementing business process management and workflow engines, and for designing, analyzing, and exchanging business processes."

While the markup languages we have discussed here are comparable to XML for text, these languages have been extended with ontologies to provide semantics for multimedia, workflow, and collaborative computing applications. For example, RDF-based languages have been developed by researchers in Scotland for collaborative and workflow applications [CHEN04].

7.2.6.3 Information Integration

While semantic web technologies were developed for machine-understandable web pages and XML in particular was developed for document exchange on the web, these technologies have extensive use for information interoperability. Syntactic heterogeneity such as data model heterogeneity was a major issue in the 1990s. Various communities were discussing the development of common object models and extended relational models for common data representation [THUR97]. However, since the development of XML, it is the language of choice for global data representations. Many organizations, including the Department of Defense (DoD), are using XML and XML schemas to publish the metadata for the individual databases. This has been a significant development toward the common data model.

While XML is ideal for representing syntax, we need RDF and OWL-like languages for representing semantics. Therefore, RDF-based languages are being used to handle semantic heterogeneity. For example, ontologies are specified to define various terms as well as to represent common semantics or to distinguish between different semantics. These ontologies are then used for information interoperability and to understand the various terms between different organizations.

7.2.6.4 Other Activities

Organizations may invoke WS for information sharing as well as for social networking and supply chain management. For example, organization A may invoke one web service to place relevant information into the shared space and another web service to retrieve information placed by another organization. An organization may request parts from a supplier by invoking a web service. That web service may invoke other WS to request additional parts.

Semantic web technologies may also be used for information sharing, social networking, and supply chain management. For example, the information to be shared may be represented in XML, RDF, or OWL. A framework based on semantic web technologies may be used as a platform for information sharing. In the case of social networking, the first ontologies may be extracted from the data to form the social networks. These ontologies may be mined to extract patterns. A good example of a semantic web-based social network is FOAF (Friend Of A Friend) that is specified in RDF.

7.2.7 Domain Web Services

In this section, we will discuss WS for the domain industries, including defense, homeland security, and healthcare. Figure 7.8 illustrates the various industries that we will explore.

7.2.7.1 Defense

One of the earliest domains to utilize WS is the defense and intelligence domain. Under the management of Dr. Jim Handler, the DAML program at DARPA developed technologies for the DoD. While security was not a consideration in that program, an ontology language called DAML was developed. This program worked closely with the W3C to develop technologies for machine-understandable web pages. DAML was then integrated with the European standard called OIL (Ontology Interface Language) to develop DAML + OIL. While the United States and Europe together developed DAML + OIL, the W3C developed OWL for ontologies. As we have mentioned earlier, OWL evolved from RDF, DAML, and OIL. In addition to representation of the data, reasoning about the data was also a focus for the DAML program.

About the time the DAML program was carried out in the late 1990s and early 2000s, the DoD was involved with the development of the GCCS (Global Command and Control System) program. Under this program, the DII COE (Defense Information Infrastructure Common Operating Environment) was developed. The DII COE essentially consisted of several working groups, including those for distributed computing systems, multimedia, and data management. However, with the emergence of WS, the DoD began to invest heavily in network-centric enterprise services (NCES) for network-centric operations. This then led to the development of the Global Information Grid, which was essentially the infrastructure for NCES. This infrastructure is based on service-oriented architecture and WS. Much

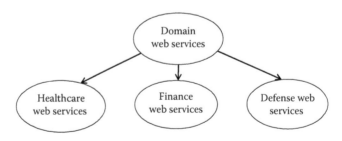

Figure 7.8 Domain web services.

of the development is influenced by XML and ontologies. Furthermore, communities of interest (COI) have been formed and these communities have developed common ontologies for their applications. WS also play a major role for applications in homeland security. For example, the use of semantic web technologies and WS for enforcing RFID (radio frequency identification) tags have been explored in [PALI04].

7.2.7.2 Healthcare and Life Sciences

W3C hosted a workshop in October 2004 to bring together researchers in life sciences to determine how semantic web technologies can be utilized. Today, several efforts are being focused on developing ontologies, WS, and markup languages for healthcare and life sciences applications. For example, ontologies are used to specify drugs and various medical terms. For example, Jonathan Borden, who is part of the W3C Web Ontology Working Group, has specified XML for healthcare applications [BORD]. He states that his goal is to use ontologies and markup languages to answer questions such as "Of all the patients I operated on for brain tumors between 1997–2000, matching severity of pathology and matching clinical status and who have the P53 mutation, did PCV chemotherapy improve the cure rate in five years?" He then illustrates how XML, RDF, and OWL could be utilized to effectively answer these questions.

Ontologies have been developed for electronic healthcare records as well as for several items in life sciences [KREM]. For example, the authors state in [LIFE], that "Contemporary life science research includes components drawn from physics, chemistry, mathematics, medicine, and many other areas, and all of these dimensions, as well as fundamental philosophical issues, must be taken into account in the construction of a domain ontology." They then describe how to go about developing domain ontologies for life sciences.

7.2.7.3 Finance

Financial domains include any domain that has to deal with finance, including banking and trading, insurance, and investment management. Almost all of these activities are now being carried out electronically. We now have electronic trading, electronic banking, and electronic insurance management among others. In this section, we will examine the applications of trustworthy semantic webs for financial domains.

Several groups are developing WS and semantic web technologies for financial domains. For example, the group in Madrid has done some very good research on applying the semantic "ontology-based platform that provides (a) the integration of contents and semantics in a knowledge base that provides a conceptual view on low-level contents, (b) an adaptive hypermedia-based knowledge visualization and navigation system and (c) semantic search facilities" [CAST]. Furthermore, they have developed a topology of economic and financial information. Another group in Belgium is developing ontologies for financial security fraud detection. They have used ontology-based knowledge engineering in projects to detect financial security fraud. In particular, they have developed a fraud forensic ontology from regulation and laws [ZHAO].

In addition, to specific projects such as the work in Madrid and Belgium to develop ontologies and semantics for financial data management, XML is being used extensively for financial services. This is now considered the norm for finance. As stated in [XML], "the Financial Services industry is creating a variety of standard XML formats to meet their special needs." The list of standards being developed include the following:

Interactive Financial Exchange (IFX) and Open Financial Exchange (OFX), which address consumer and other forms of retail banking.

Financial Information eXchange (FIX) is emerging as a standard communications protocol for equity trading data.

FIX Markup Language (FIXML) uses XML to express business messages for the FIX protocol.

Financial products Markup Language (FpML) is an XML-based interchange format for transactions in financial derivative markets.

Market Data Definition Language (MDDL) is a consortium standard for the definition and communication of market data in XML, including data required to analyze, trade, and account for market value in the handling of financial instruments.

eXtensible Business Reporting Language (XBRL) is an "XML-based specification for the preparation and exchange of financial reports and data." It is developed by a global consortium of organizations and institutions.

7.2.7.4 Telecommunication

Another domain application for WS is telecommunication. Corporations such as Ericsson, Nokia, and AT&T are developing WS for this industry. Parlay X is such an effort by the Parlay group. As stated in the Wiki article, "The Parlay Group is a technical industry consortium (founded 1998) that specifies APIs (Application Programming Interface) for the telephone network. These APIs enable the creation of services by organizations both inside and outside of the traditional carrier environment." In 2003, this group developed a new set of WS called Parlay X that is a simpler set of APIs to be used by developers. As stated in [TELE], "The Parlay X web services include Third-Party Call Control (3PCC), location and simple payment."

An interesting and useful survey on WS for the telecommunications industry is presented in [TELE]. The article states that the telecommunication industry has been in a flux over the recent years due to regulatory changes, competition, and progress in technology. The authors make a strong case for the use of WS for this industry and explain event-driven architectures and developments with Parlay X.

7.2.8 Emerging Web Services

7.2.8.1 X as a Service

What is becoming increasingly popular is using X as a service. X could be data, software platform, infrastructure, or anything of interest. With data as a service, an organization can utilize a data provider to obtain data and invoke data as a service. In the case of software, an organization can obtain a compiler, an operating system, or an application as a service from a service provider. In this section, we will elaborate on each of these services. In general, X as a service is denoted by XaaS.

7.2.8.2 Data as a Service

Data as a service has been provided for quite a while. For example, corporations such as Choice Point and Acxiom manage data for various corporations in the financial and medical industries. These data services may include data security and privacy services and data quality and cleansing services. Figure 7.9 illustrates the data as a service model. We will refer to data as a service as DaaS, although DaaS has also been used for desktop as a service.

Integrating data services with web service technology is a recent concept. As stated in [DATA], once you move past novelty WS that echo a string you sent or perform, say, a mathematical computation, services are facilitating either the insertion or retrieval of data. Whether you want to retrieve customer and product data via a service request or you want to be able to expose supply chain operations to key business partners, folding your data access layer into your SOA architecture is key. WSO2 Data Services provide a convenient and well-engineered mechanism for service-orienting your data.

The WSO2 Enterprise Service Bus enables the loose-coupling of services, connecting systems in a managed virtualized manner that allow administrators to control and direct communication without disrupting existing applications. WSO2 has many components and the data server component essentially provides data

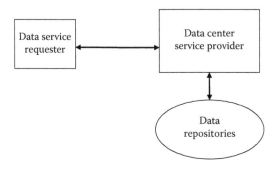

Figure 7.9   Data as a service.

services, including smashups such as integrating various data sources, database management, and related services.

Another concept that is evolving is using database management as a service. Sharad Mehrotra and his team at the University of California at Irvine, together with researchers at IBM, Purdue University, and The University of Texas at Dallas are working on this concept. The idea is to explore a new paradigm for data management in which a third-party service provider hosts "database as a service," providing its customers seamless mechanisms to create, store, and access their databases at the host site. Such a model alleviates the need for organizations to purchase expensive hardware and software, deal with software upgrades, and hire professionals for administrative and maintenance tasks, which are taken over by the service provider. Mehrotra's team has developed and deployed a database service on the Internet, called NetDB2, which is in constant use. In a sense, data management models supported by NetDB2 provide an effective mechanism for organizations to purchase data management as a service, thereby freeing them to concentrate on their core businesses. An interesting direction is to combine the WS concept that is present in WSO2 data services with the research being carried out by Mehrotra and his team to incorporate more advanced data management services into the standards.

7.2.8.3 Software as a Service

Another concept that is really exploding is the software as a service model, also referred to as SaaS. As stated in [SOFT], software as a service is a model of software deployment whereby a provider licenses an application to customers for use as a service on demand. The SaaS software vendors may host the application on their own web servers or download the application to the consumer device, disabling it after use or after the on-demand contract expires. The on-demand function may be handled internally to share licenses within a firm or by a third-party application service provider (ASP) sharing licenses between firms. Figure 7.10 illustrates SaaS.

It is also stated that SaaS can also take advantage of service-oriented architecture to enable software applications to communicate with each other. Each

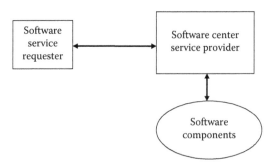

Figure 7.10   Software as a service.

software service can act as a service provider, exposing its functionality to other applications via public brokers, and can also act as a service requester, incorporating data and functionality from other services. Enterprise resource planning (ERP) software providers leverage SOA in building their SaaS offerings; an example is SAP Business ByDesign from SAP AG.

There are also those who are skeptical of SaaS as they state that this could be quite expensive and there is lot of hype. Therefore, the trade-off a corporation has to make is whether to build the software, purchase the software, or license it as part of the SaaS model, among other choices. There is still a lot to do before we see SaaS becomes a common trend. More details on such services offered via the cloud will be discussed in Part III of this book.

7.2.8.4 Other X as a Service

There are several other types of X as a service. These include desktop as a service, network as a service, platform as a service, and infrastructure as a service. We discuss two such services. As stated in the Wiki definition, "*platform as a service* (PaaS) is the delivery of a computing platform and solution stack as a service. It often goes further with the provision of a software development platform that is designed for cloud computing at the top of the cloud stack." This way an organization can invoke the service and obtain the hardware and software stack and deploy applications. In the case of infrastructure as a service (IaaS), the Wiki definition states the following: "Infrastructure as a Service (IaaS) is the delivery of computer infrastructure (typically a platform virtualization environment) as a service. These virtual infrastructure stacks are an example of the Everything as a Service trend and shares many of the common characteristics. Rather than purchasing servers, software, data center space, or network equipment, clients instead buy those resources as a fully outsourced service. The service is typically billed on a utility computing basis and amount of resources consumed (and therefore the cost) will typically reflect the level of activity. It is an evolution of web hosting and virtual private server offerings."

7.2.8.4.1 Amazon Web Services

As stated in the web pages of Amazon web services (AWS) [AMAZON], since early 2006, AWS has provided companies of all sizes with an infrastructure WS platform in the cloud. With AWS, you can requisition compute power, storage, and other services—gaining access to a suite of elastic IT infrastructure services as your business demands them. With AWS you have the flexibility to choose whichever development platform or programming model makes the most sense for the problems you are trying to solve. You pay only for what you use, with no up-front expenses or long-term commitments, making AWS the most cost-effective way to deliver your application to your customers and clients. And, with AWS, you can take advantage of Amazon.com's global computing infrastructure that is the backbone of Amazon.com's retail business.

AWS has several components, including database (called SimpleDB), storage (Amazon S3), and cloud (Amazon EC2). We will describe one such component as discussed in [AMAZON]. The details of other components are also given in the Amazon website. Amazon SimpleDB is a web service providing the core database functions of data indexing and querying. This service works in close conjunction with Amazon Simple Storage Service (Amazon S3) and Amazon Elastic Compute Cloud (Amazon EC2), collectively providing the ability to store, process, and query data sets in the cloud. It is also stated that Amazon WS provides both SOAP protocol and REST.

WS for Grids and Clouds Grid essentially consists of a collection of computers utilized to execute various applications. The goal is to optimize resource usage and schedule the machines for various tasks. The grid concept has been extended recently into clouds where there is a virtual computing space that consists of numerous virtual machines that are mapped into the physical machines. Such a concept is known as virtualization. *Information Week* [MART08] reports that cloud computing represents a new way, in some cases a better and cheaper way, of delivering enterprise IT. Often, grids and clouds are used interchangeably. However, in general, while grid focuses on scheduling resources, cloud focuses on delivering an efficient computing platform for an enterprise.

WS play a major role in grid and cloud computing. The Globus Alliance was formed with the goal to develop the Open Grid Services Architecture (OGSA). As stated in [GLOB], OGSA "represents an evolution towards a Grid system architecture based on web services concepts and technologies." The Globus Alliance has released a series of toolkits, the most recent of which is the Globus Toolkit 3.0. It consists of an "open source collection of Grid services that follow OGSA architectural principles. The Globus Toolkit also offers a development environment for producing new Grid services that follow OGSA principles."

The WS for cloud computing include AWS discussed in the previous section, Google apps, and Salesforce.com CRM. These clouds may utilize grid computing paradigms such as resource scheduling. It is expected that service virtualization will play a major role in cloud computing. In a recent article, it is stated that "Service virtualization is the ability to create a virtual service from one or more predefined service files. Service files are usually generated as a Web Service Description Language (WSDL) file by service containers running business application developed in Java, .NET, PHP type programming languages." The author further states that the services may include outsourced services such as Saas, PaaS, or IaaS or in-house services. More details will be given in Part III when we discuss cloud technologies.

7.3 Secure Specialized Web Services

7.3.1 Overview

In Section 7.3, we will discuss various types of secure specialized WS. This will include WS for secure data, information and knowledge management, as well as secure domain WS. These WS use the security standards for WS discussed in Chapter 5 such as secure SOAP, XML, UDDI, and WSDL.

The organization of this section is as follows. The WS for secure data management will be discussed in Section 7.3.2. The WS for secure complex data management such as geospatial data management will be discussed in Section 7.3.3. The WS for secure information management will be discussed in Section 7.3.4. The WS for secure knowledge management will be discussed in Section 7.3.5. The WS for secure activity management such as secure e-commerce and AIS will be discussed in Section 7.3.6. Secure domain WS will be discussed in Section 7.3.7. Some emerging secure WS will be discussed in Section 7.3.8. For more details on data and applications security, refer to [THUR05].

7.3.2 Web Services for Secure Data Management

The various secure database system functions may be invoked as WS. For example, the query manager, transaction management, and metadata manager may be executed as WS. Therefore, to query a database, the query service has to be invoked. This service may invoke the query translation service and the query optimization service. It may also invoke the metadata service to extract appropriate metadata. Security service may be invoked to check for access control policies.

Next, semantic web technologies may be utilized to develop semantic web service for secure data management. First of all, the security policies may be expressed in languages such as XML and RDF. Semantic web technologies, including the reasoning engines, may be applied to handle the inference and privacy problems. For example, languages such as RDF and OWL may be used to specify the policies and then inference controllers could be developed based on descriptive logic-based engines such as Pellet to determine whether security violations via inference occur.

In summary, in every aspect of secure data management, WS as well as semantic web technologies have applications. However, data management techniques and data mining techniques can also be applied to manage and mine the data on the web to facilitate agents to understand the web pages. Figure 7.11 illustrates WS for secure data management.

7.3.3 Web Services for Secure Complex Data Management

7.3.3.1 Secure Geospatial Data Management

Much of our discussion has been influenced by our collaborative research with Bertino at Purdue University and Gertz at the University of California Davis [BERT08]. This research is also influenced by some of our earlier research on security constraint processing and securing multimedia data [THUR95], [THUR90]. Atluri has also done some interesting research on geospatial data management and security [ATLU04], [DAMI07].

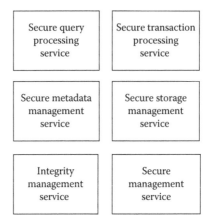

Figure 7.11   Web services for secure data management.

Geospatial data are more complex than relational data. For example, we can classify the pixels as well as classify the points and lines that make up the geospatial data. We can define policies based on content, context, and time. For example, the location and the image taken together could be classified, while individually they could be unclassified. Furthermore, the location and image could be classified at or until a particular time and after that it could be declassified. For example, satellite imagery taken over, say, Iraq could be classified for six months from the day the image was captured and unclassified after that. Bertino and her team have developed policy languages for geospatial data and a security model that they call Geo-RBAC, which integrates RBAC with geospatial data.

While there is a clear need for enforcing confidentiality policies for geospatial data, privacy remains a challenge. What does it mean to preserve privacy for geospatial data? Today, we have the capability to carry out surveillance as well as capture the images in, say, Google Maps. Therefore, we cannot expect the image of our house to remain private as the image is out there. However, the fact that it is my house could be private. We need to study the issues on privacy management for geospatial data. For our semantic web research, our goal is to develop geospatial WS that can utilize representation technologies such as GML and GRDF so that we get machine-understandable web pages. However, to secure a geospatial semantic web, we need to integrate geospatial semantic web technologies with secure geospatial data management technologies. This will be the subject of the next section. Figure 7.12 illustrates security for geospatial data management.

Geospatial data may be in the form of streams. What are the security policies for stream data? Closely related to geospatial information systems are motion databases where the data are not residing in one place. The data changes continually and this data must be captured and managed. Geospatial data may emanate from a variety of sources and therefore the data have to be integrated possibly through

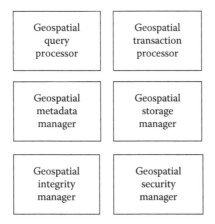

Geospatial query processor	Geospatial transaction processor
Geospatial metadata manager	Geospatial storage manager
Geospatial integrity manager	Geospatial security manager

Figure 7.12   Secure geospatial data management.

the web and by other means. Information integration has many security challenges. Some work in this area has been reported in [BERT08].

We are developing a set of policies for geospatial information systems. Data representation will be based on GML developed by OGC. The policy will include access control such as role-based and usage control, as well as trust, integrity, temporal constraints, data currency, data quality, and data provenance. Subsequently, we are designing and developing secure geospatial WS that demonstrate the interoperability with respect to security. We will examine security violations via inference for geospatial information systems. For example, inferencing techniques for intelligent data fusion have been developed. By fusing the data, security constraints may be violated. We are adapting the various techniques proposed to handle security for relational data to the handling of security for fused images. Data ownership and the need for profitability require an organization to safeguard its information bank from others. The technical complexity increases several fold when the organizational domain consists of data that is more than text or numbers. One such instance is geospatial WS that cater to queries that need information security beyond the level of a traditional RBAC mechanism. Safeguarding geospatial data requires fine granularity of access privileges, which makes RBAC a nonoptimal solution. Our goal is to harness the axiomatic framework provided through OWL to define policy assertions for potential clients and let the inference engine do the housekeeping.

Not all data housed by the geospatial agencies are considered public in nature. For instance, the data might contain critical information about people the exposure of which would jeopardize their privacy. The problem is exacerbated in a data integration environment because of the lack of a coherent security framework. If the trend toward on-the-fly data integration continues, WS providers would very soon perform complicated services that require embedding or combining geospatial data with other kinds of data. However, without an appropriate security architecture in place, there will be reluctance by clearinghouses to serve data liberally. In turn, the quality and effectiveness of the data are affected as the clients procure only partial information.

We have distinguished between two kinds of security that are most prevalent in WS and that form the foundations of semantic WS architecture as well. The first kind deals with the general authorization procedures of WS users and any subsequent execution of over-the-wire security criteria. The current set of standardized protocols for this kind of data security includes encryption methods, digital signature verification, certification generation and exchange, WS secure exchange, and so on. The second kind involves organizational protection of data from intruders or bona fide clients without proper access privileges. The most widely used defensive mechanism employed in this regard is various forms of access control languages. We are developing a semantic-rich, ontology-based access control solution for geospatial data that can have a beneficial bearing on the surge in geospatial data integration across the world.

The security for geospatial data can be compartmentalized into different logical segments based on the layer of application. Our work concentrates on secure access of geospatial resources by clients or other WS in the context of dynamic composition. In line with the vision of the semantic web, we are developing a modular access control in a language that makes the development of reasoning-enabled enforcement engines feasible. In contrast to the XML-based standards and first-order logic-based access controls, we define the axioms in OWL-DL and the emphasis on policy reuse. In our previous experience with policy-centric access control languages, it was observed that defining policies for resources on an individual basis is not well suited for integrated GIS applications. If fine-grained resource access is allowed, it amasses policies in policy files that must be navigated by the decision or enforcement module, thus degenerating overall query processing time. Our architecture is illustrated in Figure 7.13.

To improve policy decision time, our access control language keeps the collection of asserted rules as a separate unit. Then, client identities can link to appropriate rules to be applied on the client. The modular use of policies by referencing them minimizes rule duplications. Another important characteristic is the shifting of rule navigation from policies to client identities. The geospatial semantic web service agent in our framework accepts users with established identities or anonymous users.

To develop a secure geospatial semantic web, we need to incorporate security across the entire semantic web technology framework. Organizations such as OGC are examining security assertions to be specified in GML. In addition, organizations such as OASIS are developing GEO-XACML. We are developing security assertions to be specified in GRDF, which we call Secure GRDF. We are focusing on extending the secure DAGIS framework into a secure geospatial semantic web. DAGIS also has a responding component that is based on GRDF and can reason about the security policies.

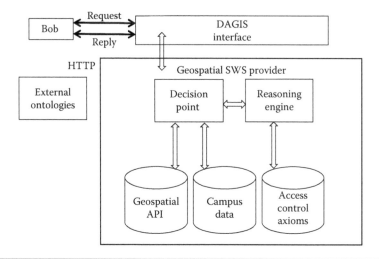

Figure 7.13   **Secure DAGIS architecture.**

7.3.3.2 Secure Multimedia Data Management

The functions for secure multimedia data management include secure query processing and secure storage management. These functions may be offered as WS. Consider the query operation. The query WS will examine the access control rules and security constraints and modify the query accordingly. For example, if the fact that the existence of Operation X is classified, then this query cannot be sent to an unclassified multimedia data collector such as a video camera to film the event. Similarly, the update processor also examines the access control rules and computes the level of the multimedia data to be inserted or modified. Security also has an impact on multimedia editing and browsing. When one is browsing multimedia data, the system must ensure that the user has the proper access to browse the link or access the data associated with the link. In the case of multimedia editing, when objects at different levels are combined to form a film, then the film object has to be classified accordingly. One may need to classify the various frames or assign the high watermark associated with the levels of the individual objects that compose the film. Furthermore, when films are edited (such as deleting certain portions of the film), one needs to recompute the level of the edited object.

Next, consider the storage manager function implemented as a web service. The storage service has to ensure that access is controlled to the multimedia database. The storage manager may also be responsible for partitioning the data according to the security levels. The security impact of access methods and indexing strategy for multimedia data are yet to be determined. Numerous index strategies have been developed for multimedia data, including those for text, images, audio, and video. We need to examine the strategies and determine the security impact. Another issue is the synchronization between storage and presentation of multimedia data. For example, we need to ensure that the video is displayed smoothly and that there are no bursts in traffic. There could be malicious programs manipulating the storage and presentation managers so that information is covertly passed from a higher-level process to lower-level processes.

7.3.4 Web Services for Secure Information Management

As in the case of data management, semantic web technologies such as XML, RDF, and OWL can be used to represent security policies, including confidentiality, privacy, and trust policies for data warehouses, information retrieval streams, and digital libraries. Furthermore, the reasoning engines based on, say, descriptive logic such as Pellet can be used to infer unauthorized conclusions via inference for data warehouse as well as information retrieval systems. Semantic web technologies can also be used to represent the nontextual data. For example, SMIL is a markup language for video while VoiceML is a markup language for audio data. The access control policies specified in, say, XML, RDF, or a more descriptive language such as REI can be enforced on video data represented in SMIL. Data mining techniques may be applied not only to relational databases but also to text, voice, video, and audio databases as well as to digital libraries. With data mining, there are privacy and security concerns. For example, data mining makes it possible to inference sensitive associations. Therefore, privacy-preserving data mining not only on relational databases but also on XML, RDF, and OWL data remains a challenge.

WS have applications in secure information management including secure data warehousing, secure data mining, secure information retrieval, and secure digital library management. For example, secure data warehouse management may be invoked as a web service. The secure warehouse manager service provider will

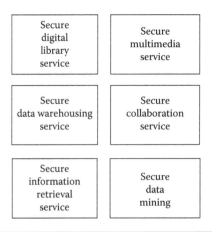

Figure 7.14 Web services for secure information management.

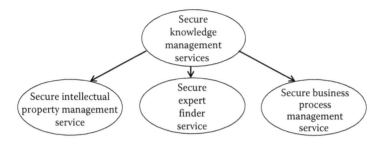

Figure 7.15 Web services for secure knowledge management.

register its services with the directory. The user who requests warehouse services will invoke the appropriate services. Figure 7.14 illustrates WS and semantic web for secure information management.

7.3.5 Web Services for Secure Knowledge Management

In an earlier section, we discussed the relationship between WS and knowledge management. That is, knowledge management services such as finding an expert and sharing a presentation can be provided as WS. Secure knowledge management includes enforcing appropriate security models for knowledge management. For example, various access control models and information sharing models have been proposed for secure knowledge management. These security services can be provided as secure WS.

Semantic web technologies can also be applied to reason about the security policies for knowledge management as well as reason about the knowledge so that unauthorized inferences may be prevented. With respect to security, in the example by Warren discussed in Section 7.2.5, confidentiality, privacy, and trust policies will determine the extent to which Sally trusts the articles and has access to the articles in putting together her report on Tony Blair's speeches. Figure 7.15 illustrates the relationships between secure knowledge management and semantic web.

7.3.6 Secure Web Services for Activity Management

Figure 7.16 illustrates secure WS for activity management. We will discuss each activity (e.g., secure e-commerce, secure collaboration, and secure information sharing) in the following sections.

7.3.6.1 Secure E-Commerce

As stated earlier, e-commerce is about organizations carrying out business transactions such as sales of goods and business agreements as well as consumers purchasing items from merchants electronically. There have been numerous

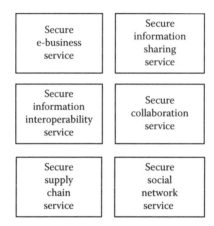

Figure 7.16   Web services for secure activity management.

developments on e-commerce and some discussions on the initial progress that were reported in [THUR00]. Owing to the fact that e-commerce may involve millions of dollars in transactions between businesses or credit card purchases between consumers and businesses, it is important that the e-commerce systems be secure. Examples of such systems include e-payment systems and supply chain management systems.

There has been some work on secure e-commerce as well as secure supply chain management (see, e.g., [GHOS98] and [ATAL03]). In the case of e-payment systems, the challenges include identification and authentication of consumers and businesses as well as tracing the purchases made by consumers. For example, it would be entirely possible for someone to masquerade as a consumer, use the consumer's credit card and make purchases electronically. Therefore, one solution proposed is for a consumer to have some credentials when he or she makes some purchases. These credentials, which may be some random numbers, could vary with each purchase. This way the malicious process that masquerades as the consumer may not have the credential and therefore may not be able to make the purchases. There will be a problem if the credentials are also stolen. Various encryption techniques are being proposed for secure e-commerce (see [HASS00]). That is, in addition to possessing credentials, the information may be encrypted, say, with the public key of the business, and only the business could get the actual data. Similarly, the communication between the business and the consumer is also encrypted. When transactions are carried out between businesses, the parties involved will have to possess certain credentials so that the transactions are carried out securely. Note that while much progress has been made on e-commerce transactions as well as secure e-commerce transactions, incorporating techniques for secure database transaction management with e-commerce is still not mature. Some work has been reported in [RAY00].

7.3.6.2 Secure Supply Chain Management

Secure supply chain management is also a key aspect of secure e-commerce. Here, the idea is for organizations to provide parts to other corporations for, say, manufacturing or other purposes. Suppose a hospital wants to order surgical equipment from a corporation; then there must be some negotiations and agreements between the hospital and the corporation. The corporation X may request some of its parts from another corporation Y and may not want to divulge the information that it is manufacturing the parts for, say, hospital A. Such sensitive information has to be protected. Supply chain management is useful in several areas of manufacturing for many domains, including medical, defense, and intelligence. Some of the information exchanged between the organizations may be highly sensitive, especially for military and intelligence applications. There needs to be a way to protect such sensitive information. Since the transactions are carried out on the web, a combination of access control rules and encryption techniques are being proposed as solutions for protecting sensitive information for supply chain management.

We have been hearing of e-commerce only since about the mid-1990s and this has been due to the explosion of the web. While much progress has been made on developing information technologies such as databases, data mining, and multimedia information management for e-commerce, there is still a lot to do on security. In addition, the information about various individuals will also have to be kept private. Many of the security technologies we have discussed in this book, including secure web data management and secure semantic web, will be applicable for secure e-commerce. For example, the semantic web can be used as a vehicle to carry out e-commerce functions. By having machine-understandable web pages, e-commerce can be automated without having a human in the loop. This means that it is critical that the semantic web be secure. As we make progress for secure web information management technologies, we can vastly improve the security of e-commerce transactions. E-commerce applications may be invoked as WS.

7.3.6.3 Secure Workflow and Collaboration

As stated earlier, collaboration technologies are important for e-commerce as organizations carry out transactions with each other. Workflow is about a process that must be followed from start to finish in carrying out an operation such as making a purchase. The steps include initiating the agreement, transferring funds, and sending the goods to the consumer. Because collaboration and workflow are part of many operations such as e-commerce and knowledge management, we need secure workflow and secure collaboration. There has been a lot of work by Bertino et al. on this topic. Most notable among the developments is the BFA model (see [BERT99]) for secure workflow management systems. Some work on secure collaborative systems was initially proposed in [DEMU93]. Since then several ideas have been developed (see IFIP Conference Series on Database Security). In this section, we will provide an overview of secure workflow and collaboration.

In the case of secure workflow management systems, the idea is for users to have the proper credentials to carry out the particular task. For example, in the case of making a purchase for a project, only a project leader could initiate the request. A secretary then types the request. Then, the administrator has to use his/her credit card and make the purchase. The mailroom has the authority to make the delivery. Essentially, what we have proposed is a role-based access control model for secure workflow. There have been several developments on this topic (see SACMAT Conference Proceedings). Various technologies such as Petri nets have been investigated for secure workflow system (see [HUAN98]).

Closely related to secure workflow is secure collaboration. Collaboration is much broader than workflow. While workflow is about a series of operations that have to be executed serially or in parallel to carry out a task, collaboration is about individuals working together to solve a problem. Object technologies in general and distributed object management technologies in particular are being used to develop collaboration systems. Here, the individual and the resources in the environment are modeled as objects. Communications between the individuals and resources are modeled as communication between the objects. This communication is carried out via object request brokers. Therefore, security issues discussed for object request brokers apply for secure collaboration. For example, should all parties involved be given the same access to the resources? If the access to resources is different, then how can the individuals work together and share data?

Workflow and collaboration are about organizations or groups working together toward a common goal such as designing a system or solving a problem. Collaboration technologies are important for e-commerce as organizations carry out transactions with each other.

Trust and negotiation systems also play an important role in workflow and collaboration systems. For example, how can the parties trust each other in solving a problem? If A gives some information to B, can B share the information with C even if A and C do not communicate with each other? Similar questions were asked when we discussed secure federations. Also, secure data management technologies are necessary to manage the data for workflow and collaboration applications. While much progress has been made, there is still a lot to do especially with the developments on the semantic web and emerging technologies such as peer to peer data management.

In Chapter 5, we discussed WS for complex activities such as workflow, choreography, and orchestration. Security for such activities is in its infancy. For example, what are the security issues in invoking the WS that comprise a workflow application? What are the security issues for orchestration and choreography? What are the security issues for WS composition?

7.3.6.3.1 Secure Information Interoperability

There are several challenges for integrating information, especially in a heterogeneous environment. One is schema heterogeneity where system A is based on a relational system and system B is based on an object system. That is, when the two systems are based on different models, we need to resolve the conflicts. One option is to have a common data model. This means that the constructs of both systems have to be transformed into the constructs of the common data model. When we consider security properties, we have to ensure that the policies enforced by the individual systems are maintained. Multiple schemas are integrated to form, say, a federated schema for a secure federated database system. Essentially, we have adopted Sheth and Larson's schema architecture for a secure federated environment. Some of the security challenges in integrating heterogeneous schemas are discussed in [THUR94]. We assume that each component exports a certain schema to the federation. Then, these schemas are integrated to form a federated policy. In a secure environment, we need to ensure that the security properties of the individual systems are maintained throughout the federation. In the next section, we will discuss security policy integration issues.

Next, we will focus on policy integration. Initial investigation of security policy integration for federated databases was reported in [THUR94]. Here, we assumed that heterogeneous database systems had to be integrated to form a secure federated database system. Our approach is very similar to the approach taken by Sheth and Larson for schema integration [SHET90]. In the case of policy integration, each system exports security policies to the federation. We assume that the component systems have more stringent access control requirements for foreign users. That is, export policies may have access control rules in addition to the rules enforced by the local system. The challenge is to ensure that there is no security violation at the federation level.

Semantic heterogeneity occurs when an entity is interpreted differently at different sites or different entities are interpreted to be the same object. For example, the term "speed" could be in miles/h in node 1 and in node 2 it could be km/day. Another example is John Smith could be Smith John at node 1 and John K Smith at node 2. In both cases, the same entity is interpreted differently. On the other hand, John Smith at node 1 could really be John J. Smith and at node 2 he is John K. Smith. They are both different people but mistakenly they are considered to be the same.

Semantic heterogeneity is one of the major challenges for data integration as well as information interoperability. They occur not only in relational databases but also in object databases, multimedia databases, and even geospatial databases. For example, when heterogeneous geospatial databases are integrated, each database could have different ways of representing the same coordinate system. Various solutions for handling heterogeneity have been proposed since the 1990s, although it is only recently with the use of semantic web technologies that we have a good handle on the problem.

WS may be invoked for integrating heterogeneous databases. That is, the agent acting on behalf of the user may invoke a web service for integration. This web service may utilize ontologies for handling semantic heterogeneity to carry out its operation. Therefore, to have secure information interoperability, we need a secure

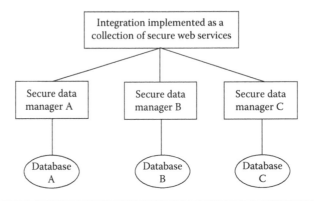

Figure 7.17 Web services for secure information interoperability.

WS. The research on WS for secure information interoperability is just beginning. Some of the challenges include privacy-preserving ontology alignment and security policy integration for WS. Figure 7.17 illustrates aspects of WS for secure information interoperability.

7.3.6.3.2 Assured (Secure) Information Sharing

Assured (secure) information sharing (AIS) is about organizations sharing information but at the same time enforcing policies and procedures so that the data are integrated and mined to extract nuggets. For example, data from the various data sources at multiple security levels as well as from different services and agencies, including the Air Force, Navy, Army, Local, State, and Federal agencies, have to be integrated so that the data can be mined, patterns and information extracted, relationships identified, and decisions made. The databases would include, for example, military databases that contain information about military strategies, intelligence databases that contain information about potential terrorists and their patterns of attack, and medical databases that contain information about infectious diseases and stock piles. Data could be structured or unstructured, including geospatial/multimedia data. Data also need to be shared between healthcare organizations such as doctors' offices, hospitals, and pharmacies. Unless the data are integrated and the big picture is formed, it will be difficult to inform all the parties concerned about the incidences that have occurred. While the different agencies have to share data and information, they also need to enforce appropriate security and integrity policies so that the data do not get into the hands of unauthorized individuals. Essentially, the agencies have to share information but at the same time maintain security and integrity requirements. A coalition consists of a set of organizations, which may be agencies, universities, and corporations that work together in a peer-to-peer environment to solve problems such as intelligence and military operations, as well as healthcare operations. Coalitions are usually dynamic in nature. That is, members may join and leave the coalition in accordance with the policies and procedures. A challenge is to ensure the secure operation of a coalition. We assume that the members of a coalition, which are also called its partners, may be trustworthy, untrustworthy, or partially (semi) trustworthy. Various aspects of coalition data sharing are discussed in the Markle report [MARK03].

There is also an urgent need for multiple organizations to share data and at the same time enforce security policies. These policies include policies for confidentiality, privacy, and trust. For example, patient data may be shared by multiple organizations, including hospitals, levels of government, and agencies. It is important to maintain the privacy of patient data. However, it is also important that there are no unnecessary access controls so that information sharing is prohibited. One needs flexible policies so that during emergency situations, it is critical that all of the data are shared for effective decisions to be made. During normal operations, it is important to maintain confidentiality and privacy. In addition, trust policies ensure that data are shared between trusted individuals. The standard efforts in this area include RBAC [SAND96] as well as P3P (platform for privacy preferences).

There are two types of conflicting requirements: one is security versus data sharing. The goal of data sharing is for organizations to share as much data as possible so that the data are mined and nuggets are obtained. However, when security policies are enforced, not all of the data are shared. The other type of conflict is between real-time processing and security. The war fighter will need information at the right time. If it is even, say, 5 min late, the information may not be useful. This means that if various security checks are to be performed, then the information may not reach the war fighter on time.

WS play a major role in information sharing. For example, an organization A may invoke a web service to obtain information from another organization B. This web service may invoke another web service to determine what the incentives are for the organization B to share the information. In the case of AIS, the organization B also examine the security policies to determine whether the information can be shared. We are building an AIS lifecycle and service-oriented architecture is central to our approach. Details are discussed in Appendix D.

7.3.6.3.3 Secure Social Networking

Social networks have exploded in recent years. We now have Facebook, Friendster, and Twitter among others. Social networks are being mined to extract useful information so that better services can be provided to the members. In addition, the mined information can also be used to help counterterrorism and law enforcement. At the same time, it is important to protect the privacy of law-abiding citizens.

There has been much interest recently on securing social networks as well as developing privacy-preserving techniques for social networks. For example, how can the members reveal the right amount of information so that their privacy is enforced? Should the system provide some feedback to the members that they are revealing too much information? WS may be invoked to manage the social networks. For example, a member may invoke a web service to post information on the network. These WS have to ensure appropriate security and privacy policies.

7.3.6.3.4 Secure Supply Chain Management

Security for supply chain management and logistics is receiving a lot of attention. With respect to logistics, a major goal is the secure movement of the objects. When items have to be moved from location A to B, the items have to be secured both physically and digitally. RFID technologies are being used to track the objects for logistics and supply chain management. It is critical that the RFID technologies be secure.

With respect to supply chain, there are also additional security considerations. For example, a product may be manufactured using several components. These components may come from different parts of the world and may be compromised. It is critical that the product be secure even if the components may be compromised. This is a very challenging problem. As discussed in Section 7.2, WS may be invoked to carry out supply chain management as well as logistics operations. These WS have to be secure to ensure secure supply chain management.

7.3.7 Secure Domain Web Services

7.3.7.1 Defense

The DoD is adopting the services technologies and the global information grid based on the service-oriented architecture paradigm. Much of the development is influenced by XML and ontologies. As we have stated, WS also play a major role for applications in homeland security. For many of the domain applications, the focus has been on implementation of attribute-based access control based on XACML security standards. The goal is for the user to present his/her credentials and request resources. The system would then make a decision as to whether the user can access the resources based on the policies enforced and the credentials of the user. This is essentially the function of the Policy Decision Point. Then the Policy Enforcement Point will enforce the access request.

7.3.7.2 Healthcare and Lifecycles

As stated earlier, semantic web technologies have played a major role in the development of healthcare information technologies. For example, ontologies have been developed for electronic healthcare records as well as for several items in life sciences. The major security challenge for healthcare information systems involves privacy. The goal is to ensure the privacy of the patient records. Typically, patients would determine what information they want to protect and under what conditions. When an organization requests data about patients, the organization will specify what its policies are. If the policies are in agreement with what the patient

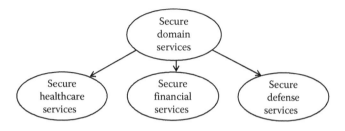

Figure 7.18   Secure domain web services.

has specified, then the information is released to the organization. W3C standards such as P3P may be utilized to enforce privacy. Furthermore, the entire operation could be implemented as WS.

7.3.7.3 Finance

Since financial domains involve money, confidentiality is critical for financial data. While it is difficult to get healthcare data due to patient privacy, we are finding that it is almost impossible to obtain financial data such as credit card data to conduct research. Several groups are developing WS and semantic web technologies for financial domains. As we have stated, the group in Madrid has done some very good research on applying the semantic "ontology-based platform that provides (a) the integration of contents and semantics in a knowledge base that provides a conceptual view on low-level contents, (b) an adaptive hypermedia-based knowledge visualization and navigation system and (c) semantic search facilities" [CAST]. The challenge we have is to integrate the security and privacy policies to protect financial data as well as the customer information into these semantic web technologies. WS will then execute the financial operations.

7.3.7.4 Other Domains

Security for domains such as telecommunications has been studied extensively. For example, WS for mobile applications, including cell phones and tablets, are being proposed. Furthermore, security efforts for the telecommunication and mobile computing domains are exploding. Secure WS for such domains are also being investigated. Figure 7.18 illustrates WS for various secure domain applications.

7.3.8 Emerging Secure Web Services

7.3.8.1 Security for X as a Service

The concept of X as a service, where X may be data, software, or some other concept such as a platform, operating system, compiler, or infrastructure, is becoming very

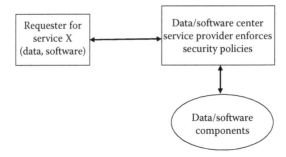

Figure 7.19 Security for X as a service.

popular. In the services computing world, everything becomes a service, including data as well as real-world services, such as healthcare and finance.

Security for data as a service has been investigated in recent years. With the explosion of outsourcing of jobs, many data-oriented jobs are being outsourced; therefore, protecting sensitive aspects of data is critical. Furthermore, when data are utilized as a service from service providers, it is important that the data be of high quality and not be corrupted. With respect to software, it is important that the software that is being utilized as a service is error-free and is not infected with worms and viruses. Figure 7.19 illustrates the notion of providing security for X as a service. More details on this topic will be discussed throughout this book.

7.3.8.2 Security for Amazon Web Services

AWS has provided companies of all sizes with an infrastructure WS platform in the cloud. With AWS, one can requisition computing power, storage, and other services. AWS provides database components called SimpleDB, which provide database functions such as querying. Amazon uses SOAP protocols for communication between the client and the service provider. Therefore, all of the security issues that pertain to SOAP are relevant. Furthermore, cloud computing security issues are also relevant to these discussions. In the case of cloud, the security concerns include enforcing appropriate access control policies as well as the secure storage of the data at multiple locations. Recently, researchers are exploring the scrutiny issues related to virtualization in a cloud. More details of cloud computing security issues will be discussed in Part V.

Our research is focusing on implementing access control and encryption for AWS. The data that is being stored in the Amazon environment is encrypted for protection. On top of that, we are also implementing role-based access control in this environment. We are also implementing XACML in the cloud environment and more details will be given in the next section. More details on this topic can be found in [PRAN09].

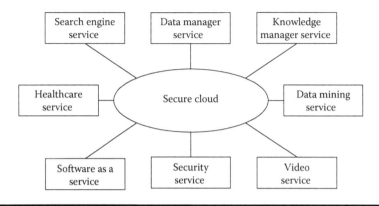

Figure 7.20 Secure cloud.

7.3.8.3 Secure Web Services for Cloud and Grid

There is a critical need to securely store, manage, share, and analyze massive amounts of complex (e.g., semistructured and unstructured) data to determine patterns and trends to improve the quality of healthcare, better safeguard the nation, and explore alternative energy. The emerging cloud computing model attempts to address the growth of web-connected devices, and handle massive amounts of data. Google has now introduced the MapReduce framework for processing large amounts of data on commodity hardware. Apache's HDFS is emerging as a superior software component for cloud computing combined with integrated parts such as MapReduce. The need to augment human reasoning, interpreting, and decision-making abilities has resulted in the emergence of the semantic web, which is an initiative that attempts to transform the web from its current, merely human-readable form to a machine-processable form. This in turn has resulted in numerous social networking sites with massive amounts of data to be shared and managed.

We are conducting extensive research in cloud computing and secure cloud computing [HAML10]. Much of the discussions of cloud computing and secure cloud computing are based on this research. Figure 7.20 illustrates a secure cloud based on Hadoop and MapReduce.

7.4 Summary and Directions

In this chapter, we discussed various types of specialized WS. First, we discussed WS for data management and complex data management. Then, we discussed WS for information management and knowledge management. Next, we discussed WS for activity management. This was followed by a discussion of domain WS. Then, we discussed some emerging WS, including the paradigm of "X as a service." Next, we described security for emerging WS, including security for WS for data, information, and knowledge, and activity management. We also discussed security for domain WS as well as for AWS and clouds. We have also examined security for X as a service.

We believe that much of the future research on WS as well as on secure WS will be on the topics we have discussed in this chapter. This is partly due to the fact that WS and secure WS are the essence of cloud computing and secure cloud computing. Cloud computing technologies are exploding due to the need for processing and analyzing massive amounts of data. The remainder of this book will be devoted to cloud computing and secure cloud computing.

References

[ALAM06] Alam, A. and B. Thuraisingham, *GRDF and Security Constructs, Computer Standards and Interfaces*, 33(1), January 2011, 35–41.

[AMAZON] http://aws.amazon.com/.

[ATAL03] Atallah, M., H. Elmongui, V. Deshpande, and L. Schwarz, Secure supply-chain protocols. *IEEE International Conference on Electronic Commerce* (CEC 2003). Newport each, CA.

[ATLU04] Atluri V. et al., An authorization model for geospatial data. *IEEE Transactions on Dependable and Secure Computing*, 238–254, December 2004.

[BERT99] Bertino, E. et al., The specification and enforcement of authorization constraints in workflow management systems. *ACM Transactions on Information and Systems Security*, 2(1), 65–104, 1999.

[BERT08] Bertino, E., B. Thuraisingham, M. Gertz, and M. Damiani, Security and privacy for geospatial data: Concepts and research directions. *Proceedings of the SIGSPATIAL ACM GIS 2008 International Workshop on Security and Privacy in GIS and LBS (SPRINGL 2008)*: 6–19, Vreine, CA.

[BORD] Borden, J., *XML Healthcare: From ASTM XML DTDs to the Semantic Web*, Technical Report, Tufts University.

[CAST] Castells, P., B. Foncillas, R. Lara, M. Rico, and J.L. Alonso, Semantic web technologies for economic and financial information management. http://nets.ii.uam.es/aniceto/publications/esws04.pdf.

[CHEN04] Chen-Burger, Y.-H., K.-Y. Hui, A.D. Preece, P.M.D. Gray, and A. Tate, Supporting collaboration through semantic-based workflow and constraint solving. http://stoater.inf.ed.ac.uk/project/ix/documents/2004/2004-ekaw-chenburger-kraft-ix.pdf.

[DAMI07] Damiani, M., E. Bertino, B. Catania, and P. Perlasca. GEO-RBAC: A spatially aware RBAC. *ACM Transactions on Information and System Security*, 10(1), 1–42, 2007.

[DATA] XML.com: http://www.xml.com/pub/a/2007/10/25/data-sources-as-web-services.html.

[DEMU93] Demurjian, S. et al., Security for collaborative computer systems, *Multimedia Review: The Journal of Multimedia Computing*, Penton Media Publishers, 4(2), 40–47, Summer 1993.

[EBXM] EBXML.org: http://www.ebxml.org/.

[GHOS98] Ghosh, A., *E-commerce Security, Weak Links and Strong Defenses*. John Wiley, New York, NY, 1998.

[GLOB] http://en.wikipedia.org/wiki/Globus_Alliance.

[HAML10] Hamlen, K. et al., *Security Issues for Cloud Computing*, Technical Report, University of Texas at Dallas, January 2010.

[HASS00] Hassler, V., *Security Fundamentals for E-Commerce*, Artech, London, UK, 2000.

[HUAN98] Huang, W. and V. Atluri, Analyzing the safety of workflow authorization models, In *Proceedings of the IFIP Database Security Conference*, Chalidiki, Greece, July 1998 (formal proceedings published by Kluwer, 1999).

[LIFE] Ontologies for the life sciences. www.jonathanborden-md.com/HealthcareSemWeb.ppt.

[KREM] Schulze-Kremer, S., Ontologies for the life sciences, Encyclopedia of Genetics, Genomics, Proteomics and Bioinformatics, 2005. Universtät Hannover, Hannover, Germany.

[MARK03] Markle Report on Assured Information Sharing, 2003.

[MART08] InformationWeek, June 2008, Guide To Cloud Computing Richard Martin and J. Nicholas Hoover, http://www.informationweek.com/services/hosted-applications/guide-to-cloud-computing/208700713

[OBEL] E3VALUE.com: http://www.e3value.com/projects/ourprojects/obelix.

[OGC] OGC White Paper, *An Introduction to GeoRSS: A Standards Based Approach for Geo-Enabling RSS Feeds*, http://www.opengeospatial.org/pressroom/papers.

[PALI04] Paliwal, A.V., N. Adam, C. Bornhövd, and J. Schaper, Semantic discovery and composition of web services for RFID applications in border control. http://www.ai.sri.com/SWS2004/final-versions/SWS2004-Paliwal-Final.pdf.

[PRAN09] Pranav, P., *Security for Amazon Web Services*, MS Thesis, University of Texas at Dallas, November 2009.

[RAY00] Ray I. et al., A fair exchange e-commerce protocol with automated dispute resolution. In *Proceedings of the IFIP Database Security Conference*, Amsterdam, The Netherlands, August 2000.

[SAND96] Sandhu, R., E. Coyne, H. Feinstein, and C. Youman, Role-based access control models. *IEEE Computer*, 29(2), 38–47, February 1996.

[SHET90] Shet, A. and J. Larson, *Federated Database Systems for Managing Distributed, Heterogeneous and Autonomous Databases*, Bellcore, Technical Report TM-STS-016302, Piscataway, NY, 1990 (also published in *ACM Computing Survey*, 9/1990).

[SING06] Singh, R. and Salam, A., Semantic information assurance for secure distributed knowledge management: A business process perspective. *IEEE Transactions Systems Man and Cybernetics*, 36(3), 472–486, 2006.

[SOFT] http://en.wikipedia.org/wiki/Software_as_a_service.

[STUD] Semantically enabled knowledge technology, http://semanticweb.org/wiki/SEKT.

[STUD] http://www.emeraldinsight.com/journals.htm?issn=0143-5124&volume=26&issue=4/5&articleid=1501536&show=html

[TELE] http://en.wikipedia.org/wiki/Parlay_X.

[THUR90] Thuraisingham, B., Multi-level Security for multimedia database systems. *IFIP Data Security Conference*, 99–116, 1990. Halifax, UK.

[THUR94] Thuraisingham, B., Security issues in federated database management systems. *Computer and Security*, 13(6): 509–525, 1994.

[THUR95] Thuraisingham, B. and W. Ford, Security constraint processing in a multilevel distributed database management system. *IEEE Transactions on Knowledge and Data Engineering*, 7(2), 278–293, April 1995.

[THUR97] Thuraisingham, B., *Data Management Systems Evolution and Interoperation*, CRC Press, Boca Raton, FL, 1997.

[THUR00] Thuraisingham, B., *Web Data Management and Electronic Commerce*, CRC Press, Boca Raton, FL, 2000.

[THUR05] Thuraisingham, B., *Database and Applications Security*, CRC Press, Boca Raton, FL, 2005.

[THUR07] Thuraisingham, B. et al., *DAGIS Architecture*, Technical Report, University of Texas at Dallas, 2007.

[THUR10] Thuraisingham, B., *Secure Semantic Service Oriented Systems*, CRC Press, Boca Raton, FL, 2010.

[TRAS] Trastour, D. et al., Semantic web support for the business-to-business e-commerce lifecycle. http://www.hpl.hp.com/techreports/2002/HPL-2002-3R1.pdf.

[WARR06] Warren, P., Knowledge management and the semantic Web: From scenario to technology. *IEEE Intelligent Systems*, 21(1): 53–59, 2006.

[WFMC] Workflow management coalition, http://xml.coverpages.org/wf-xml.html.

[XML] Thinking XML: A glimpse into XML in the financial services industry. http://www-128.ibm.com/developerworks/xml/library/x-think22.html.

[ZHAO] Zhao, G. et al., Engineering an ontology for financial securities fraud, http://www.starlab.vub.ac.be/research/projects/poirot/Publications/eofsf_20-08-final.pdf.

Conclusion to Part II

Part II provided an overview of web services and secure web services. Web services are at the heart of cloud computing as the cloud provides a collection of services to the consumer.

Chapter 5 provided an overview of the service-oriented computing paradigm and security issues for services. First, we discussed the notion of services, SOA and web services, the emerging X as a service paradigm, and SOA and design. Then, we discussed security for SOA and web services. In particular, we discussed access control for web services, standards such as SAML and XACML and some emerging security models such as models for delegation, information flow, and multilevel security. We also discussed identity management for web services.

Chapter 6 provided an overview of semantic web technologies and the notion of semantic web services. In particular, we discussed Tim Berners Lee's technology stack for the semantic web as well as XML, RDF, ontologies, and web rules. We also discussed semantic web services and how they can make use of semantic web technologies. As stated in Chapter 6, semantic web services are at the heart of semantic cloud computing.

Chapter 7 discussed various types of specialized web services. First, we discussed web services for data management and complex data management. Then, we discussed web services for information management and knowledge management. Next, we discussed web services for activity management. This was followed by a discussion of domain web services. Then, we discussed some emerging web services including the paradigm of "X as a Service."

CLOUD COMPUTING CONCEPTS

Introduction to Part III

Now that we have provided an overview of web services we are now ready to introduce cloud computing and provide an overview of the various concepts, functions, technologies, products, and standards relating to cloud computing. We will also show how the concepts discussed in Part II on web services, semantic web services, and specialized web services may be applied to provide cloud services.

Part III consists of five chapters: 8, 9, 10, 11, and 12. We provide an overview of cloud computing concepts in Chapter 8. Cloud computing functions are discussed in Chapter 9. Cloud data management, which is a main focus of our research and development, is discussed in Chapter 10. Some specialized cloud services such as mobile clouds as well as cloud applications are discussed in Chapter 11. Finally, cloud computing service providers, products, and frameworks are the subjects of Chapter 12.

Chapter 8

Cloud Computing Concepts

8.1 Overview

The emerging cloud computing model attempts to address the growth of web-connected devices, and handle massive amounts of data. Google has now introduced the MapReduce framework for processing large amounts of data on commodity hardware. Apache's HDFS is emerging as a superior software component for cloud computing combined with integrated parts such as MapReduce [HDFS], [DEAN04]. Clouds such as HP's Open Cirrus Testbed are utilizing HDFS. This in turn has resulted in numerous social networking sites with massive amounts of data to be shared and managed. For example, we may want to analyze multiple years of stock market data statistically to reveal a pattern or to build a reliable weather model based on several years of weather and related data. To handle such massive amounts of data distributed at many sites (i.e., nodes), scalable hardware and software components are needed. The cloud computing model has emerged to address the explosive growth of web-connected devices, and handle massive amounts of data. It is defined and characterized by massive scalability and new Internet-driven economics.

In this chapter, we will discuss some preliminaries in cloud computing. In this part we will discuss some of the technologies such as Hadoop and MapReduce. We will first introduce what is meant by cloud computing. While various definitions have been proposed, we will adopt the definition provided by NIST. This will be followed by a service-based paradigm for cloud computing. In particular, we will elaborate on some of the discussions in Chapter 5 (i.e., web services). Next, we will discuss the various key concepts including virtualization and data storage in the cloud.

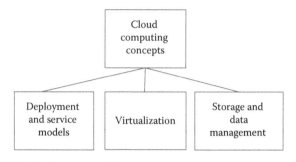

Figure 8.1   Cloud computing concepts.

The organization of this chapter is as follows. Cloud computing preliminaries will be discussed in Section 8.2. Virtualization will be discussed in Section 8.3. Cloud storage and data management issues will be discussed in Section 8.4. This chapter concludes with Section 8.5. Figure 8.1 illustrates the components addressed in this chapter. We will also point out the applicability of the concepts discussed in Part II to the concepts discussed in Part III.

8.2 Preliminaries in Cloud Computing

As stated in [CLOUD], cloud computing delivers computing as a service while in traditional computing it is provided in the form of a product. Therefore, users pay for the services based on a pay-as-you-go model. The services provided by a cloud may include hardware, systems, data, and storage. The users of the cloud need not know where the software and data are located; that is, the software and data services provided by the cloud are transparent to the user. [NIST] has defined cloud computing to be the following:

> Cloud computing is a model for enabling ubiquitous, convenient, on-demand network access to a shared pool of configurable computing resources (e.g., networks, servers, storage, applications, and services) that can be rapidly provisioned and released with minimal management effort or service provider interaction.

The cloud model is composed of multiple deployment models and service models. These models are described next.

8.2.1 Cloud Deployment Models

There are multiple deployment models for cloud computing. These include the public cloud, community cloud, hybrid cloud, and the private cloud. In a public cloud, the

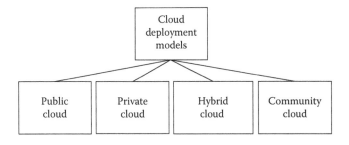

Figure 8.2 Cloud deployment models.

service provider typically provides the services over the WWW that can be accessed by the general public. Such a cloud may provide free services or pay-as-you-go services. In a community cloud, a group of organizations get together and develop a cloud. These organizations may have a common objective to provide features such as security and fault tolerance. The cost is shared among the organizations. Furthermore, the cloud may be hosted by the organizations or by a third party. A private cloud is a cloud infrastructure developed specifically for an organization. This could be hosted by the organization or by a third party. Hybrid cloud consists of a combination of public and private clouds. This way in a hybrid cloud an organization may use the private cloud for highly sensitive services while it may use the public cloud for less sensitive services and take advantage of what the WWW has to offer. Kantarcioglu and his colleagues have stated that the hybrid cloud is the deployment model of the future [KHAD12]. Figure 8.2 illustrates the cloud deployment models.

8.2.2 Service Models

As stated earlier, cloud computing provides a variety of services. These include Infrastructure as a Service (IaaS), Platform as a Service (PaaS), Software as a Service (SaaS), and Data as a Service (DaaS). In IaaS, the cloud provides a collection of hardware and networks for use by the general public or organizations. The users install operations systems and software to run the applications. The users will be billed according to the resources they utilize for their computing. In PaaS, the cloud provider will provide to their users the systems software such as operating systems (OSs) and execution environments. The users will load their applications and run them on the hardware and software infrastructures provided by the cloud. In SaaS, the cloud provider will provide the applications for the users to run. These applications could be say billing applications, tax computing applications, and sales tools. The cloud users access the applications through cloud clients. In the case of DaaS, the cloud provides data to the cloud users. Data may be stored in data centers that are accessed by the cloud users. Note that while DaaS is used to denote Desktop as a Service, more recently it denotes Data as a Service. Figure 8.3 illustrates the services models. Note that all the service-oriented concepts, technologies

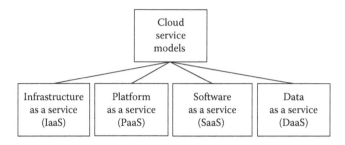

Figure 8.3   Cloud service models.

and standards discussed in Chapter 5 can be applied to develop the cloud services such as infrastructure, platform, software, applications, and data services.

8.3 Virtualization

Virtualization essentially means creating something virtual and not actual. It could be hardware, software, memory, and data. The notion of virtualization has existed for decades with respect to computing. Back in the 1960s, the concept of virtual memory was introduced. This virtual memory gives the application program the illusion that it has contiguous working memory. Mapping is developed to map the virtual memory to the actual physical memory.

Hardware virtualization is a basic notion in cloud computing. This essentially creates virtual machines hosted on a real computer with an OS. This means while the actual machine may be say an IBM PC (personal computer) running a Windows OS, through virtualization it may provide a SUN Solaris machine running Linux to the users. The actual machine is called the host machine while the virtual machine is called the guest machine.

Other types of virtualization include OS level virtualization, storage virtualization, and data/database virtualization. OS level virtualization is closely tied to hardware virtualization. In this type of virtualization, multiple virtual environments are created within a single OS. The virtual machine monitor, also known as the hypervisor, is the software that runs the virtual machine on the host computer. In storage virtualization, the logical storage is abstracted from the physical storage. Mappings have to be provided from the logical storage to the physical storage. In data/database virtualization, the data are abstracted from the underlying databases. A user has the illusion that he is working with his own database. Multiple such virtual databases may be created. The virtual databases have to be mapped to the physical database. It should be noted that while some have distinguished between data virtualization and database virtualization, we have used the terms interchangeably. In network virtualization, virtual networks are created. The virtual networks have to be mapped to the physical network. Figure 8.4 illustrates the various types of virtualization.

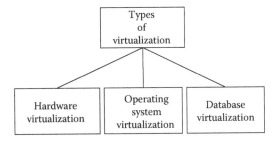

Figure 8.4 Types of virtualization.

As we have stated earlier, at the heart of cloud computing is the notion of hypervisor or the virtual machine monitor. Hardware virtualization techniques allow multiple OSs (called guests) to run concurrently on a host computer. These multiple OSs share virtualized hardware resources. Hypervisor is not a new term; it was first used in the mid-1960s in the IBM 360/65 machines. There are different types of hypervisors; in one type, the hypervisor runs on the host hardware and manages the guest OSs. Both VMware and XEN which are popular virtual machines are based on this model. In another model, the hypervisor runs within a conventional OS environment. Virtual machines are also incorporated into embedded systems and mobile phones. Embedded hypervisors have real-time processing capability. We will provide more details of hypervisors such as XEN and VMware in Chapter 9. Some details of virtualization are provided in [VIRTUAL].

8.4 Cloud Storage and Data Management

In a cloud storage model, the service providers store massive amounts of data for customers in data centers. Those who require storage space will lease the storage from the service providers who are the hosting companies. The actual location of the data is transparent to the users. What is presented to the users is virtualized storage; the storage managers will map the virtual storage with the actual storage and manage the data resources for the customers. A single object (e.g., the entire video database of a customer) may be stored in multiple locations. Each location may store objects for multiple customers. Figure 8.5 illustrates cloud storage management.

Visualizing cloud storage has many advantages. The users need not purchase expensive storage devices. The data could be placed anywhere in the cloud. Maintenance such as backup and recovery are provided by the cloud. The goal is for users to have rapid access to the cloud. However, due to the fact that the owner of the data does not have complete control of his data, there are serious security concerns with respect to storing data in the cloud.

A database that runs on the cloud is a cloud database manager. There are multiple ways to utilize a cloud database manager. In the first model, for users to run

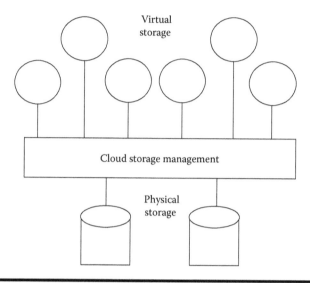

Figure 8.5   Cloud storage management.

databases on the cloud, a VirtualMachine Image must be purchased. The database is then run on the virtual machines. The second model is the Database as a Service model; the service provider will maintain the databases. The users will make use of the database services and pay for the service. An example is the Amazon relational database service which is a SQL database service and has a MySQL interface [AMAZON]. A third model is the cloud provider hosting a database on behalf of the user. The users can either utilize the database service maintained by the cloud or they can run their databases on the cloud. A cloud database must optimize its query, storage, and transaction processing to take full advantage of the services provided by the cloud. Figure 8.6 illustrates cloud data management. Note that the specialized services discussed in Chapter 6 may be utilized to develop cloud data management services. These services may include cloud query service and cloud transaction service.

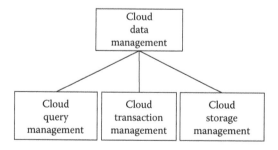

Figure 8.6   Cloud data management.

8.5 Summary and Directions

This chapter has introduced the notion of the cloud and discussed aspects of virtualization. In particular, aspects of hardware virtualization, OS virtualization, network virtualization, and database virtualization were discussed. We also discussed the various service models and deployment models for the cloud and provided a brief overview of cloud functions such as storage management and data management.

All the remaining Chapters in this part will provide more details on cloud computing concepts. In particular, we will provide some details of cloud functions as well as the products and prototypes of cloud computing systems. These chapters will lay the foundations for the discussion of security issues for the cloud as well as the experimental systems that we have developed.

References

[AMAZON] Amazon relational database service, http://aws.amazon.com/rds/

[CLOUD] Cloud computing, http://en.wikipedia.org/wiki/Cloud_computing

[DEAN04] Dean, J. and S. Ghemawat, MapReduce: Simplified data processing on large clusters, http://research.google.com/archive/mapreduce.html

[HDFS] Apache Hadoop, http://hadoop.apache.org/

[KHAD12] Khadilkar, V., K. Y. Oktay, M. Kantarcioglu, and S. Mehrotra, Secure data processing over hybrid clouds. *IEEE Data Eng. Bull.* 35(4): 46–54, 2012.

[NIST] Definition of cloud computing, National Institute of Standards and Technology, http://csrc.nist.gov/publications/nistpubs/800-145/SP800-145.pdf

[VIRTUAL] Virtualization and cloud management, http://www.vmware.com/solutions/virtualization-management/index.html

Chapter 9

Cloud Computing Functions

9.1 Overview

In Chapter 8, we provided an overview of the various concepts in cloud computing. This included a discussion of the deployment models, service models, as well as a discussion of virtualization, storage and data management in the cloud. In fact, virtualization, storage and data management can be regarded to be cloud computing functions. In this chapter, we will elaborate on the cloud computing functions.

Our approach to the discussion of the functions will be to examine the general functions of a computing system and then examine the impact of the cloud. These functions are those of OSs, storage systems, database systems, information management systems, knowledge management systems, and networking systems. The functions will be best illustrated using our cloud computing framework.

The organization of this chapter is as follows. Our cloud computing framework will be discussed in Section 9.2. OSs functions including virtualization are discussed in Section 9.3. Cloud networks will be discussed Section 9.4. Cloud data and storage management functions will be discussed in Section 9.5. Application functions will be discussed in Section 9.6. Other aspects such as policy management, backup, and recovery will be discussed in Section 9.7. This chapter is summarized in Section 9.8.

It should be noted that policy management is only briefly discussed in this chapter. Details of policy management will be provided when we give a detailed discussion of securing the cloud in Part V. Furthermore, the concepts, standards, and technologies discussed in Part II such as web services and specialized data

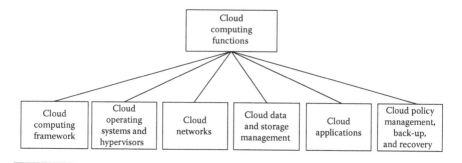

Figure 9.1   Cloud computing functions.

services may be utilized to provide the cloud services such as cloud infrastructure services and cloud data management services. The functions discussed in this chapter are illustrated in Figure 9.1.

9.2 Cloud Computing Framework

Our cloud computing framework that is based on the cloud computing functions is illustrated in Figure 9.2. We have defined a layered framework. At the lowest level is the networking layer and at the highest level is the applications layer. The applications could be any type of application, including healthcare, financial or defense and intelligence. The applications that we have hosted on the cloud are social networking, insider threat analysis, malware detection, information sharing, and ontology management. We will describe these applications in later chapters. Other applications may include information and knowledge management.

The core layers of the cloud framework are the OSs/virtualization layer, the storage layer, and the data management layer which also includes data mining functions. The OS/virtualization layer is the layer that carries out virtualization as well as memory management, scheduling, and interprocess communication management. The storage layer will manage the storage of massive amounts of data in

| Cloud application |
| Cloud data layer |
| Cloud storage layer |
| Cloud operating system and hypervisor layer |

Figure 9.2   Cloud computing framework.

the cloud. We consider the distributed file systems such as Hadoop to be part of the storage layer that will manage the distributed storage. Hadoop goes hand in hand with Google's MapReduce for analysis tasks. The data management layer will carry out cloud query processing, cloud transactions management, cloud metadata management, and cloud data mining.

Policy management, which is an aspect of security management, as well as back-up and recovery are also functions of cloud computing. Security has to be incorporated into each layer. Furthermore, the systems have to be recovered in case of failure. We will discuss security in later chapters. In the remaining sections of this chapter, we will discuss each of the other functions that we have discussed in this section. We will elaborate on cloud data management in Chapter 10 and cloud applications in Chapter 11.

9.3 Cloud OSs and Hypervisors

Essentially the cloud consists of a collection of machines. Each machine (or computer or node) has its own OS which is called the host OS. However, to enhance the computational power of the cloud, a node may have a virtual machine (VM) monitor which is also called a hypervisor. Through the hypervisor, the user is provided with the support of many virtual OSs called the guest OSs. Figure 9.3 illustrates the hypervisor concept.

In his articles for the Cloud Security Alliance, Chris Benton defined virtualization as follows: Virtualization provides the ability to emulate hardware via software [VIRT]. The article further states that some form of OS still needs to be booted from the hardware. This may be a full OS such as Linux, or it may be a stripped down system specific for virtualization. In each case, the OS is first booted and then the hypervisor (i.e., the VM monitor) is loaded. The hypervisor emulates specific hardware configurations for guest OSs. That is, when a guest OS is loaded into

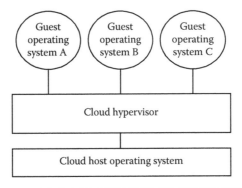

Figure 9.3   Hypervisor concept.

a VM, the hardware that hosts this guest is then simulated through the hypervisor, not the actual hardware. Ultimately of course, the multiple VMs will have to be mapped to one physical machine and this is the challenge for the hypervisor.

It should be noted that while virtualization is desirable in a cloud, it is not necessary. While many clouds utilize virtualization, especially the IaaS cloud, the SaaS-based clouds sometimes do not provide virtualization. Many cloud deployments include a virtualization component. While this is a common technique, Benton states that one can view a cloud as a house where the multiple users rent the house (i.e., the cloud). The house may have a basement (i.e., hypervisor), but it is not necessary for a house to have a basement.

There are two types of models for virtualization. One is host-based and the other is bare metal. Systems such as VMware and XEN provide host-based virtualization. That is, the hypervisor runs on the host OS. While the tools developed for applications can be used for the hypervisor, the hypervisor code may be large which is not good from a security point of view. In the bare metal case, the OS supports the virtualization. This way, while there may not be well-developed tools for the hypervisor, the code can be kept to a minimum. For more details on virtualization, we refer to [BARH03] and [VM].

9.4 Cloud Networks

In this section, we will discuss networking for the cloud. Many of the discussions about the cloud focus on virtualization and systems aspects. It is generally assumed that the commercial networks are sufficient to host the cloud. However, there are some efforts on architecting the network for the cloud. For example, in their paper on networking for the cloud, the authors state that a well-designed network to support a cloud architecture should address several challenges [BORO11]. These include routing optimization, reliability, and latency in WAN (Wide Area Networks) performance and security. We focus on the first two aspects.

With respect to routing optimization, the authors state that a key challenge for enterprises to consider is how the network can recognize, scale, and prioritize video as it is delivered through the cloud [BORO11]. In private and hybrid cloud environments, the network should be adaptable for delivering the optimal experience based on parameters such as user location, device type, or reachability. With respect to reliability and latency in WAN performance, the challenge is giving consistent, high-quality performance to applications when they are delivered from the cloud with maximum reliability and minimum latency.

Like system and data virtualization, network virtualization is also being explored in cloud computing. As stated in [BORO11], network virtualization is the process of combining hardware and software network resources and network functionality into a single, software-based administrative entity, a virtual network. Network virtualization involves platform virtualization, often combined with resource

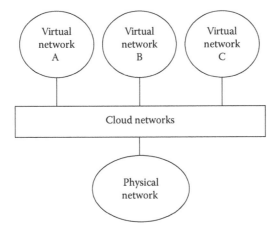

Figure 9.4 Cloud networks.

virtualization. Network virtualization is categorized as either external, combining many networks, or parts of networks, into a virtual unit, or internal, providing network-like functionality to the software containers on a single system. Analogous to the notion of the VM monitor (i.e., the hypervisor) for system virtualization, the virtual network monitor handles network virtualization. Vendors such as Cisco are now providing virtualization capabilities for networks. More work remains to be done on integrating virtualized networks into a cloud environment. Figure 9.4 illustrates cloud networking issues.

9.5 Cloud Data and Storage Management

There is some recent research on cloud data management. We will discuss details in Chapter 10. In this section, we will summarize the challenges with respect to data management functions such as query processing, transaction management, storage, metadata management, and data mining. Details on security will be provided in Part V.

Some work has been carried out on the cloud query processor. For example, we have implemented a cloud query processor using Hadoop, MapReduce, and Hive technologies. We have also implemented cloud query processing for semantic web data. Our implementations will be discussed in Part IV. The challenge is to come up with appropriate query optimization strategies for query processing. This will depend on how the data are stored across the nodes in the cloud. Kantarcioglu has investigated cloud query processing issues. In this work, he stated that one of the major challenges for cloud query processing is Dynamic Resource Allocation [OKTA12].

Some work has been carried out on transaction processing in the cloud. Most notable is that of Johannes Gehrke [GEHR11]. He stated that a major challenge in cloud data management is scaling and access. While lock-based implementations were dominant in traditional information access systems such as database systems and search engines, there has been an emergence of cloud-based systems based on Optimistic Concurrency Control (OCC).

With respect to cloud storage, the challenge is coming up with appropriate storage strategies for the cloud. How should the data be fragmented across the different nodes in the cloud? How can data virtualization be exploited to give optimum storage? Kantarcioglu and Mehrotra have developed interesting storage schemes for a hybrid cloud [OKTA12]. They state that an emerging trend in cloud computing is that of hybrid cloud wherein in-house capabilities/resources at the end-user site are seamlessly integrated with the cloud services to create a powerful cost-effective data processing solution.

Metadata management in the cloud includes not only information about the data and the resources in the cloud, it also includes information about the user accounts, usage patterns, SLAs and other cloud-specific information. Much work is required for coming up with appropriate models to store and manage the cloud metadata.

Cloud data mining is becoming an important area especially with the emergence of Big Data Analytics. Data mining algorithms have been enhanced with respect to performance with parallel data mining. The challenge is to implement these parallel data mining techniques on the cloud. Note that the difference between parallel/distributed databases and the cloud databases is that with the cloud, the data could be migrated for better resource utilization. Therefore, the data mining algorithms should take into account the location migration of the data. Figure 9.5 illustrates cloud data and storage management issues. Some interesting papers on data management in the cloud have been presented in [DMC12].

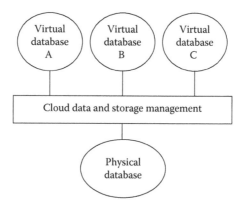

Figure 9.5 Cloud data and storage management issues.

9.6 Cloud Applications

The cloud functions are needed to host the various applications on the cloud. These applications may be domain applications such as healthcare and finance or IT applications such as information and knowledge management and social networks. In later parts of this book, we will discuss some of the applications we have developed that utilize the cloud. Our applications focus mainly on cloud data and information management. Figure 9.6 illustrates cloud applications. Some of these applications will be discussed in Chapter 11.

Next, we will discuss some examples. A healthcare organization may use a cloud to integrate the numerous data sources. These data sources may be stored in the cloud. The cloud may carry out operations such as ontology alignment (where multiple ontologies that refer to the same concept are integrated) and other data-intensive operations. A social network also may be hosted on the cloud. The cloud would provide computational resources to integrate and mine the data in the social networks. We will give examples of how we have used the cloud for applications such as social network management and query processing in Part IV. Cloud applications will also be discussed in Chapter 12.

9.7 Cloud Policy Management, Back-Up, and Recovery

Our framework also illustrates cloud policy management, back-up, and recovery. Policy management components will enforce the various policies across all the layers. These policies could be security policies or other types of policies such as administration policies. Various standards have been developed to specify and enforce the policies (e.g., SAML, XACML, WS-Security).

Back-up and recovery are important functions that the cloud service provider has to carry out. The cloud has to be up and running for the customers. Therefore, the SLAs have to specify how long the cloud will be taken down for maintenance. Also, to manage disasters the cloud data has to be backed up and possibly replicated.

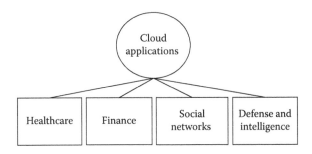

Figure 9.6   Cloud applications.

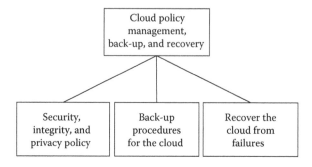

Figure 9.7   Cloud policy management, back-up, and recovery issues.

Some of the challenges will be discussed when we address cloud security. Figure 9.7 illustrates cloud policy management, back-up, and recovery issues.

9.8 Summary and Directions

This chapter has discussed various aspects of cloud computing functions. First, we presented a framework for cloud computing. This framework consists of a network layer, a virtualization layer, a storage layer, a data management layer, and an applications layer. We discussed the functions of each layer. We also discussed policy management, back-up, and recovery issues for the cloud.

Since cloud data management is our area of expertise, in the next chapter we will discuss cloud data management. We will discuss cloud applications in Chapter 11. Details of some of the prototypes we have developed for cloud data management and applications will be provided in Part IV. In Part V, we will discuss security issues for the cloud. In particular, we will discuss security for each layer of our cloud framework.

References

[BARH03] Barham, P., B. Dragovic, K. Fraser, S. Hand, T. L. Harris, A. Ho, R. Neugebauer, I. Pratt, and A. Warfield, Xen and the art of virtualization. *Proceedings of the 19th ACM Symposium on Operating Systems Principles 2003* (SOSP 2003), 164–177. Bolton Landing, NY.

[BORO11] Borovick, L., and R. Mehra, White paper. *Architecting the Network for the Cloud*, January 2011 http://www.cisco.com/en/US/solutions/collateral/ns1015/white_paper_idc-architecting_the_network_for_the_cloud.pdf

[DMC12] *Proceedings of the Workshop on Data Management in the Cloud*, http://www.nec-labs.com/dm/dmc2012.

[GEHR11] Gehrke, J., *Transaction Processing in the Cloud*, White Paper, 2011.

[OKTA12] Oktay, K. Y., V. Khadilkar, B. Hore, M. Kantarcioglu, S. Mehrotra, B., and M. Thuraisingham, Risk-aware workload distribution in hybrid clouds. *IEEE Fifth International Conference on Cloud Computing (IEEE CLOUD)*, 2012: 229–236. Honolulu, HI.

[VIRT] Cloud Security Alliance, The Basics of Virtualization Security by Chris Brenton. https://cloudsecurityalliance.org/wp-content/uploads/2011/11/virtualization-security. pdf

[VM] VMware virtualization overview. http://www.vmware.com/pdf/virtualization.pdf

Chapter 10

Cloud Data Management

10.1 Overview

Database systems technology has advanced a great deal during the past four decades from the legacy systems based on network and hierarchical models to relational and object-oriented database systems based on client–server architectures. Database systems can also now be accessed via the web and data management services have been implemented as web services. We consider a database system to include both the DBMS and the database (see also the discussion in [DATE90]). The DBMS component of the database system manages the database. The database contains persistent data. That is, the data are permanent even if the application programs go away.

In Chapter 9, we discussed cloud functions which included cloud data management functions. In this chapter, we will elaborate on cloud data management. Since this topic is still in its infancy, we will discuss various data management functions and how they may be implemented in a cloud. It should be noted that the notion of "Big Data" is increasing in popularity. That is, there are massive amounts of data in the range of exabytes and beyond that have to be processed. Many believe that cloud computing will play a major role in the big data initiatives.

The organization of this chapter is as follows. In Section 10.2, we discuss the relational data model and its implementation on the cloud. In Section 10.3, various types of architectures for database systems are described. These include an architecture for a centralized database system, schema architecture, as well as functional architecture. We then discuss data management architectures on the cloud. Database system functions are discussed in Section 10.4. These functions include query processing, transaction management, metadata management, and storage management, maintaining integrity, and fault tolerance. Note that

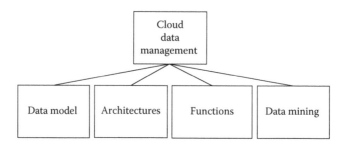

Figure 10.1   Cloud data management.

security will be the subject of several later chapters in the book and therefore we will not discuss security in this chapter. For each of the functions, the impact of the cloud will be discussed. Data mining will be the subject of Section 10.5 together with a discussion of cloud data mining. In Section 10.6, we discuss information management in the cloud. Specifically we discuss semantic web data management in the cloud. This chapter concludes with Section 10.7. It should be noted that the specialized web services discussed in Chapter 7 may be utilized for cloud data management services including cloud storage services, cloud query services, and cloud transaction services. Commercial cloud data management products will be discussed in Chapter 21. Figure 10.1 illustrates the topics addressed in this chapter.

10.2 Relational Data Model

In general, the purpose of a data model is to capture the universe that is represented as accurately, completely, and naturally as possible [TSIC82]. In this section, we discuss the essential points of the relational data model, as it is the most widely used model today. With the relational model [CODD70], the database is viewed as a collection of relations. Each relation has attributes and rows. For example, Figure 10.2

EMP			
SS#	Ename	Salary	D#
1	John	20 K	10
2	Paul	30 K	20
3	Mary	40 K	20

DEPT		
D#	Dname	Mgr
10	Math	Smith
20	Physics	Jones

Figure 10.2   Relational database.

illustrates a database with two relations, EMP and DEPT. EMP has four attributes: SS#, Ename, Salary, and D#. DEPT has three attributes: D#, Dname, and Mgr. EMP has three rows, also called tuples, and DEPT has two rows. Each row is uniquely identified by its primary key. For example, SS# could be the primary key for EMP and D# for DEPT. Another key feature of the relational model is that each element in the relation is an atomic value such as an integer or a string. That is, complex values such as lists are not supported.

Various operations are performed on relations. The SELECT operation selects a subset of rows satisfying certain conditions. For example, in the relation EMP, one may select tuples where the salary is more than 20 K. The PROJECT operation projects the relation onto some attributes. For example, in the relation EMP, one may project onto the attributes Ename and Salary. The JOIN operation joins two relations over some common attributes. A detailed discussion of these operations is given in [DATE90] and [ULLM88].

Various languages to manipulate the relations have been proposed. Notable among these languages is the ANSI (American National Standards Institute) Standard SQL (Structured Query Language). This language is used to access and manipulate data in relational databases. There is wide acceptance of this standard among DBMS vendors and users. It supports schema definition, retrieval, data manipulation, schema manipulation, transaction management, integrity, and security. Other languages include the relational calculus first proposed in the INGRES project at the University of California at Berkeley [DATE90]. Another important concept in relational databases is the notion of a view. A view is essentially a virtual relation and is formed from the relations in the database.

The challenge we are faced with today is to come up with an appropriate version of the relational model for the cloud. Vendors such as Oracle are building cloud-based relational database systems. Systems such as MySQL are being implemented in the cloud. Amazon has developed the DynamoDB database. As stated by Amazon, DynamoDB is a fully managed, NoSQL database service that provides fast and predictable performance with seamless scalability. With a few clicks in the AWS (Amazon Web Services) Management Console, customers can launch a new Amazon DynamoDB database table, scale up or down their request capacity for the table without downtime or performance degradation, and gain visibility into resource utilization and performance metrics. Researchers are investigating ways to host such a database in the cloud. In addition, special purpose data models developed specifically for the cloud are also being explored.

10.3 Architectural Issues

This section describes architectures for a database system and examines the impact of the cloud. First, we illustrate a centralized architecture for a database system. Then, we describe a distributed database architecture. Figure 10.3 is an example

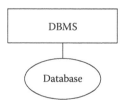

Figure 10.3 Centralized architecture.

of a centralized architecture. Here, the DBMS is a monolithic entity and manages a database, which is centralized. Functional architecture illustrates the functional modules of a DBMS. The major modules of a DBMS include the query processor, transaction manager, metadata manager, storage manager, integrity manager, and security manager. The functional architecture of the DBMS component of the centralized database system architecture (of Figure 10.3) is illustrated in Figure 10.4.

Although many definitions of a distributed database system have been given, there is no standard definition. Our discussion of distributed database system concepts and issues has been influenced by the discussion in [CERI84]. A distributed database system includes a DDBMS, a distributed database, and a network for interconnection. The DDBMS manages the distributed database. A distributed database is data that is distributed across multiple databases. Our choice architecture for a distributed database system is a multi-database architecture, which is tightly coupled. This architecture is illustrated in Figure 10.5. We have chosen such an architecture as we can explain the concepts for both homogeneous and heterogeneous systems based on this approach. In this architecture, the nodes are connected via a communication subsystem and local applications are handled by the local DBMS. In addition, each node is also involved in at least one global application,

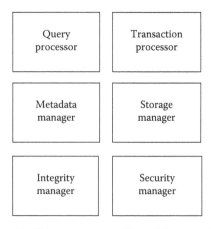

Figure 10.4 Functional architecture for a DBMS.

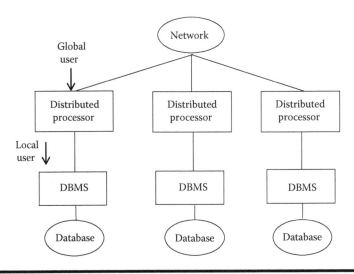

Figure 10.5   An architecture for a DDBMS.

so there is no centralized control in this architecture. The DBMSs are connected through a component called the Distributed Processor (DP). In a homogeneous environment, the local DBMSs are homogeneous while in a heterogeneous environment, the local DBMSs may be heterogeneous.

Distributed database system functions include distributed query processing, distributed transaction management, distributed metadata management, and enforcing security and integrity across the multiple nodes. The DP is an essential component of the DDBMS. It is this module that connects the different local DBMSs. That is, each local DBMS is augmented by a DP. The modules of the DP are illustrated in Figure 10.6. The components are the Distributed Metadata Manager (DMM), the Distributed Processor (DQP), the Distributed Transaction Manager (DTM), the Distributed Security Manager (DSP), and the Distributed

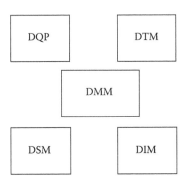

Figure 10.6   Modules of the DP.

Integrity Manager (DIM). DMM manages the global metadata. The global metadata includes information on the schemas, which describe the relations in the distributed database, the way the relations are fragmented, the locations of the fragments, and the constraints enforced. DQP is responsible for distributed query processing; DTM is responsible for distributed transaction management; DSM is responsible for enforcing global security constraints; and DIM is responsible for maintaining integrity at the global level. Note that the modules of DP communicate with their peers at the remote nodes. For example, the DQP at node 1 communicates with the DQP at node 2 for handling distributed queries.

The challenge faced by researchers is to come up with a suitable architecture for the cloud. For example, in the centralized architecture case, all the data can be hosted on one server. The processing could be distributed across multiple servers. Such an approach will not take full advantage of the capabilities provided by the cloud. In the distributed database case, each fragment of the database could be stored on a server. While this may take better advantage of the cloud, it does not take advantage of resource utilization. A cloud database architecture must use resource utilization effectively and store the data to maximize performance. Several database vendors including IBM, Oracle, and Microsoft are exploring architectures for cloud data management.

10.4 DBMS Functions

10.4.1 Overview

The functional architecture of a DBMS was illustrated in Figure 10.4 (see also [ULLM88]). The functions of a DBMS carry out its operations. A DBMS essentially manages a database, and it provides support to the user by enabling him to query and update the database. Therefore, the basic functions of a DBMS are query processing and update processing. In some applications such as banking, queries and updates are issued as part of transactions. Therefore, transaction management is also another function of a DBMS. To carry out these functions, information about the data in the database has to be maintained. This information is called the metadata. The function that is associated with managing the metadata is metadata management. Special techniques are needed to manage the data stores that actually store the data. The function that is associated with managing these techniques is storage management. To ensure that the above functions are carried out properly and that the user gets accurate data, there are some additional functions. These include security management, integrity management, and fault management (i.e., fault-tolerance).

This section focuses on some of the key functions of a DBMS. These are query processing, transaction management, metadata management, storage management, maintaining integrity, and fault-tolerance. We discuss each of these functions in Sections 10.4.2 through 10.4.7. In Section 10.4.6, the impact of the cloud will also be discussed. Figure 10.7 illustrates the concepts discussed in this section.

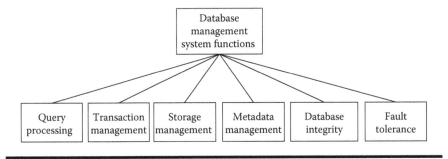

Figure 10.7   DBMS functions.

10.4.2 *Query Processing*

Query operation is the most commonly used function in a DBMS. It should be possible for users to query the database and obtain answers to their queries. There are several aspects to query processing. First of all, a good query language is needed. Languages such as SQL are popular for relational databases. Such languages are being extended for other types of databases. The second aspect is techniques for query processing. Numerous algorithms have been proposed for query processing in general and for the JOIN operation in particular. Also, different strategies are possible to execute a particular query. The costs for the various strategies are computed, and the one with the least cost is usually selected for processing. This process is called query optimization. Cost is generally determined by the disk access. The goal is to minimize disk access in processing a query.

The users pose a query using a language. The constructs of the language have to be transformed into the constructs understood by the database system. This process is called query transformation. Query transformation is carried out in stages based on the various schemas. For example, a query based on the external schema is transformed into a query on the conceptual schema. This is then transformed into a query on the physical schema. In general, rules used in the transformation process include the factoring of common subexpressions and pushing selections and projections down in the query tree as much as possible. If selections and projections are performed before the joins, then the cost of the joins can be reduced by a considerable amount.

Figure 10.8 illustrates the modules in query processing. The user interface manager accepts queries, parses the queries, and then gives them to the query transformer. The query transformer and query optimizer communicate with each other to produce an execution strategy. The database is accessed through the storage manager. The response manager gives responses to the user.

Some work has been carried out on cloud query processing. For example, we have implemented a cloud query processor using Hadoop, MapReduce, and HIVE technologies. Our implementation will be discussed in Part IV. The challenge is to

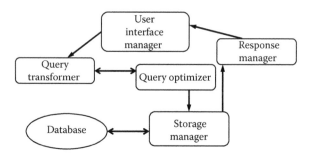

Figure 10.8   Query processor.

come up with appropriate optimization strategies for query processing. This will depend on how the data are stored across the nodes in the cloud. Researchers have also examined column-oriented databases for the cloud and state that this gives better performance. In such a database, the relations are fragmented according to the columns, that is, a table corresponding to each column of a relation. Researchers at Composite Software have taken advantage of data virtualization to develop efficient query algorithms for the cloud. They state that the strategies that data virtualization uses to achieve efficient and optimal query execution include: cost-based query plan evaluation and selection, rule-based query plan modifications, data source capability analysis, join algorithm variety and configuration, selection pooling and propagation, unnecessary operation pruning, pipelined results streaming, parallel scan execution and retrieval, blocking operator pre-processing, and redundant scan multiplexing. Essentially to take advantage of the cloud, parallel query processing has to be fully utilized [COMP].

Kantarcioglu et al. have investigated cloud query processing issues. In their work they have stated that one of the major challenges for cloud query processing is Dynamic Resource Allocation [OKTA12]. Unlike the traditional environments, cloud infrastructures generally allow applications to dynamically increase or decrease the amount of computation resources. This may have an important impact on how query processing and optimization are done. For example, if we have quality of service constraints for answering a query, we may dynamically add new computational resources to process more data. At the same time, we may reduce the used computational resources once we do not need them. Clearly, this dynamic allocation has some cost associated with it. For example, on Amazon EC2, using more machines means one will pay more for those machines. In addition, loading the images of those machines and moving necessary data to those newly initiated machines will take some time. Therefore, such costs should be considered when the query optimization is done. To address these issues, the authors have modified the existing query optimization techniques to include dynamic resource allocation costs under quality service constraints.

10.4.3 Transaction Management

A transaction is a program unit that must be executed in its entirety or not executed at all. If transactions are executed serially, then there is a performance bottleneck. Therefore, transactions are executed concurrently. Appropriate techniques must ensure that the database is consistent when multiple transactions update the database. That is, transactions must satisfy the ACID (Atomicity, Consistency, Isolation, and Durability) properties. The major aspects of transaction management are serializability, concurrency control, and recovery. We discuss them briefly in this section. For a detailed discussion of transaction management we refer to [KORT86] and [BERN87].

Serializability: A schedule is a sequence of operations performed by multiple transactions. Two schedules are equivalent if their outcomes are the same. A serial schedule is a schedule where no two transactions are executed concurrently. An objective in transaction management is to ensure that any schedule is equivalent to a serial schedule. Such a schedule is called a serializable schedule. Various conditions for testing the serializability of a schedule have been formulated for a DBMS.

Concurrency Control: Concurrency control techniques ensure that the database is in a consistent state when multiple transactions update the database. Three popular concurrency control techniques which ensure the serializability of schedules are locking, time-stamping, and validation (which is also called optimistic concurrency control).

Recovery: If a transaction aborts due to some failure, then the database must be brought to a consistent state. This is transaction recovery. One solution to handling transaction failure is to maintain log files. The transaction's actions are recorded in the log file. So, if a transaction aborts, then the database is brought back to a consistent state by undoing the actions of the transaction. The information for the undo operation is found in the log file. Another solution is to record the actions of a transaction but not make any changes to the database. Only if a transaction commits should the database be updated. This means that the log files have to be kept in stable storage. Various modifications to the above techniques have been proposed to handle the different situations.

When transactions are executed at multiple data sources, then a protocol called two-phase commit is used to ensure that the multiple data sources are consistent. Figure 10.9 illustrates the various aspects of transaction management.

Some work has been carried out on transaction processing in the cloud. Most notable is that of Johannes Gehrke. He has stated that a major challenge in cloud data management is scaling and access [GEHR11]. While lock-based implementations were dominant in traditional information access systems such as database systems and search engines, there has been an emergence of cloud-based systems based on Optimistic Concurrency Control (OCC). However, we do not know whether lock-based or OCC-based information access is superior in the cloud; there are no systematic scientific studies that can give cloud system designers a clear indication of the various tradeoffs. Gehrke and his colleagues are investigating a novel cloud

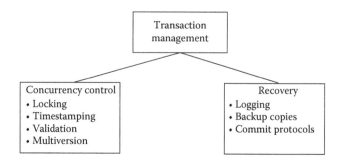

Figure 10.9   Some aspects of transaction management.

architecture based on locking *and* OCC that can scale smoothly as transaction rates increase, whose resource footprint is proportional to the load on the system, and that seamlessly integrates with the cloud query manager and enables different levels of isolation across queries and transactions.

10.4.4 Storage Management

The storage manager is responsible for accessing the database. To improve the efficiency of query and update algorithms, appropriate access methods and index strategies have to be enforced. That is, in generating strategies for executing query and update requests, the access methods and index strategies that are used need to be taken into consideration. The access methods used to access the database would depend on the indexing methods. Therefore, creating and maintaining an appropriate index file is a major issue in DBMS. By using an appropriate indexing mechanism, the query processing algorithms may not have to search the entire database. Instead, the data to be retrieved could be accessed directly. Consequently, the retrieval algorithms are more efficient. Figure 10.10 illustrates an example of an indexing strategy where the database is indexed by projects.

Much research has been carried out on developing appropriate access methods and index strategies for relational database systems. Some examples of index strategies are 10-Trees and Hashing [DATE90]. Current research is focusing on developing such mechanisms for object-oriented database systems with support for multimedia data as well as for web database systems, among others.

The challenge to developers and researchers is coming up with appropriate storage strategies for the cloud. How should the data be fragmented across the different nodes in the cloud? How can data virtualization be exploited to give optimum storage? Kantarcioglu and Mehrotra have developed interesting storage schemes for a hybrid cloud. [OKTA12]. They state that an emerging trend in cloud computing is that of hybrid cloud wherein in-house capabilities/resources at the end-user site are seamlessly integrated with cloud services to create a powerful cost-effective data processing solution. Hybrid cloud solutions offer similar benefits to cloud

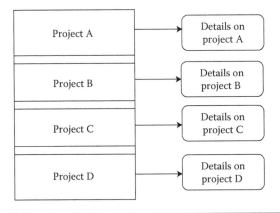

Figure 10.10   An example index on projects.

computing, for example, ability to exploit public resources when high throughput is important on a pay-as-you-use model (instead of the capital expense of creating an infrastructure for peak loads in-house). Yet, they provide opportunities to better control costs (e.g., minimize cloud resources being used if local resources suffice) and to better manage data privacy and confidentiality (e.g., exercise control on what information and processing is exposed to the public cloud). For instance, an end-user can run mission-critical tasks that depend upon sensitive information on the private cloud while outsourcing routine tasks to the public cloud. Kantarcioglu and his colleagues are exploring information management challenges in the context of hybrid clouds and propose novel solutions to address those challenges.

Kantarcioglu and Mehrotra state that information management in hybrid clouds may exploit public resources in several ways. For instance, one could partition the query workload between public and private systems to maximize system throughput by exploiting inter-query parallelism. One may further exploit inherent parallelism afforded by a hybrid cloud even in the context of a given query (intra-query parallelism) even though such a strategy may incur additional network costs. While considering various strategies in hybrid cloud architecture, we also need to consider costs and resource constraints. Cloud service providers typically support competitive cost models and provide different SLAs for data storage and processing for end-users. For example, AWS provides a tiered pricing model where the more data and processing services are used, the cheaper their prices become. AWS also provides SLAs for Elastic Compute Cloud (EC2) or Simple Storage Service (S3) that return to a user between 10% and 25% of their monthly fee if Amazon fails to meet their commitment of at least 99% up time. Similar tiered pricing models and SLAs are also provided by other cloud service providers such as Microsoft Windows Azure and Google App Engine. An information management system that leverages such hybrid cloud architectures opens several key challenges. The first question is, "How to store information in a hybrid cloud?" A good solution must take into account the chosen data representation strategy, the monetary cost associated with storage infrastructure and the query workload characteristics. The second issue is that of efficient query processing in this distributed architecture. They are exploring the issues by developing appropriate storage models for the hybrid cloud.

10.4.5 Metadata Management

Metadata describes the data in the database. For example, in the case of the relational database illustrated in Figure 10.2, metadata would include the following information: the database has two relations, EMP and DEPT; EMP has four attributes and DEPT has three attributes; and so on. One of the main issues is developing a data model for metadata. In our example, one could use a relational model to model the metadata also. The metadata relation REL shown in Figure 10.11 consists of information about relations and attributes.

In addition to information about the data in the database, metadata also includes information on access methods, index strategies, security constraints, and integrity constraints. One could also include policies and procedures as part of the metadata. Once the metadata is defined, the issues include managing the metadata. What are the techniques for querying and updating the metadata? Since all of the other DBMS components need to access the metadata for processing, what are the interfaces between the metadata manager and the other components? Metadata management is fairly well understood for relational database systems. The current challenge is in managing the metadata for more complex systems such as digital libraries and web database systems.

Metadata management in the cloud includes not only information about the data and the resources in the cloud, it also includes information about the user

Relation REL	
Relation	Attribute
EMP	SS#
EMP	Ename
EMP	Salary
EMP	D#
DEPT	D#
DEPT	Dname
DEPT	Mgr

Figure 10.11   Metadata relation.

accounts, usage patterns, SLAs, and other cloud-specific information. Much work is needed on coming with appropriate models to store and manage the cloud metadata.

10.4.6 Database Integrity

Concurrency control and recovery techniques maintain the integrity of the database. In addition, there is another type of database integrity and that is enforcing integrity constraints. There are two types of integrity constraints enforced in database systems: application-independent integrity constraints and application-specific integrity constraints. Integrity mechanisms also include techniques for determining the quality of the data. For example, what is the accuracy of the data and that of the source? What are the mechanisms for maintaining the quality of the data? How accurate is the data on output? For a discussion of integrity based on data quality, we refer to [DQ]. Note that data quality is very important for mining and warehousing. If the data that is mined is not good, then one cannot rely on the results. Application-independent integrity constraints include the primary key constraint, the entity integrity rule, referential integrity constraint, and the various functional dependencies involved in the normalization process (see the discussion in [DATE90]). Application-specific integrity constraints are those constraints that are specific to an application. Examples include "an employee's salary cannot decrease" and "no manager can manage more than two departments." Various techniques have been proposed to enforce application-specific integrity constraints. For example, when the database is updated, these constraints are checked and the data are validated. The aspects of database integrity are illustrated in Figure 10.12.

Some work on database integrity in the cloud has been carried out based on data provenance and lineage. For example, the data in the cloud may come from multiple sources over a time period. Therefore, maintaining the provenance of the data is essential. Other challenges include enforcing appropriate integrity constraints. That is, how can the integrity constraints be enforced on the data in the cloud that has to deal with data virtualization? Much research is needed on data integrity in the cloud.

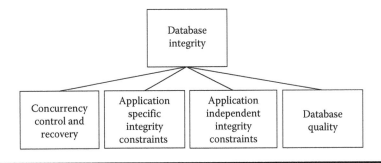

Figure 10.12 Some aspects of database integrity.

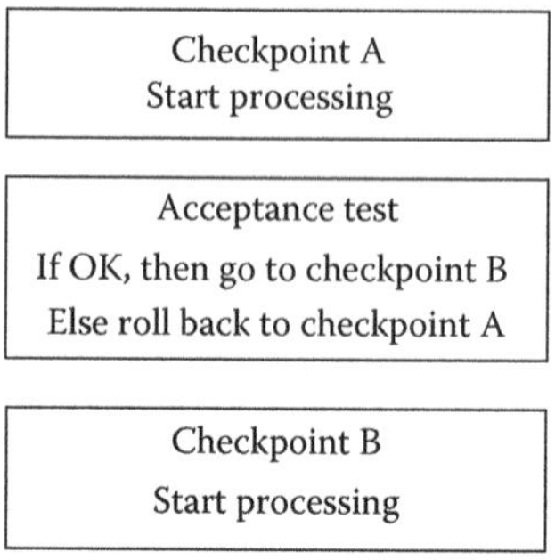

```
┌─────────────────────────────┐
│       Checkpoint A          │
│      Start processing       │
└─────────────────────────────┘

┌─────────────────────────────┐
│      Acceptance test        │
│ If OK, then go to checkpoint B │
│ Else roll back to checkpoint A │
└─────────────────────────────┘

┌─────────────────────────────┐
│       Checkpoint B          │
│      Start processing       │
└─────────────────────────────┘
```

Figure 10.13 Some aspects of fault tolerance.

10.4.7 Fault Tolerance

The previous two sections discussed database integrity and security. A closely related feature is fault tolerance. It is almost impossible to guarantee that the database will function as planned. In reality, various faults could occur. These could be hardware faults or software faults. As mentioned earlier, one of the major issues in transaction management is to ensure that the database is brought back to a consistent state in the presence of faults. The solutions proposed include maintaining appropriate log files to record the actions of a transaction in case its actions have to be retraced.

Another approach to handling faults is checkpointing. Various checkpoints are placed during the course of database processing. At each checkpoint it is ensured that the database is in a consistent state. Therefore, if a fault occurs during processing, then the database must be brought back to the last checkpoint. This way it can be guaranteed that the database is consistent. Closely associated to checkpointing are acceptance tests. After various processing steps, the acceptance tests are checked. If the techniques pass the tests, then they can proceed further. Some aspects of fault tolerance are illustrated in Figure 10.13.

Ensuring that the cloud operates continuously is one of the major challenges to the cloud service providers. The SLAs usually specify how the cloud is operated and how long it will be down for maintenance. Therefore, ensuring that the cloud databases are backed up and developing appropriate solutions for fault tolerance is crucial. This topic will also be discussed further in Part VIII when we address trustworthy clouds.

10.5 Data Mining

Data mining is the process of posing various queries and extracting useful information, patterns, and trends often previously unknown from large quantities of data possibly stored in databases. Essentially, for many organizations, the goals of data mining include improving marketing capabilities, detecting abnormal patterns, and predicting the future based on past experiences and current trends. There is clearly a need for this technology. There are large amounts of current and historical data being stored. Therefore, as databases become larger, it becomes increasingly difficult to support decision making. In addition, the data could be from multiple sources and multiple domains. There is a clear need to analyze the data to support planning and other functions of an enterprise. Various terms have been used to refer to data mining. These include knowledge/data/information discovery and knowledge/data/information extraction. Note that some define data mining to be the process of extracting previously unknown information while knowledge discovery is defined as the process of making sense out of the extracted information.

Some of the data mining techniques include those based on statistical reasoning techniques, inductive logic programming, machine learning, fuzzy sets, and neural networks, among others. The data mining outcomes include classification (finding rules to partition data into groups), association (finding rules to make associations between data), and sequencing (finding rules to order data). Essentially one arrives at some hypothesis, which is the information extracted, from examples and patterns observed. These patterns are observed from posing a series of queries; each query may depend on the responses obtained from the previous queries posed. There have been several developments in data mining. A discussion of the various tools is given in [KDN]. A good discussion of the outcomes and techniques are given in [AGRA93] and [BERR97].

Data mining is an integration of multiple technologies. These include data management such as database management, data warehousing, statistics, machine learning, decision support, and others such as visualization and parallel computing. There are a series of steps involved in data mining. These include getting the data organized for mining, determining the desired outcomes to mining, selecting tools for mining, carrying out the mining, pruning the results so that only the useful ones are considered further, taking actions from the mining, and evaluating the actions to determine benefits.

While several developments have been made, there are also many challenges. For example, due to the large volumes of data, how can the algorithms determine which technique to select and what type of data mining to do? Furthermore, the data may be incomplete and/or inaccurate. At times there may be redundant information, and at times there may not be sufficient information. It is also desirable to have data mining tools that can switch to multiple techniques and support multiple outcomes. Some of the current trends in data mining include mining web data, mining distributed and heterogeneous databases, and privacy-preserving data mining where one ensures that one can get useful results from mining and at the same time maintain the privacy of the individuals. Figure 10.14 illustrates the various aspects of data mining.

Cloud data mining is becoming an important area especially with the emergence of Big Data Analytics. Data mining algorithms have been enhanced with respect to performance with parallel data mining. The challenge is to implement these parallel data mining techniques on the cloud. Note that the difference between parallel/

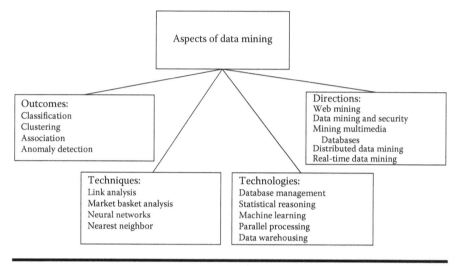

Figure 10.14   Aspects of data mining.

distributed databases and the cloud databases is that with the cloud, the data could be migrated for better resource utilization. Therefore, the data mining algorithms should take into account the location migration of the data.

10.6 Other Aspects

The explosion of the users on the web and the increasing number of WWW servers with large quantities of data are rapidly advancing database management on the web. For example, the heterogeneous information sources have to be integrated so that users access the servers in a transparent and timely manner. The need to augment human reasoning, interpreting, and decision-making abilities has resulted in the emergence of the Semantic Web, which is an initiative that attempts to transform the web from its current, merely human-readable form, to a machine processable form. Semantic web technologies have emerged to manage the massive amounts of data on the web and the cloud. These technologies include XML, RDF, and OWL.

We have developed experimental systems for managing semantic web data in the cloud. We have also developed query optimizers for semantic web data. These query optimizers have been implemented on the cloud. In addition, we are investigating social networks to be managed in the cloud. Our experimental work on query processing in the cloud with semantic web data will be discussed in Part IV. Semantic clouds are clouds that utilize semantic web technologies such as managing massive amounts of semantic web data as well as executing policies represented in semantic web languages. Semantic web services concepts discussed in Chapter 6 may be utilized to provide semantic cloud services to the consumer.

Clouds are also suitable for providing knowledge management services. Increasingly, knowledge is aggregated from online analysis of a variety of sources such as organizational data, large-scale surveillance or survey data, and social data streams. Typically, the datasets analyzed are very large. Additionally, they are typically collected by different groups within an organization, managed by different management and access policies, and maintained in different types for data repository (e.g., relational databases, RDF stores). Furthermore, they are distributed across multiple sites, each supported by its own compute clusters. Owing to the size of the data and the governance policies associated with it, taking the approach of warehousing all the data in a single location is impractical. Furthermore, knowledge management applications for a corporation, such as expert finder, may need to store massive amounts of data and perform extensive computations. Therefore, such operations may be outsourced to a cloud.

Cloud also has an impact on other aspects that we have discussed in Chapter 7 such as activity management. Activity management such as collaboration and workflow as well as e-business may be carried out in the cloud. However since e-business applications may contain sensitive data such as credit card information, security in the cloud is of utmost importance to conduct successful e-business and other applications that need to handle sensitive data. For such applications, the hybrid cloud seems to be a suitable approach where the sensitive data are stored in the private cloud while the nonsensitive data are stored in the public cloud.

Our interest is on addressing distributed querying of data across multiple, diverse processing clusters, specifically in support of large data analytics. We are specifically examining groups of clusters in a closed world, such as within a single organization, as opposed to general distributed query processing on the web. Query processing across clusters containing very large data stores is not supported with any current technology. Currently, there is no common way to summarize or catalog the data in a cluster in a way that can facilitate it being discovered by a distributed query processor. The existence of relatively slow network connections between clusters mandates the use of data-communication-efficient strategies for accessing and combining the data in the various sites efficiently. Finally, while there exists efficient mechanisms for reassembling distributed queries within the context of SQL, the distributed clusters are not necessarily relational databases, so it is necessary to develop different strategies for putting together fragments of data retrieved from nonrelational data sources. The research challenges include query decomposition and optimization as well as response assembly.

10.7 Summary and Directions

This chapter has discussed various aspects of data management systems and examined the impact of the cloud. In particular, aspects of cloud query processing, cloud transaction management, and cloud storage management are discussed. We also discussed information management, knowledge management, and activity management in the cloud. The concepts discussed in Chapter 7 on specialized services for data, information, knowledge, and activity management may be applied for cloud data information, knowledge, and activity management. Furthermore, we also discuss how semantic web services may be provided by semantic clouds.

As stated earlier, many of the applications in areas such as healthcare, finance, and defense need to handle sensitive data. Therefore, incorporating security into the cloud will be critical. In Parts V and VI of this book, we will discuss security for the cloud as well as the experimental secure cloud systems that we have developed. We will also discuss security for cloud data management functions. In the next chapter, we will discuss cloud applications which include cloud services for social networks as well as knowledge management and domain applications. We will also discuss some specialized cloud such as multimedia clouds and mobile clouds. Cloud products will be discussed in Chapter 12.

References

[AGRA93] Agrawal, A. et al., Database mining: a performance perspective. *IEEE Transactions on Knowledge and Data Engineering*, 5(6), 914–925, 1993.

[BERN87] Bernstein, P. et al., *Concurrency Control and Recovery in Database Systems*, Addison-Wesley, MA, 1987.

[BERR97] Berry, M. and G. Linoff, *Data Mining Techniques for Marketing, Sales, and Customer Support*, John Wiley, NY, 1997.

[CERI84] Ceri, S. and G. Pelagatti, *Distributed Databases, Principles and Systems*, McGraw-Hill, NY, 1984.

[CODD70] Codd, E. F., A relational model of data for large shared data banks. *Communications of the ACM*, 13(6), 1970.

[COMP] Composite software for cloud data integration, http://www.compositesw.com/solutions/cloud-data-integration/

[DATE90] Date, C., *An Introduction to Database Systems*, Addison-Wesley, Reading, MA, 1990.

[DQ] *MIT Total Data Quality Management Program*, http://web.mit.edu/tdqm/

[GEHR11] Gehrke, J., Transaction processing in the cloud, White Paper, 2011.

[KDN] Kdnuggets, http://www.kdn.com

[KORT86] Korth, H. and A. Silberschatz, *Database System Concepts*, McGraw-Hill, NY, 1986.

[OKTA12] Oktay, K. Y., V. Khadilkar, B. Hore, M. Kantarcioglu, S. Mehrotra, B. M. Thuraisingham, Risk-aware workload distribution in hybrid clouds. *Proceedings of IEEE Fifth International Conference on Cloud Computing (IEEE CLOUD)*, Honolulu, HI, 2012: 229–236.

[TSIC82] Tsichritzis, D. and F. Lochovsky, *Data Models*, Prentice-Hall, NJ, 198B.

[ULLM88] Ullman, J. D., *Principles of Database and Knowledge Base Management Systems*, Volumes I and II, Computer Science Press, MD, 1988.

Chapter 11

Specialized Clouds, Services, and Applications

11.1 Overview

We previously discussed cloud computing concepts, functions, and products. We also discussed in more detail cloud data management functions. We discussed cloud data management products as well as cloud frameworks. In addition, we provided an overview of cloud service providers. Our discussions on cloud computing concepts included the cloud deployment models as well as the cloud service models. That is, we essentially discussed the general cloud computing concepts. We also included a discussion of some of the general functions such as query processing networking and applications management.

In this chapter, we explore some of the specialized services and applications of the cloud. For example, in recent years, the use of mobile devices such as mobile phones, laptops, and more recently, the smartphone have exploded. These devices initially focused on some simple applications such as sending and receiving emails as well as making phone calls. Today these devices are being used for highly sophisticated applications such as photo sharing, video messaging, and performing process-intensive computations. There is an urgent need for these smartphone applications to access cloud for both storage and processing. The data may be streaming video data. Therefore, some specialized clouds are emerging. These include the mobile cloud and the multimedia cloud. In addition, the cloud is being used for a variety of applications in a number of fields.

In this chapter, we will provide an overview of some of the specialized clouds. In Section 11.2, we will discuss both the mobile cloud and the multimedia cloud.

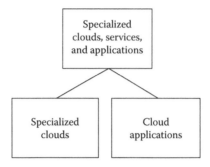

Figure 11.1   Concepts of this chapter.

In Section 11.3, we will discuss cloud applications such as healthcare, defense, and intelligence, finance, and social networking. Section 11.4 concludes this chapter. It should be noted that some of the specialized services we discussed in Chapter 7 may be utilized to provide cloud application services. These include knowledge management, social networks, and domain application services. Figure 11.1 illustrates the concepts discussed in this chapter.

11.2 Specialized Clouds

In this section we will discuss specialized clouds as illustrated in Figure 11.2.

11.2.1 Mobile Clouds

As stated in [MCC], mobile cloud computing is the usage of cloud computing in combination with mobile devices. Mobile devices such as the iPhone and Android

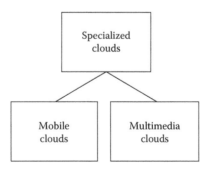

Figure 11.2   Specialized clouds.

have web-browsing capabilities. As a result, mobile cloud computing gives opportunities for mobile network providers such as Vodafone, Orange, and Verizon. For example, Verizon has made major acquisitions (e.g., Terremark and CloudSwitch) to enhance their mobile computing offerings.

Mobile cloud computing also enables the users of smartphones to store their data in a cloud. For example, one of the pioneering developments with respect to mobile computing is the Android OS. As stated in [ANDROID], Android is a Linux-based OS for mobile devices such as smartphones and tablet computers. It is developed by the Open Handset Alliance, led by Google, and other companies. Other notable smartphone devices include Apple's iPhone and iPad. Amazon Web Services (AWS) is making it possible for developers to directly integrate mobile applications for Apple's iPhone, iPad, and iPod Touch, and also apps for Android-based smartphones, with its cloud. As stated in [AWS], Amazon's aim is to make it easier for developers to build mobile applications that take advantage of its cloud-based services. Essentially with this capability, developers can integrate their applications with Amazon's cloud-based Simple Storage Service (S3), the SimpleDB database and send messages using Simple Notification Service (SNS) and Simple Queue Service (SQS).

Other cloud OSs include Alibaba, which a China-based company has released for its smartphones called Aliyun. Alibaba stated that Aliyun is the first cloud OS for smartphone. However, in an article by IBM developers [IBM], it is stated that the Android OS is ideal for cloud computing with its Linux-based architecture. They state that cloud computing, where portable devices complement powerful servers, requires an OS that maximizes what the server architects and programmers can do on a small client machine. Android is such an OS.

Smart phones, mobile OSs and especially mobile clouds are in their infancy. It will take some time for the industry to mature and we will see winners emerge in this market. Nevertheless, mobile cloud is expected to be one of the major developments in cloud computing in the near future with billions of users with smartphones (note that just in the fourth quarter of 2011, there were close to 160 million in worldwide sales).

11.2.2 Multimedia Clouds

Another type of specialized cloud that is emerging is the multimedia cloud. In a keynote lecture, Dr. Wenwu Zhu at Microsoft Research Asia introduced several options in multimedia cloud, including Multimedia-aware Cloud (Media Cloud) and Cloud-aware Multimedia (Cloud Media) [ZHU11]. He states that the Media Cloud addresses how cloud can perform distributed multimedia processing and storage as well as provide Quality of Service (QoS) provisioning for multimedia services while Cloud Media addresses how multimedia services and applications can optimally utilize cloud computing resources to achieve better Quality of Experience (QoE). The example applications he considers are eHealth Monitoring, Photosynth, and Free Viewpoint Video.

Researchers in Denmark have developed a system called i5cloud that they consider to be a mobile multimedia cloud. They state that the goal of their mobile multimedia cloud (i5Cloud) is to provide IaaS and PaaS for diverse services and applications in the domain of (mobile) multimedia and large-scale social network analysis. Their IaaS provides virtualization and utilizes Sun Solaris Container. The PaaS contains the streaming manager. Between the applications services layer and the platform later, they have the multimedia services layer that includes collaborative multimedia services and video services.

Essentially a multimedia cloud not only provides storage capabilities for massive amounts of multimedia data, including video, audio, animation, maps, photos, and text, it can also provide real-time streaming of multimedia data to the users of the data. The users could be desktop users or users of mobile devices. Therefore, the challenge is to integrate cloud computing services with mobile computing services and multimedia computing services. Just like a decade ago, the goal was to integrate the web with the mobile web and the multimedia web, while the challenge today is to develop a mobile multimedia cloud.

11.3 Cloud Applications

Cloud can be utilized for any application including defense and intelligence, healthcare and finance, accounting, and many more. They can also be utilized for IT applications, including cyber security, knowledge management, social computing, and other data and process-intensive applications. We will discuss each of the applications. Figure 11.3 illustrates the applications.

Defense and Intelligence: Massive amounts of data are being collected about various combat operations, as well as surveillance and reconnaissance operations. These data have to be processed rapidly so that appropriate decisions are made on time. Cloud computing can be used not only to store the massive amounts of data, but also to process the data (such as mine the data) so that the results can be sent to the decision makers. The major challenge is the security of the operation. Much of the data may be highly classified. Furthermore, the processing cannot be tampered with. Therefore, such data has to be managed and processed by a private cloud.

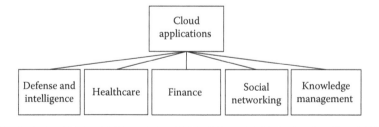

Figure 11.3   Cloud applications.

Healthcare: Massive amounts of data including patient data and administrative data are collected for storage and processing. The patient data may be analyzed to determine the conditions of the patients so that the physicians can then determine the appropriate medications to administer. Privacy is of utmost important for patient data. In addition, security of operation is also critical. Here again one needs a private cloud to store and process the data.

Finance: Banks could outsource the financial processing of their data. For example, customer account management and straight through processing applications may be outsourced to a cloud. However, the customer data have to be encrypted which means it cannot be stored on a public cloud. Also critical banking operations cannot be outsourced to a public cloud as any error could be catastrophic to the bank.

Social networking: Here, an organization such as Facebook can host its massive social network on a cloud. Owing to the fact that the information that is entered by an individual is in general not considered to be private, such social networks could utilize a public cloud. However, there are privacy concerns. This is because Facebook has the notion of friends where one may only want to share information with friends. This means that one could hack into a public cloud and extract information about Facebook users. This is a topic that is being debated quite a bit these days.

Knowledge Management: A corporation can outsource its knowledge management operations to a cloud service provider. That is, all the relevant information that is needed to enhance the organization's business strategy is stored in a cloud. The information is analyzed using techniques such as data mining so that the senior management is notified of any changes that is needed to be made. Here again, confidentiality is an issue. An organization will not want its secrets and intellectual property to be made public. Therefore, the organization may employ a private cloud for its use.

In summary, many of the applications that utilize the cloud need to be secure, ensure the privacy of the individuals and in many cases ensure the confidentiality of the data. Therefore, private cloud seems to be most appropriate for many such applications. However, private clouds are expensive to host and implement. One would like to take advantage of the public cloud as much as possible. Therefore, to use a public cloud, security is critical. Another option is to use a hybrid cloud. That is, use the public cloud for nonsensitive applications and a private cloud for sensitive applications.

11.4 Summary and Directions

In this chapter, we have discussed two main topics: specialized cloud and cloud applications. In particular, we discussed mobile cloud and specialized clouds as well as applications such as defense, finance, social networks, and knowledge management. We essentially examined some of the specialized web services discussed in

Chapter 7 and applied them to provide cloud application service. Our experimental cloud systems as well as applications will be discussed in Parts IV, VI, and VII. These include cloud-based malware detection, cloud-based insider threat detection, and cloud-based social networking. We will also discuss secure query processing in the cloud.

Note that Chapters 10 and 11 have discussed the data management and application layers of the framework were discussed in Chapter 9. We briefly discussed the other layers of the framework such as virtualization, storage, and the network layers. In Chapter 12, we discuss the various cloud products that are being offered. Security issues for the topics discussed in Part III will be provided in Part V.

References

[ANDROID] Android operating system, http://google.about.com/od/socialtoolsfromgoogle/p/android_what_is.htm
[AWS] i-Phone application hosting, http://aws.amazon.com/iphone-application-hosting/
[IBM] IBM developerWorks http://www.ibm.com/developerworks/topics/android/
[MCC] Mobile Cloud Computing, http://en.wikipedia.org/wiki/Mobile_cloud_computing
[ZHU11] Zhu, W., C. Luo, J. Wang, and S. Li, Multimedia cloud computing, *IEEE Signal Processing Magazine*, 28(3), 59–69, May 2011.

Chapter 12

Cloud Service Providers, Products, and Frameworks

12.1 Overview

Numerous cloud service providers have emerged since around 2007. Notable among them are Amazon web services, Google's app engine, Microsoft's azure, proofpoint, rightscale, salesforce.com, sun's open cloud platform, and workday [AWS], [GOOG], [WIND]. In addition, numerous cloud products have emerged not only from service providers such as Amazon, Google, and Microsoft, but also from vendors such as oracle, VMWARE and IBM [IBM] [ORAC1], [ORAC2], [VM]. Cloud frameworks have also emerged. These include storm, Hadoop/Mapreduce, and HIVE [HIVE], [HADOOP], [STORM]. Research prototypes such as XEN hypervisor are also being commercialized [BARH03].

Grouping the products is a difficult task as service providers also market products. For example, Amazon's Elastic Computer Cloud (EC2) works in conjunction with Amazon Simple Storage Service (Amazon S3), Amazon Relational Database Service (Amazon RDS), Amazon SimpleDB, and Amazon Simple Queue Service (Amazon SQS) to provide solutions for computing, query processing, and storage across a wide range of applications. Therefore, we have combined the offerings by service providers such as Amazon, Microsoft, and Google, products such as Oracle Enterprise Edition, IBM SmartCloud, VMware, and XEN as well as frameworks such as Hadoop, MapReduce, Storm, and Hive and discussed them as products.

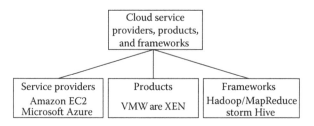

Figure 12.1 **Cloud service providers, products, and frameworks.**

It should be noted that we have only selected the service providers, products, and frameworks that we are most familiar with and those that we have examined in our work. Describing all of the service providers, products, and frameworks is beyond the scope of this book.

The organization of this chapter is as follows. In Section 12.2, we will describe the various cloud service providers: Amazon, Microsoft, and Google, producers such as those by Oracle, IBM, VMware, and Citrix (i.e., XEN) as well as frameworks such as Hadoop, MapReduce, Storm, and Hive. This chapter is summarized in Section 12.3. Figure 12.1 illustrates the concepts discussed in this chapter.

12.2 Cloud Service Providers, Products, and Frameworks

12.2.1 Cloud Service Providers

This section discusses the cloud service providers as illustrated in Figure 12.2.

Amazon Elastic Compute Cloud (Amazon EC2) as stated in [AWS], Amazon Elastic Compute Cloud (Amazon EC2) is a web service that provides resizable compute capacity in the cloud. Its web service interface allows one to obtain

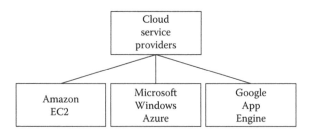

Figure 12.2 **Cloud service providers.**

and configure capacity. It provides the user with complete control of his/her computing resources. It also enables one to pay only for capacity used. Finally, it provides developers the tools to build failure-resilient applications. Amazon EC2 presents a virtual computing environment and allows the user to access web service interfaces to launch instances with a variety of OSs, load them with custom application environment, and manage the network's access permissions, and run images.

The services provided by this cloud are the following:

Elasticity: Amazon EC2 enables one to increase or decrease capacity within minutes.

Control: The user has control of his/her instances.

Flexibility: The user has the choice of multiple instance types, OSs, and software packages.

Integration with Amazon Web Services (AWS): Amazon EC2 works in conjunction with Amazon Simple Storage Service (Amazon S3), Amazon Relational Database Service (Amazon RDS), Amazon SimpleDB, and Amazon Simple Queue Service (Amazon SQS) to provide solutions for computing, query processing, and storage across a wide range of applications.

Reliability: Amazon EC2 offers a highly reliable environment where replacement instances can be commissioned.

Security: Amazon EC2 has mechanisms for securing the user's computer resources.

The features of Amazon EC2 include the following:

■ *Amazon Elastic Block Store:* Amazon Elastic Block Store (EBS) offers persistent storage for Amazon EC2 instances. Amazon EBS provides off-instance storage that persists independently from the life of an instance.

■ *Multiple Locations:* Amazon EC2 provides the ability to place instances in multiple locations. Amazon EC2 locations are composed of Regions and Availability Zones.

■ *Elastic IP Addresses:* Elastic IP addresses are static IP addresses designed for dynamic cloud computing. An Elastic IP address is associated with an account, not a particular instance, and the account owner controls that address until it is explicitly released.

■ *Amazon Virtual Private Cloud:* Amazon VPC is a secure and seamless bridge between a company's existing IT infrastructure and the AWS cloud. Amazon VPC enables enterprises to connect their existing infrastructure to a set of isolated AWS compute resources via a Virtual Private Network (VPN) connection, and to extend their existing management capabilities such as security services, firewalls, and intrusion detection systems to include their AWS resources.

■ *Amazon Cloud Watch:* Amazon CloudWatch is a web service that provides monitoring for AWS cloud resources and applications. It provides a user with visibility into resource utilization, operational performance, and overall demand patterns.

■ *Auto Scaling:* Auto Scaling allows a user to automatically scale his/her Amazon EC2 capacity up or down according to conditions defined.

■ *Elastic Load Balancing:* Elastic Load Balancing automatically distributes incoming application traffic across multiple Amazon EC2 instances. It enables fault-tolerance in the applications.

■ *High-Performance Computing (HPC) Clusters:* Customers with complex computational workloads such as tightly coupled parallel processes can achieve the same high compute and network performance provided by custom-built infrastructure.

■ *VM Import/Export:* VM Import/Export enables one to easily import VM images from the existing environment to Amazon EC2 instances and export them back at any time.

■ *AWS Marketplace:* AWS Marketplace is an online store that helps a customer to find, buy, and quickly deploy software that runs on AWS.

12.2.1.1 Windows Azure

As stated in [WIND], Windows Azure is an open and flexible cloud platform that enables a customer to quickly build, deploy, and manage applications across a global network of Microsoft-managed datacenters. One can build applications using any language, tool, or framework and can integrate public cloud applications with an existing IT environment. It is stated in [WIND] that Windows Azure delivers a 99.95% monthly SLA and enables one to build and run highly available applications without focusing on the infrastructure. It provides automatic OS and service patching, built-in network load balancing and resiliency to hardware failure. It supports a deployment model that enables one to upgrade an application without downtime.

Windows Azure enables one to use any language, framework, or tool to build applications. Features and services are exposed using open REST protocols. The Windows Azure client libraries are available for multiple programming languages, and are released under an open source license. It is also stated in [WIND] that Windows Azure enables one to easily scale the applications to any size. It is an automated self-service platform that allows the customer to provision resources within minutes. Customers can grow or shrink resource usage and pay for only the resources utilized.

With Windows Azure, data can be stored using relational SQL databases, NoSQL table stores, and unstructured blob stores, and can also optionally use Hadoop and business intelligence services for data mining. Windows Azure's distributed caching allows a customer to reduce latency. Furthermore, each compute instance is a VM that isolates a customer from other customers. Once compute resources are assigned to customer application, Windows Azure automatically handles network load balancing and failover to provide continuous availability.

The components of Windows Azure include SQL Azure and Windows Azure Storage. As stated in [WIND], SQL Azure is a highly available and scalable cloud database service built on SQL Server technologies. With SQL Azure, developers do not have to install, setup, or manage any database. High availability and fault-tolerance is built-in and no physical administration is required. SQL Azure is a managed service that is operated by Microsoft and has a 99.9% monthly SLA. SQL Azure provides a full featured relational database and enables different types of applications including business applications and business intelligence. As stated in [WIND], Windows Azure Storage provides secure, scalable and easily accessible storage services that remain highly available and durable. The Storage service supports multiple storage formats such as structured and unstructured data, NoSQL databases, and queues. Storage is a managed service and has a 99.9% monthly SLA. Other components of Azure include those for networking, business intelligence, content delivery, and security. More details can be found in [MATH09].

12.2.1.2 Google App Engine

As stated in [GOOG], the Google App Engine enables the customer to use web applications on Google's infrastructure. App Engine applications are easy to build, easy to maintain, and easy to scale as traffic and data storage needs grow. With App Engine, there are no servers to maintain; one uploads his/her application and it runs on the cloud. Google App Engine supports apps written in several programming languages. With App Engine's Java runtime environment, one can build apps using standard Java technologies, including the JVM, Java servlets, and the Java programming language. App Engine also features two dedicated Python runtime environments. With App Engine, a customer pays only for the usage.

As stated in [GOOG], App Engine includes the following features:

■ Dynamic web serving, with full support for common web technologies
■ Persistent storage with queries, sorting, and transactions
■ Automatic scaling and load balancing
■ APIs for authenticating users and sending email using Google Accounts
■ A fully featured local development environment that simulates Google App Engine on your computer
■ Task queues for performing work outside of the scope of a web request
■ Scheduled tasks for triggering events at specified times and regular intervals

The App Engine environment provides a range of options for data storage including the following:

■ App Engine Datastore provides a NoSQL schemaless object datastore, with a query engine and atomic transactions.

■ GoogleCloudSQL provides a relational SQL database service for an App Engine application, based on MySQL.
■ GoogleCloudStorage provides a storage service for objects and files up to terabytes in size, accessible from Python and Java applications.

More details of the Apps Engine can be found in [MATH09].

12.2.2 Cloud Products

This section discusses cloud products as illustrated in Figure 12.3.

12.2.2.1 Oracle Enterprise Manager

It is stated in [ORAC1] that Oracle Enterprise Manager is Oracle's integrated enterprise IT management product line, and provides a cloud lifecycle management solution. It enables a customer to set up, manage, and support enterprise clouds. It is also stated in [ORAC1] that Oracle Enterprise Manager is Oracle's premiere cloud management solution. It provides self-service provisioning balanced against centralized, policy-based resource management, integrated chargeback and capacity planning and visibility of the physical and virtual environment from applications to disk. Essentially, the Enterprise Manager provides Database as a Service Cloud for users in an enterprise.

As stated in [ORAC2], Oracle Cloud Management Pack for Oracle Database delivers capabilities spanning the entire Database cloud lifecycle. It lets cloud administrators identify pooled resources, configure role-based access, define the service catalog, and the related chargeback plans. It allows cloud users to request database services, and consume them on-demand. It also allows users to scale up and down their platforms to adapt to changes in workload. Finally, it lets both parties understand the costs of the service delivered, and establishes accountability for consumption of resources.

It is stated in [ORAC1], that Enterprise Manager has associated with it an out-of-box self-service portal that allows developers, testers, DBAs, and other self-service

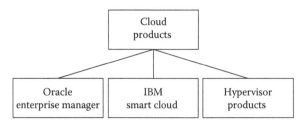

Figure 12.3 Cloud products.

users to log on and request new Single Instance (SI) and Real Application Clusters (RAC) databases, as well as perform lifecycle operations such as start/stop, status, and health monitoring on them. One can also deploy Virtual Assemblies containing databases on an Oracle VM virtualized server infrastructure. The portal provides access to a service catalog which lists various published service templates for standardized database configuration and versions. The users can review their past and outstanding requests, resource quotas, current utilization as well as chargeback information for the databases they own. The portal also allows users to automatically backup their databases on a daily basis or take on-demand backups. Users can restore the database to any of these backups. The self-service portal is the user's view into the cloud.

Oracle has also released a number of cloud products that complement the enterprise manager including the Oracle File Systems. In addition, Oracle has announced that it will release a suite of cloud-based products including customer relationship management for the cloud.

12.2.2.2 IBM Smart Cloud

As stated in [IBM], SmartCloud is the IBM vision for cloud computing. IBM SmartCloud Foundation infrastructure offerings include servers, storage, and virtualization components for building your private and hybrid cloud computing environment. It provides infrastructure-as-a-service solution that allows quick cloud deployment. It also provides automated provisioning, parallel scalability, integrated fault-tolerance, and a foundation for more advanced cloud capabilities.

IBM SmartCloud Provisioning provides:

- A low-cost, easy-to-use private cloud solution that can be deployed within hours.
- Reliable, nonstop operation capable of automatically tolerating and recovering from software and hardware failures.
- Rapid scalability to meet business growth with near-instant deployment of hundreds of VMs.
- Low-touch infrastructure that helps reduce errors, enhance security and compliance, and increase administrator productivity.

IBM SmartCloud Monitoring monitors the health and performance of a private cloud infrastructure, including environments containing both physical and virtualized components. This solution provides the tools needed to assess current capacity and model expansion, as needed.

Associated with SmartCloud are a suite of tools for integration among multiple clouds, data management, and security. For example, IBM's DB2.9 is a database server for managing relational and XML data and is suited for cloud deployments.

12.2.2.3 Hypervisor Products

Several hypervisor products have been released since the late 1990s. One of the early hypervisors was the product by VMware. It started off as a Stanford University Research project that was then commercialized. Essentially, VMware developed one of the early virtualization software for the cloud. As stated in [VM], VMware software provides a completely virtualized set of hardware to the guest OS. VMware software virtualizes the hardware for a video adapter, a network adapter, and hard disk adapters. The host provides pass-through drivers for guest USB, serial, and parallel devices. Thus, VMware VMs are portable between computers because every host looks nearly identical to the guest. VMware provides desktop virtualization, server virtualization, cloud virtualization, and applications. Its desktop product suite includes VMwareWorkstation and VMwareFusion. Its server products include VMwareESX and VMotion. Its cloud products include VMwarevCloud. Its application products include VMware vFabric tc Server.

Another notable hypervisor product is XEN. Like VMware, it started as a research project at the University of Cambridge, England and is marketed through Citrix. XEN Hypervisor runs just on top of the hardware and traps all calls by VMs to access the hardware. Domain 0 (Dom0) is a modified version of Linux that is used to manage the other VMs. Domain U (DomU) is the user domain in XEN. DomU is where all of the untrusted guest OSs reside. DomU is broken into two parts: Para-virtualized Domains (PV) and Hardware Assisted Virtualized Machine (HVM) Domains. A Para-virtualized domain is a modified OS which is aware that it is a VM and can achieve near-native performance. HVM Domain is a VM that runs OSs that have not been modified to work with Dom0. PVs are given read-only access to memory and any updates are controlled by the hypervisor. HVMs are given a shadow page table because they do not know how to work with noncontiguous physical address spaces. I/O (input/output) management is controlled by Dom0. PVs share memory with Dom0 through which they can pass messages.

There are several white papers and articles on both VMware and XEN. Details can be found in [MATH09]. We will discuss security details of these hypervisors in Chapter 17.

12.2.3 Cloud Frameworks

This section discusses the cloud service providers as illustrated in Figure 12.4. We have utilized these frameworks in our experimental work. Our experimental systems will be discussed in Part IV.

12.2.3.1 Hadoop, MapReduce Framework

As stated in [AWS], Apache Hadoop is a software framework that supports data-intensive distributed applications under a free license. It enables applications to

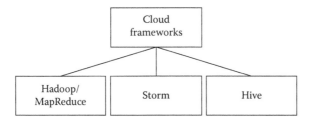

Figure 12.4   Cloud frameworks.

work on numerous machines and generates massive amounts of data. Hadoop was derived from Google's MapReduce and GoogleFileSystem (GFS) papers. Hadoop is written in Java.

Hadoop consists of the Hadoop Common, which provides access to the file systems supported by Hadoop. For effective scheduling of work, every Hadoop-compatible file system should provide location awareness: the name of the rack where a worker node is. Hadoop applications can use this information to run work on the node where the data is, and, failing that, on the same rack/switch, so reducing backbone traffic. HDFS uses this when replicating data, to try to keep different copies of the data on different racks. The goal is to reduce the impact of a rack power outage or switch failure so that even if these events occur, the data may still be readable.

A small Hadoop cluster will include a single master and multiple worker nodes. The master node consists of a JobTracker, TaskTracker, NameNode, and DataNode. A slave or *worker node* acts as both a DataNode and TaskTracker, though it is possible to have data-only worker nodes, and compute-only worker nodes; these are normally only used in nonstandard applications. In a larger cluster, the HDFS is managed through a dedicated NameNode server to host the file system index, and a secondary NameNode that can generate snapshots of the namenode's memory structures. This prevents file system corruption and reduces loss of data.

HDFS is a distributed, scalable, and portable file system written in Java for the Hadoop framework. Each node in a Hadoop instance typically has a single datanode; a cluster of datanodes form the HDFS cluster. Above the file systems comes the MapReduce engine, which consists of one JobTracker, to which client applications submit MapReduce jobs. The JobTracker pushes work out to available TaskTracker nodes in the cluster, striving to keep the work as close to the data as possible. With a rack-aware file system, the JobTracker knows which node contains the data, and which other machines are nearby. If the work cannot be hosted on the actual node where the data reside, priority is given to nodes in the same rack. This reduces network traffic on the main backbone network. If a TaskTracker fails or times out, that part of the job is rescheduled.

We have used the Hadoop/MapReduce framework in all of our cloud implementations to be discussed in later chapters. That is, many of our prototypes including cloud data managers and social networks are hosted on the Hadoop/ MapReduce framework.

12.2.3.2 Storm

Storm is an open source distributed real-time computation system. Storm is similar to Hadoop in the sense that it provides users with a general framework for performing computations in real time, much like Hadoop provides users with a general framework for performing batch processing operations. Storm provides the following key properties: (i) Support for a broad range of use cases such as stream processing and continuous computation; (ii) Storm is scalable and has the ability to process massive numbers of messages per second; (iii) Storm guarantees that every message will be processed and thereby ensures that there is no data loss; (iv) Storm clusters are easily manageable and extremely robust; (v) Storm ensures fault-tolerance by automatically reassigning tasks that fail during execution; and (vi) Storm's components are programming language agnostic and therefore can be utilized by nearly anyone.

A Storm cluster is made up of two kinds of nodes: the master node and the worker nodes. The master node runs a daemon called "Nimbus" that is responsible for distributing code around the cluster, assigning tasks to machines and monitoring for failures. Every worker node runs a daemon called "Supervisor" that listens to the work assigned to it by Nimbus and starts/stops worker processes to accomplish this work. The coordination between Nimbus and Supervisors is done through a Zookeeper cluster.

Storm uses the concept of a "topology" to perform real-time computation. A Storm topology is analogous to a MapReduce job, however, a key difference is that a MapReduce job eventually finishes while a topology runs forever or until it is killed. A topology is a directed graph of spouts and bolts that are connected together with stream groupings. Note that the stream is the core abstraction in Storm and represents an unbounded sequence of tuples that is created and processed in a parallel fashion using a distributed cluster. A spout acts as a source of streams for a topology and usually reads tuples from an external source and emits them into the topology. A bolt is used to perform the desired processing within a topology such as initiating connections with a database, performing operations such as filtering, aggregations, and joins. A stream grouping defines how a stream that is being input to a particular bolt is partitioned between that bolt's tasks. Finally, Storm guarantees that every spout tuple will be fully processed by the topology and also provides several configurations for customizing the behavior of the nimbus, supervisors, and running topologies.

12.2.3.3 HIVE

Hive is an open source system by Apache. As stated in [HIVE], Hive is a data warehouse system for Hadoop that facilitates easy data summarization, ad-hoc queries, and the analysis of large datasets stored in Hadoop compatible file systems. Hive provides a mechanism to project structure onto this data and query the data using a SQL-like language called HiveQL. At the same time, this language also allows traditional map/reduce programmers to plug in their custom mappers and reducers when it is inconvenient or inefficient to express this logic in HiveQL. That is, Hive supports data queries in an SQL-like language that are converted into map/reduced tasks, which are then executed by the Hadoop framework. Using HDFS as data storage, Hive inherits all of Hadoop's fault tolerance and scalability, and the ability to handle huge data sets.

As stated in [HIVE], the major difference between a Hive query language and an SQL query is that a Hive query executes on a Hadoop cluster (instead of a platform that uses expensive hardware for large data sets). This allows Hive to scale to handle massive data sets. The internal execution of the Hive query is via a series of automatically generated MapReduce jobs.

Hive is the foundation through which Hive queries are executed. It consists of three major components: (i) Hadoop Cluster, (ii) Metadata Store, and (iii) Warehouse Director. The Hadoop cluster is the cluster of inexpensive commodity computers on which the large data set is stored and all processing is performed. The Metadata Store is the location in which the description of the structure of the large datasets is kept. The Warehouse Directory is the storage location that Hive uses to store/cache working files.

One of the notable implementations of Hive is that from the developers at Facebook. In an article [THUS09], Facebook developers have described the Hive as, an open-source data warehousing solution built on top of Hadoop. They state that in Facebook, the Hive warehouse contains tens of thousands of tables and stores over 700 terabytes of data and is being used extensively for both reporting and ad-hoc analyses by more than 200 users per month. We have utilized Hive extensively in our implementations of cloud query processing. We will discuss our implementation in Chapter 22.

12.3 Summary and Directions

In this chapter we have discussed various cloud service providers, products, and frameworks. These include service providers such as Amazon, Microsoft and Google, products such as Oracle, IBM, VMware, and XEN and frameworks such as Hadoop, MapReduce, Storm, and Hive. Note that we have selected these service providers, products, and frameworks as we are familiar with them and have utilized them in our work. There are many more good service providers, products, and frameworks for clouds, but discussing all of them are beyond the scope of this book. An overview is also given in [MATH09].

Part III has essentially provided information on some of the key concepts in cloud computing, including deployment and service models, functions, and applications. Some details of how we have used the various products, frameworks, and services will be discussed in Part IV. Security issues for the cloud as well as our experimental secure cloud computing systems will be the subject of Parts V, VI, VII, VIII, and IX. In particular, we will discuss security for the various cloud services, products, and frameworks.

References

[AWS] Amazon Web Services: http://www.aws.amazon.com/ec2/

[BARH03] Barham, P., B. Dragovic, K. Fraser, S. Hand, T. L. Harris, A. Ho, R. Neugebauer, I. Pratt and A. Warfield, Xen and the art of virtualization. *Proceedings of the 19th ACM Symposium on Operating Systems Principles 2003 (SOSP 2003)*, Bolton Landing, NY, 164–177.

[GOOG] Google Apps Engine, http://www.oracle.com/technetwork/oem/pdf/512029.pdf

[HADOOP] Hadoop, http://hadoop.apache.org/

[HIVE] The HIVE system, http://hive.apache.org/

[IBM] IBM cloud computing, http://www.ibm.com/cloud-computing/us/en/

[MATH09] Mather, T., S. Kumaraswamy, S. Latif, *Cloud Security and Privacy*, O'Reilly, Sebastopol, CA, 2009.

[ORAC1] Oracle enterprise manager, http://www.oracle.com/us/products/enterprise-manager/index.html

[ORAC2] Oracle cloud management pack for Oracle database, http://www.oracle.com/technetwork/oem/pdf/512029.pdf

[STORM] Twitter storm: Open source real-time Hadoop, http://www.infoq.com/news/2011/09/twitter-storm-real-time-hadoop

[THUS09] Thushoo, A., Hive—A petabyte scale data warehouse using Hadoop, http://www.facebook.com/note.php?note—-id=89508453919

[VM] VMware virtualization overview, http: //www. vmware.com/pdf/virtualization.pdf

[WIND] Windows Azure, http://www.windowsazure.com/en-us/develop/overview/

Conclusion to Part III

While Part II discussed web services which are at the heart of cloud computing, in Part III we provided an overview of cloud computing concepts, technologies, and products. We also showed how the concepts in Part II on web services, semantic web services, and specialized web services may be utilized to provide cloud services to the consumer.

Chapter 8 introduced the notion of the cloud and discussed aspects of virtualization. In particular, aspects of hardware virtualization, operating system virtualization, network virtualization, and data virtualization were discussed. We also discussed the various service models and deployment models for the cloud.

Chapter 9 discussed various aspects of cloud computing functions. First, we presented a framework for cloud computing. This framework consists of a network layer, a virtualization layer, a storage layer, a data management layer, and an applications layer. We discussed the functions of each layer. We also discussed policy management, back-up, and recovery issues for the cloud.

Chapter 10 discussed various aspects of data management systems and examined the impact of the cloud. In particular, aspects of cloud query processing, cloud transaction management, and cloud storage management were discussed. We also discussed information management, knowledge management, and activity management in the cloud.

Chapter 11 discussed two main topics: specialized cloud and cloud applications, In particular, we discussed mobile cloud and specialized clouds as well as cloud applications such as defense, finance, social networks, and knowledge management.

Chapter 12 discussed various cloud service providers, products, and frameworks. These include service providers such as Amazon, Microsoft, and Google, products such as Oracle, IBM, VMware, and XEN, and frameworks such as Hadoop, MapReduce, Storm, and Hive.

EXPERIMENTAL CLOUD COMPUTING SYSTEMS

IV

Introduction to Part IV

Now that we have provided an overview of cloud computing, we will describe some experimental cloud computing systems that we have developed. This will give the reader a better understanding of how we have utilized technologies such as Hadoop, MapReduce, and Storm that we discussed in Part III in developing our prototypes.

Part IV consists of three chapters: 13, 14, and 15. Chapter 13 discusses our prototype system on semantic web-based cloud query processing. Chapter 12 discusses our work on hosting social networks on the cloud. Chapter 15 discusses multiple prototypes that we have developed, including cloud computing for social networks, cloud computing for semantic web data storage, and cloud computing for ontology-based query processing.

Chapter 13

Experimental Cloud Query Processing System

13.1 Overview

As mentioned previously, cloud computing is an emerging paradigm in the IT and data processing communities. Enterprises utilize cloud computing services to outsource data maintenance, which can result in significant financial benefits. Businesses store and access data at remote locations in the cloud. As the popularity of cloud computing grows, the service providers face ever-increasing challenges. They have to maintain large quantities of heterogeneous data while providing efficient information retrieval. Thus, the key emphasis for cloud computing solutions is scalability and query efficiency. Semantic web technologies are being developed to present data in a standardized way such that such data can be retrieved and understood by both humans and machines. Historically, web pages were published in plain HTML (Hypertext Markup Language) files, which are not suitable for reasoning. Instead, the machine treats these HTML files as a bag of keywords. Researchers are developing semantic web technologies that have been standardized to address such inadequacies. The most prominent standards are the RDF [W3b], SPARQL (SPARQL Protocol and RDF Query Language) Protocol, and RDF Query Language [W3c] (SPARQL). RDF is the standard for storing and representing data and SPARQL is a query language to retrieve data from an RDF store. Cloud computing systems can utilize the power of these semantic web technologies to provide the user with the capability to efficiently store and retrieve data for data-intensive applications.

Semantic web technologies could be especially useful for maintaining data in the cloud. These technologies provide the ability to specify and query heterogeneous data in a standardized manner. Moreover, via the Web Ontology Language

(OWL) ontologies, different schemas, classes, data types, and relationships can be specified without sacrificing the standard RDF/SPARQL interface. Conversely, cloud computing solutions could be of great benefit to the semantic web community. Semantic web data sets are growing exponentially. More than any other arena, in the web domain, scalability is paramount. At the same time, high-speed response time is also vital in the web community. This is because there are a large number of clients (i.e., users) accessing massive amounts of web data. We believe that the cloud computing paradigm offers a solution that can achieve both these goals.

The existing commercial tools and technologies do not scale well in cloud computing settings. Researchers have started to focus on these problems recently. They are proposing systems built from the scratch. In [WANG10], researchers propose an indexing scheme for a new distributed database [COMP], which can be used as a cloud system. When it comes to semantic web data such as RDF, we are faced with similar challenges. With storage becoming cheaper and the need to store and retrieve large amounts of data, developing systems to handle billions of RDF triples requiring tera- and even petabytes of disk space is no longer a distant prospect. Researchers are already working on billions of triples [NEWM08], [ROHL07]. Competitions are being organized to encourage researchers to build efficient repositories [CHAL]. At present, there are just a few frameworks (e.g., RDF-3X [NEUM08], Jena [CARR04], Sesame [OPEN], BigOWLIM [KIRY05]) for semantic web technologies, and these frameworks have limitations for large RDF graphs. Therefore, storing a large number of RDF triples and efficiently querying them is a challenging and important problem.

In this chapter, we discuss a query processing system that functions in the cloud and manages a large number of RDF triples. The organization of this chapter is as follows. Our approach is discussed in Section 13.2. In Section 13.3, we discuss related work. In Section 13.4, we discuss our system architecture. In Section 13.5, we discuss how we answer a SPARQL query. In Section 13.6, we present the results of our experiments. Finally, in Section 13.7, we draw some conclusions and discuss

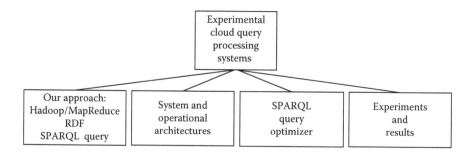

Figure 13.1 Cloud query processing. (Husain, M.F., J.P. McGlothlin, M.M. Masud, L.R. Khan, and B.M. Thuraisingham, Heuristics-based query processing for large RDF graphs using cloud computing, *IEEE Transactions on Knowledge and Data Engineering*, 23(9): 1312–1327. © (2011) IEEE.)

areas we have identified for improvement in the future. The contents of this chapter are illustrated in Figure 13.1. A more detailed discussion of the concepts, architectures, and experiments are provided in [HUSA11a] and [HUSA11b].

13.2 Our Approach

A distributed system can be built to overcome the scalability and performance problems of current semantic web frameworks. Databases are being distributed to provide such scalable solutions. However, to date, there is no distributed repository for storing and managing RDF data. Researchers have only recently begun to explore the problems and technical solutions that must be addressed to build such a distributed system. One promising line of investigation involves making use of readily available distributed database systems or relational databases. Such database systems can use a relational schema for the storage of RDF data. SPARQL queries can be answered by converting them to SQL first [CHEB07], [CHON05], [CYGA05]. Optimal relational schemas are being probed for this purpose [ABAD07]. The main disadvantage with such systems is that they are optimized for relational data. They may not perform well for RDF data, especially because RDF data are sets of triples [W3a] (an ordered tuple of three components called subject, predicate, and object), which form large directed graphs. In a SPARQL query, any number of triple patterns (TPs) [W3e] can join on a single variable [W3d], which makes a relational database query plan complex. Performance and scalability will remain a challenging issue due to the fact that these systems are optimized for relational data schemata and transactional database usage.

Yet another approach is to build a distributed system for RDF from scratch. Here, there will be an opportunity to design and optimize a system with specific application to RDF data. However, this approach is highly customized and it will be difficult to adapt to new standards. Instead of starting with a blank slate, we built a solution with a generic distributed storage system that utilizes a cloud computing platform. We then tailored the system and schema specifically to meet the needs of semantic web data. Finally, we built a semantic web repository using such a storage facility.

Hadoop [HADOa] is a distributed file system where files can be saved with replication. It is an ideal candidate for building a storage system. Hadoop features high fault tolerance and great reliability. In addition, it also contains an implementation of the MapReduce [DEAN04] programming model, a functional programming model that is suitable for the parallel processing of large amounts of data. Through partitioning data into a number of independent chunks, MapReduce processes run against these chunks, making parallelization simpler. Moreover, the MapReduce programming model facilitates and simplifies the task of joining multiple triple patterns.

In this chapter, we will describe a schema to store RDF data in Hadoop, and we will detail a solution to process queries against these data. In the preprocessing stage, we process RDF data and populate files in the distributed file system. This

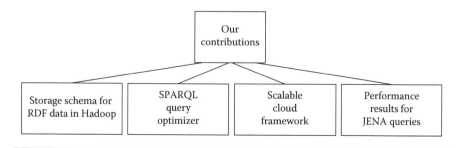

Figure 13.2 Our contributions.

process includes partitioning and organizing the data files and executing dictionary encoding. We will then detail a query engine for information retrieval. We will
specify exactly how SPARQL queries will be satisfied using MapReduce programming. Specifically, we must determine the Hadoop "jobs" that will be executed to
solve the query. We will present a greedy algorithm that produces a query plan with
the minimal number of Hadoop jobs. This is an approximation algorithm using
heuristics, but we will prove that the worst case has a reasonable upper bound.
Finally, we will utilize two standard benchmark data sets to run experiments. We
will present results for data sets ranging from 0.1 to more than 6.6 billion triples.
We will show that our solution is exceptionally scalable. We will also show that our
solution outperforms the leading state-of-the-art semantic web repositories, using
standard benchmark queries on very large data sets. Our contributions are listed
below and illustrated in Figure 13.2. More details are given in [HUSA11a].

1. We designed a storage scheme to store RDF data in HDFS [HADOb].
2. We developed an algorithm that is guaranteed to provide a query plan whose
   cost is bounded by the log of the total number of variables in the given SPARQL
   query. It uses summary statistics for estimating join selectivity to break ties.
3. We built a framework that is highly scalable and fault tolerant and supports
   data-intensive query processing.
4. We demonstrated that our approach performs better than Jena for all queries.
   It performed better than BigOWLIM and RDF-3X for complex queries with
   large result sets.

13.3 Related Work

MapReduce, though a programming paradigm, is rapidly being adopted by researchers. This technology is becoming increasingly popular in the community that handles
large amounts of data. It is the most promising technology to solve the performance
issues researchers are facing in cloud computing. In [ABAD09a], the author discusses
how MapReduce can satisfy most of the requirements to build an ideal cloud DBMS.
Researchers and enterprises are using MapReduce technology for web indexing,

searches, and data mining. In this section, we will first investigate the research related to MapReduce. Next, we will discuss works related to the semantic web.

Google uses MapReduce for web indexing, data storage, and social networking [CHAN06]. Yahoo! uses MapReduce extensively in its data analysis tasks [OLST08]. IBM has successfully experimented with a scale-up scale-out search framework using MapReduce technology [MORE07]. In a recent work [SISM10], they have reported how they integrated Hadoop and System R. Teradata did a similar work by integrating Hadoop with a parallel DBMS [XU10].

Researchers have used MapReduce to scale up classifiers for mining petabytes of data [MORE08]. They have worked on data distribution and partitioning for data mining, and have applied three data mining algorithms to test the performance. Data mining algorithms are being rewritten in different forms to take advantage of the MapReduce technology. In [CHU07], researchers rewrite well-known machine learning algorithms to take advantage of multicore machines by leveraging MapReduce programming paradigm. Another area where this technology is being successfully used is simulation [MCNA07]. In [ABOU09], researchers reported an interesting idea of combining MapReduce with existing relational database techniques. These works differ from our research in that we use MapReduce for semantic web technologies. Our focus is on developing a scalable solution for storing RDF data and retrieving them with SPARQL queries.

In the semantic web arena, there has not been much work done with MapReduce technology. We have found two related projects: the BioMANTA [ITEE] project and the Scalable, High-Performance, Robust, and Distributed (SHARD) project [CLOU]. BioMANTA proposes extensions to RDF molecules [DING05] and implements a MapReduce-based molecule store [NEWM08]. They use MapReduce to answer the queries. They have queried a maximum of four million triples. Our work differs in the following ways: First, we have queried one billion triples. Second, we have devised a storage schema that is tailored to improve the query execution performance for RDF data. We store RDF triples in files based on the predicate of the triple and the type of the object. Finally, we also have an algorithm to determine a query processing plan whose cost is bounded by the log of the total number of variables in the given SPARQL query. By using this, we can determine the input files of a job and the order in which they should be run. To the best of our knowledge, we are the first ones to come up with a storage schema for RDF data using flat files in HDFS, and a MapReduce job determination algorithm to answer a SPARQL query.

SHARD is an RDF triple store using the Hadoop Cloudera distribution. This project shows initial results demonstrating Hadoop's ability to improve scalability for RDF data sets. However, SHARD stores its data only in a triple store schema. It currently does no query planning or reordering, and its query processor will not minimize the number of Hadoop jobs. There has been significant research into semantic web repositories, with particular emphasis on query efficiency and scalability. In fact, there are too many such repositories to fairly evaluate and discuss each. Therefore, we will pay attention to semantic web repositories that are open source or available for download, and which have received favorable recognition in the semantic web and database communities.

In [ABAD09b] and [ABAD07], researchers reported a vertically partitioned DBMS for storage and retrieval of RDF data. Their solution is a schema with a two-column table for each predicate. Their schema is then implemented on top of a column-store relational database such as CStore [STON05] or MonetDB [BONC06]. They observed performance improvement with their scheme over traditional relational database schemes. We have leveraged this technology in our predicate-based partitioning within the MapReduce framework. However, in the vertical partitioning research, only small databases (<100 million) were used. Several papers [SIDI08], [MCGL09], [WEIS08] have shown that the performance of the vertical partitioning method is drastically reduced as the data set size is increased.

Jena [CARR04] is a semantic web framework for managing RDF data. True to its framework design, it allows integration of multiple solutions for persistence. It also supports inference through the development of reasoners. However, Jena is limited to a triple store schema. In other words, all data are stored in a single three-column table. Jena has very poor query performance for large data sets. Furthermore, any change to the data set requires complete recalculation of the inferred triples.

BigOWLIM [KIRY05] is among the fastest and most scalable semantic web frameworks available. However, it is not as scalable as our framework and requires very high end and costly machines. It requires expensive hardware (a lot of main memory) to load large data sets and it has a long loading time. As our experiments show, it does not perform well when there is no bound object in a query. However, the performance of our framework is not affected in such a case.

RDF-3X [NEUM08] is considered the fastest existing semantic web repository. In other words, it has the fastest query times. RDF-3X uses histograms, summary statistics, and query optimization to enable high-performance semantic web queries. As a result, RDF-3X is generally able to outperform any other solution for queries with bound objects and aggregate queries. However, RDF-3X's performance degrades exponentially for unbound queries, and queries with even simple joins if the selectivity factor is low. This becomes increasingly relevant for inference queries, which generally require unions of subqueries with unbound objects. Our experiments show that RDF-3X is not only slower for such queries but it also often aborts and cannot complete the query. For example, consider the simple query "Select all students." This query in LUBM (Lehigh Benchmark) requires us to select all graduate students, select all undergraduate students, and combine the results together. However, there are a very large number of results in this union. While both subqueries complete easily, the union will abort in RDF-3X for LUBM (data set 30,000) with 3.3 billion triples.

RDF Knowledge Base (RDFKB) [MCGL10] is a semantic web repository using a relational database schema built upon bit vectors. RDFKB achieves better query performance than RDF-3X or vertical partitioning. However, RDFKB aims to provide knowledge base functions such as inference forward chaining, uncertainty reasoning, and ontology alignment. RDFKB prioritizes these goals ahead of scalability. RDFKB is not able to load LUBM (30,000) with three billion triples, so it cannot compete with our solution for scalability.

Hexastore [WEIS08] and BitMat [ATRE08] are the main memory data structures optimized for RDF indexing. These solutions may achieve exceptional performance on hot runs, but they are not optimized for cold runs from persistent storage. Furthermore, their scalability is directly associated with the quantity of the main memory RAM available. These products are not available for testing and evaluation.

In our previous work [HUSA09], [HUSA10], we developed a greedy and an exhaustive search algorithm to generate a query processing plan. However, the exhaustive search algorithm was expensive and the greedy one was not bounded and its theoretical complexity was not defined. In this chapter, we present a new greedy algorithm with an upper bound. Also, we did observe scenarios in which our old greedy algorithm failed to generate the optimal plan. The new algorithm is able to obtain the optimal plan in each of these cases. The Join Executer component runs the jobs using the MapReduce framework. It then relays the query answer from Hadoop to the user.

13.4 Architecture

Our system architecture is illustrated in Figure 13.3. It essentially consists of a SPARQL query optimizer and a RDF data manager implemented in the cloud.

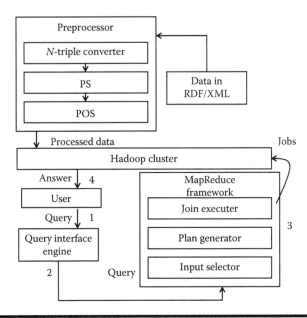

Figure 13.3   System architecture.

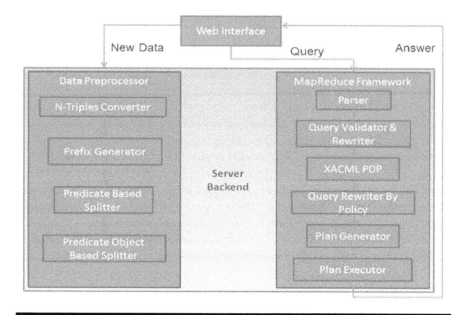

Figure 13.4 Operational architecture.

The operational architecture is illustrated in Figure 13.4. It consists of two components. The left side of Figure 13.4 depicts the data preprocessing component while the right side shows the query answering component. We have three subcomponents for data generation and preprocessing. We convert RDF/XML [W3f] to N-Triples [W3a] serialization format using our N-Triples Converter component. The Predicate Split (PS) component takes the N-Triples data and splits it into predicate files. The predicate files are then fed into the Predicate Object Split (POS) component, which splits the predicate files into smaller files based on the type of objects. These steps are described below.

13.4.1 Data Generation and Storage

For our experiments, we use the LUBM [GUO05] data set. It is a benchmark data set designed to enable researchers to evaluate a semantic web repository's performance [GUO04]. The LUBM data generator generates data in RDF/XML serialization format. This format is not suitable for our purpose because we store data in HDFS as flat files and so to retrieve even a single triple, we would need to parse the entire file. Therefore, we convert the data to N-Triples to store the data because with that format we have a complete RDF triple (subject, predicate, and object) in one line of a file, which is very convenient to use with MapReduce jobs. The processing steps to go through to get the data into our intended format are described in the following sections.

13.4.2 File Organization

We do not store the data in a single file because in the Hadoop and MapReduce Framework, a file is the smallest unit of input to a MapReduce job and in the absence of caching, a file is always read from the disk. If we have all the data in one file, the whole file will be input to jobs for each query. Instead, we divide the data into multiple smaller files. The splitting is done in two steps, which we discuss in the following sections.

13.4.3 Predicate Split

In the first step, we divide the data according to the predicates. This division immediately enables us to cut down the search space for any SPARQL query that does not have a variable predicate. For such a query, we can just pick a file for each predicate and run the query on these files only. For simplicity, we name the files with predicates, for example, all the triples containing a predicate p1:pred go into a file named p1-pred. However, in case we have a variable predicate in a triple pattern [W3e] and if we cannot determine the type of the object, we have to consider all files. If we can determine the type of the object, then we consider all files having that type of the object. We discuss more on this in Section 13.5. In real-world RDF data sets, the number of distinct predicates is in general not a large number [STOC08]. However, there are data sets having many predicates. Our system performance does not vary in such a case because we just select files related to the predicates specified in a SPARQL query.

13.4.4 Split Using Explicit-Type Information of Object

In the next step, we work with the explicit-type information in the rdf_type file. The predicate rdf:type is used in RDF to denote that a resource is an instance of a class. The rdf_type file is first divided into as many files as the number of distinct objects the rdf:type predicate has. For example, if in the ontology, the leaves of the class hierarchy are $c_1, c_2, \ldots, c_n$ then we will create files for each of these leaves and the file names will be like type_c_1, type_c_2, ..., type_c_n. Note that the object values $c_1, c_2, \ldots, c_n$ are no longer needed to be stored within the file as they can be easily retrieved from the file name. This further reduces the amount of space needed to store the data. We generate such a file for each distinct object value of the predicate rdf:type.

13.4.5 Split Using Implicit-Type Information of Object

We divide the remaining predicate files according to the type of the objects. Not all the objects are URIs (uniform resource identifier); some are literals. The literals remain in the file named by the predicate; no further processing is required for them. The type information of a URI object is not mentioned in these files but they can be retrieved from the type_*files. The URI objects move into their respective file named as predicate_type. For example, if a triple has the predicate p and the type of the URI object is c_i, then the subject and object appear in one line in the file p_c_i. To do this split, we need to join a predicate file with the type_*files to retrieve the type information.

Our MapReduce framework, described in Section 13.5, has three subcomponents in it. It takes the SPARQL query from the user and passes it to the Input and Plan Generator. This component selects the input files, by using our algorithm described in Section 13.5, decides how many MapReduce jobs are needed, and passes the information to the Join Executer component that runs the jobs using the MapReduce framework. It then relays the query answer from Hadoop to the user.

13.5 MapReduce Framework

13.5.1 Overview

The MapReduce framework is at the heart of our cloud computing efforts. We will discuss MapReduce in various chapters of this book as it relates to the contents of that chapter. In this section, we discuss how we answer SPARQL queries with our MapReduce framework component.

Section 13.5.2 discusses our algorithm to select input files for answering the query. Section 13.5.3 describes the cost estimation needed to generate a plan to answer a SPARQL query. It introduces few terms that we use in the following discussions. We also describe the ideal model that we should follow to estimate the cost of a plan, and introduce the heuristics-based model we use in practice. Section 13.5.4 presents our heuristics-based greedy algorithm to generate a query plan that uses the cost model introduced in Section 13.5.3. We face tie situations to generate a plan in some cases. In Section 13.5.5 we discuss how we handle these special cases. Section 13.5.6 shows how we implement a Join in a Hadoop MapReduce job by working through an example query.

13.5.2 Input Files Selection

Before determining the jobs, we select the files that need to be input to the jobs. We have some query rewriting capability that we apply at this step of query processing. We take the query submitted by the user and iterate over the triple patterns. We may encounter the following cases:

1. In a triple pattern, if the predicate is a variable, we select all the files as input to the jobs and terminate the iteration.

2. If the predicate is rdf:type and the object is concrete, we select the type file having that particular type. For example, for the LUBM query 9 (Listing 1), we could select file type_Student as part of the input set. However, this brings up an interesting scenario. In our data set, there is actually no file named type_Student because Student class is not a leaf in the ontology tree. In this case, we consult the LUBM ontology [LEHI] to determine the correct set of input files. We add the files type_GraduateStudent, type_ UndergraduateStudent, and type_ResearchAssistant as GraduateStudent, UndergraduateStudent, and ResearchAssistant are the leaves of the subtree rooted at node Student.

3. If the predicate is rdf:type and the object is a variable, then if the type of the variable is defined by another triple pattern, we select the type file having that particular type. Otherwise, we select all type files.

4. If the predicate is not rdf:type and the object is a variable, then we need to determine if the type of the object is specified by another triple pattern in the query. In this case, we can rewrite the query eliminate some joins. For example, in LUBM Query 9 (Listing 1), the type of Y is specified as Faculty and Z as Course and these variables are used as objects in last three triple patterns. If we choose files advisor_Lecturer, advisor_PostDoc, advisor_FullProfessor, advisor_AssociateProfessor, advisor_AssistantProfessor, and advisor_ VisitingProfessor as part of the input set, then the triple pattern in line 2 becomes unnecessary. Similarly, triple pattern in line 3 becomes unnecessary if files takesCourse_Course and takesCourse_ GraduateCourse are chosen. Hence, we get the rewritten query shown in Listing 2. However, if the type of the object is not specified, then we select all files for that predicate.

5. If the predicate is not rdf:type and the object is concrete, then we select all files for that predicate.

```
Listing 1. LUBM Query 9
SELECT ?X ?Y ?Z WHERE {
?X rdf:type ub:Student.
?Y rdf:type ub:Faculty.
?Z rdf:type ub:Course.
?X ub:advisor ?Y.
?Y ub:teacherOf ?Z.
?X ub:takesCourse ?Z}

Listing 2. Rewritten LUBM Query 9
SELECT ?X ?Y ?Z WHERE {
?X rdf:type ub:Student.
?X ub:advisor ?Y.
?Y ub:teacherOf ?Z.
?X ub:takesCourse ?Z}
```

13.5.3 Cost Estimation for Query Processing

We run Hadoop jobs to answer a SPARQL query. In this section, we discuss how we estimate the cost of a job. However, before doing that, we introduce some definitions that we will use later:

Definition 13.1

Triple Pattern, TP: A triple pattern is an ordered set of subject, predicate, and object that appears in a SPARQL query WHERE clause. The subject, predicate, and object can be either a variable (unbounded) or a concrete value (bounded).

Definition 13.2

Triple Pattern Join, TPJ: A triple pattern join is a join between two TPs on a variable.

Definition 13.3

MapReduceJoin, MRJ: A MapReduceJoin is a join between two or more triple patterns on a variable.

Definition 13.4

Job, JB: A job JB is a Hadoop job where one or more MRJs are done. JB has a set of input files and a set of output files.

Definition 13.5

Conflicting MapReduceJoins, CMRJ: Conflicting MapReduceJoins is a pair of MRJs on different variables sharing a triple pattern.

Definition 13.6

Nonconflicting MapReduceJoins, NCMRJ: Nonconflicting MapReduceJoins is a pair of MRJs either not sharing any triple pattern or sharing a triple pattern and the MRJs are on the same variable.

An example will illustrate these terms better. In Listing 3, we show LUBM Query 12. Lines 2, 3, 4, and 5 each have a triple pattern. The join between TPs in lines 2 and 4 on variable ?X is an MRJ. If we do two MRJs, one between TPs in lines 2 and 4 on variable ?X and the other between TPs in lines 4 and 5 on variable ?Y, there will be a CMRJ as TP in line 4 (?X ub:worksFor ?Y) takes part in two MRJs on two different variables ?X and ?Y. This type of join is called CMRJ because in a Hadoop job, more than one variable of a TP cannot be a key at the same time and MRJs are performed on keys. An NCMRJ, shown would be one MRJ between triple patterns in lines 2 and 4 on variable ?X and another MRJ between triple patterns in lines 3 and 5 on variable ?Y. These two MRJs can make up a JB.

```
Listing 3. LUBM Query 12
SELECT ?X WHERE {
?X rdf:type ub:Chair.
?Y rdf:type ub:Department.
?X ub:worksFor ?Y.
?Y ub:subOrganizationOf http://www.U0.edu}
```

13.5.3.1 Ideal Model

To answer a SPARQL query, we may need more than one job. Therefore, in an ideal scenario, the cost estimation for processing a query requires individual cost estimation of each job that is needed to answer that query. A job contains three main tasks, which are reading, sorting, and writing. We estimate the cost of a job based on these three tasks. For each task, a unit cost is assigned to each triple pattern it deals with. In the current model, we assume that the costs for reading and writing are the same.

$$\text{Cost} = \left(\sum_{i=1}^{n-1} MI_i + MO_i + RI_i + RO_i \right) + MI_n + MO_n + RI_n \qquad (13.1)$$

$$= \left(\sum_{i=1}^{n-1} Job_i \right) + MI_n + MO_n + RI_n \qquad (13.2)$$

$$Job_i = +MI_i + MO_i + RO_i + RI_i \quad (\text{if } i < n) \qquad (13.3)$$

where
  MI_i = Map Input phase for job i
  MO_i = Map Output phase for job i
  RI_i = Reduce Input phase for job i
  RO_i = Reduce Output phase for job i

Equation 13.1 is the total cost of processing a query. It is the summation of the individual costs of each job and only the map phase of the final job. We do not consider the cost of the reduce output of the final job because it would be the same for any query plan as this output is the final result that is fixed for a query and a given data set. A job essentially performs a MapReduce task on the file data. Equation 13.2 shows the division of the MapReduce task into subtasks. Hence, to estimate the cost of each job, we will combine the estimated cost of each subtask.

Map Input (MI) phase. This phase reads the triple patterns from the selected input files stored in the HDFS. Therefore, we can estimate the cost for the MI phase to be equal to the total number of triples in each of the selected files.

Map Output (MO) phase. The estimation of the MO phase depends on the type of query being processed. If the query has no bound variable (e.g., [?X ub:worksFor?Y]), then the output of the map phase is equal to the input. All of the triple patterns are transformed into key-value pairs and given as output. Therefore, for such a query, the MO cost will be the same as the MI cost. However, if the query involves a bound variable (e.g., [?Y ub:subOrganizationOf <http://www.U0.edu>]), then, before making the key-value pairs, a bound component selectivity estimation can be applied. The resulting estimate for the triple patterns will account for the cost of the MO phase. The selected triples are written to a local disk.

Reduce Input (RI) phase. In this phase, the triples from the MO phase are read via HTTP and then sorted based on their key values. After sorting, the triples with identical keys are grouped together. Therefore, the cost estimation for the RI phase is equal to the MO phase. The number of key-value pairs that are sorted in the RI phase is equal to the number of key-value pairs generated in the MO phase.

Reduce Output (RO) phase. The RO phase deals with performing the joins. Therefore, it is in this phase that we can use the join triple pattern selectivity summary statistics to estimate the size of its output. Below, we discuss in detail about the join triple pattern selectivity summary statistics needed for our framework.

However, in practice, the above discussion is applicable for the first job only. For subsequent jobs, we lack both the precise knowledge and the estimate of the number of triple patterns selected after applying the join in the first job. Therefore, for these jobs, we can take the size of the RO phase of the first job as an upper bound on the different phases of the subsequent jobs.

Equation 13.3 shows a very important postulation. It illustrates the total cost of an intermediate job, when $i < n$, includes the cost of the RO phase in calculating the total cost of the job.

13.5.3.2 Heuristic Model

In this section, we show that the ideal model is not practical or cost effective. There are several issues that make the ideal model less attractive in practice. First, the ideal model considers simple abstract costs, namely, the number of triples read and written by the different phases ignoring the actual cost of copying, sorting, and so on, these triples, and the overhead for running jobs in Hadoop. But incorporating these costs accurately in the model is a difficult task. Even making reasonably good estimation may be nontrivial. Second, to estimate intermediate join outputs, we need to maintain comprehensive summary statistics. In a MapReduce job in Hadoop, all the joins on a variable are joined together. For example, in the rewritten LUBM Query 9 (Listing 2), there are three joins on variable X. When a job is run to do the join on X, all the joins on X between triple patterns 1, 2, and 4 are done. If there were more than three joins on X, all will still be handled in one job. This shows that to gather summary statistics to estimate join selectivity, we face an exponential number of join cases. For example, between triple patterns having p_1, p_2, and p_3, there may be 23 types of joins because in each triple pattern, a variable can occur either as a subject or as an object. In the case of the rewritten Query 9, it is a subject–subject–subject join between 1, 2, and 4. There can be more types of join between these three, for example, subject–object–subject, object–subject–object, and so on. That means, between P predicates, there can be 2^P type of joins on a single variable (ignoring the possibility that a variable may appear both as a subject and as an object in a triple pattern). If there are P predicates in the data set, the total number of cases for which we need to collect summary statistics can be calculated by the formula

$$2^2 \times C_2^P + 2^3 \times C_3^P + \cdots + 2^P \times C_P^P$$

In the LUBM data set, there are 17 predicates. So, in total, there are 129,140,128 cases, which is a large number. Gathering summary statistics for such a large number of cases would be very much time and space consuming. Hence, we took an alternate approach.

We observe that there is significant overhead for running a job in Hadoop. Therefore, if we minimize the number of jobs to answer a query, we get the fastest plan. The overhead is incurred by several disk I/O and network transfers that are an integral part of any Hadoop job. When a job is submitted to the Hadoop cluster, at least the following set of actions take place:

1. The Executable file is transferred from the client machine to the Hadoop JobTracker [WIKIa].
2. The JobTracker decides which TaskTrackers [WIKIb] will execute the job.
3. The Executable file is distributed to the TaskTrackers over the network.
4. Map processes start by reading data from HDFS.
5. Map outputs are written to disks.
6. Map outputs are read from disks, shuffled (transferred over the network to TaskTrackers, which would run Reduce processes), sorted, and written to disks.
7. Reduce processes start by reading the input from the disks.
8. Reduce outputs are written to disks.

These disk operations and network transfers are expensive operations even for a small amount of data. For example, in our experiments, we observed that the over head incurred by one job is almost equivalent to reading a billion triples. The reason is that in every job, the output of the map process is always sorted before feeding the reduce processes. This sorting is unavoidable even if it is not needed by the user. Therefore, it would be less costly to process several hundred million more triples in n jobs, rather than processing several hundred million less triples in $n + 1$ jobs.

To further investigate, we did an experiment where we used the query shown in Listing 4. Here, the join selectivity between TPs 2 and 3 on ?Z is the highest. Hence, a query plan generation algorithm that uses selectivity factors to pick joins would select this join for the first job. As the other TPs 1 and 4 share variables with either TP 2 or 3, they cannot take part in any other join; moreover, they do not share any variables so the only possible join that can be executed in this job is the join between TPs 2 and 3 on ?X. Once this join is done, the two joins left are between TP 1 and the join output of the first job on variable ?X and between TP 4 and the join output of the first job on variable ?Y. We found that the selectivity of the first join is greater than the latter. Hence, the second job will do this join and TP 4 will again not participate. In the third and last job, the join output of the second job will be joined with TP 4 on ?Y. This is the plan generated using join selectivity estimation. But the minimum job plan is a two-job plan where the first job joins TPs 1 and 2 on ?X and TPs 3 and 4 on ?Y. The second and final job joins the two join outputs of the first job on ?Z. The query runtimes we found are given in [HUSA11a].

```
Listing 4. Experiment Query
?S1 ub:advisor ?X.
?X ub:headOf ?Z.
?Z ub:subOrganizationOf ?Y.
?S2 ub:mastersDegreeFrom ?Y
```

For each data set, we found that the two-job plan is faster than the three-job plan even though the three-job plan produced less intermediate data because of the join selectivity order. We can explain this by an observation we made in another small experiment. We generated files of sizes 5 and 10 MB containing random integers. We put the files in HDFS. For each file, we first read the file by a program and recorded the time needed to do it. While reading, our program reads from one of the three available replica of the file. Then, we ran a MapReduce job that rewrites the file with the numbers sorted. We utilized MapReduces sorting to have the sorted output. Note that when it writes the file, it writes three replications of it. We found that the MapReduce job, which does reading, sorting, and writing, takes 24.47 times longer to finish for 5 MB. For 10 MB, it is 42.79 times. This clearly shows how the write and data transfer operations of a MapReduce job are more expensive than a simple read from only one replica. Because of the number of jobs, the three-job plan is doing much more disk read and write operations as well as network data transfers and as a result is slower than the two-job plan even if it is reading less input data.

Because of these reasons, we do not pursue the ideal model. We follow the practical model, which is to generate a query plan having minimum possible jobs. However, while generating a minimum job plan, whenever we need to choose a join to be considered in a job among more than one joins, instead of choosing randomly, we use the summary join statistics. This is described in Section 13.5.4. More details of our experimental results with the charts are provided in [HUSA11a].

13.5.4 Query Plan Generation

In this section, we first define the query plan generation problem, and show that generating the best (i.e., least cost) query plan for the ideal model as well as for the practical model is computationally expensive. Then, we will present a heuristic and a greedy approach to generate an approximate solution to generate the best plan.

RUNNING EXAMPLE

We will use the following query as a running example in this section:

```
Listing 5. Running Example
SELECT ?V,?X,?Y,?Z WHERE{
?X rdf:type ub:GraduateStudent
?Y rdf:type ub:University
?Z ?V ub:Department
?X ub:memberOf ?Z
?X ub:undergraduateDegreeFrom ?Y}
```

To simplify the notations, we will only refer to the TPs by the variable in that pattern. For example, the first TP (?X rdf:type ub:GraduateStudent) will be represented as simply X. Also, in the simplified version, the whole query would be represented as follows: {X,Y,Z,XZ,XY}. We will use the notation join(XY,X) to denote a join operation between the two TPs XY and X on the common variable X.

Definition 13.7

(The Minimum Cost Plan Generation Problem). (Bestplan Problem). For a given query, the Bestplan problem is to generate a job plan so that the total cost of the jobs is minimized. Note that Bestplan considers the more general case where each job has some cost associated with it (i.e., the ideal model).

EXAMPLE

Given the query in our running example, two possible job plans are as follows:

Plan1. $job_1 = \{X, XY, XZ\}$,
resultant TPs = $\{YZ, YZ\}$. $job_2 = \{Y, YZ\}$,
resultant TPs = $\{Z, Z\}$. $job_3 = \{Z, Z\}$. Total cost = $cost(job_1) + cost(job_2)$.

Plan 2. $job_1 = \{XZ, Z\}$ and $join(XY, Y)$
resultant TPs = $\{X, X, X\}$. $job_2 = join(X, X, X)$.
Total cost = $cost(job_1) + cost(job_2)$.

The Bestplan problem is to find the least cost job plan among all possible job plans. Next, we define some related terms and discuss the complexity of our approach.

Definition 13.8

(Joining Variable). A variable that is common in two or more triple patterns. For example, in the running example query, X, Y, Z are joining variables, but V is not.

Definition 13.9

(Complete Elimination). A join operation that eliminates a joining variable. For example, in the example query, Y can be completely eliminated if we join (XY, Y).

Definition 13.10

(Partial Elimination). A join operation that partially eliminates a joining variable. For example, in the example query, if we perform join(XY, Y) and join(X, ZX) in the same job, the resultant triple patterns would be $\{X, Z, X\}$. Therefore, Y will be completely eliminated but X will be partially eliminated. So, the join(X, ZX) performs a partial elimination.

Definition 13.11

(E-Count(v)). E-count(v) is the number of joining variables in the resultant triple pattern after a complete elimination of variable v. In the running example, join(X, XY, XZ) completely eliminates X, and the resultant triple pattern (YZ) has two joining variables Y and Z. So, E-count$(X) = 2$. Similarly, E-count$(Y) = 1$ and E-count$(Z) = 1$.

13.5.4.1 Computational Complexity of Bestplan

It can be shown that generating the least cost query plan is computationally expensive since the search space is exponentially large. At first, we formulate the problem and then show its complexity.

13.5.4.1.1 Problem Formulation

We formulate Bestplan as a search problem. Let $G = (V, E)$ be a weighted directed graph, where each vertex $v_i \in V$ represents a state of the triple patterns, and each edge $e_i \in (v_{i_1}, v_{i_2}) \in E$ represents a job that makes a transition from state v_{i_1} to state v_{i_2}. v_0 is the initial state, where no joins have been performed, that is, the given query. Also, v_{goal} is the goal state, which represents a state of the triple pattern where all joins have been performed. The problem is to find the shortest weighted path from v_0 to v_{goal}.

For example, in our running example query, the initial state $v_0 = \{X, Y, Z, XY, XZ\}$, and the goal state, $v_{goal} = \emptyset$, that is, no more triple patterns left. Suppose the first job (job1) performs $join(X, XY, XZ)$. Then, the resultant triple patterns (new state) would be $v_1 = \{Y, Z, YZ\}$, and job1 would be represented by the edge (v_0, v_1). The weight of edge (v_0, v_1) is the cost of $job_1 = cost(job_1)$, where the cost is the given cost function. Figure 13.4 shows the partial graph for the example query.

13.5.4.1.2 Search Space Size

Given a graph $G = (V, E)$, Dijkstra's shortest path algorithm can find the shortest path from a source to all other nodes in $O(|V| log |V| + |E|)$ time. However, for Bestplan, it can be shown that in the worst case, $|V| \geq 2^K$, where K is the total number of joining variables in the given query. Therefore, the number of vertices in the graph is exponential, leading to an exponential search problem. In [HUSA11a], we have shown that the worst-case complexity of the Bestplan problem is exponential in K, the number of joining variables in the given query.

13.5.4.2 Relaxed Bestplan Problem and Approximate Solution

In the Relaxed Bestplan problem, we assume uniform cost for all jobs. Although this relaxation does not reduce the search space, the problem is reduced to finding a job plan having the minimum number of jobs. Note that this is the problem for the practical version of the model.

Definition 13.12

(Relaxed Bestplan Problem). The Relaxed Bestplan problem is to find the job plan that has the minimum number of jobs.

Next, we show that if joins are reasonably chosen, and no eligible join operation is left undone in a job, then we may set an upper bound on the maximum number of jobs required for any given query. However, it is still computationally expensive to generate all possible job plans. Therefore, we resort to a greedy algorithm (Algorithm 1) that finds an approximate solution to the Relaxed Bestplan problem but is guaranteed to find a job plan within the upper bound.

Definition 13.13 (Early Elimination Heuristic). The early elimination heuristic makes as many complete eliminations as possible in each job.

This heuristic leaves the fewest number of variables for join in the next job. To apply the heuristic, we must first choose the variable in each job with the least E-count. This heuristic is applied in Algorithm 1.

Algorithm 1: Relaxed-Bestplan (Query Q)

1: $Q \leftarrow$ Remove non $-$ joining variables(Q)
2: **while** $Q \neq$ Empty **do**
3: $J \leftarrow 1//$Total number of jobs
4: $U = \{u_1,\ldots,u_K\} \leftarrow$ All variables sorted in non-decreasing order of their E-counts
5: $Job_J \leftarrow$ Empty //List of join operations in the
//current job
6: $tmp \leftarrow$ Empty //Temporarily stores resultant
//triple patterns
7: **for** $i = 1$ *to* K **do**
8: **if** $Can - Eliminate(Q,u_i) = true$ **then**
//complete or partial elimination possible
9: $tmp \leftarrow tmp \cup Join - result(TP(Q,u_i))$
10: $Q \leftarrow Q - TP(Q,u_i)$
11: $Job_J \leftarrow Job_J \cup join(TP(Q,u_i))$
12: **end if**
13: **end for**
14: $Q \leftarrow Q \cup tmp$
15: $J \leftarrow J + 1$
16: **end while**
17: $return \{Job_1,\ldots, Job_{J-1}\}$

Description of Algorithm 1. The algorithm starts by removing all the nonjoining variables from the query Q. In our running example, $Q = \{X,Y,VZ,XY,XZ\}$, and removing the nonjoining variable V makes $Q = \{X,Y,Z,XY,XZ\}$. In the while loop, the job plan is generated, starting from Job_1. In line 4, we sort the variables according to their E-count. The sorted variables are $U = \{Y,Z,X\}$, since Y and Z have E-count $= 1$ and X has E-count $= 2$. For each job, the list of join operations is stored in the variable Job_J, where J is the ID of the current job. Also, a temporary variable *tmp* is used to store the resultant triples of the joins to be performed in the current job (line 6). In the for loop, each variable is checked to see if the variable can be completely or partially eliminated (line 8). If yes, we store the join result in the temporary variable (line 9), update Q (line 10), and add this join to the current job (line 11). In our running example, this results in the following operations: Iteration 1 of the for loop: $u_1 = (Y)$ can be completely eliminated. Here, $TP(Q,Y)$, the triple patterns in Q containing Iteration 3 of the for loop: $u_3 = (X)$ cannot be completely or partially eliminated since there is no other TP left to join with it. Therefore, when the for loop terminates, we have $job_1 = \{join(Y,XY), join(Z,XZ)\}$, and $Q = \{X,X,X\}$. In the second iteration of the while loop, we will have $\{job_2 = \{X,X,X\}$. Since after this join, Q becomes Empty, the while loop is exited. Finally, $\{job_1, job_2\}$ are returned from the algorithm.

In [HUSA11a], we have proved that for any given query Q, containing K joining variables and N triple patterns, Algorithm Relaxed-Bestplan (Q) generates a job plan containing at most J jobs, where

$$
J = \begin{cases} 0 & N = 0 \\ 1 & N = 1 \text{ or } K = 1 \\ \min(\lceil 1.71 \log_2 N \rceil, K) & N, K > 1 \end{cases} \tag{13.4}
$$

13.5.5 Breaking Ties by Summary Statistics

We frequently face situations where we need to choose a join for multiple join options. These choices can occur when both query plans (i.e., join orderings) require the minimum number of jobs. For example, the query shown in Listing 6 poses such a situation.

```
Listing 6. Query Having Tie Situation
?X rdf:type ub:FullProfessor.
?X ub:advisorOf ?Y.
?Y rdf:type ub:ResearchAssistant.
```

The second triple pattern in the query makes it impossible to answer and solve the query with only one job. There are only two possible plans: we can join the first two triple patterns on X first and then join its output with the last triple pattern on Y or we can join the last two patterns first on Y and then join its output with the first pattern on X. In such a situation, instead of randomly choosing a join variable for the first job, we use join summary statistics for a pair of predicates. We select the join for the first job, which is more selective to break the tie. The join summary statistics we use are described in [STOC08].

13.5.6 MapReduce Join Execution

In this section, we discuss how we implement the joins needed to answer the SPARQL queries using the MapReduce framework of Hadoop. Algorithm 1 determines the number of jobs required to answer a query. It returns an ordered set of jobs. Each job has associated input information. The Job Handler component of our MapReduce framework runs the jobs in the sequence they appear in the ordered set. The output file of one job is the input of the next. The output file of the last job has the answer to the query.

```
Listing 7. LUBM Query 2
SELECT ?X, ?Y, ?Z WHERE {
?X rdf:type ub:GraduateStudent.
?Y rdf:type ub:University.
?Z rdf:type ub:Department.
?X ub:memberOf ?Z.
?Z ub:subOrganizationOf ?Y.
?X ub:undergraduateDegreeFrom ?Y}
```

Listing 7 shows LUBM Query 2, which we will use to illustrate the way we do a join using map and reduce methods. The query has six triple patterns and nine joins between them on the variable X, Y, and Z.

Our input selection algorithm selects files *type_GraduateStudent, type_University, type_Department,* all files having the prefix *memberOf,* all files having the prefix *subOrganizationOf,* and all files having the prefix *underGraduateDegreeFrom* as the input to the jobs needed to answer the query.

The query plan has two jobs. In job 1, triple patterns of lines 2, 5, and 7 are joined on X and triple patterns of lines 3 and 6 are joined on Y. In job 2, triple pattern of line 4 is joined with the outputs of previous two joins on Z and also the join outputs of job 1 are joined on Y.

The input files of job 1 are type_GraduateStudent, type_University, all files having the prefix memberOf, all files having the prefix subOrganizationOf, and all files having the prefix underGraduateDegreeFrom. In the map phase, we first tokenize the input value, which is actually a line of the input file. Then, we check the input file name and, if the input is from type_GraduateStudent, we output a key-value pair having the subject URI prefixed with X# the key and a flag string GS# as the value. The value serves as a flag to indicate that the key is of type GraduateStudent. The subject URI is the first token returned by the tokenizer. Similarly, for input from file type_University, output a key-value pair having the subject URI prefixed with Y# the key and a flag string U# as the value. If the input from any file has the prefix memberOf, we retrieve the subject and object from the input line by the tokenizer and output a key-value pair having the subject URI prefixed with X# the key and the object value prefixed with MO# as the value. For input from files having the prefix subOrganizationOf, we output key-value pairs making the object prefixed with Y# the key and the subject prefixed with SO# the value. For input from files having the prefix underGraduate DegreeFrom, we output key-value pairs making the subject URI prefixed with X# the key and the object value prefixed with UDF# the value. Hence, we make either the subject or the object a map output key based on which we are joining. This is the reason why the object is made the key for the triples from files having the prefix subOrganizationOf because the joining variable Y is an object in the triple pattern in line 6. For all other inputs, the subject is made the key because the joining variables X and Y are subjects in the triple patterns in lines 2, 3, 5, and 7.

In the reduce phase, Hadoop groups all the values for a single key and for each key provides the key and an iterator to the values collection. Looking at the prefix, we can immediately tell if it is a value for X or Y because of the prefixes we used. In either case, we output a key-value pair using the same key and concatenating all the values to make a string value. So, after this reduce phase, the join on X is complete and the join on Y is partially complete.

The input files of job 2 are type_Department file and the output file of job 1, job1.out. Like the map phase of job 1, in the map phase of job 2, we also tokenize the input value, which is actually a line of the input file. Then, we check the input file name and, if the input is from type_Department, we output a key-value pair having the subject URI prefixed with Z# the key and a flag string D# as the value. If the input is from job1.out, we find the value having the prefix Z#. We make this value the output key and concatenate the rest of the values to make a string and make it the output value. Basically, we make the Z# values the keys to join on Z.

In the reduce phase, we know that the key is the value for Z. The values collection have two types of strings. One has X values, which are URIs for graduate students and also Y values from which they got their undergraduate degree. The Z value, that is, the key, may or may not be a subOrganizationOf the Y value. The other types of strings have only Y values that are universities and of which the Z value is a suborganization. We iterate over the values collection and then join the two types of tuples on Y values. From the join output, we find the result tuples that have values for X, Y, and Z.

13.6 Results

Before we present our evaluation result, we first present the benchmark data sets with which we experimented with, the alternative repositories we evaluated for comparison, and our detailed experimental setup.

13.6.1 Data Sets, Frameworks, and Experimental Setup

13.6.1.1 Data Sets

In our experiments with SPARQL query processing, we use two synthetic data sets: LUBM [GUO05] and SP2B [SCHM09]. The LUBM data set generates data about universities by using an ontology [LEHI]. It has 14 standard queries. Some of the queries require inference to an answer. The LUBM data set is very good for both inference and scalability testing. For all LUBM data sets, we used the default seed. The SP2B data set is good for scalability testing with complex queries and data access patterns. It has 16 queries most of which have complex structures.

13.6.1.2 Baseline Frameworks

We compared our framework with RDF-3X [NEUM08], Jena [JENA], and BigOWLIM [ONTO]. RDF-3X is considered the fastest semantic web framework with persistent storage. Jena is an open source framework for semantic web data. It has several models that can be used to store and retrieve RDF data. We chose Jena's in-memory and SDB models to compare our framework with. As the name suggests, the in-memory model stores the data in the main memory and does not persist data. The SDB model is a persistent model and can use many off-the-shelf database management systems. We used MySQL database as SDB's backend in our experiments. BigOWLIM is a proprietary framework that is the state-of-the-art significantly fast framework for semantic web data. It can act both as a persistent and as a nonpersistent storage. All of these frameworks run in a single machine setup.

13.6.1.3 Experimental Setup

Hardware: We have a 10-node Hadoop cluster that we use for our framework. Each of the nodes has the following configuration: Pentium IV 2.80 GHz processor, 4 GB main memory, and 640 GB disk space. We ran Jena, RDF-3X, and BigOWLIM frameworks on a powerful single machine having 2.80 GHz quad core processor, 8 GB main memory, and 1 TB disk space.

Software: We used hadoop-0.20.1 for our framework. We compared our framework with Jena-2.5.7, which used MySQL 14.12 for its SDB model. We used BigOWLIM version 3.2.6. For RDF-3X, we utilized version 0.3.5 of the source code.

13.6.2 Evaluation

We present performance comparison between our framework, RDF-3X, Jena In-Memory and SDB models, and BigOWLIM. More details are found in [HUSA11a]. We used three LUBM data sets: 10,000, 20,000, and 30,000, which have more than 1.1, 2.2, and 3.3 billion triples, respectively. The initial population time for RDF-3X took 655, 1756, and 3353 min to load the data sets, respectively. This shows that the

RDF-3X load time is increasing exponentially. LUBM (30,000) has three times as many triples as LUBM (10,000), yet it requires more than five times as long to load.

For evaluation purposes, we chose LUBM Queries 1, 2, 4, 9, 12, and 13 to be reported in this work. These queries provide a good mixture and include simple and complex structures, inference, and multiple types of joins. They are representatives of other queries of the benchmark and so reporting only these covers all types of variations found in the queries we left out and also saves space. Query 1 is a simple selective query. RDF-3X is much faster than HadoopRDF for this query. RDF-3X utilizes six indexes [NEUM08] and these six indexes actually make up the data set. The indexes provide RDF-3X a very fast way to look up triples, similar to a hash table. Hence, a highly selective query is efficiently answered by RDF-3X. Query 2 is a query with complex structures, low selectivity, and no bound objects. The result set is quite large. For this query, HadoopRDF outperforms RDF-3X for all three data set sizes. RDF-3X fails to answer the query at all when the data set size is 3.3 billion triples. RDF-3X returns memory segmentation fault error messages and does not produce any query results. Query 4 is also a highly selective query, that is, the result set size is small because of a bound object in the second triple pattern but it needs inferencing to answer it. The first triple pattern uses the class Person, which is a superclass of many classes. No resource in the LUBM data set is of type Person, rather, there are many resources that are its subtypes. RDF-3X does not support inferencing, so we had to convert the query to an equivalent query having some union operations. RDF-3X outperforms HadoopRDF for this query. Query 9 is similar in structure to Query 2 but it requires significant inferencing. The first three triple patterns of this query use classes that are not explicitly instantiated in the data set. However, the data set includes many instances of the corresponding subclasses. This is also the query that requires the largest data set join and returns the largest result set out of the queries we evaluated. RDF-3X is faster than HadoopRDF for 1.1 billion triples data set but it fails to answer the query at all for the other two data sets. Query 12 is similar to Query 4 because it is selective and has inferencing in one triple pattern. RDF-3X beats HadoopRDF for this query. Query 13 has only two triple patterns. Both of them involve inferencing. There is a bound subject in the second triple pattern. It returns the second largest result set. HadoopRDF beats RDF-3X for this query for all data sets. RDF-3X's performance is slow because the first triple pattern has very low selectivity and requires low selectivity joins to perform inference via backward chaining.

These results lead us to some simple conclusions. RDF-3X achieves the best performance for queries with high selectivity and bound objects. However, HadoopRDF outperforms RDF-3X for queries with unbound objects, low selectivity, or large data set joins. RDF-3X cannot execute the two queries with unbound objects (Queries 2 and 9) for a 3.3 billion triples data set. This demonstrates that HadoopRDF is more scalable and handles low selectivity queries more efficiently than RDF-3X.

We also compared our implementation with the Jena In-Memory model and the SDB models and BigOWLIM. Owing to space and time limitations, we performed these tests only for the LUBM Queries 2 and 9 from the LUBM data set. We chose these queries because they have complex structures and require inference. It is to be noted that BigOWLIM needed 7 GB of Java heap space to successfully load the billion triples data set. We ran BigOWLIM only for the largest three data sets as we are interested in its performance with large data sets. For each set, we obtained the results for the Jena In-Memory model, the Jena SDB model, our Hadoop implementation, and BigOWLIM, respectively. At times, the query could not complete or it ran out of memory. In most of the cases, our approach was the fastest. For Query 2, the Jena In-Memory model and the Jena SDB model were faster than our approach, giving results in 3.9 and 0.4 s, respectively. However, as the size of the data set grew, the Jena In-Memory model ran out of memory space. Our implementation was much faster than the Jena SDB model for large data sets. For example, for 110 million triples, our approach took 143.5 s as compared to about 5000 s for the Jena SDB model. We found that the Jena SDB model could not finish answering Query 9. The Jena In-Memory model worked well for small data sets but became slower than our implementation as the data set size grew and eventually ran out of memory.

For Query 2, BigOWLIM was slower than us for the 110 and 550 million data sets. For 550 million data sets, it took 22693.4 s, which is very high compared to its other timings. For the billion triple data sets, BigOWLIM was faster. It should be noted that our framework does not have any indexing or triple cache, whereas BigOWLIM exploits indexing, which it loads into the main memory when it starts. It may also prefetch triples into the main memory. For Query 9, our implementation is faster than BigOWLIM in all experiments.

It should be noted that our RDF-3X queries and HadoopRDF queries were tested using cold runs. What we mean by this is that the main memory and the file system cache were cleared prior to execution. However, for BigOWLIM, we were forced to execute hot runs. This is because it takes a significant amount of time to load a database into BigOWLIM. Therefore, we will always easily outperform BigOWLIM for cold runs. So, we actually tested BigOWLIM for hot runs against HadoopRDF for cold runs. This gives a tremendous advantage to BigOWLIM, yet for large data sets, HadoopRDF still produced much better results. This shows that HadoopRDF is much more scalable than BigOWLIM, and provides more efficient queries for large data sets.

The final tests we have performed are an in-depth scalability test. For this, we repeated the same queries for eight different data set sizes, all the way up to 6.6 billion.

In our experiments, we found that Query 1 is simple and requires only one join; thus, it took the least amount of time among all the queries. Query 2 is one of the two queries having the greatest number of triple patterns. Even though it has three times more triple patterns, it does not take thrice the Query 1 answering time because of our storage schema. Query 4 has one less triple pattern than Query 2, but it requires inferencing. As we determine inferred relations on the fly, queries requiring inference take longer times in our framework. Queries 9 and 12 also require inferencing. The details are given in [HUSA11a].

As the size of the data set grows, the increase in time to answer a query does not grow proportionately. The increase in time is always less. For example, there are 10 times as many triples in the data set of 10,000 universities than 1000 universities, but for Query 1, the time only increases by 3.76 times and for query 9 by 7.49 times. The latter is the highest increase in time, yet it is still less than the increase in the size of the data sets. Owing to space limitations, we do not report query runtimes with PS schema here. We found that the PS schema is much slower than the POS schema.

13.7 Summary and Directions

We have presented a framework capable of handling massive amounts of RDF data. Since our framework is based on Hadoop, which is a distributed and highly fault-tolerant system, it inherits these two properties automatically. The framework is highly scalable. To increase the capacity of our system, all that needs to be done is to add new nodes to the Hadoop cluster. We have proposed a schema to store RDF data, an algorithm to determine a query processing plan, whose worst case is bounded, to answer a SPARQL query and a simplified cost model to be used by the algorithm. Our experiments demonstrate that our system is highly scalable. If we increase the data volume, the delay introduced to answer a query does not increase proportionally. The results indicate that for very large data sets (over one billion triples), HadoopRDF is preferable and more efficient if the query includes low selectivity joins or significant inference. Other solutions may be more efficient if the query includes bound objects that produce high selectivity.

In the future, we would like to extend the work in multiple directions. First, we will investigate a more sophisticated query model. We will cache statistics for the most frequent queries and use dynamic programming to exploit the statistics. Second, we will evaluate the impact of the number of reducers, the only parameter of a Hadoop job specifiable by user, on the query runtimes. Third, we will investigate indexing opportunities and further usage of binary formats. Finally, we will handle more complex SPARQL patterns, for example, queries having OPTIONAL blocks.

References

[ABAD07] Abadi, D.J., A. Marcus, S.R. Madden, and K. Hollenbach, Scalable semantic web data management using vertical partitioning, *Proceedings of the 33rd International Conference on Very Large Data Bases*, 2007, Vienna, Austria.

[ABAD09a] Abadi, D.J. Data management in the cloud: Limitations and opportunities, *IEEE Data Engineering Bulletin*, 32(1): 3–12, March 2009.

[ABAD09b] Abadi, D.J., A. Marcus, S.R. Madden, and K. Hollenbach, SW-store: A vertically partitioned DBMS for semantic web data management, *VLDB Journal*, 18(2): 385–406, April 2009.

[ABOU09] Abouzeid, A., K. Bajda-Pawlikowski, D.J. Abadi, A. Silberschatz, and A. Rasin. HadoopDB: An architectural hybrid of MapReduce and DBMS technologies for analytical workloads, *Proceedings of VLDB Endowment*, 2, 922–933, 2009.

[ATRE08] Atre, M., J. Srinivasan, and J.A. Hendler, BitMat: A main-memory bit matrix of RDF triples for conjunctive triple pattern queries, *Proceedings of the International Semantic Web Conference*, 2008, Karlsruhe, Germany.

[BONC06] Boncz, P., T. Grust, M. van Keulen, S. Manegold, J. Rittinger, and J. Teubner, MonetDB/XQuery: A fast XQuery processor powered by a relational engine, *Proceedings of the ACM SIGMOD International Conference on Management of Data*, pp. 479–490, 2006, Chicago, IL.

[CARR04] Carroll, J.J., I. Dickinson, C. Dollin, D. Reynolds, A. Seaborne, and K. Wilkinson, Jena: Implementing the semantic web recommendations, *Proceedings of the 13th International World Wide Web Conference on Alternate Track Papers and Posters*, pp. 74–83, 2004, New York, NY.

[CHAL] Semantic Web Challenge http://challenge.semanticweb.org.

[CHAN06] Chang, F., J. Dean, S. Ghemawat, W.C. Hsieh, D.A. Wallach, M. Burrows, T. Chandra, A. Fikes, and R.E. Gruber, Bigtable: A distributed storage system for structured data, *Proceedings of the Seventh USENIX Symposium on Operating System Design and Implementation*, November 2006, 205–218, Seattle, WA.

[CHEB07] Chebotko, A., S. Lu, and F. Fotouhi, *Semantics Preserving SPARQL-to-SQL Translation*, Technical Report TR-DB-112007-CLF, 2007.

[CHON05] Chong, E.I., S. Das, G. Eadon, and J. Srinivasan, An efficient SQL-based RDF querying scheme, *Proceedings of the International Conference on Very Large Data Bases (VLDB '05)*, 2005, 1216–1227, Trondheim, Norway.

[CHU07] Chu, C.T., S.K. Kim, Y.A. Lin, Y. Yu, G. Bradski, A.Y. Ng, and K. Olukotun, MapReduce for machine learning on multicore, *Proceedings of Neural Information Processing Systems (NIPS)*, 2006, Vancouver, BC, Canada.

[CLOU] Cloudera University: http://www.cloudera.com/blog/2010/03/how-raytheon-researchers-are-using-hadoop-to-build-a-scalable-distributed-triple-store.

[COMP] National University of Singapore School of Computing: http://www.comp.nus.edu.sg/~epic/.

[CYGA05] Cyganiak, R. *A Relational Algebra for SPARQL*, Technical Report HPL-2005-170, 2005.

[DEAN04] Dean, J. and S. Ghemawat, MapReduce: Simplified data processing on large clusters, *Proceedings of the Sixth Conference Symposium on Operating Systems Design and Implementation*, 2004, 137–150, San Francisco, CA.

[DING05] Ding, L., T. Finin, Y. Peng, P.P. da Silva, and D.L. Mcguinness, Tracking RDF graph provenance using RDF molecules, *Proceedings of the Fourth International Semantic Web Conference*, 2005, Galway, Ireland.

[ELMA94] Elmasri, R. and B. Navathe, *Fundamentals of Database Systems*. Pearson Education, 1994., Boston, MA.

[GUO04] Guo, Y., Z. Pan, and J. Heflin, An evaluation of knowledge base systems for large OWL datasets, *Proceedings of the International Semantic Web Conference*, 2004, Hiroshima, Japan.

[GUO05] Guo, Y., Z. Pan, and J. Heflin, LUBM: A benchmark for OWL knowledge base systems, *Web Semantics: Science, Services and Agents on the World Wide Web*, 3, 158–182, 2005.

[GUO06] Guo, Y. and J. Heflin, A scalable approach for partitioning OWL knowledge bases, *Proceedings of the Second International Workshop on Scalable Semantic Web Knowledge Base Systems*, 2006, Athens, GA.

[HADOa] Apache Software Foundation: http://hadoop.apache.org.

[HADOb] Apache Software Foundation: http://hadoop.apache.org/core/docs/r0.18.3/hdfs_design.html.

[HUSA09] Husain, M.F., P. Doshi, L. Khan, and B. Thuraisingham, Storage and retrieval of large RDF graph using Hadoop and MapReduce, *Proceedings of the First International Conference on Cloud Computing*, http://www.utdal- las.edu/mfh062000/techreport1.pdf, 2009, Beijing, China.

[HUSA10] Husain, M.F., L. Khan, M. Kantarcioglu, and B. Thuraisingham, Data intensive query processing for large RDF graphs using cloud computing tools, *Proceedings of the IEEE International Conference on Cloud Computing*, pp. 1–10, July 2010, Miami, FL.

[HUSA11a] Husain, M.F., J.P. McGlothlin, M.M. Masud, L.R. Khan, and B.M. Thuraisingham, Heuristics-based query processing for large RDF graphs using cloud computing, *IEEE Transactions on Knowledge and Data Engineering*, 23(9): 1312–1327, 2011.

[HUSA11b] Husain, M.F., *Data Intensive Query Processing for Semantic Web Data Using Hadoop and MapReduce*, PhD Thesis, University of Texas at Dallas, May 2011.

[ITEE] The University of Queensland Australia, School of Information Technology and Electrical Engineering: http://www.itee.uq.edu.au/eresearch/projects/biomanta.

[JENA] Apache Software Foundation: http://jena.sourceforge.net.

[KIRY05] Kiryakov, A., D. Ognyanov, and D. Manov, OWLIM: A pragmatic semantic repository for OWL, *Proceedings of the International Workshop on Scalable Semantic Web Knowledge Base Systems (SSWS)*, 2005, New York, NY.

[LEHI] Lehigh University: http://www.lehigh.edu/~zhp2/2004/0401/univ-bench.owl.

[MCGL09] McGlothlin, J.P. and L.R. Khan, RDFKB: Efficient support for RDF inference queries and knowledge management, *Proceedings of the International Database Engineering and Applications Symposium (IDEAS)*, 2009, Cetraro, Italy.

[MCGL10] McGlothlin, J.P. and L. Khan, Materializing and persisting inferred and uncertain knowledge in RDF datasets, *Proceedings of the AAAI Conference on Artificial Intelligence*, 2010, Atlanta, GA.

[MCNA07] Mcnabb, A.W., Monson, C.K., and K.D. Seppi, MRPSO: MapReduce particle swarm optimization, *Proceedings of the Annual Conference on Genetic and Evolutionary Computation (GECCO)*, 2007, London, England, UK.

[MIKA08] Mika, P. and G. Tummarello, Web semantics in the clouds, *IEEE Intelligent Systems*, 23(5), 82–87, Sept./Oct. 2008.

[MORE07] Moreira, J.E., M.M. Michael, D.D. Silva, D. Shiloach, P. Dube, and L. Zhang, Scalability of the Nutch search engine, *Proceedings of the 21st Annual International Conference on Supercomputing (ICS '07)*, pp. 3–12, June 2007, Rotterdam, The Netherlands.

[MORE08] Moretti, C., K. Steinhaeuser, D. Thain, and N. Chawla, Scaling up classifiers to cloud computers, *Proceedings of the IEEE International Conference on Data Mining (ICDM '08)*, 2008, Pisa, Italy.

[NEUM08] Neumann, T. and G. Weikum, RDF-3X: A RISC-Style Engine for RDF, *Proceedings of VLDB Endowment*, 1(1), 647–659, 2008.

[NEWM08] Newman, A., J. Hunter, Y.F. Li, C. Bouton, and M. Davis, A scale-out RDF molecule store for distributed processing of biomedical data, *Proceedings of the Semantic Web for Health Care and Life Sciences Workshop*, 2008, Karlsruhe, Germany.

[OLST08] C. Olston, B. Reed, U. Srivastava, R. Kumar, and A. Tomkins, Pig latin: A not-so-foreign language for data processing, *Proceedings of the ACM SIGMOD International Conference on Management of Data*, 2008, Vancouver, BC, Canada.

[ONTO] Ontotext AD: http://www.ontotext.com/owlim/big/index.html.

[OPEN] OpenRDF: http://www.openrdf.org.

[PANT07] Pantel, P. Data catalysis: Facilitating large-scale natural language data processing, *Proceedings of the International Symposium on Universal Communication*, 2007, Kuoto, Japan.

[ROHL07] Rohloff, K., M. Dean, I. Emmons, D. Ryder, and J. Sumner, An evaluation of triple-store technologies for large data stores, *Proceedings of the OTM Confederated International Conference on the Move to Meaningful Internet Systems*, 2007, Vilamoura, Portugal.

[SCHM09] Schmidt, M., T. Hornung, G. Lausen, and C. Pinkel, SP2Bench: A SPARQL performance benchmark, *Proceedings of the 25th International Conference on Data Engineering (ICDE '09)*, 2009, Shanghai, China.

[SIDI08] Sidirourgos, L., R. Goncalves, M. Kersten, N. Nes, and S. Manegold, Column-store support for RDF data management: Not all swans are white, *Proceedings of VLDB Endowment*, 1(2): 1553–1563, August 2008.

[SISM10] Sismanis, Y., S. Das, R. Gemulla, P. Haas, K. Beyer, and J. McPherson, Ricardo: Integrating R and Hadoop, *Proceedings of the ACM SIGMOD International Conference on the Management of Data (SIGMOD)*, 2010, Indianapolis, IN.

[STOC08] Stocker, M., A. Seaborne, A. Bernstein, C. Kiefer, and D. Reynolds, SPARQL basic graph pattern optimization using selectivity estimation, *WWW '08: Proceedings of the 17th International Conference on World Wide Web*, 2008, Beijing, China.

[STON05] Stonebraker, M., D. Abadi, A. Batkin, X. Chen, M. Cherniack, M. Ferreira, E. Lau et al., C-store: A column-oriented DBMS, *VLDB '05: Proceedings of the 31st International Conference on Very Large Data Bases*, pp. 553–564, 2005, Trondheim, Norway.

[URBA09] Urbani, J., S. Kotoulas, E. Oren, and F. van Harmelen, Scalable distributed reasoning using MapReduce, *Proceedings of the International Semantic Web Conference*, 2009, Linz, Austria.

[W3a] World Wide Web Consortium: http://www.w3.org/2001/sw/RDFCore/ntriples.

[W3b] World Wide Web Consortium: http://www.w3.org/TR/rdf-concepts/#dfn-rdf-triple.

[W3c] World Wide Web Consortium: http://www.w3.org/TR/rdf-primer.

[W3d] World Wide Web Consortium: http://www.w3.org/TR/rdf-sparql-query/#defn_QueryVariable.

[W3e] World Wide Web Consortium: http://www.w3.org/TR/rdf-sparql-query/#defn_TriplePattern.

[W3f] World Wide Web Consortium: http://www.w3.org/TR/rdf-syntax-grammar.

[WANG10] Wang, J., S. Wu, H. Gao, J. Li, and B.C. Ooi, Indexing multi-dimensional data in a cloud system, *Proceedings of the ACM SIGMOD International Conference on Management of Data (SIGMOD)*, 2010, Indianapolis, IN.

[WEAV09] Weaver, J. and J.A. Hendler, Parallel materialization of the finite RDFS closure for hundreds of millions of triples, *Proceedings of the Eighth International Semantic Web Conference*, 2009, Linz, Austria.

[WEIS08] Weiss, C., P. Karras, and A. Bernstein, Hexastore: Sextuple indexing for semantic web data management, *Proceedings of VLDB Endowment*, 1(1): 1008–1019, 2008.

[WIKIa] http://wiki.apache.org/hadoop/JobTracker.

[WIKIb] http://wiki.apache.org/hadoop/TaskTracker.

[XU10] Xu, Y., P. Kostamaa, and L. Gao, Integrating Hadoop and parallel DBMs, *Proceedings of the ACM SIGMOD International Conference on Management of Data (SIGMOD)*, 2010, Indianapolis, IN.

Chapter 14

Social Networking on the Cloud

14.1 Overview

This chapter describes a cloud-based system called SNODSOC (stream-based novel class detection for social network analysis) that we are developing to detect evolving patterns and trends in social blogs. SNODSOC extends our powerful data mining system called SNOD (stream-based novel class detection) for detecting classes of blogs. We also describe SNODSOC++, which is an extended version of SNODSOC for detecting multiple novel classes.

Social media such as Facebook, Twitter, and YouTube have become the most popular ways for groups to communicate and share information with each other. Social media communication differs from traditional data communication in many ways. For example, with social media communication, it is possible to exchange numerous messages in a very short period of time, Furthermore, the communication messages (e.g., blogs and tweets) are often abbreviated and difficult to follow. To understand the motives, sentiments, and behavior of the various social media groups, some of them malicious, tools are needed to make sense out of the social network communication messages often represented as graphs. To address this need, we have designed a semantic framework for analyzing stream-based social media communication data.

We have developed a powerful machine learning tool called SNOD. SNOD is a unique data stream classification technique that can classify and detect novel classes in data streams. SNOD has been successfully applied on NASA's Aviation Safety Reporting System (ASRS) data set. SNOD has many potential applications such as analyzing social networks, credit card fraud detection, blogs and tweets detection, and text stream classification. We utilized SNOD to develop a sophisticated social

269

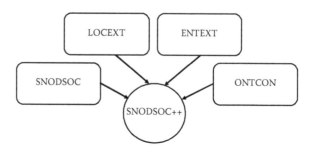

Figure 14.1   Framework. (From Abrol,S., Khan, L., Khadilkar, V., Cadenhead, T. Design and implementation of SNODSOC: Novel class detectionfor social network analysis, *Proceedings of the 2012 International Conference on Intelligence and Security Informatics,* **p. 215–220. © (2012) IEEE. With permission.)**

network analysis system called SNODSOC. Mining blogs and twitter messages can be modeled as a data stream classification problem. SNODSOC analyzes social network data such as blogs and twitter messages. We are implementing SNODSOC utilizing our cloud computing framework. Owing to the massive amounts of social media data that has to be processed, a cloud-based implementation is needed for scalability and performance.

In addition to SNODSOC, we are also developing tools for location extraction (LOCEXT), concept/entity extraction (ENTEXT), and ontology construction (ONTCON). These tools are being integrated to develop a semantic framework for analyzing social media communication data. The integrated system is called SNODSOC++. Figure 14.1 illustrates our framework.

This chapter is organized as follows. Section 14.2 discusses the foundational technologies that we have used to develop scalable solutions for SNODSOC, LOCEXT, ENTEXT, and ONTCON. These include SNOD as well as our preliminary tools for location extraction, entity extraction, ontology construction, as well as cloud query processing. SNODSOC will be discussed in Section 14.3. SNODSOC++ will be discussed in Section 14.4. Cloud-based social network analysis (SNA) is

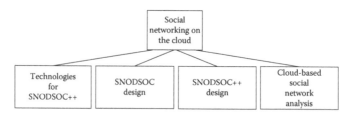

Figure 14.2   Social networking on the cloud. (From Abrol,S., Khan, L., Khadilkar, V., Cadenhead, T. Design and implementation of SNODSOC: Novel class detectionfor social network analysis, *Proceedings of the 2012 International Conference on Intelligence and Security Informatics,* **p. 215–220. © (2012) IEEE. With permission.)**

discussed in Section 14.5. Related work is discussed in Section 14.6. This chapter concludes with Section 14.7. Figure 14.2 illustrates the contents of this chapter.

14.2 Foundational Technologies for SNODSOC and SNODSOC++

In this section, we describe the several tools that we have developed that form the basis for the components illustrated in Figure 14.1. These components are discussed in Section 14.3.

14.2.1 SNOD

SNOD uses our data stream learning algorithms to detect novel classes [MASU11a], [MASU11b], [MASU12], [MASU10]. Three major challenges in data stream classification are infinite stream length, concept-drift, and concept-evolution. SNOD addresses the infinite stream length and concept-drift problems by applying a hybrid batch-incremental process, which is carried out as follows. The data stream is divided into equal-sized chunks and a classification model is trained from each chunk.

An ensemble of L such models is used to classify the unlabeled data. When a new model is trained from a data chunk, it replaces one of the existing models in the ensemble. In this way, the ensemble is kept current. The infinite stream length problem is addressed by maintaining a fixed-sized ensemble, and the concept-drift is addressed by keeping the ensemble current. SNOD solves the concept-evolution problem by automatically detecting novel classes in the data stream. To detect a novel class, it first builds a decision boundary around the training data. During the classification of unlabeled data, it first identifies the test data points that are outside the decision boundary. Such data points are called *filtered outliers (F-outliers)*; they represent data points that are well separated from the training data. If a sufficient number of F-outliers are found that show strong cohesion among themselves (i.e., they are close together), the F-outliers are classified as novel class instances.

Figure 14.3 summarizes the SNOD algorithm proposed by [MASU11a]. A classification model is trained from the last labeled data chunk. This model is used to update the existing ensemble. The latest data point in the stream is tested by the ensemble. If it is found to be an outlier, it is temporarily stored in a buffer. Otherwise, it is classified immediately using the current ensemble. The temporary buffer is processed periodically to detect whether the instances in the buffer belong to a novel class.

14.2.2 Location Extraction

We will discuss some of our prior work on location extraction and social network analysis. Our first related work, MapIt [ABRO09], uses an efficient algorithm and heuristics to identify and disambiguate the correct location from the unstructured text present in Craigslist advertisements. The major challenge associated with geo-parsing

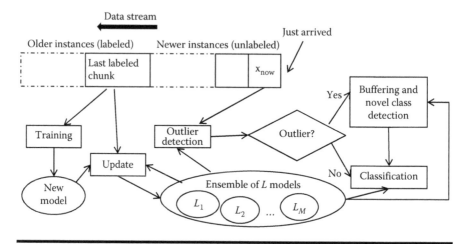

Figure 14.3 SNOD algorithm.

(determining geographic coordinates of textual words and phrases that occur in unstructured content) is the resolution of ambiguity. There are two types of ambiguities that exist: geo/nongeo and geo/geo ambiguities. Geo/nongeo ambiguity is the case of a place name having another, nongeographic meaning, for example, Paris might be the capital of France or might refer to the socialite Paris Hilton. Geo/geo ambiguity arises from the two having the same name but different geographic locations. For example, Paris is the capital of France and is also a city in Texas. Smith et al. report that 92% of all names occurring in their corpus are ambiguous. MapIt resolves this ambiguity by using a nine-point heuristic algorithm that goes beyond the previous work to identify the location up to the street level with 85% accuracy. We have developed a fully functional prototype and tested on real data set collected from the Craigslist website.

In our second related work [CHAN11], we use a probabilistic framework (PDF) to estimate the city-level Twitter user location for each user. The probabilities are based on the contents of the tweet messages with the aid of reply-tweet messages generated from the interaction between different users in the Twitter social network. The use of reply-tweet messages provides better association of words with the user location, thus reducing the noise in the spatial distribution of terms. We also provide the top K list of most probable cities for each user. We find that our estimation of the user location is within 100 miles of the actual user location 22% of the time, as compared to the previous work that had an accuracy of about 10%, using a similar PDF.

14.2.3 Entity/Concept Extraction and Integration

We have developed a machine learning approach to entity and relation extraction. In particular, we investigated two types of extensions to existing machine learning approaches.

14.2.3.1 Linguistic Extensions

These extensions are concerned with incorporating additional linguistic knowledge sources into the existing machine learning framework for entity and relation extraction. First, we examined how the information is derived from the fixed ontology (and can be profitably integrated with the learned classifiers for making classification decisions). We represented such information as features for training classifiers; we also classified an entity or relation directly using the available ontologies and resorted to the learned classifiers only if the desired information is absent from the ontologies.

14.2.3.2 Extralinguistic Extensions

While supervised machine learning approaches reduce a system's reliance on ontology, the performance of a learning-based system depends heavily on the availability of a large amount of annotated data, which can be expensive to obtain. Consequently, we developed three extralinguistic extensions that aim to improve the robustness of an extraction system in the face of limited annotated data. They are (i) combining knowledge-based and learning-based approaches to entity extraction and relation extraction, (ii) incorporating domain adaptation techniques, and (iii) automatically generating additional training data.

14.2.3.3 Entity Integration

Once entities and relations are extracted from free text, they have to be integrated to create a combined semantic representation. During entity extraction, some extracted entities may be erroneous/irrelevant and some extracted ones relevant. Hence, we discarded irrelevant entities and keep relevant ones. Next, we consolidated the entities that will come from multiple documents. It is possible that an entity may have multiple references in various documents that refer to the same entity in real life. We solved the following two relevant challenges: (1) remove irrelevant entities in a document generated by information extraction techniques and (2) consolidate the extracted entities among documents so that we can establish a "same as" relationship between entities that are indeed the same entity.

14.2.4 Ontology Construction

We are developing a potentially powerful and novel approach for the automatic construction of domain-dependent ontologies based on the work discussed in [KHAN02]. The crux of our approach is the development of a hierarchy, and the concept selection from generic ontology for each node in the hierarchy. For developing a hierarchy, we have modified the existing self-organizing tree algorithm (SOTA) that constructs a hierarchy from top to bottom.

Next, we need to assign a concept for each node in the hierarchy. For this, we deploy two types of strategy and adopt a bottom-up concept assignment mechanism. First, for each cluster consisting of a set of documents, we assign a topic based on a modified Rocchio algorithm for topic tracking. However, if multiple concepts are candidates for a topic, we propose an intelligent method for arbitration. Next, to assign a concept to an interior node in the hierarchy, we use WordNet, a linguist ontology. Descendant concepts of the internal node will also be identified in WordNet. From these identified concepts and their hypernyms, we can identify a more generic concept that can be assigned as a concept for the interior node [MCGL10] [ALIP10].

14.2.5 Cloud Query Processing

As discussed in Chapter 13, we have developed a SPARQL query processing system on the cloud. Essentially, we have developed a framework to query RDF data stored over Hadoop. We used the Pellet reasoner to reason at various stages. We carried out real-time query reasoning using the pellet libraries coupled with Hadoop's MapReduce functionalities. Our RDF query processing is composed of two main steps: (1) the preprocessing and (2) the query optimization and execution (Figure 14.4).

14.2.5.1 Preprocessing

To execute a SPARQL query on RDF data, we carried out data preprocessing steps and stored the preprocessed data in HDFS. A separate MapReduce task was written

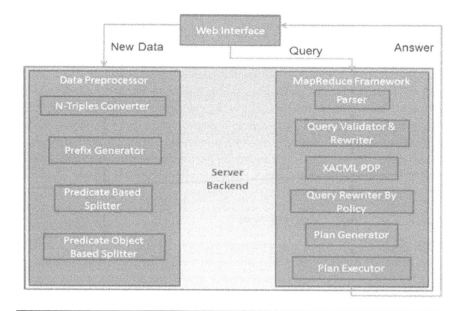

Figure 14.4   Cloud query processing.

to perform the conversion of RDF/XML data into N-Triples as well as for prefix generation. Our storage strategy is based on predicate splits [HUSA11].

14.2.5.2 Query Execution and Optimization

We have developed a SPARQL query execution and optimization module for Hadoop. As our storage strategy is based on predicate splits, first, we examine the predicates present in the query. Second, we examine a subset of the input files that are matched with predicates. Third, SPARQL queries generally have many joins in them and all of these joins may not be possible to perform in a single map-reduce job. Therefore, we have developed an algorithm that decides the number of jobs required for each kind of query. As part of optimization, we applied a greedy strategy and cost-based optimization to reduce the query processing time [HUSA11].

14.3 Design of SNODSOC

14.3.1 Overview of the Modules

Internet social media services, such as microblogging and social networking, which are offered by platforms such as Twitter, have seen a phenomenal growth in their user bases. This microblogging phenomenon has been discussed as early as the mid-2000s noting that users use the service to talk about their daily activities and to seek or share information. This growth has spurred an interest in using the data provided by these platforms for extracting various types of information. We have designed the following tools for social network analysis (as illustrated in Figure 14.1).

a. Trend analysis, including SNODSOC
b. Geographic location extraction of the users from the blogs and tweets (LOCEXT)
c. Message categorization and entity extraction (ENTEXT)
d. Ontology construction (ONTCON)

These tools will form the framework for SNODSOC++ that will carry out sophisticated social network analysis. In particular, we developed a set of techniques that will facilitate (a) emerging trend analysis; (b) geographic location extraction; (c) message categorization and entity extraction; and (d) ontology construction. The mentioned extraction process will be time consuming. Hence, we are exploiting a cloud-computing solution to speed up the extraction process. The extracted knowledge can be used to provide users with personalized services, such as local news, local advertisements, application sharing, and so on. With more than 200 million accounts on Twitter in diverse geographical locations, the short messages, or tweets, form a huge data set that can be analyzed to extract such geographic information.

14.3.2 SNODSOC and Trend Analysis

Twitter has emerged as not only a major form of social networking, but also as a new and growing form of communication. Twitter continues to increase both its number of users and its number of tweets. Tweets quickly reflect breaking news stories. Often, the first source of news about a natural disaster, a crime, or a political event is tweets. Twitter also serves as the communication mechanism for groups and community organizations. Twitter has had significant impact in political events and protest groups.

Recently, Twitter communications were credited for their significant influence in the toppling of political regimes in Egypt and Libya. Twitter can provide a way for individuals to communicate without depending on traditional media outlets. This new paradigm of communication via Twitter services provides new challenges for stream data mining. Tweets flow in a continuous stream. Our goal is to decipher and monitor the topics in these tweets as well as detect when trends emerge. This includes general changes in topics such as sports or fashion and it includes new, quickly emerging trends such as deaths or catastrophes. This is a challenging problem to correctly associate tweet messages with trends and topics. These challenges are best addressed with a streaming model due to the continuous and large volume of incoming messages.

At the heart of our system is the classification model of SNOD (Figure 14.5). To build this model, we can use K-NN approach or multilabel text classification. This model will be incrementally updated with feature data obtained from new twitter messages. When a new message (i.e., tweet) is chosen as a training example, it will be analyzed and its features will be recorded. This recorded data will be stored in a temporal database that will hold the data for a batch of N messages at a time. When

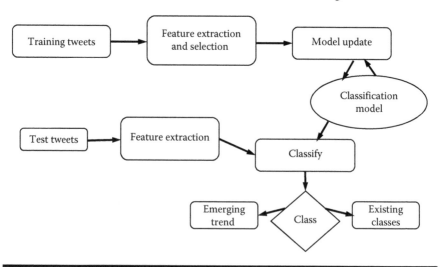

Figure 14.5   Classification model.

a batch of data has been processed, it will be discarded, and a new batch will be stored. Each batch of data will undergo a feature extraction and selection phase. The selected features will be used to compute feature vectors (one vector per message). These vectors will be used to update the existing classification model using an incremental learning technique. When an unknown executable appears in the system, at first its runtime and network behavior will be monitored and recorded. This data will then undergo a similar feature extraction phase, but no feature selection will be needed here because the same features selected in the training/update phase will be used to build the feature vector. This feature vector will be classified using the classification model. Based on the class label, appropriate measures will be taken.

14.3.2.1 Novel Class Detection

The feature extraction and categorization process discussed above generates feature vectors for fixed-sized training data. To cope with the ever-growing volume of tweets, we must extend this to a data stream framework. Our data stream classifier [MASU11a, MASU10, MASU11b, MASU12] can handle massive volumes of training and test data, as well as concept-drift, novel classes, and feature-evolution in the stream. Recall that we assume that the data stream is divided into equal-sized chunks. The heart of this system is an ensemble L of M classifiers $\{L_1,\ldots, L_M\}$. When a new unlabeled executable (test instance) arrives, the ensemble is used to classify the instance. If the test instance is identified as outlier, it is temporarily stored in a buffer *buf* for further inspection. Otherwise, if it is not outlier, then it is classified as either *benign* or *malicious*. The buffer is periodically checked to see if a novel class has appeared. If a novel class is detected, the instances belonging to the novel class are identified and tagged accordingly. As soon as a new labeled data chunk arrives, it is used to train a classifier L'. Then, the existing ensemble is updated by choosing the best M classifiers from the $M + 1$ classifiers $L \cup \{L'\}$ based on their accuracies on the latest labeled data chunk D_n (see Algorithm A).

The central concept of our novel class detection technique is that the data points belonging to a common class should be closer to each other (cohesion) and should be far apart from the data points belonging to other classes (separation). When the *buf* is examined for novel classes, we look for strong cohesion among the outliers in *buf*, and large separation between the outliers and training data. If such strong cohesion and separation is found, we declare it a novel class. When the true labels of the novel class instances are revealed by human experts, these instances are used as training data, and a new model is trained. Finally, the existing ensemble is updated with that model. Therefore, the ensemble of models is continuously enriched with new classes. Algorithm A summarizes the technique.

Creating decision boundary during training: The training data are clustered using K-means and the summary of each cluster is saved as a *pseudopoint*. Then the raw training data are discarded. These pseudopoints form a decision boundary for the training data.

14.3.2.2 Storing the Cluster Summary Information

For each cluster, we store the following summary information in a pseudopoint data structure: (i) *weight w*: the total number of points in the cluster, (ii) *centroid μ*, (iii) *radius r*: the distance between the centroid and the farthest data point in the cluster, and (iv) *mean distance μd*: the mean distance from each point to the cluster centroid. Thus, notation $w(h)$ denotes the weight value of a pseudopoint h, and so on. After computing the cluster summaries, the raw data are discarded and only the pseudopoints are stored in memory. Any pseudopoint having too few (less than three) instances is considered as noise and is also discarded. Thus, the memory requirement for storing the training data becomes constant, namely, $O(K)$.

Outlier detection and filtering: Each pseudopoint h corresponds to a hypersphere in the feature space having center $\mu(h)$ and radius $R(h)$. The portion of the feature space covered by a pseudopoint h is the pseudopoint's *region RE(h)*. The union of the regions of all pseudopoints in classifier L_i is the decision boundary for the training data of L_i. The decision boundary for the ensemble of classifiers L is the union of the decision boundaries of all classifiers in the ensemble. The decision boundary plays an important role in novel class detection. It defines the physical boundary of existing class instances.

Each test instance is first tested to see if it is outside the decision boundary of the existing class instances. To compute this, we find the nearest pseudopoint from the test instance in each classifier. If the test instance is outside the radius of each of the pseudopoints in all the classifiers, it is considered as an outlier. We refer to any test instance outside the decision boundary as an *F-outlier*.

Algorithm A: Stream-based Novel Class Detection
Input: L: Current ensemble of best M classifiers
x: an unknown instance to be classified
Output: Class label of x or detection of novel class

1. *outlier* ← detectOutlier(x, L)
2. **if** (*outlier* = *false*) **then**
3. classify(x, L)   //classify as benign or malicious
4. **else** *buf* ⇐ x //save in outlier buffer
5: **if** time to check *buf* **then**
found ← *DetectNovelClass*(*buf*, L)
6: **if** *found* **then** {Y ← Novel_instances(D_n);} //tag novel instances
//if a new labeled chunk D_n is ready for training
7: L' ← *Train-new-model*(D_n)
8: L ← *Update*(L,$L\,\square$,D_n)

Novel class detection: We perform several computations on the *F*-outliers to detect the arrival of a new class. For every *F*-outlier *x*, we define its λ_c-neighborhood $\lambda_c(x)$ to be the set of *N*-nearest neighbors of *x* belonging to class *c*. Here, *N* is a user-defined parameter. For example, neighborhood $\lambda_+(x)$ is the set of *N* instances of class c_+ nearest *x*. Similarly, $\lambda_o(x)$ refers to the set of *N* *F*-outliers nearest *x*.

Using this neighborhood information, we compute the *N*-neighborhood Silhouette Coefficient (N-NSC) metric as follows: Let $a(x)$ be the average distance from an *F*-outlier *x* to the instances in $\lambda_o(x)$, and let $b_c(x)$ be the average distance from *x* to the instances in $\lambda_c(x)$ (where *c* is an existing class). Let $b_{min}(x)$ be the minimum $b_c(x)$ for all classes *c*. Then, metric $N - NSC(x)$ is given by

$$N - NSC(x) = \frac{b_{min}(x) - a(x)}{\max(b_{min}(x), a(x))}$$

According to this definition, the value of *N*-NSC is between −1 and +1. It is actually a unified measure of cohesion and separation. A negative value indicates that *x* is closer to the other classes (less separation) and farther away from its own class (less cohesion). We declare a *new class* if for all the classifiers L_i, there are at least *N′* (>*N*) *F*-outliers whose *N*-NSC is positive.

It should be noted that the larger the value of *N*, the greater the confidence with which we can decide whether a novel class has arrived. However, if *N* is too large, then we may also fail to detect a new class if the total number of instances belonging to the novel class in the corresponding data chunk is ≤*N*. Therefore, it will be important to determine an optimal value of *N* through experimental testing on realistic data sets.

Novel Class Detection with Feature-Evolution: The feature space that represents a data point in the stream may change over time; we call these phenomena "feature-evolution" [LIN11, GOYA09]. For example, consider a text stream where each data point is a tweet message, and each word is a feature. Since it is impossible to know which words will appear in the future, the complete feature space is unknown. Besides, it is customary to use only a subset of the words as the feature set because most of the words are likely to be redundant for classification. Therefore at any given time, the feature space is defined by the useful words (i.e., features) selected using some selection criteria. Since in the future, new words may become useful and old useful words may become redundant, the feature space changes dynamically. To cope with feature-evolution, the classification model should be able to correctly classify a data point having a different feature space than the feature space of the model. The following example demonstrates the feature-evolution in two continuous data chunks. In the *i*th chunk, the key feature set is {runway, climb}, and in the (*i* + 1)th chunk, the key feature set is {runway, clear, ramp}. Apparently, the key feature set in two different chunks is different, while the new key features come with the novel class emerged in (*i* + 1)th chunk. If we use the feature set of the *i*th chunk to test the instances of the (*i* + 1)th chunk, we might not be able to detect the novel class.

Most of the existing data stream classification techniques assume that the feature space of the data points in the stream is static. As seen in the above example, this assumption may be impractical for some data streams, such as text stream. Our technique will consider the dynamic nature of the feature space and provide an elegant solution for classification and novel class detection when the feature space is dynamic. If the feature space is dynamic, then we would have different feature sets in different data chunks. As a result, each model in the ensemble would be trained on different feature sets. Besides, the feature space of the test instances would also be different from the feature space of the models. When we need to classify an instance, we need to come up with a homogeneous feature space for the model and the test instances. There are three possible alternatives: (i) Lossy fixed conversion (or *Lossy-F* conversion in short): Here, we use the same feature set for the entire stream, which had been selected for the first data chunk (or first *n* data chunks). This will make the feature set fixed, and therefore all the instances in the stream, whether training or testing, will be mapped to this feature set. We call this a lossy conversion because future models and instances may lose important features due to this conversion; (ii) Lossy local conversion (or *Lossy-L* conversion in short): In this case, each training chunk, as well as the model built from the chunk, will have its own feature set selected using the feature extraction and selection technique. When a test instance is to be classified using a model M_j, the model will use its own feature set as the feature set of the test instance. This conversion is also lossy because the test instance might lose important features as a result of this conversion; and (iii) Lossless homogenizing conversion (or *Lossless* conversion in short): Here, each model has its own selected set of features. When a test instance x is to be classified using a model M_j, both the model and the instance will convert their feature sets to the union of their feature sets. We call this conversion "loss-less homogenizing" since both the model and the test instance preserve their dimensions (i.e., features), and the converted feature space becomes homogeneous for both the model and the test instance. Therefore, no useful features are lost as a result of the conversion. Since an instance may not have a fixed predetermined feature vector and due to the text we end up with variable-length high-dimensional features. Therefore, we apply feature selection to select the best features for each chunk and apply the above-mentioned techniques to make a homogeneous feature space. To tackle sparsity, we are examining the following option. To track topics/trends in a continuous stream having short messages, we are examining a hybrid model based on the combination of a foreground model and a background model. The foreground model will capture "what's happening right now" based on the ensemble-based technique as described above and a background model will combat data sparsity [LIN11].

14.3.3 Content-Driven Location Extraction

Twitter allows its users to specify their geographical location as user information (Meta-Data). This location information is manually entered by the user or updated with a GPS-enabled device. The feature to update the user location with a GPS-enabled device has not been adopted by a significant number of users [CHEN10]. Hence, this geographic location data for most users may be missing or incorrect. There are several drawbacks to relying on a user's manual update of the location.

1. Users may have incorrect geographic location data. For example, a Twitter user may enter his/her location as "Krypton." This may not be the name of a real geographic location.
2. Users may not always have a city-level location. Users can input location names vaguely, such as the name of a state (e.g., Arizona) or the name of a country (e.g., United States). These location names cannot be directly used in determining the city-level location of the user.
3. Users may have multiple locations. If a user travels to different locations, he/she might mention more than one location in the Meta-Data of his/her Twitter page. This makes it very difficult to determine their current, singular city-level geographic location.
4. Users may have incomplete location data. A user may have specified an ambiguous name that may refer to different locations. For example, if a user specifies a location such as "Washington," this name can be related to a state name or a city name (Washington DC). These types of ambiguous names make it difficult to determine the exact user location.

Therefore, the reliability of such data for determining a city-level geographic location of a user is low. To overcome this problem of sparsely available geo-location information of users, we evaluate the Twitter user's city-level geographic location based purely on his/her tweet content along with the content of the related reply-tweet messages. We use a PDF that considers a distribution of terms used in the tweet messages of a certain conversation containing reply-tweet messages, initiated by the user. Our tool is built on our foundational work discussed in Section 14.2.

14.3.3.1 Motivation

On Twitter, users can post microblogs known as tweets, which can be read by other users. Along with this microblogging service, Twitter also provides a social network-ing service where a user *(follower)* can "follow" another user *(followee)*. Each edge of the social network is formed by this "follow" relationship. As a *follower*, a user receives all the tweets posted by the *followee*, and in turn can reply to these tweets with a reply-tweet. This reply-tweet is received by the *followee* from the *follower*. This forms the basis of a conversation between two different users. Huberman et al. [HUBE09] analyzed more than 300 thousand users and found that reply-tweets and directed tweets constitute about 25.4% of all posts on Twitter. This shows that the reply-tweet feature is used widely among Twitter users. (Figure 14.6 illustrates an example tweet).

Figure 14.6 Example tweet.

Our intuition is that a conversation between users can be related to a set of top-ics such as weather, sports, and so on, including certain location-specific topics such as an event related to a city or a reference to a specific place or an entity in a city. We assume this set of topics remains constant during a conversation. When a user posts a tweet message, it can be seen as the start of a conversation. This conversation can continue when another user posts a reply-tweet to the original tweet. Without detailing the topic of the reply-tweet, it can be assumed that the topic is the same as the original tweet message. Under this assumption, any content of the reply-tweet can be related back to the topic of the original tweet message. For example, consider the tweet messages exchanged by two users in Figure 14.6. A user posts a tweet message, and another user replies back with a reply-tweet message. Note that the topic of conversation remains the same during the conversation. So, by combining the above assumption, with the use of tweet content that may have location-specific data, we should obtain a better result than if we considered tweets in isolation, or if we just relied on user-specified location.

14.3.3.2 Challenges: Proposed Approach

The use of pure tweet content for estimating the Twitter user location, along with the above-mentioned intuition, presents some challenges. These challenges are based on the semantic complexities of the natural language used in tweets. Some users may use nonstandard vocabulary in their tweets. Users from a city may refer to the same location-specific entity with different names. For example, a user from

Los Angeles can refer to the name of the city as LA, L.A., City of Los Angeles, and so on. Users may also refer to different locations with the same name. For example, a user from New York can refer to 6th Street as a street name in New York, whereas a user from Austin may refer to the street with the same name in Austin. These examples can dilute the spatial distribution of the terms.

The tweets do not always contain location-specific terms. They may contain many general words from a natural language, as users tweet about general topics. Hence, the content of the tweets are considered noisy.

A tweet can have terms referencing to multiple locations. This reduces the ability to estimate a specific location of the user. When considering a conversation, the topic of a conversation may not remain the same throughout the conversation, as assumed. A change of topic in a reply-tweet may result in multiple location-specific terms or dilution of the spatial distribution of terms. Taking note of these challenges, we propose two approaches to extract city-level home location of a user from his messages or blog.

In the first approach, we use a PDF to estimate the city-level Twitter user location for each user. The probabilities are based on the contents of the tweet messages with the aid of reply-tweet messages generated from the interaction between different users in the Twitter social network. The use of reply-tweet messages provides better association of words with the user location, thus reducing the noise in the spatial distribution of terms. We also provide the top K list of most probable cities for each user.

As noted earlier, extracting geographic location-specific information from the tweet content alone is challenging. With the social interaction model, we use the content of the tweets in any interaction between users to determine the probability distribution of terms used during the conversation. In the second approach, we examine a user-centric location mining approach that looks to identify a single city-level home location of a particular user from his messages. Unlike the first approach, which is specific to messages originating from social interactions, this approach is a more general approach that works for all social media, including Twitter, blogs, and so on.

Social interactions–probability distribution model (PDM): In this probability distribution technique, each user can be assumed to belong to a particular city. Hence, the tweets of the user can be assumed to be related to a particular city, specifically the geographical location of the user who posted the tweet, that is, the terms occurring in the user's tweet can be assigned as terms related to the user's city. This forms the basic distribution of terms for the set of cities considered in the complete data set. The probability distribution of term t over the entire data set, for each city c, is given as

$$p(t|c) = |\{t|t \in \text{terms} \wedge t \text{ occurs in city } c\}|/|t|$$

A probability distribution matrix of size $n \times m$ is formed, where n is the size of the term list, that is, the size of the dictionary, and m is the total number of cities in the data set that is considered for evaluation.

Reply-based probability distribution model (RBPDM): In the basic probability distribution calculation of PDM, the terms used by a user in his/her tweet is assigned to a city to which the user belongs. It does not consider the relation between different tweet messages.

Twitter offers a feature to tag another user in a tweet called a *reply tag.* This tag directs the message to the user who is addressed in the tweet. With this in mind, a tweet message can be classified into three different types:

1. The first type of tweet message is a general message that a user typically posts on Twitter. These tweet messages do not contain any reply tag. The terms used in this type of tweet message can be used to form a direct relation with that of the user's city in evaluating the spatial distribution of terms.
2. The second kind of tweet message is one that contains the reply tag addressing a user. This type of message is called a *reply-tweet.* This message is used generally to reply to a certain tweet posted by another user. The reply-tweet message will be directed to the user who is being replied to, that is, to the user who had posted the original tweet message. This tweet will generally contain the reply tag at the beginning of the tweet message.
3. The third type of tweet message is one that has a reply tag but may not be a reply-tweet. It may be a tweet message that may be directed to a user but need not be a reply to a tweet from that user. This message may contain the reply tag in between the tweet words. It can also be a re-tweet where users repost the tweet message of a user so that his/her followers can receive the tweet message.

The relationship between two tweet messages occurs when the reply tag in a tweet is taken into consideration. The reply-tweet will have a direct relationship with the original tweet that generated the reply-tweet message from a user. The PDM distribution ignores all relationships between tweet messages. The relationship between two tweet messages occurs when the reply tag in a tweet is taken into consideration. The reply-tweet will have a direct relationship with the original tweet that generated the reply-tweet message from a user. Here, we consider this relationship between different tweet messages while calculating the probability distribution of terms from the data set. This relationship forms the basis of a conversation between different users, that is, a tweet message and its reply messages can be considered as a dialogue between the users. Hence, with the application of the assumption that the topic of a conversation is to remain constant in the reply-tweet messages, the terms used in the conversation can be related to the topic of the conversation. The conversation may involve location-specific terms related to the topic. Instead of plainly assigning the terms used in a tweet to the user who posts the tweet, the terms occurring in the complete conversation can be assigned to the user who initiated the conversation since the initiator may initiate a conversation topic involving his/her geographic location. Thus, when a reply-tweet is encountered in the data set, we assign the terms involved in the tweet to the user to which the tweet is addressed rather than to the user who posted the reply-tweet message. With this assignment of terms to different users, we evaluate the probability distribution that does not ignore recognizing the different types of tweet messages and the relationship between them. Hence, the social structure of the network is considered while estimating the geographic location of a user in the Twitter social network.

Term Distribution Estimator: Using the distribution of terms across the cities considered in the data set, the probability of a city c given a term t can be calculated based on maximum likelihood estimation.

$$p(c|t) = \max_{\forall c \in cities} p(t|c)$$

The probability estimate of the user u being located in the city c is the total probability of the terms extracted from the user tweet for the city c, that is

$$p(c|u) = \sum_{(w \in terms)} p(c|w)*p(w)$$

Using this equation, the probability estimation matrix is obtained as mentioned previously, which has size $p \times q$, where p is the size of the user list being considered and q is the size of the city list being considered in the data set. The city-level geographic location estimation can be obtained by considering the city with the highest probability for that user. A list of top k estimated cities can also be obtained by sorting the probability estimation matrix for each user, and listing the top k most probable cities from it.

14.3.3.3 Using Gazetteer and Natural Language Processing

Before running the actual algorithm (see Algorithm B), we need to perform preprocessing of data, which initially involves using an external dictionary such as the urban dictionary to understand slang words and replace them with appropriate phrases to obtain grammatically correct sentences. After this, we remove all those words from the messages that are not references to geographic locations (Figure 14.7).

For this, we use Part of Speech (POS) tagger for English. The POS tagger identifies all the proper nouns from the text and terms them as keywords $\{K_1, K_2, \ldots, K_n\}$. In the next step, the TIGER (Topologically Integrated Geographic Encoding and Referencing system) data set is searched for identifying the city names from among them. The TIGER data set is an open source gazetteer consisting of topological records and shape files with coordinates for cities, counties, zip codes, street segments, and so on for the entire United States.

We search the TIGER gazetteer for the concepts $\{C_1, C_2, \ldots, C_n\}$ pertaining to each keyword. Now, our goal for each keyword would be to pick out the right concept among the list, in other words, disambiguate the location. For this, we use a weight-based disambiguation method. We assign the weight to each concept based

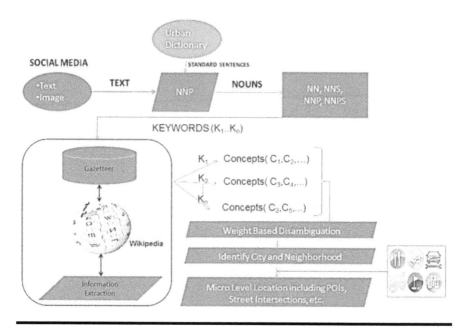

Figure 14.7 Using gazetteer and natural language processing approach.

on the occurrence of its terms in the text (phase 1). Specific concepts are assigned a greater weight as compared to the more general ones. We check for correlation between concepts, in which one concept subsumes the other (phase 2). In that case, the more specific concept gets the boosting from the more general concept. If a more specific concept C_i is part of another C_j, then the weight of C_j is added to that of C_i.

Algorithm B: Location Identification (User_Messages)
Input: UM: *All Messages of User*
Output: Vector (C, S): Concepts and Score vector

```
1: for each keyword, Kᵢ              //Phase 1
2:    for each Cⱼ ∈ Kᵢ    //Cⱼ - City Concept
3:       for each Tᶠ∈ Cⱼ
4:          type = Type (Tᶠ)
5:             If (Tᶠoccurs in UM) then S_Cj = S_Cj + S_type
6: for each Kᵢ //Phase 2
7:    for each Cⱼ ∈ Kᵢ
8:    for Tᶠ∈ Cⱼ, Tₛ∈ C_L
9:       If (Tᶠ = Tₛ) and (Cⱼ ≠ C_L) then
10:            type = Type (Tᶠ)
```

11:                    $S_{Sj} = S_{Cj} + S_{type}$
12: return (C, S)

For example, city carries 15 points, state 10, and a country name carries 5 points. For the keyword "Dallas," consider the concept of {City} Dallas/{State} Texas/{Country} USA. The concept gets 15 points because Dallas is a city name, and it gets an additional 10 points if Texas is also mentioned in the text. In phase 2, we consider the relation between two keywords. Considering the previous example, if {Dallas, Texas} are the keywords appearing in the text, then among the various concepts listed for "Dallas" would be {City} Dallas/{State} Texas/{Country} USA and one of the concepts for "Texas" would be {State} Texas/{Country} USA. Now, in phase 2, we check for such correlated concepts, in which one concept subsumes the other. In that case, the more specific concept gets the boosting from the more general concept. Here, the above-mentioned Texas concept boosts up the more specific Dallas concept. After the two phases are complete, we reorder the concepts in descending order of their weights. Next, each concept is assigned a probability depending on their individual weights.

Once the city-level location has been identified, the algorithm will next focus on identifying micro-level locations that may be mentioned in the text (blogs, tweets, etc.). For this, we would use geospatial proximity and context-based disambiguation algorithm, which uses a rich Point of Interest (POI) database (the Foursquare Venue data set is an example) to identify potential micro-level places such as coffee shops, schools, restaurants, places of worship, and so on. The algorithm would return a list of places, which match that particular keyword and are located in the city determined by us previously. Now, our goal for each keyword would be to pick out the right concept among the list, in other words, identify the correct POI the user is referring to. For this, we use a two-phase disambiguation process. The first phase consists of context-based scoring. Each POI entry in the gazetteer is associated with tags, and by using Wordnet Semantic Similarity measure, we compute the similarity between the message and the POI entry. This serves the purpose of disambiguating the correct POI based on the type of place the user might be referring to. After which, in phase 2, we simply boost the scores based on the proximity of each POI candidate to previously determined POIs for that particular user. So, if for a user, there are multiple Starbucks coffee shops returned in the Los Angeles area, the algorithm would choose the Starbucks closer to his comfort zone (probably his home or office).

14.3.4 Categorization

A major objective of our work is to extract entities from tweets and categorize the messages. Then, we provide *semantic* representation of the knowledge buried in the tweets. This would enable an analyst to interact more directly with the hidden knowledge. We build on the foundational work discussed in Section 14.2 for categorization.

Entity Extraction Entities are basic elements in knowledge representation. We have developed techniques to recognize several important entities in the messages, including event, location, people, organization, and so on. Entity extraction has been extensively studied in the literature. The most effective methods tend to cast the problem as a classification problem and apply supervised learning methods. We adopt the same strategy and leverage the many tools that are publicly available to perform this task. We start with using FEX (available at http://l2r.cs.uiuc.edu/cogcomp/asoftware.php?skey=FEX) for feature extraction and BBR (available at http://www.stat.rutgers.edu/~madigan/BBR/) for logistic regression to recognize interesting entities in the tweets. We have successfully used FEX and BBR to recognize names in NASA ASRS reports [AHME10a].

While some existing algorithms and tools are available for us to use, a major challenge we have to solve is to create labeled data for training. Labeling data is in general an expensive process. We propose to study two strategies for solving this problem: (1) we adopt a bootstrapping approach, in which we would first rely on linguistic rules to recognize easy-to-recognize instances of a given type of entity and then use the rule-based recognizer to generate training data for supervised learning; and (2) we apply domain adaptation techniques based on some existing work to leverage training data that already exists in other related domain (e.g., news domain); these techniques can effectively avoid overfitting when we reuse some existing training data. Since the extracted entities are meant to be used for data mining, we expect that we can tolerate some errors in entity recognition. In case we need to further improve accuracy, we explore possibilities to manually label some examples. The strategies discussed above can help generate the most promising positive examples for labeling. In general, active learning can be applied to selecting examples for users to judge.

Multi-Label Text Classification: The classification of social communication data and related messages plays an important role in such data analysis. To find a classification technique that is well suited for social media data, we first need to find out how such data is different from its nontext counterpart. First of all, messages in such data sets are usually written nonformally. These include very high and sparse dimensionality, as the dimension or feature space consists of all the distinct words appearing in the vocabulary of the corresponding natural language.

The second difference that we consider is its increasing tendency to associate with multiple classes for classification. Text data sets can be binary, multiclass, or multilabel in nature. For the binary and multiclass categories, only a single class label can be associated with a document and the class label association is mutually exclusive. However, in case of multilabel data, more than one class label can be associated with a message at the same time.

In multilabeled data classification, class labels can co-occur and the frequency with which different class labels co-occur indicates that the class labels are not independent of each other. Also, not all class label combinations occur in the data set. Hence, making an assumption that class labels are independent is inherently incorrect during the classification process. For example, in the *ASRS NASA* data set, we consider a total of 21 classes. There are class label combinations that can never occur together. For instance, given the label for two attributes, *Aircraft equipment problem: Critical* and *Less severe and Conflict: Less Severe* and *Critical*, we know that the labels *Aircraft equipment problem: Critical* and *Conflict: Less Severe* can never occur together, which is apparent from their names. However, an *Aircraft equipment problem: Critical* and *Conflict: Critical* classes can co-occur. During classification, considering the probability of such varying co-occurrence can, to some extent, allow us to generate clusters where such class label pairs do not co-occur.

To categorize tweets, we exploit text classification. For this, we use SISC algorithm [AHME09, AHME10a, AHME10b] that uses subspace clustering in conjunction with K-NN approach along with a semisupervised learning approach, under small or limited amount of labeled training data sets. To correctly interpret the multilabel property of such data, fuzzy clustering can perform this interpretation in a more meaningful way. In fact, the notion of fuzzy subspace clustering matches that of text data, that is, having high and sparse dimensionality and multilabel property. Subspace clustering allows us to find clusters in a weighted hyperspace [FRIG04] and can aid us in finding documents that form clusters in only a subset of dimensions. SISC [AHME09] is one such algorithm that we use in our experiments.

14.3.5 Ontology Construction

Ontology is a collection of concepts and their interrelationships, which can collectively provide an abstract view of an application domain [KHAN02]. There are two distinct problem/tasks for an ontology-based model: one is the extraction of semantic concepts from the keywords and the other is the actual construction of the ontology. With regard to the first problem, the key issue is to identify appropriate concepts that describe and identify messages (as described before). In this way, it is important to make sure that irrelevant concepts will not be associated and matched, and that relevant concepts will not be discarded. With regard to the second problem, we would like to construct the ontology automatically. Here, we address these two problems together by proposing a new method for the automatic construction of the ontology.

We build on the foundation work discussed in Section 14.2 for ontology construction. Our method constructs ontology automatically in a bottom-up fashion. For this, we first construct a hierarchy using some clustering algorithms. Recall that if documents are similar to each other in content, they will be associated with the same concept in ontology. Next, we need to assign a concept for each node in the hierarchy. As stated earlier, for this, we deploy two types of strategies and adopt a bottom-up concept assignment mechanism. First, for each cluster consisting of a set of documents, we assign a topic based on a modified Rocchio algorithm for topic tracking. However, if multiple concepts are candidates for a topic, we propose an intelligent method for arbitration. Next, to assign a concept to an interior node in the hierarchy, we use WordNet, a linguist ontology. Descendant concepts of the

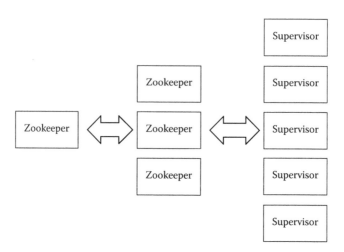

Figure 14.8   Ontology construction.

internal node will also be identified in WordNet. From these identified concepts and their hypernyms, we can identify a more generic concept that can be assigned as a concept for the interior node.

With regard to the hierarchy construction, we construct ontology automatically. For this, we rely on a SOTA that constructs a hierarchy from top to bottom. We modify the original algorithm, and propose an efficient algorithm that constructs hierarchy with better accuracy as compared to hierarchical agglomerative clustering algorithm [LUO04]. To illustrate the effectiveness of the method of automatic ontology construction, we have explored our ontology construction in the text documents. The Reuters21578 text document corpus has been used. We have observed that our modified SOTA outperforms agglomerative clustering in terms of accuracy. The main contributions of this work will be as follows:

1. We propose a new mechanism that can be used to generate ontology automatically to make our approach scalable. For this, we modify the existing SOTA that constructs a hierarchy from top to bottom.
2. Furthermore, to find an appropriate concept for each node in the hierarchy we developed an automatic concept selection algorithm from WordNet, linguistic ontology.

Figure 14.8 illustrates an example of ontology construction.

14.4 Toward SNODSOC++

We are examining the integration of multiple tools to develop SNODSOC++. Note that SNODSOC is based on SNOD and has several limitations. First, SNOD does not consider the *feature-evolution* problem (to be explained shortly), which occurs because of the dynamic nature of the stream. Second, if more than one novel class appears in the stream, SNOD cannot detect them. Third, SNOD does not address the problem of high-dimensional feature spaces, which may lead to higher training and classification error. Finally, SNOD does not apply any optimizations for feature extraction and classification. Therefore, we are developing a practical and robust blogs and tweets detection tool, which we call SNODSOC. To develop SNODSOC++ from SNODSOC, we first need to extend SNOD to SNOD++. That is, we propose to enhance SNOD into SNOD++, which is more practical and robust than SNOD. In addition to addressing the infinite-length, concept-drift, and concept-evolution problems, SNOD++ addresses feature-evolution and multiple novel classes, as well as applying subspace clustering and other optimizations, all of which improve the robustness, power, and accuracy of the algorithm. All of the tools that we have developed (e.g., LOCEXT, ONTCON, and ENTEXT) are being integrated with SNODSOC in the development of SNODSOC++. SNODSOC++ will essentially combine SNODSOC with the semantic knowledge extracted from the tweets and blogs.

14.4.1 Benefits of SNOD++

SNODSOC++ will be useful in social network analysis applications, including detecting reactively adaptive blogs and tweets. SNODSOC++ will be capable of handling massive volumes of training data and will also be able to cope with concept-drift in the data. These attributes make it more practical and robust than blogs and tweets detectors that are trained with static data. Furthermore, it can be used in detecting one or more novel classes of blogs and tweets. Also, recall that existing blogs and tweets detection techniques may fail to detect completely new patterns, but SNODSOC++ should be able to detect such novel classes and raise an alarm. The blogs would be later analyzed and characterized by human experts. In particular, SNODSOC++ will be more robust and useful than SNODSOC because SNODSOC++ will be capable of detecting multiple novel blogs and tweets in the stream, and will also exhibit a much higher classification accuracy and a faster training time because of its robustness to higher feature dimensions and application of distributed feature extraction and selection.

14.5 Cloud-Based Social Network Analysis

As previously stated, cloud computing is growing in popularity as a design model for enabling extreme scalability for data-intensive applications. In the cloud computing paradigm, data storage and retrieval operations are performed in parallel over clusters of commodity hardware. Cloud computing solutions have been used in production at major industry leaders such as Google, Amazon, and Facebook. Our goal is to integrate multiple social networks and analyze the data in the cloud as illustrated in Figure 14.9.

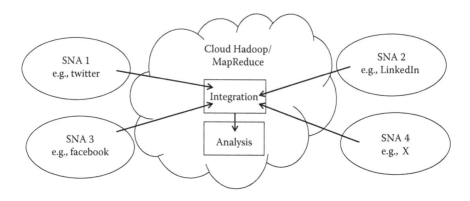

Figure 14.9   Cloud-based social network analysis.

To develop scalable SNODSOC and SNODSOC++, we are using Twitter Storm, which is a distributed, fault-tolerant, real-time computation system, at GitHub under the Eclipse Public License 1.0. Storm is a real-time processing system developed by BackType, which is now under the Twitter umbrella. It can be thought to be the Hadoop of real-time processing. That is, it does for real-time processing what Hadoop does for batch processing.

14.5.1 Stream Processing

Storm can be used to process a stream of new data and update databases in real time. Unlike the standard approach of doing stream processing with a network of queues and workers, Storm is fault-tolerant and scalable. A Storm cluster is superficially similar to a Hadoop cluster. Whereas on Hadoop you run "MapReduce jobs," on Storm you run "topologies." "Jobs" and "topologies" themselves are very different; one key difference is that a MapReduce job eventually finishes, whereas a topology processes messages forever (or until you kill it). There are two kinds of nodes on a Storm cluster: the master node and the worker nodes. The master node runs a daemon called "Nimbus" that is similar to Hadoop's "JobTracker." Nimbus is responsible for distributing code around the cluster, assigning tasks to machines, and monitoring for failures.

Each worker node runs a daemon called the "Supervisor." The supervisor listens for work assigned to its machine and starts and stops worker processes as necessary based on what Nimbus has assigned to it. Each worker process executes a subset of a topology; a running topology consists of many worker processes spread across many machines. All coordination between Nimbus and the Supervisors is done through a Zookeepercluster. Additionally, the Nimbus and Supervisor daemons are fail-fast and stateless; all state is kept in Zookeeper or on local disk. This means you can kill −9 Nimbus or the Supervisors and they will start back up like nothing happened. This design leads to Storm clusters being incredibly stable. We have had topologies running for months without requiring any maintenance.

14.5.2 *Twitter Storm for SNODSOC*

A data loading module will add Twitter user data into a cloud-based semantic web database. For this part, a vocabulary of terms that Twitter uses will be created. This vocabulary is the simplest way of moving into the semantic web world; a vocabulary is the least expressive of all semantic web languages but is the most efficient in terms of processing. The idea is to build such vocabularies for all other data sources we wish to use such as Google Plus, LinkedIn, and so on, and then perform a certain amount of automated integration of data based on these vocabularies. To perform complex reasoning over the data, which is our eventual goal, we later refine these vocabularies into more complicated ontologies that are far more expressive but require a longer processing effort. Twitter Storm would provide a framework for near real-time processing of tweets and other social media messages for entity extraction, location mining, and more importantly novel class detection. Our SPARQL query processor discussed in Section 14.2 is being examined for querying the semantic web database. At present, we are implementing SNODSOC using the Twitter Storm framework. We are also developing a second social network system using the Twitter Storm framework and the latter system is called StormRider. StormRider will be discussed in Chapter 15.

14.6 Related Work

Other works that have influenced our approach include those of Goyal et al., Katakis et al., Lin et al., Markou et al., Smith et al., Spinosa et al., Frigui et al., Backstrom et al., and Wenerstrom et al. ([GOYA09] [KATA06] [LIN11] [MARK03] [SMIT01] [SPIN08] [WENE06] [BACK08] [FRIG04]).

Many tools exist for entity extraction and location identification from web pages and other structured text. Although the details of some of these detection strategies are proprietary, it is well known that all of them use standard natural language processing or machine learning techniques that assume that the text is structured and consists of complete sentences with correct grammar. Our work on the other hand focuses on unstructured text consisting of slangs and incomplete sentences that are usually associated with the social media. With regard to cloud-based stream mining and novel class detection framework, to the best of our knowledge, there is no significant commercial competition for a cloud-centric trend detection tool. The current work on trend detection (TwitterMonitor and Streaming Trend Detection in Twitter by James Benhardusis) is primitive and makes use of a keyword-based approach instead of choosing feature vectors. Additionally, since we have taken a modular approach to the creation of our tools, we can iteratively refine each component (novel class detection for trend analysis, entity extraction, scalability on cloud, and ontology construction) separately. All the frameworks and tools that we are using for the development of the SNODSOC++ are open source and have been extensively used in our previous research and hence our tools will be able to accommodate any changes to the platform.

14.7 Summary and Directions

This chapter has described the design of SNODSOC. SNODSOC will be a great asset to the analysts who have to deal with billions of blogs and messages. For example, by analyzing the behavioral history of a particular group of individuals, analysts will be able to predict behavioral changes in the near future and take necessary measures. This line of research will stimulate a new branch of social network analysis technology and inspire a new field of study. We have also discussed how cloud computing may be used to implement SNODSOC.

New blogs swarm the cyberspace every day. Analyzing such blogs and updating the existing classification models is a daunting task. Most existing behavior-profiling techniques are manual, which require days to analyze a single blog sample and extract its behavioral profile. Even existing automated techniques have been tested only on a small sample of training data. By integrating our approach with a cloud computing framework, we overcome this barrier and will provide a highly scalable behavior modeling tool, thereby achieving higher accuracy in detecting new patterns. Furthermore, no existing profiling (manual or automated) technique addresses the evolving characteristics of blogs and messages. Therefore, our product will have a tremendous advantage over other behavior-based products by quickly responding to the dynamic environment.

While SNODSOC is a considerable improvement over currently available SNA tools, the underlying SNOD technology has some limitations. For example, SNOD lacks the ability to detect multiple novel classes emerging simultaneously. Since blogs and messages could have multiple concurrent evolutions, we need a system that can detect multiple novel classes. Therefore, we are extending SNOD to achieve a more powerful detection strategy (SNOD++) that addresses these limitations. Our goal is to develop a fully functional and robust blog analysis system called SNODSOC++. We believe that SNODSOC++ will be a novel for social network analysis due to the fact that it can handle dynamic data, changing patterns, and dynamic emergence of novel classes. We will utilize our cloud computing framework to develop SNODSOC++. Based on the initial experiments with the SNOD technology, we believe that both SNODSOC and SNODSIC++ will provide a high degree of accuracy, be scalable and operate in real time. SNODSOC++ will also integrate the tools LOCEXT, ENTEXT, and ONTCON so that highly accurate and evolving patterns and trends can be detected with the semantic knowledge extracted. Finally, using our cloud computing framework, we can develop scalable solutions for mining social network data.

Securing social networks is also one of our our major goals. We have carried out some investigation on security and privacy for social networks [CARM11]. Our systems have to be implemented on the cloud. A first step toward such an implementation is to develop assured information sharing capabilities in the cloud. We discuss some of our experimental systems in this area in Part VII.

References

[ABRO09] Abrol, S., L. Khan and T. M. Al-Khateeb. MapIt: Smarter searches using location driven knowledge discovery and mining, *1st SIGSPATIAL ACM GIS 2009 International Workshop on Querying and Mining Uncertain Spatio-Temporal Data (QUeST)*, Seattle, November 2009.

[ABRO12] Abrol,S., Khan, L., Khadilkar, V., Cadenhead, T. Design and implementation of SNODSOC: Novel class detectionfor social network analysis, Proceedings of the 2012 International Conference on Intelligence and Security Informatics, p. 215--220, 2012.

[AHME09] Ahmed, M. S. and L. Khan. SISC: A text classification approach using semi supervised subspace clustering. *ICDM Workshops* 2009, pp. 1–6, Miami, FL.

[AHME10a] Ahmed, M. S., L. Khan and M. Rajeswari. Using correlation based subspace clustering for multi-label text data classification. *ICTAI*, 2, 296–303, 2010.

[AHME10b] Ahmed, M. S., L. Khan, N. C. Oza and M. Rajeswari. Multi-label ASRS dataset classification using semi supervised subspace clustering. *Proceedings of Conference on Intelligent Data Understanding (CIDU)*, Mountain View, CA, 285–299, 2010.

[ALIP10] Alipanah, N., P. Parveen, S. Menezes, L. Khan, S. Seida and B. M. Thuraisingham. Ontology-driven query expansion methods to facilitate federated queries. *Proceedings of IEEE Intl. Conference on Service-Oriented Computing and Applications (SOCA)*, Perth, Australia, 2010.

[BACK08] Backstrom, L., J. Kleinberg, R. Kumar and J. Novak. Spatial variation in search engine queries. In WWW, *Proceedings of World Wide Web Conference (WWW)*, Beijing, China, 2008.

[CARM11] Carminati, B., Ferrari, E., Heatherly, R., Kantarcioglu, M. and B. M. Thuraisingham. Semantic web-based social network access control. *Computers & Security*, 30(2–3): 108–115, 2011.

[CHAN11] Chandra, S. and L. Khan, Estimating twitter user location using social interactions ⊥Ö a content based approach, *The Third IEEE International Conference on Social Computing*, MIT, Boston, USA, October 9–11, 2011.

[CHEN10] Cheng, Z., J. Caverlee and K. Lee. You are where you tweet: A content-based approach to geo-locating twitter users. *Proceeding of the 19th ACM Conference on Information and Knowledge Management (CIKM)*, Toronto, October 2010.

[FRIG04] H. Frigui and O. Nasraoui. Unsupervised learning of prototypes and attribute weights. *Pattern Recognition*, 37(3): 567–581, 2004.

[GOYA09] Goyal, A., H. Daum and S. Venkatasubramanian. Streaming for large scale NLP: Language modeling. *Proceedings of Human Language Technologies: The 2009 Annual Conference of the North American Chapter of the Association for Computational Linguistics*, Boulder, Colorado, 2009, pp. 512–520.

[HUBE09] Huberman, B. and D. R. F. Wu. Social networks that matter: Twitter under the microscope. *First Monday*, 14, 2009.

[HUSAIN11] Husain, M. F., McGlothlin, J. P., Masud, M. M., Khan, L. R. and B. M. Thuraisingham. Heuristics-based query processing for large RDF graphs using cloud computing. *IEEE Transactions on Knowledge and Data Engineering*, 23(9): 1312–1327, 2011.

[FRIG04] Frigui, H. and O. Nasraoui, Unsupervised learning of prototypes and attribute weights, *Pattern Recognition*, 37(3): 567–581, 2004.

[GOYA09] Goyal, M. A., H. Daum and S. Venkatasubramanian, Streaming for large scale NLP: Language modeling, *Human Language Technologies: The 2009 Annual Conference of the North American Chapter of the Association for Computational Linguistics*, Boulder, Colorado, 2009, pp. 512–520.

[KATA06] Katakis, I., G. Tsoumakas and I. Vlahavas. Dynamic feature space and incremental feature selection for the classification of textual data streams. *Proceedings of European Conference on Machine Learning and Principles and Practice of Knowledge Discovery (ECML PKDD)*, 102–116, 2006, Berlin, Germany.

[KHAL10] Khaled, A., M. F. Husain, L. Khan, K. W. Hamlen and B. M. Thuraisingham, A token-based access control system for RDF data in the clouds. *Proceedings of IEEE Intl. Conference on Cloud Computing Technology and Science,* Indianapolis, IN, *CloudCom,* 2010, 104–111.

[KHAN02] Khan, L. and F. Luo. Ontology construction for information selection. *Proceedings of IEEE Intl. Conference on Tools with Artificial Intelligence (ICTAI)*, 122-, Washington, DC, 2002.

[LIN11] Lin, J., R. Snow and W. Morgan. Smoothing techniques for adaptive online language models: Topic tracking in tweet streams, *Proceedings of ACM SIGKDD Conference on Knowledge Discovery and Data Mining*, San Diego, CA, August 2011.

[LUO04] Luo, F., L. Khan, F. B. Bastani, I.-L. Yen and J. Zhou. A dynamically growing self-organizing tree (DGSOT) for hierarchical clustering gene expression profiles. *Bioinformatics*, 20(16): 2605–2617, 2004.

[MARK03] Markou, M. and S. Singh. Novelty detection: A review. Part 1: Statistical approaches, Part 2: Neural network based approaches. *Signal Processing*, 83, 2481–2497, 2499–2521, 2003.

[MASU10] Masud, M. M., Q. Chen, L. Khan, C. C. Aggarwal, J. Gao, J. Han and B. M. Thuraisingham. Addressing concept-evolution in concept-drifting data streams. *Proceedings of ICDM'10*, pp. 929–934.

[MASU11a] Masud, M. M., T. M. Al-Khateeb, L. Khan, C. C. Aggarwal, J. Gao, J. Han and B. M. Thuraisingham. Detecting recurring and novel classes in concept-drifting data streams. *Proceedings of Intl. Conference on Data Mining*, Vancouver, BC, Canada.

[MASU11b] Masud, M. M., J. Gao, L. Khan, J. Han and B. M. Thuraisingham. Classification and novel class detection in concept-drifting data streams under time constraints. *IEEE TKDE*, 23(1): 859–874, 2011.

[MASU12] M. M. Masud, J. Gao, L. Khan, J. Han, K. W. Hamlen and N. C. Oza. Facing the reality of data stream classification: Coping with scarcity of labeled data. *International Journal of Knowledge and Information Systems (KAIS)*, 33(1), 213–244, Springer, 2012.

[MCGL10] McGlothlin, J. P. and L. R. Khan. Materializing and persisting inferred and uncertain knowledge in RDF datasets. *Proceedings of AAAI Conference on Artificial Intelligence*, Atlanta, GA, 2010.

[SMIT01] D. A. Smith and G. Crane. Disambiguating geographic names in a historical digital library, *5th European Conference on Research and Advanced Technology for Digital Libraries (ECDL 2001), Lecture Notes in Computer Science*, Darmstadt, Germany, September 2001, pp. 127–136.

[SPIN08] Spinosa, E. J., A. P. de Leon, F. de Carvalho and J. Gama. Cluster-based novel concept detection in data streams applied to intrusion detection in computer networks. *Proceedings of ACM SAC*, 2008, pp. 976–980.

[WENE06] Wenerstrom, B. and C. Giraud-Carrier. Temporal data mining in dynamic feature spaces. *ICDM*, 2006, pp. 1141–1145.

Chapter 15

Experimental Semantic Web-Based Cloud Computing Systems

15.1 Overview

In this chapter, we describe three additional experimental cloud computing systems that utilize semantic web technologies. The first system, called Jena-HBase, is a storage system for RDF triples. The second system, called StormRider, uses the Storm framework for hosting social networks in the cloud. StormRider also uses Jena-HBase in its implementation. The third system is an ontology-driven query processing system that utilizes the MapReduce framework. We describe the motivation behind the three systems.

First, the lack of scalability is one of the most significant problems faced by single-machine RDF data stores. The advent of cloud computing has paved the way for a distributed ecosystem of RDF triple stores that can potentially allow up to a planet-scale storage along with distributed query processing capabilities. Toward this end, we present Jena-HBase, a HBase backed triple store that can be used with the Jena framework. Jena-HBase provides end users with a scalable storage and querying solution that supports all features from the RDF specification.

Second, the focus of online social media providers today has shifted from "content generation" toward finding effective methodologies for "content storage, retrieval and analysis" in the presence of evolving networks. Toward this end, we present StormRider, a framework that uses the existing cloud computing and semantic web technologies to provide application programmers with automated

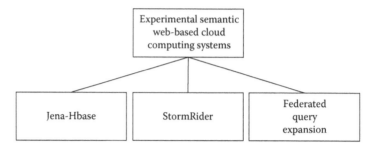

Figure 15.1 Experimental semantic web-based cloud computing systems. (Adapted from Khadilkar, V., M. Kantarcioglu, and B. Thuraisingham, StormRider: Harnessing "Storm" for social networks. Technical report, 543–544, 2012. http://www.utdallas.edu/vvk072000/Research/StormRider/tech-report.pdf)

support for these tasks, thereby allowing a richer assortment of use cases to be implemented on the underlying evolving social networks.

Third, in view of the need for a highly distributed and federated architecture, a robust query expansion has great impact on the performance of information retrieval. We determine ontology-driven query expansion terms using different weighting techniques. For this, we consider each individual ontology and user query keywords to determine the basic expansion terms (BETs) using a number of semantic measures including betweenness measure (BM) and semantic similarity measure (SSM). We develop a Map/Reduce distributed algorithm for calculating all the shortest paths in the ontology graph. Map/Reduce algorithm will considerably improve the efficiency of BET calculation for large ontologies.

The organization of this chapter is as follows. We discuss Jena-HBase that is discussed in Section 15.2. StormRider is discussed in Section 15.3. The ontology-driven query processing tool implemented with MapReduce is discussed in Section 15.4. Section 15.5 concludes this chapter. The contents of this chapter are illustrated in Figure 15.1.

15.2 Jena-HBase: A Distributed, Scalable, and Efficient RDF Triple Store

The simplest way to store RDF triples comprises a relation/table of three columns, one each for *subjects*, *predicates*, and *objects*. However, this approach suffers from the lack of scalability and abridged query performance, as the single table becomes long and narrow when the number of RDF triples increases [ERET09]. The approach is not scalable since the table is usually located on a single machine. The cloud computing paradigm has made it possible to harness the processing power of multiple machines in parallel. Tools such as Hadoop and HBase provide advantages such as fault tolerance and optimizations for real-time queries. In this section, we present Jena-HBase, a HBase backed triple store that can be used with the Jena framework along with a preliminary experimental evaluation of our prototype.

Our work focuses on the creation of a distributed RDF storage framework, thereby mitigating the scalability issue that exists with single-machine systems. The motivation to opt for Jena is its widespread acceptance, and its built-in support for manipulating RDF data as well as developing ontologies. Further, HBase was selected for the storage layer for two reasons: (i) HBase is a column-oriented store and in general, a column-oriented store performs better than row-oriented stores; and (ii) Hadoop comprises HDFS, a distributed file system that stores data, and MapReduce, a framework for processing the data stored in HDFS. HBase uses HDFS for data storage but does not require MapReduce for accessing data. Thus, Jena-HBase does not require the implementation of a MapReduce-based query engine for executing queries on RDF triples. In contrast, the existing systems that use a MapReduce-based query engine for processing RDF data are optimized for query performance; however, currently, they are unable to support all features from the RDF specification. Our motivation with Jena-HBase is to provide end users with a cloud-based RDF storage and querying API that supports all features from the RDF specification.

Jena-HBase provides the following: (a) a variety of custom-built RDF data storage layouts for HBase that provide a trade-off in terms of query performance/storage; and (b) support for reification, inference, and SPARQL processing through the implementation of appropriate Jena interfaces. Figure 15.2 presents an overview of

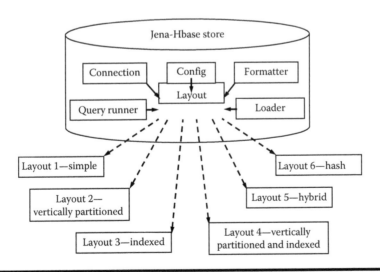

Figure 15.2   Jena-HBase architecture. (Adapted from Khadilkar, V., M. Kantarcioglu, P. Castagna, and B. Thuraisingham, Jena-HBase: A distributed, scalable and effcient RDF triple store. Technical report, 2012. http://www.utdallas.edu/~vvk072000/ Research/Jena-HBase-Ext/tech-report.pdf)

the architecture employed by Jena-HBase. Jena-HBase uses the concept of a store to provide data manipulation capabilities on the underlying HBase tables. A store represents a single RDF dataset and can be composed of several RDF graphs, each with its own storage layout. A layout uses several HBase tables with different schemas to store RDF triples; each layout provides a trade-off in terms of query performance/ storage. All operations on an RDF graph are implicitly converted into operations on the underlying layout. These operations include (a) formatting a layout, that is, deleting all triples while preserving tables (**Formatter** block); (b) loading–unloading triples into a layout (**Loader** block); (c) querying a layout for triples that match a given (*S, P, O*) pattern (**Query Runner** block); and (d) the additional operations include the following: (i) Maintaining an HBase connection (**Connection** block) and (ii) Maintaining configuration information for each RDF graph (**Config** block).

We have performed benchmark experiments using SP²Bench (noninference queries) [POTA09] and LUBM (inference queries) [BRAN01] to determine the best layout currently available in Jena-HBase, as well as to compare the performance of the best layout with Jena TDB. We have compared Jena-HBase only with Jena TDB and not with other Hadoop-based systems for the following reasons: (i) Jena TDB gives the best query performance of all available Jena storage subsystems, and (ii) The available Hadoop-based systems do not implement all features from the RDF specification. As part of the procedure to determine the best layout, we ran both benchmarks over several graph sizes and our results are given in [KHAD12a], [KHAD12b]. Since LUBM contains inference queries, we used the Pellet Reasoner (v2.3.0) to perform inferencing.

15.3 StormRider: Harnessing "Storm" for Social Networks

The rise of social media applications has turned the once privileged realm of web authoring and publishing into a commonplace activity. This has led to an explosion in the amount of user-generated content online. The main concern for social media providers is no longer "content generation" but finding effective methodologies for "content storage, retrieval and analysis." There has been a significant amount of research (see, e.g., [ERET09]) that addresses this issue. However, the existing work views a network as a series of snapshots, where a snapshot represents the state of a network in a given time period. Therefore, different network operations need to be individually performed over each snapshot. In reality, online social networks are continuously evolving entities and therefore, network operations should be automatically performed as they evolve. Moreover, viewing the problem from this perspective allows us to create a solution that supports advanced, real-world use cases such as the following: (a) Tracking the neighborhood of a given node. This use case is relevant in law enforcement, for example, to track the activities of potential criminals/terrorists; and (b) Being able to store and access the prior snapshots of a network for auditing and verification tasks. Such a use case is relevant in health care, for example, in tracing the medical history of a patient.

In this section, we present StormRider, a framework that uses a combination of cloud-based and semantic web-based tools to allow for the storage, retrieval, and analysis of the evolving social networks. In addition, users can perform these operations on networks of their choice by creating custom-built implementations of the interfaces provided in StormRider. The StormRider framework makes use of the following existing tools as the basic building blocks: (i) The Storm framework allows StormRider to automatically store, query, and analyze data as the underlying network evolves over time. Storm was selected because it is a real-time computation system that guarantees message processing and is scalable, robust, and fault-tolerant. (ii) The Jena-HBase framework [KHAD12a] allows the storage of network data in an RDF representation as well as to query the data using SPARQL. (iii) Apache HBase was used to construct materialized views that store metadata related to nodes in the network. These views allow faster analytics to be performed on the network.

StormRider provides the following novel contributions: (i) the Jena-HBase framework facilitates the use of several semantic web features with social networks such as the application of reasoning algorithms, reification, and so on; (ii) the ability to store, query, and analyze the evolving networks through the use of novel algorithms (e.g., approximation algorithms for centrality estimation) implemented in Storm; and (iii) application programmers are provided with simple interfaces through which they can interact with social networks of their choice.

Figure 15.3 presents an architectural overview of StormRider. The user applications interact with an abstract social network model (Model-SN) that translates

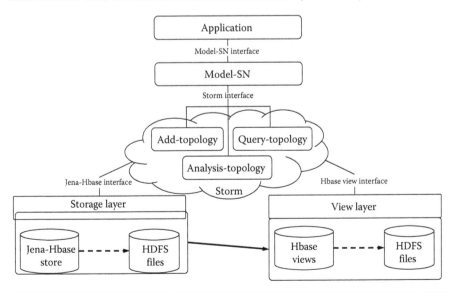

Figure 15.3   StormRider architecture.

high-level user-defined network operations (viz., store, query, and analyze) into low-level operations on the underlying network representations used by StormRider. The low-level operations are implemented as Storm topologies and are designed to support the evolving social networks. A Storm topology represents a graph of computation, where nodes contain the logic of the computation whereas links between nodes denote how data are passed from one node to another. Storm internally interfaces with the storage layer (Jena-HBase), through the Jena-HBase interface, and the view layer (HBase tables used as materialized views), through the HBase view interface, to execute topologies on the underlying networks.

The storage layer, composed of Jena-HBase, is used to store networks in an RDF representation in a cloud-based framework. The storage of networks in RDF when combined with topologies defined in Storm allows us to support realistic uses cases such as those given previously (e.g., [a] and [b] in the introduction) through the use of concepts such as property-path queries and reification. For additional details about Jena-HBase, an interested reader is referred to our detailed technical report [KHAD12a]. The view layer is used to store metadata about nodes that make up a network. The metadata is mainly used to facilitate a speedup in performance during the analysis of a network.

The additional details of the architecture along with a detailed description of sample add-, query-, and analyze-topologies for the Twitter network are given in [KHAD12c]. Note that these topologies are only provided as examples with the StormRider framework. Consequently, an application programmer needs to define custom topologies based on their requirements to interact with networks they want to examine.

The sample topologies in StormRider have been implemented for Twitter. The add-topology is used to add data to the storage layer as well as to update node-related information in the view layer. The analyze-topology is then used to compute degree, closeness, and betweenness centrality using the metadata from the view layer. Some of these metrics require shortest path computations that we perform using the landmark-based approximation technique [POTA09]. As a part of our experimental evaluation, we evaluated the effectiveness of this method versus the exact method given in [BRAN01] for computing closeness and betweenness centrality on a maximum of 500,000 Twitter users. The number of nodes in the landmarks set was set to (total no. of users)/100, where the factor 100 was randomly selected, whereas the elements in the landmarks set were selected as the top-k nodes with the highest degree. Finally, each experiment was conducted along the following dimensions: (i) approximation error: This metric measures the accuracy of StormRider in computing the centrality value versus the exact method and is computed as $|\hat{l} - l|$ where l is the actual centrality value and $\hat{l}$ is the approximation; and (ii) execution time: This metric measures the time required to perform the approximate and exact calculations of the centrality values. The time for the approximate case is computed as the sum of both the time required to update the views and the time required to perform the actual centrality computation. Our experimental results are given in [KHAD12c] and [KHAD12d].

Note that in Chapter 14, we described the design of SNODSOC, a social network that operates in the cloud. SNODSOC utilizes Twitter Storm for its cloud implementation. Currently, SNODSOC and StormRider are two separate systems being developed independent of each other on different projects. In the future, we will explore the integration of SNODSOC and StormRider.

15.4 Ontology-Driven Query Expansion Using Map/Reduce Framework

Distributed and parallel computing continues to solve efficiency problems for many web applications in a federated architecture. Since data applications use distributed data sources in such architecture, it is required to enrich the original user query and cover the gap between the user query and required information by query expansion. The goal of many researchers is to discriminate between different expansion terms and improve the robustness of query expansion. In our previous work [ALIP10a], we developed a novel weighting mechanism for ontology-driven query expansion called the BETs and new expansion terms (NETs). For each user query, BET is calculated in each ontology based on some metrics namely semantic similarity, density, and betweenness. NET is determined by aligning ontologies to find robust expansion terms between different ontologies. BET metrics are defined using the shortest paths calculation in ontology graphs. The problem of finding the number of shortest path that goes through every entity in ontology graph is not practical especially for large ontologies. Therefore, in this section, we concentrate on Map/Reduce algorithm for BET calculation in each ontology. More details are given in [ALIP10a], [ALIP10b], [ALIP11a], [ALIP11b], [ALIP12a], and [ALIP12b]. Our architecture for query expansion is illustrated in Figure 15.4.

15.4.1 BET Calculation Using MapReduce Distributed Computing

In our BET calculation [ERET09], we use BM, centrality, density measure (DM), and SSM metrics. For this, first we determine the central entity (CE) using BM in each ontology. Next, we use the CE and calculate SSM for each of the expansion terms in BET. In both BM and SSM metrics, we need to determine the shortest paths between different entities of each ontology several times as follows. BM and CE: Betweenness (BM) assigns the number of shortest paths that pass through each node in the ontology graph when calculating the expansion terms. The node that occurs on many shortest paths for expanding user terms is considered as the central keyword in each ontology [ERET09]. Let $e_i, e_j \in O_k$. BM(e) is the BM of entity e.

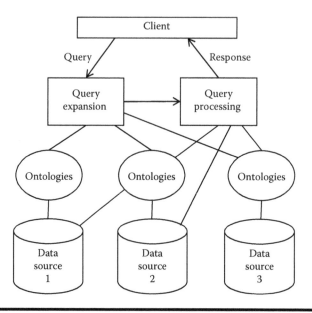

Figure 15.4 Architecture for query expansion.

$$BM(e) = \sum_{e_i \neq e_j \neq e} \left(\frac{\text{shortestpath}(e_i, e_j)\text{pas sin g } e}{\text{shortestpath}(e_i, e_j)} \right) \qquad (15.1)$$

BM determines the central keyword that is used in SSM for finding BET. The central keyword has the highest BM value. SSM: SSM uses ontology graph as a semantic presentation of a domain to determine weights for all expansion terms in every ontology. The entities that are closer to the central node have more weights. SSM is calculated using the shortest path measure. The more relationships entities have in common, the closer they will be in the ontology [ERET09]. If any entity is positioned relatively far from the central node, then it has a smaller weight. Therefore, we use the shortest path measure as weights for the ontology vocabulary.

Let entities e_j, $c \in O_i$ and there is a path between c (central) and e_j.

$$SSM(c, e_j) = \begin{cases} \dfrac{1}{\text{lenghth}(\text{minpath}(c, e_j))} & c \neq e_j \\ 1 & c = e_j \end{cases} \qquad (15.2)$$

BET in this method, is all entities in the shortest path from the central keyword to e_j. The shortest paths in BM and SSM calculations are determined by Breadth First Search (BFS). Given a branching factor *b* and graph depth *d* in ontology graph, the asymptotic space and time complexity is the number of nodes at the deepest level, $O(b^d)$ that is exponential. For large ontologies, shortest path calculation is not practical. Therefore, in the next section, we explain about the Map/Reduce distributed algorithm that optimizes our federated query expansion.

15.4.1.1 Shortest Path Calculation Using Iterative MapReduce Algorithm

Map/Reduce programming model is a powerful interface for automatic parallelization and distribution of large-scale computations. In this model, Map and Reduce functions are defined as follows:

$$\text{Map}(\langle in_{key}, in_{Value} \rangle) \rightarrow \langle out_{key}, intermediate_{Value} \rangle list$$
$$\text{Reduce}(\langle out_{key}, intermediate_{Value} \rangle list) \rightarrow out_{Value} list \tag{15.3}$$

The data from data sources are fed into Map function as a pair of $\langle in_{Key}, in_{Value} \rangle$. Map function produces one or more intermediate values along with the $output_{key}$ from the input. After the Map phase, all intermediate values for any given out_{Key} are combined together into a list. Reduce function combines $intermediate_{Value}$ into one or more final values for that same output out_{key}. In our BET calculation, we are using the ontology graph illustrated in Figure 15.5 as the input for the system. The ontol-

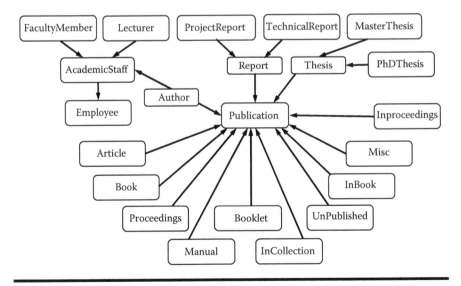

Figure 15.5   Karlsruhe bibliography ontology.

ogy graph needs a transformation from graph to adjacency list to be used by Map function. Step 1 explains the transformation and $\langle in_{key}, in_{Value} \rangle$ for the Map function.

Step 1: Given an ontology O_1, the algorithm constructs adjacency matrix for each entity $e_i \in O_1$. Each e_i is considered as in_{key}. For each entity e_i, we first determine the neighbors of e_i and store them as a comma delimited *NeighbourList(NL)* that is connected to this entity. We also specify *Distance–From–Source(DFS)*, *Path–From–Source(PFS)* and color for each entity. There are three possible *EntityColors(EC)* for each entity. Source entities are determined using *Gray* color, whereas visited entities are defined by *Black* and not visited entities are defined by *White* color. We use $DFS = 0$ for the source entity and $DFS = Int.Maxval$ for other entities because we are using BFS for source entity. Also, for the source entity, $PFS = in_{key}$ of the source, whereas *PFS* is empty for other entities. The concatenation of *NL*, *DFS*, *PFS*, and *EC* is considered as in_{Value} for the Map function. Considering Figure 15.5 ontology graph, suppose that *MasterThesis* is the source entity in the graph; thus, some sample keys and values are

$\langle$*Masterthesis," Thesis*$|0|$*Masterthesis*$|$*Gray*"$\rangle$,

$\langle$*Author,"Publication,AcademinStaff*$\backslash$*Int.Maxval*$|-|$*White*"$\rangle$,

$\langle$*Report"Publication*$|$*Int.Maxval*$|-|$*White*"$\rangle$,

$\langle$*Thesis,"Publication*$|$*Int.Maxval*$|-|$*White*"$\rangle$

Step 2: In this step, mappers produce *intermediate$_{Value}$* for each source entity in_{Key}. For each source entity Si in the ontology graph with the *Gray* color, the mappers first change its color to *Black*. Then it creates some new nodes based on the number of neighbors with $DFS = DFS + 1$. $PFS = in_{Key} \cup in_{Keynewword}$ and color $=$ *Gray*. Since the mappers do not have the information about the next neighbors for new nodes, it considers the next neighbors as *NULL*. Also, it assumes $PFS = "-"$ for non-gray nodes. Back to our example, below is the result after the first iteration:

$\langle$*Masterthesis," Thesis*$|0|$*Masterthesis*$|$*Black*"$\rangle$

$\langle$*Thesis,"Null*$|1|$*Masterthesis–Thesis*$|$*Gray*"$\rangle$,

$\langle$*Author,"Publication,AcademinStaff*$\backslash$*Int.Maxval*$|-|$*White*"$\rangle$,

$\langle$*Report"Publication*$|$*Int.Maxval*$|-|$*White*"$\rangle$,

$\langle$*Thesis,"Publication*$|$*Int.Maxval*$|-|$*White*"$\rangle$.

Step 3: In this step, the reducer uses one out_{Key} and the list of all *intermediate$_{Value}$* to calculate the final out_{Value}. Each reducer takes all *intermediate$_{Value}$* of each *Key* and constructs a new node using the *"Not–Null"* list of edges, the minimum DFS, *"Not–Null"* value for PFS, and the darkest color. That is, for the above example

⟨*Thesis,*" *Publication*|1|*Masterthesis–Thesis*|*Gray*"'⟩.

After reducing the *intermediate$_{Value}$* in step 3, the algorithm continues for the next iteration to explode new *Gray* nodes in step 2. This iteration continues until it expands all possible paths for each source examined and all nodes change to black color.

15.4.1.2 Betweenness and Centrality Measures Using Map/Reduce Computation

In BET calculation, first, for each $q_i \in query_{keywords}$, we calculate BM measure. Second, we determine the central $query_{keywords}$(i.e.,q_c) among all $query_{keywords}$. As discussed in the previous section, in each iteration, the *intermediate$_{Value}$* is updated and the PFS is determined. For betweenness of each q_i, we find the number of times the q_i appears in the shortest paths between entities of ontology in the last iteration of Map-Reduce step. After determining the BM(q_i), we specify the q_i with the maximum value of betweenness as the central keyword.

15.4.1.3 SSMs Using Map/Reduce Algorithm

We use the CE from the previous section and calculate SSM for all the BET. For SSM calculation, we use the result of Map/Reduce-ShortestPath (MRSP) algorithm as explained in Algorithm 1. In line 2 and 3, the algorithm uses MRSP and SSM using Map/Reduce-ShortestPath and returns SSM for each *entity* $\in$ *BET*.

Algorithm 1: SSMs Using Map/Reduce Computation
Require: BET $\{b_1, b_2, \ldots, b_n\}$, CE, and ontology O
Ensure: SSM for each b_i

1: **For all** $b_i \in B$ **do**
2:   MRSP = Map/Reduce-ShortestPath result (b_i)
3:   SSM(b_i) = $\dfrac{1}{\text{lengthofMRSP}}$
4: **end for**
5: return SSM(b_i)

15.5 Summary and Directions

In this chapter, we have described three separate experimental cloud-based semantic web data management systems. The first system integrated a distributed RDF storage framework with the existing cloud computing tools resulting in a scalable data-processing solution. Our solution maintains a reasonable query execution time overhead when compared with a single-machine RDF storage framework (viz., Jena TDB). Next, we presented StormRider, a framework that uses a novel combination of the existing cloud computing and semantic web technologies to allow for the "storage, retrieval and analysis" of the evolving online social networks, thus enabling the support for several new, realistic use cases. Finally, we discussed an ontology-driven query expansion system in the cloud.

There are many areas for further research. First, we need to conduct extensive experiments with our systems to see if they scale. Next, we need to develop more robust algorithms that operate on the cloud. Finally, we need to test our system with some real-world examples.

References

[ABAD07] Abadi, D.J., A. Marcus, S. Madden, and K.J. Hollenbach, Scalable semantic web data management using vertical partitioning. In *Proceedings of Very Large Database Conference (VLDB)*, Vienna, Austria, 411–422, 2007.

[ALIP10a] Alipanah, N., P. Srivastava, P. Parveen, and B.M. Thuraisingham, Ranking ontologies using verified entities to facilitate federated queries. *Proceedings of Web Intelligence Conference*, Toronto, Canada, 332–337, 2010.

[ALIP10b] Alipanah, N., P. Parveen, L. Khan, and B. Thuraisingham, Ontology-driven query expansion methods to facilitate federated queries. *Proceedings of 2010 IEEE International Conference on Service Oriented Computing and Applications (SOCA10)*, Perth, Australia, 2010.

[ALIP11a] Alipanah, N., L. Khan, and B. Thuraisingham, Ontology-driven query expansion methods to facilitate federated queries, Technical Report, UTDCS-30-11, The University of Texas at Dallas, 2011.

[ALIP11b] Alipanah, N., P. Parveen, L. Khan, and B.M. Thuraisingham, Ontology-driven query expansion using Map/Reduce framework to facilitate federated queries. *Proceedings of International Conference on Web Services (ICWS)*, Washington, DC, 712–713, 2011.

[ALIP12a] Alipanah, N., L. Khan, and B.M. Thuraisingham, Optimized ontology-driven query expansion using Map-Reduce framework to facilitate federated queries. *Intl. Journal of Computer Systems Science and Engineering*, 27(2), 2012.

[ALIP12b] Alipanah, N., Federated query processing using Ontology structure and ranking in a service oriented environment, PhD thesis, The University of Texas at Dallas, 2012.

[BRAN01] Brandes, U., A faster algorithm for betweenness centrality. *Journal of Mathematical Sociology*, 25(2):163–177, 2001.

[ERET09] Erétéo, G., M. Buffa, F. Gandon, and O. Corby, Analysis of a real online social network using semantic web frameworks. In *Proceedings of IEEE Intl. Semantic Web Conference (ISWC)*, Chantilly, VA, 180–195, 2009.

[KHAD12a] Khadilkar, V., M. Kantarcioglu, P. Castagna, and B. Thuraisingham, Jena-HBase: A distributed, scalable and effcient RDF triple store. Technical report, 2012. http://www.utdallas.edu/~vvk072000/Research/Jena-HBase-Ext/tech-report.pdf.

[KHAD12b] Khadilkar, V., M. Kantarcioglu, B.M. Thuraisingham, and P. Castagna, Jena-HBase: A distributed, scalable and efficient RDF triple store. *International Semantic Web Conference (Posters & Demos)*, Boston, MA, 2012.

[KHAD12c] Khadilkar, V., M. Kantarcioglu, and B. Thuraisingham, StormRider: Harnessing "Storm" for social networks. Technical report, 543–544, 2012. http://www.utdallas.edu/~vvk072000/Research/StormRider/tech-report.pdf.

[KHAD12d] Khadilkar, V., M. Kantarcioglu, and B.M. Thuraisingham, StormRider: Harnessing "storm" for social networks. *Proceedings of World Wide Web Conference (WWW)*, Lyon, France, 543–544, 2012.

[POTA09] Potamias, M., F. Bonchi, C. Castillo, and A. Gionis, Fast shortest path distance estimation in large networks. In *Proceedings of Conference on Information and Knowledge Management (CIKM)*, Hong Kong, China, 867–876, 2009.

Conclusion to Part IV

While Part III discussed cloud computing concepts, Part IV discussed experimental cloud computing systems. These are systems that we have developed at the UTD.

In Chapter 13, we presented a framework capable of handling large amounts of RDF data. Since our framework is based on Hadoop, which is a distributed and highly fault-tolerant system, it is highly scalable. To increase capacity of our system, all that needs to be done is to add new nodes to the Hadoop cluster. We developed a schema to store RDF data and an algorithm to determine a query processing plan to answer an SPARQL query.

Chapter 14 described the design of SNODSOC, a social network system based on a data mining algorithm that we have developed called SNOD (Stream-based novel class detection). SNODSOC will be a great asset to the analysts who have to deal with billions of blogs and messages. For example, by analyzing the behavioral history of a particular group of individuals, analysts will be able to predict behavioral changes in the near future and take necessary measures.

Chapter 15 described three cloud-based tools we have developed. We first presented StormRider, a framework that uses a novel combination of existing cloud computing and semantic web technologies to allow for the "storage, retrieval and analysis" of evolving online social networks, thus enabling support for several new, realistic use cases. Second, we showed that creating a distributed RDF storage framework with existing cloud computing tools results in a scalable data processing solution. Additionally, our solution maintains a reasonable query execution time overhead when compared with a single-machine RDF storage framework. Third, we discussed ontology-based query expansion in the cloud.

SECURE CLOUD COMPUTING CONCEPTS

Introduction to Part V

Now that we have provided an overview of cloud computing as well as discussed some of our experimental cloud computing systems, we will discuss security issues for the cloud. In particular, the concepts, functions, guidelines, and products for secure cloud computing will be discussed.

Part V consists of six chapters: 16, 17, 18, 19, 20, and 21. Chapter 16 provides an overview of secure cloud computing concepts. Secure cloud computing functions are discussed in Chapter 17. Secure cloud data management is the subject of Chapter 18. Secure cloud computing guidelines are discussed in Chapter 19. The notion of security-as-a-service is discussed in Chapter 20. Secure cloud computing products are discussed in Chapter 21.

Chapter 16

Secure Cloud Computing Concepts

16.1 Overview

One of the major hurdles in deploying the cloud for many applications is security. As we have discussed in the earlier parts of this book, with the cloud, not only is the processing outsourced to the cloud service providers (CSPs), the data are also outsourced. Therefore, many organizations are reluctant to place their data in the cloud, especially if the data is sensitive. Furthermore, even if the data are to be encrypted in the cloud, with current technology, it has to be decrypted before operations are performed on the data. Storing and managing unencrypted data in any form is usually not acceptable to many organizations. As a result, these organizations cannot take advantage of the cloud.

Owing to these challenges, securing the cloud has become an urgent need for many organizations. A significant amount of resources has been expended to secure the cloud. In this chapter, we will examine the security issues surrounding the cloud. Our work has been influenced by the 10 CISSP (Certified Information Systems Security Professional) modules that discuss security [HARR10], as well as the excellent book on cloud security by Mather et al. [MATH09]. Specifically, we will review the 10 CISSP modules that discuss security concepts and examine them for the cloud. These modules are the following:

- Information systems security and governance
- Security architectures
- Security/access control models

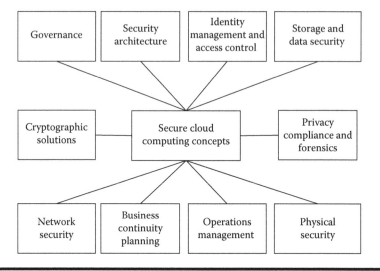

Figure 16.1   Secure cloud computing concepts.

- Cryptography
- Network security
- Data and applications security
- Legal aspects including privacy and forensics
- Business continuity planning and disaster recovery
- Physical security
- Operations management

The organization of this chapter is as follows. Cloud computing security and governance will be discussed in Section 16.2. Security architecture for cloud computing will be discussed in Section 16.3. Access control and identity management for the cloud will be discussed in Section 16.4. Data and applications security issues for the cloud will be discussed in Section 16.5. Privacy, compliance, and forensics for the cloud will be discussed in Section 16.6. Cryptographic solutions will be discussed in Section 16.7. Network security issues for the cloud will be discussed in Section 16.8. Business continuity planning will be discussed in Section 16.9. Operations security will be discussed in Section 16.10. Physical security issues will be discussed in Section 16.11. This chapter is summarized in Section 16.12. Figure 16.1 illustrates the various aspects discussed in this chapter.

16.2 Secure Cloud Computing and Governance

Recall that the cloud framework consists of three major models. They are the following:

- SaaS
- PaaS
- Iaas

Furthermore, there are three deployment models. They are the following:

- The public cloud
- The private cloud
- The hybrid cloud

Our discussion of the security issues will be influenced by the cloud framework and the deployment models discussed in Part IV.

As stated in [MATH09], five layers of governance for IT are the following:

- Network
- Storage
- Server
- Services
- Applications

For on-premise hosting, an organization has control over storage, server, services, and applications while the vendor and organization have shared control over networks. For example, for on-premise hosting, the organization will typically purchase the hardware and software as well as the applications. Therefore, the organization has control over these resources. With respect to network, the organization will work with a vendor to provide network services.

For the SaaS model, all layers are controlled by the vendor. This is because the vendor is hosting the networks, the platforms, the infrastructure, and the applications. The organization will run the vendor-provided applications on the vendor infrastructure and software. For the IaaS model, the applications are controlled by the organization while the services are controlled by both the organization and the vendor. This is because to host the organization's applications, the organization will have to provide some services. However, the remaining layers such as storage and network are provided by the vendor. For the PaaS model, applications and services are controlled by both, while servers, storage, and network are controlled by the vendor.

Other aspects of cloud security and governance include risk assessment. One of the first steps in deploying a cloud is to analyze the risks involved. This would involve carrying out a thorough risk analysis by an independent team including assessing the vulnerabilities of the cloud. If the cloud is to be deployed in a public environment, then the security risks are greater than deploying it in a private environment. The traditional risk analysis methods for IT systems have to be examined for a cloud.

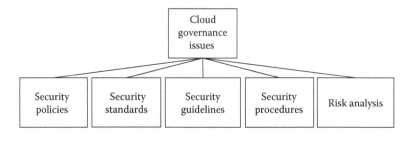

Figure 16.2 Cloud governance issues.

Another aspect of governance is formulating a security policy for the cloud. This would include the definition of the roles and responsibilities of the organization versus those of the CSP. In addition, the issues surrounding asset management, human resource security, physical and environmental security, communications and operations management, access control, information systems acquisition, development and maintenance, information security incident management, compliance and key management have to be clearly articulated and documented. For example, access control management aspects include: Who should have access and why? How is a resource accessed? How is the access monitored? Add the impact of access control on SaaS, PaaS, and IaaS. These aspects will be discussed in the ensuing sections.

Standards also play a major role in managing security in IT systems. These include security management standards such as ITIL (Information Technology Infrastructure Library) and ISO (International Standards Organization) 27001/27002. These standards discuss the policies, procedures, and processes for security. These standards also include those for availability management, access control, vulnerability management, patch management, configuration management incident response and system use, and access monitoring.

In summary, several policies, processes, standards, guidelines and technologies have been developed for the governance of information systems. They have to be examined and possibly expanded for the cloud. Appropriate risk analysis techniques should also be developed for the cloud. Figure 16.2 illustrates governance issues.

16.3 Security Architecture

Security architecture consists of the security critical components of the system architecture. For example, the trusted computing base (TCB) is a computing system consisting of the part of the system that is responsible for enforcing the security critical functions. The reference monitor is the part of the system that implements the trusted computing base. We need to examine these concepts for the cloud. Specifically, we need to determine the security architecture of the cloud with respect to Iaas, Paas, and SaaS.

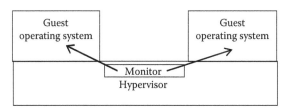

Figure 16.3   Hypervisor monitoring.

Security of the cloud will impact different levels including the network, the host, and the applications. We will discuss the network level security issues in a later section. With respect to host security, both the PaaS and SaaS hide the host OS from end users. That is, the host security responsibilities in SaaS and PaaS are transferred to the CSP. The host security at the IaaS level is due to virtualization. Essentially, it deals with security at the hypervisor level and security at the guest OS level.

One of the major issues is whether the hypervisor should monitor the guest operations systems or should there be a monitor for each guest OS? If the hypervisor is monitoring the guest OSs, then the hypervisor code could be large and this is not desirable. Furthermore, it will be hard to migrate to a new hypervisor if the hypervisor is changed. The advantage with this approach is that the hypervisor can determine the security of all of the guest OSs. On the other hand, if the guest OS is carrying out the monitoring, then it is easier to migrate to a new hypervisor. These are tradeoffs that have to be carried out at the design level of the virtualization component. Figure 16.3 illustrates the hypervisor monitoring the guest OSs while Figure 16.4 illustrates the guest OSs carrying out the monitoring.

Next, let us examine application security at the level of SaaS, PaaS, and IaaS. SaaS providers are responsible for providing application security. With respect to PaaS, security has to be provided at the PaaS platform level as well as at the level of the customer applications deployed on a PaaS platform. With respect to IaaS, customer applications are treated as a blackbox. That is, IaaS is not responsible for applications security.

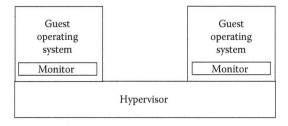

Figure 16.4   Guest OS monitoring.

We started this section stating that security architecture usually consists of the security critical components of the system architecture. Therefore, the main questions are: What is the TCB of the cloud? How much of the hypervisor should be trusted? The challenge for the security architect is to design software for the cloud that will minimize the TCB and yet provide maximum security.

16.4 Identity Management and Access Control

In this section, we will discuss technologies for identity management and access control and their applicability for cloud computing. The first question in identity management is the trust boundary. In a traditional environment, trust boundary is within the control of the organization. This includes the governance of the networks, servers, services, and applications. In a cloud environment, the trust boundary is dynamic and moves within the control of the service provider as well as organizations. Identity federation is an emerging industry best practice for dealing with dynamic and loosely coupled trust relationships in the collaboration model of an organization. The core of the identity federation architecture is the directory service which is the repository for the identity, credentials, and user attributes. Identity management enables organizations to achieve access control and operational security.

In [MATH09] various cloud use cases that need identity management are discussed. These include the following: organization employees accessing SaaS using identity federation; developers creating accounts for partner users in PaaS; end users access storage service in a cloud; applications residing in a CSP; access storage from another cloud service; and provisioning resources to users rapidly to accommodate their changing roles.

The three major components of identity management are authentication, authorization, and auditing. Authentication verifies the identity of a user, system, or service. Authorization gives privileges that a user or system or service has after being authenticated (e.g., access control). Auditing examines what the user, system, or service has carried out and checks for compliance. The identity management process consists of user management (for managing identity lifecycles), authentication management, authorization management, access management, monitoring and auditing, provisioning, credential and attribute management, entitlement management, compliance management, and identity federation management. For example, as stated in [MATH09], organizations using a cloud must plan for user account provisioning such as authenticating a user in a cloud. Identity management can also be provided as a service.

16.4.1 Cloud Identity Administration

In cloud-based identity management, lifecycle management of user identities has to be carried out. Federated identity management with Single Sign-On is being explored for the cloud. What is the responsibility of the CSP and the responsibility of the organization/enterprise? Enterprise Identity and Access Management (IAM) requirements include provisioning of cloud service accounts to users. Current investigation on cloud-based identity management includes how enterprises can expand their identity management requirements to SaaS, PaaS, and IaaS.

Several standards have been developed for identity management. Standards for federated identity management include SAML (Security Assertions Markup Language), WS-Federation, Liberty Alliance, SPML (Service Provisioning Markup Language), XACML (eXtensible Access Control Markup Language), OAuth (Open Authorization), OpenID, Information Cards, and Open Authentication (OAUTH). In this section we will briefly discuss these standards.

SAML: As stated in [SAML], the Security Assertion Markup Language (SAML) is an XML-based open standard data format for exchanging authentication and authorization of data between an identity provider and a service provider.

WS-Federation: As stated in [FEDE], WS-Federation is an Identity Federation specification developed by various corporations such as IBM and Microsoft and is part of the Web Services Security framework. It defines mechanisms for allowing disparate security realms to broker information on identities, identity attributes, and authentication.

Liberty Alliance: As stated in [LIBE], The Liberty Alliance, formed in September 2001 by various organizations, establishes open standards, guidelines, and best practices for identity management.

SPML: As stated in [SPML], Service Provisioning Markup Language (SPML) is an XML-based framework for exchanging user, resource, and service provisioning information between cooperating organizations.

XACML: As stated in [XACM], the eXtensible Access Control Markup Language (XACML) is a standard that defines a declarative access control policy language implemented in XML and a processing model that describes how to evaluate authorization requests according to the rules defined in the policies.

OAuth (Open Authorization): As stated in [OAUT1], OAuth is an open standard for authorization and allows users to share their private resources (e.g., photos, videos) stored on one site with another site without having to give out their credentials. Instead, users would typically provide their username and password tokens. OAuth provides the capability for cloud service X to access data from cloud service Y without disclosing credentials.

OpenID: As stated in [OPEN], OpenID is an open standard that describes how users can be authenticated in a decentralized manner. It eliminates the need for services to provide their own systems and allows users to consolidate their digital identities.

Information Card: As stated in [INFO], an Information Card is a personal digital identity that a person can use online. It is a major component of the Identity metasystem which is an interoperable architecture for digital identity that enables people to use a collection of digital identities based on multiple technologies.

> • SAML
>
> • WS-Federation
>
> • SPML
>
> • XACML
>
> • O Auth
>
> • Open ID
>
> • Information cards
>
> • Open authenticate
>
> • Open authentication API

Figure 16.5   Identity management and access control standards.

Open Authentication (OAUTH): As stated in [OAUT2]. OAUTH is an industry wide collaboration to develop open reference architecture by leveraging existing open standards for the universal adoption of strong authentication.

In summary, we have discussed the various aspects of identity management for the cloud. Figure 16.5 illustrates these aspects.

16.5 Cloud Storage and Data Security

In securing the data for the cloud, one first needs to identify the different types of data. These include data in transit and data at rest. The data are moved from node to node in a cloud. The data in transit have to be secure. Data that are stored in the cloud also have to be secured. Other data security concerns include data lineage and provenance. That is, where does the data come from? Can we trust the data? Are the data accurate? Data remnants are also an important aspect for the cloud. That is, once the customer removes the data from the cloud, the CSP has to ensure that no data of this customer remains in the cloud.

Data security solutions include encryption, identity management, and sanitization. Even though data in transit is encrypted, the use of the data in the cloud will require decryption. That is, the cloud will have unencrypted data. As long as the data is unencrypted, there will be major security concerns. As a result, sensitive data cannot be stored in the public cloud. The homomorphic encryption solution being developed at Stanford University by Craig Gentry [GENT09] is a future solution for the cloud. In this approach, the authors have proved that one does not have to decrypt the data to perform operations.

One of the major challenges is what data does the provider collect—for example, metadata, and how can these data be secured? Other data security issues include

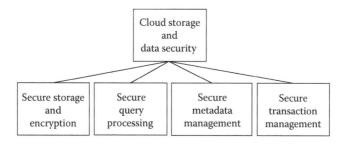

Figure 16.6   Cloud storage and data security.

access control and key management for encrypting. Confidentiality, integrity, and availability are objectives of data security in the cloud.

Data security also includes data management security. That is, how can the database that operates on the cloud be secured? Much of our research is on developing secure cloud data managers for query processing. We will discuss our prototypes in Part VI. Figure 16.6 illustrates the various aspects of storage and data security for the cloud.

16.6 Privacy, Compliance, and Forensics for the Cloud

We will separate the legal issues into three components. One is privacy, another is the various regulations for auditing and compliance and the third is forensics.

16.6.1 Privacy

Privacy is a major concern in the cloud. The question is: Who is responsible for privacy? Is it the owner of the data or is it the cloud? Data lifecycle is an important aspect of privacy. This includes generation, use, transfer, transformation, storage, archival, and destruction of the data. We need policies for each of these operations in the data lifecycle.

Several questions need to be answered. These include who owns the data? Is it the organization that collected the information in the first place, the person about whom the data was collected or the CSP? If the CSP is not the owner of the data, then what is the role of the CSP? Note that organizations can transfer liability but not accountability. Risk assessment and mitigation have to be carried out throughout the data lifecycle. Furthermore, the organization and CSP have to be knowledgeable about the legal obligations.

Various principles have been developed with respect to data lifecycle. These include Collection Limitation Principle; Use Limitation Principle; Security Principle; Retention and Destruction Principle; Transfer Principle and Accountability Principle. These principles have to be examined for the cloud.

16.6.2 Regulations and Compliance

Several regulations both within and outside the United States have been developed for protecting data and information as well as the IT systems. The US regulations for privacy management include the Federal Rules of Civil Procedure, the US Patriot Act, the Electronic Communications Privacy Act, FISMA (Financial Services and Markets Act), GLBA (Gramm–Leach–Bliley Act), HIPAA (Health Insurance Portability and Accountability Act), and HITECH (Health Information Technology for Economic and Clinical Health) Act. The International Regulations include the EU (European Union) Directive and APEC (Asia Pacific Economic Cooperation) Privacy Framework. These regulations have to be examined for cloud security.

Auditing and compliance have been major aspects of IT security. The steps include: define a strategy, define requirements (provide services to clients), define architecture (i.e., architect and structure services to meet requirements), define policies, define processes and procedures, ongoing operations, ongoing monitoring, and continuous improvement. Regulations for auditing include the Sarbanes–Oxley Act, PCI DSS (Payment Card Industry Data Security Standard), HIPAA and COBIT (Control Objectives for Information and Related Technology). There are several questions that need to be answered for cloud computing. These include: What is the impact of cloud computing on the above regulations? What are the internal and external audits for a cloud? What is an appropriate audit framework for the cloud?

16.6.3 Cloud Forensics

The third component of the legal aspects related to the cloud is conducting cloud forensics. There are two issues. One is to use the cloud to conduct forensics. This is because forensics data analysis could be extremely time consuming. Therefore, using the cloud, one can obtain forensics as a service. The other aspect is analyzing the cloud that has been attacked. This is a major challenge as the attack could occur anywhere in the cloud. The examiner should figure out the node that has been compromised and determine when, where, and why the attack occurred. Also with virtualization technologies, the hypervisor as well as the guest OSs have to be monitored. Some of the challenges have been discussed under the section on security architectures. Figure 16.7 illustrates the various legal aspects for the cloud.

16.7 Cryptogaphic Solutions

We discuss encryption as part of our overview on cloud data security and storage. As stated earlier, all sensitive data, whether they are in transit or at rest,

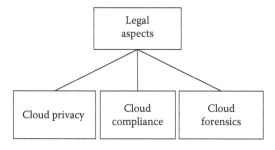

Figure 16.7   Legal aspects of the cloud.

have to be encrypted in the cloud. The major challenge is decryption of the data when performing operations. Whenever decrypted data has to be stored in the cloud even temporarily, this is a major vulnerability. While the homomorphic encryption is a promising solution, the practical implementation of this solution is years away.

Currently, the data stored in the cloud or transmitted across the cloud use traditional encryption techniques. These could include symmetric key or asymmetric key-based encryption algorithms. For example, to ensure confidentiality, the sender may encrypt the data with the receiver's public key. The receiver decrypts the data with his private key. To ensure integrity, the sender may encrypt the data with his private key. The receiver will decrypt the data with the sender's public key. Research is needed to develop cloud-specific cryptographic solutions. Figure 16.8 illustrates cryptographic solutions.

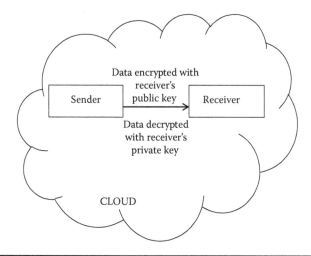

Figure 16.8   Cryptographic solutions.

16.8 Network Security

Network security solutions have to ensure data confidentiality and integrity of the organization's data in transit to and from the public cloud provider. This includes ensuring proper access control (authentication, authorization, and auditing) to resources in the public cloud, ensuring availability of the Internet-facing resources of the public cloud used by the organization, and replacing the established network zones and tiers with domains. That is, the network of the cloud is divided into domains and security has to be provided within a domain as well as across domains. One key is to mitigate the risk factors.

Much of the security for the cloud has focused on architectures, data and storage security as well as identity management. Some of the existing network security protocols are being applied to secure the cloud networks. Research needs to be done on developing special network security protocols for the cloud. Figure 16.9 illustrates network security aspects for the cloud.

16.9 Business Continuity Planning

One of the challenges of an IT organization is business continuity planning and disaster recovery. The disasters could include natural ones such as earthquakes, hurricanes and tornados or manmade ones such as bombing and terrorism. After 9/11 and Katrina, many IT organizations found it extremely difficult to maintain the continuity of operations. Therefore, proper planning is essential.

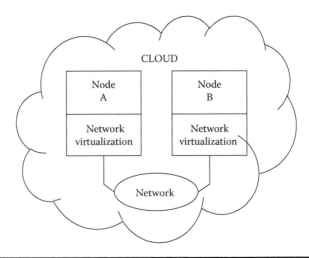

Figure 16.9   Network security.

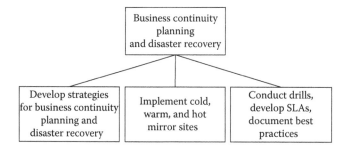

Figure 16.10 Business continuity planning.

The steps in business continuity planning and disaster recovery include having mirror sites that will duplicate the IT environment. These sites could be cold sites with minimum equipment or warm/hot sites with complete duplication. It is not simply sufficient to have back-up sites. The organization has to carry out drills to determine potential issues that could arise. In addition, the organization must have appropriate disaster recovery plans.

In a cloud environment, one major aspect is having everything documented in the SLAs. For example, the CSP may specify that the cloud will be down for a certain number of hours per week for maintenance. This has to be documented in the SLA. Finally, the business continuity plan and disaster management steps have to be extended to include the cloud. That is, should the entire cloud be replicated for back-up or should certain parts of the cloud be replicated? There is not much work done in this area. Figure 16.10 illustrates aspects of business continuity planning.

16.10 Operations Management

Operations management in an IT organization will include managing and maintaining the numerous computers and networks in the organization. For example, all of the machines have to be kept up to date with the latest patch releases. This activity typically comes under the management of the organization's chief security officer. The systems and databases have to be backed up regularly. Furthermore, the legacy systems have to be migrated to modern platforms from time to time.

Operations management in the cloud is a relatively unexplored area. How can the operations management practices in an IT organization be migrated to a cloud? Who is responsible for operations management in the cloud? Is there a cloud security officer? What is the role of the service provider? When and how should the systems in a cloud be backed up? What is the impact of operations management on SaaS, PaaS, and IaaS as well as the deployment models? More investigation is needed to provide answers to the above questions. Figure 16.11 illustrates aspects of operations management.

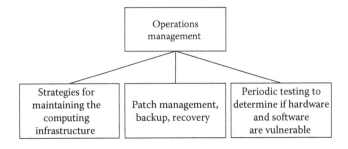

Figure 16.11 Operations management.

16.11 Physical Security

Last but not the least, the physical security of the cloud is critical. Physical security for an IT organization will include protecting the systems and data against natural disasters such as fire and manmade disasters such as terrorism and vandalism. Physical security measures include proper locks and lighting as well as using appropriate material for the fences, walls, windows, and doors. Employees should have proper access to the buildings. Furthermore, in addition to security guards monitoring entry points, security cameras need to be installed.

The question is how should the physical security measures be extended to a cloud environment? The cloud components could be scattered across geographical locations. Therefore, who should guard the cloud? What is the responsibility of the service provider? What happens if the components of the cloud are stolen? We need more work to determine answers to the above questions. Figure 16.12 illustrates aspects of physical security.

16.12 Summary and Directions

This chapter has discussed various secure cloud computing concepts. First, we discussed cloud computing security and governance. Next, we discussed aspects of

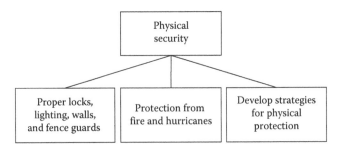

Figure 16.12 Physical security.

security architecture for the cloud. This was followed by a discussion of access control and identity management for the cloud. Data and storage security issues for the cloud were discussed next. Following this, we provided an overview of privacy, compliance, and forensics for the cloud. Finally, aspects such as cryptographic solutions, network security issues, business continuity, operations security, and physical security issues for the cloud were discussed.

Many of the concepts discussed in this chapter are still premature for the cloud. For example, with respect to identity management, we discussed several standards that have been developed for identity management in IT systems. These include SAML, SPML, and XACML. The applicability of these standards for the cloud has to be carried out. A major challenge in applying the standards and technologies for the cloud is scalability. That is, a cloud could have hundreds of nodes and could carry out extensive computations and yet ensure that the clients get the responses in a timely manner. That is, performance of the cloud is a major issue. As stated earlier, research in secure cloud computing is just beginning. A lot more needs to be done before secure clouds can be deployed.

References

[FEDE] WS-Federation, http://en.wikipedia.org/wiki/WS-Federation

[GENT09] Craig Gentry, Fully homomorphic encryption using ideal lattices: http://www.informatik.uni-trier.de/~LEY/db/conf/stoc/stoc2009.html. STOC 2009: 169-178.

[HARR10] Harris, S., *CISSP Exam Guide*, McGraw-Hill, New York, NY, 2010.

[INFO] Information Card, http://en.wikipedia.org/wiki/Information_Card

[LIBE] The Liberty Alliance, http://en.wikipedia.org/wiki/Liberty_Alliance

[MATH09] Mather, T., Kumaraswamy, S., and Latif, S., *Cloud Security and Privacy: An Enterprise Perspective on Risks and Compliance,* O'Reilly, Sebastopol, CA, 2009.

[OAUT1] Open Authorization, http://en.wikipedia.org/wiki/OAuth

[OAUT2] Open Authentication, http://www.openauthentication.org/

[OPEN] OpenID, http://en.wikipedia.org/wiki/OpenID

[SAML] Security Assertion Markup Language, http://en.wikipedia.org/wiki/Security_Assertion_Markup_Language

[SPML] Services Provisioning Markup Language, http://en.wikipedia.org/wiki/Service_Provisioning_Markup_Language

[XACML] eXtensible Access Control Markup Language, http://en.wikipedia.org/wiki/XACML

Chapter 17

Secure Cloud Computing Functions

17.1 Overview

In Chapter 8, we provided an overview of the various concepts about the cloud. This included a discussion on the deployment models and service models. In Chapter 9, we discussed cloud computing functions. In particular, we described a cloud computing framework and then discussed the various layers of the framework. In Chapter 16, we discussed secure cloud computing concepts. In particular, we examined the CISSP modules and explored the impact of the cloud on these modules. In this chapter, we will continue along the lines and discuss secure cloud computing functions. Specifically we will examine the cloud computing functions discussed in Chapter 9 and examine the security impact on the functions. These functions include those for:

- Cloud OSs
- Cloud storage systems
- Cloud database systems
- Cloud networking systems

The secure cloud computing functions will be best illustrated using our secure cloud computing framework. In addition, we will also discuss integrity management in the cloud. Finally, we will discuss cloud applications such as cloud information and knowledge management.

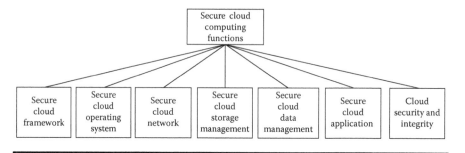

Figure 17.1   Secure cloud computing functions.

The organization of this chapter is as follows. Our secure cloud computing framework will be discussed in Section 17.2. Secure OS functions, including secure virtualization is discussed in Section 17.3. Secure cloud networks will be discussed in Section 17.4. Secure cloud storage management functions will be discussed in Section 17.5. Secure cloud data management functions will be discussed in Section 17.6. Other aspects such as access control and identity management will be discussed in Section 17.7. Application functions will be discussed in Section 17.8. This chapter is summarized in Section 17.9. The concepts discussed in this chapter are illustrated in Figure 17.1. More details on security issues for cloud computing can be found in [HAML10] and [MATH09].

17.2 Secure Cloud Computing Framework

Our secure cloud computing framework is illustrated in Figure 17.2. We have defined a layered framework. At the lowest level is the networking layer and at the highest level is the applications layer. The applications could be any type of application including healthcare, financial and defense and intelligence. The applications that we have hosted on the cloud include threat analysis, malware detection, and

Secure Cloud Application
Secure Cloud Data Management
Secure Cloud Storage Management
Secure Cloud Operating System Virtualization
Secure Cloud Network Virtualization

Figure 17.2   Secure cloud computing framework.

assured information sharing and ontology management. We will describe these applications in later chapters.

The core layers of the secure cloud framework are the secure OS/virtualization layer, the secure storage layer, the secure data management layer which also includes data mining functions. The secure OS/virtualization layer is the layer that carries out virtualization as well as memory management, scheduling, and interprocess communication management. The secure storage layer will manage the massive storage of data in the cloud and its functions include encryption and decryption of the data. We have explored aspects of securing Hadoop for managing distributed storage securely. As stated earlier, Hadoop goes hand-in-hand with Google's MapReduce for analysis tasks. Our current research is exploring ways to secure MapReduce functions. The secure data management layer will carry out secure cloud query processing, secure cloud transactions management, secure cloud metadata management, and secure cloud data mining.

Security management which is an aspect of policy management was discussed in Chapter 9. Identity management includes identification, authentication, and authorization and some of these concepts were discussed in Chapter 16. Integrity management will include maintaining the accuracy and quality of the data. Other security-related functions include governance, risk management, and backup and recovery. Since we discussed many of the secure cloud computing concepts in Chapter 16, we will not discuss them here. In the remaining sections of this chapter, we will discuss each of the functions that we have mentioned in this section including secure OSs and hypervisors, secure data storage, secure data management, secure networks, security and integrity management, and secure applications.

17.3 Secure Cloud OSs and Hypervisors

Securing the cloud OS involves two aspects. One is securing the host OS and the other is securing the hypervisors. Securing the host OS involves enforcing an appropriate security policy as well as securing functions such as memory management, interprocess communications, and scheduling. For example, the host OS may enforce access control policies based on access control lists or capability lists. In the case of multilevel security, the host OS may enforce a policy such as the Bell and LaPadula policy. Interprocess communication between the processes is determined by the policies. That is, can a process P1 send a message to process P2? Access control policies will determine the access that a process has to a file. Usually with OSs, access is at the file level while in a database system, finer granularity of access is provided. Scheduling tasks will involve executing tasks that have higher priority first. However, if the higher priority task is at a higher security level than a lower level task which has lower priority, it may have to be aborted so that resources are given to the higher priority process. This could result in a covert channel. Such security considerations have to be examined when scheduling the tasks. Memory management involves allocating memory space for process execution. This action has to be carried out without violating the security policies.

We discussed virtualization in Chapter 9. Securing the hypervisor is a major challenge. It is the hypervisor that keeps the guest OSs separate. That is, the hypervisor has to ensure that the guest OSs are allocated resources in such a way that the OSs do not interfere with each other. Furthermore, a guest OS cannot corrupt the resources of another guest OS. Therefore, if the hypervisor is compromised then the entire cloud can be compromised. As a result, it is desirable to have the hypervisor code as small as possible.

The main question is: who should monitor the guest OSs? If the hypervisor is to monitor all the guest OSs, then the guest OSs cannot be ported to a new hypervisor easily. Furthermore, the hypervisor code could be complex. However, all of the monitoring resides in the hypervisor which means each VM (virtual machine) does not have to do expensive computations. The hypervisor carrying out the monitoring is called Virtual Machine Introspection (VMI). If the guest OSs do their own monitoring, then the hypervisor code will be less complex, but each VM has to carry out its own monitoring which could be computationally expensive. Furthermore, the virtual agents in the VMs have to be managed by the host OS which means much of the security is the responsibility of the host OS.

In his article, Chris Benton has explained these concepts very well. He states that one of the biggest security issues is kernel level rootkits [BENT]. This is because a kernel level rootkit effectively turns the core OS into malware. The result is that the rootkit has the highest level of system permissions, and can leverage these to hide itself from detection. With introspection, the VM is run at a lower level of permissions than the hypervisor. This means that if a rootkit infects a VM, our ability to detect the presence of the rootkit is improved.

Chris Benton states that executing antivirus software is computationally intensive. Therefore, if multiple VMs initiate a full disk scan at the same time, an IaaS cloud can become extremely unresponsive. He calls this situation "an AV (anti-virus) storm." Therefore, having an AV instance at the hypervisor level could monitor the entire IaaS. While in many ways hypervisors providing security is desirable, it also enables attacks to the hypervisor as it carries out more functions. Furthermore, the hypervisor will have full access to the entire cloud since it has access to all the VMs. This could be a problem.

The debate continues whether to implement the hypervisor code or enhance the host OSs to operate in the cloud. OSs such as the Android now have support to function in the cloud. More recently there has been some work on investigating attacks on the cloud as well as solutions to the attacks. For example, Michael Reiter and his team at the University of North Carolina are investigating side channel attacks on hypervisors such as XEN. Zhiqiang Lin and his colleagues at the University of Texas at Dallas are developing solutions to VMI including the VM Space Traveler. Details can be found at [ZHAN12] and [FU12].

17.4 Secure Cloud Networks

In Chapter 9, we discussed network virtualization issues for the cloud. As in the case of hypervisor security, security for virtual networks remains a challenge. Should the virtualization software for the networks monitor all the virtual networks, or should each virtual network have its own monitor? Such individual monitors are hosted on the physical network. Another challenge to secure cloud networks is extending the secure network protocols to the cloud. Networking protocols include the TCP/IP protocols. The question is what extensions should be made to these protocols to operate in the cloud?

Chris Benton has discussed the challenges in firewall management in a cloud. In a regular networked environment, usually there are well-organized firewall policies. However, in a cloud there could be multiple firewalls provided by multiple vendors. Managing all the firewall policies could become a nightmare. The policies are inconsistent and have different representations. The challenge is to come up with some uniform mappings between the different policies. These are virtual firewalls.

Mather, Kumaraswamy, and Latif argue that the traditional network zones and tiers have to be replaced by security domains or security groups in the cloud environment [MATH09]. They state that the security group feature of Amazon's AWS enables VMs to communicate with each other through virtual firewalls that filter traffic based on IP addresses, ports, and firewalls.

In summary, the security challenges include securing the virtual networks, defining the notion of domains, determining the communications between VMs via virtual networks and firewalls, and examining the network protocols to determine the impact of cloud computing.

17.5 Secure Cloud Storage Management

With respect to secure cloud storage, the challenge is coming up with appropriate storage strategies for the cloud without violating the policies. For example, how should the data be fragmented across the different nodes in the cloud without any information leakage? How can data virtualization be exploited to give optimum storage and yet maintain security? Kantarcioglu and Mehrotra have developed interesting secure storage schemes for a hybrid cloud [OKTA12]. Their storage schemes take into consideration the query execution costs with sensitive data residing in the private cloud and unclassified data residing in the public cloud.

Encryption is another major challenge for secure storage. All sensitive data such as patient data and financial data have to be encrypted. The encrypted data has to be manipulated. While the work at Stanford University has shown how to manipulate encrypted data computationally (i.e., homomorphic encryption), feasible solutions are yet to be developed. Therefore, at present the sensitive data have to be stored in a private cloud.

Our research is also examining security for both Hadoop and MapReduce. We are examining how policy models such as XACML can be implemented on the Hadoop framework. At present, our XACML policies are enforced on the data and not at the Hadoop level. We are exploring implementations of the models at the Hadoop level. Furthermore, our recent work includes examining security for the MapReduce framework.

17.6 Secure Cloud Data Management

Secure cloud data management issues include secure cloud query processing and secure cloud transaction processing. We have carried out a lot of work on secure cloud data management. In later chapters we will discuss the prototypes we have developed for secure cloud query processing. All of our prototypes utilize the Hadoop/MapReduce Framework for distributed storage. In our first prototype, we built an XACML policy engine on top of the HIVE framework. Here, we assume that the data resides in relational databases in the cloud. In our second prototype, we have developed a SPARQL query optimizer to operate in the cloud to store and manage RDF data. Queries are posed in SPARQL. The policies are specified in XACML. We have developed query rewriting strategies that enforce the XACML policies on RDF data. More details can be found in [THUR10] and [HUSA11].

Our third prototype implements an RDF-based policy engine on top of our SPARQL query optimizer. This way there is a seamless integration between the data and policies, both expressed in RDF. The policy engine will enforce information-sharing policies as well as handle problems such as the inference problem. We will discuss this policy engine when we discuss assured information sharing in the cloud in Part VII.

We also have developed a prototype of a hybrid cloud that utilizes tools such as HBASE for query processing. Here, we assume that sensitive data are placed in a private cloud while unclassified data are placed in a public cloud. We have come up with algorithms for secure query processing in such an environment. Details can be found in [OKTA12].

Other secure cloud data management functions include secure transaction processing, data interoperability in the cloud, and cloud data mining. More discussions on some of these functions will be given in Chapter 18 when we discuss secure cloud data management.

17.7 Cloud Security and Integrity Management

Cloud security includes confidentiality, privacy, and trust. Several standards have been developed to provide cloud security. We discussed these standards in Chapter 16. For example, standards such as SAML are being explored for authentication.

Scalability of SAML to operate in a cloud is a challenge. Standards such as XACML are being explored for authorization. That is, once the user is authenticated, the next step is to determine the resources that the user can access. Provisioning the resources of the cloud to the users is provided by standards such as SPML. We discussed these standards as well as others such as OpenID in Chapter 16.

To ensure the integrity of the data and the processing, various integrity policies have to be enforced. Enforcing policies such as a full-time employee must work at least 40 h have been studied extensively in a database. These integrity enforcement techniques have to be studied for a cloud environment. Furthermore, the provenance of the data becomes critical as the data could come from any application from multiple clouds. Thus, the amount of provenance data gathered and/or generated could be massive. Appropriate strategies have to be developed to process such massive data in the cloud. Other integrity management techniques include fault tolerance computing, backup, and recovery. Some aspects of these techniques were discussed in Chapter 16 and will be revisited in Chapter 18.

17.8 Secure Cloud Applications

In Chapter 12, we discussed some cloud applications such as healthcare, financial, and social networking. More details on securing these applications will be discussed in Chapter 18. Consider for example, knowledge management for an organization. Secure knowledge management which involves controlling access to intellectual property and resources of an organization is usually provided as a collection of web services. For example, an organization may want to find experts for a particular project. The expert finder web service may be involved and this service can find the experts via the corporate Intranet. These web services may be implemented on the cloud for improved performance. That is, the knowledge management services can be implemented as SaaS. Security for web services is essential for securing the knowledge management services.

While the framework we have defined (i.e., OS and database system) provides security at the file and data (e.g., relational table) level, the applications enforce application-specific policies. These policies are unique to the applications. For example, in the case of cloud-based workflow applications, the policies will specify the authorization that a person has to carry out a specific activity. These policies are enforced at the workflow management (i.e., application) level.

17.9 Summary and Directions

This chapter has discussed various aspects of cloud computing functions. We provided an overview of our secure cloud computing framework and then discussed security for virtualization, network, data storage, and management for the cloud.

Essentially, we examined the functions for the cloud discussed in Part III and described security for these functions. There is a lot of work that remains to be done. First, we need to examine each layer of the framework and determine the attacks that could occur. As we stated, Reiter and his team are investigating side challenge attacks at the virtualization layer. These attacks could occur not just at the virtualization layer, but also at the storage and data layers. We need to carry out a comprehensive investigation of the potential attacks and the solutions to these attacks.

In the next chapter, we will elaborate on secure cloud data management functions. Secure cloud products will be discussed in Chapter 21. We will also describe some of the prototypes we have developed for secure cloud data management in Part VI.

References

[BENT] Benton, C., *The Basics of Virtualization Security, Cloud Security Alliance*, https://cloudsecurityalliance.org/wp-content/uploads/2011/11/virtualization-security.pdf

[HAML10] Hamlen, K. W., M. Kantarcioglu, L. Khan and B. M. Thuraisingham, Security issues for cloud computing. *International Journal of Information Security and Privacy*, 4(2): 36–48, 2010.

[HUSA11] Husain, M. F., J. P. McGlothlin, M. M. Masud, L. R. Khan, B. M. Thuraisingham, Heuristics-based query processing for large RDF graphs using cloud computing. *IEEE Trans. Knowl. Data Eng.* (TKDE) 23(9): 1312–1327, 2011.

[FU12] Fu, Y. and Z. Lin, Space traveling across VM: Automatically bridging the semantic gap in virtual machine introspection via online kernel data redirection. *IEEE Symposium on Security and Privacy*, San Francisco, CA, 2012: 586–600.

[MATH09] Mather, T., et al., *Cloud Security and Privacy: An Enterprise Perspective on Risks and Compliance*, O'Reilly, Sebastopol, CA, 2009.

[OKTA12] Oktay, K. Y., V. Khadilkar, B. Hore, M. Kantarcioglu, S. Mehrotra and B. M. Thuraisingham, *Risk-Aware Workload Distribution in Hybrid Clouds*, IEEE CLOUD, Honolulu, HI, 2012, pp. 229–236.

[THUR10] Thuraisingham, B. M., V. Khadilkar, A. Gupta, M. Kantarcioglu and L. Khan, Secure data storage and retrieval in the cloud. Collaborate Com 2010: 1–8.

[ZHAN12] Zhang, Y., A. Juels, M. K. Reiter, T. Ristenpart, Cross-VM side channels and their use to extract private keys. *ACM Conference on Computer and Communications Security*, Raleigh, NC, 2012: 305–316.

Chapter 18

Secure Cloud Data Management

18.1 Overview

In the previous two chapters, we discussed secure cloud computing concepts as well as secure cloud computing functions. For example, in Chapter 16, we discussed the impact of the cloud on the 10 CISSP topics, including governance and risk management, access control, security architecture, cryptography, data and applications security, network security, physical security, legal implications and forensics, business continuity management, and operations management. In Chapter 17, we discussed the secure cloud computing functions including secure virtualization, secure cloud data and storage management, secure cloud networking, and secure cloud applications. In this chapter, we will elaborate on secure cloud data management. We will also include concepts in secure cloud information management and secure cloud knowledge management.

In our terminology, data are managed by a data manager. Information is extracted from the data and knowledge is about understanding the information and taking actions. Data management technologies include database management and data administration. Information management technologies include multimedia information management and collaborative information management. Knowledge management is about reusing the knowledge and expertise of an organization to improve profits and other benefits. In this chapter, we will examine security issues for data, information and knowledge management and then discuss how cloud computing technologies may be applied for managing data, information and knowledge. Some of the prototypes we have implemented for secure cloud

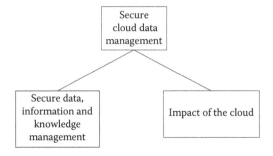

Figure 18.1   Secure cloud data management.

query processing as well as secure cloud-based assured information sharing will be discussed in later chapters.

The organization of this chapter is as follows. In Section 18.2, we discuss secure data management that also include discussions of secure information and knowledge management. In Section 18.3, we discuss how cloud computing may be utilized for secure data, information, and knowledge management. This chapter is summarized in Section 18.4. Figure 18.1 illustrates the concepts discussed in this chapter. More details on secure data management are provided in Appendix C.

18.2 Secure Data Management

18.2.1 Access Control

Access control deals with granting access to the data depending on the users, user groups, and other factors such as roles of users. Access control-based security was initially investigated for secure OSs where access was granted to files depending on the kinds of processes. The types of access included read and write operations. Then the concept was extended to databases where access was granted say to relations, attributes, and elements. Now, access control-based security is part of discretionary security and also includes the handling of complex security policies, granting access to data based on roles and functions, and also both positive and negative authorization policies. One of the techniques for enforcing security policies in data management systems is query modification, also known as query rewriting. In this approach, the query is modified according to the policies and the modified query is executed. Figure 18.2 illustrates various types of discretionary access control mechanisms. Query modification is illustrated in Figure 18.3. More details are also given in [THUE05].

18.2.2 Inference Problem

Inference is the process of posing queries and deducing unauthorized information from the legitimate responses received. The inference problem exists for all types

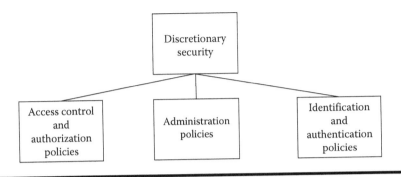

Figure 18.2   Discretionary security.

of database systems and has been studied extensively within the context of multi-level databases. Early developments on the inference problem focused on statistical database security. Then the focus was on security constraint processing to handle the inference problem. Researchers also used conceptual structures to design the database application and detect security violations via inferences during the design time. There are many technical challenges for the inference problem including the insolvability and the complexity of the problem. The developments on the inference problem are illustrated in Figure 18.4. Recently, the inference problem is receiving much attention within the context of privacy. Technologies such as data mining are being used extensively for national security. This is causing privacy concerns. The privacy problem is a form of the inference problem where one deduces highly private information from the public information.

Query Modification Algorithm:

Input: Query, security constraints
Output: Modified query

For constraints that are relevant to the query, modify the where clause of the query via a Negation.

For example: If salary should not be released to Jane and if Jane requests information from employee, then modify the query to retrieve information from employee where attribute is not salary.

Repeat the process until all relevant constraints are processed.

The end result is the modified query.

Figure 18.3   Query modification.

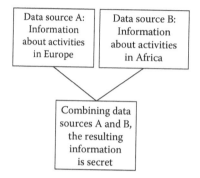

Figure 18.4 Aspects of the inference problem.

18.2.3 Secure Distributed/Heterogeneous Data Management

Security for distributed, heterogeneous, and federated database systems is critical for many operational environments. For example, the individual's data management systems could enforce their own policies. These policies have to be integrated to form the global policy. Policy integration is a major challenge in heterogeneous and federated data management systems. Figure 18.5 illustrates policy integration.

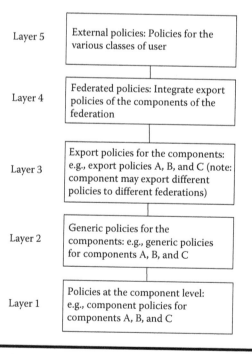

Figure 18.5 Policy integration.

18.2.4 Secure Object Data Systems

Object technology is important for many applications including programming languages, design and analysis for applications and systems, interconnection and databases. For example, programming languages such as Java are based on objects. Distributed object management systems connect heterogeneous databases and applications. Databases and applications are modeled using objects. Large systems are created using object components. Finally, object technology is very popular for modeling and design. It is critical that objects be secure. That is, we need secure object programming languages, secure object databases, secure distributed object systems, and secure object components and using objects to model secure applications. In [THUR05], we discussed various types of secure object technologies relevant to databases and applications. For example, in a secure object model, access may be controlled to the object instances, the attributes, the methods, and the classes. Figure 18.6 illustrates access control on objects.

18.2.5 Data Warehousing, Data Mining, Security, and Privacy

Many organizations are now developing data warehouses. Warehouses essentially provide different views of the data to different users. For example, a president of a company may want to see quarterly sales figures while a manager of a department may want to see the daily sales numbers. These data warehouses have to be secure. Figure 18.7 illustrates security aspects of data warehouses. For example, based on the security policies of the individual databases, a policy for the warehouse has to be developed.

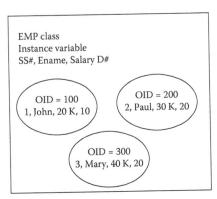

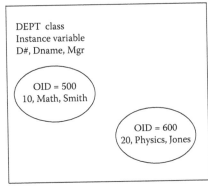

Figure 18.6   Access control on objects.

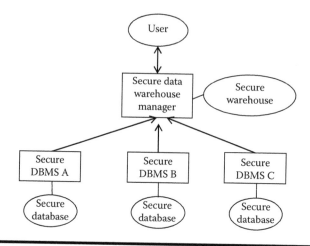

Figure 18.7 Secure data warehousing.

In [THUR05], we discussed the relationship between data mining and security. For example, data mining could be used to handle security problems such as intrusion detection and auditing. On the other hand, data mining also exacerbates the inference and privacy problems. This is because a user can use the various data mining tools and combine different pieces of information and deduce new information that may be sensitive and private. This is illustrated in Figure 18.8. Recently there has been much discussion on privacy violations that result due to data mining. We discussed privacy issues as well as the notion of privacy-preserving data mining in [THUR05].

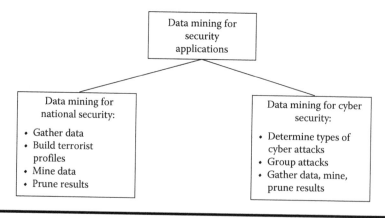

Figure 18.8 Data mining and security.

18.2.6 Secure Information Management

Security has an impact on the functions of information management systems such as multimedia information management and workflow/collaborative information management. For example, consider the query operation in a multimedia data manager. The query processor has to examine the access control rules and security and modify the query accordingly. For example, if the fact that the existence of Operation X is classified, then this query cannot be sent to an unclassified multimedia data collector such as a video camera to film the event. Security also has an impact on multimedia editing and browsing. When one is browsing multimedia data, the system must ensure that the user has the proper access to browse the link or access the data associated with the link. In the case of multimedia editing, when objects at different levels are combined to form a film, then the film object has to be classified accordingly. One may need to classify the various frames or assign the high water mark associated with the levels of the individual objects that compose the film. Furthermore, when films are edited (such as deleting certain portions of the film) then one needs to recompute the level of the edited object.

Next, consider workflow systems where the objective is for users to have the proper credentials to carry out the particular task. For example, in the case of making a purchase for a project, only a project leader could initiate the request. A secretary then types the request. Then the administrator has to use his/her credit card and make the purchase. The mailroom has the authority to make the delivery. In a collaborative environment, trust and negotiation play an important role. For example, how can the parties trust each other in solving a problem? If A gives some information to B, can B share the information with C even if A and C do not communicate with each other? Also secure data management technologies are necessary to manage the data for workflow and collaboration applications. Figure 18.9 illustrates secure collaboration.

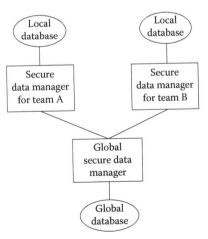

Figure 18.9   Secure collaboration.

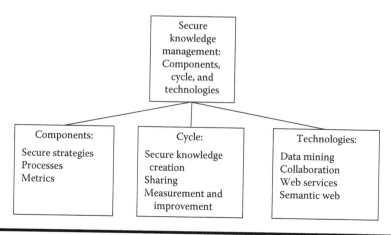

Figure 18.10   Secure knowledge management.

18.2.7 Secure Knowledge Management

This is about corporations sharing the resources and expertise, as well as building intellectual capital so that it can increase its competitiveness. One of the challenges in knowledge management is maintaining security. Trade secrets have to be kept highly confidential so that competitors do not have any access to them. This means one needs to enforce some form of access control such as role-based access control, credential mechanism, or encryption.

To have secure knowledge management, we need to have secure strategies, processes, and metrics [BERT06]. That is, metrics must include support for security-related information. Processes must include secure operations. Strategies must include security strategies. When knowledge is created, the creator may specify to whom the knowledge can be transferred. Additional access control techniques may be enforced by the manager of the knowledge. Knowledge sharing and knowledge transfer operations must also enforce the access control and security policies. Secure knowledge management architecture may be built around the corporation's Intranet. Figure 18.10 illustrates the various information that must be protected to ensure secure knowledge management.

18.3 Impact of the Cloud

In this section, we will discuss the impact of the cloud on the secure data management functions discussed in Section 18.2.

18.3.1 Discretionary Security

Much of the work on secure cloud data management has focused on secure cloud query processing. For example, in the prototypes that we have developed, the

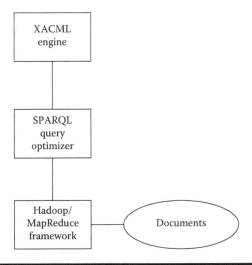

Figure 18.11   XACML policy engine.

policies are expressed in XACML. The query is modified according to the policies and executed on the cloud. We have utilized the Hadoop/MapReduce framework as well the HIVE framework for distributed storage management and relational data management. We have also implemented query rewriting for queries specified in XACML and implemented the queries using our SPARQL query processor on the cloud for semantic web data. The query processor is hosted on the Hadoop/MapReduce framework. The challenge in query processing is to exploit the distributed processing and resource utilization capability provided by the cloud. We have also implemented an XACML-based policy engine on the cloud for secure query processing. This policy engine is discussed in [HUSA11]. Figure 18.11 illustrates our policy engine.

18.3.2 Inference Problem

With respect to the inference problem, the cloud platform provides an ideal solution. To handle the inference problem, massive amounts of data that include history information as well as external knowledge have to be processed. Such massive amounts of data can be stored and processed in a cloud. As stated earlier, we have developed an RDF-based policy engine for handling the inference problem. This policy engine now operates on the cloud [CADE12]. Figure 18.12 illustrates our policy engine.

18.3.3 Secure Distributed and Heterogeneous Data Management

Since cloud computing is essentially based on distributed computing, it lends itself naturally to distributed data management. For example, the data as well as

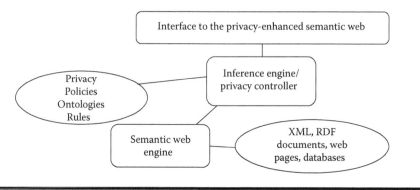

Figure 18.12 RDF policy engine.

processing is distributed across the cloud. For integrating heterogeneous databases, one needs to match the schemas as well as align the ontologies. For example, for the entity resolution problem, schema matching and ontology alignment have been explored as solutions. These schema matching and ontology management algorithms have been implemented on the cloud [ALIP11]. The challenge is to implement the policy integration algorithms on the cloud. In one of our prototypes, we have assumed that each organization stores its data and policies on the cloud. Organizations share the data according to the policies.

18.3.4 Secure Object Systems

The policies enforced on the object model can be handled the same way query rewriting is handled for relational systems. With respect to objects for integrating the various components, organizations such as Object Management Group (OMG) are exploring implementations of object request brokers on the cloud. The security properties that have been developed for such systems have to be implemented on the cloud.

18.3.5 Data Warehousing, Data Mining, Security, and Privacy

Data management corporations such as Oracle and IBM are implementing their data warehousing products on the cloud. The challenge is to implement the policies enforced in data warehouses on the cloud. Data mining on the cloud has received a lot of attention. One challenge with data mining is to ensure the privacy of the individuals. Privacy-preserving data mining algorithms have emerged during the past decade. Many of the solutions, such as multiparty computation, are processing intensive and are ideal for cloud implementations.

18.3.6 Secure Information Management

Secure Information management applications such as insider threat detection and information sharing are being implemented on the cloud. Furthermore, managing multimedia data on the cloud has received a lot of attention. Multimedia services have been implemented at a layer between PaaS and SaaS. Such clouds are called multimedia clouds. These clouds provide quality of service as well as streaming video for mobile applications. Incorporating security services with the multimedia services remains a challenge.

Workflow applications have been implemented in Enterprise Resource Planning systems such as PeopleSoft and SAP. These systems have also implemented access control policies such as role-based access control. With companies such as Oracle and SAP moving their data and applications to the cloud, we can expect secure workflow processing to be provided on the cloud. With respect to collaboration, individuals or groups of individuals work together to solve a problem. They could store their data and policies on the cloud and work together utilizing the cloud.

18.3.7 Secure Knowledge Management

Secure knowledge management is usually provided as a collection of web services. For example, an organization may want to find experts for a particular project. The expert finder web service may be involved and this service can find the experts via the corporate Intranet. These web services may be implemented on the cloud for improved performance. That is, the knowledge management services can be implemented as SaaS.

18.4 Summary and Directions

In this chapter, we have discussed secure data management functions and then described the impact of the cloud on these functions. In particular, we discussed discretionary security, multilevel security, and inference problem, secure objects, secure multimedia systems, secure distributed data management secure heterogeneous data integration, secure data warehousing, data mining, secure information, and knowledge management. Securing the cloud for managing data, information and knowledge will continue to be a critical area in IT due to the need for storing, mining, and mining massive amounts of data.

Our work has focused on developing prototypes mainly for cloud data management systems. We have also developed systems for secure information sharing in the cloud. We will discuss some of the prototypes we have developed for secure cloud data management in Parts VI and VII of this book.

References

[ALIP11] Alipanah, N., P. Parveen, L. Khan, and B. M. Thuraisingham, Ontology-driven query expansion using map/reduce framework to facilitate federated queries. *In Proceedings of International Conference on Web Services* (ICWS 2011), Washington, DC, 712–713.

[BERT06] Bertino, E. et al., Secure knowledge management, *IEEE Transactions on Systems, Man and Cybernetics*, May 2006.

[CADE12] Cadenhead, T., V. Khadilkar, M. Kantarcioglu, and B. M. Thuraisingham, A cloud-based RDF policy engine for assured information sharing. *In Proceedings of ACM Symposium on Access Control Models and Technologies* (SACMAT 2012), Newark, NJ, 113–116.

[HUSA11] Husain, M. F., J. P. McGlothlin, M. M. Masud, L. R. Khan, and B. M. Thuraisingham, Heuristics-based query processing for large RDF graphs using cloud computing. *IEEE Trans. Knowl. Data Eng.*, 23(9), 1312–1327, 2011.

[THUR05] Thuraisingham, B., *Database and Applications Security*, CRC Press, Boca Raton, FL, 2005.

Chapter 19

Secure Cloud Computing Guidelines

19.1 Overview

In this chapter, we will provide an overview of the guidelines for cloud computing security. These guidelines have been developed by the NIST. We have essentially summarized the discussions in the NIST document. For more details of the guidelines, we will refer the reader to [NIST]. For completion of the guidelines as discussed by NIST, we have included the definition of cloud computing, cloud computing service models, deployment models, and security issues.

The guidelines discussed by NIST cover several topics. These include the service and deployment models, architecture governance, data protection, security and privacy, availability, and incident response. Since secure cloud computing is still evolving, the reader should note that these guidelines will also evolve. Nevertheless, we have found these guidelines to be very useful to understand secure cloud computing. The guidelines discuss the service and deployment models, identity management as well as availability.

The organization of this chapter is as follows. The guidelines will be summarized in Section 19.2. This chapter is summarized in Section 19.3. Figure 19.1 illustrates the guidelines discussed in this chapter. An overview of secure cloud computing can be found in [MATH09]. White papers on secure cloud computing have been posted on the website of the Cloud Security Alliance [CSA].

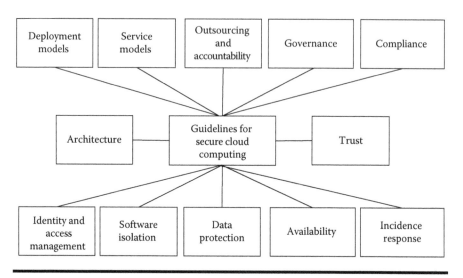

Figure 19.1 Guidelines for secure cloud computing.

19.2 The Guidelines

Definition: Cloud computing has been defined by NIST as a

> model for enabling convenient, on-demand network access to a shared pool of configurable computing resources (e.g., networks, servers, storage, applications, and services) that can be rapidly provisioned and released with minimal management effort or cloud provider interaction. [NIST]

Deployment models: As stated by [NIST], there are multiple deployment models.

> Public cloud is one in which the infrastructure and computational resources that it comprises are made available to the general public over the Internet. It is owned and operated by a cloud provider delivering cloud services to consumers and is external to the customer organization. A private cloud is one in which the computing environment is operated exclusively for a single organization. It may be managed by the organization or by a third party, and may be hosted within the organization's data center or outside of it. A private cloud may give the organization more control over the resources and operation of the cloud. Hybrid clouds involve a composition of two or more clouds at least one of which is public and one of which is private. A community cloud is a cloud managed by a collection of organizations referred to as the community.

Service models: As stated by NIST, the service model specifies the control the organization has over the cloud resources. There are three main service models.

Software-as-a-Service (SaaS) is a model of service delivery where the cloud service provider provides all the applications to run on the cloud. These applications may include financial applications and health-care applications. Security is provided by the cloud service provider. Platform-as-a-Service (PaaS) is a model of service delivery where the computing platform is provided so that applications can be developed and deployed. That is, programming tools and databases are examples of service provided by the Platform. Security provisions are split between the cloud provider and the cloud consumer. Infrastructure-as-a-Service (IaaS) is a model of service delivery where the basic computing infra-structure of servers, software, and network equipment is provided as a service upon which their platform and applications can be hosted.

Outsourcing and accountability: With cloud computing, an organization may outsource its applications, data, and processing. As stated by NIST, due to out-sourcing, there is concern about security and privacy. What are the risks associated with moving data to the public cloud?

There are three types of public cloud. One type provides no cost to the consumer and gets revenue through advertising. The second type of public cloud charges a fee but does not include any advertisements. The third type is also fee based, but the terms are negotiated between the consumer and the provider.

It is stated by NIST that the organization is ultimately responsible for the secu-rity of its data and processing and each type of public cloud brings different security challenges.

Governance: We addressed governance in the previous chapter. Here, we will discuss governance as defined by NIST.

Governance is about control and oversight by the organization over poli-cies, procedures, and standards for application development, acquisition design, implementation, testing, use, and monitoring of the services.

The challenge is to develop appropriate methods for governance for the cloud services. This will involve determining the roles and responsibilities of the cloud service provider and the organizations as well as determining the risks, conducting a risk-analysis process, and managing and mitigating the risks.

Compliance: As stated by NIST,

compliance refers to an organization's responsibility to operate in agree-ment with established laws, regulations, standards, and specifications. Since cloud crosses organizational boundaries and in many cases it spans multiple counties, the different laws have to be analyzed and enforced.

Therefore, data security and privacy become the critical issues. Appropriate audit mechanisms are also needed to ensure that the regulations and laws are properly enforced.

Trust: As stated by NIST,

> with cloud computing, an organization gives up control over its data and processing and as a result much of the security and privacy controls are in the hands of the service provider.

Therefore, the organization has to trust the service provider. However, there are regulations that protect sensitive data. For example, sensitive data usually must be encrypted, and therefore cannot be placed in a public cloud. Insider threat is also a possibility in a cloud computing paradigm as the service provider will have access to the resources and the data. Moving data in the cloud also increases the security risks. Data ownership has to be firmly established between the organization and the service provider. For example, if a user stores data in the cloud, who owns these data? Cloud services can be transposed into multiple services. Therefore, security issues for service composition have to be examined [THUR10]. Another challenge is protecting the metadata. This would involve information about the users, the account contact information, and the various types of contracts. Such metadata could violate user privacy.

Risk: As with any IT system, risk management for cloud-based services is essential. As stated by NIST,

> risk management is the process of identifying and assessing risk to organizational operations, organizational assets, or individuals resulting from the operation of an information system, and taking the necessary steps to reduce it to an acceptable level.

Architecture: In this section, we will discuss architectural issues as given by the NIST guidelines. Virtual machines are at the heart of the cloud. As stated by NIST,

> virtual machines typically serve as the abstract unit of deployment for IaaS clouds and are loosely coupled with the cloud storage architecture.

The hypervisor (also called the virtual machine monitor) is an additional layer of software between an operating system and hardware platform that is used to operate multitenant virtual machines (called guest operating systems). These hypervisors are prone to attack. It is also stated by NIST that

> most virtualization platforms have the ability to create software-based switches and network configurations as part of the virtual environment to allow virtual machines on the same host to communicate more directly and efficiently.

These virtual networks may also be under attack. Finally, it is stated that both the clients and the servers in the cloud have to be protected.

Identity and access management: Identity management ensures that users can access only authorized information. The challenge is to develop the appropriate access control procedures for the cloud. As stated by NIST,

> identity federation allows the organization and cloud provider to trust and share digital identities and attributes across both the organization and the service provider domains and to provide a means for single sign-on.

The various standards such as SAML and OpenID are being examined for the cloud. Authentication is the process of establishing user identities and SAML is becoming a popular authentication standard for the cloud. SAML request and response messages are typically mapped over SOAP, which relies on XML for its format. SOAP messages are digitally signed. Access control ensures that a user can access the resources that he/she is authorized to access. XACML standard for access control is becoming popular among the cloud providers. In fact, many of our experimental systems have implemented XACML-based access control for various types of data managers.

Software isolation: Owing to the fact that multiple users (i.e., tenants) share the cloud, process isolation is essential. As stated by NIST,

> multi-tenancy in IaaS cloud computing environments is typically done by multiplexing the execution of virtual machines from potentially different consumers on the same physical server. Applications deployed on guest virtual machines can be attacked.

Software isolation for multitenancy in PaaS and SaaS is also being explored. A crucial element is the security of the hypervisor. It is the hypervisor who provides isolation between the guest operating systems. Therefore, if the hypervisor is attacked, then the entire cloud may be compromised. The NIST document states that

> multi-tenancy in virtual machine-based cloud infrastructures gives rise to new threats. The most serious threat is that malicious code can escape the confines of its virtual machine and interfere with the hypervisor or other guest virtual machines.

Data protection: Data stored in a public cloud are in a shared environment. Then data may belong to multiple customers. Storing sensitive data in a public cloud is a major challenge. The typical attacks include attacks to the cryptographic protocols and attacks to the passwords. There is also the issue of who owns the data. Is it the organization that created the data or the cloud service provider? Typically, it is the organization that owns the data. Therefore, it is the responsibility of the organization to ensure data security and privacy. NIST has identified data security techniques, including data isolation, proper access controls, and data sanitization. After the data are removed by the organization, the service provider must ensure that there is no residual data in the cloud.

Availability: Availability of the cloud is important for the customer. The service provider has to specify availability details in the SLAs. There may be temporary outages to the cloud or prolonged outages. In this case, appropriate backup procedures are needed so that the service is not disrupted. There is also the danger of the service provider going out of business. Finally, the cloud may be subject to denial of service attacks. Therefore, such attacks have to be detected before they cause damage.

Incident response: As stated by NIST,

> incident response involves an organized method for dealing with the consequences of an attack against the security of a computer system. It is the responsibility of the cloud service provider to ensure that the system is in operation including the applications, network operating systems and the database systems.

The log files of the cloud have to be examined so that the systems can be recovered. The log data have to be made available in a timely manner. The service provider has to work with the organization as well as with the incident analysis and response team to determine the problem, fix the problem, and carry out a forensics analysis.

19.3 Summary and Directions

This chapter has provided an overview of the security guidelines for cloud computing as discussed by NIST. The guidelines include those for the deployment models, web services, as well as governance, compliance, availability, identity and access management, architecture, incident response, trust, software isolation, and data protection. We have essentially summarized the guidelines provided by NIST. More details can be found in [NIST]. It should be noted that cloud computing will continue to evolve. Therefore, the security issues will also evolve. As a result, these guidelines will continue to evolve. Nevertheless, these guidelines are an excellent starting point for deploying a secure cloud.

Now that we have provided an overview of security issues for the cloud as well as secure cloud computing functions with an emphasis on secure cloud data management, we will provide an overview of (i) using the cloud to carry out security functions in Chapter 20 and (ii) the various security offerings in the cloud computing products and services in Chapter 21.

References

[CSA] Cloud Security Alliance, https://cloudsecurityalliance.org/

[MATH09] Mather, T., Kumaraswamy, S., and Latif, S., *Cloud Security and Privacy: An Enterprise Perspective on Risks and Compliance*, O'Reilly, Sebastopol, CA, 2009.

[NIST] Guidelines on security and privacy in public cloud computing, *National Institute of Standards and Technology*, http://www.nist.gov/customcf/get_pdf.cfm?pub_id=909494

[THUR10] Thuraisingham, B., *Secure Semantic Service-Oriented Systems*, CRC Press, Boca Raton, FL, 2010.

Chapter 20

Security as a Service

20.1 Overview

Chapters 16 to 19 discussed security issues for cloud computing. For example, the various aspects on securing cloud infrastructures were discussed. While cloud computing technologies have to be secure, cloud computing can be used for security services. These include data mining for malware detection services, email spam detection services, and digital forensics services. Using the cloud for security applications has come to be known as "Security-as-a-Service." In this chapter, we will discuss examples of clouds that provide security as a service. Our main focus is on data mining services. An overview of secure cloud computing products including security as a service product will be discussed in Chapter 21.

Data mining has many applications in security including in national security (e.g., surveillance) as well as in cyber security (e.g., virus detection). The threats to national security include attacking buildings, destroying critical infrastructures such as power grids and telecommunication systems [BOLZ05]. Data mining techniques are being investigated to find out who the suspicious people are and who is capable of carrying out terrorist activities. Data mining is also being applied to provide solutions such as intrusion detection and auditing. In this chapter, we will focus mainly on data mining for cyber security applications.

To understand the mechanisms to be applied to safeguard the nation and the computers and networks, we need to understand the types of threats. In [THUR03], we described real-time threats as well as non-real-time threats. A real-time threat is a threat that must be acted upon within a certain time to prevent some catastrophic situation. Note that a nonreal-time threat could become a real-time threat over time. For example, one could suspect that a group of terrorists will eventually perform some act of terrorism. However, when we set time bounds such as a threat

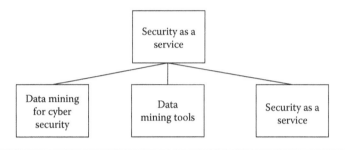

Figure 20.1 Security-as-a-service.

will likely occur say before July 1, 2004, then it becomes a real-time threat and we have to take actions immediately. If the time bounds are tighter such as "a threat will occur within two days," then we cannot afford to make any mistakes in our response.

There has been a lot of work on applying data mining for both national security and cyber security. However, data mining techniques are computationally intensive. Therefore, the data mining services for security applications are the prime candidates for implementation in the cloud.

The organization of this chapter is as follows. In Section 20.2, we will discuss data mining services for cyber security applications. In particular, we will discuss the threats to the computers and networks and describe the applications of data mining to detect such threats and attacks. Some of our current research at UTD will be discussed in Section 20.3. Some other services that fall into the category of security as a service will be discussed in Section 20.4. This chapter is summarized in Section 20.5. Figure 20.1 illustrates the concepts discussed in this chapter. More details can also be found in [THUR04].

20.2 Data Mining Services for Cyber Security Applications

20.2.1 Overview

In this section, we will describe data mining services for security. First, we will provide an overview of the various types of threats. These include cyber terrorism as well as security violations through access control, Trojan horses, and viruses. Then we will describe how data mining techniques may be developed as services to detect security violations. Here is an example of how the data mining service will work. When an organization wants to check whether their networks have been intruded, they will invoke a cloud data mining service to work on their audit data. The data mining service will determine whether there are any intrusions. In Part VII, we described data mining services for intrusion detection and malware detection.

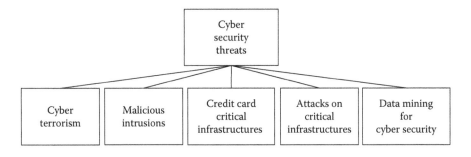

Figure 20.2   Cyber security threats.

The organization of this section is as follows. In Section 20.2.2, we give an overview of cyber terrorism and then discuss insider threats and external attacks. Malicious intrusions are the subject of Section 20.2.3. Credit card and identity theft are discussed in Section 20.2.4. The attacks on critical infrastructures will be discussed in Section 20.2.5. Data mining for cyber security will be discussed in Section 20.2.6. Figure 20.2 illustrates cyber security threats.

20.2.2 Cyber Terrorism, Insider Threats, and External Attacks

Cyber terrorism is one of the major terrorist threats posed to our nation today. As we have mentioned earlier, there is now so much information available electronically and on the web. The attack on our computers as well as networks, databases, and the Internet could be devastating to businesses. It is estimated that cyber terrorism could cost billions of dollars to businesses. For example, consider a banking information system. If terrorists attack such a system and deplete accounts of the funds, then the bank could lose millions and perhaps billions of dollars. By crippling the computer system, millions of hours of productivity could be lost and that equates to money in the end. Even a simple power outage at work through some accident could cause several hours of productivity loss and as a result, a major financial loss. Therefore, it is critical that our information systems must be secure. We discuss the various types of cyber-terrorist attacks. One is spreading viruses and Trojan horses that can wipe away files and other important documents; another is intruding into computer networks.

Note that threats can occur from the outside or from the inside of an organization. Outside attacks are attacks on computers from someone outside the organization. We hear of hackers breaking into computer systems and causing havoc within an organization. There are hackers who start spreading viruses and these viruses cause great damage to the files in various computer systems. But a more sinister problem is the insider threat. There are people inside an organization who have studied the business practices and developed schemes to cripple the organization's information assets. These people could be regular employees or even those working at computer centers. The problem is quite serious as someone may be masquerading as someone else and causing all kinds of damage. In the next few sections, we will examine how data mining could detect and perhaps prevent such attacks.

20.2.3 Malicious Intrusions

Malicious intrusions may include intruding into the networks, web clients and servers, databases, and the operating systems. Many of the cyber-terrorism attacks are due to malicious intrusions. We hear much about network intrusions. What happens here is that intruders try to tap into the networks and get the information that is being transmitted. These intruders may be human intruders or Trojan horses set up by humans. Intrusions could also happen on files. For example, one can masquerade as someone else and log into someone else's computer system and access the files. Intrusions can also occur on databases. The intruders posing as legitimate users can pose queries such as SQL queries and access the data that they are not authorized to know.

Essentially, cyber terrorism includes malicious intrusions as well as sabotage through malicious intrusions or otherwise. Cyber security consists of security mechanisms that attempt to provide solutions to cyber attacks or cyber terrorism. When we discuss malicious intrusions or cyber attacks, we may need to think about the noncyber world, that is, noninformation-related terrorism, and then translate those attacks to attacks on computers and networks. For example, a thief could enter a building through a trapdoor. In the same way, a computer intruder could enter the computer or network through some sort of a trap door that has been intentionally built by a malicious insider and left unattended through perhaps careless design. Another example is a thief entering the bank with a mask and stealing money. The analogy here is an intruder masquerades as someone else, legitimately enters the system, and takes all the information assets. Money in the real world would translate to information assets in the cyber world. That is, there are many parallels between noninformation-related attacks and information-related attacks. We can then proceed to develop countermeasures for both types of attacks.

20.2.4 Credit Card Fraud and Identity Theft

We are hearing a lot these days about credit card fraud and identity theft. In the case of credit card fraud, others get hold of a person's credit card and make all kinds of purchases; by the time the owner of the card finds out, it may be too late. The thief may have left the country by then.

A more serious theft is identity theft. Here, one assumes the identity of another person, say by getting hold of the social security number and essentially carries out all the transactions under the other person's name. This could even be selling houses and depositing the income in a fraudulent bank account. By the time the owner finds out, it will be far too late. It is very likely that the owner may have lost millions of dollars due to the identity theft.

We need to explore the use of data mining for both credit card fraud detection and for identity theft. There have been some efforts on detecting credit card fraud [CHAN99]. We need to start working actively on detecting and preventing identity thefts.

20.2.5 Attacks on Critical Infrastructures

The attacks on critical infrastructures could cripple a nation and its economy. Infrastructure attacks include attacking the telecommunication lines, electronic, power, gas, reservoirs and water supplies, food supplies, and other basic entities that are critical for the operation of a nation.

The attacks on critical infrastructures could occur during any type of attack whether they are noninformation-related, information-related, or bioterrorism attacks. For example, one could attack the software that runs the telecommunications industry and closedown all the telecommunication lines. Similarly, software that runs the power and gas supplies could be attacked. Attacks could also occur through bombs and explosives. That is, the telecommunication lines could be attacked through bombs. Attacking transportation lines such as highways and railway tracks are also attacks on infrastructures.

Infrastructures could also be attacked by natural disasters such as hurricanes and earthquakes. Our main interest here is the attacks on infrastructures through malicious attacks, both information related and noninformation related. Our goal is to examine data mining and related data management technologies to detect and prevent such infrastructure attacks. Figure 20.3 illustrates attacks on critical infrastructures.

20.2.6 Data Mining Services for Cyber Security

Data mining is being applied to problems such as intrusion detection and auditing. For example, anomaly detection techniques could be used to detect unusual

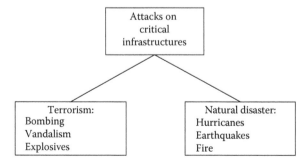

Figure 20.3 Attacks on critical infrastructures.

patterns and behaviors. Link analysis may be used to trace the viruses to the perpetrators. Classification may be used to group the various cyber attacks and then use the profiles to detect an attack when it occurs. Prediction may be used to determine the potential future attacks depending on a way on information learned about terrorists through email and phone conversations. Also, for some threats, nonreal-time data mining may suffice whereas for certain other threats such as for network intrusions, we may need real-time data mining. Many researchers are investigating the use of data mining for intrusion detection. While we need some form of real-time data mining, that is, the results have to be generated in real time, we also need to build models in real time. For example, credit card fraud detection is a form of real-time processing. However, here, models are usually built ahead of time. Building models in real time remains a challenge. Data mining can also be used for analyzing web logs as well as analyzing the audit trails. On the basis of the results of the data mining tool, one can then determine whether any unauthorized intrusions have occurred and/or whether any unauthorized queries have been posed.

Other applications of data mining for cyber security include analyzing the audit data. One could build a repository or a warehouse containing the audit data and then conduct an analysis using various data mining tools to see if there are potential anomalies. For example, there could be a situation where a certain user group may access the database between 3 and 5 a.m. in the morning. It could be that this group is working in the night shift, in which case there may be a valid explanation. However, if this group is working between say 9 a.m. and 5 p.m., then this may be an unusual occurrence. Another example is when a person accesses the databases always between 1 and 2 p.m., but for the last 2 days, he has been accessing the database between 1 and 2 a.m. This could then be flagged as an unusual pattern that would need further investigation.

Insider threat analysis is also a problem both from a national security and from a cyber security perspective. That is, those working in a corporation who are considered to be trusted could commit espionage. Similarly, those with proper access to the computer system could plant Trojan horses and viruses. Catching such terrorists is far more difficult than catching terrorists outside an organization. One may need to monitor the access patterns of all the individuals of a corporation even if they are system administrators, to see whether they are carrying out cyber-terrorism activities. There is some research now on applying data mining to such applications by various groups. Figure 20.4 illustrates data mining for cyber security.

While data mining can be used to detect and prevent cyber attacks, data mining also exacerbates some security problems such as the inference and privacy problems. With data mining techniques, one could infer sensitive associations from the legitimate responses. For more details on privacy and data mining, we refer to [THUR05].

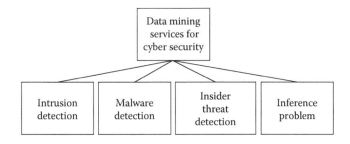

Figure 20.4   Data mining services for cyber security.

20.3 Current Research on Security as a Service

We are developing a number of tools on data mining for cyber security applications at the UTD. In the previous chapter, we discussed one such tool for intrusion detection [AWAD09]. An intrusion can be defined as any set of actions that attempts to compromise the integrity, confidentiality, or availability of a resource. As systems become more complex, there are always exploitable weaknesses due to the design and programming errors, or through the use of various "socially-engineered" penetration techniques. Computer attacks are split into two categories, host-based attacks and network-based attacks. Host-based attacks target a machine and try to gain access to privileged services or resources on that machine. Host-based detection usually uses routines that obtain system call data from an audit process that tracks all system calls made on behalf of each user.

Network-based attacks make it difficult for legitimate users to access various network services by purposely occupying or sabotaging network resources and services. This can be done by sending large amounts of network traffic, exploiting well-known faults in networking services, overloading network hosts, and so on. Network-based attack detection uses network traffic data (i.e., tcpdump) to look at traffic addressed to the machines being monitored. Intrusion detection systems are split into two groups: anomaly detection systems and misuse detection systems.

Anomaly detection is the attempt to identify malicious traffic based on deviations from established normal network traffic patterns. Misuse detection is the ability to identify intrusions based on a known pattern for the malicious activity. These known patterns are referred to as signatures. Anomaly detection is capable of catching new attacks. However, new legitimate behavior can also be falsely identified as an attack, resulting in a false positive. The focus with the current state-of-the-art technologies is to reduce the false-negative and false-positive rate.

Our current tools, discussed in our recent book, include those for email worm detection, malicious code detection, buffer overflow detection, and botnet detection, as well as analyzing firewall policy rules [MASU11]. Figure 20.5 illustrates the various tools we have developed. For example, for email worm detection, we

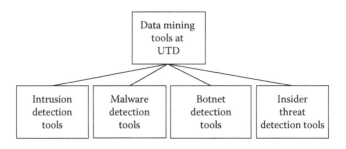

Figure 20.5 Data mining tools at UTD.

examine emails and extract features such as "number of attachments" and then train data mining tools with techniques such as SVM or naive Bayesian classifiers and develop a model. Then we test the model and determine whether the email has a virus/worm or not. We use training and testing data sets posted on various websites. Similarly, for malicious code detection, we extract n-gram features both with the assembly code and binary code. We first train the data mining tool using the SVM technique and then test the model. The classifier will determine whether the code is malicious or not. For buffer overflow detection, we assume that malicious messages contain the code whereas normal messages contain data. We train SVM and then test to see if the message contains the code or data. A discussion of the various data mining techniques that we have utilized to provide security as a service in the cloud is given in Appendix B. Some details can also be found in [AWAD09].

20.4 Other Services for Cyber Security Applications

Other services that are candidates to be hosted on the cloud include email filtering, identity management, and digital forensics. Each of these services is computationally intensive. In the case of email filtering services, the organization will outsource this service to a cloud. The cloud will examine the email, possibly apply data mining techniques, and filter out the suspicious emails. We have developed such data mining tools for email worm detection. In the case of identity management, the organization will outsource the processing of identifying and authenticating the user to the cloud. Note that this is not cloud authentication where the user has to be authenticated to access a cloud. This is essentially about accessing the organization's resources. However, authenticating the user is left to the cloud instead of the organization. With respect to conducting forensics, the tools will be hosted on the cloud. The organization will send all the relevant data to carry out forensics to the cloud. Here again, this is not about cloud forensics where the intrusions on the cloud have to be examined. This is about the organization outsourcing its forensics activities to the cloud.

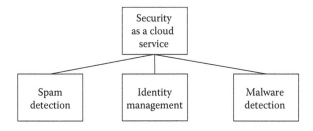

Figure 20.6   Security as a cloud service.

The major obstacle to implement security as a service is security itself. That is, the security services implemented by the cloud have to be secure. For example, if the cloud is to carry out identity management, it has to ensure that the process is correct. Therefore, outsourcing a highly secure function to the cloud remains a challenge. Figure 20.6 illustrates these other security services that can be implemented on a cloud.

20.5 Summary and Directions

This chapter has discussed data mining services for security applications. These data mining services are the ideal candidates to be implemented on a cloud as they are computationally intensive. Such services that perform security-critical functions are called security as a service. We first started with a discussion of data mining for cyber security applications and then provided a brief overview of the tools we are developing. We also discussed some other services such as email filtering, forensics, and identity management.

We will discuss some of the cloud-based tools we have developed for security as a service. These include malware detection on the cloud, cloud-based assured information sharing, and cloud-based insider threat detection. We will discuss these tools in Part VII. Some of the security as a service cloud products will be discussed in the next chapter.

References

[AWAD09] Awad, M., L. Khan, B. Thuraisingham, and L. Wang, *Design and Implementation of Data Mining Tools*, CRC Press, Boca Raton, FL, 2009.

[BOLZ05] Bolz, F., K. Dudonis, and D. Schulz, *The Counterterrorism Handbook: Tactics, Procedures, and Techniques, Third Edition Practical Aspects of Criminal & Forensic Investigations*, CRC Press, Boca Raton, FL, 2005.

[CHAN99] Chan, P., W. Fan, A. Prodromidis, and S. Stolfo, Distributed data mining in credit card fraud detection, *IEEE Intelligent Systems*, 14(6), 47–74, 1999.

[MASU11] Masud, M., L. Khan, and B. Thuraisingham, *Data Mining Tools for Malware Detection*, CRC Press, Boca Raton, FL, 2011.

[THUR03] Thuraisingham, B., *Web Data Mining Technologies and Their Applications in Business Intelligence and Counter-Terrorism*, CRC Press, Boca Raton, FL, 2003.

[THUR04] Thuraisingham, B., *Managing Threats to Web Databases and Cyber Systems, Issues, Solutions and Challenges* (eds: V. Kumar, J. Srivastava, Al. Lazarevic), Kluwer, MA, 2004.

[THUR05] Thuraisingham, B., *Database and Applications Security*, CRC Press, Boca Raton, FL, 2005.

Chapter 21

Secure Cloud Computing Products

21.1 Overview

Since the inception of the cloud as we know it in the mid-2000s, numerous cloud security solutions have emerged. These solutions can be grouped into two categories. The products in the first category essentially provide security for the cloud. That is, these products secure the cloud infrastructure, platform, or the application. The products in the second category provide security as a service in the cloud. These services include email security service, web-filtering service, and malware detection service.

While some of the companies such as Symplified have developed solutions mainly for the cloud, some other companies have adopted their security solutions for the cloud. Such companies include large computer companies such as IBM. Some other companies such as McAfee and Symantec are general security solution providers and these companies now provide security solutions implemented in the cloud. That is, they provide security as a service solution.

In this chapter, we provide an overview of a variety of cloud security offerings. We have obtained the list from a survey carried out in [TECH]. We have carried out our own survey of these products. The taxonomy of the cloud security offerings is given in Figure 21.1. The organization of this chapter is as follows. In Section 21.2, we will provide an overview of several cloud security products including those by large companies such as IBM and Novell, security solutions companies such as McAfee and Symantec, and cloud security companies such as Symplified and CloudPassage. This chapter is summarized in Section 21.3.

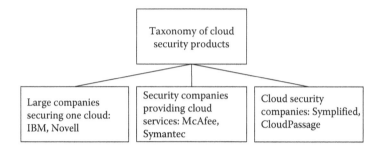

Figure 21.1   Taxonomy of cloud security products.

21.2 Overview of the Products

Trend Micro: Trend Micro is a Japanese-based security company and provides security solutions that include antivirus and antispam products [TREND]. These products provide security solutions to networks, the web, and mobile applications. The company made entry into cloud security with their product Smart Protection Network in 2008. The goals of this product are to protect clients from web-based malware. In recent years, this product has been extended to secure the cloud and to provide a wide range of cloud security features, including virtualization security, cloud data security, policy management, and encryption.

McAfee: McAfee is a U.S-based security company and provides security solutions to home users as well as to businesses and the government. Its products include those for virus scans, email and web security as well as encryption. For example, McAfee Total Solution consists of a variety of security tools and protects against malware. More recently, McAfee provides solutions for security-as-a-service [MCAF]. With this service, customers can obtain cloud-based solutions for data protection, email protection, and virus scanning. McAfee is now part of Intel Corporation.

CA Technologies: CA Technologies Inc. was formerly known as Computer Associates International and is a large software company. It develops systems software and prior to that applications software for a number of platforms including the mainframe and personal computers. By acquiring several companies, it ventured into the cloud computing market in recent years. Their main product is called CA Cloud Minder and provides solutions for authentication, identity management, and single sign-on [CA].

Symplified: While Trend Micro and McAfee are security solutions companies and CA Technologies is a software company, Symplified was formed in 2006 to provide cloud security solutions. Its major focus is on providing identity management solutions for the cloud, including authentication and single sign-on with SAML technologies [SYMP].

Symantec: Symantec started off as an artificial intelligence and database software company and then migrated into providing security solutions. It is one of the largest security solutions company. It markets the Norton antivirus products and, through the acquisition of Veritas, provides storage solutions. Symantec provides cloud-based security solutions, including virus scans, email, and web security [SYMA].

Zscaler: Zscaler was founded in 2008 to provide cloud-based security as a service for web traffic. The product provides malware protection for web traffic. It essentially provides policy-based web access. The services provided include antivirus scan, antispam filtering, antispyware detection, and URL filtering [ZSCA]. Note that while Symplified provides identity and access management for the cloud, Zscaler, like Symantec and McAfee, provides security as a service in the cloud. However, unlike Symantec and McAfee, Zscaler is not a general security solutions company.

Panda Security: Panda Security is a security company based in Spain and founded in 1990. Its products include antivirus software, spam detection software, firewall applications, and cyber-crime prevention solutions. More recently, it provides cloud-based security solutions. That is, it provides security as service solutions for email and Internet traffic protection [PAND].

WhiteHat: WhiteHat Inc. is a security solutions provider to businesses as well as to the government. It also provides solutions for website risk management. In 2010, WhiteHat joined the Cloud Security Alliance. More recently, WhiteHat provides a cloud-based solution called Sentinel that provides compressive security for websites [WHIT].

CipherCloud: CipherCloud provides security solutions for the cloud. In particular, it provides encryption solutions for the cloud so that cloud customers can securely store their data in the cloud. It provides security solutions for cloud systems such as SalesForce.com, Amazon EC2, Amazon S3, and Forcel.com [CIPH]. Note that while companies such as WhiteHat and Zscaler provide security as a service to businesses, Symplified and CipherCloud provide security solutions for the cloud.

SecureAuth: SecureAuth was founded in 2005 and develops identity provider solutions for organizations across borders. It is stated in [SECU] that the company combines single sign-on with two-factor authentication. More recently, SecureAuth provides identity management solutions as a cloud service to organizations.

CloudPassage: CloudPassage [CLOU] was founded in 2010 and provides security for the cloud servers including virtualization security. Its security solutions can be incorporated into public, private as well as hybrid clouds. Like Symplified, CloudPassage was founded to provide security for the cloud.

Dome9 Security: As stated in [DOME], Dome9 Security provides security for the cloud stack so that hackers cannot penetrate. It provides a variety of security solutions including policy management, role-based access control, security auditing, and strong two-factor authentication. Like CloudPassage, Dome9 security provides security solutions for the cloud.

IBM: IBM is the largest computer company and offers a variety of products including mainframes, database applications, and security solutions. Its cloud security solutions include data protection, server security as well as policy management [IBM]. IBM also provides consulting services for securing the cloud.

Novell: Novell is a very large software and networking company and provides a variety of solutions for collaboration and networking. Novell's cloud security solution is called the Novell Cloud Security Service [NOVE] and it enables an organization's identity management solutions to be provided through the cloud providers at IaaS, SaaS, and PaaS levels.

ThreatMetrix: As stated in [THRE], ThreatMetrix provides a variety of security solutions including (i) determining whether an online visitor is legitimate, (ii) malware detection, and (iii) defense of mobile applications from fraud and misuse. Its cloud-based solutions provide fraud detection via the cloud. That is, like Panda Security, it provides security services through the cloud.

Okta: As stated in [OKTA], Okta provides directory services, single sign-on, strong authentication, provisioning, workflow, and built-in reporting. These services are provided via the cloud and are integrated with the organization's identity management services. Corporations such as SAP and Informatica use Okta security services.

Dell Data Protection: Credant Dell provides enterprise-wide data protection. It essentially provides encryption solutions. As stated in [DELL], their product protects system disks and external media, and includes powerful remote management, audit and policy-setting capabilities.

Awareness Technologies: Awareness Technologies provides security solutions for employee monitoring as well as insider threat protection. In addition, its InterGuard product suite provides solutions for web filtering, data loss prevention, laptop recovery monitoring, email, and text messages [AWAR]. The security services are provided through the cloud.

HyTrust: HyTrust provides security for virtualization software. As stated in [HYTR], it enforces policies on the control plane of VMware-based virtualization infrastructure. HyTrust is a virtual appliance and assigns labels to virtual objects and subsequently enforces policies on the labels.

Vyatta: As stated in [VYAT], Vyatta provides VPN products as well as virtual firewalls and virtual routers for the Internet protocol. Its on-demand network security solutions are being incorporated into virtualization, multicore, and cloud computing platforms.

StillSecure: As stated in [STIL], StillSecure provides network access control and managed security services. These managed security services protect the network and the data. More recently, StillSecure has launched a cloud monitoring service product that customers can download and install in their cloud platform.

SafeNet: As stated in [SAFE], SafeNet provides data protection solutions for various enterprises. It essentially provides encryption technologies. SafeNet's cloud security product called ProcutV provides encryption solutions for data centers as well as for data in the cloud.

Proofpoint: As stated in [PROO], Proofpoint provides security as a service solution for protecting the enterprise data. It also ensures that the governance, compliance, and regulatory requirements are met for the data. The security solutions provided enable the organizations to keep malicious content out of the data as well as to prevent the theft or loss of sensitive data.

Commtouch: Commtouch is a company founded in Germany and provides email security. It also provides antivirus protection as well as spam filtering and web filtering. As stated in [COMM], Commtouch's Global View Cloud Technology provides security as a service by analyzing web traffic as well as email traffic. The results of the analysis are incorporated into the solutions provided for email and web security as well as for antivirus protection.

21.3 Summary and Directions

This chapter has provided an overview of the various commercial products that either provide security solutions for the cloud or provide security as a service to various businesses. Some of these products have been developed mainly for the cloud or to function in the cloud. Some other solutions have taken general security products and applied them to the cloud. The security solutions for the cloud include encryption, virtualization security, and cloud monitoring. Security as a service includes identity management, malware detection, web, and email filtering.

We selected the products listed in the survey of commercial cloud products provided in [TECH]. However, we have carried out our own survey of these products. We expect the number of products to grow rapidly as cloud technologies are developed. These products will provide solutions to secure the cloud or will utilize the cloud to provide security services.

References

[AWAR] Awareness Technologies, http://www.awarenesstechnologies.com/
[CA] CA Technologies, http://www.ca.com/us/cloud.aspx
[CIPH] Cipher Cloud, http://www.ciphercloud.com/
[CLOU] Cloud Passage, http://www.cloudpassage.com/about/
[COMM] Commtouch, http://www.commtouch.com/#
[DELL] Dell Data Protection Solutions, http://www.dell.com/learn/us/en/04/campaigns/
    dell-data-protection-solutions
[DOME] Dome9 Security, http://www.dome9.com/about-us
[HYTR] Hytrust, http://www.hytrust.com/
[IBM] IBM, http://www-03.ibm.com/security/cloud-security.html
[MCAF] McAfee, http://www.mcafee.com/us/solutions/cloud-security/cloud-security.aspx
[NOVE] Novell Cloud Security, http://en.wikipedia.org/wiki/Novell_Cloud_Security_Service
[OKTA] Okta Service, http://www.okta.com/company/

[PAND] Panda Security, http://www.pandasecurity.com/usa/

[PROO] Proofpoint, http://www.proofpoint.com/about-us/index.php\

[SAFE] Safenet, http://www.safenet-inc.com/

[SECU] Secure Auth, http://www.gosecureauth.com/company/

[STIL] Still Secure, http://www.stillsecure.com/

[SYMA] Symantec, http://www.symantec.com/products-solutions/families/?fid=symantec-cloud

[SYMP] Symplified, http://www.symplified.com/

[TECH] Technavio Insights, Global Cloud Security Market, 2010–2014.

[THRE] ThreatMatrix, http://threatmetrix.com/datasheets/ThreatMetrix-SmartID-Datasheet.pdf

[TREND] Trend Micro, http://www.trendmicro.com/us/index.html

[VYAT] Vyatta, http://www.vyatta.com/

[WHIT] White Hat Security, https://www.whitehatsec.com/sentinel_services/sentinel_services.html

[ZSCA] Zscalar, http://en.wikipedia.org/wiki/Zscaler

Conclusion to Part V

While Part III described cloud computing concepts and Part IV described experimental cloud computing systems, the chapters in this part describe secure cloud computing concepts, technologies, and products.

Chapter 16 discussed various secure cloud computing concepts. First, we discussed cloud computing security and governance. Next, we discussed security architectures for the cloud. This was followed by a discussion of access control and identity management for the cloud. Data security issues for the cloud were discussed next. Following this, we provided an overview of privacy, compliance, and forensics for the cloud. Finally, aspects such as cryptographic solutions, network security issues, business continuity, operations security, and physical security for the cloud were discussed.

Chapter 17 discussed various aspects of cloud computing functions. We provided an overview of our cloud computing framework and then discussed security for virtualization, network, data storage, and management for the cloud.

Chapter 18 discussed secure data management functions and then described the impact of the cloud on these functions. In particular, we discussed discretionary security, secure objects, secure distributed data management, and secure heterogeneous data integration for the cloud.

Chapter 19 provided an overview of the security guidelines for cloud computing as discussed by NIST. The guidelines include those for the deployment models, web services, as well as governance, compliance, availability, identity and access management, architecture, incident response, trust, software isolation, and data protection.

Chapter 20 discussed the notion of security as a service and explained the concept with data mining services for security applications as examples. These data mining services are ideal candidates to be implemented on a cloud as they are computationally intensive. We first started with a discussion of data mining for cyber security applications and then provided a brief overview of the tools we are developing.

Chapter 21 provided an overview of the various commercial products that either provide security solutions for the cloud or provide security as a service to various businesses. Some of these products have been developed mainly for the cloud or to function in the cloud. Some other solutions have taken general security products and applied them to the cloud. The security solutions for the cloud include encryption, virtualization security, and cloud monitoring. Security as a service includes identity management, malware detection, and web and email filtering.

EXPERIMENTAL SECURE CLOUD COMPUTING SYSTEMS

VI

Introduction to Part VI

Now that we have provided an overview of secure cloud computing, we will give some experimental secure cloud computing systems that we have developed. This will give the reader a better understanding of how we have utilized various access control models for cloud systems. Part VI consists of three chapters: 22, 23, and 24. Our secure relational data query processor in the cloud is discussed in Chapter 24. Our secure semantic web data query processor in the cloud is discussed in Chapter 25. Our work on secure information integration in the cloud is discussed in Chapter 26.

Our cloud-based secure relational data manager makes use of HIVE for data management and builds an XACML-based policy engine for access control. With respect to secure semantic web data processing in a cloud, we have built a SPARQL query optimizer and developed an XACML-based access control model. Finally for secure information integration in the cloud, we have built a security module for storing data on AMAZON S3. The experimental systems we have developed are among the early secure cloud data management systems to be discussed in the literature.

Chapter 22

Secure Cloud Query Processing with Relational Data

22.1 Overview

The WWW is envisioned as a system of interlinked hypertext documents that are accessed using the Internet [WWW]. With the emergence of organizations that provide e-commerce such as Amazon.com and social network applications such as Facebook and Twitter on the WWW, the volume of data generated by them daily is massive [AXON10]. It was estimated that the amount of data that would be generated by individuals in 2009 would be more than that generated in the entire history of mankind through 2008 [WEIG09]. The large amount of data generated by one organization could be valuable to other organizations or researchers if it can be correlated with the data that they have. This is especially true for various governmental intelligence organizations. This has led to another trend of forming partnerships between business organizations and universities for research collaborations [NOKI] and between business organizations for data sharing to create better applications [SALE08].

The two main obstacles to this process of collaboration among organizations are arranging a large, common data storage area and providing secure access to the shared data. Organizations across the world invest a great deal of resources in minimizing storage costs and with the introduction of cloud-based services, it is estimated that this cost would be reduced further [ALL10]. Additionally, organizations spend a large amount of their yearly budget on security but this is still

379

not sufficient to prevent security breaches [SAWY10, FIRS10]. In this chapter, we present a web-based system (Hive access control) that aims to achieve the previously stated goals by combining cloud computing technologies with policy-based security mechanisms. This idea comes in part from the recommendations of the Cloud Security Alliance for Identity and Access Management [KUMA10] and our previous work using XACML policies [PARO09]. We have combined the HDFS [BORT10] with Hive [APACa] to provide a common storage area for participating organizations. Further, we have used an XACML [MOSE05] policy-based security mechanism to provide fine-grained access controls over the shared data. The users of our system are divided into groups based on the kinds of queries that they can run such as SELECT and INSERT. Our system provides a secure log-in feature to users based on a salted hash technique. When a user logs into our system, based on the group that the user belongs to, he/she is provided with different options. We allow collaborating organizations to load data to the shared storage space in the form of relational tables and views. Users can also define fine-grained XACML access control policies on tables/views for groups of users. Users can then query the entire database based on the credentials that they have. We have provided some basic query rewriting rules in our system that abstract users from the query language of Hive (HiveQL). This allows them to enter the regular SQL queries in the web application that are translated into HiveQL using the basic rewriting rules. Our system also allows new users to register, but only a designated special user "admin" can assign these users to the appropriate groups. Our contributions include the following:

- The mechanism to load and query shared data securely that are stored in HDFS using Hive.
- Additional layer of security above HDFS and Hive using an XACML policy-based mechanism.

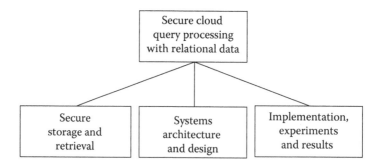

Figure 22.1 Secure cloud query processing with relational data. (Adapted from Thuraisingham, B., M. V. Khadilkar, A. Gupta, M. Kantarcioglu, and L. Khan, Secure data storage and retrieval in the cloud. *CollaborateCom*, Chicago, IL, 1–8, 2010.)

- Basic query rewriting rules that abstract a user from HiveQL and allow him/her to enter SQL queries.
- Incorporation of the above mechanisms into a web-based system.

This chapter is organized as follows: Section 22.2 presents the related work in the area of secure storage and retrieval of information in the cloud. In Section 22.3, we present our architecture for solving the problem of secure large-scale data sharing based on combining cloud computing technologies with XACML policy-based security mechanisms. Further, in Section 22.4, we present the details of our implementation. Finally, Section 22.5 presents our conclusions and future work. Figure 22.1 illustrates the contents of this chapter.

22.2 Related Work

We combine cloud computing technologies with security mechanisms so that cooperating organizations can share vast amounts of data securely. Since the birth of cloud computing technologies, there has been much interest generated among researchers, business organizations, and media outlets about security issues with these technologies [TALB09, MITC096]. This interest has resulted in large-scale research and development efforts from business organizations [WIND, AMAZ09, OMAL09]. A part of the work related to security in the cloud has been focused on implementing security at the infrastructure level. In [OMAL09], the authors present their vision for security in Hadoop. Their work presents a few security risks with Hadoop and outlines solutions to them. These solutions have been implemented in beta versions of Hadoop v0.20. This development effort is an important step toward securing cloud infrastructures but is only in its inception stage. The goal of our system is to add another layer of security above the security offered by Hadoop. Once the security offered by Hadoop becomes robust, it will only strengthen the effectiveness of our system.

AWS is a web services infrastructure platform in the cloud [AMAZ]. [AMAZ09] offers an overview of security aspects that are relevant to AWS such as physical security, network security, and AWS security. Our system is different from AWS in the sense that our cloud infrastructure is completely private *versus* AWS's infrastructure that is in the public domain. This distinguishing factor makes our infrastructure "trusted" over the AWS infrastructure where data must be stored in an encrypted format since AWS is in the public domain. In the future, we plan to extend our work to include both public and private clouds.

The Windows Azure platform is an Internet-scale cloud computing services platform hosted in Microsoft data centers [WIND]. [MARS10] provides an overview of the security challenges and recommended approaches to design and develop more secure applications for the Windows Azure platform. However, according to [BROD10], the Windows Azure platform is suitable for building new applications, but it is not optimal to migrate the existing applications. The main reason that we did not use the Windows Azure platform is that we wanted to port our existing application to an open-source system instead of writing our code from scratch as would be needed with Windows Azure. We also did not want to be tied to the Windows framework but rather allow our work to be used on any kind of system. We will be able to test our system on the Windows Azure platform once the platform supports the use of VMs to run the existing applications [BROD10].

22.3 System Architecture

In this section, we present our architecture that securely provides access to a large common storage space (the "Cloud") thus allowing cooperating organizations to share data reliably. We begin by giving an overview of the architecture followed by a discussion of each of its component layers.

Figure 22.2 shows the architecture of our system. Each rectangle in the figure represents a different component of our framework. The various line styles for arrows indicate the flow of control for a specific task that can be accomplished with this system. Next, we present each of the component layers in the architecture.

22.3.1 The Web Application Layer

The web application layer is the only interface provided by our system to the user to access the cloud infrastructure. We provide different functions based on the permissions assigned to a user. The web application provides a log-in page that can be used by any user to log into the system. We used the Java-simplified encryption (JASYPT) library's [JASY] salted hash technique to store usernames and passwords in a file. Further, that file is stored in a secure location that is not accessible to any user. Currently, the system supports three types of users:

- Users who can only query the existing tables/views
- Users who can create tables/views and define XACML policies on them in addition to querying all tables/views, and finally
- A special "admin" user who in addition to the previous functions can also assign new users to either of the above categories

22.3.2 The ZQL Parser Layer

The ZQL Parser [ZQL] layer takes as input any query submitted by a user and either proceeds to the XACML policy evaluator if the query is successfully parsed or returns an error message to the user. The ZQL Parser is an SQL parser written in Java that takes an SQL query as input and fills different Java vectors with different parts of the query [ZQL]. For example, consider the following query:

SELECT a.id, a.name FROM a WHERE a.id > 5.

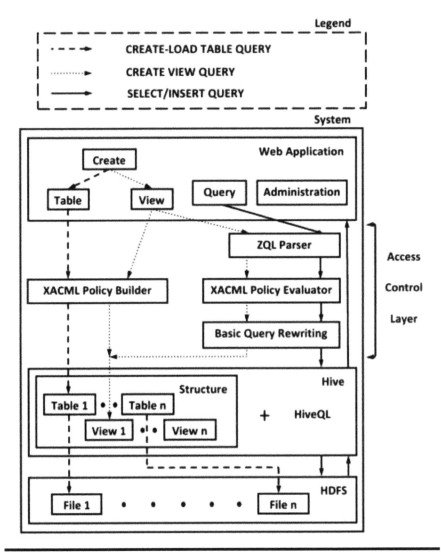

Figure 22.2 System architecture.

The ZQL Parser parses the query and constructs different Java vectors for every part of the query (SELECT, FROM, and WHERE). In our system, the vector of attribute names in the SELECT clause for the query above is returned to the web application layer to be used in displaying the results returned by the query. The vector of table/view names in the FROM clause is passed to the XACML policy evaluator to ensure that the current user has permissions to access all tables/ views specified in the query. If the evaluator determines that the current user has the required permissions, the query is processed further, else an error message is returned to the web application layer. Currently, the ZQL Parser supports the SQL DELETE, INSERT, SELECT, and UPDATE statements. Our future work involves adding support for other keywords such as CREATE, DROP, and so on.

22.3.3 The XACML Policy Layer

The XACML is an XML-based language that is used to define access control policies on resources. The same language is also used to determine whether access is allowed for a particular resource based on the policy defined for that resource [ZQL]. Next, we explain how we have defined and used XACML policies in our framework.

22.3.3.1 XACML Policy Builder

In our framework, the tables and views defined by users are treated as resources for building XACML policies. Further, we have defined role-based access control [FERR92, SAND96] policies on these resources based on the kinds of queries that are provided by our system. For every type of query supported by our framework, we define a mapping between this type and all users who are allowed to run that kind of query. A sample listing of such a mapping is given below:

    INSERT admin user1 user2
    SELECT admin user1 user3

In our system for every table/view that a user wants to create, they are given the option of uploading their own predefined XACML policy or having the framework build a policy for them. If a user selects the latter option, they must also specify the kinds of queries (e.g., INSERT, SELECT, etc.) that will be allowed on the table/view. We then use Sun's XACML implementation [SUN] to build a policy for that table/view with the groups specified by that particular user.

22.3.3.2 XACML Policy Evaluator

Our system uses Sun's XACML implementation [SUN] to evaluate if the current user has access to all tables/views that are defined in any user query. If permission is granted for all tables/views, then the query is processed further, else an error message is returned to the user. The policy evaluator is used both during regular user query execution, as well as during view creation, since the only way to create a view in Hive is by specifying a SELECT query on the existing tables/views. The current user must have access to all tables/views specified in this SELECT query before the view can be created.

22.3.3.3 The Basic Query Rewriting Layer

This layer enables us to add another layer of abstraction between the user and HiveQL by allowing users to enter SQL queries that are rewritten according to

HiveQL's syntax. In our current system, we provide two basic rewriting rules for user-specified SQL queries.

HiveQL does not allow multiple tables in the FROM clause of a query, but rather expects this kind of query to be given as a sequence of JOIN statements. The user is abstracted from this fact by allowing him/her to enter a regular SQL query with multiple tables in the FROM clause that we transform to a sequence of JOIN statements in conformance with HiveQL's syntax. The following is an example:

SELECT a.id, b.age FROM a, b; → SELECT a.id, b.age FROM a JOIN b;

HiveQL uses a modified version of SQL's INSERT-SELECT statement, INSERT OVERWRITE TABLE <tablename> SELECT rather than INSERT INTO <tablename> SELECT. Again, we abstract this from the user by allowing him/her to enter the traditional INSERT INTO <tablename> SELECT that we then rewrite into HiveQL's INSERT OVERWRITE TABLE <tablename> SELECT. The following is an example:

INSERT INTO a SELECT * FROM b; → INSERT OVERWRITE TABLE a SELECT * FROM b.

As a part of our future work, we plan to extend these basic rewriting rules with more complicated rules in a complete query rewriting engine.

22.3.3.4 The Hive Layer

Hive is a data warehouse infrastructure built on top of Hadoop [HIVE]. Hive provides the ability to structure the data in the underlying HDFS as well as to query these data. The arrows in Figure 22.2 between the tables in this layer and the files in the HDFS layer indicate that each table in Hive is stored as a file in the HDFS. These files contain the data that this table represents. There are no arrows between the views in this layer and the files in the HDFS layer since a view is only a logical concept in Hive that is created with a SELECT query. In our framework, Hive is used to structure the data that will be shared by collaborating organizations. Further, we use Hive's SQL-like query language, HiveQL, to enable access to these data. The advantage of using Hive in our system is that users can query the data using a familiar SQL-like syntax.

22.3.3.5 HDFS Layer

HDFS is a distributed file system that is designed to run on basic hardware [BORT10]. The HDFS layer in our framework stores the data files corresponding to tables that are created in Hive [THUS09]. Our security assumption is that these files can neither be accessed using Hadoop's [APACb] web interface nor Hadoop's Command Line Interface (CLI) but only by using our system.

22.4 Implementation Details and Results

In this section, we present the implementation of our system by providing performance graphs for the insert and query processes for tables with different sizes. The details of our experiments and performance graphs are given in [THUR10]. We begin by giving a brief description of our implementation setup followed by the implementation details.

22.4.1 Implementation Setup

Our implementation was carried out on a 19-node cluster with a mix of two different configurations for nodes. Furthermore, all the nodes are in the same rack. Out of 19 nodes, 11 nodes ran Ubuntu v10.04 Lucid Lynx on an Intel Pentium 4, 3.2 GHz central processing unit (CPU) with 4 GB SDRAM 400 MHz memory and a 40 GB Western Digital WDC WD400BB-75FJ SATA hard drive as the primary drive and a 250 GB Western Digital WD2500AAJB-0 SATA hard drive as the secondary drive. The other eight nodes ran Ubuntu v9.04 Jaunty Jackalope on an Intel Pentium 4, 2.8 GHz CPU with 4 GB SDRAM 333 MHz memory and two 40 GB Western Digital WDC WD400BB-75FJ SATA hard drives. We used the Java version JRE v1.6.0_18 for our implementation. For the cloud infrastructure, we used Hadoop version v0.19.1, with a 1000 MB heap space and Hive version v0.5, with the default heap space. We also used Apache Tomcat v7.0.0 as the web server for our application with a 2 GB heap space. We also used default values for all parameters that are provided by Hadoop and Hive. We understand that we will have a performance gain when we set optimal values for these parameters. But since this is a preliminary work, we have chosen not to focus on these parameters that will be done in the future.

22.4.2 Experimental Datasets

We have used two different datasets to test the performance of our system *versus* Hive. The first dataset is the Freebase [FREE] system that is an open repository of structured data that has approximately 12 million topics or entities. An entity is a person, place, or thing with a unique identifier. We wanted to simulate an environment of cooperating organizations by using people, business, film, sports, organization, and awards datasets from the Freebase system. We assume that each dataset is loaded into our system by a different organization and further, users can run various queries across these datasets based on their permissions. The queries we have used to test our implementation were created by us based on the datasets of the Freebase system.

The second dataset we have used to test our system is the well-known TPC-H benchmark [TPC]. The TPC-H benchmark is a decision-support benchmark that consists of a schema that is typical to any business organization. The benchmark contains eight tables and provides 22 queries with a high degree of complexity. We have used this benchmark to test the performance of our system *versus* Hive in performing complex queries. The TPC-H benchmark provides a tool for data generation (DBGEN) and a tool for query generation (QGEN). We have used DBGEN to generate datasets with varying scale factors (SFs) from 1 to 1000 as specified in the benchmark document. The reader should note that a scale factor of 1 is approximately 1 GB of data. Thus, we have tested our system with data sizes varying from 1 to 1000 GB. The smaller datasets (SF = 1, SF = 10, and SF = 30) are used to test the loading performance of our system *versus* Hive. On the other hand, the larger datasets (SF = 100, SF = 300, and SF = 1000) are used to run a few of the benchmark queries. We have used queries Q1, Q3, Q6, and Q13 of the TPC-H benchmark to test our system. These queries were randomly selected after applying the following criterion to the study given in [JIA09]. The original query does not need to be divided into subqueries manually since our web application does not support this feature. We also think that the results obtained by running the queries selected above are indicative of the performance of all the other TPC-H benchmark queries that can be run on our system.

22.4.3 Implementation Results

We have tested our web-based system for performance metrics such as data loading and querying times. Further, we have compared these metrics with the Hive CLI. All query times that are used in performance graphs and result tables in this subsection are averaged over three separate runs. We ran two sets of experiments, one using the Freebase system and the other using the TPC-H benchmark.

We have compared the time it takes to load and query the data for our application *versus* Hive for the Freebase datasets. The data loading time for our application is almost the same as Hive's time for small tables (0.1 and 0.3 million tuples). As the number of tuples increases to 0.5 million and then to 1.67 million tuples, our system gets slower than Hive by loading tuples. This is primarily because of the overhead associated with establishing a connection with the Hive database as well as the time associated with building an XACML policy for the table being loaded.

In addition, we have compared the running time for a simple "SELECT * FROM" query between our application and Hive. We have run the query on the same tables that were used for data loading but we restricted our results by using the LIMIT clause to only the first 100 tuples. This was done to avoid the large time difference that would occur between our application and Hives CLI since we have implemented a paging mechanism on the results whereas Hive's CLI would display all the results on the screen. Our application running time is slightly faster than the running time for the query on the Hive CLI. This difference is due to the time taken by the Hive

CLI to display the results of the query on the screen. Both running times are fast because Hive does not need to run a MapReduce [APACc] job for this query, but simply needs to return the whole file for the corresponding table from the HDFS.

We have also run a number of other queries and compared the running times of these queries on our system *versus* Hive for the Freebase system. These queries test the performance of our system in creating and querying views/tables *versus* Hive. We have tested a variety of queries, including insert, create, select, aggregate, and join queries.

We have also compared the data loading time of our application *versus* Hive for the "Customer" and "Supplier" tables for SF = 1, 10, and 30 from the TPC-H benchmark. Currently, our system allows users to upload data files that are at most 1 GB in size. The TPC-H benchmark's DBGEN tool generates files for the "Customer" and "Supplier" tables for SF = 1, 10, and 30 that are less than 1 GB in size. These are the reasons why we have selected the "Customer" and "Supplier" tables with SF = 1, 10, and 30 to compare the data loading performance of our system *versus* Hive. Our system performs similar to Hive at the smallest SF of 1 and as the SF increases, our system gets slower than Hive for data loading. Again, this difference in execution performance is because of the overhead associated with the Hive database connection and XACML policy generation. The trend for both, our system and Hive is linear as expected, since the size of these tables increases linearly with the SF.

Finally, we have compared the performance of four TPC-H benchmark queries on our system *versus* Hive. Our system performs as well as the Hive CLI for the selected queries. On the basis of query performance times for both, our system and Hive, as the size of the tables increases, the time for benchmark query execution also increases as expected. In a production environment, such queries would not be performed at runtime on large datasets. We would rather run these queries off-line and could store the results in Hive as views. We could then use a query rewriting mechanism to return these results efficiently.

22.5 Summary and Directions

In this chapter, we have presented a system that allows cooperating organizations to securely share large amounts of data. We have ensured that the organizations have a large common storage area by using Hadoop. Further, we have used Hive to present users of our system with a structured view of the data and to also enable them to query the data with an SQL-like language. We have used a simple salted hash mechanism to authenticate users in the current version of our system. We plan to implement a more sophisticated technique for authentication in future versions of our system. In this chapter, we have used the ZQL Parser to parse any SQL query that is input by the user. We plan to extend this parser with support for keywords such as DESCRIBE, JOIN, and so on that are currently not supported in ZQL. We have abstracted the user from the use of Hive by implementing some basic query rewriting rules. A part of our future work is to implement materialized views in Hive and extend the basic query rewriting rules into a complete engine for Hive that takes into account all the existing tables/materialized views and the XACML policies defined on them. We have provided fine-grained access control on the shared data using XACML policies. We have also incorporated role-based access control in our framework based on the kinds of queries that users will submit to our system. In the current version of our system, we only provide support for two types of keywords, INSERT and SELECT, as groups for XACML policies.

In the future, we plan to extend our system to include other keyword-based groups such as DELETE, UPDATE, and so on. We also plan to test the impact of using different values for parameters provided by Hadoop and Hive on query execution performance. Finally, the current system is implemented in a private cloud that will be extended to include public clouds such as AWS and Amazon simple storage services in future versions.

References

[ALL10] All, A., Cloud data storage: It'll still cost you, so give it some thought, http://www.itbusinessedge.com/cm/blogs/all/cloud-data-storage-itll-still-cost-you-so-give-it-some-thought/?cs=38733, January 2010.

[AMAZ] Amazon Web Services, http://aws.amazon.com/.

[AMAZ09] Amazon Web Services: Overview of security processes, http://awsmedia.s3.amazonaws.com/pdf/AWS_Security_Whitepaper.pdf, November 2009.

[APACa] Apache Hive, https://cwiki.apache.org/confluence/display/Hive/Home%3bjsessionid=8946C5F66E7FBD0CE2466BAA5C699289.

[APACb] Apache Hadoop, http://hadoop.apache.org/.

[APACc] Apache MapReduce, http://hadoop.apache.org/mapreduce/.

[AXON10] Axon, S., Facebook will celebrate 500 million users next week, http://mashable.com/2010/07/17/facebook-500-million/, July 2010.

[BORT10] Borthakur, D., HDFS architecture, http://hadoop.apache.org/common/docs/r0.19.2/hdfs_design.pdf, 2010.

[BROD10] Brodkin, J., Microsoft Windows Azure and Amazon EC2 on collision course, http://www.networkworld.com/news/2010/062510-microsoft-azure-amazon-ec2.html, June 2010.

[FERR92] Ferraiolo, D. F. and D. R. Kuhn, Role-based access controls. In *National Computer Security Conference*, pp. 554–563, Baltimore, MD, 1992.

[FIRS10] First annual cost of cyber crime security, Technical report, Ponemon Institute, July 2010.

[FREE] Freebase, http://www.freebase.com/.

[JASY] JASYPT—Java simplified encryption, http://www.jasypt.org/index.html.

[KUMA10] Kumaraswamy, S., S. Lakshminarayanan, M. Reiter, J. Stein, and Y. Wilson, Domain 12: Guidance for Identity & Access Management V2.1, April 2010.

[MARS10] Marshall, A., M. Howard, G. Bugher, and B. Harden, Security best practices for developing Windows Azure applications, June 2010, http://download.microsoft.

com/download/7/3/E/73E4EE93–559F-4D0F-A6FC-7FEC5F1542D1/SecurityBest
PracticesWindowsAzureApps.docx

[MITC096] Mitchell, R. L., Cloud storage triggers security worries, http://www.computer-world.com/s/article/340438/Confidence in the Cloud?, July 2009.

[MOSE05] Moses, T., eXtensible access control markup language (XACML) Version 2.0, http://docs.oasis-open.org/xacml/2.0/access_control-xacml-2.0-core-spec-os.pdf, February 2005.

[NOKI] Nokia Research Center—Open innovation, http://research.nokia.com/openinnovation.

[OMAL09] O'Malley, O., K. Zhang, S. Radia, R. Marti, and C. Harrell, Hadoop security design, http://bit.ly/75011o, October 2009.

[SALE08] Salesforce.com and Facebook create new opportunities for enterprise applications to serve Facebook's 120 million users, http://www.salesforce.com/company/news-press/press-releases/2008/11/081103-4.jsp, November 2008.

[SAND96] Sandhu, R. S., E. J. Coyne, H. L. Feinstein, and C. E. Youman, Role-based access control models. *IEEE Computer*, 29(2): 38–47, 1996.

[SAWY10] Sawyer, J., Tech insight: How to cut security costs without a lot of pain, http://www.darkreading.com/smb-security/security/management/showArticle.jhtml?articleID=226200159, July 2010.

[SUN] Sun XACML implementation, http://sunxacml.sourceforge.net/.

[TALB09] Talbot, D., How secure is cloud computing? http://www.technologyreview.com/computing/23951/, November 2009.

[THUR10] Thuraisingham, B., M. V. Khadilkar, A. Gupta, M. Kantarcioglu, and L. Khan, Secure data storage and retrieval in the cloud. *CollaborateCom*, Chicago, IL, 1–8, 2010.

[THUS09] Thusoo, A., J. S. Sarma, N. Jain, Z. Shao, P. Chakka, S. Anthony, H. Liu, P. Wyckoff, and R. Murthy, Hive—A warehousing solution over a map-reduce framework. *PVLDB*, 2(2): 1626–1629, 2009.

[TPC] TPC BENCHMARK H, http://tpc.org/tpch/spec/tpch2.11.0.pdf.

[WEIG09] Weigend, A., The social data revolution(s), http://blogs.hbr.org/now-new-next/2009/05/the-social-data-revolution.html, May 2009.

[WIND] Windows Azure platform—Whitepapers, http://www.windowsazure.com/en-us/develop/net/other-resources/white-papers/

[WWW] World Wide Web, http://en.wikipedia.org/wiki/World Wide Web.

[ZQL] Zql: A Java SQL parser, http://zql.sourceforge.net/.

Chapter 23

Secure Cloud Query Processing with Semantic Web Data

23.1 Overview

The semantic web is becoming increasingly ubiquitous. Most small and large businesses, such as Oracle, IBM, Adobe, Software AG, and many others, are actively using semantic web technologies [W3C09], and broad application areas such as Healthcare and Life Sciences are considering their possibilities for data integration [W3C09]. Sir Tim Berners-Lee originally envisioned the semantic web as a machine-understandable web [LEE98]. The power of the semantic web lies in its codification of relationships among web resources [W3C09].

Semantic web, along with ontologies, is one of the most robust ways to represent knowledge. An ontology formally describes the concepts or classes in a domain, various properties of the classes, the relationships between classes, and restrictions. A knowledge base can be constructed by an ontology and its various class instances. An example of a knowledge base (ontology and its instance) is presented in Figure 23.1.

RDF is widely used for the semantic web due to its expressive power, semantic interoperability, and reusability. Most RDF stores in current use, including Apache Jena Fuseki [APAC], Kowari [KOWA], 3store [HARR05], and Sesame [BROE02], are not primarily concerned with security. Efforts have been made to incorporate security, especially in Jena [JAIN06] [REDD05]; however, one drawback of Jena is that it lacks scalability. Its execution times can become quite slow with larger

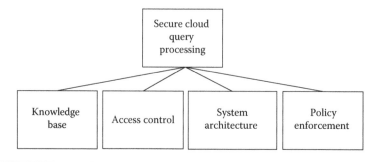

Figure 23.1 Secure cloud query processing.

datasets, making certain queries over large stores intractable (e.g., those with 10 million triples or more) [HUSA09] [HUSA10].

On the other hand, large RDF stores can be stored and retrieved from cloud computers due to their scalability, parallel processing ability, cost-effectiveness, and availability. Hadoop (Apache) [APAC]—one of the most widely used cloud computing environments—uses Google's MapReduce framework. MapReduce splits large jobs into smaller jobs and combines the results of these jobs to produce the final output once the subjobs are complete. Prior work has demonstrated that large RDF graphs can be efficiently stored and queried in these clouds [CHOI09], [HUSA09], [HUSA10], and [MIKA08]. While storing and managing, large RDF graphs have received some attention; access control for RDF stores in Hadoop has received very little attention. In this chapter, we describe a system that implements access control for RDF data on Hadoop.

Our system implements a token-based access control system. System administrators grant Access Tokens (ATs) for security-relevant data according to agents' needs and security levels. The conflicts that might arise due to the assignment of conflicting ATs to the same agent are resolved using the time stamps of the access tokens. We use the LUBM [GUO05] test instances for experiments. A few sample scenarios have been generated and implemented in Hadoop.

We have made several contributions. First, we designed an architecture that scales well to extremely large datasets. Second, we addressed access control not only at the level of users but also at the level of subjects, objects, and predicates, making policies fine grained and more expressive than the past work. Third, a time stamp-based conflict detection and resolution algorithm were designed. Fourth, the architecture was implemented and tested on benchmark data in several alternative stages: query rewriting (preprocessing phase), embedded enforcement (MapReduce execution phase), and postprocessing enforcement (data display phase). Finally, the entire system is being implemented on Hadoop—an open-source cloud computing environment. This chapter is beneficial for others considering access control for RDF data in Hadoop.

The organization of this chapter is as follows. In Section 23.2, we present the related work and a brief overview of Hadoop and MapReduce. Section 23.3

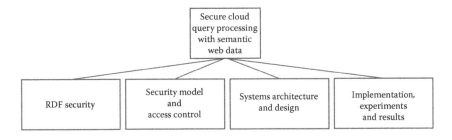

Figure 23.2 Secure cloud query processing with semantic web data. (Adapted from Khaled, A., Husain, M.F., Khan, L., Hamlen, K.W. A Token-Based Access Control System for RDF Data in the Clouds, *Proceedings of the 2010 IEEE Second International Conference on Cloud Computing Technology and Science* **(CloudCom), p. 104–111, 2010. © (2010) IEEE.)**

introduces access tokens, AT tuples, conflicts, and our conflict-resolution algorithm. We describe the architecture of our system in Section 23.4. In Section 23.5, we describe the impact of assigning ATs to agents, including experiments and their running times. Finally, Section 23.6 concludes with a summary and suggestions for future work. Figure 23.2 illustrates the contents of this chapter.

23.2 Background

23.2.1 Related Work

We begin by describing the prior work on RDF security for single machines. We then summarize some of the cloud computing architectures that store RDF data. Finally, we provide a summary of our own prior work.

Although extensive research has been undertaken on storing, representing, and reasoning about RDF knowledge, research on security and access control issues for RDF stores are comparatively sparse [REDD05]. Reddivari et al. [REDD05] have implemented access control based on a set of policy rules. They address insertion/deletion actions of triples, models, and sets in RDF stores, as well as see and use actions. Jain and Farkas [JAIN] have described RDF protection objects as RDF patterns and designed security requirements for them. They show that the security level of a subclass or subproperty should be at least as restricted as the supertype. The RDF triple-based access control model discussed in [KIM08] considers explicit and implicit authorization propagation.

Most of these works are implemented in Jena. However, Jena scales poorly in that it runs on single machines and is unable to handle large amounts of data [HUSA09] [HUSA10]. Husain et al. [HUSA09] [HUSA10] design and implement an architecture to store and query large RDF graphs. Mika and Tummarello [MIKA08] store RDF data in Hadoop. The SPIDER system [CHOI09] stores and processes large RDF datasets, but lacks an access control mechanism.

Our architecture supports access control for large datasets by including an access control layer in the architecture discussed in [HUSA10]. Instead of assigning access controls directly to users or agents, our method generates tokens for specific access levels and assigns these tokens to agents, considering the business needs and security levels of the agents. Although tokens have been used by others for access control to manage XML documents [BOUG04] and digital information [HOLM99], these have not been used for RDF stores. One of the advantages of using tokens is that they can be reused if the needs and security requirements for multiple agents are identical.

23.2.1.1 Hadoop and MapReduce

Next, we provide a brief overview of Hadoop [APAC] and MapReduce. In Hadoop, the unit of computation is called a job. The users submit jobs to Hadoop's JobTracker component. Each job has two phases: Map and Reduce. The Map phase takes as input a key-value pair and may output zero or more key-value pairs. In the Reduce phase, the values for each key are grouped together into collections traversable by an iterator. These key-iterator pairs are then passed to the Reduce method, which also outputs zero or more key-value pairs. When a job is submitted to the JobTracker, Hadoop attempts to position the Map processes near the input data in the cluster. Each Map process and Reduce process works independently without communicating. This lack of communication is advantageous for both speed and simplicity.

23.3 Access Control

23.3.1 Model

Definition 23.1

ATs permit access to security-relevant data. An agent in possession of an AT may view the data permitted by that AT. We denote ATs by positive integers.

Definition 23.2

Access token tuples (ATTs) have the form ⟨*AccessToken*, *Element*, *ElementType*, and *ElementName*⟩, where *Element* can be *Subject*, *Object*, or predicate, and *ElementType* can be described as *URI*, DataType, *Literal*, *Model*, or *BlankNode*. Model is used to access subject models and will be explained later in the section.

For example, in the ontology in Figure 23.1, *David* is a subject and ⟨1, *Subject*, *URI*, *David*⟩ is an ATT. Any agent having AT 1 may retrieve *David*'s information over all files (subject to any other security restrictions governing access to URIs, literals, etc., associated with *David*'s objects). While describing ATTs for *icates*, we leave the *ElementName* blank (_).

On the basis of record organization, we support six access levels along with a few subtypes described below. The agents may be assigned one or more of the following access levels. Access levels with a common AT combine conjunctively, whereas those with different ATs combine disjunctively.

1. *Predicate data access:* If an object type is defined for one particular predicate in an access level, then an agent having that access level may read the whole predicate file (subject to any other policy restrictions). For example, ⟨1, *Predicate, isPaid, _*⟩ is an ATT that permits its possessor to read the entire predicate file *isPaid*.

2. *Predicate and subject data access:* Agents possessing a subject ATT may access data associated with a particular subject, where the subject can be either a *URI* or a *DataType*. Combining one of these subject ATTs with a predicate data access, ATT having the same AT grants the agent access to a specific subject of a specific predicate. For example
   a. *Predicate and subject as URIs:* Combining ATT's ⟨1, *Predicate, isPaid*⟩, and ⟨1, *Subject, URI, MichaelScott*⟩ (drawn from the ontology in Figure 23.1) permits an agent with AT 1 to access a subject with URI *MichaelScott* of predicate *isPaid*.
   b. *Predicate and subject as DataTypes:* Similarly, predicate and datatype ATTs can be combined to permit access to subjects of a specific data type over a specific predicate file.
   For brevity, we omit descriptions of the different subject and object variations of each of the remaining access levels.

3. *Predicate and object:* This access level permits a principal to extract the names of subjects satisfying a particular predicate and object. For example, with ATT's ⟨1, *Predicate, hasVitamins, _*⟩, and ⟨1, *Object, URI, E*⟩, an agent possessing AT 1 may view the names of subjects (e.g., foods) that have vitamin *E*. More generally, if X_1 and X_2 are the set of triples generated by predicate and object triples (respectively) describing an AT, then agents possessing the AT may view set $X1 \cap X2$ of triples. An illustration of this example is displayed in Figure 23.3. The conjunctive combination of ATTs is with a common AT.

4. *Subject access:* With this access level, an agent may read the subject's information over all the files. This is one of the less-restrictive access levels. The subject can be a *DataType* or *BlankNode*.

5. *Object access:* With this access level, an agent may read the object's subjects over all the files. Like the previous level, this is one of the less-restrictive access levels. The object can be a *URI, DataType, Literal,* or *BlankNode*.

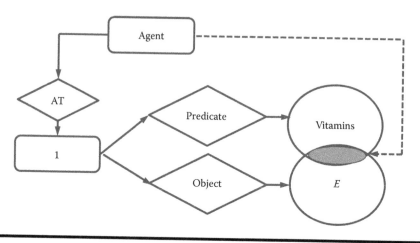

Figure 23.3 Conjunctive combination of ATTs with a common AT. (Adapted from Khaled, A., Husain, M.F., Khan, L., Hamlen, K.W. A Token-Based Access Control System for RDF Data in the Clouds, *Proceedings of the 2010 IEEE Second International Conference on Cloud Computing Technology and Science* (CloudCom), p. 104–111, 2010. © (2010) IEEE.)

6. *Subject model level access:* Model level access permits an agent to read all the necessary predicate files to obtain all objects of a given subject. Of these objects, the ones that are URIs are next treated as subjects to extract their respective predicates and objects. This process continues iteratively until all objects finally become literals or blank nodes. In this manner, agents possessing model level access may generate models on a given subject.

The following example drawn from Figure 23.1 illustrates *David* lives in *LongIsland*. *LongIsland* is a subject with an *Avg_Summer_ Temp* predicate having object 75°F. An agent with model level access of *David* reads the average summer temperature of *Island*.

23.3.2 AT Assignment

Definition 23.3

An *access token list* (AT-list) is an array of one or more ATs granted to a given agent, along with a time stamp identifying the time at which each AT was granted. A separate AT-list is maintained for each agent.

When a system administrator decides to add an AT to an agent's AT-list, the AT and time stamp are first stored in a temporary variable *AT*. Before committing the change, the system must first detect the potential conflicts in the new AT-list.

23.3.2.1 Final Output of an Agent's ATs

Each AT permits access to a set of triples. We refer to this set as the AT's *result set*. The set of triples accessible by an agent is the union of the result sets of the ATs in the agent's AT-list. Formally, if $Y_1, Y_2, \ldots, Y_n$ are the result sets of ATs AT_1, $AT_2, \ldots, AT_n$ (respectively) in an agent's AT-list, then the agent may access the triples in set $Y_1 \cup Y_2 \cup \ldots \cup Y_n$.

23.3.2.2 Security Level Defaults

An administrator's AT assignment burden can be considerably simplified by conservatively choosing default security levels for data in the system. In our implementation, all items in the data store have default security levels. The personal information of individuals is kept private by denying access to any URI of the data type *Person* by default. This prevents agents from making inferences about any individual to whom they have not been granted explicit permission. However, if an agent is granted explicit access to a particular type or property, the agent is also granted default access to the subtypes or subproperties of that type or property.

As an example, consider a predicate file *Likes* that lists elements that an individual likes. Assume further that *Jim* is a person who likes *Flying*, *SemanticWeb*, and *Jenny*, which are URIs of type *Hobby*, *ResearchInterest*, and *Person*, respectively, and 1 is an AT with ATTs ⟨1, *Subject*, *URI*, *Jim*⟩ and ⟨1, *Likes*, *Predicate*, _⟩. By default, agent *Ben* having only AT 1 cannot learn that *Jenny* is in *Jim* 's *Likes* -list since *Jenny*'s data type is *Person*. However, if *Ben* also has AT 2 described by ATT ⟨2, *Object*, *URI*, *Jenny*⟩, then *Ben* will be able to see *Jenny* in *Jim*'s *Likes* list.

23.3.3 Conflicts

A conflict arises when the following three conditions occur: (1) An agent possesses two ATs 1 and 2, (2) the result set of AT 2 is a proper subset of AT 1, and (3) the time stamp of AT 1 is earlier than the time stamp of AT 2. In this case, the latter, more specific AT supersedes the former; so, AT 1 is discarded from the AT list to resolve the conflict. Such conflicts arise in two varieties, which we term *subset conflicts* and *subtype conflicts*.

A subset conflict occurs when AT 2 is a conjunction of ATTs that refines those of AT 1. For example, suppose AT 1 is defined by ATT ⟨1, *Subject*, *URI*, *Sam*⟩ and AT 2 is defined by ATT's ⟨2, *Subject*, *URI*, *Sam*⟩ and ⟨2, *Predicate*, *HasAccounts*, _⟩. In this case, the result set of AT 2 is a subset of the result set of AT 1. Therefore, a conflict will occur if an agent possessing AT 1 is later assigned AT 2. When this occurs, AT 1 is discarded from the agent's AT-list to resolve the conflict.

Subtype conflicts occur when the ATTs in AT 2 involve data types that are subtypes of those in AT 1. The data types can be those of subjects, objects, or both.

Conflict resolution is summarized by Algorithm 1. Here, subset (AT_1, AT_2) is a function that returns true if the result set of AT_1 is a proper subset of the result set of AT_2, and SubjectSubType (AT_1, AT_2) returns true if the subject of AT_1 is a subtype of the subject of AT_2. Similarly, ObjectSubType (AT_1, AT_2) decides subtyping relations for objects instead of subjects.

Algorithm 1: Conflict detection and resolution
Input: AT *newAT* with timestamp TS_{newAT}
Result: Detect conflict and, if none exists, add
      (newAT, TS_{newAT}) to the agent's AT-list

1 *currentAT[]* ← the AT's and their timestamps;
2 if (!Subset(newAT, tempATTS) AND
    !Subset(tempATTS, newAT) AND
    !SubjectSubType(newAT, tempATTS)) AND
    !SubjectSubType(tempATTS, newAT) AND
    !ObjectSubType(newAT, tempATTS)) AND
    !ObjectSubType (tempATTS, newAT)) then
3   *currentAT*[*length$_{currentAT}$*].*AT* ← *newAT*;
4   *currentAT*[*length$_{currentAT}$*].*TS* ← *TS newAT* ;
5 else
6 *count* ← 0;
7 **while** *count < length$_{currentAT}$* **do**
8   *AT tempATTS* ← *currentAT* [*count*].*AT* ;
9   *tempTS* ← *currentAT* [*count*].*TS* ;
10   /* the timestamp during the AT assignment */
11   **if** (*Subset(newAT, tempATTS)* AND ($TS_{newAT} \geq tempTS$)) **then**
12   /* a conflict occurs */
13   *currentAT*[*count*].*AT* ← *newAT* ;
14   *currentAT*[*count*].*TS* ← *TSnewAT* ;
15   **else if** ((*Subset(tempATTS, newAT)*)AND(*tempTS < TS_{newAT}*)) **then**
16   *currentAT*[*count*].*AT* ← *newAT* ;
17   *currentAT*[*count*].*TS* ← *TSnewAT* ;
18   **else if** ((*SubjectSubType(newAT, tempATTS)* OR
              ObjectSubType (newAT,tempATTS)) AND $TS_{newAT} \geq tempTS$) **then**
19   /* a conflict occurs */
20   *currentAT*[*count*].*AT* ← *newAT* ;
21   *currentAT*[*count*].*TS* ← *TSnewAT* ;
22 **else if** ((*SubjectSubType(tempATTS, newAT)* OR *ObjectSubType (tempATTS, newAT)*) AND (*tempATTS < TS_{newAT}*)) **then**

```
23        currentAT[count].AT ← newAT ;
24        currentAT[count].TS ← TSnewAT ;
25      end
26      count ← count + 1;
27    end
28  end
```

23.4 System Architecture

23.4.1 Overview of the Architecture

Our architecture consists of two components. The upper part of Figure 23.4 depicts the data preprocessing component and the lower part shows the components responsible for answering queries.

Three subcomponents perform data generation and preprocessing. We convert RDF/XML [BECK04] into *N*-triples serialization format [GRAN04] using our

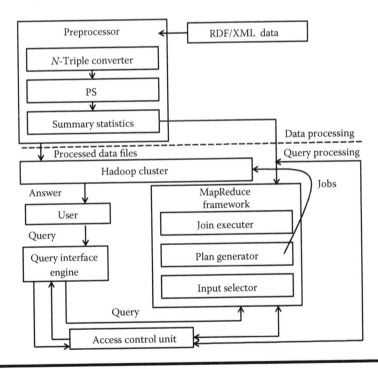

Figure 23.4 System architecture. (Adapted from Khaled, A., Husain, M.F., Khan, L., Hamlen, K.W. A Token-Based Access Control System for RDF Data in the Clouds, *Proceedings of the 2010 IEEE Second International Conference on Cloud Computing Technology and Science* **(CloudCom), p. 104–111, 2010. © (2010) IEEE.)**

N-triples converter component. The PS component takes the *N*-triples data and splits them into predicate files. These steps are described in this section. The output of the last component is then used to gather summary statistics, which are delivered to the HDFS.

The bottom part of the architecture shows the access control unit and the MapReduce framework. The access control unit takes part in different phases of query execution. When the user submits a query, the query is rewritten (if possible) to enforce one or more access control policies. The MapReduce framework has three subcomponents. It takes the rewritten SPARQL query from the query interface engine and passes it to the input selector and plan generator. This component selects the input files, decides how many jobs are needed, and passes the information to the job executor component, which submits the corresponding jobs to Hadoop. The job executor component communicates with the access control unit to get the relevant policies to enforce, and runs jobs accordingly. It then relays the query answer from Hadoop to the user. To answer queries that require inferencing, we use the Pellet OWL Reasoner. The policies are stored in the HDFS and loaded by the access control unit each time the framework loads.

23.4.1.1 Data Generation and Storage

We use the LUBM [GUO05] dataset for our experiments. This benchmark dataset is widely used by researchers [GUO04]. The LUBM data generator generates data in RDF/XML serialization format. This format is not suitable for our purpose because we store data in HDFS as flat files. If the data are in RDF/XML format, then to retrieve even a single triple, we need to parse the entire file. Also, RDF/XML format is not suitable as an input for a MapReduce job. Therefore, we store data as *N*-triples because with that format, we have a complete RDF triple (subject, predicate, and object) in one file line, which is very convenient for MapReduce jobs. Therefore, we convert the data into *N*-triple format, partitioning the data by the predicate. This step is called PS. In real-world RDF datasets, the number of distinct predicates is not more than 10 or 20 [STOC08]. This partitioning reduces the search space for any SPARQL query that does not contain a variable predicate [PRUD08]. For such a query, we can just pick a file for each predicate and run the query only on those files. We name the files by the predicate for simplicity; for example, all the triples containing predicate p1:pred are stored in a file named p1-pred. A more detailed description of this process is provided in [HUSA10].

23.4.1.2 Example Data

Table 23.1 shows the sample data for three predicates. The leftmost column shows the type of file for student objects after the PS step. It lists only the subjects of the triples having rdf:type predicate and student object. The rest of the columns

Table 23.1 Sample Data for an LUBM Query

Type		*ub: advisor*		*ub: takescourse*		*ub: teacherOf*	
GS_1	Student	GS_2	A_2	GS_1	C_2	A_1	C_1
GS_2	Student	GS_1	A_1	GS_3	C_1	A_2	C_2
GS_3	Student	GS_3	A_3	GS_3	C_3	A_3	C_3
GS_4	Student	GS_4	A_4	GS_2	C_4	A_4	C_4
				GS_1	C_1	A_5	C_5
				GS_4	C_2		

Source: Adapted from Khaled, A., Husain, M.F., Khan, L., Hamlen, K.W. A Token-Based Access Control System for RDF Data in the Clouds, *Proceedings of the 2010 IEEE Second International Conference on Cloud Computing Technology and Science* (CloudCom), p. 104–111, 2010. © (2010) IEEE.

show the advisor, takesCourse, and teacherOf predicate files after the PS step. Each row has a subject–object pair. In all cases, the predicate can be retrieved from the filename.

23.5 Policy Enforcement

Our MapReduce framework enforces policies in two phases. Some policies can be enforced by simply rewriting an SPARQL query during the query parsing phase. The remaining policies can be enforced in the query answering phase in two ways. First, we can enforce the policies as we run MapReduce jobs to answer a query. Second, we can run the jobs for a query as if there is no policy to enforce, and then take the output and run a set of jobs to enforce the policies. These postprocessing jobs are called filter jobs. In both cases, we enforce predicate-level policies while we select the input files by the input selector. In the following sections, we discuss these approaches in detail.

23.5.1 Query Rewriting

Policies involving predicates can be enforced by rewriting an SPARQL query. This involves replacing predicate variables by the predicates to which a user has access. An example illustrates. Suppose a user's AT-list consists of AT 1 described by ATT ⟨1, *Predicate, takesCourses*⟩ (i.e., the user may only access the predicate file *takes-Course*). If the user submits the query on the left of Figure 23.5, we can replace the predicate variable ?p with *takesCourse*. The rewritten query is shown on the right of Figure 23.5. After the query is rewritten, we can answer the query in two ways, detailed in the following two sections.

$$
\begin{array}{ccc}
\text{SELECT ?o WHERE} & & \text{SELECT ?o WHERE} \\
\{A ?p\ ?o\} & \Rightarrow & \{A\ takesCourse\ ?o\}
\end{array}
$$

Figure 23.5 SPARQL query before and after rewriting.

23.5.2 Embedded Enforcement

In this approach, we enforce the policies as we answer a query by Hadoop jobs. We leverage the query language's join mechanism to do this kind of enforcement. The policies involving URIs, literals, and so on, can be enforced in this way. For example, suppose access to data for some confidential courses is restricted to only a few students. If an unprivileged user wishes to list the courses a student has taken, we can join the file listing the confidential courses with the file takesCourse, and thereby enforce the desired policy within the Reduce phase of a Hadoop job. Suppose courses C3 and C4 are confidential courses. If an unprivileged user wishes to list the courses taken by GS 3, then we can answer the query by the Map and Reduce code shown in Algorithms 2 and 3.

Algorithm 2: Pseudocode for EEMAP

   1: *splits ← value . split* ()
   2: **if** *Input file = sensitiveCourses* **then**
   3:   *output* (*splits* [0], "*S*")
   4:   else if *splits* [0] = GS_3 then
   5:   *output* (*splits* [1], "*T*")
   6: **end if**

Algorithm 3: Pseudocode for EEREDUCE

   1: *count ← 0*
   2: *iter ← values . iterator* ()
   3: **while** *iter . hasNext* () **do**
   4:   *count + +*
   5:   *t ← iter . next* ()
   6: **end while**
   7: **if** *count = 1 AND t = "T"* **then**
   8:   *output* (*key*)
   9: **end if**

Algorithm 2 shows the code of the Map phase. It first splits each line into a key and a value. If the input is from a confidential course file, it outputs the course and a flag ("S" for "secret") denoting a confidential course as the output whether the

Table 23.2   EEMap Output and EEReduce Input

EEMap Output		EEReduce Input	
Key	*Value*	*Key*	*Values*
C_1	T	C_1	T
C_3	S	C_3	S,T
C_3	T	C_4	S
C_4	S		

Source: Adapted from Khaled, A., Husain, M.F., Khan, L., Hamlen, K.W. A Token-Based Access Control System for RDF Data in the Clouds, *Proceedings of the 2010 IEEE Second International Conference on Cloud Computing Technology and Science* (CloudCom), p. 104–111, 2010. © (2010) IEEE.

subject is GS 3 in line 4. If so, it outputs the course as the key and a flag ("T" for "takes") indicating that the course is of student GS 3. The left half of Table 23.2 shows the output of Algorithm 2 on the example data.

Algorithm 3 shows the code of the Reduce phase. It gets a course as the key and the flag strings as the value. The right half of Table 23.2 shows the input of Algorithm 2 on the example data. The code simply counts the number of student GS 3 (line 7), then it outputs the course (line 8). A confidential course that is taken by the student GS 3 has an additional flag, raising the count to 2 and preventing those courses from being reported. A confidential course not taken by the student will also have one flag indicating that it is a confidential course. The check whether the flag is the one for the course taken by student GS 3 prevents such courses from being reported. These two checks together ensure that only nonconfidential courses taken by GS 3 are divulged in the output. Hence, only course C1 appears in the output.

23.5.3 Postprocessing Enforcement

The second approach runs jobs as if there are no access controls, and then runs one or more additional jobs to filter the output in accordance with the policy. The advantage of this approach is that it is simple to implement, but it may take longer to answer the query. We can use the previous example to illustrate this approach. We first run the job as if there is no restriction on courses. Then we run one extra job to enforce the policy. The extra job takes two files as the input: the output of the first job and the confidentialCourses file containing the URIs of confidential courses. In the Map phase, we output the course as the key and depending on the input file, a flag string. The Map code is largely the same as Algorithm 2. The only difference is that we do not need to check the URI identifying the student, since the output of the first job will contain the courses taken by only that student. The code for the Reduce phase remains the same. Hence, at the end of the second job, we get the output that does not contain any confidential courses.

23.6 Experimental Setup and Results

We ran our experiments in a Hadoop cluster of 10 nodes. Each node had a Pentium IV 2.80 GHz processor, 4 GB main memory, and 640 GB disk space. The operating system was Ubuntu Linux 9.04. We compared our embedded enforcement approach with our postprocessing enforcement approach. We used the LUBM100, LUBM500, LUBM1000, LUBM2000, LUBM6000, and LUBM9000 datasets for the experiments.

We experimented with these approaches using two scenarios: takeCourse and displayTeachers. In the takeCourse scenario, a list of confidential courses cannot be viewed by an unprivileged user for any student. A query was submitted to display the courses taken by one particular student. In the displayTeachers scenario, an unprivileged user may view information only about the lecturers. A query was submitted to display the URI of people who are employed in a particular department. Even though professors, assistant professors, associate professors, and so on are employed in that department, only URIs of lecturers are returned because of the policy. The detailed results are given in [KHAL10]. We observed that postprocessing enforcement always takes 20–80% more time than the embedded enforcement approach. This can be easily explained by the extra job needed in postprocessing. Hadoop takes roughly equal times to set up jobs regardless of the input and output data sizes of the jobs. The postprocessing enforcement approach runs more jobs than the embedded enforcement approach, yielding the observed overhead.

23.7 Summary and Directions

The access controls for RDF data on single machines have been widely discussed in the literature, but these systems scale poorly owing to large datasets. The amount of RDF data in the web is growing rapidly; so, this is a serious limitation. One of the most efficient ways to handle these data is to store them in cloud computers. However, access control has not yet been adequately addressed for cloud-resident RDF data. Our implemented mechanism incorporates a token-based access control system where users of the system are granted tokens based on business needs and authorization levels. Currently, we are building a generic system that incorporates tokens and resolves policy conflicts. Our goal is to implement subject model level access that recursively extracts objects of subjects and treats these objects as subjects as long as these objects are URIs. This will allow agents possessing model level access to generate models on a given subject.

Our current work also examines secure query processing in hybrid clouds [OKTA12]. In the future, we will explore the various types of access control models for cloud query processing and evaluate them. This will give us a better idea of the most suitable access control models for cloud query processing.

References

[APAC] Apache Hadoop. http://hadoop.apache.org/

[APAC] Apache Jena Fuseki. http://jena.apache.org/documentation/serving_data/

[BECK04] Beckett, D., RDF/XML syntax specification (revised). Technical report, W3C, February 2004.

[LEE98] Berners-Lee, T., Semantic web road map. http://www.w3.org/DesignIssues/Semantic.html, 1998.

[BOUG04] Bouganim, L., F.D. Ngoc, and P. Pucheral, Client-based access control management for XML documents. In: *Proceedings of the 20émes Journées Bases de Données Avancées (BDA)*, pp. 65–89, Montpellier, France, October 2004.

[BROE02] Broekstra, J., A. Kampman, and F. van Harmelen, Sesame: A generic architecture for storing and querying RDF. In: *Proceedings of the 1st International Semantic Web Conference (ISWC)*, pp. 54–68, Sardinia, Italy, June 2002.

[CHOI09] Choi, H., J. Son, Y. Cho, M.K. Sung, and Y.D. Chung, SPIDER: A system for scalable, parallel/distributed evaluation of large-scale RDF data. In: *Proceedings of the 18th ACM Conference on Information and Knowledge Management (CIKM)*, pp. 2087–2088, Hong Kong, China, November 2009.

[GRAN04] Grant, J. and D. Beckett, RDF test cases. Technical report, W3C, February 2004.

[GUO04] Guo, Y., Z. Pan, and J. Heflin, An evaluation of knowledge base systems for large OWL datasets. In: *Proceedings of the 3rd International Semantic Web Conference (ISWC)*, pp. 274–288, Hiroshima, Japan, November 2004.

[GUO05] Guo, Y., Z. Pan, and J. Heflin, LUBM: A benchmark for OWL knowledge base systems. *Journal of Web Semantics*, 3(2–3): 158–182, 2005.

[HARR05] Harris, S. and N. Shadbolt, SPARQL query processing with conventional relational database systems. In: *Proceedings of the Web Information Systems Engineering (WISE) International Workshop on Scalable Semantic Web Knowledge Base Systems (SSWS)*, pp. 235–244, New York, NY, November 2005.

[HOLM99] Holmquist, L. E., J. Redström, and P. Ljungstrand, Token-based access to digital information. In: *Proceedings of the 1st International Symposium on Handheld and Ubiquitous Computing (HUC)*, pp. 234–245, Karlsruhe, Germany, September 1999.

[HUSA09] Husain, M. F., P. Doshi, L. Khan, and B. M. Thuraisingham, Storage and retrieval of large RDF graph using Hadoop and MapReduce. In *Proceedings of the 1st International Conference on Cloud Computing (CloudCom)*, pp. 680–686, Beijing, China, December 2009.

[HUSA10] Husain M. F., L. Khan, M. Kantarcioglu, and B. Thuraisingham, Data intensive query processing for large RDF graphs using cloud computing tools. In: *Proceedings of the IEEE 3rd International Conference on Cloud Computing (CLOUD)*, pp. 1–10, Miami, Florida, July 2010.

[JAIN06] Jain, A. and C. Farkas, Secure resource description framework: An access control model. In *Proceedings of the 11th ACM Symposium on Access Control Models and Technologies (SACMAT)*, pp. 121–129, Lake Tahoe, California, June 2006.

[KHAL10] Khaled, A., M.F. Husain, L. Khan, K.W. Hamlen, and B.M. Thuraisingham, A Token-Based Access Control System for RDF Data in the Clouds. *IEEE Cloud Com*, Indianapolis, IN, December 2010.

[KIM08] Kim, J., K. Jung, and S. Park, An introduction to authorization conflict problem in RDF access control. In: *Proceedings of the 12th International Conference on Knowledge-Based Intelligent Information and Engineering Systems (KES)*, pp. 583–592, Zagreg, Croatia, September 2008.

[KOWA] Kowari. http://kowari.sourceforge.net.

[MIKA08] Mika, P. and G. Tummarello, Web semantics in the clouds. *IEEE Intelligent Systems*, 23(5): 82–87, 2008.

[OKTA12] Oktay, K.Y., V. Khadilkar, B. Hore, M. Kantarcioglu, S. Mehrotra, and B. M. Thuraisingham, Risk-Aware Workload Distribution in Hybrid Clouds. *IEEE Cloud*, Honolulu, HI, June 2012.

[PRUD08] Prud'hommeaux, E. and A. Seaborne, SPARQL query language for RDF. Technical report, W3C, January 2008.

[REDD05] Reddivari, P., T. Finin, and A. Joshi, Policy based access control for an RDF store. In: *Proceedings of the Policy Management for the Web Workshop*, Chiba, Japan, 2005.

[STOC08] Stocker, M., A. Seaborne, A. Bernstein, C. Kiefer, and D. Reynolds, SPARQL basic graph pattern optimization using selectivity estimation. In: *Proceedings of the 17th International Conference on World Wide Web (WWW)*, pp. 595–604, Beijing, China, April 2008.

[W3C09] W3C. Semantic web frequently asked questions. http://www.w3.org/RDF/FAQ, 2009.

Chapter 24

Secure Cloud-Based Information Integration

24.1 Overview

Cloud computing services such as Amazon S3 [AMAZ] are gaining a lot of popularity because of factors such as cost efficiency and ease of maintenance. We have evaluated the feasibility of using S3 storage services for storing semantic web data using the Intelligence Community's Blackbook system. Blackbook was an initiative by IARPA (Intelligence Advanced Research Project Activity) toward building a semantic web-based data integration framework [BLAC]. The main purpose of the Blackbook system is to provide intelligence analysts an easy-to-use tool to access data from disparate data sources, make logical inferences across the data sources, and share this knowledge with other analysts using the system. Besides providing a web application interface, it also exposes its services by means of web services. Blackbook integrates data from different data sources, thereby making it prudent to store the data sources in a shared environment such as the one provided by cloud computing services. Blackbook essentially uses several semantic data sources to produce search results. But storing shared data in cloud environments in a secure manner is a big challenge. Our approach to solve this problem is discussed in this chapter.

In our approach, we stored one of the Blackbook data sources on Amazon S3 in a secure manner, thus leveraging cloud computing services within a semantic web-based framework. We encrypted the data source using Advanced Encryption Standard [AES] before storing it on Amazon S3. Also, we do not store the original key anywhere in our system. Instead, the key is generated by two separate components, each called a "Key Server." Then, the generated key is used to encrypt the data.

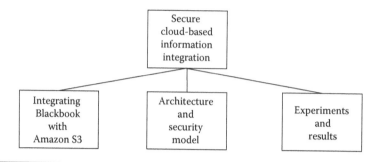

Figure 24.1 Secure cloud-based information integration. (Parikh, P., M. Kantarcioglu, V. Khadilkar, B. M. Thuraisingham, and L. Khan: Secure information integration with a semantic web-based framework. *Proceedings of the IEEE 13th International Conference on Information Reuse and Integration (IRI2012),* **Las Vegas, NV, 659–663. © (2012) IEEE.)**

To prevent replay attacks, we used the Lamport one time password (OTP) [LAMP81] scheme to generate the passwords that are used by the client for authentication with the "Key Servers." We used the RBAC model [SAND96] to restrict system access to authorized users and implemented the RBAC policies using Sun's implementation of XACML [OASI].

In this chapter, we describe the design and implementation of a secure information integration framework that uses Blackbook. The organization of this chapter is as follows. In Section 24.2, we present a detailed description of our implementation. Section 24.3 presents our experimental results. The chapter summary and future directions are presented in Section 24.4. The additional details of our work can be found in [PARI09] and [PARI12]. Figure 24.1 illustrates the contents of this chapter. The details of Blackbook can be found in [BLAC].

24.2 Integrating Blackbook with Amazon S3

As stated earlier, Blackbook, a semantic web-based data integration framework, allows data integration from various data sources. We have found that RDF resources are the perfect candidates for the publication via RESTful web services. Since both RESTful web services and semantic web deal with resources, it makes sense to expose RDF resources via RESTful interface. Technologies such as semantic web can only work with web services that identify resources with URIs and hence, REST is an ideal platform for implementing web services for semantic web-based systems [PARI09].

As discussed in Part III, cloud computing is a paradigm of computing in which dynamically scalable and often virtualized resources are provided as a service over the Internet [CLOU]. The concept incorporates the following combinations:

- IaaS
- PaaS
- SaaS

The economic advantage is one of the main motivations behind the cloud computing paradigm, since it promises the reduction of capital expenditure (CapEx) and operational expenditure (OpEx) [JENS09]. Various organizations can share data and computational power using the cloud computing infrastructure. For instance, salesforce.com is an industry leader in CRM products and is one of the pioneers to leverage the cloud computing infrastructure on a massive scale. Since Blackbook is a data integration framework, it can search and integrate data from various data sources that may be located on local machines or remote servers. We utilized the data storage services provided by Amazon S3 to store data sources used by Blackbook.

The reasons we chose Amazon S3 are as follows:

- Cost effective—Storage price as low as $0.125 per GB per month.
- Ease of use—Can be invoked via both REST and SOAP web services.
- Reliability—Amazon is a big player in cloud computing and is known for providing reliable cloud computing services.

One of the major challenges for the current cloud computing systems is privacy risk. That is, privacy is an important concern for cloud computing services in terms of legal compliance and user trust. In [PEAR09], the author provides some interesting insights about how privacy issues should be taken into consideration when designing cloud computing services. The main privacy risks identified in [PEAR09] include the following:

- For the cloud service user—being forced to be tracked or give personal information against his/her will.
- For the organization using cloud service—noncompliance to enterprise policies, loss of reputation, and credibility.
- For implementers of cloud platforms—exposure of sensitive information stored on the platforms, loss of reputation, and credibility.
- For providers of applications on top of cloud platforms—legal noncompliance, loss of reputation.
- For the data subject—exposure of personal information.

We have used Amazon S3 in our implementation. As stated in [AMAZ],

Amazon S3 is storage for the Internet. It is designed to make web-scale computing easier for developers. Amazon S3 provides a simple web services interface that can be used to store and retrieve any amount of data, at any time, from anywhere on the web. It gives any developer access to the same highly scalable, reliable, fast, inexpensive data storage infrastructure that Amazon uses to run its own global network of web sites. The service aims to maximize benefits of scale and to pass those benefits on to developers.

Many organizations use services such as Amazon S3 for data storage. Some important questions that need to be addressed include: Is the data we store on S3, secure? Is it accessible by any user outside our organization? How do we restrict access to files for users within the organization? To keep our data secure, we propose to encrypt the data using AES before uploading the data files on Amazon S3. To restrict access to files to users within the organization, we propose to implement role-based access control policies using XACML. In RBAC, permissions are associated with roles and users are made members of the appropriate roles. This simplifies the management of permissions [SAND96]. Our system architecture is illustrated in Figure 24.2.

The data sources are stored on an Amazon S3 server in an encrypted form. The two keys used to encrypt the data source are stored on two servers—key server 1 and key server 2. The policies associated with the data sources for different users are also stored on these servers.

The system uses the OTP for authentication. It is a password that is only valid for a single session or transaction. OTPs avoid the shortcomings associated with static passwords [ONE]. Unlike static passwords, they are not vulnerable to replay

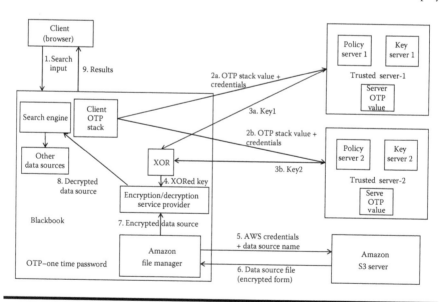

Figure 24.2   System architecture. (Parikh, P., M. Kantarcioglu, V. Khadilkar, B. M. Thuraisingham, and L. Khan. Secure information integration with a semantic web-based framework. *Proceedings of the IEEE 13th International Conference on Information Reuse and Integration (IRI2012),* **Las Vegas, NV, 659–663. © (2012) IEEE.)**

attacks. So, if an intruder manages to get hold of an OTP that was used previously to log into a service or carry a transaction, the system's security would not be compromised since that password will no longer be valid. The only drawback of OTP is that humans cannot memorize it and hence require additional technology to work.

OTP generation algorithms make use of randomness to prevent the prediction of future OTPs based on the previously observed OTPs. Some of the approaches to generate OTPs are as follows:

■ The use of a mathematical algorithm to generate a new password based on the previous passwords.
■ On the basis of time synchronization between the authentication server and the client providing the password.
■ The use of a mathematical algorithm where the new password is based on a challenge (e.g., a random number chosen by the authentication server or transaction details) and/or a counter.

We use Lamport's OTP scheme for authentication. The Lamport OTP approach is based on a mathematical algorithm for generating a sequence of "passkey" values and each successor value is based on the value of the predecessor. The core of Lamport's OTP scheme requires that cooperating client/service components agree to use a common sequencing algorithm to generate a set of expiring OTPs (client side) and validate client-provided passkeys included in each client-initiated request (service side). In our case, the client is the Blackbook system and the service components are the "Key Servers." The client generates a finite sequence of values starting with a "seed" value and each successor value is generated by applying some transformation algorithm (or F(S) function) to the previous sequence value:

$$S1 = seed, S2 = F(S1), S3 = F(S2), S4 = F(S3) \ldots S[n] = F(S[n-1])$$

We use the "password" of the user that is salted with some randomly generated bytes (using SHA1PRNG) as a key to generate the seed value using SHA-256 [SECU02]. The next values in the sequence are generated using the obtained seed value using SHA-256. All these generated values are stored in a stack on the client machine. The topmost value on the stack is stored on both the "Key Servers" (1 & 2). If the client sends a request for the first time, the topmost value of the client stack is compared with the value on the "Key Servers" (1 & 2). If the values match, the client is authenticated and the topmost value on the client stack is removed. For subsequent requests, the topmost value on the client stack is used to compute the successor value using the hash function (used to build the stack). If the generated value and the value on the "Key Servers" match, the user is authenticated; the topmost value on the client stack is stored on the "Key Servers" and subsequently removed from the client stack. If the client stack gets exhausted, a new stack is generated and the topmost value on the stack is stored on the "Key Servers." Once the user is authenticated using the OTP scheme, the user request is evaluated against the policies applicable for the resource (data source in our case) requested by the user for access. The predefined policies are stored in the "Policy Server" component of the "Key Servers." If the policies for the resource are applicable for the user request, the "Key Server" sends the keys used to encrypt the resource requested by the user.

We use XACML to implement the access control using the policies defined in an XML file. After the user gets authenticated with the system, the system checks if the user is authorized to access the requested resource. The user request is handled by the PEP that converts the users' request into an XACML request and sends it to the PDP for further evaluation. The PDP evaluates the request and sends back a response, which can be either "access permitted" or "access denied," with the appropriate obligations. (We are not considering obligations for our system.) A policy is a collection of several subcomponents: target, rules, rule combining algorithms, and obligations.

Target: Each policy has only one target that helps in determining whether the policy is relevant for the request. The policy's relevance for the request determines if the policy is to be evaluated for the request, which is achieved by defining attributes of three categories in the target—subject, resource, and action. For example, we have specified the value "testadmin@blackbook.jhuapl.edu" for the subject and "Amazons3" for the resource.

Rules: We can associate multiple roles with the policy. Each rule consists of a condition, an effect, and a target.

Conditions are statements about attributes that return true, false, or indeterminate upon evaluation.

Effect is the consequence of the satisfied rule that assumes the value permit or deny. We have specified the value as permit.

Target helps in determining if the rule is relevant for the request.

Rule combining algorithms: As a policy can have various rules, it is possible for different rules to generate conflicting results. Rule combining algorithms resolve such conflicts to arrive at one outcome per policy per request. Only one rule combining algorithm is applicable to one policy.

Obligations: Obligations allow the mechanism to provide a finer level of access control than to merely permit and deny decisions. They are the actions that must be performed by the PEP in conjunction with the enforcement of an authorization decision.

After successful authentication and authorization, the Amazon File Manager downloads the requested resource from Amazon S3 server. More specifically, key server—1 sends key1 and the key server—2 sends key2 to the Amazon File Manager. These keys are XORED to get keyorg, that is,

$$\text{keyorg} = \text{key1 XOR key2}$$

Then, keyorg is used to decrypt the resource by the encryption/decryption service provider.

The main motive behind using the two key servers is to avoid a single point of failure. If any of the key servers gets hacked, the data are not compromised as two keys, one from each of the key servers are needed to decrypt the data sources. In case one of the key servers is hacked and the keys stored on that server are compromised, we run into the risk of rendering the data source stored on Amazon useless as we need two keys, one from each key server, to retrieve the original key used to encrypt the data source. To avoid this, we propose to take periodic backups of the keys on each of the key server.

Scenario: We now describe a sample scenario, depicting an interaction with the Amazon S3 storage service, with respect to the Blackbook system:

1. The user U fires a search query to Blackbook (step 1 in Figure 24.2). Blackbook federates the query across various data sources, including the data source F that is securely stored on Amazon S3.
2. We follow the OTP scheme to authenticate the client (Blackbook in this case) for using the AWS S3 service. The client machine sends the topmost value on the OTP stack along with the user credentials and the request to key servers 1 and 2 (steps 2a and 2b in Figure 24.2).
3. If the value passed by the client matches the value on the OTP stack of the key servers and the policies applicable for the user are valid for the request, the key servers send the "key" used to decrypt the data source (steps 3a and 3b in Figure 24.1).
4. The keys, key1 and key2, obtained from the key servers 1 and 2 are/ XOR-ed to obtain the original key used to decrypt the data source F (step 4 in Figure 24.2).
5. The Amazon File Manager passes the Amazon account credentials and the data source name to retrieve the data source (steps 5 and 6 in Figure 24.2).
6. The encryption/decryption service manager retrieves the encrypted data source and then, using the XOR-ed key, decrypts the data source (steps 7 and 8 in Figure 24.2).
7. Blackbook performs a search on the data source retrieved from Amazon along with other data sources and returns the results to the user (step 9 in Figure 24.2).

A sample XACML request: The subject, testadmin@blackbook.jhuapl.edu, which belongs to the users group (attribute of the subject), is trying to perform a read action on the resource Amazons3. To create such a request, we need two subject attributes, one resource attribute, and one action attribute. The two subject attributes are rfc822Name (email ID) and the group to which the subject belongs. The one resource attribute is the URI of the resource and the one action attribute is the read action on the resource. The complete listing that demonstrates the creation of the PEP with all these attributes can be found in [PARI09].

24.3 Experiments

In our approach, we have used the AES to encrypt data before storing them on Amazon S3 server. Uploading the data on the Amazon server are a one-time process. The data source needs to be uploaded again only when the stored data needs to be modified. But the data source stored on Amazon S3 needs to be downloaded every time the user issues a search query to the Blackbook system. Since the data source needs to be decrypted every time a query is issued, it may affect performance since encryption and decryption are costly operations.

We ran the experiments on a Dell desktop computer running on Ubuntu Gutsy 7.10 with the following hardware configuration:Intel® Pentium® 4 CPU 3.00 GHZ, 1 GB RAM. The network bandwidth while running the experiments varied between 250 and 300 Mbps. We generated the data files using the triple-generation program provided by SP2B, the SPARQL Performance Benchmark [SPAR]. We experimented with 30 files of different sizes, ranging from 1 to 30 MB. The details of the experiments are given in [PARI09].

24.4 Summary and Directions

Cloud computing paradigm is becoming increasingly important in today's world. Therefore, issues such as data security and privacy in the context of cloud computing have gained a lot of attention. In this chapter, we described techniques to protect our data by encrypting them before storing on cloud computing servers such as Amazon S3. Our approach is novel as we propose to use two key servers to generate and store the keys. Also, we assure more security than some of the other known approaches as we do not store the actual key used to encrypt the data. This assures the protection of our data even if one or both key servers are compromised. Our implementation utilizes Blackbook, a semantic web-based data integration framework, which integrated data from various data sources.

In our current approach, we download the data source for every request from the user. In the future, we can make the provision to cache the data source requested by the user on our local server and provide the results to the user from the cached data source by treating it as a local data source. This approach will help to enhance performance. Also, we can divide the data source in chunks and then upload it. Since the search process takes place in an asynchronous manner, we can download the chunks, search for results, and display them to the user, one at a time. Meanwhile, the application can keep downloading other chunks. We can also keep a track of the search history for the user. When the user logs into the system, we can download chunks that a user is most likely to query.

References

[AES] Advanced encryption standard, http://en.wikipedia.org/wiki/Advanced_Encryption_Standard

[AMAZ] Amazon S3, http://aws.amazon.com/s3/

[BLAC] http://info.publicintelligence.net/IARPA_overview_UMD.pdf

[CLOU] Cloud computing, http://en.wikipedia.org/wiki/Cloud_computing

[LAMP81] Lamport, L., Password authentication with insecure communication. *Communications of the ACM*, 24(11): 770–772, 1981.

[JENS09] Jensen, M., J. S. Jensen, N. Gruschka, and L. L. Iacono, On technical security issues in cloud computing, *Proceedings of IEEE International Conference on Cloud Computing*, Bangalore, India, 2009.

[OASI] OASIS, http://www.oasis-pen.org/committees/xacml/repository/cs-xacml-specification-1.1.pdf

[ONE] One time password, http://en.wikipedia.org/wiki/One-time_password

[PARI09] Parikh, P., Masters thesis, *Secured Information Integration with a Semantic Web-Based Framework*, 2009, the University of Texas at Dallas.

[PARI12] Parikh, P., M. Kantarcioglu, V. Khadilkar, B. M. Thuraisingham, and L. Khan, Secure information integration with a semantic web-based framework. *Proceedings of the IEEE 13th International Conference on Information Reuse and Integration (IRI2012)*, Las Vegas, NV, 659–663.

[PEAR09] Pearson, S., HP labs—Taking account of privacy when designing cloud computing services, *Proceedings of IEEE ICSE Cloud09*, Vancouver, IEEE, May 2009.

[SAND96] Sandhu, R., E. J. Coyne, H. L. Feinstein, and C. Youman, Role based access control models. *IEEE Computer,* 29(2): 38–47, 1996.

[SECU02] Secure hash standard, http://csrc.nist.gov/publications/fips/fips180-2/fips180-2.pdf, 2002.

[SPAR] SPARQL performance benchmark http://www.openlinksw.com/dataspace/vdb/weblog/vdb%27s%20BLOG%20%5B136%5D/1423.

Conclusion to Part VI

The chapters in this part have described the experimental secure cloud systems that we have developed including secure cloud query processing and secure information integration.

In Chapter 22, we presented a system that allows cooperating organizations to securely share large amounts of data. We have ensured that the organizations have a large common storage area by using Hadoop. Further, we have used Hive to present users of our system with a structured view of the data and to also enable them to query the data with a SQL-like language.

In Chapter 23, we have described access control mechanisms for semantic web data stored in the cloud. Our implemented mechanism incorporates a token-based access control system where users of the system are granted tokens based on business needs and authorization levels.

In Chapter 24, we described techniques to protect our data by encrypting it before storing on cloud computing servers like Amazon S3. Our approach is novel as we propose to use two key servers to generate and store the keys. Also, we provide more security than some of the other known approaches as we do not store the actual key used to encrypt the data. This assures the protection of our data even if one or both key servers are compromised.

EXPERIMENTAL CLOUD SYSTEMS FOR SECURITY APPLICATIONS

Introduction to Part VII

In Part VI, we discussed our prototypes on secure cloud computing systems, in Part VII, we will discuss the use of cloud computing for security functions. That is, we will describe the systems we have developed that illustrate how cloud systems provide security-as-a-service.

Part VII consists of four chapters: 25, 26, 27, and 28. Our cloud-based malware detection system is discussed in Chapter 25. Our cloud-based insider threat detection is discussed in Chapter 26. Our assured information-sharing system in the cloud is discussed in Chapter 27. We described the design and implementation of a semantic-cloud-based information-sharing system in Chapter 28. A semantic cloud is a cloud that provides semantic web services to the consumer.

Chapter 25

Cloud-Based Malware Detection for Evolving Data Streams

25.1 Overview

Malware is a potent vehicle for many successful cyber-attacks every year, including data and identity theft, system and data corruption, and denial of service; it therefore constitutes a significant security threat to many individuals and organizations. The average direct malware cost damages worldwide per year from 1999 to 2006 have been estimated at $14 billion [COMP07]. This includes labor costs for analyzing, repairing, and disinfecting systems, productivity losses, revenue losses due to system loss or degraded performance, and other costs directly incurred as the result of the attack. However, the direct cost does not include the prevention cost, such as antivirus software, hardware, and IT (information technology) security staff salary, and so on. Aside from these monetary losses, individuals and organizations also suffer identity theft, data theft, and other intangible losses due to successful attacks.

Malware includes viruses, worms, Trojan horses, time and logic bombs, botnets, and spyware. A number of techniques have been devised by researchers to counter these attacks; however, the more successful the researchers become in detecting and preventing the attacks, the more sophisticated malicious code appears in the wild. Thus, the arms race between malware authors and malware defenders continues to escalate. One popular technique applied by the antivirus community to detect malicious code is *signature detection*. This technique matches untrusted executables

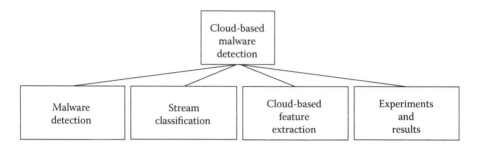

Figure 25.1   Cloud-based malware detection for evolving data streams.

against a unique telltale string or byte pattern known as a *signature*, which is used as an identifier for a particular malicious code. Although signature detection techniques are widely used, they are not effective against zero-day attacks (new malicious code), polymorphic attacks (different encryptions of the same binary), or metamorphic attacks (different code for the same functionality) [CRAN05]. There has therefore been a growing need for fast, automated, and efficient detection techniques that are robust to these attacks.

This chapter describes a data mining technique that is dedicated to the automated generation of signatures to defend against these kinds of attacks. Owing to the need for near real-time performance of the malware detection tools, we have developed our data mining tool in the cloud. We describe the detailed design and implementation of this cloud-based tool in the remaining sections of this chapter.

The organization of this chapter is as follows: Section 25.2 discusses malware detection. Section 25.3 discusses related work. Section 25.4 discusses the classification algorithm and proves its effectiveness analytically. Section 25.5 then describes the feature extraction and selection technique using cloud computing for malware detection, and Section 25.6 discusses data collection, experimental setup, evaluation techniques, and results. Section 25.7 discusses several issues related to our approach. Section 25.8 summarizes our conclusions. Figure 25.1 illustrates the concepts of this chapter.

25.2 Malware Detection

25.2.1 Malware Detection as a Data Stream Classification Problem

The problem of detecting malware using data mining [SCHU01], [KOLT04], [MASU08a] involves classifying each executable as either *benign* or *malicious*. Most past work has approached the problem as a static data classification problem, where the classification model is trained with fixed training data. However, the escalating rate of malware evolution and innovation is not well suited to static training. Detection of continuously evolving malware is better treated as a *data stream* classification problem. In this paradigm, the data stream is a sequence of executables in which each data point is one executable. The stream is of *infinite-length*. It also observes *concept-drift* as attackers relentlessly develop new techniques to avoid detection, changing the characteristics of the malicious code. Similarly, the characteristics of benign executables change with the evolution of compilers and operating systems.

Data stream classification is a major area of active research in the data mining community, and requires surmounting at least three challenges: First, the storage and maintenance of potentially unbounded historical data in an infinite-length, concept-drifting stream for training purposes is infeasible. Second, the classification model must be adapted continuously to cope with concept-drift. Third, if there is no predefined feature space for the data points in the stream, new features with high discriminating power must be selected and extracted as the stream evolves, which we call *feature evolution*.

Solutions to the first two problems are related. Concept-drift necessitates refinement of the hypothesis to accommodate the new concept; most of the old data must be discarded from the training set. Therefore, one of the main issues in mining concept-drifting data streams is the selection of training instances adequate to learn the evolving concept. Solving the third problem requires a feature selection process that is ongoing, since new and more powerful features are likely to emerge and old features are likely to become less dominant as the concept evolves. If the feature space is large, then the running time and memory requirements for feature extraction and selection becomes a bottleneck for the data stream classification system.

One approach to addressing concept-drift is to select and store the training data that are most consistent with the current concept [FAN04]. Other approaches, such as Very Fast Decision Trees (VFDTs) [Domingos and HULT00], update the existing classification model when new data appear. However, past work has shown that ensemble techniques are often more robust for handling unexpected changes and concept-drifts [WANG03], [SCHO05], [KOLT05]. These maintain an ensemble of classifiers and update the ensemble when new data appear.

We design and develop a multipartition, multichunk ensemble classification algorithm that generalizes the existing ensemble methods. The generalization leads to significantly improved classification accuracy relative to the existing single-partition, single-chunk ensemble approaches when tested on real-world data streams. The ensemble in our approach consists of Kv classifiers, where K is a constant and v is the number of partitions, to be explained shortly.

Our approach divides the data stream into equal-sized *chunks*. The chunk size is chosen so that all data in each chunk fits into the main memory. Each chunk, when *labeled*, is used to train classifiers. Whenever a new data chunk is labeled, the ensemble is updated as follows. We take the r most recent labeled consecutive data chunks, divide these r chunks into v *partitions*, and train a classifier with each partition. Therefore, v classifiers are trained using the r consecutive chunks. We then update the ensemble by choosing the best Kv classifiers (based on accuracy) among the newly trained v classifiers and the existing Kv classifiers. Thus, the total number of classifiers in the ensemble remains constant. Our approach is therefore parameterized by the number of partitions v, the number of chunks r, and the ensemble size K.

Our approach does not assume that new data points appearing in the stream are immediately labeled. Instead, it defers the ensemble updating process until labels for the data points in the latest data chunk become available. In the meantime, new unlabeled data continue to be classified using the current ensemble. Thus, the approach is well suited to applications in which misclassifications solicit corrected labels from an expert user or other source. For example, consider the online credit card fraud detection problem. When a new credit card transaction takes place, its class (*fraud* or *authentic*) is predicted using the current ensemble. Suppose a fraudulent transaction is misclassified as *authentic*. When the customer receives the bank statement, he identifies this error and reports it to the authority. In this way, the actual labels of the data points are obtained and the ensemble is updated accordingly.

25.2.2 Cloud Computing for Malware Detection

If the feature space of the data points is not fixed, a subproblem of the classification problem is the extraction and selection of features that describe each data point. As in earlier work (e.g., [KOLT04]), we use binary n-grams as features for malware detection. However, since the total number of possible n-grams is prohibitively large, we judiciously select n-grams that have the greatest discriminatory power. This selection process is ongoing; as the stream progresses, newer n-grams appear that dominate the older n-grams. These newer n-grams replace the old in our model in order to identify the best features for a particular period.

Naïve implementation of the feature extraction and selection process can be both time- and storage-intensive for large datasets. For example, our previous work [MASU08a] extracted roughly a quarter billion n-grams from a corpus of only 3500 executables. This feature extraction process required extensive virtual memory (with associated performance overhead), since not all of these features could be stored in the main memory. Extraction and selection required about 2 h of computation and many gigabytes of disk space for a machine with a quad-core processor and 12 GB of memory. This is despite the use of a purely static dataset; when the dataset is a dynamic stream, extraction and selection must recur, resulting in a major bottleneck. In this chapter, we consider a much larger dataset of 105 thousand executables for which our previous approach is insufficient.

We therefore design and develop a scalable feature selection and extraction solution that leverages a cloud computing framework [DEAN08]. We show that depending on the availability of cluster nodes, the running time for feature extraction and selection can be reduced by a factor of m, where m is the number of nodes in the cloud cluster. The nodes are machines with inexpensive commodity hardware. Therefore, the solution is also cost effective as high-end computing machines are not required.

25.2.3 *Our Contributions*

Our contributions can therefore be summarized as follows. We design and develop a generalized multipartition, multichunk ensemble technique that significantly reduces the expected classification error over existing single-partition, single-chunk ensemble methods. A theoretical analysis justifies the effectiveness of the approach. We then formulate the malware detection problem as a data stream classification problem and identify drawbacks of traditional malicious code detection techniques relative to our data mining approach.

We design and develop a scalable and cost-effective solution to this problem using a cloud computing framework. Finally, we apply our technique to synthetically generated data as well as real botnet traffic and real malicious executables, achieving better detection accuracy than other stream data classification techniques. The results show that our ensemble technique constitutes a powerful tool for intrusion detection based on data stream classification.

25.3 Related Work

Our work is related to both malware detection and stream mining. Both are discussed in this section. Traditional *signature-based* malware detectors identify malware by scanning untrusted binaries for distinguishing byte sequences or *features*. Features unique to malware are maintained in a *signature database*, which must be continually updated as new malware is discovered and analyzed. Traditionally, signature databases have been manually derived, updated, and disseminated by human experts as new malware appears and is analyzed. However, the escalating rate of new malware appearances and the advent of self-mutating, polymorphic malware over the past decade have made manual signature updating less practical. This has led to the development of automated data mining techniques for malware detection (e.g., [KOLT04], [SCHU01], [MASU08a], and [HAML09]) that are capable of automatically inferring signatures for previously unseen malware.

Data-mining-based approaches analyze the content of an executable and classify it as malware if a certain combination of features are found (or not found) in the executable. These malware detectors are first trained so that they can generalize the distinction between malicious and benign executables, and thus detect future instances of malware. The training process involves feature extraction and model building using these features. Data-mining-based malware detectors differ mainly on how the features are extracted and which machine learning technique is used to build the model. The performance of these techniques largely depends on the quality of the features that are extracted.

In the work reported in [SCHU01], the authors extract DLL call information (using *GNU binutils*) and character strings (using *GNU strings*) from the headers of Windows PE executables, as well as 2-byte sequences from the executable content. The DLL calls, strings, and bytes are used as features to train models. Models are trained using two different machine learning techniques, RIPPER [COHE96] and Naïve Bayes (NB) [MICH94], to compare their relative performances. In [KOLT04], the authors extract binary n-gram features from executables and apply them to different classification methods, such as k-nearest neighbor (KNN) [AHA91], NB, support vector machines (SVM) [BOSE92], decision trees [QUIN03], and boosting [FREU96]. Boosting is applied in combination with various other learning algorithms to obtain improved models (e.g., boosted decision trees). Our previous work on data-mining-based malware detection [MASU08a] extracts binary n-grams from the executable, assembly instruction sequences from the disassembled executables, and DLL call information from the program headers. The classification models used in this work are SVM, decision tree, NB, boosted decision tree, and boosted NB.

Hamsa and Polygraph [LI06], [NEWS05] apply a simple form of data mining to generate worm signatures automatically using binary n-grams as features. Both identify a collection of n-grams as a worm signature if they appear only in malicious binaries (i.e., positive samples) and never in benign binaries. This differs from the traditional data mining approaches already discussed (including ours) in two significant respects: First, Polygraph and Hamsa limit their attention to n-grams that appear only in the malicious pool, whereas traditional data mining techniques also consider n-grams that appear in the benign pool to improve the classification accuracy. Second, Polygraph and Hamsa define signature matches as simply the presence of a set of n-grams, whereas traditional data mining approaches build classification models that match samples based on both the presence and absence of features. Traditional data mining approaches therefore generalize the approaches of Polygraph and Hamsa, with corresponding increases in power.

Almost all past work has approached the malware detection problem as a static data classification problem in which the classification model is trained with fixed training data. However, the rapid emergence of new types of malware and new obfuscation strategies adopted by malware authors introduces a dynamic component to the problem that violates the static paradigm. We therefore argue that effective malware detection must be increasingly treated as a data stream classification problem in order to keep pace with attacks.

Many existing data stream classification techniques target infinite-length data streams that exhibit concept drift [AGRA06], [WANG03], [YANG05] [KOLT05], [HULT01], [FAN04], [GAO07], [HASH09], and [ZANG09]. All of these techniques adopt a one-pass incremental update approach, but with differing approaches to the incremental updating mechanism. Most can be grouped into two main classes: single-model incremental approaches and hybrid batch-incremental approaches.

Single-model incremental updating involves dynamically updating a single model with each new training instance. For example, decision tree models can be incrementally updated with incoming data [HULT01]. In contrast, hybrid batch-incremental approaches build each model from a batch of training data using a traditional batch learning technique. Older models are then periodically replaced by newer models as the concept drifts [WANG03], [BIFF09]. [YANG05], [FAN04], [GAO07]. Some of these hybrid approaches use a single model to classify the unlabeled data (e.g., [YANG05] and [CHEN08]) while others use an ensemble of models (e.g., [WANG03] and [SCHO05]). Hybrid approaches have the advantage that model updates are typically far simpler than in single-model approaches; for example, classifiers in the ensemble can simply be removed or replaced. However, other techniques that combine the two approaches by incrementally updating the classifiers within the ensemble can be more complex [KOLT05].

Accuracy Weighted Classifier Ensembles (AWE) [WANG03], [SCHO05] are an important category of hybrid-incremental updating ensemble classifiers that use weighted majority voting for classification. These divide the stream into equal-sized chunks, and each chunk is used to train a classification model. An ensemble of K such models classifies the unlabeled data. Each time a new data chunk is labeled, a new classifier is trained from that chunk. This classifier replaces one of the existing classifiers in the ensemble. The replacement victim is chosen by evaluating the accuracy of each classifier on the latest training chunk. These ensemble approaches have the advantage that they can be built more efficiently than a continually updated single model, and they observe higher accuracy than their single-model counterparts [TUME96].

Our ensemble approach is most closely related to AWE, but with a number of significant differences. First, we apply multipartitioning of the training data to build v classifiers from that training data. Second, the training data consists of r consecutive data chunks (i.e., a multichunk approach) rather than from a single chunk. We have proved both analytically and empirically that both of these enhancements, that is, multipartitioning and multichunk, significantly reduces ensemble classification error [MASU11]. Third, when we update the ensemble, v classifiers in the ensemble are replaced by v newly trained classifiers. The v classifiers that are replaced may come from different chunks; thus, although some classifiers from a chunk may have been removed, other classifiers from that chunk may still remain in the ensemble. This differs from AWE, in which removal of a classifier means total removal of the knowledge obtained from one whole chunk. Our replacement strategy also contributes to error reduction. Finally, we use simple majority voting rather than weighted voting, which is more suitable for data streams, as shown in [GAO07]. Thus, our multipartition, multichunk ensemble approach is a more generalized and efficient form of that implemented by AWE.

Our work extends our previously published work [MASU09]. Most existing data stream classification techniques, including our previous work, assume that the feature space of the data points in the stream is fixed. However, in some cases, such as text data, this assumption is not valid. For example, when features are words, the feature space cannot be fully determined at the start of the stream since new words appear frequently. In addition, it is likely that much of this large lexicon of words has low discriminatory power, and is therefore best omitted from the feature space. It is therefore more effective and efficient to select a subset of the candidate features for each data point. This feature selection must occur incrementally as newer, more discriminating candidate features arise and older features become outdated. Therefore, feature extraction and selection should be an integral part of data stream classification. In this chapter, we describe the design and implementation of an efficient and scalable feature extraction and selection technique using a cloud computing framework [ZHAO09], [DEAN08]. This approach supersedes our previous work in that it considers the real challenges in data stream classification that occur when the feature space cannot be predetermined. This facilitates application of our technique to the detection of real malicious executables from a large, evolving dataset, showing that it can detect newer varieties of malware as malware instances evolve over time.

25.4 Design and Implementation of the System

25.4.1 Ensemble Construction and Updating

Our *Extended, MultiPartition, Multi-Chunk (EMPC)* ensemble learning approach maintains an ensemble $A = \{A1, A2,\ldots, AKv\}$ of the most recent, best Kv classifiers. Each time a new data chunk Dn arrives, it tests the data chunk with the ensemble A. The ensemble is updated once chunk Dn is labeled. The classification process uses simple majority voting.

The ensemble construction updating process is illustrated in Figure 25.2 and summarized in Algorithm 1. Lines 1–3 of the algorithm compute the error of each classifier $A_i \in A$ on chunk D_n, where D_n is the most recent data chunk that has been labeled. Let D be the data of the most recently labeled r data chunks, including Dn. Line 5 randomly partitions D into v equal parts $\{d1,\ldots, dv\}$ such that all the parts have roughly the same class distributions. Lines 6–9 train a new batch of v classifiers, where each classifier A^n is trained with dataset $D - d_j$. The error of each classifier

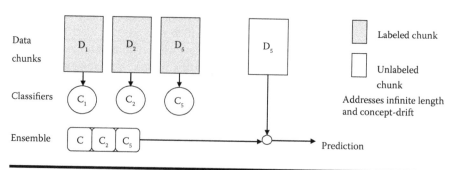

Figure 25.2 Ensemble construction.

$A^n \in A^n$ is computed by testing it on its corresponding test data. Finally, line 10 selects the best Kv classifiers from the $Kv + v$ classifiers in $A^n \cup A$ based on the errors of each classifier computed in lines 2 and 8. Note that any subset of the nth batch of v classifiers may be selected for inclusion in the new ensemble.

25.4.2 *Error Reduction Analysis*

As explained in Algorithm 1, we build ensemble A of Kv classifiers. A test instance x is classified using a majority vote of the classifiers in the ensemble. We use simple majority voting rather than weighted majority voting (refer to [WANG03]), since simple majority voting has been theoretically proven the optimal choice for data streams [GAO07]. Weighted voting can be problematic in these contexts because it assumes that the distribution of training and test data are the same. However, in data streams, this assumption is violated because of concept-drift. Simple majority voting is therefore a better alternative. Our experiments confirm this in practice, obtaining better results with simple rather than weighted majority voting.

We have shown in [MASU11] that EMPC can further reduce the expected error in classifying concept-drifting data streams compared to *Single-Partition, Single-Chunk (SPC)* approaches, which use only one data chunk for training a single classifier (i.e., $r = v = 1$). Intuitively, there are two main reasons for the error reduction. First, the training data per classifier is increased by introducing the multichunk concept. Larger training data naturally leads to better trained model, reducing the error. Second, rather than training only one model from the training data, we partition the data into v partitions, and train one model from each partition. This further reduces error because the mean expected error of an ensemble of v classifiers is theoretically v times lower than that of a single classifier [TUME96]. Therefore, both the multichunk and multipartition strategy contribute to error reduction.

Algorithm 1: Updating the classifier ensemble
Input: $\{D_{n-r+1}, \ldots, D_n\}$ the r most recently labeled data chunks
A: the current ensemble of best Kv classifiers
Output: an updated ensemble A

1: **for** each classifier $A_i \in A$ **do**
2:     $e(A_i) \leftarrow$ *error of* A_i on D_n // test and compute error
3: **end for**
4: $D \leftarrow \cup_{j=n-r+1}^{n} D_j$
5: Partition D into equal parts $\{d_1, d_2, \ldots, d_v\}$
6: **for** $j = 1$ to v **do**
7:     $A_j^n \leftarrow n$ newly trained classifier from data $D - d_j$
8:     $e(A_j) \leftarrow$ error of A_j on d_j // test and compute error
9: **end for**
10: $A \leftarrow$ best Kv from $A^n \cup A$ *based on computed error* $e(.)$

25.4.3 Empirical Error Reduction and Time Complexity

For a given partition size v, increasing the window size r only yields reduced error up to a certain point. After that, increasing r actually hurts the performance of our algorithm, because inequality (18) is violated. The upper bound of r depends on the magnitude of drift ρd. We have shown in [MASU11] the relative error *ER* for $v = 2$, and different values of ρd, for increasing r. It is clear from the graph that for lower values of ρd, increasing r reduces the relative error by a greater margin. However, in all cases after r exceeds a certain threshold, *ER* becomes greater than 1. Although it may not be possible to know the actual value of ρd from the data, we may determine the optimal value of r experimentally. In our experiments, we found that for smaller chunk sizes, higher values of r work better, and vice versa. However, the best performance-cost trade-off is found for $r = 2$ or $r = 3$. We have used $r = 2$ in our experiments. Similarly, the upper bound of v can be derived from inequality (18) for a fixed value of r. It should be noted that if v is increased, running time also increases. From our experiments, we obtained the best performance-cost trade-off for $v = 5$.

The time complexity of the algorithm is $O(vn(Ks + f(rs)))$, where n is the total number of data chunks, s is the size of each chunk, and $f(z)$ is the time required to build a classifier on a training data of size z. Since v is constant, the complexity becomes $O(n(Ks + f(rs)))$. This is at most a constant factor rv slower than the closest related work [WANG03], but with the advantage of significantly reduced error.

25.4.4 Hadoop/MapReduce Framework

We used the open-source Hadoop [APAC10] MapReduce framework to implement our experiments. Here, we provide some of the algorithmic details of the Hadoop MapReduce feature extraction and selection algorithm. The *Map* function in a MapReduce framework takes a key-value pair as input and yields a list of intermediate key-value pairs for each.

$$\textit{Map: (MKey} \times \textit{MVal)} \rightarrow \textit{(RKey} \times \textit{RVal)}*$$

All the *Map* tasks are processed in parallel by each node in the cluster without sharing data with other nodes. Hadoop collates the output of the *Map* tasks by grouping each set of intermediate values $V \subseteq RVal$ that share a common intermediate key $k \in RKey$. The resulting collated pairs (k, V) are then streamed to *Reduce* nodes. Each reducer in a Hadoop MapReduce framework therefore receives a list of multiple (k, V) pairs, issued by Hadoop one at a time in an iterative fashion. *Reduce* can therefore be understood as a function having signature

$$\textit{Reduce: (RKey} \times \textit{RVal}*)* \rightarrow \textit{Val.}$$

Codomain *Val* is the type of the final results of the MapReduce cycle.

In our framework, *Map* keys (*MKey*) are binary file identifiers (e.g., filenames), and *Map* values (*MVal*) are the file contents in bytes. *Reduce* keys (*RKey*) are *n*-gram features, and their corresponding values (*RVal*) are the class labels of the file instances where they were found. Algorithm 2 shows the feature extraction procedure that *Map* nodes use to map the former to the latter.

Lines 5–10 of Algorithm 3 tally the class labels reported by *Map* to obtain positive and negative instance counts for each *n*-gram. These form a basis for computing the information gain of each *n*-gram in line 11. Lines 12–16 use a min-heap data structure *h* to filter all but the best *S* features as evaluated by information gain. The final best *S* features encountered are returned by lines 18–20.

The *q* reducers in the Hadoop system therefore yield a total of *qS* candidate features and their information gains. These are streamed to a second reducer that simply implements the last half of Algorithm 3 to select the best *S* features.

Algorithm 2: *Map(file_id, bytes)*
Input: file file id with content bytes
Output: list of pairs (*g*, *l*), where *g* is an n-gram and *l* is file id's label

1: $T \leftarrow \varnothing$
2: **for all** *n*-grams *g* in bytes **do**
3: $T \leftarrow T \cup \{g, labelof\,(file\;id)\}$ $\{(g, labelof(fil\_id))\}$
4: **end for**
5: **for all** $(g, l) \in T$ **do**
6: **print** (*g*, *l*)
7: **end for**

Algorithm 3: $Reduce_{p,t}(F)$
Input: list *F* of (*g*, *L*) pairs, where g is an n-gram and L is a list of class labels; total size t of original instance set; total number p of positive instances
Output: S pairs (g, i), where i is the information gain of n-gram g

1: **heap** *h*/* empty min-heap */
2: **for all** (g, L) in **F do**
3: $t' \leftarrow 0$
4: $p' \leftarrow 0$
5: **for all** *l* **in** *L* **do**
6: $t' \leftarrow t' + 1$
7: **if** $l = +$ **then**
8: $p \leftarrow p + 1$
9: **end if**
10: **end for**
11: $i \leftarrow \hat{G}(p', t', p, t)$/* see Equation 21 */

12: **if** $h.\ size < S$ **then**
13: $h.\ insert(i_{(g)})$
14: **else if** ($h.\ root < i$) **then**
15: $h.\ replace(h.\ root, i_{(g)})$
16: **end if**
17: **end for**
18: **for all** $i_{(g)}$ in h do
19: print $(g,\ i)$
20: **end for**

25.5 Malicious Code Detection

25.5.1 Overview

Malware is a major source of cyber-attacks. Some malware varieties are purely static; each instance is an exact copy of the instance that propagated it. These are relatively easier to be detected and filtered once a single instance has been identified. However, a much more significant body of current-day malware is polymorphic. Polymorphic malware self-modifies during propagation so that each instance has a unique syntax but carries a semantically identical malicious payload. The antivirus community invests significant effort and manpower toward devising, automating, and deploying algorithms that detect particular malware instances and polymorphic malware families that have been identified and analyzed by human experts. This has led to an escalating arms race between malware authors and antiviral defenders, in which each camp seeks to develop offenses and defenses that counter the recent advances of the other. With the increasing ease of malware development and the exponential growth of malware variants, many believe that this race will ultimately prove to be a losing battle for the defenders.

The malicious code detection problem can be modeled as a data mining problem for a stream having both infinite length and concept-drift. Concept-drift occurs as polymorphic malware mutates, and as attackers and defenders introduce new technologies to the arms race. This conceptualization invites application of our stream classification technique to automate the detection of new malicious executables.

Feature extraction using n-gram analysis involves extracting all possible n-grams from the given dataset (training set), and selecting the best n-grams among them. Each such n-gram is a feature. That is, an n-gram is a sequence of n bytes. Before extracting n-grams, we preprocess the binary executables by converting them into hexdump files. Here, the granularity level is 1 byte. We apply the UNIX hexdump utility to convert the binary executable files into text files (*hexdump files*) containing the hexadecimal numbers corresponding to each byte of the binary. This process is performed to ensure safe and easy portability of the binary executables. In a nondistributed framework, the feature extraction process consists of two phases: feature extraction and feature selection, described shortly. Our cloud computing variant of this traditional technique is presented in this chapter.

25.5.2 Nondistributed Feature Extraction and Selection

In a nondistributed setting, feature extraction proceeds as follows. Each hexdump file is scanned by sliding an n-byte window over its content. Each n-byte sequence that appears in the window is an n-gram. For each n-gram g, we tally the total number tg of file instances in which g appears, as well as the total number $pg \leq tg$ of these that are positive (i.e., malicious executables).

This involves maintaining a hash table T of all n-grams encountered so far. If g is not found in T, then g is added to T with counts $tg = 1$ and $pg \in \{0, 1\}$ depending on whether the current file has a negative or positive class label. If g is already in T, then tg is incremented and pg is conditionally incremented depending on the file's label. When all hexdump files have been scanned, T contains all the unique n-grams in the dataset along with their frequencies in the positive instances and in total.

It is not always practical to use all n-gram features extracted from all the files corresponding to the current chunk. The exponential number of such n-grams may introduce unacceptable memory overhead, slow the training process, or confuse the classifier with large numbers of noisy, redundant, or irrelevant features. To avoid these pitfalls, candidate n-gram features must be sorted according to a selection criterion so that only the best ones are selected.

We choose *information gain* as the selection criterion, because it is one of the most effective criteria used in literature for selecting the best features. Information gain can be defined as a measure of the effectiveness of an attribute (i.e., feature) for classifying the training data. If we split the training data based on the values of this attribute, then information gain measures the expected reduction in entropy after the split. The more an attribute reduces entropy in the training data, the better that attribute is for classifying the data.

We have shown in [MASU11] that as new features are considered, their information gains are compared against the heap's root. If the gain of the new feature is greater than that of the root, the root is discarded and the new feature inserted into the heap. Otherwise, the new feature is discarded and feature selection continues.

25.5.3 Distributed Feature Extraction and Selection

There are several drawbacks related to the nondistributed feature extraction and selection approach just described.

- The total number of extracted n-gram features might be very large. For example, the total number of 4-grams in one chunk is around 200 million. It might not be possible to store all of them in the main memory. One obvious solution is to store the *n*-grams in a disk file, but this introduces unacceptable overhead due to the cost of disk read/write operations.

■ If colliding features in hash table *T* are not sorted, then a linear search is required for each scanned *n*-gram during feature extraction to test whether it is already in *T*. If they are sorted, then the linear search is required during insertion. In either case, the time to extract all *n*-grams is worst-case quadratic in the total number *N* of *n*-grams in each chunk, an impractical amount of time when $N \approx 108$. Similarly, the nondistributed feature selection process requires a sort of the *n*-grams in each chunk. In general, this requires $O(N \log N)$ time, which is impractical when *N* is large.

To efficiently and effectively tackle the drawbacks of the nondistributed feature extraction and selection approach, we leverage the power of cloud computing. This allows feature extraction, *n*-gram sorting, and feature selection to be performed in parallel, utilizing the Hadoop *MapReduce* framework.

MapReduce [DEAN08] is an increasingly popular distributed programming paradigm used in cloud computing environments. The model processes large datasets in parallel, distributing the workload across many nodes (machines) in a share-nothing fashion. The main focus is to simplify the processing of large datasets using inexpensive cluster computers. Another objective is ease of usability with both load balancing and fault tolerance.

MapReduce is named for its two primary functions. The *Map* function breaks jobs down into subtasks to be distributed to available nodes, whereas its dual, *Reduce*, aggregates the results of completed subtasks. We will henceforth refer to nodes performing these functions as *mappers* and *reducers*, respectively. The details of the MapReduce process for *n*-gram feature extraction and selection are explained in the Appendix. In this section, we give a high-level overview of the approach.

Each training chunk containing *N* training files are used to extract the *n*-grams. These training files are first distributed among *m* nodes (machines) by HDFS (Figure 25.3, step 1). Quantity *m* is selected by HDFS depending on system availability. Each node then independently extracts *n*-grams from the subset of training files supplied to the node using the technique [MASU11] (Figure 25.3, step 2). When all nodes finish their jobs, the *n*-grams extracted from each node are collated (Figure 25.3, step 3).

For example, suppose Node 1 observes *n*-gram *abc* in one positive instance (i.e., a malicious training file) while Node 2 observes it in a negative (i.e., benign) instance. This is denoted by pairs *abc*, + and *abc*, − under Nodes 1 and 2 (respectively) in Figure 25.3. When the *n*-grams are combined, the labels of instances containing identical *n*-grams are aggregated. Therefore, the aggregated pair for *abc* is *abc*, + −. The combined *n*-grams are distributed to *q* reducers (with *q* chosen by HDFS based on system availability). Each reducer first tallies the aggregated labels to obtain a positive count and a total count. In the case of *n*-gram *abc*, we obtain tallies of $pabc = 1$ and $tabc = 2$. The reducer uses these tallies to choose the best *S* *n*-grams (based on Equation 21) from the subset of *n*-grams supplied to the node

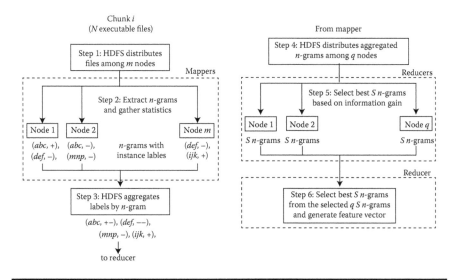

Figure 25.3 Distributed feature extraction and selection.

(Figure 25.3, step 5). This can be done efficiently using a min-heap of size S; the process requires $O(W \log S)$ time, where W is the total number of n-grams supplied to each reducer. In contrast, the nondistributed version requires $O(W \log W)$ time. Thus, from the q reducer nodes, we obtain qS n-grams. From these, we again select the best S by running another round of the MapReduce cycle in which the Map phase does nothing but the Reduce phase performs feature selection using only one node (Figure 25.3, step 6). Each feature in a feature set is binary; its value is 1 if it is present in a given instance (i.e., executable) and 0 otherwise. For each training or testing instance, we compute the feature vector whose bits consist of the feature values of the corresponding feature set. These feature vectors are used by the classifiers for training and testing.

25.6 Experiments

We evaluated our approach on synthetic data, botnet traffic generated in a controlled environment, and a malware dataset. The results of the experiments are compared with several baseline methods.

25.6.1 Data Sets

25.6.1.1 Synthetic Dataset

To generate synthetic data with a drifting concept, we use a moving hyperplane, given by $\sum_{i=1}^{d} a_i x_i = a_0$ [WANG03]. If $\sum_{i=1}^{d} a_i x_i \leq a_0$, then an example is negative;

otherwise it is positive. Each example is a randomly generated d dimensional vector $\{x_1,\ldots,x_d\}$ where $x_i \in [0,1]$ eights $\{a_1,\ldots,a_d\}$ are also randomly initialized with a real number in the range $[0,1]$ the value of a_0 is adjusted so that roughly the same number of positive and negative examples are generated. This can be done by choosing $a_0 = (1/2)\sum_{i=1}^{d} a_i$. We also introduce noise randomly by switching the labels of percent of the examples, where $p = 5n$ in our experiments. There are several parameters that simulate concept-drift. We use parameters identical to those in [WANG03]. In total, we generate 250,000 records and four different datasets having chunk sizes 250, 500, 750, and 1000, respectively. Each dataset has 50% positive instances and 50% negative.

25.6.1.2 Botnet Dataset

Botnets are networks of compromised hosts known as *bots*, all under the control of a human attacker known as the *botmaster* [BARF06]. The botmaster can issue commands to the bots to perform malicious actions, such as launching DDoS attacks, spamming, spying, and so on. Botnets are widely regarded as an enormous emerging threat to the Internet community. Many cutting-edge botnets apply peer-to-peer (P2P) technology to reliably and covertly communicate as the botnet topology evolves. These botnets are distributed and small, making them more difficult to detect and destroy. Examples of P2P bots include Nugache [LEMO06], Sinit [STEW03], and Trojan.Peacomm [GRIZ07].

Botnet traffic can be viewed as a data stream having both infinite length and concept-drift. Concept-drift occurs as the bot undertakes new malicious missions or adopts differing communication strategies in response to new botmaster instructions. We therefore consider our stream classification technique to be well suited to detecting P2P botnet traffic.

We generate real P2P botnet traffic in a controlled environment using the Nugache P2P bot [LEMO06]. The details of the feature extraction process are discussed in Masud et al. [MASU08b]. There are 81 continuous attributes in total. The whole dataset consists of 30,000 records, representing one week's worth of network traffic. We generate four different datasets having chunk sizes of 30, 60, 90, and 120 min, respectively. Each dataset has 25% positive (botnet traffic) instances and 75% negative (benign traffic).

25.6.1.3 Malware Dataset

We extract a total of 38,694 benign executables from different Windows machines, and a total of 66,694 malicious executables collected from an online malware repository VX Heavens [VX10], which contains a large collection of malicious executables (viruses, worms, trojans, and back-doors). The benign executables include various applications found at the Windows installation folder, as well as other executables in the default program installation directory.

We select only the Win32 Portable Executables (PE) in both cases. Experiments with the ELF executables are a potential direction of future work. The collected 105,388 files (benign and malicious) form a data stream of 130 chunks, each consisting of 2000 instances (executable files). The stream order was chosen by sorting the malware by version and discovery date, simulating the evolving nature of Internet malware. Each chunk has 1500 benign executables (75% negative) and 500 malicious executables (25% positive). The feature extraction and selection process for this dataset is described in earlier sections.

Note that all these datasets are dynamic in nature. Their unbounded (potentially infinite-length) size puts them beyond the scope of purely static classification frameworks. The synthetic data also exhibits concept-drift. Although it is not possible to accurately determine whether the real datasets have concept-drift, theoretically the stream of executables should exhibit concept-drift when observed over a long period of time. The malware data exhibits feature evolution as evidenced by the differing set of distinguishing features identified for each chunk.

25.6.2 Baseline Methods

For classification, we use the Weka machine learning open-source package [HALL09]. We apply two different classifiers: J48 decision tree and Ripper. We then compare each of the following baseline techniques to our EMPC algorithm.

BestK. This is an SPC ensemble approach, where an ensemble of the best K classifiers is used. The ensemble is created by storing all the classifiers seen so far, and selecting the best K based on expected error on the most recent training chunk. An instance is tested using simple majority voting.

Last. In this case, we only keep the classifier trained on the most recent training chunk. This can be considered an SPC approach with $K = 1$.

AWE. This is the SPC method implemented using Accuracy-Weighted classifier Ensembles [WANG03]. It builds an ensemble of K models, where each model is trained from one data chunk. The ensemble is updated as follows. Let Cn be the classifier built on the most recent training chunk. From the existing K models and the newest model Cn, the K best models are selected based on their error on the most recent training chunk. Selection is based on weighted voting where the weight of each model is inversely proportional to the error of the model on the most recent training chunk.

All. This SPC uses an ensemble of all the classifiers seen so far. The new data chunk is tested with this ensemble by simple voting among the classifiers. Since this is an SPC approach, each classifier is trained from only one data chunk.

We obtain the optimal values of r and v to be between 2 and 3, and between 3 and 5, respectively, for most datasets. Unless and otherwise, we use $r = 2$ and $v = 5$ in our experiments. To obtain a fair comparison, we use the same value for K (ensemble size) in EMPC and all baseline techniques.

25.6.2.1 Hadoop Distributed System Setup

The distributed system on which we performed our experiments consists of a cluster of 10 nodes. Each node has the same hardware configuration: an Intel Pentium IV 2.8 GHz processor, 4 GB main memory, and 640 GB hard disk space. The software environment consists of a Ubuntu 9.10 operating system, the Hadoop-0.20.1 distributed computing platform, the JDK 1.6 Java development platform, and a 100 MB LAN network link.

25.7 Discussion

Our work considers a feature space consisting of purely syntactic features: binary n-grams drawn from executable code segments, static data segments, headers, and all other contents of untrusted files. Higher-level structural features such as call- and control-flow graphs, and dynamic features such as runtime traces, are beyond our current scope. Nevertheless, n-gram features have been observed to have very high discriminatory power for malware detection, as demonstrated by a large body of prior work as well as our experiments. This is in part because n-gram sets that span the entire binary file content, including headers and data tables, capture important low-level structural details that are often abstracted away by higher-level representations. For example, malware often contains hand-written assembly code that has been assembled and linked using nonstandard tools. This allows attackers to implement binary obfuscations and low-level exploits not available from higher-level source languages and standard compilers. As a result, malware often contains unusual instruction encodings, header structures, and link tables whose abnormalities can only be seen at the raw binary level, not in assembly code listings, control-flow graphs, or system API call traces. Expanding the feature space to include these additional higher-level features requires an efficient and reliable method of harvesting them and assessing their relative discriminatory power during feature selection, and is reserved as a subject of future work.

The empirical results reported in [MASU11] confirm our analysis that shows that multipartition, multichunk approaches should perform better than single-chunk, single-partition approaches. Intuitively, a classifier trained on multiple chunks should have better prediction accuracy than a classifier trained on a single chunk because of the larger training data. Furthermore, if more than one classifier is trained by multipartitioning the training data, the prediction accuracy of the resulting ensemble of classifiers should be higher than a single classifier trained from the same training data because of the error reduction power of an ensemble over single classifier. In addition, the accuracy advantages of EMPC can be traced to two important differences between our work and that of AWE. First, when a classifier is removed during ensemble updating in AWE, all information obtained from the corresponding chunk is forgotten; but in EMPC, one or more classifiers from an earlier chunk may survive. Thus, EMPC ensemble updating tends to retain more information than that of AWE, leading to a better ensemble. Second, AWE requires at least Kv data chunks, whereas EMPC requires at least $K + r - 1$ data chunks to obtain Kv classifiers. Thus, AWE tends to keep much older classifiers in the ensemble than EMPC, leading to some outdated classifiers that can have a negative effect on the classification accuracy.

However, the higher accuracy comes with an increased cost in running time. Theoretically, EMPC is at most rv times slower than AWE, its closest competitor in accuracy. This is also evident in the empirical evaluation, which shows that the running time of EMPC is within 5 times that of AWE (for $r = 2$ and $v = 5$). However, some optimizations can be adopted to reduce the runtime cost. First, parallelization of training for each partition can be easily implemented, reducing the training time by a factor of v. Second, classification by each model in the ensemble can also be done in parallel, thereby reducing the classification time by a factor of Kv. Therefore, parallelization of training and classification should reduce the running time at least by a factor of v, making the runtime close to that of AWE. Alternatively, if parallelization is not available, parameters v and r can be lowered to sacrifice prediction accuracy for lower runtime cost. In this case, the desired balance between runtime and prediction accuracy can be obtained by evaluating the first few chunks of the stream with different values of v and r and choosing the most suitable values.

25.8 Summary and Directions

Many intrusion detection problems can be formulated as classification problems for infinite-length, concept-drifting data streams. Concept-drift occurs in these streams as attackers react and adapt to defenses. We formulated both malicious code detection and botnet traffic detection as such problems, and introduced EMPC, a novel ensemble learning technique for automated classification of infinite-length, concept-drifting streams. Applying EMPC to real data streams obtained from polymorphic malware and botnet traffic samples yielded better detection accuracies than other stream data classification techniques. This shows that the approach is useful and effective for both intrusion detection and more general data stream classification.

EMPC uses generalized, multipartition, multichunk ensemble learning. Both theoretical and empirical evaluation of the technique show that it significantly reduces the expected classification error over existing single-partition, single-chunk ensemble methods. Moreover, we show that EMPC can be elegantly implemented in a cloud computing framework based on MapReduce [DEAN08]. The result is a low-cost, scalable stream classification framework with high classification accuracy and low runtime overhead.

At least two extensions to our technique offer promising directions of future work. First, our current feature selection procedure limits its attention to the best

S features based on information gain as the selection criterion. The classification accuracy could potentially be improved by leveraging recent work on supervised dimensionality reduction techniques [RISH08], [SAJA05] for improved feature selection. Second, the runtime performance of our approach could be improved by exploiting additional parallelism available in the cloud computing architecture. For example, the classifiers of an ensemble could be run in parallel as mappers in a MapReduce framework, with reducers that aggregate the results for voting. Similarly, the candidate classifiers for the next ensemble could be trained and evaluated in parallel. Reformulating the ensemble components of the system in this way could lead to significantly shortened processing times, and hence opportunities to devote more processing time to classification for improved accuracy.

References

[AGGR06] Aggarwal, C.C., J. Han, J. Wang, and P. S. Yu, A framework for on-demand classification of evolving data streams. *IEEE Trans. Knowl. Data Eng.* 18(5): 577–589, 2006.

[AHA91] Aha, D.W., D. Kibler, and M.K. Albert, Instance-based learning algorithms. *Mach. Learn.* 6: 37–66, 1991.

[APAC10] Hadoop. hadoop.apache.org., 2010.

[BARF06] Barford, P. and V. Yegneswaran, An inside look at botnets. In *Malware Detection, Advances in Information Security* (Editors: M. Christodorescu, S. Jha, D. Maughan, D. Song, and C. Wang,), Springer, 171–192. 2006.

[BIFF09] Bifet, A., G. Holmes, B. Pfahringer, R. Kirkby, and R. Gavaldà, New ensemble methods for evolving data streams. In *Proceedings of the 15th ACM International Conference on Knowledge Discovery and Data Mining (KDD)*, Paris, France, 139–148, 2009.

[BOSE92] Boser, B.E., I.M. Guyon, and V.N. Vapnik, A training algorithm for optimal margin classifiers. In *Proceedings of the 5th ACM Workshop on Computational Learning Theory.* 144–152, Pittsburgh, PA, 1992.

[CHEN08] Chen, S., H. Wang, S. Zhou, and P.S. Yu, Stop chasing trends: Discovering high order models in evolving data. In *Proceedings of the 24th IEEE International Conference on Data Engineering (ICDE).* 923–932, 2008.

[COHE96] Cohen, W.W., Learning rules that classify e-mail. In *Proceedings of the AAAI Spring Symposium on Machine Learning in Information Access*, Palo Alto, CA, 18–25, 1996.

[COMP07] Computer Economics, Inc. Malware report: The economic impact of viruses, spyware, adware, botnets, and other malicious code. http://www.computereconomics.com/article.cfm?id=1225, 2007.

[CRAN05] Crandall, J. R., Z. Su, S. F. Wu, and F.T. Chong, On deriving unknown vulnerabilities from zero-day polymorphic and metamorphic worm exploits. In *Proceedings of the 12th ACM Conference on Computer and Communications Security (CCS'05).* 235–248, 2005.

[DEAN08] Dean, J. and S. Ghemawat, MapReduce: Simplified data processing on large clusters. *Commun. ACM* 51(1): 107–113, 2008.

[DOMI00] Domingos, P. and G. Hulten, Mining high-speed data streams. In *Proceedings of the 6th ACM International Conference on Knowledge Discovery and Data Mining (KDD)*, Boston, MA, 71–80, 2000.

[FAN04] Fan, W. Systematic data selection to mine concept-drifting data streams. In *Proceedings of the 10th ACM International Conference on Knowledge Discovery and Data Mining (KDD)*. 128–137, Seattle, WA, 2004.

[FREU96] Freund, Y. and R.E. Schapire, Experiments with a new boosting algorithm. In *Proceedings of the 13th International Conference on Machine Learning*. 148–156, Bari, Italy, 1996.

[GAO07] Gao, J., W. Fan, and J. Han, On appropriate assumptions to mine data streams: Analysis and practice. In *Proceedings of the 7th IEEE International Conference on Data Mining (ICDM)*. 143–152, Omaha, NE, 2007.

[GRIZ07] Grizzard, J. B., V. Sharma, C. Nunnery, B.B. Kang, and D. Dagon, Peer-to-peer botnets: Overview and case study. In *Proceedings of the 1st Workshop on Hot Topics in Understanding Botnets (HotBots)*. 1–8, Cambridge, MA, 2007.

[HALL09] Hall, M., E. Frank, G. Holmes, B. Pfahringer, P. Reutemann, and I. H. Witten, The WEKA data mining software: An update. *ACM SIGKDD Explor.* 11 (1): 10–18, 2009.

[HAML09] Hamlen, K.W., V. Mohan, M.M. Masud, L. Khan, and B.M. Thuraisingham., Exploiting an antivirus interface. *Comput. Stand. Interfaces* 31(6): 1182–1189, 2009.

[HASH09] Hashemi, S., Yang, Y., Mirzamomen, Z., and Kangavari, M. R. Adapted one-versus-all decision trees for data stream classification. *IEEE Trans. Knowl. Data Engin.* 21(5):624–637, 2009.

[HULT01] Hulten, G., L. Spencer, and P. Domingos. Mining time-changing data streams. In *Proceedings of the 7th ACM International Conference on Knowledge Discovery and Data Mining (KDD)*. 97–106, San Francisco, CA, 2001.

[KOLT04] Kolter, J. and M.A. Maloof, Learning to detect malicious executables in the wild. In *Proceedings of the 10th ACM International Conference on Knowledge Discovery and Data Mining (KDD)*. Seattle, WA, 470–478, 2004.

[KOLT05] Kolter, J. Z. and M.A. Maloof, Using additive expert ensembles to cope with concept drift. In *Proceedings of the 22nd International Conference on Machine Learning (ICML)*. Bonn, Germany, 449–456, 2005.

[LEMO06] Lemos, R., Bot software looks to improve peerage. *Security Focus*. http://www.securityfocus.com/news/11390.

[LI06] Li, Z., Sanghi, M., Y. Chen, M.-Y. Kao, and B. Chavez, Hamsa: Fast signature generation for zero-day polymorphic worms with provable attack resilience. In *Proceedings of the IEEE Symposium on Security and Privacy (S&P)*. Berkeley, CA, 32–47, 2006.

[MASU08a] Masud, M. M., J. Gao, L. Khan, J. Han, and B. Thuraisingham, Mining concept-drifting data stream to detect peer to peer botnet traffic. Tech. rep. UTDCS-05-08, The University of Texas at Dallas, Richardson, Texas. http://www.utdallas.edu/~bxt043000/Publications/Technical-Reports/UTDCS-05-08.pdf, 2008a.

[MASU08b] Masud, M.M., L. Khan, and B. Thuraisingham., A scalable multi-level feature extraction technique to detect malicious executables. *Inf. Syst. Frontiers,* 10(1):33–45, 2008b.

[MASU09] Masud, M. M., J. Gao, L. Khan, J. Han, and B. M. Thuraisingham, 2009. A multi-partition multi-chunk ensemble technique to classify concept-drifting data streams. In *Proceedings of the 13th Pacific-Asia Conference on Advances in Knowledge Discovery and Data Mining*. Bangkok, Thailand.

[MASU11] Masud, M. M.,T. Al-Khateeb, K. W. Hamlen, J. Gao, L. Khan, J. Han, B.M. Thuraisingham, Cloud-based malware detection for evolving data streams. *ACM Trans. Management Inf. Syst.* 2(3): 16, 2011.

[MICH94] Michie, D., D. J. Spiegelhalter, and C. C. Taylor, Eds. *Machine Learning, Neural and Statistical Classification*. Ellis Horwood Series in Artificial Intelligence. Morgan Kaufmann, 50–83, 1994.

[NEWS05] Newsome, J., B. Karp, and D. Song, Polygraph: Automatically generating signatures for polymorphic worms. In *Proceedings of the IEEE Symposium on Security and Privacy (S&P)*. 226–241, 2005.

[QUIN03] Quinlan, J. R., *C4.5: Programs for Machine Learning* 5th Ed. Morgan Kaufmann, San Francisco, CA.

[RISH08] Rish, I., Grabarnik, G., Cecchi, G. A., Pereira, Gordon, G., Closed-form supervised dimensionality reduction with generalized linear models. In *Proceeding of Intl. Conf. on Maching Learning* (*ICML 2008*), Helsinki, Finland, 832–839, 2008.

[SAJA05] Sajama and A. Orlitsky, Supervised dimensionality reduction using mixture models. In *Proceedings of the 22nd ACM International Conference on Machine Learning (ICML)*. 768–775, Bonn, Germany, 2005.

[SCHO05] Scholz, M. and R. Klinkenberg, An ensemble classifier for drifting concepts. In *Proceedings of the 2nd International Workshop on Knowledge Discovery in Data Streams (IWKDDS)*. 53–64, 2005.

[SCHU01] Schultz, M. G., E. Eskin, E. Zadok, and S. J. Stolfo, Data mining methods for detection of new malicious executables. In *Proceedings of the IEEE Symposium on Security and Privacy (S&P)*. 38–49, 2001.

[STEW03] Stewart, J. Sinit P2P trojan analysis. http://www.securiteam.com/securityreviews/6J0022A95E.html, 2003.

[TUME96] Tumer, K. and J. Ghosh, Error correlation and error reduction in ensemble classifiers. *Connect. Sci.* 8(3):385–404, 1996.

[VX10] VX Heavens 2010. VX Heavens. vx.netlux.org.

[WANG03] Wang, H., W. Fan, P. S. Yu, and J. Han, Mining concept-drifting data streams using ensemble classifiers. In *Proceedings of the 9th ACM International Conference on Knowledge Discovery and Data Mining (KDD)*. Washington, DC, 226–235, 2003.

[YANG05] Yang, Y., X. Wu, and X. Zhu, Combining proactive and reactive predictions for data streams. In *Proceedings of the 11th ACM International Conference on Knowledge Discovery and Data Mining (KDD)*. Chicago, IL, 710–715, 2005.

[ZHAN09] Zhang, P., X. Zhu, and L. Guo, Mining data streams with labeled and unlabeled training examples. In *Proceedings of the 9th IEEE International Conference on Data Mining (ICDM)*. Miami, FL, 627–636, 2009.

[ZHAO09] Zhao, W., H. Ma, and Q. He, Parallel *K*-means clustering based on MapReduce. In *Proceedings of the 1st International Conference on Cloud Computing (CloudCom)*. Beijing, China, 674–679, 2009.

Chapter 26

Cloud-Based Data Mining for Insider Threat Detection

26.1 Overview

Effective detection of insider threats requires monitoring mechanisms that are far more fine grained than for external threat detection. These monitors must be efficiently and reliably deployable in the software environments where actions endemic to malicious insider missions are caught in a timely manner. Such environments typically include user-level applications, such as word processors, email clients, and web browsers for which reliable monitoring of internal events by conventional means is difficult.

To monitor the activities of the insiders, tools are needed to capture the communications and relationships between the insiders, store the captured relationships, query the stored relationships, and ultimately analyze the relationships so that patterns can be extracted that would give the analyst better insights into the potential threats. Over time, the number of communications and relationships between the insiders could be in billions. Using the tools developed under our project, billions of relationships between the insiders can be captured, stored, queried, and analyzed to detect malicious insiders.

In this chapter, we will discuss how data mining technologies may be applied for insider threat detection in the cloud. First, we will discuss how semantic web technologies may be used to represent the communication between insiders. Next, we will discuss our approach to insider threat detection. Finally, we will provide an

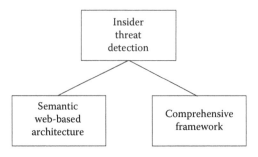

Figure 26.1   Cloud-based data mining for insider threat detection.

overview of our framework for insider threat detection that also incorporates some other techniques.

The organization of this chapter is as follows. In Section 26.2, we will discuss the challenges, related work, and our approach to this problem. Our approach will be discussed in detail in Section 26.3. Our framework will be discussed in Section 26.4. This chapter concludes with Section 26.5. Figure 26.1 illustrates the contents of this chapter.

26.2 Challenges, Related Work, and Our Approach

The insiders and the relationships between the insiders are presented as nodes and links in a graph. Therefore, the challenge is to represent the information in graphs, develop efficient storage strategies, develop query processing techniques for the graphs, and subsequently develop data mining and analysis techniques to extract information from the graphs. In particular, there are three major challenges:

1. Storing these large graphs in an expressive and unified manner in a secondary storage.
2. Devising scalable solutions for querying the large graphs to find the relevant data.
3. Identifying the relevant features for the complex graphs and subsequently detecting insider threats in a dynamic environment that changes over time.

The motivation behind our approach is to address the three challenges we have mentioned above. We are developing solutions based on cloud computing (i) to characterize graphs containing up to billions of nodes and edges between nodes representing activities (e.g., credit card transactions), email, or text messages. Since the graphs will be massive, we will develop technologies for efficient and persistent storage. (ii) To facilitate the novel anomaly detection, we require an efficient interface to fetch the relevant data in a timely manner from this persistent storage.

Therefore, we will develop efficient query techniques on the stored graphs. (iii) The fetched relevant data can then be used for further analysis to detect anomalies. To do this, first, we have to identify the relevant features from the complex graphs and subsequently develop techniques for mining large graphs to extract the nuggets.

As stated in Chapter 1, insider threat detection is a difficult problem [MAYB05]. The problem becomes increasingly complex with more data originating from heterogeneous sources and sensors. Recently, there are some that focus on anomaly-based insider threat detection from graphs [EBER09]. This method is based on Minimum Description Length (MDL) principle. The solution discussed by [EBER09] has some limitations. First, with their approach, scalability is an issue. In other words, they have not discussed any issue related to large graphs. Second, the heterogeneity issue has not been addressed. Finally, it is unclear how their algorithm will deal with a dynamic environment that changes over time.

There are also several graph mining techniques that have been developed especially for social network analysis [COOK06], [TONG09], [CARM09], and [THUR09]. The scalability of these techniques is still an issue. There is some work from the mathematics research community to apply linear programming techniques for graph analysis [BERR07]. Whether these techniques will work in a real-world setting are not clear.

For a solution to be viable, it must be highly scalable and must support multiple heterogeneous data sources. The current state-of-the-art solutions do not scale well and preserve accuracy. By leveraging Hadoop technology, our solution will be highly scalable. Furthermore, by utilizing the flexible semantic web RDF data model, we are able to easily integrate and align heterogeneous data. Thus, our approach will create a scalable solution in a dynamic environment. No existing threat detection tools offer this level of scalability and interoperability. We will combine these technologies with the novel data mining techniques to create a complete insider threat detection solution.

We have exploited the cloud computing framework based on Hadoop/MapReduce technologies. The insiders and their relationships are represented by nodes and links in the form of graphs. In particular, in our approach, billions of nodes and links are represented as RDF graphs. By exploiting RDF representation, we will address heterogeneity. We will develop mechanisms to efficiently store the RDF graphs, query the graphs using SPARQL technologies, and mine the graphs to extract patterns within the cloud computing framework.

26.3 Data Mining for Insider Threat Detection

26.3.1 Our Solution Architecture

Figure 26.2 shows the architectural view of our solution. Our solution will pull the data from multiple sources and then extract and select features. After feature

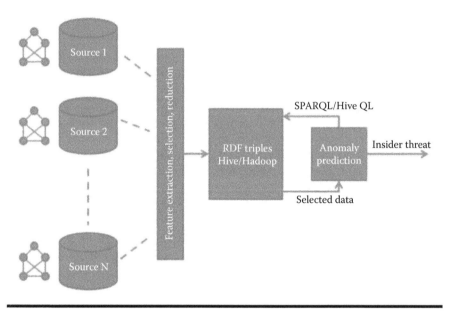

Figure 26.2 Solution architecture.

reduction, the data are stored in our hardtop repository. The data are stored in the RDF format; so, a format conversion may be required if the data are in any other format. RDF is the data format for the semantic web and is very much capable of representing graph data. The anomaly prediction component will submit SPARQL to the repository to select data. It will then output any detected insider threats. SPARQL is the query language for RDF data. It is similar to SQL in syntax. The details of each of the components are given in the following sections. For choosing RDF representation for graphs over relational data models, we will address the heterogeneity issue effectively (semistructured data model). For querying, we will exploit the standard query language, SPARQL, instead of starting from scratch. Furthermore, inferencing is a feature provided by our framework.

We are assuming that the large graphs already exist. To facilitate persistent storage and efficient retrieval of these data, we use a distributed framework based on the Hadoop cloud computing framework [HADO]. By leveraging the Hadoop technology, our framework is readily fault-tolerant and scalable. To support large amounts of data, we can simply add more nodes to the Hadoop cluster. All the nodes of a cluster are commodity-class machines; there is no need to buy expensive server machines. To handle large complex graphs, we exploit the HDFS and the MapReduce framework. The former is the storage layer that stores data in multiple nodes with replication. The latter is the execution layer where MapReduce jobs can be run. We use HDFS to store RDF data and the MapReduce framework to answer queries.

26.3.2 Feature Extraction and Compact Representation

In traditional graph analysis, an edge represents a simple number that represents strength. However, we may face additional challenges in representing link values due to the unstructured nature of the content of the text and email messages. One possible approach is to keep the whole content as a part of link values that we call explicit content (EC). EC will not scale well, even for a moderate size graph. This is because the content representing a link between two nodes will require a lot of main memory space to process the graph in the memory. We use a vector representation of the content (VRC) for each message. In RDF triple representation, this will simply be represented as a unique predicate. We keep track of the feature vector along with the physical location or URL of the original raw message in a dictionary-encoded table.

VRC: During the preprocessing step for each message, we extract keywords and phrases (*n*-grams) as features. Then if we want to generate vectors for these features, the dimensionality of these vectors will be very high. Here, we observe the curse of dimensionality (i.e., sparseness and processing time will increase). Therefore, we can apply feature reduction as well as feature selection (e.g., methods include principal component analysis, support vector machine). Since feature reduction maps high-dimensional feature spaces to a space of fewer dimensions and new feature dimension may be the linear combination of old dimensions that may be difficult to interpret, we exploit feature selection.

With regard to feature selection, we need to use a class label for supervised data. Here, for the message, we may not have a class label; however, we know the source/sender and the destination/recipient of a message. Now, we would like to use this knowledge to construct an artificial label. The sender and destination pair will form a unique class label and all messages sent from this sender to the recipient will serve as data points. Hence, our goal is to find the appropriate features that will have discriminating power across all these class labels based on these messages. There are several methods for feature selection that are widely used in the area of machine learning, such as IG [MITC97], [MASU10a], [MASU10b], Gini index, chi-square statistics, subspace clustering [AHME09], and so on. Here, we present information gain, which is very popular and for the text domain, we can use subspace clustering for feature selection.

IG can be defined as a measure of the effectiveness of a feature in classifying the training data [MITC97]. If we split the training data on these attribute values, then IG provides the measurement of the expected reduction in entropy after the split. The more an attribute can reduce entropy in the training data, the better the attribute in classifying the data. IG of an attribute A on a collection of examples S is given by Equation 26.1

$$\text{Gain}(S, A) \equiv \text{Entropy}(S) - \sum_{V \in Values(A)} \frac{|S_v|}{|S|} \text{Entropy}(S_v) \qquad (26.1)$$

where *values* (*A*) is the set of all possible values for attribute *A* and S_v is the subset of *S* for which attribute *A* has value *v*. The entropy of *S* is computed using the following Equation 26.2:

$$\text{Entropy}(S) = -\sum_{i=1}^{n} p_i(S)\log_2 p_i(S) \tag{26.2}$$

where $p_i(S)$ is the prior probability of class *i* in the set *S*.

26.3.2.1 Subspace Clustering

Subspace clustering can be used for feature selection. Subspace clustering is appropriate when the clusters corresponding to a data set form a subset of the original dimensions. On the basis of how these subsets are formed, a subspace clustering algorithm can be referred to as soft or hard subspace clustering. In the case of soft subspace clustering, the features are assigned weights according to the contribution each feature/dimension plays during the clustering process for each cluster. In the case of hard subspace clustering, however, a specific subset of features is selected for each cluster and the rest of the features are discarded for that cluster. Therefore, subspace clustering can be utilized for selecting which features are important (and discarding some features if their weights are very small for all clusters). One such soft subspace clustering approach is SISC [AHME09]. The following objective function is used in that subspace clustering algorithm. An *E–M* formulation is used for the clustering. In every iteration, the feature weights are updated for each cluster and by selecting the features that have higher weights in each cluster, we can select a set of important features for the corresponding data set.

$$F(W,Z,\Lambda) = \sum_{l=1}^{k}\sum_{j=1}^{n}\sum_{i=1}^{m} w_{lj}^{f}\lambda_{li}^{q}D_{lij} * (1 + \text{Im } pl) + r\sum_{l=1}^{k}\sum_{i=1}^{m}\lambda_{li}^{q}\chi_{li}^{2}$$

where

$$D_{lij} = (z_{li} - x_{ji})^2$$

subject to

$$\sum_{l=1}^{k} w_{lj} = 1, \quad 1 \le j \le n, \quad 1 \le l \le k, \quad 0 \le w_{lj} \le 1$$

$$\sum_{i=1}^{m} \lambda_{li} = 1, \quad 1 \le i \le m, \quad 1 \le l \le k, \quad 0 \le \lambda_{li} \le 1$$

In this objective function, W, Z, and Λ represent the cluster membership, cluster centroid, and dimension weight matrices respectively. Also, the parameter f controls the fuzziness of the membership of each data point, q further modifies the weight of each dimension of each cluster (λ_{lj}) and finally, γ controls the strength of the incentive given to the *chi-square* component and dimension weights. It is also assumed that there are n documents in the training data set, m features for each of the data points, and k subspace clusters are generated during the clustering process. Imp_l indicates the cluster impurity whereas χ^2 indicates the *chi-square statistic*. The details about these notations and how the clustering is done can be found in our prior work [AHME09]. It should be noted that feature selection using subspace clustering can be considered as an unsupervised approach toward feature selection as no label information is required during an unsupervised clustering process.

Once we select features, a message between two nodes is represented as a vector using these features. Each vector's individual value can be binary or weighted. Hence, this will be a compact representation of the original message and it can be loaded into the main memory along with the graph structure. In addition, the location or URL of the original message is kept in the main memory data structure. If needed, we fetch the message. Over time, the feature vector may be changed due to the dynamic nature of the content [MASU10a], and hence, the feature set may evolve. On the basis of our prior work for the evolving streams with dynamic feature sets [MASU10b], we investigate the alternative options.

26.3.3 RDF Repository Architecture

RDF is the data format for semantic web. However, it can be used to represent any linked data in the world. RDF data are actually a collection of triples. Triples consist of three parts: subject, predicate, and object. In RDF, almost everything is a resource and hence the name of the format. Subject and predicate are always resources. The objects may be either a resource or a literal. Here, RDF data can be viewed as a directed graph where predicates are edges that flow from subjects to objects. Therefore, in our research to model any graph, we exploit RDF triple format. Here, an edge from the source node to the destination node in the graph dataset is represented as predicate, subject, and object of an RDF triple respectively. To reduce the storage size of RDF triples, we exploit dictionary encoding, that is, replace each unique string with a unique number and store the RDF data in the binary format. Hence, RDF triples will have subject, predicate, and object in an encoded form. We maintain a separate table/file for keeping track of dictionary-encoding information. To address the dynamic nature of the data, we extend RDF triple to quad by adding a time stamp along with subject, predicate, and object representing information in the network.

Figure 26.3 shows our repository architecture that consists of two components. The upper part of Figure 26.3 depicts the data preprocessing component and the lower part shows the component that answers a query. We have three subcomponents

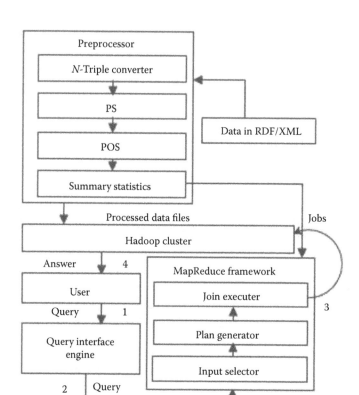

Figure 26.3 RDF repository architecture.

for data generation and preprocessing. If the data are not in *N*-triples, we convert them into *N*-triples serialization format using the *N*-triples converter component. The PS component takes the *N*-triples data and splits them into predicate files. The predicate-based files are fed into the POS component that would split the predicate files into smaller files based on the type of objects.

Our MapReduce framework has three subcomponents in it. It takes the SPARQL query from the user and passes it to the input selector and plan generator. This component will select the input files, decide how many MapReduce jobs are needed, and pass the information to the join executor component that runs the jobs using MapReduce framework. It will then relay the query answer from Hadoop to the user.

26.3.4 Data Storage

We store the data in *N*-triples format because in this format, we have a complete RDF triple (subject, predicate, and object) in one line of a file, which is very convenient to use with MapReduce jobs. We carry out dictionary encoding of the data for increased efficiency. Dictionary encoding means replacing text strings with a unique binary number. This not only reduces the disk space required for storage but also query answering will be fast because handling the primitive data type is much faster than string matching. The processing steps to obtain the data in our intended format are described below.

26.3.4.1 File Organization

We do not store the data in a single file because, in Hadoop and MapReduce framework, a file is the smallest unit of input to a MapReduce job and, in the absence of caching, a file is always read from the disk. If we have all the data in one file, the entire file is input to jobs for each query. Instead, we divide the data into multiple smaller files. The splitting is done in two steps that we discuss in the following sections.

26.3.4.2 Predicate Split

In the first step, we divide the data according to the predicates. In real-world RDF datasets, the number of distinct predicates is not more than 100. This division will immediately enable us to cut down the search space for any SPARQL query that does not have a variable predicate. For such a query, we can just pick a file for each predicate and run the query only on those files. For simplicity, we name the files with predicates, for example, all the triples containing a predicate *p1:pred* go into a file named *p1-pred*. However, in case we have a variable predicate in a triple pattern and if we cannot determine the type of the object, we have to consider all the files. If we can determine the type of the object, then we consider all files having that type of object.

26.3.4.3 Predicate Object Split

In the next step, we work with the explicit type of information in the *rdf_type* file. The file is first divided into as many files as the number of distinct objects the *rdf:type* predicate has. The object values will no longer be needed to be stored inside the file as they can be easily retrieved from the file name. This will further reduce the amount of space needed to store the data.

Then, we divide the remaining predicate files according to the type of the objects. Not all the objects are URIs, some are literals. The literals will remain in the file named by the predicate: no further processing is required for them. The type of information of a URI object is not mentioned in these files but they can be retrieved from the *rdf-type_** files. The URI objects will move into their respective file named as *predicate_type*.

26.3.5 Answering Queries Using Hadoop MapReduce

For querying, we can utilize HIVE, an SQL-like query language and SPARQL, the query language for RDF data. When a query is submitted in HiveQL, Hive, which runs on top of the Hadoop installation, can answer that query based on our schema presented above. When a SPARQL query is submitted to retrieve relevant data from the graph, first, we generate a query plan having the minimum number of Hadoop jobs possible.

Next, we run the jobs and answer the query. Finally, we convert the numbers used to encode the strings back to the strings when we present the query results to the user. We focus on minimizing the number of jobs because in our observation, we have found that setting up Hadoop jobs is very costly and is the dominant factor (time-wise) in query answering. The search space for finding the minimum number of jobs is exponential; so, we try to find a greedy-based solution or, generally speaking, an approximation solution. Our approach will be capable of handling queries involving inference. We can infer on the fly and if needed, we can materialize the inferred data.

26.3.6 Data Mining Applications

To detect anomaly/insider threat, we are examining machine learning and domain knowledge-guided techniques. Our goal is to create a comparison baseline to assess the effectiveness of chaotic attractors. Rather than modeling normal behavior and detecting changes as anomaly, we apply a holistic approach based on a semisupervised model. In particular, first, in our machine learning technique, we apply a sequence of activities or dimensions as features. Second, domain knowledge (e.g., adversarial behavior) will be a part of semisupervised learning and will be used for identifying the correct features. Finally, our techniques will be able to identify an entirely brand-new anomaly. Over time, activities/dimensions may change or deviate. Hence, our classification model needs to be adaptive and identify new types or brand-new anomalies. We develop adaptive and novel class detection techniques so that our insider threat detection can cope with changes and identify or isolate new anomalies from the existing ones.

We apply a classification technique to detect insider threat/anomaly. Each distinct insider mission is treated as class and dimension and/or activities are treated as features. Since classification is a supervised task, we require a training set. Given a training set, feature extraction will be a challenge. We apply *N*-gram analysis to extract features or generate a number of sequences based on temporal property. Once a new test case comes, first, we test it against our classification model. For the classification model, we can apply the support vector machine, K-NN, and Markovian model.

From a machine learning perspective, it is customary to classify behavior as either anomalous or benign. However, the behavior of a malevolent insider (i.e., insider threat) may not be immediately identified as malicious and it should also have subtle differences from benign behavior. A traditional machine learning-based classification model is likely to classify the behavior of a malevolent insider as benign. It will be interesting to see whether a machine learning-based novel class detection technique [MASU10a] can detect the insider threat as a novel class, and therefore trigger a warning.

The novel class detection technique is applied on the massive amounts of data that are being generated from user activities. Since these data have temporal properties and are produced continuously, they are usually referred to as data streams. The novel class detection model is updated incrementally with the incoming data. This will allow us to keep the memory requirement within a constant limit, since the raw data will be discarded, but the characteristic/pattern of the behaviors will be summarized in the model. Besides, this incremental learning will also reduce the training time, since the model need not be built from scratch with the new incoming data. Therefore, this incremental learning technique will be useful in achieving scalability.

We are examining the techniques that we have developed as well as other relevant techniques for modeling and anomaly detection. In particular, we are developing:

- Tools that will analyze and model benign and anomalous mission.
- Techniques to identify the right dimensions and activities and apply pruning to discard irrelevant dimensions.
- Techniques to cope with changes and novel class/anomaly detection.

In a typical data stream classification task, it is assumed that the total number of classes is fixed. This assumption may not be valid in insider threat detection cases, where new classes may evolve. The traditional data stream classification techniques are not capable of recognizing novel class instances until the appearance of the novel class is manually identified, and labeled instances of that class are presented to the learning algorithm for training. The problem becomes more challenging in the presence of concept drift, when the underlying data distribution changes over time. We have developed a novel and efficient technique that can automatically detect the emergence of a novel class (i.e., brand-new anomaly) by quantifying cohesion among unlabeled test instances and separating the test instances from training instances. Our goal is to use the available data and build this model.

One interesting aspect of this model is that it should capture the dynamic nature of dimensions of the mission as well as filter out the noisy behaviors. The dimensions (both benign and anomalous) have dynamic nature because they tend to change over time, which we denote as concept drift. A major challenge of the novel class detection is to differentiate the novel class from concept drift and noisy data. We are exploring this challenge in our current work.

26.4 Comprehensive Framework

As we stated in Section 26.2, insider threat detection is an extremely challenging problem. In the previous section, we discussed our approach to handle this problem. Insider threat does not occur only at the application level, it happens at all levels including the operating system, database system, and the application.

Furthermore, due to the fact that the insider will be continually changing patterns, it will be impossible to detect all types of malicious behavior using a purely static algorithm; a dynamic learning approach is required. Essentially, we need a comprehensive solution to the insider threat problem. However, to provide a more comprehensive solution, we need a more comprehensive framework. Therefore, we are proposing a framework for insider threat detection. Our framework will implement a number of interrelated solutions to detect malicious insiders. Figure 26.4 illustrates such a framework. We are examining four approaches to this problem. At the heart of our framework is the module that implements in-line reference monitor-based techniques for feature collection. This feature-collection process is aided by two modules; one uses game-theory approach and the other uses the natural language-based approach to determine which features could be collected. The fourth module implements machine learning techniques to analyze the collected features. In summary, the relationship between the four approaches can be characterized as follows:

- In-line reference monitors (IRMs) perform covert, fine-grained feature collection.
- Game theoretic techniques will identify which features should be collected by the IRMs.
- Natural language processing techniques in general and honey token generation in particular, will take an active approach to introduce additional useful features (i.e., honey token accesses) that can be collected.
- Machine learning techniques will use the collected features to infer and classify the objectives of malicious insiders.

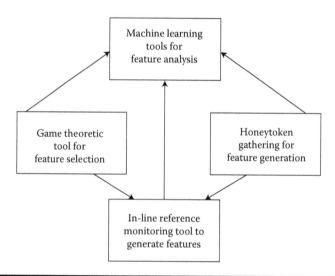

Figure 26.4 Framework for insider threat detection.

The details of our framework are provided in [HAML11]. We assume that the in-line reference monitor tool, game theoretic tool, and honey token generation tool will select and refine the features we need. Our data mining tools will analyze the features and determine whether there is a potential for insider threat.

We have started implementing parts of the framework. In particular, we have developed a number of data and stream mining techniques for insider threat detection. The evidence of malicious insider activity is often buried within large data streams, such as system logs accumulated over months or years. Ensemble-based stream mining leverages multiple classification models to achieve highly accurate anomaly detection in such streams even when the stream is unbounded, evolving, and unlabeled. This makes the approach effective for identifying insider threats that attempt to conceal their activities by varying their behaviors over time. Our approach applies ensemble-based stream mining, unsupervised learning, supervised learning, and graph-based anomaly detection to the problem of insider threat detection, demonstrating that the ensemble-based approach is significantly more effective than traditional single-model methods. We further investigate the suitability of various learning strategies for evolving insider threat data. We also developed unsupervised machine learning algorithms for insider threat detection. Our implementation is being hosted on the cloud. More information can also be found in [PALL12]. For more information on ensemble-based stream mining applications, see Chapter 25. The details of our algorithms are presented in [MASU10a].

26.5 Summary and Directions

In this chapter, we have discussed our approach to insider threat detection. We represent the insiders and their communication as RDF graphs and then query and mine the graphs to extract the nuggets. We also provided a comprehensive framework for insider threat detection.

The insider threat problem is a challenging one. Research is only beginning. The problem is that the insider may change his/her patterns and behaviors. Therefore, we need tools that can be adaptive. For example, our stream mining tools discussed in Chapter 25 may be used for detecting such threats and we have developed some initial stream mining tools [PALL12]. Because of the massive amounts of data to be analyzed, cloud-based data mining would be a suitable approach for insider threat detection. Our approach is essentially for insider threat detection to be offered as a security-as-a-service solution.

References

[AHME09] Ahmed, M.S. and L. Khan, SISC: A text classification approach using semi supervised subspace clustering. *DDDM '09: The 3rd International Workshop on Domain Driven Data Mining in Conjunction with ICDM 2009,* December 6, 2009, Miami, Florida.

[BERR07] Berry, M.W., M. Browne, A. Langville, V.P. Pauca, and R.J. Plemmons, Algorithms and applications for approximate nonnegative matrix factorization. *Computational Statistics and Data Analysis*, 52(1): 155–173, 2007.

[CARM09] Carminati, B., E. Ferrari, R. Heatherly, M. Kantarcioglu, and B. Thuraisingham, A semantic web based framework for social network access control. *Proceedings of Symposium on Access Control Models and Technologies (SACMAT)*, Stresa, Italy, 177–186, 2009.

[COOK06] Cook, D. and L. Holder, *Mining Graph Data*, Wiley Interscience, New York, NY, 2006.

[EBER09] Eberle, W. and L. Holder, Applying graph-based anomaly detection approaches to the discovery of insider threats, *IEEE International Conference on Intelligence and Security Informatics (ISI)*, Dallas, TX, June 2009.

[HADO] http://hadoop.apache.org/

[HAML11] Hamlen, K., L. Khan, M. Kantarcioglu, V. Ng, and B. Thuraisingham, Insider threat detection, White paper, The University of Texas at Dallas, April 2011.

[MASU10a] Masud, M., J. Gao, L. Khan, J. Han, and B. Thuraisingham, Classification and novel class detection in concept-drifting data streams under time constraints. *IEEE Transactions on Knowledge and Data Engineering (TKDE), April 2010, IEEE Computer Society.*

[MASU10b] Masud, M., Q. Chen, J. Gao, L. Khan, J. Han, and B. Thuraisingham, Classification and novel class detection of data streams in a dynamic feature space, In: *Proceedings of European Conference on Machine Learning and Knowledge Discovery in Databases, ECML PKDD 2010*, Barcelona, Spain, September 20–24, 2010, Springer 2010, ISBN 978-3-642-15882-7, 2: 337–352.

[MAYB05] Maybury, M., P. Chase, B. Cheikes, D. Brackney, S. Matzner, T. Hetherington, B. Wood et al., *Analysis and Detection of Malicious Insiders,* In: *2005 International Conference on Intelligence Analysis*, McLean, VA.

[MITC97] Mitchell, T., *Machine Learning*. McGraw-Hill, 1997.

[NEUM08] Neumann, T. and G. Weikum, RDF-3X: A RISC-style engine for RDF, *Proceedings of the VLDB Endowment*, 1(1): 647–659, 2008.

[PALL12] Parveen, P., N. McDaniel, V.S. Hariharan, B.M. Thuraisingham, and L. Khan, Unsupervised ensemble based learning for insider threat detection. *SocialCom/PASSAT Conference,* 718–727, Amsterdam, the Netherlands, 2012.

[THUR09] Thuraisingham, B., M. Kantarcioglu, and L. Khan, Building a geosocial semantic web for military stabilization and reconstruction operations. *PAISI*, Bangkok, Thailand, 1: 2009.

[TONG09] Tong, H., Fast algorithms for querying and mining large graphs. CMU Report, ML-09-112, September 2009.

Chapter 27

Cloud-Centric Assured Information Sharing

27.1 Overview

The advent of *cloud computing* and the continuing movement toward *software as a service* (SaaS) paradigms has posed an increasing need for *assured information sharing* (AIS) as a service in the cloud. The urgency of this need has been voiced as recently as in April 2011 by NSA (National Security Agency) CIO (Chief Information Officer) Lonny Anderson in describing the agency's focus on a "cloud-centric" approach to information sharing with other agencies [NSA11]. Likewise, the DoD has been embracing cloud computing paradigms more efficiently, economically, flexibly, and scalably to meet its vision of "delivering the power of information to ensure mission success through an agile enterprise with freedom of maneuverability across the information environment" [DoD, DoD07, DoD09]. Both agencies therefore have a tremendous need for effective AIS technologies and tools for cloud environments.

Although a number of AIS tools have been developed over the past five years for policy-based information sharing [FINI09, THUR08, AWAD10, RAO08], to our knowledge none of these tools operate in the cloud and hence do not provide the scalability needed to support large numbers of users utilizing massive amounts of data. Our recent prototype systems for supporting cloud-based AIS have applied cloud-centric engines that query large amounts of data in relational databases via non-cloud policy engines that enforce policies expressed in XACML [THUR10, THUR11]. While this is a significant improvement over prior efforts (and has given us insights into implementing cloud-based solutions), it nevertheless has at least three significant limitations. First, XACML-based policy specifications are not expressive enough to support many of the complex policies needed for AIS missions like those of the NSA and DoD. Second, to meet the scalability and efficiency requirements of mission-critical tasks, the policy engine needs to operate in the cloud. Third, secure query processing based on relational technology has limitations in representing and processing unstructured data needed for many applications.

To share the large amounts of data securely and efficiently, there clearly needs to be a seamless integration of the policy and data managers in the cloud. Therefore, in order to satisfy the cloud-centric AIS needs, we need (i) a cloud-resident policy manager that enforces information-sharing policies expressed in a semantically rich language, and (ii) a cloud-resident data manager that securely stores and retrieves data and seamlessly integrates with the policy manager. To our knowledge, no such system currently exists. Therefore, our project to design and develop such cloud-based AIS system is proceeding in two phases.

We have designed a system and implemented a version of a cloud-centric assured information sharing system (CAISS) that utilizes the technology components we have designed in-house as well as some open source tools. CAISS consists of two components: a cloud-centric policy manager that enforces policies specified in RDF, and a cloud-centric data manager that will store and manage data also specified in RDF. This RDF data manager is essentially a query engine for SPARQL, a language widely used by the semantic web community to query RDF data. RDF is a semantic web language that is considerably more expressive than XACML for specifying and reasoning about policies. Furthermore, our policy manager and data manager will have seamless integration since they both manage RDF data. We have chosen this RDF-based approach for cloud-centric AIS during Phase 1 because it satisfies the two necessary conditions stated earlier, and we have already developed an RDF-based noncloud centric policy manager [CADE11a] and an RDF-based cloud-centric data manager [HUSA11]. Specifically, we are enhancing our RDF-based policy engine to operate on a cloud, extend our cloud-centric RDF data manager to integrate with the policy manager, and build an integrated framework for CAISS. We describe the detailed implementation of a version of CAISS in Chapter 28.

While our CAISS design and implementation will be the first system supporting cloud-centric AIS, it will operate only on a single trusted cloud and will therefore not support information sharing across multiple clouds. Furthermore, while CAISS's RDF-based, formal semantics approach to policy specification will be significantly more expressive than XACML-based approaches, it will not support an enhanced machine interpretability of content since RDF does not provide a sufficiently rich vocabulary (e.g., support for classes and properties). We have therefore designed a fully functional and robust AIS system called CAISS++ that addresses these deficiencies. CAISS is an important stepping-stone toward CAISS++ because CAISS can be used as a baseline framework against which CAISS++ can be compared along several performance dimensions, such as storage model efficiency and OWL-based policy expressiveness. Furthermore, since CAISS and CAISS++ share the same core components (policy engine and query processor), the lessons learned from the implementation and integration of these components in CAISS will be invaluable during the development of CAISS++. Finally, the evaluation and testing of CAISS will provide us with important insights into the shortcomings of CAISS, which can then be systematically addressed in the implementation of CAISS++.

We will also conduct a formal analysis of policy specifications and the software-level protection mechanisms that enforce them to provide exceptionally high-assurance security guarantees for the resulting system. We envisage CAISS++ to be used in highly mission-critical applications. Therefore, it becomes imperative to provide guarantees that the policies are enforced in a provably correct manner. We will utilize our work in formal policy analysis [JONE10], [JONE11] and their enforcement via machine-certified, in-line reference monitors [HAML06a], [HAML06b], [SRID10] in the analysis of CAISS++. Such analyses will be of use to model and certify security properties enforced by core software components in the trusted computing base of CAISS++.

CAISS++ will be a critical technology for information sharing due to the fact that it uses a novel combination of cloud-centric policy specification and enforcement along with a cloud-centric data storage and efficient query evaluation. CAISS++ will make use of ontologies, a sublanguage OWL, to build policies. A mixture of such ontologies with a semantic web-based rule language (e.g., SWRL) facilitates distributed reasoning on the policies to enforce security. Additionally, CAISS++ will include an RDF processing engine that provides cost-based optimization for evaluating SPARQL queries based on information-sharing policies.

The organization of this chapter is as follows. We will discuss the design of CAISS in Section 27.2.1 and the design of CAISS++ in Section 27.2.2. Formal policy analysis and the implementation approach for CAISS++ will be provided in Sections 27.2.3 and 27.2.4, respectively. Related efforts are discussed in Section 27.3. This chapter concludes with Section 27.4. Figure 27.1 illustrates the contents

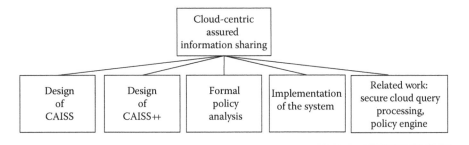

Figure 27.1 Cloud-centric assured information sharing. (With kind permission from Springer Science+Business Media: Khadilkar, V ., Rachapalli, J., Cadenhead, T., Kantarcioglu, M., Hamlen, K.W., Khan, L., and Husain, M.F. Media from Lecture Notes in Computer Science, *Proceedings of Intelligence and Security Informatics–Pacific Asia Workshop*, PAISI 2012, Kuala Lumpur, Malaysia, 7299, 2012, p. 1–26, © Springer, ISBN 978-3-642-30427-9.)

of this chapter. Details of our work can also be found in [THUR12]. Our approach to AIS is given in Appendix D. Note that a version of the implementation of CAISS as a collection of semantic web services will be discussed in Chapter 28.

27.2 System Design

27.2.1 Design of CAISS

We are enhancing our tools on (i) secure cloud query processing with semantic web data, and (ii) semantic web-based policy engine to develop CAISS. Details of our tools are given in Section 27.4 (under related work). In this section, we will discuss the enhancements to be made to our tools to develop CAISS.

First, our RDF-based policy engine enforces access control, redaction, and inference control policies on data represented as RDF graphs. Second, our cloud SPARQL query engine for RDF data uses the Hadoop/MapReduce framework. Note that Hadoop is the Apache distributed file system and MapReduce sits on top of Hadoop and carries out job scheduling. As in the case of our cloud-based relational query processor prototype [THUR10], our SPARQL query engine also handles policies specified in XACML and the policy engine implements the XACML protocol. The use of XACML as a policy language requires extensive knowledge about the general concepts used in the design of XACML. Thus, policy authoring in XACML requires a steep learning curve, and is therefore a task that is left to an experienced administrator. A second disadvantage of using XACML is related to performance. Current implementations of XACML require an access request to be evaluated against every policy in the system until a policy applies to the incoming request. This strategy is sufficient for systems with relatively few users and policies. However, for systems with a large number of users and a substantial number of access requests, the aforementioned strategy becomes a performance bottleneck. Finally, XACML is not sufficiently expressive to capture the semantics of information-sharing policies. Prior research has shown that semantic web-based policies are far more expressive. This is because semantic web technologies are based on description logic and have the power to represent knowledge as well as reason about knowledge. Therefore, our first step is to replace the XACML-based policy engine with a semantic web-based policy engine. Since we already have our RDF-based policy engine, for the Phase 1 prototype, we will enhance this engine and integrate it with our SPARQL query processor. Since our policy engine is based on RDF and our query processor also manages large RDF graphs, there will be no impedance mismatch between the data and the policies.

27.2.1.1 Enhanced Policy Engine

Our current policy engine has a limitation in that it does not operate in a cloud. Therefore, we will port our RDF policy engine to the cloud environment and integrate it with the SPARQL query engine for federated query processing in the cloud. Our policy engine will benefit from the scalability and the distributed platform offered by Hadoop's MapReduce framework to answer SPARQL queries over large distributed RDF triple stores (billions of RDF triples). The reasons for using RDF as our data model are: (1) RDF allows us to achieve data interoperability between the seemingly disparate sources of information that are catalogued by each agency/organization separately; (2) the use of RDF allows participating agencies to create data-centric applications that make use of the integrated data that is now available to them; and (3) since RDF does not require the use of an explicit schema for data generation, it can be easily adapted to ever-changing user requirements. The policy engine's flexibility is based on its accepting high-level policies and executing them as query rules over a directed RDF graph representation of the data. While our prior work focuses on provenance data and access control policies, our CAISS prototype will be flexible enough to handle data represented in RDF and will include information-sharing policies. The strength of our policy engine is that it can handle any type of policy that could be represented using RDF and horn logic rules.

The second limitation of our policy engine is that it currently addresses certain types of policies such as confidentiality, privacy, and redaction policies. We need to incorporate information-sharing policies into our policy engine. We have however conducted simulation studies for incentive-based AIS as well as AIS prototypes in the cloud. We have defined a number of information-sharing policies such as "US gives information to UK provided UK does not share it with India." We specify such policies in RDF and incorporate them to be processed by our enhanced policy engine.

27.2.1.2 Enhanced SPARQL Query Processor

While we have a tool that will execute SPARQL queries over large RDF graphs on Hadoop (discussed in Chapter 13), there is still the need for supporting path queries (i.e., SPARQL queries that provide answers to a request for paths in an RDF graph). An RDF triple can be viewed as an arc from the Subject to Object with the Predicate used to label the arc. The answers to the SPARQL query are based on reachability (i.e., the paths between a source node and a target node). The concatenation of the labels on the arcs along a path can be thought of as a word belonging to the answer set of the path query. Each term of a word is contributed by some predicate label of a triple in the RDF graph. We have designed an algorithm to determine the candidate triples as an answer set in a distributed RDF graph. First, the RDF document is converted to an *N*-triple file that is split based on predicate labels. A term in a word could correspond to some predicate file. Second, we form the word by tracing an appropriate path in the distributed RDF graph. We use MapReduce jobs to build the word and to get the candidate RDF triples as an order set. Finally, we return all of the set of ordered RDF triples as the answers to the corresponding SPARQL query.

27.2.1.3 Integration Framework

Figure 27.2 provides an overview of the CAISS architecture. The integration of the cloud-centric RDF policy engine with the enhanced SPARQL query processor must address the following. First, we need to make sure that RDF-based policies can be stored in the existing storage schema used by the query processor. Second, we need to ensure that the enhanced query processor is able to efficiently evaluate policies (i.e., path queries) over the underlying RDF storage. Finally, we need to conduct a performance evaluation of CAISS to verify that it meets the performance requirements of various participating agencies. Figure 27.3 illustrates the concept of operation of CAISS. Here, multiple agencies will share data in a single cloud. The enhanced policy engine and the cloud-centric SPARQL query processor will enforce the information-sharing policies.

There are several benefits in developing a proof of concept prototype such as CAISS before we embark on CAISS++. First, CAISS itself is useful to share data within a single cloud. Second, we will have a baseline system that we can compare against with respect to efficiency and ease-of-use when we implement CAISS++. Third, this will give us valuable lessons with respect to the integration of the different pieces required for AIS in the cloud. Finally, by running different scenarios on CAISS, we can identify potential performance bottlenecks that need to be addressed in CAISS++.

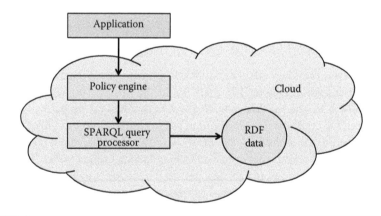

Figure 27.2 CAISS prototype overview. (With kind permission from Springer Science+Business Media: Khadilkar, V ., Rachapalli, J., Cadenhead, T., Kantarcioglu, M., Hamlen, K.W., Khan, L., and Husain, M.F. Media from Lecture Notes in Computer Science, *Proceedings of Intelligence and Security Informatics–Pacific Asia Workshop*, PAISI 2012, Kuala Lumpur, Malaysia, 7299, 2012, p. 1–26, © Springer, ISBN 978-3-642-30427-9.)

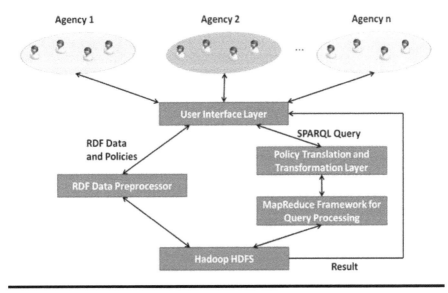

Figure 27.3 Operation of CAISS. (With kind permission from Springer Science+Business Media: Khadilkar, V ., Rachapalli, J., Cadenhead, T., Kantarcioglu, M., Hamlen, K.W., Khan, L., and Husain, M.F. Media from Lecture Notes in Computer Science, *Proceedings of Intelligence and Security Informatics–Pacific Asia Workshop*, PAISI 2012, Kuala Lumpur, Malaysia, 7299, 2012, p. 1–26, © Springer, ISBN 978-3-642-30427-9.)

27.2.2 Design of CAISS++

We have examined alternatives and carried out a preliminary design of CAISS++. On the basis of the lessons learned from the CAISS prototype and the preliminary design of CAISS++, we will carry out a detailed design of CAISS++ and subsequently implement an operational prototype of CAISS++ during phase 2. In this section, we will first discuss the limitations of CAISS and then discuss the design alternatives for CAISS++.

27.2.2.1 Limitations of CAISS

1. *Policy engine:* CAISS uses an RDF-based policy engine which has limited expressivity. The purpose of RDF is to provide a structure (or framework) for describing resources. OWL is built on top of RDF and it is designed for use by applications that need to process the content of information instead of just presenting information to human users. OWL facilitates greater machine interpretability of content than that supported by RDF by providing additional vocabulary for describing properties and classes along with a formal

semantics. OWL has three increasingly expressive sublanguages: OWL Lite, OWL DL, and OWL Full and one has the freedom to choose a suitable sublanguage based on application requirements. In CAISS++, we plan to make use of OWL which is much more expressive than RDF to model security policies through organization-specific domain ontologies as well as a system-wide upper ontology (note that CAISS++ will reuse an organization's existing domain ontology or facilitate the creation of a new domain ontology if it does not exist. Additionally, we have to engineer the upper ontology that will be used by the centralized component of CAISS++). Additionally, CAISS++ will make use of a distributed reasoning algorithm that will leverage ontologies to enforce security policies.

2. *Hadoop storage architecture:* CAISS uses a static storage model wherein a user provides the system with RDF data only once during the initialization step. Thereafter, a user is not allowed to update the existing data. On the other hand, CAISS++ attempts to provide a flexible storage model to users. In CAISS++, a user is allowed to append new data to the existing RDF data stored in HDFS. Note that only allowing a user to append new data rather than deleting/modifying existing data comes from the append-only restriction for files that is enforced by HDFS.

3. *SPARQL query processor:* CAISS only supports simple SPARQL queries that make use of basic graph patterns (BGP). In CAISS++, support for other SPARQL query operators such as FILTER, GROUP BY, ORDER BY, and so on will be added. Additionally, CAISS uses a heuristic query optimizer that aims to minimize the number of MapReduce jobs required to answer a query. CAISS++ will incorporate a cost-based query optimizer that will minimize the number of triples that are accessed during the process of query execution.

27.2.2.2 Design of CAISS++

CAISS++ overcomes the limitations of CAISS. The detailed design of CAISS++ and its implementation will be carried out during phase 2. The lessons learned from CAISS will also drive the detailed design of CAISS++. We assume that the data are encrypted with appropriate DoD encryption technologies and therefore will not conduct research on encryption in this project. The concept of operation for CAISS++ is shown in interaction with several participating agencies in Figure 27.4 where multiple organizations share data in a single cloud.

The design of CAISS++ is based on a novel combination of an OWL-based policy engine with an RDF processing engine. Therefore, this design is composed of several tasks, each of which is solved separately after which all tasks are integrated into a single framework: (1) *OWL-based policy engine:* The policy engine uses a set of agency-specific domain ontologies as well as an upper ontology to construct policies for the task of AIS. The task of enforcing policies may require

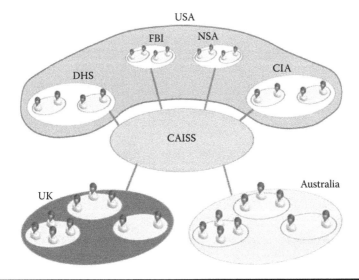

Figure 27.4 CAISS++ scenario. (With kind permission from Springer Science+Business Media: Khadilkar, V ., Rachapalli, J., Cadenhead, T., Kantarcioglu, M., Hamlen, K.W., Khan, L., and Husain, M.F. Media from Lecture Notes in Computer Science, *Proceedings of Intelligence and Security Informatics–Pacific Asia Workshop*, PAISI 2012, Kuala Lumpur, Malaysia, 7299, 2012, p. 1–26, © Springer, ISBN 978-3-642-30427-9.)

the use of a distributed reasoner, therefore, we will evaluate the existing distributed reasoners; (2) *RDF processing engine:* The processing engine requires the construction of sophisticated storage architectures as well as an efficient query processor; and (3) *Integration Framework:* The final task is to combine the policy engine with the processing engine into an integrated framework. The initial design of CAISS++ will be based on a trade-off between simplicity of design versus its scalability and efficiency. The first design alternative is known as centralized CAISS++ and it chooses simplicity as the trade-off whereas the second design alternative (known as decentralized CAISS++) chooses scalability and efficiency as the trade-off. Finally, we also provide a Hybrid CAISS++ architecture that tries to combine the benefits of both, centralized and decentralized CAISS++. Since CAISS++ follows a requirements-driven design, the division of tasks that we outlined above to achieve AIS are present in each of the approaches that we present next.

27.2.2.3 Centralized CAISS++

Figure 27.5 illustrates two agencies interacting through centralized CAISS++. Centralized CAISS++ consists of shared cloud storage to store the shared data. All the participating agencies store their respective knowledge bases consisting of

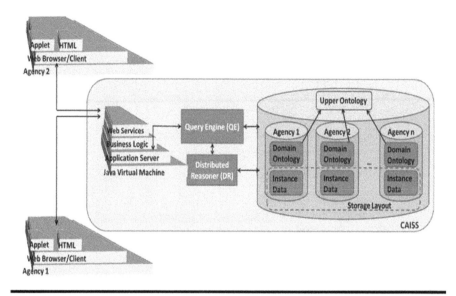

Figure 27.5 Centralized CAISS++. (With kind permission from Springer Science+Business Media: Khadilkar, V ., Rachapalli, J., Cadenhead, T., Kantarcioglu, M., Hamlen, K.W., Khan, L., and Husain, M.F. Media from Lecture Notes in Computer Science, *Proceedings of Intelligence and Security Informatics–Pacific Asia Workshop,* **PAISI 2012, Kuala Lumpur, Malaysia, 7299, 2012, p. 1–26, © Springer, ISBN 978-3-642-30427-9.)**

domain ontology with corresponding instance data. Centralized CAISS++ also consists of an upper ontology, a query engine (QE), and a distributed reasoner (DR). The upper ontology is used to capture the domain knowledge that is common across the domains of participating agencies whereas, domain ontology captures the knowledge specific to a given agency or a domain. Note that the domain ontology for a given agency will be protected from the domain ontologies of other participating agencies. Policies can either be captured in the upper ontology or in any of the domain ontologies depending on their scope of applicability. Note that the domain ontology for a given agency will be protected from domain ontologies of other participating agencies.

The design of an upper ontology as well as domain ontologies that capture the requirements of the participating agencies is a significant research area and is the focus of the ontology engineering problem. Ontologies will be created using suitable dialects of OWL which are based on Description Logics. Description Logics are usually decidable fragments of First Order Logic and will be the basis for providing sound formal semantics. Having represented knowledge in terms of ontologies, reasoning will be done using existing optimized reasoning algorithms. Query answering will leverage reasoning algorithms to formulate and answer intelligent queries. The encoding of policies in OWL will ensure that they are enforced in a provably correct manner. Later, we present an ongoing research project at the University of Texas at Dallas that focuses on providing a general framework for enforcing policies in a provably correct manner using the same underlying technologies. This work can be leveraged toward modeling and enforcement of security policies in CAISS++. The instance data can choose between several available data storage formats (discussed later on). The QE receives queries from the participating agencies, parses the query, and determines whether or not the computation requires the use of a DR. If the query is simple and does not require the use of a reasoner, the query engine executes the query directly over the shared knowledge base. Once the query result has been computed, the result is returned to the querying agency. If however, the query is complex and requires inferences over the given data, the query engine uses the distributed reasoner to compute the inferences and then returns the result to the querying agency. A distributed DL reasoner differs from a traditional DL reasoner in its ability to perform reasoning over cloud data storage using the MapReduce framework. During the preliminary design of CAISS++ in phase 1, we will conduct a thorough investigation of the available distributed reasoners using existing benchmarks such as LUBM [Guo05]. The goal of this investigation is to determine if we can use one of the existing reasoners or whether we need to build our own distributed reasoner. In Figure 27.4, an agency is illustrated as a stack consisting of a web browser, an applet, and HTML. An agency uses the web browser to send the queries to CAISS++ which are handled by the query processor.

The main differences between centralized CAISS++ and CAISS are: (1) CAISS will use RDF to encode security policies whereas centralized CAISS++ will use a suitable sublanguage of OWL which is more expressive than RDF and can therefore capture the security policies better; (2) the SPARQL query processor in CAISS will support a limited subset of SPARQL expressivity, that is, it will provide support only for Basic Graph Patterns (BGP), whereas the SPARQL query processor in centralized CAISS++ will be designed to support maximum expressivity of SPARQL; and (3) the Hadoop storage architecture used in CAISS only supports data insertion during an initialization step. However, when data needs to be updated, the entire RDF graph is deleted and a new dataset is inserted in its place. On the other hand, centralized CAISS++, in addition to supporting the previous feature, also opens up Hadoop HDFS's append-only feature to users. This feature allows users to append new information to the data that they have previously uploaded to the system.

27.2.2.4 Decentralized CAISS++

Figure 27.6 illustrates two agencies in interaction with decentralized CAISS++. Decentralized CAISS++ consists of two parts, namely global CAISS++ and local CAISS++. Global CAISS++ consists of a shared cloud storage which is used by the participating agencies to store only their respective domain ontologies and not the

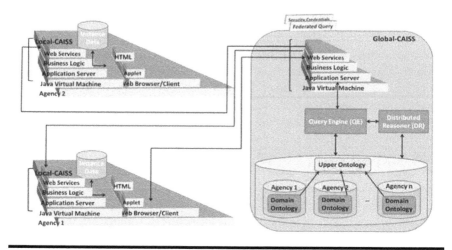

Figure 27.6 Decentralized CAISS++. (With kind permission from Springer Science+Business Media: Khadilkar, V ., Rachapalli, J., Cadenhead, T., Kantarcioglu, M., Hamlen, K.W., Khan, L., and Husain, M.F. Media from Lecture Notes in Computer Science, *Proceedings of Intelligence and Security Informatics–Pacific Asia Workshop,* **PAISI 2012, Kuala Lumpur, Malaysia, 7299, 2012, p. 1–26, © Springer, ISBN 978-3-642-30427-9.)**

instance data unlike centralized CAISS++. Note that domain ontologies for various organizations will be sensitive, therefore, CAISS++ will make use of its own domain ontology to protect a participating agency from accessing other domain ontologies. When a user from an agency queries the CAISS++ data store, Global CAISS++ processes the query in two steps. In the first step, it performs a check to verify whether the user is authorized to perform the action specified in the query. If the result of step 1 verifies the user as an authorized user, then it proceeds to step 2 of query processing. In the second step, global CAISS++ federates the actual query to the participating agencies. The query is then processed by the local CAISS++ of a participating agency. The result of computation is then returned to the global CAISS++ which aggregates the final result and returns it to the user. Step 2 of query processing may involve query splitting if the data required to answer a query spans multiple domains. In this case, the results of sub-queries from several agencies (their local CAISS++) will need to be combined for further query processing. Once the results are merged and the final result is computed, the result is returned to the user of the querying agency. The figure illustrates agencies with a set of two stacks, one of which corresponds to the local CAISS++ and the other consisting of a web browser, an applet, and HTML, which is used by an agency to query global CAISS++. Table 27.1 shows the pros and cons of the centralized CAISS++ approach while Table 27.2 shows the pros and cons of the decentralized CAISS++ approach.

Table 27.1 Pros and Cons of Centralized CAISS++

Pros	Cons
Simple approach	Difficult to update data. Expensive approach as data needs to be migrated to central storage on each update or a set of updates.
Ease of implementation	Leads to data duplication
Easier to query	If data are available in different formats they needs to be homogenized by translating it to RDF

Source: With kind permission from Springer Science+Business Media: Khadilkar, V ., Rachapalli, J., Cadenhead, T., Kantarcioglu, M., Hamlen, K.W., Khan, L., and Husain, M.F. Media from Lecture Notes in Computer Science, *Proceedings of Intelligence and Security Informatics–Pacific Asia Workshop*, PAISI 2012, Kuala Lumpur, Malaysia, 7299, 2012, p. 1–26, © Springer, ISBN 978-3-642-30427-9.

Table 27.2 Pros and Cons of Decentralized CAISS++

Advantages	Disadvantages
No duplication of data	Complex query processing
Scalable and flexible	Difficult to implement
Efficient	May require query rewriting and query splitting

Source: With kind permission from Springer Science+Business Media: Khadilkar, V ., Rachapalli, J., Cadenhead, T., Kantarcioglu, M., Hamlen, K.W., Khan, L., and Husain, M.F. Media from Lecture Notes in Computer Science, *Proceedings of Intelligence and Security Informatics–Pacific Asia Workshop*, PAISI 2012, Kuala Lumpur, Malaysia, 7299, 2012, p. 1–26, © Springer, ISBN 978-3-642-30427-9.

27.2.2.5 Hybrid CAISS++

Figure 27.7 illustrates an overview of hybrid CAISS++ which leverages the benefits of centralized CAISS++ as well as decentralized CAISS++. Hybrid CAISS++ architecture is illustrated in Figure 27.8. It is a flexible design alternative as the users of the participating agencies have the freedom to choose between centralized CAISS++ or decentralized CAISS++. Hybrid CAISS++ is made up of global CAISS++ and a set of local CAISS++'s located at each of the participating agencies. Global CAISS++ consists of a shared cloud storage which is used by the participating agencies to store the data they would like to share with other agencies.

A local CAISS++ of an agency is used to receive and process a federated query on the instance data located at the agency. A participating group is a group comprised

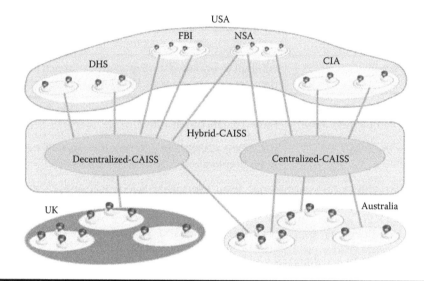

Figure 27.7 Hybrid CAISS++ overview. (With kind permission from Springer Science+Business Media: Khadilkar, V ., Rachapalli, J., Cadenhead, T., Kantarcioglu, M., Hamlen, K.W., Khan, L., and Husain, M.F. Media from Lecture Notes in Computer Science, *Proceedings of Intelligence and Security Informatics–Pacific Asia Workshop*, PAISI 2012, Kuala Lumpur, Malaysia, 7299, 2012, p. 1–26, © Springer, ISBN 978-3-642-30427-9.)

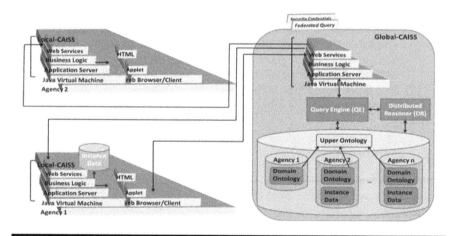

Figure 27.8 Hybrid CAISS++ architecture. (With kin permission from Springer Science+Business Media: *Proceedings of Intelligence and Security Informatics–Pacific Asia Workshop, PAISI 2012, Kuala Lumpur, Malaysia,* Media from Lecture Notes in Computer Science 7299, 2012, p. 1–26, Khadilkar, V ., Rachapalli, J., Cadenhead, T., Kantarcioglu, M., Hamlen, K.W., Khan, L., and Husain, M.F. © Springer, ISBN 978-3-642-30427-9.)

of users from several agencies who want to share information with each other. The members of a group arrive at a mutual agreement on whether they opt for centralized or decentralized approach. Additional users can join a group at a later point in time if the need arises. Hybrid CAISS++ will be designed to simultaneously support a set of participating groups. Additionally, a user can belong to several participating groups at the same time. We describe a few use-case scenarios which illustrates the operation.

1. The first case corresponds to the scenario where a set of users who want to securely share information with each other opt for a centralized approach. Suppose users from agency 1 want to share information with users of agency 2 and vice versa, then both the agencies store their knowledge bases comprising of domain ontology and instance data on the shared cloud storage located at global CAISS++. The centralized CAISS++ approach works by having the participating agencies arrive at mutual trust on using the central cloud storage. Subsequently, information sharing proceeds as in centralized CAISS++.

2. The second corresponds to the scenario where a set of users opt for a decentralized approach. For example, agencies 3, 4, and 5 wish to share information with each other and mutually opt for the decentralized approach. All the three agencies store their respective domain ontologies at the central cloud storage and this information is only accessible to members of this group. The subsequent information-sharing process proceeds in the manner proceeds as in the decentralized CAISS++ approach.

3. The third corresponds to the scenario where a user of an agency belongs to multiple participating groups, some of which opt for the centralized approach and others for the decentralized approach. Since the user is a part of a group using the centralized approach to sharing, he/she needs to make his/her data available to the group by shipping his/her data to the central cloud storage. Additionally, since the user is also a part of a group using the decentralized approach for sharing, he/she needs to respond to the federated query with the help of the local CAISS++ located at his/her agency.

Table 27.3 shows the trade-offs between the different approaches and this will enable users to choose a suitable approach of AIS based on their application requirements. Next, we describe details of the cloud storage mechanism that makes use of Hadoop to store the knowledge bases from various agencies and then discuss the details of distributed SPARQL query processing over the cloud storage.

In Figure 27.9, we present an architectural overview of our Hadoop-based RDF storage and retrieval framework. We use the concept of a "Store" to provide data loading and querying capabilities on RDF graphs that are stored in the underlying HDFS. A store represents a single RDF dataset and can therefore contain several RDF graphs, each with its own separate layout. All operations on a RDF graph are

Table 27.3 A Comparison of the Three Approaches Based on Functionality Hadoop Storage Architecture

Functionality	Centralized CAISS++	Decentralized CAISS++	Hybrid CAISS++
No data duplication	X	√	Maybe
Flexibility	X	X	√
Scalablility	X	√	√
Efficiency	√	√	√
Simplicity—no query rewriting	√	X	X
Trusted centralized cloud data storage	√	X	X

Source: With kind permission from Springer Science+Business Media: Khadilkar, V ., Rachapalli, J., Cadenhead, T., Kantarcioglu, M., Hamlen, K.W., Khan, L., and Husain, M.F. Media from Lecture Notes in Computer Science, *Proceedings of Intelligence and Security Informatics–Pacific Asia Workshop,* PAISI 2012, Kuala Lumpur, Malaysia, 7299, 2012, p. 1–26, © Springer, ISBN 978-3-642-30427-9.

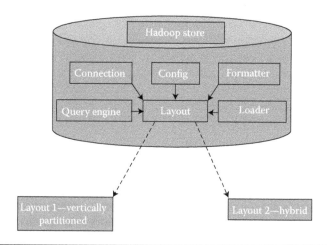

Figure 27.9 Hadoop storage architecture used by CAISS++. (With kind permission from Springer Science+Business Media: Khadilkar, V ., Rachapalli, J., Cadenhead, T., Kantarcioglu, M., Hamlen, K.W., Khan, L., and Husain, M.F. Media from Lecture Notes in Computer Science, *Proceedings of Intelligence and Security Informatics–Pacific Asia Workshop*, PAISI 2012, Kuala Lumpur, Malaysia, 7299, 2012, p. 1–26, © Springer, ISBN 978-3-642-30427-9.)

then implicitly converted into operations on the underlying layout including the following:

- *Layout formatter:* This block performs the function of formatting a layout, which is the process of deleting all triples in a RDF graph while preserving the directory structure used to store that graph.
- *Loader:* This block performs loading of triples into a layout.
- *Query engine:* This block allows a user to query a layout using a SPARQL query. Since our framework operates on the underlying HDFS, the querying mechanism on a layout involves translating a SPARQL query into a possible pipeline of MapReduce jobs and then executing this pipeline on a layout.
- *Connection:* This block maintains the necessary connections and configurations with the underlying HDFS.
- *Config:* This block maintains configuration information such as graph names for each of the RDF graphs that make up a store.

Since RDF data will be stored under different HDFS folders in separate files as a part of our storage schema, we need to adopt certain naming conventions for such folders and files.

27.2.2.6 Naming Conventions

A Hadoop Store can be composed of several distinct RDF graphs in our framework. Therefore, a separate folder will be created in HDFS for each such Hadoop Store. The name of this folder will correspond to the name that has been selected for the given store. Furthermore, an RDF graph is divided into several files in our framework depending on the storage layout that is selected. Therefore, a separate folder will be created in HDFS for each distinct RDF graph. The name of this folder is defined to be "default" for the default RDF graph while for a named RDF graph, the URI of the graph is used as the folder name. We use the abstraction of a store in our framework for the reason that this will simplify the management of data belonging to various agencies. Two of the layouts to be supported by our framework are given below. These layouts use a varying number of HDFS files to store RDF data.

27.2.2.7 Vertically Partitioned Layout

Figure 27.10 presents the storage schema for the vertically partitioned layout. For every unique predicate contained in an RDF graph, this layout creates a separate file using the name of the predicate as the file name, in the underlying HDFS. Note that only the local name part of a predicate URI (Universal Resource Identifier) is used in a file name and a separate mapping exists between a file name and the predicate URI. A file for a given predicate contains a separate line for every triple that contains that predicate. This line stores the subject and object values that make up the triple. This schema will lead to significant storage space savings since

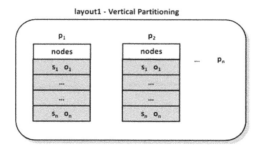

Figure 27.10 Vertically partitioned layout. (With kind permission from Springer Science+Business Media: Khadilkar, V ., Rachapalli, J., Cadenhead, T., Kantarcioglu, M., Hamlen, K.W., Khan, L., and Husain, M.F. Media from Lecture Notes in Computer Science, *Proceedings of Intelligence and Security Informatics–Pacific Asia Workshop*, PAISI 2012, Kuala Lumpur, Malaysia, 7299, 2012, p. 1–26, © Springer, ISBN 978-3-642-30427-9.)

moving the predicate name to the name of a file completely eliminates the storage of this predicate value. However, multiple occurrences of the same resource URI or literal value will be stored multiple times across all files as well as within a file. Additionally, a SPARQL query may need to lookup multiple files to ensure that a complete result is returned to a user, for example, a query to find all triples that belong to a specific subject or object.

27.2.2.8 Hybrid Layout

Figure 27.11 presents the storage schema for the hybrid layout. This layout is an extension of the vertically partitioned layout, since in addition to the separate files

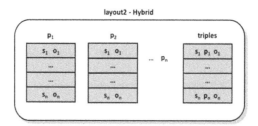

Figure 27.11 Hybrid layout. (With kind permission from Springer Science+Business Media: Khadilkar, V ., Rachapalli, J., Cadenhead, T., Kantarcioglu, M., Hamlen, K.W., Khan, L., and Husain, M.F. Media from Lecture Notes in Computer Science, *Proceedings of Intelligence and Security Informatics–Pacific Asia Workshop*, PAISI 2012, Kuala Lumpur, Malaysia, 7299, 2012, p. 1–26, © Springer, ISBN 978-3-642-30427-9.)

that are created for every unique predicate in an RDF graph, it also creates a separate triples file containing all the triples in the SPO (Subject, Predicate, Object) format. The advantage of having such a file is that it directly gives us all triples belonging to a certain subject or object. Recall that such a search operation required scanning through multiple files in the vertically partitioned layout. The storage space efficiency of this layout is not as good as the vertically partitioned layout due to the addition of the triples file. However, a SPARQL query to find all triples belonging to a certain subject or object could be performed more efficiently using this layout.

27.2.2.9 Distributed Processing of SPARQL

Query processing in CAISS++ comprises of several steps (Figure 27.12). The first step is query parsing and translation where a given SPARQL query is first parsed to verify syntactic correctness and then a parse tree corresponding to the input query is built. The parse tree is then translated into a SPARQL algebra expression. Since a given SPARQL query can have multiple equivalent SPARQL algebra expressions, we annotate each such expression with instructions on how to evaluate each operation in this expression. Such annotated SPARQL algebra expressions correspond to query-evaluation plans which serve as the input to the optimizer. The optimizer

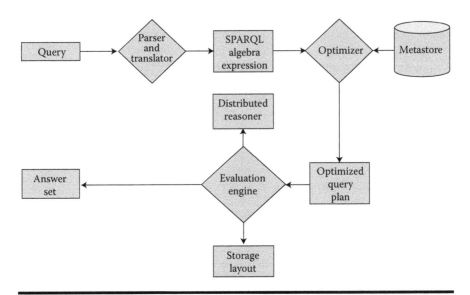

Figure 27.12 Distributed processing of SPARQL in CAISS++. (With kind permission from Springer Science+Business Media: Khadilkar, V ., Rachapalli, J., Cadenhead, T., Kantarcioglu, M., Hamlen, K.W., Khan, L., and Husain, M.F. Media from Lecture Notes in Computer Science, *Proceedings of Intelligence and Security Informatics–Pacific Asia Workshop*, PAISI 2012, Kuala Lumpur, Malaysia, 7299, 2012, p. 1–26, © Springer, ISBN 978-3-642-30427-9.)

selects a query plan that minimizes the cost of query evaluation. To optimize a query, an optimizer must know the cost of each operation. To compute the cost of each operation, the optimizer uses a Metastore that stores statistics associated with the RDF data. The cost of a given query-evaluation plan is alternatively measured in terms of the number of MapReduce jobs or the number of triples that will be accessed as a part of query execution. Once the query plan is chosen, the query is evaluated with that plan and the result of the query is output. Since we use a cloud-centric framework to store RDF data, an evaluation engine needs to convert SPARQL algebra operators into equivalent MapReduce jobs on the underlying storage layouts. Therefore, in CAISS++ we will implement a MapReduce job for each of the SPARQL algebra operators. Additionally, the evaluation engine uses a distributed reasoner to compute inferences required for query evaluation.

27.2.2.10 Framework Integration

The components that we have outlined that are a part of CAISS++ need to be integrated to work with another. Furthermore, this process of integration depends on a user's selection of one of the three possible design choices provided with CAISS++, namely, centralized CAISS++, decentralized CAISS++, or hybrid CAISS++. The integration of the various pieces of CAISS++ that have been presented so far needs to take into account several issues. First, we need to make sure that our ontology engineering process has been successful in capturing an agency's requirements and additionally, the ontologies can be stored in the storage schema used by the Hadoop Storage Architecture. Second, we need to ensure that the distributed SPARQL query processor is able to efficiently evaluate queries (i.e., user-generated SPARQL queries as well as SPARQL queries that evaluate policies) over the underlying RDF storage. Finally, we need to conduct a performance evaluation of CAISS++ to verify that it meets the performance requirements of various participating agencies as well as leads to significant performance advantages when compared with CAISS.

27.2.2.11 Policy Specification and Enforcement

The users of CAISS++ can use a language of their choice (e.g., XACML, RDF, Rei, etc.) to specify their information-sharing policies. These policies will be translated into a suitable sub-language of OWL using existing or custom-built translators. We will extend our policy engine for CAISS to handle policies specified in OWL. In addition to RDF policies, our current policy engine can handle policies in OWL for implementing role-based access control, inference control, and social network analysis.

27.2.3 Formal Policy Analysis

Our framework is applicable to a variety of mission-critical, high-assurance applications that span multiple possibly mutually distrusting organizations. To provide

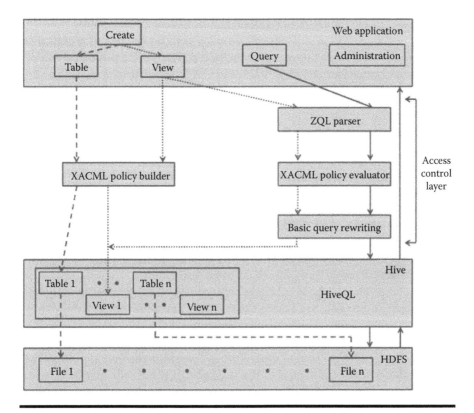

Figure 27.13 HIVE-based assured cloud query processing. (With kind permission from Springer Science+Business Media: Khadilkar, V ., Rachapalli, J., Cadenhead, T., Kantarcioglu, M., Hamlen, K.W., Khan, L., and Husain, M.F. Media from Lecture Notes in Computer Science, *Proceedings of Intelligence and Security Informatics–Pacific Asia Workshop*, PAISI 2012, Kuala Lumpur, Malaysia, 7299, 2012, p. 1–26, © Springer, ISBN 978-3-642-30427-9.)

maximal security assurance in such settings, it is important to establish strong formal guarantees regarding the correctness of the system and the policies it enforces. To that end, we examined the development of an infrastructure for constructing formal, machine-checkable proofs of important system properties, and policy analyses for our system. While machine-checkable proofs can be very difficult and time-consuming to construct for many large software systems, our choice of SPARQL, RDF, and OWL as query, ontology, and policy languages, opens unique opportunities to elegantly formulate such proofs in a logic programming environment. We will encode policies, policy-rewriting algorithms, and security properties as a rule-based, logical derivation system in Prolog, and will apply model-checking and theorem-proving systems such as ACL2 to produce machine-checkable proofs that these properties are obeyed by the system. Properties that we intend to consider in our model include soundness, transparency, consistency, and completeness. The results of our formal policy analysis will drive our detailed design and implementation of CAISS++. To our knowledge, none of the prior work has focused on such formal policy analysis for SPARQL, RDF, and OWL. Our extensive research on formal policy analysis with in-line reference monitors is discussed under related work.

27.2.4 Implementation Approach

The implementation of CAISS is being carried out in Java and is based on a flexible design where we can plug and play multiple components. A service provider and/or user will have the flexibility to use the SPARQL query processor as well as the RDF-based policy engine as separate components or combine them. The open source component used for CAISS will include the Pellet reasoner as well as our in-house tools such as the SPARQL query processor on the Hadoop/MapReduce framework and the cloud-centric RDF policy engine. CAISS will allow us to demonstrate basic AIS scenarios on our cloud-based framework.

In the implementation of CAISS++, we will again use Java as the programming language. We will use Protégé as our ontology editor during the process of ontology engineering which includes designing domain ontologies as well as the upper ontology. We will also evaluate several existing distributed reasoning algorithms such as WebPIE and QueryPIE to determine the best algorithm that matches an agency's requirements. The selected algorithm will then be used to perform reasoning over OWL-based security policies. Additionally, the design of the Hadoop Storage Architecture is based on Jena's SPARQL Database (SDB) architecture and will feature some of the functionalities that are available with Jena SDB. The SPARQL query engine will also feature a code written in Java. This code will consist of several modules including query parsing and translation, query optimization, and query execution. The query execution module will consist of MapReduce jobs for the various operators of the SPARQL language. Finally, our web-based user interface will make use of several components such as JBoss, EJB, JSF, among others.

27.3 Related Work

We will first provide an overview of our research directly relevant to our project and then discuss overall related work. We will also discuss product/technology competition.

27.3.1 Our Related Research

Note that much of our related research has been discussed in Chapters 13, 22, and 23. We summarize this research as well as discuss some other related research.

27.3.1.1 Secure Data Storage and Retrieval in the Cloud

We have built a web-based application that combines existing cloud computing technologies such as Hadoop, an open source distributed file system and Hive data warehouse infrastructure built on top of Hadoop with a XACML policy-based security mechanism to allow collaborating organizations to securely store and retrieve large amounts of data [THUR10], [HUSA11], [UTD1]. Figure 27.13 presents the architecture of our system. We use the services provided by the HIVE layer and Hadoop including the *Hadoop Distributed File System (HDFS)* layer that makes up the storage layer of Hadoop and allows the storage of data blocks across a cluster of nodes. The layers we have implemented include the web application layer, the ZQL parser layer, the XACML policy layer, and the query rewriting layer. The *Web Application layer* is the only interface provided by our system to the user to access the cloud infrastructure. The *ZQL Parser* [ZQL] layer takes as input any query submitted by a user and either proceeds to the XACML policy evaluator if the query is successfully parsed or returns an error message to the user. The *XACML Policy Layer* is used to build (XACML Policy Builder) and evaluate (XACML Policy Evaluation) XACML policies. The *Basic Query Rewriting Layer* rewrites SQL queries entered by the user. The *Hive* layer is used to manage relational data that is stored in the underlying Hadoop HDFS [THUS09]. In addition, we have also designed and implemented secure storage and query processing in a hybrid cloud [KHAD11].

27.3.1.2 Secure SPARQL Query Processing on the Cloud

We have developed a framework to query RDF data stored over Hadoop as shown in Figure 27.14. We used the Pellet reasoner to reason at various stages. We carried out real-time query reasoning using the pellet libraries coupled with Hadoop's MapReduce functionalities. Our RDF query processing is composed of two main steps: (1) the preprocessing and (2) the query optimization and execution.

27.3.1.2.1 Pre-Processing

To execute a SPARQL query on RDF data, we carried out data pre-processing steps and stored the pre-processed data in HDFS. A separate MapReduce task was written to perform the conversion of RDF/XML data into *N*-Triples as well as for prefix generation. Our storage strategy is based on predicate splits [HUSA11].

27.3.1.2.2 Query Execution and Optimization

We have developed a SPARQL query execution and optimization module for Hadoop. As our storage strategy is based on predicate splits, first, we examine the predicates present in the query. Second, we examine a subset of the input files that are matched with predicates. Third, SPARQL queries generally have many joins in them and all these joins may not be possible to be performed in a single map-reduce

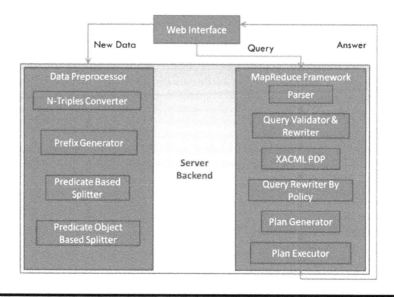

Figure 27.14   SPARQL-based assured cloud query processing. (With kind permission from Springer Science+Business Media: Khadilkar, V ., Rachapalli, J., Cadenhead, T., Kantarcioglu, M., Hamlen, K.W., Khan, L., and Husain, M.F. Media from Lecture Notes in Computer Science, *Proceedings of Intelligence and Security Informatics–Pacific Asia Workshop,* **PAISI 2012, Kuala Lumpur, Malaysia, 7299, 2012, p. 1–26, © Springer, ISBN 978-3-642-30427-9.)**

job. Therefore, we have developed an algorithm that decides the number of jobs required for each kind of query. As part of optimization, we applied a greedy strategy and cost-based optimization to reduce query processing time. We have also developed a XACML-based centralized policy engine that will carry out federated RDF query processing on the cloud. Details of the enforcement strategy are given in [HUSA11], [KHAL10], [HAMLl10a].

27.3.1.3 RDF Policy Engine

In our earlier work [CADE11a], we have developed a policy engine to process RDF-based access control policies for RDF data. The policy engine is designed with the following features on mind: scalability, efficiency, and interoperability. This framework (Figure 27.15) can be used to execute various policies, including access control policies and redaction policies. It can also be used as a testbed for evaluating different policy sets over RDF data and to view the outcomes graphically. Our framework presents an interface that accepts a high-level policy, which is then translated into the required format. It takes a user's input query and returns a response which has been pruned using a set of user-defined policy constraints. The architecture is built using a modular approach, therefore it is very flexible in that

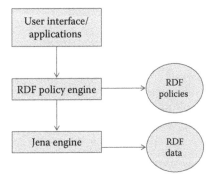

Figure 27.15   RDF policy engine.

most of the modules can be extended or replaced by another application module. For example, a policy module implementing a Discretionary Access Control (DAC) could be replaced entirely by a RBAC module or we may decide to enforce all our constraints based on a generalized redaction model. It should be noted that our policy engine also handles role-based access control policies specified in OWL and SWRL [CADE10]. In addition, it handles certain policies specified in OWL for inference control such as association-based policies where access to collections of entities is denied and logical policies where A implies B and if access to B is denied then access to A should also be denied [CADE10], [CADE11b], [CARM09]. This capability of our policy engine will be useful in our design and implementation of CAISS++ where information is shared across multiple clouds.

27.3.1.4 AIS Prototypes

We have developed multiple systems for AIS at UTD. In particular, we developed an XACML-based policy engine to function on top of relational databases and demonstrated the sharing of (simulated) medical data [THUR08]. In this implementation, we specified the policies in XACML and stored the data in multiple Oracle databases. When one organization requests data from another organization, the policies are examined and authorized data are released. In addition, we also conducted simulation studies on the amount of data that would be lost by enforcing the policies while sharing information. We have also conducted simulation studies for incentive-based information sharing [KANT10]. In addition, we have examined risk-based access control in an information-sharing scenario [CELI07]. In addition to access control policies, we have specified different types of policies including need-to-share policies and trust policies (e.g., A shared data with B provided B does not share the data with C). Note that the 9/11 commission report calls for the migration from the more restrictive need-to-know to the less restrictive need-to-share policies. These policies are key to support the specification of directive concerning AIS obligations. We have discussed our work on AIS in Appendix D.

27.3.1.5 Formal Policy Analysis

By reducing high-level security policy specifications and system models to the level of the denotational and operational semantics of their binary-level implementations, our past work has developed formally machine-certifiable security enforcement mechanisms of a variety of complex software systems, including those implemented in.NET [HAML06b], ActionScript [SRID10], Java [JONE10], and native code [HAML10b]. Working at the binary level provides extremely high formal guarantees because it permits the tool chain that produces mission-critical software components to remain untrusted; the binary code produced by the chain can be certified directly. This strategy is an excellent match for CAISS++ because data security specification languages such as XACML and OWL can be elegantly reflected down to the binary level of bytecode languages with XML-aware system APIs, such as Java bytecode. Our past work has applied binary-instrumentation (e.g., in-lined reference monitoring) and a combination of binary type-checking [HAML06b], model-checking [SRID10], and automated theorem proving (e.g., via ACL2) to achieve fully automated machine certification of binary software in such domains.

27.3.2 Overall Related Research

While there are some related efforts, none of the efforts have provided a solution to AIS in the cloud, nor have they conducted such a formal policy analysis.

27.3.2.1 Secure Data Storage and Retrieval in the Cloud

Security for cloud has received recent attention [TALB09]. Some efforts on implementing at the infrastructure level have been reported [OMAL09]. Such development efforts are an important step toward securing cloud infrastructures but are only in their inception stages. The goal of our system is to add another layer of security above the security offered by Hadoop [UTD1]. Once the security offered by Hadoop becomes robust, it will only strengthen the effectiveness of our system. Similar efforts have been undertaken by Amazon and Microsoft for their cloud computing offerings [AMAZ09], [MARS10]. However, this work falls in the public domain whereas our system is designed for a private cloud infrastructure. This distinguishing factor makes our infrastructure "trusted" over public infrastructures where the data must be stored in an encrypted format.

27.3.2.2 SPARQL Query Processor

Only a handful of efforts have been reported on SPARQL query processing. These include BioMANTA [BIOM11] and SHARD [SHAR11]. BioMANTA proposes extensions to RDF Molecules [DING05] and implements a MapReduce-based Molecule store [NEWM08]. They use MapReduce to answer the queries. They have queried a maximum of 4 million triples. Our work differs in the following ways: first, we have queried 1 billion triples. Second, we have devised a storage schema which is tailored to improve query execution performance for RDF data. To our knowledge, we are the first to come up with a storage schema for RDF data using flat files in HDFS, and a MapReduce job determination algorithm to answer a SPARQL query. SHARD (Scalable, High-Performance, Robust and Distributed) is an RDF triple store using the Hadoop Cloudera distribution. This project shows initial results demonstrating Hadoop's ability to improve scalability for RDF datasets. However, SHARD stores its data only in a triple store schema. It does no query planning or reordering, and its query processor will not minimize the number of Hadoop jobs. None of the efforts have incorporated security policies.

27.3.2.3 RDF-Based Policy Engine

There exists prior research devoted to the study of enforcingpolicies over RDF stores. These include the work in [CARM04], which uses RDF for policy specification and enforcement. In addition, the policies are generally written in RDF. In [JAIN06], the authors propose an access control model for RDF. Their model is based on RDF data semantics and incorporates RDF and RDF Schema (RDFS) entailments. Here, protection is provided at the resource level, which adds granularity to their framework. Other frameworks enforcing policies over RDF\OWL include [USZO04], [KAGA02]. [USZO04] describes KAoS, a policy and domain services framework that uses OWL, both to represent policies and domains. [KAGA02] introduces Rei, a policy framework that is flexible and allows different kinds of policies to be stated. Extensions to Rei have been proposed recently [KHAN10]. The policy specification language allows users to develop declarative policies over domain specific ontologies in RDF, DAML + OIL, and OWL. The authors in [REDD05] also introduced a prototype, RAP, for implementation of an RDF store with integrated maintenance capabilities and access control. These frameworks, however, do not address cases where the RDF store can become very large or the case where the policies do not scale with the data. Under an IARPA funded project, we have developed techniques for very large RDF graph processing [UTD2].

27.3.2.4 Hadoop Storage Architecture

There has been significant interest in large-scale distributed storage and retrieval techniques for RDF data. The theoretical designs of a parallel processing framework for RDF data are presented in the work done by Castagna et al. [CAST09]. This work advocates the use of a data distribution model with varying levels of granularity such as triple level, graph level, and dataset level. A query over such a distributed model is then divided into a set of sub-queries over machines containing the distributed data. The results of all sub-queries will then be merged to return a complete result to a user application. Several implementations of this theoretical concept exist in the research community. These efforts include the work done by

Choi et al. [CHOI09] and Abraham et al. [ABRA10]. A separate technique that has been used to store and retrieve RDF data makes use of peer-to-peer systems [ABER04], [CAI04], [HART07], and [VALL06]. However, there are some drawbacks with such systems as peer-to-peer systems need to have super peers that store information about the distribution of RDF data among the peers. Another disadvantage is a need to federate a SPARQL query to every peer in the network.

27.3.2.5 Distributed Reasoning

InteGrail system uses distributed reasoning, whose vision is to shape the European railway organization of the future [INTE09]. In [URBA09], authors have shown a scalable implementation of RDFS reasoning based on MapReduce which can infer 30 billion triples from a real-world dataset in less than 2 h, yielding an input and output throughput of 123.000 triples/s and 3.27 million triples/s, respectively. They have presented some nontrivial optimizations for encoding the RDFS ruleset in MapReduce and have evaluated the scalability of their implementation on a cluster of 64 compute nodes using several real-world datasets.

27.3.2.6 Access Control and Policy Ontology Modeling

There have been some attempts to model access control and policy models using semantic web technologies. In [CIRI07], authors have shown how OWL and Description Logic can be used to build an access control system. They have developed a high-level OWL-DL ontology that expresses the elements of a role-based access control system and have built a domain-specific ontology that captures the features of a sample scenario. Finally, they have joined these two artifacts to take into account attributes in the dentition of the policies and in the access control decision. In [REUL10], authors first presented a security policy ontology based on the DOGMA which is a formal ontology engineering framework. This ontology covers the core elements of security policies (i.e., Condition, Action, Resource) and can easily be extended to represent specific security policies, such as access control policies. In [ANDE09], the authors present an ontologically motivated approach to multi-level access control and provenance for information systems.

27.3.3 Commercial Developments

27.3.3.1 RDF Processing Engines

Research and commercial RDF processing engines include Jena by HP labs, BigOWLIM and RDF-3X. Although the storage schemas and query processing mechanisms for some of these tools are proprietary, they are all based on some type of indexing strategy for RDF data. However, only a few tools exist that use a cloud-centric architecture for processing RDF data and moreover, these tools are not scalable to a very large number of triples. In contrast, our query processor in CAISS++ will be built as a planet-scale

RDF processing engine that supports all SPARQL operators and will provide optimized execution strategies for SPARQL queries and can scale to billions of triples.

27.3.3.2 Semantic Web-Based Security Policy Engines

As stated in Section 27.3.2, the current work on semantic web-based policy specification and enforcement does not address the issues of policy generation and enforcement for massive amounts of data and support large number of users.

27.3.3.3 Cloud

To the best of our knowledge, there is no significant commercial competition for cloud-centric AIS. Since we have taken a modular approach to the creation of our tools, we can iteratively refine each component (policy engine, storage architecture, and query processor) separately. Owing to the component-based approach we have taken, we will be able to adapt to changes in the platforms we use (e.g., Hadoop, RDF, OWL, and SPARQL) without having to depend on the particular features of a given platform.

27.4 Summary and Directions

This chapter has described our design of a cloud-based information-sharing system called CAISS. CAISS utilizes several of the technologies we have developed as well as open source tools. We also described the design of an ideal cloud-based assured information-sharing system called CAISS++.

We have implemented versions of CAISS. In the first implementation of CAISS we utilized our SPARQL query processor with the policies specified in XACML. This is more or less the system described in Chapter 23. In the second prototype we specified policies in RDF, developed the policy engine in the cloud and integrated it with the data engine. This system is discussed in Chapter 28 (see also [CADE12a], [CADE12b]). In the future we will continue to enhance our prototype by implementing more complex policies. Pour policies include both access control policies as well as information-sharing policies. We will also carry out a formal analysis of the execution of the policies. Our ultimate goal is to implement CAISS++.

References

[ABRA10] Brazier, A., C. Navarro, and A. Piazza. Distributed storage and querying techniques for a semantic web of scientific workflow provenance. *Proceedings IEEE SCC*, Miami, FL, 2010.

[ABER04] Aberer, K. P., P. Cudfe-Mauroux, M. Hauswirth, and T. Van Pelt. GridVine: Building Internet-scale semantic overlay networks. *International Semantic Web Conference*, Hiroshima, Japan, 2004.

[AMAZ09] Amazon Web Services: Overview of Security Processes. http://awsmedia.s3.amazonaws.com/pdf/AWSSecurityWhitepaper.pdf

[ANDE09] Andersen, B. and F. Neuhaus. An ontological approach to information access control and provenance. *Proceedings of Ontology for the Intelligence Community*, Fairfax, VA, October 2009.

[AWAD10] Khan, A. and B. M. Thuraisingham. Policy enforcement system for inter-organizational data sharing. *Journal of Information Security and Privacy*, 4(3): 22–39, 2010.

[BIOM11] BioMANTA: Modelling and analysis of biological network activity. http://www. itee.uq.edu.au/reresearch/projects/biomanta.

[CADE10] Cadenhead, T., M. Kantarcioglu, and B. M. Thuraisingham. Scalable and efficient reasoning for enforcing role-based access control. *Proceedings of Data and Applications Security and Privacy XXIV, 24th Annual IFIP Working Group 11.3 Working Conference*, Rome, Italy, p. 209–224, 2010.

[CADE11a] Cadenhead, T., V. Khadilkar, M. Kantarcioglu, and B. M. Thuraisingham. Transforming provenance using redaction. *Proceedings of ACM Symposium on Access Control Models and Technologies*, Innsbruck, Austria, p. 93–102, 2011.

[CADE11b] Cadenhead, T., V. Khadilkar, M. Kantarcioglu, and B. M. Thuraisingham. A language for provenance access control. *Proceedings of ACM Conference on Data Application Security and Privacy*, San Antonio, TX, 133–144, 2011.

[CADE12a] Cadenhead, T., V. Khadilkar, M. Kantarcioglu, and B. M. Thuraisingham. A cloud-based RDF policy engine for assured information sharing. *Proceedings of ACM Symposium on Access Control Models and Technologies*, Newark, NJ, 113–116, 2012.

[CADE12b] Cadenhead, T., M. Kantarcioglu, V. Khadilkar, and B. M. Thuraisingham. Design and implementation of a cloud-based assured information sharing system. *Proc. of Intl. Conf. on Mathematical Methods, Models and Architectures for Computer Network Security*, St. Petersburg, Russia, 36–50, 2012.

[CARM04] Carminati, B., E. Ferrari, and B. M. Thuraisingham. Using RDF for policy specification and enforcement. *Proc. of Intl. Workshop on Database and Expert Systems Applications*, Zaragoza, Spain, p. 163–167, 2004.

[CARM09] Carminati, B., E. Ferrari, R. Heatherly, M. Kantarcioglu, and B. M. Thuraisingham. A semantic web based framework for social network access control. *Proc. of ACM Symposium on Access Control Models and Technologies*, Stresa, Italy, 177–186, 2009.

[CAI04] Cai, M. and M. Frank. RDFPeers: A scalable distributed RDF repository based on a structured peer-to-peer network. *Proceedings ACM World Wide Web Conference*, New York, NY, 2004.

[CELI07] Celikel, E., M. Kantarcioglu, and B. M. Thuraisingham, ElisaBertino. Managing risks in RBAC employed distributed environments. *On the Move to Meaningful Internet Systems*, Vilamoura, Portugal, (2): 2007.

[CAST09] Castagna, P., A. Seaborne, and C. Dollin. A parallel processing framework for RDF design and issues. Technical report, HP Laboratories, HPL-2009-346, 2009.

[CHOI09] Choi, H., J. Son, Y. Cho, M. Sung, and Y. Chung. SPIDER: A system for scalable, parallel/distributed evaluation of large-scale RDF data. *Proceedings ACM Conference on Information and Knowledge Management (CIKM)*, Hong Kong, China, 2087–2088, 2009.

[CIRI07] Cirio, L., I. Cruz, and R. Tamassia. A role and attribute based access control system using semantic web technologies. *IFIP Workshop on Semantic Web and Web Semantics*, Vilamoura, Algarve, Portugal, 2007.

[DING05] Ding, L., T. Finin, Y. Peng, P. da Silva, and D. Mcguinness. Tracking RDF graph provenance using RDF molecules. *Proc. International Semantic Web Conference*, Galway, Ireland, 2005.

[DoD] DoD Information Enterprise Strategic Plan, 2010-2012, http://cio-nii.defense.gov/docs/DodIESP-r16.pdf

[DoD07] Department of Defense Information Sharing Strategy, 2007.

[DoD09] DoD mbraced Cloud Computing, http://www.defensemarket.com/?p=67

[FINI09] Finin, T., A. Joshi, H. Kargupta, Y. Yesha, J. Sachs, E. Bertino, Li et al., Assured information sharing life cycle. *Proc. Intelligence and Security Informatics*, 2009.

[GUO05] Guo, Y., J. Heflin, and Z. Pan. LUBM: A benchmark for OWL knowledge base systems. *Web Semantics*, 3(2-3), 158–182, 2005.

[HAML06a] Hamlen, K., G. Morrisett, and F. Schneider. Computability classes for enforcement mechanisms. *ACM Transactions on Programming Languages and Systems*, 28(1): 175–205, 2006.

[HAML06b] Hamlen, K., G. Morrisett, and F. Schneider. Certified in-lined reference monitoring on.NET. *Proc. ACM Workshop on Prog. Lang. and Analysis for Security*, pp. 7–16, Ottawa, Canada, 2006.

[HAML10b] Hamlen, K., V. Mohan, and R. Wartell. Reining in Windows API abuses with in-lined reference monitors. Tech. Rep. UTDCS-18–10, Computer Science Dept., University of Texas at Dallas, 2010.

[HART07] Harth, A., J. Umbrich, A. Hogan, and S. Decker. YARS2: A federated repository for searching and querying graph structured data. *Intl. Semantic Web Conference*, Busan, Korea, 2007.

[HUSA11] Husain, M., J. McGlothlin, M. Masud, L. Khan, and B. M. Thuraisingham. Heuristics-based query processing for large RDF graphs using cloud computing. *IEEE Trans. Knowl. Data Eng.*, 23, 1312–1327, 2011.

[INTE09] Distributed reasoning: Seamless integration and processing of distributed knowledge. http://www.integrail.eu/documents/fs04.pdf.

[JAIN06] Jain, A. and C. Farkas. Secure resource description framework: An access control model. *ACM Symposium on Access Control Models and Technologies*, Lake Tahoe, CA, 2006.

[JONE10] Jones, M. and K. Hamlen. Disambiguating aspect-oriented security policies. *Proc. 9th Int. Conf. Aspect-Oriented Software Development*, Rennes and St. Malo, France, pp. 193–204, 2010.

[JONE11] Jones, M. and K. Hamlen. A service-oriented approach to mobile code security. *Proc. 8th Int. Conf. Mobile Web Information Systems*, (MobiWIS) Niagara Falls, Ontario, Canada, 2011.

[KAGA02] Kagal, L. REI., A policy language for the project, http://www.hpl.hp.com/techreports/2002/HPL-2002-270.pdf. 2002

[KANT10] Kantarcioglu, M. Incentive-based assured information sharing, *AFOSR MURI Review*, October 2010.

[KHAD11] Khadilkar, V., M. Kantarcioglu, and B. M. Thuraisingham. Mehrotra: Secure data processing in a hybrid cloud. *Proc. Computing Research Repository/1105.1982*, May 2011.

[KHAL10] Khaled, A., M. Husain, L. Khan, K. Hamlen, and B. M. Thuraisingham. A token-based access control system for RDF data in the clouds. *CloudCom2010*, Indianapolis, IN.

[KHAN10] Khandelwal, A., J. Bao, L. Kagal, I. Jacobi, L. Ding, and J. Hendler. Analyzing the AIR language: A semantic web (production) rule language. *Intl. Conf. on Web Reasoning and Rule Systems*, Bressanone, Brixen, Italy, 58–72, 2010.

[MARS10] Marshall, A., M. Howard, G. Bugher, and B. Harden. Security best practices in developing Windows Azure applications. *Microsoft Corp.* 2010.

[MEWM08] Newman, A., J. Hunter, Y. Li, C. Bouton, and M. Davis. A scale-out RDF molecule store for distributed processing of biomedical data. *Semantic Web for Health Care and Life Sciences Workshop, World Wide Web Conference*, Beijing, China, 2008.

[NSA11] *Information Week*, NSA pursues intelligence-sharing architecture, http://www.informationweek.com/news/government/cloud-saas/229401646. 2011.

[OMAL09] O'Malley, D., K. Zhang, S. Radia, R. Marti, and C. Harrell. Hadoop Security Design. http://techcat.org/wp-content/uploads/2013/04/hadoop-security-design.pdf. 2009.

[RAO08] Rao, P., D. Lin, E. Bertino, N. Li, and J. Lobo. EXAM: An environment for access control policy analysis and management. *IEEE Workshop on Policies for Distributed Systems and Networks (POLICY)*, Palisades, NY, 2008.

[REDD05] Reddivari, P., A. Joshi, and T. Finin. Policy-based access control for an RDF store. *Policy Management for the Web, IJCAI Workshop*, Chiba, Japan, 2005.

[REUL10] Reul, Q., G. Zhao, and R. Meersman. Ontology-based access control policy interoperability. *Proc. 1st Conference on Mobility, Individualisation, Socialisation and Connectivity*, MISC, London, UK, 2010.

[SHAR11] SHARD. http://www.cloudera.com/blog/2010/03/how-raytheonresearchers-are-using-hadoop-to-build-a-scalable-distributed-triplestore.

[SRID10] Sridhar, M. and R. Hamlen. Model-checking in-lined reference monitors. *Proc. 11th Int. Conf. on Verification, Model Checking, and Abstract Interpretation*, Madrid, Spain, pp. 312–327, 2010.

[TALB09] Talbot, D. How secure is cloud computing, 2009, http://www.technologyreview.com/computing/23951/

[THUR08] Thuraisingham, B. M., H. Kumar, and L. Khan. Design and implementation of a framework for assured information sharing across organizational boundaries. *Journal of Information Security and Privacy*, 2(4): 67–90, 2008.

[THUR10] Thuraisingham, B. M., V. Khadilkar, A., Gupta, M. Kantarcioglu, and Khan. Secure data storage and retrieval in the cloud. *CollaborateCom*, Chicago, IL, 2010.

[THUR11] Thuraisingham, B. M. and V. Khadilkar. Assured information sharing in the cloud. *UTD Tech. Report.* Sept. 2011.

[THUS09] Thusoo, A., J. Sharma, N. Jain, Z. Shao, P. Chakka, S. Anthony, H. Liu, P. Wyckoff, and R. Murthy. Hive—A warehousing solution over a map-reduce framework. *Proceedings of VLDB Endowment*, 2009.

[THUR12] Thuraisingham, B. M., V. Khadilkar, J. Rachapalli, T. Cadenhead, M. Kantarcioglu, K. W. Hamlen, L. Khan, and M. F. Husain. Cloud-centric assured information sharing. *PAISI*, Kuala Lumpur, Malaysia, 2012, 1–26.

[URBA09] Urbani. Scalable Distributed Reasoning using MapReduce. http://www.few.vu.nl/~jui200/papers/ISWC09-Urbani.pdf.

[USZO04] Uszok, Bradshaw, Johnson, Jeffers, Tate, Dalton, and Aitken. KAoS policy management for semantic web services. *IEEE Intelligent Systems*, 19(4): 32–41, 2004.

[UTD1] UTD Secure Cloud Repository, http://cs.utdallas.edu/secure-cloud-repository/

[UTD2] UTD Semantic Web Repository, http://cs.utdallas.edu/semanticweb/

[VALL06] Valle, E., A. Turati, and A. Ghioni. AGE: A distributed infrastructure for fostering RDF-based interoperability. *Proceedings Distributed Applications and Inter-Operable Systems (DAIS)*, Bologna, Italy, 2006.

[ZQL] Zql: A Java SQL parser. http://www.gibello.com/code/zql/

Chapter 28

Design and Implementation of a Semantic Cloud-Based Assured Information Sharing System

28.1 Overview

The cloud computing paradigm enables the sharing of large amounts of data securely and efficiently. Furthermore, the advent of *cloud computing* and the continuing movement toward *software as a service* (SaaS) paradigms has posed an increasing need for *assured information sharing* (AIS) as a service in the cloud. To satisfy the cloud-centric AIS needs of coalition organization, there is a critical need to develop an AIS framework that operates in the cloud. To our knowledge, no such system currently exists. In Chapter 27 [THUR12], we described the design of a system called CAISS: a Cloud Centric Assured Information Sharing System (CAISS) that utilizes the technology components we have designed in-house as well as open source tools. CAISS consists of two components: a cloud-centric policy manager that enforces policies specified in RDF [KLYN04], and a cloud-centric data manager that will store and manage data also specified in RDF. This RDF data manager is essentially a query engine for SPARQL, a language widely used by the semantic web community to query RDF data. RDF is a semantic web language that is considerably more expressive than XML-based policy languages for specifying and reasoning about policies. Furthermore, our policy manager and data manager will have seamless integration since they both manage RDF data.

While the systems discussed in the previous chapter (e.g., CAISS, CAISS++) were in the design stages, in this chapter, we describe the detailed design and implementation of AIS in a semantic cloud. That is, we have used semantic web technologies for providing cloud-based semantic web services. These semantic web services enable information sharing. This is more or less the CAISS system described in Chapter 27. We have essentially developed a comprehensive AIS framework that seamlessly operates in the cloud. Our framework consists of a three-layer architecture that comprises of a user interface layer, a policy engine layer, and a data connection layer that integrates multiple data sources in the cloud. To our knowledge this is the first of its kind of AIS framework that operates in the cloud. We describe the detailed design and implementation of our system in Section 28.2. In particular, the system architecture, its operations, its modules, and usage are discussed. This chapter concludes with a discussion of future work in Section 28.3.

28.2 Architecture

28.2.1 Overview

Our policy engine framework is driven by RDF configuration documents, which encode the logic of the policy engines and their usage, the user interface layouts and customizable parameters, and the mappings of dereferenceable Uris to the data stores using the available data connections. Our policy engine framework can be used as a key enabler in augmenting security for RDBMS's (Relational Database Management System), as well as cloud-based systems. RDBMS's are developed with atomicity, concurrency, and durability in mind, but are normally shipped with limited support for access control. A cloud storage layer allows the agencies to store and scale policies with finer levels of control over RDF resources. The cloud was developed with scalability and availability in mind, but security considerations were neglected. Our policy engine can be configured to complement policies in a RDBMS system with an entry point for supporting security policies over cloud-based backends. We first present an overview of the configuration of the framework. Then we define the layers in our architecture, and finally, we provide a description of the novel features of our implementation. Figure 28.1 illustrates our architecture and Figure 28.2 illustrates our configuration framework.

28.2.2 Framework Configuration

A loosely coupled system provides easy configuration and flexibility to our RDF policy engine framework. Each component is abstracted from the others by

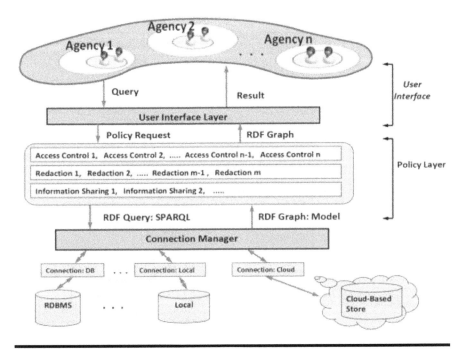

Figure 28.1 Architecture. (With kind permission from Springer Science+Business Media: Cadenhead, T., Kantarcioglu, M., and Khadilkar, V., Design and Implementation of a Cloud-Based Assured Information Sharing System, Media from Lecture Notes in Computer Science, *Proceedings of Computer Network Security–6th International Conference on Mathematical Methods, Models and Architectures for Computer Network Security, MMM-ACNS 2012*, St. Petersburg, Russia, 7531, 2012, p. 36–50. © Springer.)

employing RDF documents consisting of an agency's preferences for a policy or data connection to a data store. Furthermore, a loosely coupled web front-end promotes easier maintenance and reusability of the policy framework, since an adapter pattern abstracts the mapping of the web interfaces (and communications) to the other layers. An abstraction hides the actual implementation and intricacies of the policy engine manager and data managers from the agencies. This therefore allows agencies to specify their policies in any representation languages, such as XML, RDF, or REI [KAGA02]; an adapter hides the translation of high-level policy specification to policy implementation.

28.2.3 Modules in our Architecture

Our system architecture consists of three layers. At the front end, we have a user interface; the middle layer consists of our policy engine logic; and at the backend, we have our data stores. We provide a discussion of these modules next.

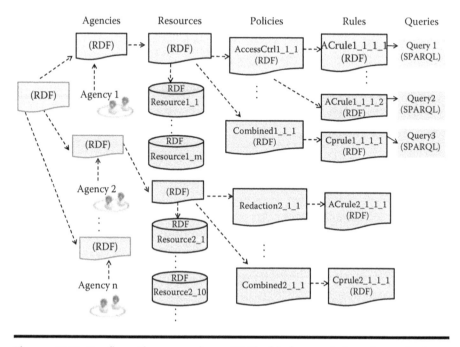

Figure 28.2 Configuration overview. (With kind permission from Springer Science+Business Media: Cadenhead, T., Kantarcioglu, M., and Khadilkar, V., Design and Implementation of a Cloud-Based Assured Information Sharing System, Media from Lecture Notes in Computer Science, *Proceedings of Computer Network Security–6th International Conference on Mathematical Methods, Models and Architectures for Computer Network Security, MMM-ACNS 2012*, St. Petersburg, Russia, 7531, 2012, p. 36–50. © Springer.)

28.2.3.1 User Interface Layer

To enable a one-to-one interaction with our framework, a web-based user interface is built on top of the policy layer. Rich client and open source web technologies simplify the interactions between users, web pages, and the underlying policy and data layers. This integration has many advantages. The policy framework operates in a distributed environment and has a greater geographical spread; therefore, agencies and users have mobility. The web interface requires users to create an account (also a registration) and choose unique credentials, which will then be used by the users to identify them to the policy framework. A form-based authentication pattern, as well as a challenge-response test distinguishes legitimate users from robots (which may pose as normal users). The legitimate users are presented with a querying screen that allows them to compose SPARQL queries once they have been authenticated. Note that SPARQL [PRUD06] is a query language for RDF and is used for retrieving data from triple stores. The SPARQL queries are validated and then sent to our policy engine layer, which in turn returns a resultant RDF graph that is then displayed on a web page.

28.2.3.1.1 User Registration

The User Registration presents the user the opportunity to register with the system using a web registration form. The registration form captures the user's name, password, and other metadata about the user. Metadata could be an agency that the user is a part of, or data that is used for mapping the user's credentials to a role, which is to be performed by the user. The following RDF graph displays contents from a user configuration file. The final triple in the RDF graph contains a dereferenceable *URI* to another RDF graph, which then contains a list of dereferenceable Uris of the actual resources that the user is allowed to query.

```
<http://policy.org/agency/pol#users>
    pol:user <http://policy.org/agency/pol#user1>.

# resources
<http://policy.org/agency/pol#user1>
  pol:name "user1";
  pol:passwd "_:b1";
    pol:organization <http://policy.org/agency/pol#Agency1>;
    pol:resourcelist <http://example/users/resources/user1>.
```

28.2.3.1.2 Agency Registration

The Agency Registration comprises a sequence of web pages, each being a child page of the previous one. The process commences with an agency registering information to describe itself. First, an agency registers important metadata about itself. This metadata is an RDF document, which can be used to introduce one agency to another, and therefore, should be self-describing. Some example triples in this metadata could assert an agency's name, address, industry, affiliations, and so on. Second, an agency records its resources. A resource has a unique *URI*, which is a dereferenceable *URI* to an agency's RDF document, which contains both the sensitive and nonsensitive data for the agency; this is the information that is normally stored in a relational database, but is now migrated to the cloud. Third, an agency defines the policies for its resources. An agency may choose among the various policies that are supported at the policy engine layer. Examples of policies are access control, redaction, information sharing, and so on. Fourth, an agency describes various policy rules for a policy. Note that an agency may use access control to protect its resources; however, the agency may need more than one rule for a particular policy choice. For example, one access control rule may specify a positive authorization, while another may specify a negative authorization on the same resource. Finally, an agency specifies queries. It is a very popular technique to write policy rules as views (i.e., SPARQL queries) over a data store. An agency may specify in its policy rule configuration document that queries be materialized or that they be nonmaterialized. A materialized query may speed up the policy execution, while a nonmaterialized query refreshes the result set in real time.

28.2.3.2 Policy Engines

The *Policy Engine Layer* first evaluates the user queries against the stored data resources (which can be traditional data, or provenance metadata). A data resource is characterized by a uniform resource identifier (URI), which connects to an actual RDF graph in the data storage layer. The policy layer uses a factory object to create the underlying policies. The factory exposes a policy through a consistent interface, thus making it easy to extend our policy engine to support other types of policies in the future. We currently support access control, redaction, and information-sharing policies. To support traditional policies, we use SPARQL queries to define views over resources, where a view can be associated with positive and negative authorizations or a target in a subgraph replacement procedure. An important metadata is provenance, which records the history of a piece of data item. However, provenance takes on a Directed Acyclic Graph (DAG) structure, and as such requires its own policies [BRAU08]. Therefore, we support the use of regular expression SPARQL queries for access control policies [CADE11a], as well as redaction policies [CADE11b]. We have also implemented information-sharing policies over data and provenance that allow cooperating agencies to share information based on mutual agreements [CADE12].

An agile environment pushes policy designers to constantly fine tune or extend their policies to rapidly adapt to ever-changing conditions, thus ensuring that data integrating and combinations does not violate data confidentiality, especially when quick actions are critical (e.g., in intelligence). To meet this demand, our policy engine layer supports many policy engines, while the cloud supports many policy configuration documents.

A policy engine takes as input a user's credential and a dereferenceable *URI*; it then evaluates the underlying logic of a policy before returning a new RDF graph (or model) to the user interface layer. The dereferenceable *URI* points to a configuration document, which itself contains other dereferenceable Uris to the policies about an agency's resource and to the agency's resource at the data layer. An agency's resource is an RDF document, with triples at one or more classification levels; for example, an entire RDF document would be classified as sensitive in case it contains intelligence information, or some subset of triples may have actual intelligence information. An agency therefore requires more than one type of policy to achieve fine grain control over its resources. A policy is therefore defined by an interface, which allows the implementation of the logic of each policy. The policy engine evaluates the underlying logic of a policy before returning a new RDF graph (or model) to the user interface layer. By migrating its policies to the cloud, an agency overcomes the restriction on the number of policy definitions previously possible. The following subsections summarize various policy types. In the subsections below, we discuss the details of the policy engine layer. This layer comprises of many policy types, for example, access control, redaction, information sharing, to name a few. We will also motivate the need for a flexible policy engine by discussing each of these policy types in turn.

28.2.3.2.1 Access Control Policy Engine

An access control policy authorizes a set of *users* to perform a set of *actions* on a set of *resources* within an *environment*. Unless authorized through one or more access control policies, users have no access to any resource of the system. There are different kinds of access control policies, which can be grouped into three main classes [SAMA01]. These policies differ by the constraints they place on the sets of *users*, *actions*, and *objects* (access control models often refer to *resources* as *objects*). These classes are (1) RBAC, which restricts access based on roles; (2) discretionary access control (DAC), which controls access based on the identity of the user; and (3) mandatory access control (MAC), which controls access based on mandated regulations determined by a central authority.

Policies based on RBAC are often used to simplify the management of policy mappings, which is a common feature in the three classes of access control policies. Policy creation and manageability are important in getting finer levels of access control over the shared resources. We use the convention that a permission is a unique pair of (*action, resource*). Given n resources, m users, and a set of only two actions (read, write), we have a maximum of $2 \times n$ possible permissions. This gives $m \times (2 \times n) = c_1 n$ mappings. A further improvement of RBAC is the case where there is at least one role with two or more users assigned to it, from a possible set of r roles. Therefore, we have $r \times (2 \times n) = c_2 n$ mappings and we also assume that $c_2 \leq c_1$. However, even with this simplification, the number of policies needed to achieve finer levels of access control in a dynamic and agile community may be intractable. Our cloud-centric policy framework addresses this by providing the agencies the ability to support and scale their access control policies to meet their ever-growing security needs.

28.2.3.2.2 Redaction Policy Engine

A redaction policy identifies and removes sensitive information from a document before releasing it to a user. Unlike access control policies, which restricts access, redaction policies encourage sharing of information, by ensuring that sensitive or proprietary information is removed (or obscured) before providing the final RDF graph (referred to as a redacted graph) to a user's query. Redaction policies rely on a transformation operation to circumvent any identifying or sensitive information. The redaction policy engines currently supported rely on a graph transformation technique that is based on a graph grammar approach (which is presented in [EHRI06], [ROZE97]. Basically, there are two steps to applying a redaction policy over a directed labeled RDF graph: (i) Identify a resource (or subgraph) in the original RDF graph that we want to protect. This can be done with a graph query (i.e., a query equipped with regular expressions). (ii) Apply a redaction policy to this identified resource in the form of a graph transformation rule. An implementation of this graph transformation is used in [CADE11b] for redacting provenance graphs.

28.2.3.2.3 Information-Sharing Policy Engine

An information-sharing policy allows agencies to determine the context in which their resources are shared or combined with resources from other agencies. An information-sharing policy engine has logic for processing a query requesting information on two or more RDF graphs simultaneously. We illustrate this using the following SPARQL query.

SELECT $\vec{B}$ FROM NAMED uri1 FROM NAMED uri2 WHERE P,

where P is a graph pattern, $\vec{B}$ is a tuple of variables appearing in P and uri1 and uri2 are dereferenceable URIs for two resources, R1 and R2. Resources R1 and R2 may be from the same agency, in case an agency strictly requires a partitioning of its resources based on confidentiality concerns or they could belong to two agencies, agency 1 and agency 2, respectively. Therefore, each of these resources may define individual information-sharing policy rules. We define an operator ⊙, so that an information-sharing policy is now evaluated over uri1 ⊙ uri2. The operator ⊙ can be implemented as a graph operation over a RDF graph. Note that, ⊙, could be one of the following operators: ∩, ∪, or − and can also be applied to an original RDF graph or to previous one, which resulted from the operator, ⊙. In order to execute the operator, ⊙, we define a graph recursively as follows.

- ε is a graph.
- The set of graphs are closed under intersection, union, and set difference. Let G_1 and G_1 be two graphs, then $G_1[G_2, G_1\backslash G_2$ and $G_1 - G_2$ are graphs, such that if $t \in G_1[G_2$ then $t \in G_1$ or $t \in G_2$; if $t \in G_1[G_2$ then $t \in G_1$ and $t \in G_2$; or if $t \in G_1 - G_2$ then $t \in G_1$ and $t \notin G_2$.

The following RDF graph lists the triples of a combined policy configuration document containing policies with embedded logic for sharing two resources, R1 and R2, which belong to two agencies, agency 1 and agency 2, respectively.

```
# entity
<http://policy.org/entity/pol#Combined1_1_1>
  pol:owner <http://policy.org/entity/pol#Agency1>;
    pol:rule <http://policy.org/entity/pol#Cprule1_1_1_1>.

# mappings
<http://policy.org/entity/pol#Cprule1_1_1_1>
  pol:agency < http://policy.org/entity/pol#Agency2 >;
    pol:operator "UNION";
    pol:type "combined1".
```

This policy works at the level of the agencies. For example, agency 1 shares all its resources as a union with all of agency 2 resources. The policy type allows an agency to have modes of sharing. For example, a type *combined*1 provides sharing at the agency level, while another policy type, *combined*2, could offer a finer level of control in determining how agency 1 shares each of its resources with a classification of a resource for agency 2. In other words, information-sharing policies can incorporate contextual information about an agency and metadata about each of its resources at the resource level. The following shows two policy types for our information-sharing policies:

1. *Combined 1.* $\forall r1 \in Agency1, \forall r2 \in Agency2$, use r1 $\cup$ r2. This policy states that Agency 1 shares all its resources with agency 2 as a union of the resources.
2. *Combined 2.* let $r1_1, r1_2, \ldots, r1_n \in$ Agency1, use, $r1_1[r2, r1_1 \backslash r2 \; \forall r2 \in Agency2$. This policy offers a finer level of control.

28.2.3.2.4 Provenance Policy Engines

Sometimes the relationships among the triples in an RDF graph need be taken into consideration, when defining policies. The three policy types discussed so far, fail to address the cases where sensitive information is implicit in the various paths within a RDF graph. We will explore other policy engines in this section. The focus will be on the definition of policy engines tailored to the execution of access control and redaction policies over a provenance graph. We will base the logic of these policy engines on [CADE11a], which discusses an access control policy language for provenance and [CADE12], which discusses how to perform redaction over provenance. We will first give an example of a provenance graph and the type of provenance information which may exist in the example provenance graph. Then we will present brief definitions of some of the theory behind executing policies over a provenance graph.

Figure 28.3 shows an intelligence example as a provenance graph using a RDF representation that outlines a flow of a document through a server located in some unfriendly territory (or at another agency posing a potential threat). This document was given to a journalist. The contents of this provenance graph could serve to evaluate the trustworthiness of the servers (i.e., processes in the example graph) from which the document originated. This example provenance graph also shows the base skeleton of the actual provenance, which is usually annotated with RDF triples indicating contextual information, for example, time and location. Note that the predicates (i.e., arcs) are labeled with the OPM abstract predicate [MORE10] labels and that the final report can be traced back to a CIA agent.

The information embedded in the graph in Figure 28.2 represents a directed RDF graph. A provenance path in Figure 28.3 is defined as follows:

Definition 28.1

(Provenance Path) Given a provenance graph, a provenance path (s p o) is a path $s \xrightarrow{p} o$ *that is defined over the provenance vocabulary V using regular expressions.*

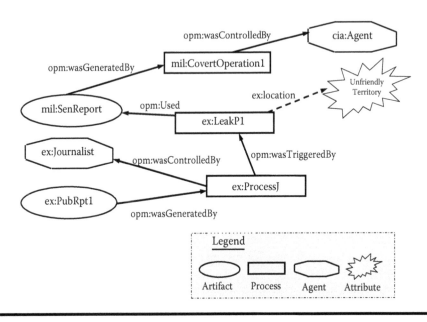

Figure 28.3 Provenance graph. (With kind permission from Springer Science+Business Media: Cadenhead, T., Kantarcioglu, M., and Khadilkar, V., Design and Implementation of a Cloud-Based Assured Information Sharing System, Media from Lecture Notes in Computer Science, *Proceedings of Computer Network Security–6th International Conference on Mathematical Methods, Models and Architectures for Computer Network Security*, MMM-ACNS 2012, St. Petersburg, Russia, 7531, 2012, p. 36–50. © Springer.)

Definition 28.2

(Regular Expressions) Let Σ *be an alphabet of terms in V, then the set RE(Σ) of regular expressions is inductively defined by:*

- $\forall x \in \Sigma, x \in RE(\Sigma)$;
- $\Sigma \in RE(\Sigma)$;
- $\varepsilon \in RE(\Sigma)$;
- If $A \in RE(\Sigma)$ and $B \in RE(\Sigma)$ then:
- $A|B, A/B, A^*, A^+, A? \in RE(\Sigma)$

The symbols | and/are interpreted as logical OR and composition, respectively.

Our intention is to define paths between two nodes by edges equipped with*for paths of arbitrary length, including length 0 or + for paths that have at least length 1. Therefore, for two nodes x, y, and predicate name p, $x(\overset{p}{\rightarrow})^* y$ and $x(\overset{p}{\rightarrow})^+ y$ are paths in G.

A SPARQL query extended with regular expressions [HARRI10] can define a resource (or subgraph) of the provenance graph in Figure 28.3 as follows:

EXAMPLE 28.1 (PROVENANCE PATH QUERY)

Select ?x
    {ex:PubRpt1 arq:OnPath("([opm:WasGeneratedBy]/
       [opm:WasTriggeredBy]/[ex:location])" ?x).}

This query would return the location as a binding to the variable *x* and could be used to pinpoint the origin of a compromise (and leakage) of the original report. This could also serve to alert policy designers to add appropriate policies for reports and servers in their respective agencies.

28.2.3.2.5 Policy Sequence

The execution of the policies over an agency's resource results in a policy sequence. In particular, a protected resource could employ the services of multiple policy engines and policy types. Each policy type produces a new subgraph of its input RDF graph. It is important to note that the effect of a policy is directly dependent on the RDF graph it receives as input, and furthermore, the effect may be different from the original effect the policy was intended to achieve. A sequence takes the original input graph through a series of transformations until a final RDF graph is returned to the user. Note that the success of a policy rule (which is implemented as a SPARQL query) returning a particular set of RDF triples is dependent on the transformation step at which the rule was applied in a policy sequence. We illustrate this using the following SPARQL query:

CONSTRUCT G WHERE P,

G is a newly constructed graph, which contains a set of triples that satisfy condition *P* in the input graph. A policy protecting the following RDF triples,
<http://cs.utdallas.edu/semanticweb/Prov-AC/agency#agent_1 >
    foaf:name "John brown";
    foaf:projectHomepage <http://www.agency1.gov/>.
will fail if either the name or project home page triple was earlier removed or altered by a previous policy rule.

A policy precedence feature in the framework helps an agency determine the ordering of its policies. In the user interface layer, an agency configures the ordering of its policies. The policy sequence is then stored in a RDF sequence file (using the "rdf:seq" feature of the RDF specification). When a query is evaluated, the policy framework will in turn invoke each policy in the intended order.

28.2.3.2.6 Rule Sequence

In a similar way, a policy may be implemented using a set of rules. For example, to fully redact a shared resource, an agency may need a separate rule to redact each sensitive triple in an RDF graph. Each rule is triggered when a triple (or set of triples) meet some specified criteria in the input graph. Note that each rule transforms the current state of a shared resource. Therefore, each sequencing of the rules will impact the final graph (also called the redacted graph).

28.2.3.3 Data Layer

At the data layer is a connection factory, which acts as a facade, for creating connection objects. These connection objects expose the same properties (functionally) as public methods to the policy designer. This makes it easier for the policy designer to concentrate on the policy engine design. The policy designer makes a call to an RDF Policy Factory, which returns an RDF model object. This RDF model object is backed by a connection store, which can be a local connection, a relational database connection, or a cloud connection. During the registration process, an agency is given an opportunity to decide where it wants to store its resources and configuration documents. It is recommended that the smaller configuration documents be stored locally on disk (or in a local database) to enable quick access to them. Local connections also consume lower bandwidth, offer real-time access, and enable development before deployment. However, an agency may decide to store them in a private cloud (or on a remote database server) to take advantage of the added protection there.

The connection factory also enables agencies to store their resources in any cloud infrastructure. For example an agency's resources could reside on a private could, or a community cloud or a public cloud. A private cloud deployment provides more control, in that agencies could house their own cloud. A community cloud is provisioned for exclusive access by a specific community, thus serving the common interest of cooperating agencies. A public cloud is open to the public and thus susceptible to more vulnerabilities due to the loss of control over the data uploaded onto the public cloud. Agencies may choose to use a mixture of connections and also employ more than one deployment simultaneously (e.g., a hybrid cloud model).

28.2.4 Features of our Policy Engine Framework

In the subsections below, we present some novel features of our policy engine framework.

28.2.4.1 Policy Reciprocity

Policy Reciprocity enables agencies to specify policies when knowledge of the other agencies, their resources, or policy specification are available. This is made possible via the registration process, where agencies make metadata available about themselves, their recourses and associated policies. The following discussion provides scenarios for policy reciprocity.

*Agency*1 wishes to share its resources if *Agency*2 also shares its resources with it. Current access control and redaction policies do not provide for this reciprocity.

Our framework provides information-sharing policies, which allow agents to define policies based on reciprocity and mutual interest among cooperating agencies.

We present two sample information-sharing policies below:

1. $\forall r1 \in Agency1, \forall r2 \in Agency2$, use $r1 \cup r2$.
   This policy states that *Agency1* shares all its resources with any resource of *Agency2* as a union of the resources (i.e., $\odot \in \{\cup\}$).
2. Let $r1_1, r1_2, \ldots, r1_n \Box Agency1$. *Agency1* can use $r1_1 \cup r2, r1_2 \cap r2, \forall r2 \in Agency2$.
   This policy offers a finer level of control and defines the combined operator, $\odot \in \{\cap, \cup\}$.

28.2.4.2 Conditional Policies

A consequence of policy reciprocity is allowing the use of conditional sharing policies. For example, *Agency1* shares its resources with *Agency2* if *Agency2* does not share *Agency1*'s resources with *Agency3*. We present a sample information-sharing policy below:

1. $\forall r1 \in Agency1, \forall r2 \in Agency2$, *Agency1* defines $r1 \cap r2$. If $\forall r3 \in Agency3$, then
   - *Agency2* does not define any sharing policy of the form $r1 \cap r3$,
   - or *Agency2* does not define any sharing policy of the form $r1 \subseteq r2 \odot r3$, where $\odot \in \{\cup, \cap\}$.

28.2.4.3 Policy Symmetry

Another consequence of policy reciprocity is to have symmetry in the sharing of policies. For example, *Agency1* shares its resources with *Agency2* with a combined operator, $\odot$, if *Agency2* also shares its resources with *Agency1* using the same combined operator, $\odot$. We present a sample information-sharing policy below:

1. $\forall r1 \in Agency1, \forall r2 \in Agency2$, *Agency1* uses $r1 \cup r2$ if *Agency2* also uses $r2 \cup r1$.

28.2.4.4 Develop and Scale Policies

To enable freedom of maneuverability across the information environment and to deliver the power of information to ensure mission success, an agency should be able to rapidly develop policies and deploy them as needed. Next, we discuss the features that are available to an agency during and after development of its policies.

28.2.4.4.1 Policy Development

Agency1 wishes to simulate a live environment and create test scenarios to visualize the results of each policy configuration. Our policy framework provides three configurations: (i) a stand-alone version for development and testing; (ii) a version backed by a relational database; and (iii) a cloud-based version that achieves high availability and scalability while maintaining low setup and operation costs.

28.2.4.4.2 Sequencing Effects

Agency1 wishes to vary the result set to a user's query based on the user's credentials. The policy sequence feature can be used to configure different outcomes by permuting the policies and their respective rules.

28.2.4.4.3 Rapid Elasticity

Agency1 identifies recent security vulnerabilities in its existing policy configurations and wishes to extend (or grow) its existing policy set with support for policies at a finer granularity. Our policy engine provides a policy interface that should be implemented by all policies; therefore, we can add newer types of policies as needed. In addition, our policy engine gives an agency rapid elasticity, whereby the capabilities available by our policy framework appear unlimited.

28.2.4.4.4 Location Independence

Agency1 wishes to store its resources closer to where it is consumed, but with little or no change at the policy layer. Our policy engine provides location independence whereby the policy engine has no control or knowledge over the exact location of the resources, but may be able to access the resources through a specified location using the connection manager. Note that an agency's resources can be in any cloud, geographically. The ability to locate any resource by a dereferenceable *URI* provides much flexibility.

28.2.4.4.5 Deployment Models

Agency1 can take advantage of different deployment models. For example, a private cloud, a hybrid cloud, a community, or a public cloud. The connection manager allows an agency to choose among a list of connection types based on different risk factors and objectives to protect data confidentiality.

28.2.4.5 Justification of Resources

Provenance makes available an explanation about why information was manipulated and a trace to the source of the information manipulation. This establishes trust among agencies, thus facilitating partnerships for common goals.

Agency1 asks *Agency2* for a justification of resource R2. The current commercial access control policies are mainly designed to protect single data items, while current redaction policies are designed for redacting text and images. Our policy engine allows agents to define policies over provenance; therefore, *Agency2* can provide the provenance to *Agency1*, but protect it by using access control or redaction policies.

28.2.4.6 Policy Specification and Enforcement

Our architectural design supports a high-level specification of policies, thus separating the business layer from a specific policy implementation.

Agency1 wishes to express its policies in a high-level language (e.g., XACML), and would prefer not learning RDF or any of its variations. The framework exposes a web interface layer between the users and the policy engine layer, whereby the users can specify their policies independent of the actual implementation of the policy. A suitable adapter, also known as a data translator, will translate each high-level policy specification into the appropriate RDF representation used by the appropriate policy, which protects an agency's resources.

Policies may be specified using more expressive languages than RDF, by extending RDF with a formal vocabulary, in particular a sub-language of OWL. OWL has a formal semantics that is based on description logics, a decidable fragment of first-order logic. Thus, by supporting this adapter pattern, our framework is extended to handle semantic policies specified in OWL and high-level policies can be translated into a suitable sub-language of OWL using existing or custom-built translators.

28.3 Summary and Directions

This chapter has described the design and implementation of the first of its kind AIS framework that operates in the cloud. As stated earlier, the idea is for each organization to store their data and the information-sharing policies in a cloud. The information is shared according to the policies. We described a cloud-based information-sharing framework that utilized semantic web technologies, our framework consists of a policy engine that reasons about the policies for information-sharing purposes and a secure data engine that stores and queries data in the cloud. We also described the operation of our system with example policies.

Our framework is flexible so that additional data sources and cloud can be added. Furthermore, by using RDF for a policy engine, we can add more sophisticated policies for information sharing. This is one of the major strengths of our system. Future directions include specifying and reasoning about more sophisticated policies as well as testing our system in a real-world environment.

References

[BRAU08] Braun, U., A. Shinnar, and M. Seltzer, Securing provenance. In *Proceedings of the 3rd Conference on Hot Topics in Security*, USENIX Association, San Jose, CA, 2008, Article No. 4.

[CADE11a] Cadenhead, T., Khadilkar, V., Kantarcioglu, M. and B. Thuraisingham, A language for provenance access control. In *Proceedings of the first ACM Conference on Data and Application Security and Privacy*, San Antonio, TX, pp. 133–144, 2011.

[CADE11b] Cadenhead, T., V. Khadilkar, M. Kantarcioglu, and B. M. Thuraisingham, Transforming provenance using redaction. In *Proceedings of the 16th ACM Symposium on Access Control Models and Technologies*, Innsbruck, Austria, pp. 93–102, 2011.

[CADE12] Cadenhead, T., V. Khadilkar, M. Kantarcioglu, and B. Thuraisingham, A cloud-based RDF policy engine for assured information sharing. In *Proceedings of the 17th ACM Symposium on Access Control Models and Technologies*, Newark, NJ, pp. 113–116, 2012.

[CADE12] Cadenhead, T., Kantarcioglu, M., and Khadilkar, V., Design and Implementation of a Cloud-Based Assured Information Sharing System, Media from Lecture Notes in Computer Science, *Proceedings of Computer Network Security-6th International Conference on Mathematical Methods, Models and Architectures for Computer Network Security, MMM-ACNS 2012*, St. Petersburg, Russia, 7531, 2012, p. 36–50. © Springer.

[EHRI06] Ehrig, H., *Fundamentals of Algebraic Graph Transformation*. Springer-Verlag, New York Inc, 2006.

[HARR10] Harris, S. and A. Seaborne, SPARQL 1.1 Query Language. *W3C Working Draft*, 2010, www.w3.org/TR/spargl11-query/

[KAGA02] Kagal, L. REI., A policy language for the project, http://www.hpl.hp.com/techreports/2002/HPL-2002-270.pdf. 2002.

[KLYN04] Klyne, G., J. J. Carroll, and B. McBride, Resource description framework (RDF): Concepts and abstract syntax. *W3C Recommendation*, 10, 2004, www.w3.org/TR/rdf-concepts/

[MORE10] Moreau, L., Clifford, B., Freire, J. et al. The open provenance model core specification (v1. 1). *Future Generation Computer Systems*, 27(6), 743–756, 2011.

[PRUD06] Prud'hommeaux, E., A. Seaborne, (Eds.). SPARQL query language for RDF. *W3C Working Draft*, 4, 2006, www.w3.org/TR/rdf-spargl-query/

[ROZE97] Rozenberg, G. and H. Ehrig, *Handbook of Graph Grammars and Computing by Graph Transformation*. World Scientific, River Edge, NJ, 1997.

[SAMA01] Samarati, P. and Vimercati, S. de. Access control: Policies, models, and mechanisms. *Foundations of Security Analysis and Design*, 137–196, 2001.

Conclusion to Part VII

The chapters in this part have described the experimental cloud systems we have developed for implementing security applications. These applications are malware detection, insider threat detection, and assured information sharing.

In Chapter 25, we introduced EMPC, a novel ensemble learning technique for automated classification of infinite-length, concept-drifting streams. We showed that by applying EMPC to real data streams obtained from polymorphic malware and botnet traffic samples yielded better detection accuracies than other stream data classification techniques. Our implementation of the algorithms was carried out on the cloud.

In Chapter 26, we discussed our approach to insider threat detection. We represented the insiders and their communication as RDF graphs and then queried and mined the graphs to extract the nuggets. We also provided a comprehensive framework based on the cloud for insider threat detection.

In Chapter 27, we described our approach to developing a cloud-based assured information-sharing system called CAISS. CAISS utilizes several of the technologies we have developed as well as open source tools. We also described the design of an ideal Cloud Based Assured Information Sharing System called CAISS++.

In Chapter 28, we described the design and implementation of the first of its kind assured information-sharing framework that operates in the semantic cloud. A semantic cloud is a cloud that provides semantic web services to the consumer. The idea is for each organization to store their data and the information-sharing policies in a cloud. The information is shared according to the policies. We described a cloud-based information-sharing framework that utilized semantic web technologies. Our framework consists of a policy engine that reasons about the policies for information-sharing purposes and a secure data engine that stores and queries data in the cloud. We also described the operation of our system with example policies.

TOWARD A TRUSTWORTHY CLOUD

Introduction to Part VIII

Most of the discussions in the previous parts focused on security for the cloud. Note that while security in general encompasses confidentiality, integrity, and trust, our focus on security has mainly been on confidentiality. In Part VIII, we discuss other aspects toward developing a trustworthy cloud, including trust, privacy, and integrity.

Part VIII consists of three chapters: 29, 30, and 31. Chapter 29 discusses trust management and cloud services. Trust is essentially about how much confidence you place on what a person says or whether that person can keep a secret. Trust can also be a measure of whether a person will keep his commitments. In general, before I give out information to a person, I determine whether that person can be trusted, even though he is authorized to get that information from me. Chapter 30 focuses on privacy and cloud services. Note that different definitions of privacy have been proposed. The definition we will use here is that a person must decide what information to release about him/her. Therefore, any organization that violates the will of this person violates this person's privacy. Chapter 31 focuses on integrity and cloud services. Integrity for us includes accuracy of the data, and quality of the data, as well as the provenance of the data.

Chapter 29

Trust Management and the Cloud

29.1 Overview

This chapter focuses on trust management for cloud services. Trust has been discussed a great deal in developing secure systems. Much of the early focus was on trusting the software to develop high-assurance systems. For example, in designing say a multilevel system that has to be evaluated at say A1 level according to the TCSEC (Trusted Computer Systems Evaluation Criteria), the software has to go through a formal verification process to ensure that there are no covert channels. Such software is called trusted software. However, as data and applications security became prominent over the last decade, the focus was on trusting the individuals or processes acting on behalf of the individuals. Here, we had to determine the trust that had to be placed on the individuals. Furthermore, the data also had to be assigned trust values. That is, the data could have a high trust value if it emanated from a trustworthy individual or source (e.g., a file or database).

Cloud services also need to have trust to carry out certain operations. Some cloud services that carry out critical functions such as command and control and patient monitoring have to be more trustworthy than say other cloud services that search for a company that sells shoes. In this chapter, we will discuss issues related to trust management and then discuss trust-based cloud services. We will also discuss trust for semantic cloud services. Note that such cloud services utilize semantic web technologies for tasks such as data, policy representation, and reasoning.

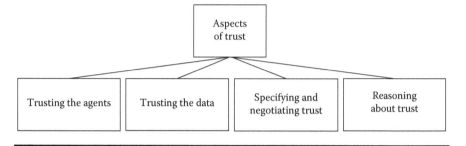

Figure 29.1   Aspects of trust.

The organization of this chapter is as follows. Trust management, including trusting individuals as well as data, will be discussed in Section 29.2. In particular, trust management and trust negotiation will be discussed in Section 29.2.1. Note that trust and risk have a relationship between them. That is, if a person is not trustworthy and if you have to give him/her some data, you are taking a risk. Therefore, some of the developments on correlating trust and risk are discussed in Section 29.2.2. Reputation-based trust is discussed in Section 29.2.3. Then in Section 29.3, we will discuss trust management and cloud services. In particular, trust management as a cloud service will be discussed in Section 29.3.1. Trust for cloud services will be discussed in Section 29.3.2. This chapter concludes with Section 29.3. Figure 29.1 illustrates the various aspects of trust.

29.2 Trust Management

29.2.1 Trust Management and Negotiation

Before we discuss aspects of trust management and describe the relationship to the semantic cloud service, we need to determine what is meant by trust. Trust has been defined by philosophers and it relates to the amount of value that one would place on another. This value will depend on whether the person can keep secrets or carry out safe activities, among others. On the basis of trust that is placed on a person, the data that are emanating from that person would also be assigned a trust value. We will address data trust later. First, we will focus on trusting an individual. We can extend the arguments to include not only an individual but also a group of individuals or even a website or an organization.

The work on trust initially focused on the amount of verification or testing that has to be carried out to ensure that the software meets the specification. If the software has a Trojan horse, then it is not trusted. If the software is trusted, then depending on the techniques used to trust the software (e.g., formal verification vs. testing), one could then determine the assurance that is placed on the software. Later on, with the prominence of data security, trust was assigned to individuals or organizations. In such cases, two approaches were used to define trust; one was based on credentials and the other was based on reputation. Both schools of thought have received attention in the research community working on trust.

Bertino and her team have conducted extensive research on credential-based trust management. The idea here is to exchange credentials between individuals and depending on the type of credentials, trust is established between two parties. Credentials are initially obtained through some credential authority. Therefore, if John wants to see Jane's personal data, he has to present Jane with his credentials that were given to him by a credential authority. The other noted research on credential-based trust management is the work of Winslett and coworkers and Winsborough et al., among others. Numerous papers on credential-based trust management have appeared in the proceedings of conferences such as ACM, SACMAT, and IEEE policy (see also [BERT03], [YU03], [WINS04]).

In the reputation-based systems, trust is assigned based on the reputation that one gets based on his past behavior. For example, if Jane applies for a position as a teacher, then those who have heard about Jane will discuss her reputation such as she is not reliable and misses classes a great deal of the time. If this is the case, then Jane's reputation as a teacher is not good; so, Jane will not be trusted to be given the job. We use reputation all the time in our daily lives. That is, we trust an individual or an organization based on its reputation. It is usually very hard to improve the reputation. However, it does not take much to ruin the reputation and as a result to decrease the trust value. Reputation-based trust systems are discussed in [SHMA].The third type of trust is to determine the confidence value that one places on the data. In other words, how much do you trust the data? To give an answer, we need to determine who has produced the data? Who has accessed the data? Have the data gone through an organization that is untrustworthy? We will discuss data trust when we address data quality and data provenance in Chapter 31.

Once trust values are assigned, what does it take to manage trust? This involves exchanging data depending on the trust values, as well as increasing and decreasing trust values based on credentials received or subtracted or the reputation that has changed. For example, if John is entrusted with some critical data and if it is known that John has misused the data, the trust value will be decreased. There is research on formalizing the notion of trust and performing operations on trust. Algebras for trust management are also being developed. One important aspect of trust management is trust negotiation. Here, two parties may negotiate with each other; the trust values and the data to be shared among them. Trust negotiation is an active research area in trust management [WINS04]. Figure 29.1 illustrates the various aspects of trust. Trust-negotiation process is illustrated in Figure 29.2.

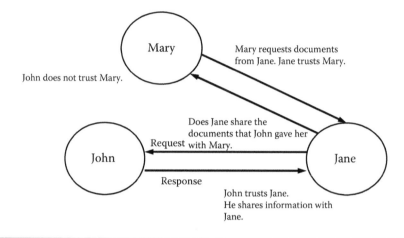

Figure 29.2 Trust negotiation.

29.2.2 Trust and Risk Management

We need to have an understanding of the risk factors in order to manage the risk in data sharing. Although trust and risk are related, they are not one and the same. For example, the more you trust someone, the more you share the data with that person. However, there is also the situation that a hospital A trusts hospital B, but A does not share the data with B as B's systems are not secure. One could argue that since B's computers are not secure, then B cannot be trusted. In some cases, sharing data with untrustworthy parties may not be risky. For example, a hospital may share its data with a drug company to find a cure, even though the hospital does not trust the company. Here again, one could argue that the hospital places some trust that the company will find a cure for the disease even if it may not use the data appropriately. However, if the data are not sensitive, then sharing them may not be an issue. Therefore, one can treat trust and risk to be interrelated but different concepts.

Although different models for the relationship between trust and risk have been proposed, the exact relationship between trust and risk in data-sharing applications is yet to be made clear. What we need is an appropriate model to specify trust and risk relationships. Trust is not the only factor that affects risk. Our research is involved with understanding trust and risk and developing a trust-based risk model. In order to create a trust based risk model, we need to capture all the risks associated with trust misjudgments. Furthermore, he states that cost–benefit analysis has to be carried out whether to share the data even if the risks are high. Trust-based risk management is illustrated in Figure 29.3.

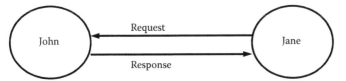

Jane request document from John.
John calculates the risk of sharing the document.
Risk is determined on the trust John places on Jane.
Depending on the risk, John determines whether or not to share the document.

Figure 29.3   Trust and risk.

29.2.3 *Reputation-Based Systems*

Trust may be established using what is called a reputation network. As stated in [GOLB03], a reputation-based network is a distributed, web-based social network. Reputation rating is inferred from one user to another. Individuals are connected to each person they rate and that results in a large interconnected network of users. The only requirement is that the individuals should assert their reputation ratings for one another in the network. Individuals control their own data. Data are maintained in a distributed manner. Data can be stored anywhere and integrated through a common foundation.

The FOAF [RDF] project illustrates the relationship between the semantic web and reputation networks. An ontological vocabulary is used for describing people and their relationships. This is extended by providing a mechanism describing the reputation relationships and allows people to rate the reputation or trustworthiness of another person.

Algorithms are being developed to infer reputations. As stated in [GOLB03], recommendations are made to one person (source) about the reputation of another person. Trust and reputation literature contain many different metrics. These metrics are categorized according to the perspective used for making calculations. For example, global metrics calculate a single value for each entity in the network. Local metrics calculate a reputation rating for an individual in the network. In the global system, an entity will always have the same inferred rating. In the local system, an entity could be rated differently depending on the node the inference is made for.

An example of a reputation system is TrustMail. It is a message-scoring system and adds reputation ratings to the folder views of a message. It helps to sort messages accordingly by the user after he sees the reputation ratings. It highlights the important and relevant messages. Figure 29.4 illustrates a reputation network.

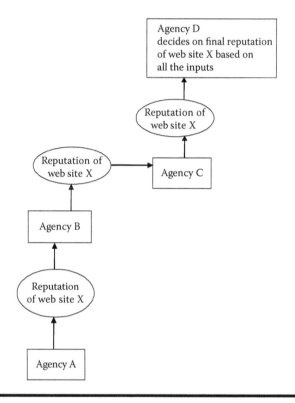

Figure 29.4 Reputation network.

29.3 Trust and Cloud Services

29.3.1 Trust Management as a Cloud Service

There are two aspects here. One is to implement trust management as a cloud service or as a collection of cloud services. The other is to explore trust management for cloud services. We illustrate the case of implementing trust management as a cloud service (or web service) in Figure 29.5. A user issues a request to a web server or a CSP to obtain a resource. The query service will issue a request to the trust management service provided by a cloud to determine the trust level of the user. On the basis of this trust level, appropriate resources are then given to the user.

Figure 29.5 Cloud services for trust management.

There is also an interest in the use of semantic web technologies for trust management and negotiation. While several trust policy languages have been developed, a notable system that takes advantage of XML for policy representation is the system developed at the University of Milan and Purdue by Bertino and her group. The system developed is called Trust-X and is based on XML. A trust policy language based on XML is used by Trust-X that is a credential-based system [BERT04]. Recall that a cloud service that utilizes semantic web technologies to represent and reason about the policies is a semantic cloud service.

While XML is a suitable policy language, it suffers from the drawbacks in that it cannot adequately represent semantics. For example, statements such as A trusts B only if B does not trust C or A trusts B and B trusts C does not mean that A trusts C. It is difficult to express such statements in XML. Note that unlike XML, RDF can express class–subclass relationships and languages such as OWL can represent relationships such as union and intersection. Therefore, we need rich policy languages to represent trust. Furthermore, since the 9/11 commission report (http://www.9-11commission.gov/report/911Report.pdf) the environment is migrating from a need-to-know to a need-to-share environment. Therefore, it is important to represent trust relationships in such an environment. We need policy languages to represent statements of the form "in emergency situations, one needs to share all the data and then determine the consequences of data sharing with respect to trust." Finin and coworkers are investigating the use of language such as REI for need-to-share environments [KAGA03].

The advantage of using semantic web-based policy languages is that one could use reasoning capabilities based on descriptive logic to reason about trust statements and make inferences about trust that is not explicitly specified. The reasoning engines such as JENA and PELLET are also being explored for representing and reasoning about semantic web-based policy specifications. The policy-aware web project being carried out at MIT (Massachusetts Institute of Technology) is also developing specification languages and reasoning engines for trust policies.

Note that one of the layers of the semantic web is logic, proof, and trust. This type of trust is different from trust as we have discussed in this chapter. The trust layer for the semantic web is essentially about reasoning about the trustworthiness of statements. For example, how much trust do you place on statements such as "John and James are best friends." Trusting this statement depends on the source of the statement. We will discuss this type of trust when we discuss data quality and provenance in a later chapter.

While there is lot of research now on the specification of policy languages, the advantage of web languages is that we can utilize the reasoning tools being developed to reason about the policies so that we can check for the consistency of the policies. We also want to ensure that trust policies do not divulge sensitive information that is classified or private. Research along these lines has been carried out by Bertino and her group [SQUI06]. Figure 29.5 illustrates cloud services for trust management whereas Figure 29.6 illustrates semantic cloud services for trust management.

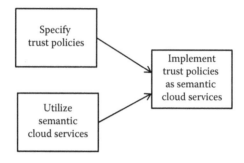

Figure 29.6   Semantic cloud services for trust management.

29.3.2 Trust Management for Cloud Services

In the previous subsection, we discussed the application of cloud services and semantic cloud services for trust management. Essentially, the idea here is to implement trust management as a cloud service, use languages such as XML, RDF, and OWL to specify policies, and reason about policies based on descriptive logic as well as invoke cloud services for managing trust. In this section, we discuss how trust management techniques may be applied for cloud services as well as for semantic cloud services. Note that the semantic web is a collection of technologies that give us machine understandable web pages. Therefore, the challenge here is how do we trust the reasoning that is carried out to obtain machine understandable web pages? Furthermore, do we trust the web pages that are produced? With respect to trust management for cloud services, the idea is to determine how much trust we place on the cloud services. Has the cloud service been authenticated? If so, what is the level of authentication? Figure 29.7 illustrates trust for cloud services whereas Figure 29.8 illustrates trust for semantic cloud services.

Figure 29.7   Trust management for cloud services.

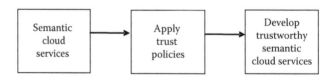

Figure 29.8   Trust management for the semantic cloud services.

One of the layers of the semantic cloud service is the logic, proof, and trust layer. Here, we need technologies to reason about the accuracy of the web pages. Do we trust the data that are produced? Do we trust the decisions that are made by the agents who carry out the activities on behalf of the user? Trusting the web pages will also determine who produced the web pages. If the agents who produced the web pages are highly trustworthy, then we may place higher trust on the results. We will discuss this aspect under data quality and data provenance in Chapter 30.

Another aspect is about trusting the agents, implemented as a collection of web/cloud services, which make use of semantic web technologies such as XML and RDF based to carry out their activities. Do we trust the answers produced by the agents? Do these agents carry out trust negotiations between them? That is, trust established between agents is essentially the trust that is established between people. This trust may depend on credentials or may be based on reputation. For example, in providing a travel service, the agent has to make reservations, book hotels as well as make arrangements for the client to participate in tours. The agent who acts on behalf of the client will read the web pages in XML or RDF and then contact the agent who is acting on behalf of the airlines and hotels. The trust that the first agent places on the other may depend on the credential or the reputation that the travel agent has.

Therefore, when we discuss trust, there are two major aspects. One is the trust placed on the data and the other is trust placed on the agents. The trust placed on the data will depend on the trust placed on the agent. Similarly, an agent who consistently produces trustworthy data can be regarded to have a higher trust value.

29.4 Summary and Directions

In this chapter, we have discussed trust management and its connection to cloud services and semantic cloud services. We first discussed the aspects of trust management, including defining trust and also describing trust negotiations. Then we discussed enforcing trust within the context of the semantic cloud service. Furthermore, we also discussed the use of semantic cloud service technologies for specifying trust policies. Next, we discussed the related concepts, including risk-based trust management and reputation networks.

Our goal is to provide a high-level overview of what the challenges are and what is going on in trust related to web services. Trust management is a fledging research area and several researchers including Bertino at Purdue, Berners Lee at MIT, Finin at UMBC (University of Maryland, Baltimore County), and Winslett at UIUC (University of Illinois, Urbana Champaign), among others are conducting extensive research on this topic. For example, Finin and coworkers at UMBC have pioneered techniques for specifying and reasoning about trust using a language called REI. We are collaborating with UMBC on trust management in a need-to-share environment. While numerous trust-negotiation approaches have been proposed, we need research on evaluating these approaches and determining which approaches are appropriate and under what context. Therefore, while much has been done on trust management during the past decade, much still remains to be done for specific applications and domains including cloud services.

References

[BERT03] E. Bertino, E. Ferrari, and A. C. Squicciarini, Trust-Chi: An XML framework for trust negotiations. *Communications and Multimedia Security*: 146–157, 2003, Torino, Italy.

[BERT04] E. Bertino, E. Ferrari, and A. C. Squicciarini, Trust-X: A peer-to-peer framework for trust establishment. *IEEE Transactions on Knowledge of Data Engineering* 16(7): 827–842, 2004.

[GARC06] R. García and R. Gil, An OWL copyright ontology for semantic digital rights management, *Workshop on Ontology Content and Evaluation in Enterprise*, 2, 2006, Montpellier, France.

[GOLB03] G. Jennifer, B. Parsia, and J. Hendler, Trust networks on the semantic cloud service, *Proceedings of Cooperative Information Agents*, August 27–29, 2003, Helsinki, Finland.

[KAGA03] L. Kagal, T. W. Finin, and A. Joshi, A policy based approach to security for the semantic web. *International Semantic Web Conference* 2003: 402–418, White Maris, NY.

[RDF] RDFWeb: FOAF: The Friend Of A Friend vocabulary. http://xmlns.com/foaf/0.1/.

[SHMA06] V. Shmatikov and C. Talcott, Reputation-based trust management. http://www.cs.utexas.edu/~shmat/shmat_rtm.pdf

[SQUI06] A. C. Squicciarini, E. Bertino, E. Ferrari, and I. Ray, Achieving privacy in trust negotiations with an ontology-based approach. *IEEE Transactions on Dependable Security Computing* 3(1): 13–30, 2006.

[WINS04] W. H. Winsborough and N. Li, Safety in automated trust negotiation. *IEEE Symposium on Security and Privacy* 2004, Berkeley, CA.

[YU03] T. Yu and M. Winslett, A unified scheme for resource protection in automated trust negotiation. *IEEE Symposium on Security and Privacy* 2003: 129–132, Berkeley, CA.

Chapter 30

Privacy and Cloud Services

30.1 Overview

While confidentiality is about the cloud releasing data/information only to those who are authorized according to the policies, privacy is about a person determining what information should be released about him. Therefore, if the CSP's privacy policies are not acceptable to this user, then he/she can decide whether he/she wants to store the information in the cloud.

However, note that while privacy has been discussed a great deal even at the congressional levels, not everyone agrees with this definition. For example, I teach data mining, national security, and privacy at the unclassified level at the Armed Forces Communication and Electronics Association in Washington, DC. The students who take my courses mainly work for the Department of Defense and Intelligence agencies. For them, privacy is not the same as one feels about releasing say his or her medical records. It is my understanding that FBI's (Federal Bureau of Investigation) idea of privacy is to ensure that the personal information of the U.S. citizens does not get into the wrong hands. Even to other agencies, the FBI will release private information only if the agency is authorized to get that information. In a way, privacy becomes more or less like confidentiality for such organizations.

Much work has been carried out on privacy including specification and enforcement of privacy policies, developing techniques for privacy preserving, data mining, and specifying standards for privacy. One of the significant developments with W3C is the specification of standards that a website (or CSP) can use to specify its privacy policies that is called P3P. Another challenge is to ensure that private information is not released as a result of semantic web mining (mining data in the cloud). Finally, cloud services have to ensure that private information is not leaked. Likewise, cloud services that carry out cloud mining have to ensure that privacy of individuals is protected.

The organization of this chapter is as follows. In Section 30.2, we discuss privacy management in general. In particular, privacy issues are discussed in Section 30.2.1. The privacy problem via inference including privacy constraint processing and data mining will be discussed in Section 30.2.2. P3P will be discussed in Section 30.2.3. The relationship between privacy and cloud services is discussed in Section 30.3. In particular, privacy as a cloud service will be discussed in Section 30.3.1. Privacy for cloud services will be discussed in Section 30.3.2. This chapter concludes with Section 30.4.

30.2 Privacy Management

30.2.1 Privacy Issues

Social scientists have studied privacy for several years and policy specialists have developed privacy policies for agencies and corporations. However, it is only recently that security specialists have started focusing on privacy. Furthermore, the Terrorism Information Awareness program at DARPA together with the focus on data mining has resulted in efforts on privacy preserving data mining and privacy preserving data management. Today, privacy is an important area of information security. However, it has been difficult to give a precise definition of privacy as each organization and agency has a different view.

So, the question is what is privacy? The general notion is that a person should decide what personal information should be released about him or her. Such a definition was fine before we had tools for data analysis, data mining, and the WWW. Through such tools, it may now be possible for someone to infer private information about another person. Therefore, we need to perhaps redefine the notion of privacy. On the other hand, some organizations want to control personal information about the community and decide who they should release the personal information to. That is, my understanding is that the FBI has information about various individuals; they will determine whether to release the information to say CIA. Initially, I argued that this is essentially ensuring confidentiality and not privacy. However, after working more on privacy issues and reading about the subject, I now believe that there can be no universal definition of privacy. Privacy has to be defined by an organization. That is, one organization may define privacy policies as policies protecting its sensitive information. Another organization may define privacy policies to be those that are specified by those who work for the organization as to what information can be released by them. Therefore, whether privacy policies

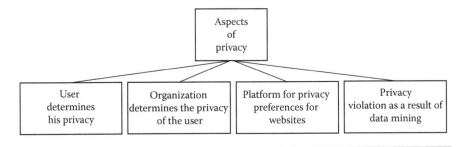

Figure 30.1   Privacy management.

are a subset of confidentiality policies or whether they are separate policies is left to an organization to be determined.

Our interest also lies in the relationship between privacy, confidentiality, and trust. As we have discussed in the earlier chapters, in our work we have made the following assumption. Trust is established between say a CSP and a user based on credentials or reputations. When a user logs into a cloud to make a purchase, the CSP will specify what its privacy policies are. The user will then determine whether he wants to enter personal information. That is, if the CSP will give out say the user's address to a third party, then the user can decide whether to enter this information. However, before the user enters the information, the user has to decide whether he trusts the CSP. This can be based on the credential and reputation. If the user trusts the CSP, then the user can enter his private information if he is satisfied with the policies. If not, he can choose not to enter the information.

We have given a similar reasoning for confidentiality. Here, the user is requesting information from the CSP; the CSP checks its confidentiality policies and decides what information to release to the user. The CSP can also check the trust it has on the user and decide whether to give the information to the user. One can also determine the quality of the data based on the trust placed on the user or on the CSP.

More details on the specific aspects of privacy and semantic cloud services will be discussed in the next several sections. In particular, applying semantic web technologies for privacy management, privacy issues for the semantic cloud service, P3P, privacy problem that occurs via inference, and privacy preserving cloud mining will be discussed. Figure 30.1 illustrates the aspects of privacy management.

30.2.2 Privacy Problem through Inference

We have conducted extensive research on the inference problem for secure databases. Much of our work focused on security constraint processing, which has now come to be known as policy management. The policies included those for content- and context-dependent constraints as well as dynamic- and event-based constraints.

For example, the ship's mission becomes classified after the war begins [THUR90]. We have therefore adopted this approach for privacy constraint processing where security levels would now become privacy levels (public, private, semipublic, etc.) and the security constraint would become a privacy constraint such as names and health-care records taken together. It should be noted that with this approach, we are assuming that privacy and confidentiality are one and the same. Now, this agrees with say FBI's notion of privacy where it has to protect the private information of U.S. citizens. But this is not consistent with medical privacy where in this context, privacy is specified by an individual, that is, an individual determines the information he has to keep private. In this case, the privacy controller is managed by the individual. That is, the client will determine that if it gives out say his/her genetic information, then an insurance company can figure out the illnesses he/she may be prone to. Therefore, the privacy controller will guide the client as to what information to release about him/her.

Figure 30.2 illustrates the privacy controller. Here, data represented using semantic web technologies such as XML, RDF, and ontologies are augmented with inference engines. These engines may carry out rule processing or utilize ontology-based reasoning to deduce new data from the existing data. If the new data are private, then they can give advice to the client as to what information should be kept private. Note that under the FBI scenario, the privacy controller is essentially the confidentiality controller (that we have called the inference controller) and therefore, it acts on the server side and determines what information it has to release to the client (such as the CIA).

Note that we have proved that the inference problem is unsolvable [THUR90]. We have applied similar techniques to prove that the privacy problem is unsolvable [THUR06b]. Figure 30.2 illustrates the architecture of a privacy controller.

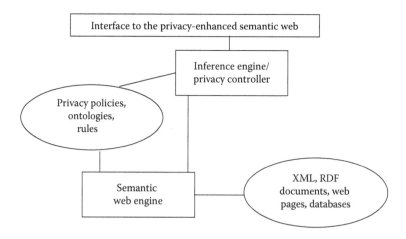

Figure 30.2   Privacy controller architecture.

30.2.3 *Platform for Privacy Preferences*

P3P is an emerging industry standard that enables CSPs to express their privacy practices in a standard format. The format of the policies can be automatically retrieved and understood by user agents. It is a product of W3C (www.w3c.org). As we have stated, the main difference between privacy and security as considered in many domains is the following: (1) The user is informed of the privacy policies enforced by the CSP; (2) The user is not informed of the security (or confidentiality) policies in general; (3) When a user enters a cloud, the privacy policies of the CSP are conveyed to the user; and (4) If the privacy policies are different from user preferences, the user is notified. The user can then decide how to proceed.

Several major corporations are working on P3P standards including Microsoft, IBM, HP, NEC Nokia, and NCR. Several websites have also implemented P3P. Semantic web groups have adopted P3P. The initial version of P3P used RDF to specify policies; the recent version has migrated to XML. P3P policies use XML with namespaces for encoding policies.

EXAMPLE: CATALOG SHOPPING. YOUR NAME WILL NOT BE GIVEN TO A THIRD PARTY BUT YOUR PURCHASES WILL BE GIVEN TO A THIRD PARTY

```
<POLICIES xmlns=http://www.w3.org/2002/01/P3Pv1>
    <POLICY name=- - - -
    </POLICY>
    </POLICIES>
```

P3P has its own statements and data types expressed in XML. P3P schemas utilize XML schemas. XML is a prerequisite to understand P3P. P3P specification released in January 2005 uses an example of catalog shopping to explain concepts. P3P is an international standard and is an ongoing project.

Note that P3P does not replace the laws. P3P works together with the law. What happens if the websites do not honor their P3P policies? Then appropriate legal actions will have to be taken. Today, XML is the technology to specify P3P policies. Policy experts will have to specify the policies. Technologies will have to develop the specifications. Legal experts will have to take actions if the policies are violated.

30.2.4 *Privacy Preserving Cloud Mining*

In our previous chapter [THUR05], we discussed privacy preserving data mining. The idea is as follows. Using the data mining tools, even the naive users can make unauthorized inferences that could be highly sensitive or private. Furthermore, the goal is to hide the private data such as the disease of a particular person while giving out the general trends and associations. That is, we could give out the information that "people living in California are more prone to Asthma" without giving out the fact that John has asthma. Privacy preserving data mining techniques work with perturbed or randomized data without revealing the actual data.

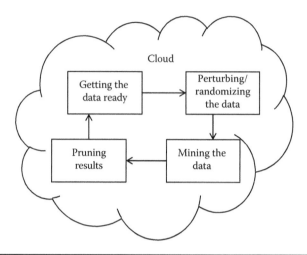

Figure 30.3   Privacy preserving cloud data mining.

Recently, there have been reports on semantic cloud mining. There are two aspects here. One is to mine the data on the cloud represented using semantic web technologies such as XML, RDF, and OWL. Note that much of the work has focused on mining relational data. More recently, there is work on mining unstructured data such as text, audio, images, and video. The challenge is to mine the databases that store and manage XML and RDF documents. The other aspect is to mine the XML and RDF documents without revealing the actual data but giving out correlations and trends. The former is an aspect of data mining whereas the latter is an aspect of privacy preserving data mining. There is yet a third aspect and that is to use ontologies to help the mining process. For example, the data mining tool may need clarifications about the meaning of a cloud page. Here, ontologies expressed in OWL may be used to clarify the concepts to facilitate the mining process (Figure 30.3).

30.3 Privacy Management and the Cloud

30.3.1 Cloud Services for Privacy Management

Privacy management can be implemented as a collection of cloud services. For example, when a user requests a resource from a cloud, the cloud service for privacy management is invoked. This service will present the privacy policies of the CSP to the user and the user can subsequently determine whether to request the resource or not. Figure 30.4 illustrates cloud services for privacy management whereas Figure 30.5 illustrates semantic cloud services for privacy management.

The major contributions of semantic web technologies for privacy management are in specifying policies in semantic web technologies. These policies could be

Figure 30.4 Cloud services for privacy.

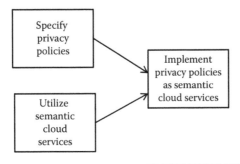

Figure 30.5 Semantic cloud services for privacy.

specified in XML, RDF, OWL, or related semantic web languages. Another contribution is the P3P. CSPs could utilize these semantic web technologies to represent and reason about the privacy policies.

As in the case of trust management, one needs to decide the appropriate language to specify privacy polices. XML is becoming a popular language for this purpose. Even the P3P standards that initially focused on using RDF for privacy policy specification switched to XML. However, if one needs to represent the semantics of the privacy policies and reason about privacy, then RDF or OWL would be more appropriate.

In specifying privacy policies, one also needs to determine whether sensitive or private information could be leaked. Therefore, the appropriate confidentiality or privacy policies may be enforced on the original privacy policies themselves. Therefore, we may want to control access to various parts of the privacy policy specifications that describe the policies.

30.3.2 Privacy for Cloud Services and Semantic Cloud Services

Privacy for cloud services is about ensuring the privacy of cloud services. For example, a cloud service may be processing highly sensitive information or carrying out surveillance. Private and sensitive information such as the social security numbers and/or the location of the individuals may have to be protected via the appropriate policy enforcement. Figure 30.6 illustrates privacy for cloud services.

Figure 30.6 Privacy for cloud services.

Privacy for the semantic cloud services is essentially about ensuring that private information is not divulged by these semantic cloud services. Note that semantic cloud services are services that utilize cloud-based WS and semantic web technologies for representing and reasoning about the cloud data and the policies. Our goal is not to reveal private information. For this, we need to ensure that privacy policies are enforced properly on XML and RDF documents as well as OWL ontologies. Furthermore, the goal of the reasoning engines that are developed based on descriptive logic is such that private information cannot be inferred by deduction.

Privacy for cloud services has received little attention. Bertino and coworkers have investigated privacy for XML and have also examined aspects of privacy violations that result from trust management based on their Trust-X system [SQUI07]. Finin et al. are examining privacy for their research on semantic web although their research is focusing mainly on trust management. In our investigation of CPT (confidentiality, privacy, and trust) for the semantic cloud services, we have privacy enforcement both based on what we call the basic system and the advanced system [THUR06]. Note that the advanced system consists of a privacy engine that will focus on privacy violations via inference. With the semantic cloud services, the idea is for the machine to examine the semantic data in the cloud and determine whether any private information is revealed. Furthermore, while in an ordinary cloud, the CSP will display its privacy policies to the user and the user determines whether to store his/her private information in the cloud; with semantic cloud services, the CSP may examine the privacy policies and the user preferences and may give advice to the user as to whether he/she should store his private information. Figure 30.7 illustrates privacy management for the semantic cloud.

Figure 30.7 Privacy for semantic cloud services.

30.4 Summary and Directions

In this chapter, we have discussed the various notions of privacy and provided an overview of privacy management. Then, we discussed the privacy management and cloud services. For example, cloud services have to maintain privacy. Privacy controllers may be implemented as cloud services. We also discussed privacy for the semantic cloud for specifying privacy policies.

Much of the discussion in this chapter is in the early stages of research. We have not attempted to discuss the correct definition of privacy. Our goal is to illustrate the connection between privacy management and the semantic cloud. As we have mentioned, the semantic web technologies are useful in the specification and reasoning of the privacy policies. Furthermore, we have discussed that the data represented by XML and RDF could be mined and the privacy of individuals may be violated as a result.

We have stressed in our work that technology alone is not sufficient to protect the privacy of the individuals. We need social scientists, technologists, and policy makers to work together. It is also important to bring in the legal specialists. Some have said that it will be impossible to prevent privacy violations and legal measures are the only viable solution. However, our view is "some privacy is better than nothing," but we have to be careful not to inflict a false sense of privacy or security.

References

[P3P] Platform for privacy preferences, www.w3c.org

[SQUI07] Squicciarini, A. C., E. Bertino, E. Ferrari, F. Paci, and B. Thuraisingham, PP-Trust-XA system for privacy preserving trust negotiations. ACM TISSEC—*Transactions on Systems and Information Security*, 10(3), Article 12, 2007.

[THUR90] Thuraisingham, B., Recursion theoretic complexity of the inference problem, *Computer Security Foundations Workshop*, 1990 (also, Technical report, The MITRE Corporation, MTP-291), Franconia, NH.

[THUR05] Thuraisingham, B., *Database and Applications Security: Integrating Data Management and Information Security*, CRC Press, Boca Raton, FL, 2005.

[THUR06a] Thuraisingham, B., N. Tsybulnik, and A. Alam, Administering the semantic web: Confidentiality, privacy and trust management. *Journal of Information Security and Privacy*, 1(1): 18–34, 2007.

[THUR06b] Thuraisingham, B., On the complexity of the privacy problem, Technical report, The University of Texas at Dallas, 2006.

[W3C] World Wide Web Consortium: www.w3c.org

Chapter 31

Integrity Management, Data Provenance, and Cloud Services

31.1 Overview

In this chapter, we will discuss integrity management for cloud services. Integrity includes several aspects. In the database world, integrity includes concurrency control and recovery as well as enforcing integrity constraints. For example, when multiple transactions are executed at the same time, the consistency of the data has to be ensured. When a transaction aborts, it has to be ensured that the database is recovered from the failure into a consistent state. Integrity constraints are rules that have to be satisfied by the data. The rules include "salary value has to be positive" and "age of an employee cannot decrease over time." More recently, integrity has included data quality, data provenance, data currency, real-time processing, and fault tolerance.

In this chapter, we discuss the aspects of integrity for cloud services as well as implementing integrity management as cloud services. For example, how do we ensure the integrity of the data and the processes? How do we ensure that data quality is maintained? The organization of this chapter is as follows. In Section 31.2, we discuss the aspects of integrity, data quality, and provenance. In particular, integrity aspects will be discussed in Section 31.2.1. Data quality and provenance will be discussed in Section 31.2.2. Detecting security threats and misuse with data provenance will be discussed in Section 31.2.3. Cloud services and integrity

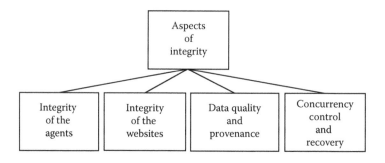

Figure 31.1 Aspects of integrity.

management are discussed in Section 31.3. In particular, data integrity and provenance as cloud services will be discussed in Section 31.3.1. Data integrity for cloud services will be discussed in Section 31.3.2. This chapter concludes with Section 31.4. The aspects of integrity are illustrated in Figure 31.1.

31.2 Integrity, Data Quality, and Provenance

31.2.1 Aspects of Integrity

There are many aspects of integrity. For example, concurrency control, recovery, data accuracy, meeting real-time constraints, data accuracy, data quality, data provenance, fault tolerance, and integrity constraint enforcement are all aspects of integrity management. This is illustrated in Figure 31.1. In this section, we will examine each aspect of integrity.

Concurrency control: In data management, concurrency control is about transactions that are executed at the same time and ensuring the consistency of the data. Therefore, transactions have to obtain locks or utilize time stamps to ensure that the data are left in a consistent state when multiple transactions attempt to access the data at the same time. Extensive research has been carried out on concurrency-control techniques for transaction management both in centralized and in distributed environments [BERN87].

Data recovery: When transactions abort before they complete execution, the database should be recovered to a consistent state such as its state before the transaction started execution. Several recovery techniques have been proposed to ensure the consistency of the data.

Data authenticity: When the data are delivered to the user, their authenticity has to be ensured. That is, the user should get the accurate data and the data should not be tampered with. We have conducted research on ensuring authenticity of XML data during third-party publishing [BERT04].

Data completeness: The data that a user receives should not only be authentic but should also be complete. That is, everything that the user is authorized to see has to be delivered to the user.

Data currency: The data have to be current. That is, data that are outdated have to be deleted or archived and the data that the user sees have to be the current data. Data currency is an aspect of real-time processing. If a user wants to retrieve the temperature, he has to be given the current temperature, not the temperature that is 24-h old.

Data accuracy: The question is how accurate is the data? This is also closely related to data quality and data currency. That is, accuracy depends on whether the data have been maliciously corrupted or whether they have come from an untrusted source.

Data quality: Are the data of high quality? This includes data authenticity, data accuracy, and whether the data are complete or certain. If the data are uncertain, then can we reason under uncertainty to ensure that the operations that use the data are not affected? Data quality also depends on the data source.

Data provenance: This has to do with the history of the data, that is, from the time the data originated such as emanating from the sensors until the current time when they are given to the decision maker. The question is who has accessed the data? Who has modified the data? How has the data traveled? This will determine whether the data have been misused.

Integrity constraints: These are rules that the data have to satisfy such as that the age of a person cannot be a negative number. This type of integrity has been studied extensively by the database and the artificial intelligence communities.

Fault tolerance: As in the case of data recovery, the processes that fail have to be recovered. Therefore, fault tolerance deals with data recovery as well as process recovery. The techniques for fault tolerance include check pointing and acceptance testing.

Real-time processing: Data currency is one aspect of real-time processing where the data have to be current. Real-time processing also has to deal with transactions meeting timing constraints. For example, stock quotes have to be given within say 5 min. If not, it will be too late. Missing timing constraints could cause integrity violations.

31.2.2 Inferencing, Data Quality, and Data Provenance

Some researchers feel that data quality is an application of data provenance. Furthermore, they have developed theories for inferring data quality. In this section, we will examine some of the developments keeping in mind the relationship between data quality, data provenance, and the semantic cloud services.

Data quality is about accuracy, timeliness, and dependability (i.e., trustworthiness) of the data. However, it is subjective and depends on the users and the domains. Some of the issues that have to be answered include the creation of the data, that is, where did they come from and why and how was the data obtained? Data quality information is stored as annotations to the data and should be part of data provenance. One could ask the question as to how we can obtain the trustworthiness of the data. This could depend on how the source is ranked and the reputation of the source. Note that we discussed reputation in Chapter 29.

As we have stated, researchers have developed theories for inferring data quality [PON]. The motivation is due to the fact that data could come from multiple sources; they are shared and prone to errors. Furthermore, data could be uncertain. Therefore, theories of uncertainty such as statistical reasoning, Bayesian theories, and Dempster–Schafer theory of evidence are being used to infer the quality of the data. With respect to security, we need to ensure that the quality of the inferred data does not violate the policies. For example, at the unclassified level, we may say that the source is trustworthy but at the secret level, we know that the source is not trustworthy. The inference controllers that we have developed could be integrated with the theories of inferencing developed for data quality to ensure security.

Next, let us examine data provenance. For many of the domains including medical and health care, as well as defense where the accuracy of the data is critical, we need to have a good understanding as to where the data came from and who may have tampered with the data. As stated in [SIMM05], data provenance, a kind of metadata, sometimes called "lineage" or "pedigree" is the description of the origin of a piece of data and the process by which it arrived in a database. Data provenance is information that helps to determine the derivation history of a data product, starting from its original source.

Provenance information can be applied to data quality, auditing, and ownership, among others. By having records of who accessed the data, data misuse can be determined. Usually, annotations are used to describe the information related to the data (e.g., who accesses the data? Where did the data come from?) The challenge is to determine whether one needs to maintain coarse-grained provenance data or fine-grained provenance data. For example, in a coarse-grained situation, the tables of a relation may be annotated whereas in a fine-grained situation, every element may be annotated. There is of course the storage overhead to consider for managing provenance. XML, RDF, and OWL have been used to represent provenance data and this way, the tools developed for the semantic web technologies may be used to manage the provenance data.

There is much interest in using data provenance for misuse detection. For example, by maintaining the complete history of the data such as who accessed the data, when and where was the data accessed, one can answer queries such as "who accessed the data between January and May 2010?" Therefore, if the data are corrupted, one can determine who corrupted the data or when the data were corrupted. Figure 31.2 illustrates the aspects of data provenance. We have conducted extensive research on representing and reasoning about provenance data and policies represented using semantic web technologies [CADE11a], [CADE11b].

Data provenance

Who created the data?

Where has the data come from?

Who accessed the data?

What is the complete history of the data?

Has the data been misused?

Figure 31.2 Data provenance.

31.3 Integrity Management and Cloud Services

31.3.1 Cloud Services for Integrity Management

There are two aspects here. One is that integrity management may be implemented with cloud services and the other is ensuring that the cloud services have high integrity. For implementing integrity management as cloud services, the idea is to invoke cloud services to ensure data quality as well as the integrity of the data and the system. Figure 31.3 illustrates implementing integrity management as a cloud service.

Like confidentiality, privacy, and trust, semantic web technologies such as XML and RDF may be used to specify integrity policies. Integrity policies may include policies for specifying integrity constraints as well as policies for specifying timing constraints, data currency, and data quality. Here are some examples of the policies:

Integrity constraints: The age of an employee has to be positive. In a relational representation, one could specify this policy as

EMP.AGE > 0.

In XML, this could be represented as the following:

```
<Condition Object="//Employee/Age">
  <Apply FunctionId="greater-than">
    <AttributeValue DataType="http://www.w3.org/2001/XMLSchema#integer">0
```

Figure 31.3 Cloud service for integrity management.

```
    </AttributeValue>
  </Apply>
</Condition>
```

Data quality policy: The quality of the data in the employee table is LOW. In the relational model, this could be represented as

EMP.Quality = LOW.

In XML, this policy could be represented as

```
<Condition Object="//Employee/Quality">
  <Apply FunctionId="equal">
    <AttributeValue DataType="http://www.w3.org/2001/XMLSchema#string">
LOW
    </AttributeValue>
  </Apply>
</Condition>
```

Data currency: An example is the salary value of EMP cannot be more than 365-days old. In a relational representation, this could be represented as

AGE (EMP.SAL) <= 365 days.

In XML, this is represented as

```
<Condition Object="//Employee/Salary">
  <Apply FunctionId="AGE">
    <Apply FunctionId="less-than-or-equal">
      <AttributeValue DataType="http://www.w3.org/2001/XMLSchema#integer"
>365
      </AttributeValue>
    </Apply>
  </Apply>
</Condition>
```

The above examples have shown how certain integrity policies may be specified. Note that there are many other applications of semantic web technologies to ensure integrity. For example, to ensure data provenance, the history of the data has to be documented. Semantic web technologies such as XML are being used to represent the data annotations that are used to determine the quality of the data or whether the data have been misused. That is, the data captured are annotated with metadata information such as what the data are about, when they were captured, and who captured them. Then as the data move from place to place or from person to person,

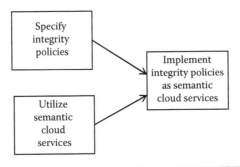

Figure 31.4   Semantic cloud services for integrity management.

the annotations are updated so that at a later time, the data may be analyzed for misuse. These annotations are typically represented in semantic web technologies such as XML, RDF, and OWL.

Another application of semantic web technologies for integrity management is the use of ontologies to resolve semantic heterogeneity. That is, semantic heterogeneity causes integrity violations. This happens when the same entity is considered to be different at different sites and therefore compromises integrity and accuracy. Through the use of ontologies specified in say OWL, it can be expressed that the ship in one site and submarine in another site are one and the same.

Semantic web technologies also have applications in making inferences and reasoning under uncertainty. For example, the reasoning engines based on RDF, OWL, or say rules may be used to determine whether the integrity policies are violated. We have discussed inference and privacy problems and building inference engines in this part. These techniques have to be investigated for violation integrity policies. In the case of semantic cloud services, these services are invoked to enforce or determine whether the data have been corrupted. Figure 31.4 illustrates the use of semantic cloud services for integrity management.

31.3.2 Integrity for the Cloud and Semantic Cloud Services

While we discussed the use of cloud services and semantic cloud services for integrity management, in this section, we examined issues to ensure that the cloud services have high integrity. The idea here is to ensure that the cloud service is not malicious and does not corrupt the data or other services. This means that the cloud services have to be verified or tested that they do not contain the malicious code. Figure 31.5 illustrates integrity management for cloud services.

We also need to ensure that integrity is maintained for semantic web technologies. The annotations that are used for data quality and provenance are typically represented in XML or RDF documents. These documents have to be accurate, complete, and current. Therefore, the semantic cloud services have to ensure that the documents maintain integrity. Another aspect of integrity is managing databases

Figure 31.5   Integrity for cloud services.

Figure 31.6   Integrity for semantic cloud services.

that consist of XML or RDF documents. These databases have all the issues and challenges that are present for say relational databases. That is, the queries have to be optimized and transactions should execute concurrently. Therefore, concurrency control and recovery for XML and RDF documents become a challenge for managing XML and RDF databases. In this case, the semantic cloud services carry out secure data management functions.

The agents, implemented as semantic cloud services, which carry out operations such as searching, querying, and integrating heterogeneous databases have to ensure that the integrity of the data is maintained. These agents cannot maliciously corrupt the data. They have to ensure that the data are accurate, complete, and consistent. Finally, when integrating heterogeneous databases, semantic web technologies such as OWL ontologies are being used to handle semantic heterogeneity. These ontologies have to be accurate and complete and cannot be tampered with.

In summary, for the semantic web technologies to be useful, they have to enforce integrity. Furthermore, semantic web technologies themselves are being used to specify and reason about integrity policies. Figure 31.6 illustrates integrity management for the semantic cloud services.

31.4 Summary and Directions

In this chapter, we have provided an overview of data integrity that includes data quality and data provenance. We discussed the applications of semantic web technologies for data integrity as well as discussed integrity for semantic web technologies. Finally, we provided an overview of the relationship between data quality and data provenance.

Data provenance and data quality while important, are only recently receiving attention. This is due to the fact that there are vast quantities of information on the cloud and it is important to know the accuracy of the data and whether the data are copied or plagiarized. We also need to have answers to questions such as who owns the data. Have the data been misused? Therefore, data provenance is important to determine the security of the data.

Cloud services should have high integrity. Furthermore, integrity techniques can be implemented as cloud services. Semantic web technologies provide a way to represent and store data quality and provenance data. As we make progress with these technologies, we will have improved solutions for data quality and data provenance management. Essentially, data quality and data provenance are part of data security and semantic web technologies are very useful to manage data quality and data provenance information.

References

[BERT04] Bertino, E., B. Carminati, E. Ferrari, B. Thuraisingham, and A. Gupta, Selective and authentic third party distribution of XML documents, *IEEE Transactions on Knowledge and Data Engineering*, 2004, 16(10), 1263–1278.

[BERN87] Bernstein, P. et al., *Concurrency Control and Recovery in Database Systems*, Addison-Wesley, MA, 1987.

[CADE11a] Cadenhead, T., V. Khadilkar, M. Kantarcioglu, and B.M. Thuraisingham, A language for provenance access control. CODASPY2011: 133–144.

[CADE11b] Cadenhead, T., V. Khadilkar, M. Kantarcioglu, and B. M. Thuraisingham, Transforming provenance using redaction. SACMAT2011: 93–102.

[PON] Pon, R. K. and A. F. Cárdenas, Data quality inference, UCLA Report.

[SIMM05] Simmhan, Y. L., B. Plale, and D. Gannon, *A Survey of Data Provenance in e-Science*; Indiana University Technical Report, also in SIGMOD record, 34(3), 2005.

Conclusion to Part VIII

While the previous parts focused mainly on access control models and confidentiality for cloud services, in Part VIII we discussed trust, privacy, and integrity issues for cloud services. In particular, we discussed privacy control, data quality as well as managing trust. Features such as confidentiality, trust, privacy, and integrity incorporated into the cloud will result in trustworthy clouds.

In Chapter 29, we discussed trust management and its connection to cloud services and semantic cloud services. We first discussed aspects of trust management, including defining trust and also describing trust negotiations. Then, we discussed aspects of enforcing trust within the context of the semantic cloud service. We also discussed the use of semantic cloud service technologies for specifying trust policies. In addition, related concepts including risk-based trust management and reputation networks were also discussed.

In Chapter 30, we discussed the various notions of privacy and provided an overview of privacy management. Then, we discussed the privacy management for cloud services. For example, cloud services have to maintain privacy. Furthermore, privacy controllers may be implemented as cloud services. We also discussed privacy for the semantic cloud and the use of semantic web technologies for specifying and reasoning about privacy policies.

In Chapter 31, we provided an overview of data integrity which includes data quality and data provenance. We discussed the applications of semantic cloud services for data integrity as well as discussed integrity for the semantic cloud. We also provided an overview of the relationship between data quality and data provenance.

BUILDING AN INFRASTRUCTURE, AN EDUCATION INITIATIVE, AND A RESEARCH PROGRAM FOR A SECURE CLOUD

IX

Introduction to Part IX

Now that we have provided an overview of the systems we have developed in cloud computing and secure cloud computing, we will describe the infrastructure, education initiative, and research program that we are developing that forms the foundation for our work in secure cloud computing.

Part IX consists of three chapters: 32, 33, and 34. Chapter 32 discusses the secure cloud computing infrastructure that we are developing at the UTD. Our educational program in secure cloud computing is discussed in Chapter 33. The collaborative research program that we have been leading for the past five years is discussed in Chapter 34. Many of the prototypes that we have discussed in the previous chapters have resulted from our research program. These prototypes are helping us to not only build secure infrastructures and enhancing our research, but also to build a strong education program in secure cloud computing.

Chapter 32

An Infrastructure for a Secure Cloud

32.1 Overview

As we have previously discussed, there is a critical need to securely store, manage, share, and analyze massive amounts of complex (e.g., semistructured and unstructured) data to determine patterns and trends to improve the quality of health care, safeguard the nation better, and explore alternative energy. However, to the best of our knowledge, there is no off-the-shelf infrastructure that addresses the above need. Therefore, we at UTD are developing an infrastructure that queries massive amounts of complex (e.g., semantic web and geospatial) data and maintains the confidentiality of these data and the privacy of individuals.

The emerging cloud computing model attempts to address the growth of web-connected devices and handle massive amounts of data. Google has now introduced the MapReduce framework for processing large amounts of data on commodity hardware. Apache's HDFS is emerging as a superior software component for cloud computing combined with integrated parts such as MapReduce. The need to augment human reasoning, interpreting, and decision-making abilities has resulted in the emergence of the semantic web, which is an initiative that attempts to transform the web from its current, merely human-readable form, to a machine-processable form. This in turn has resulted in numerous social-networking sites with massive amounts of data to be shared and managed. Therefore, we urgently need an infrastructure that can scale to handle a large number of sites and process massive amounts of data. However, state-of-the-art infrastructures utilizing HDFS and MapReduce are not sufficient due to the fact that (i) they do not provide adequate security mechanisms to protect sensitive data and (ii) they do not have the capability to process massive amounts of semantic web and geospatial data.

We are utilizing the state-of-the-art hardware, software, and data components and building an infrastructure that handles the inadequacies of the current cloud computing infrastructures. In particular, we (i) use modern hardware parts (e.g., secure coprocessors) to improve the performance due to incorporating additional security functionalities, (ii) integrate open-source software parts as well as custom-developed software parts to support query operations on complex data, (iii) support fine-grained access control and reference monitor support to provide security for complex data, and (iv) provide strong authentication mechanisms for cloud computing. The infrastructure facilitates several areas of computer and information science as well as social science research, including security and privacy, semantic web, geospatial information management, and social network analysis.

The technical contribution of our work is a cloud that supports fine-grained access control, storage of encrypted and sensitive data, complex query processing for massive data sets, and authentication mechanisms. This cloud is the first of its kind that we have developed for applications such as assured information sharing with massive amounts of data and consists of state-of-the-art hardware, software, and data components. It is utilized by our research projects on semantic web data management, assured information sharing, and automated reference monitors, among others. It should be noted that the development of our infrastructure is being carried out with funding from the AFOSR as well as the NSF and it is a work in progress.

The organization of this chapter is as follows: in Section 32.2, we will describe our infrastructure. Integrating with other infrastructures will be discussed in Section 32.3. Research enhancement with our infrastructure is discussed in Section 32.4. Education and performance aspects are discussed in Section 32.5. This chapter is summarized in Section 32.6. Figure 32.1 illustrates the contents of this chapter. Figure 32.2 illustrates the components of the infrastructure.

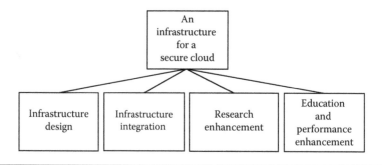

Figure 32.1 An infrastructure for a secure cloud.

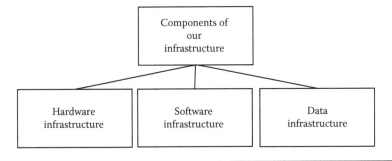

Figure 32.2 Components of our infrastructure. (From Hamlen, K.W., Kantarcioglu, M., and Khan, L. Security Issues for Cloud Computing, *This paper appears in the International Journal of Information Security and Privacy,* **Namati, H. (ed.), 4(2), 36–48. © 2010, IGI Global. With permission.)**

32.2 Description of the Research Infrastructure

32.2.1 Background

32.2.1.1 The Need for Our Infrastructure

There is a need to securely store, manage, share, and analyze massive amounts of data. For example, we may want to analyze multiple years of stock market data statistically to reveal a pattern or to build a reliable weather model based on several years of weather and related data. To handle such massive amounts of data distributed at many sites (i.e., nodes), we need an infrastructure with scalable hardware and software components. The cloud computing model has emerged to address the explosive growth of web-connected devices and handle massive amounts of data. It is defined and characterized by massive scalability and new Internet-driven economics. Hadoop is emerging as a superior software solution for cloud computing together with the integrated software parts such as Mahout, Hama, and MapReduce [MAHO, HAMA, CHU07, DEAN04]. Infrastructures such as HP's Open Cirrus test bed are utilizing HDFS. However, while such infrastructures have the advantages that come with Hadoop, they also have the limitations of Hadoop. These include the inability to handle complex data and have inadequate security protections. Owing to the fact that there is no infrastructure that can handle petabyte data sets consisting of semantic web and geospatial data as well as to provide secure storage and access to these data, we are developing such an infrastructure. Our infrastructure consists of a hardware component, a software component, and a data component.

32.2.1.2 Hadoop for Cloud Computing

A major part of the software component of our infrastructure is HDFS that is a distributed Java-based file system with the capacity to handle a large number of nodes storing

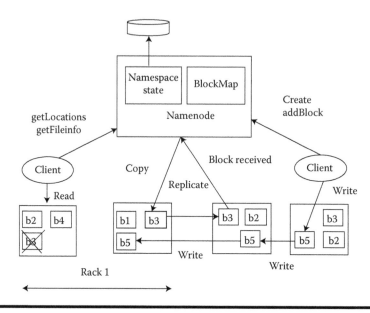

Figure 32.3   HDFS architecture.

petabytes of data. Ideally, a file size is a multiple of 64 MB. Reliability is achieved by replicating the data across several hosts. The default replication value is 3 (i.e., data are stored on three nodes). Two of these nodes reside on the same rack whereas the other node is on a different rack. A cluster of data nodes constructs the file system. The nodes transmit data over HTTP and clients access the data using a web browser. The data nodes communicate with each other to regulate, transfer, and replicate data.

HDFS architecture is based on the master–slave approach (Figure 32.3). The master is called a Namenode and contains metadata. It keeps the directory tree of all files and tracks from which data are available which node across the cluster. This information is stored as an image in the memory. Data blocks are stored in Datanodes. The Namenode is the single point of failure as it contains the metadata. So, there is an optional secondary Namenode that can be setup on any machine. The client accesses the Namenode to get the metadata of the required file. After getting the metadata, the client directly talks to the respective Datanodes to obtain data or to perform IO (input/output) actions [HADO]. On top of the file systems, there exists the *Map/ Reduce engine*. This engine consists of a JobTracker. The client applications submit Map/Reduce jobs to this engine. The JobTracker attempts to place the work near the data by pushing the work out to the available Task Tracker nodes in the cluster.

32.2.1.3 Inadequacies of Hadoop

At the time of writing, the current infrastructures utilizing Hadoop have the following limitations:

1. *No facility to handle encrypted sensitive data:* Sensitive data ranging from medical records to credit card transactions need to be stored using encryption techniques for additional protection. Currently, HDFS does not perform secure and efficient query processing over encrypted data.

2. *Semantic web data management:* There is a need for viable solutions to improve the performance and scalability of queries against semantic web data such as RDF. The number of RDF datasets is increasing. The problem of storing billions of RDF triples and the ability to efficiently query them is yet to be solved [MUYS06, TESW07, RAMA09a-c]. Currently, there is no support to store and retrieve RDF data in HDFS.

3. *No fine-grained access control:* HDFS does not provide fine-grained access control. There is some work to provide access control lists for HDFS [ZHAN09]. For many applications such as assured information sharing, access control lists are not sufficient and there is a need to support more complex policies.

4. *No strong authentication:* A user who can connect to the JobTracker can submit any job with the privileges of the account used to set up the HDFS. Future versions of HDFS will support network authentication protocols such as Kerberos for user authentication and encryption of data transfers [ZHAN09]. However, for some assured information-sharing scenarios, we need PKIs to provide digital signature support.

32.2.2 Infrastructure Development

We are developing an infrastructure for secure cloud computing. It consists of a hardware component (includes 800 TB—terabytes) of data storage on a mechanical disk drive, 2400 GB (gigabytes) of memory and 100 commodity computers, a software component (includes Hadoop), and a data component (includes a semantic web data repository). This infrastructure provides the following support to researchers: (a) efficient storage of encrypted sensitive data, (b) store, manage, and query massive amounts of data, (c) fine-grained access control, and (d) strong authentication. The development of the infrastructure consists of four parts to address each of the limitations of HDFS (as shown in Figure 32.4):

1. Incorporate secure coprocessor (SCP) parts to the hardware component to enable efficient encrypted storage of sensitive data.

2. Incorporate several parts to the software component including Mahout [MAHO], Hama [HAMA], Jena [JENA], and Pellet [PELL] as well as develop parts for SPARQL query processing over HDFS.

3. Incorporate an XACML [MOSE05] implementation part to the software component for fine-grained access control.

4. Incorporate a part for flexible authentication mechanisms.

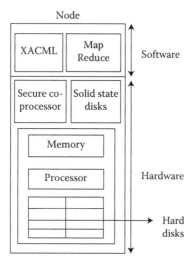

Figure 32.4   Secure coprocessor.

Note that while items (2), (3), and (4) are part of the software component, (1) is part of the hardware component.

One could ask us the question, why not implement your software component on a hardware component provided by the current cloud computing infrastructures such as Open Cirrus? We have explored this option. First, Open Cirrus provides limited access based on their economic model (e.g., virtual cash). Furthermore, Open Cirrus does not provide the hardware support we need (e.g., secure coprocessors). However, we are having discussions with HP on integrating our infrastructure into Open Cirrus.

32.2.3 Hardware Component of the Infrastructure

32.2.3.1 Cluster Part of the Hardware Component

At UTD, we already have substantial hardware to support our research. This hardware is part of the hardware component of the infrastructure. The hardware that we have currently includes three major clusters having different configurations. The first cluster is very small in size and is generally used as our test cluster. It consists of four nodes. Each node has Pentium-IV machines with 80 GB of hard disk space and 1 GB of main memory. We use the sample data in this cluster to test our code and carry out various optimization algorithms. The second cluster is placed in SAIAL (Security Analysis and Information Assurance Lab with lab support) lab and has a total of 32 nodes. All the nodes in this cluster run on commodity-class hardware on which Hadoop runs as well. This 32-node cluster has a mixed collection of hardware; 10 nodes have some high-end configuration such as Pentium-IV machines with 500 GB of disk space and 4 GB of main memory in each of them.

The remaining 22 nodes are also Pentium-IV machines having about 80 GB of hard disk space and 2 GB of main memory in each. All these nodes are connected to each other via 48-port Cisco switch on an internal network. Only the master node is accessible from the public network. The third cluster to which we have access is the Open Cirrus test bed infrastructure from HP Labs. We can use up to 30 nodes from their test bed. Each node has high-end configuration such as quad-core processor with 8 GB of main memory and more than 1 TB of hard disk space.

We considered three possible configurations for our project. They are the following:

1. Normal Dell precision machines (commodity hardware but less storage space per machine).
2. Assembled servers from different vendors that can support more disks per machine (commodity hardware).
3. SAN storage for data storage and 90 computers for computing (costs around 3–4 million dollars for a petabyte of data).

Since option 3 was too expensive, we did not investigate this option any further. Therefore, we further explored options 1 and 2.

Option 1: Dell machine configuration—An instance of each node of the cluster is a Dell precision machine having single quad-core Intel Xeon Processor E5502 with 4.8 GT/s. It has 24 GB of main memory DDR3, 1066 MZ, and 6 DIMM. Such a configuration allows us to use up to 6 GB of memory per core. Each of these nodes can store up to a maximum of four hard disks of 1.5 TB each and scaling up to 6 TB per node. Considering the replication factor of 3 for Hadoop, each node can actually store up to 2 TB of data at a maximum. So, if we had opted for these machines to scale our cloud and to store 800 TB of data, then we need 400 machines for which physical storage would have been an issue.

Option 2: Assembled server configuration—An instance of each node in the cluster is a 2U Rack Mount server. Each contains a two quad-core Intel Xeon Processor 5500 sequence with quick path interconnect (QPI) up to 6.4 GT/s. Moreover, each server contains 24 GB (12× MEM DDRIII 1333 2 GB ECC/REG) of memory. Thus, this kind of configuration allows us to use about 12 GB of memory per processor and 3 GB per core. We have room to extend the memory up to 48 GB. Furthermore, each server has Infiband 20 Gbps controller with SATA supporting RAID 5 for hard disk. The network controllers are Intel® 82576 dual-port Gigabit Ethernet controllers and also support 10BASE-T, 100BASE-TX, and 1000BASE-T, RJ45 output that reduces the chance for bottlenecks while there are IO operations or data transfers over the network. Hadoop is a distributed file system and thus, each node is a combination of solid-state drives as well as traditional storage devices. Each server may include a 128 GB solid-state disk (SSD) along with 12 disks with the traditional storage feature. It has a 12 × 3.5" hot-swap SAS/SATA drive trays. We are using a 12× HD WD20EADS SATA2 2 TB low power that gives us a total of 24 TB of physical available disk space per node. Hadoop is reliable because it maintains the replication of data. With the default replication factor being 3, each node can store up to 8 TB of data at a maximum. Out of these data, about 5–10% is used by the Hadoop temporary directory and the swap space needed for Map-Reduce functionality.

Once completed, our cloud will consist of 100 such nodes across in at most five racks. These nodes are a combination of storage nodes and compute nodes with some that serve as both. We are providing a Cisco 6509 switch for intra-rack communication for better throughput. In addition, according to the configuration discussed above for each node, we have 2400 TB (2.4 PB) of traditional disk storage and about 3.2 TB of SSD (assuming that 25 SSDs are deployed for 100 nodes). Considering the replication factor of Hadoop, our cloud is able to store up to 800 TB of data at a maximum.

Next, we compared our HDFS specification with benchmark hardware. Benchmark hardware on Hadoop–Apache Wiki provides two clusters for benchmark named as Herd 1 and Herd 2. For example, each node in Herd 1 consists of Intel Xeon LV 2.0 GHz, quad core, 4 GB RAM, and four disks each one of 0.25 TB SATA. Herd 1 consists of 35 nodes in total across two racks. In our cloud, each node has two quad-core processors and a high amount of RAM (24 GB) that is better than the benchmark hardware. Hence, we expect obviously good results on our cloud.

32.2.3.2 Secure Coprocessor Part of the Hardware Component

We are implementing this component mainly in hardware as follows. An SCP is embedded to handle encrypted data efficiently (see Figure 32.5). Basically, SCP is a tamper-resistant hardware capable of limited general-purpose computation. For example, IBM 4758 cryptographic coprocessor [IBM04] is a single-board computer consisting of a CPU, memory, and special-purpose cryptographic hardware contained in a tamper-resistant shell, certified to level 4 under FIPS PUB 140-1. When installed on the server, it is capable of performing local computations that are completely hidden from the server. If tampering is detected, then the SCP clears the internal memory. Since the SCP is tamper resistant, one could be tempted to run the entire sensitive data storage server on SCP. Pushing the entire data storage functionality into an SCP is not feasible due to many reasons.

First of all, due to the tamper-resistant shell, SCPs usually have limited memory (only a few megabytes of RAM and a few kilobytes of nonvolatile memory) and computational power [SMIT99]. The performance will improve over time, but problems such as heat dissipation/power use (that must be controlled to avoid disclosing processing) will force a gap between general purpose and secure computing. Another issue is that the software running on the SCP must be totally trusted and verified. This security requirement implies that the software running on the SCP should be kept as simple as possible. So, how does this hardware help in storing large sensitive data sets? We can encrypt the sensitive data sets using random private keys and to

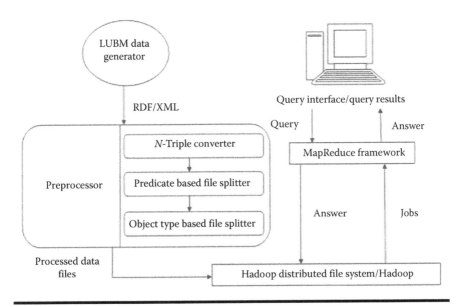

Figure 32.5 SPARQL query processing. (From Hamlen, K.W., Kantarcioglu, M., and Khan, L. Security Issues for Cloud Computing, *This paper appears in the International Journal of Information Security and Privacy,* **Namati, H. (ed.), 4(2), 36–48. © 2010, IGI Global. With permission.)**

alleviate the risk of key disclosure, we can use tamper-resistant hardware to store some of the encryption/decryption keys (i.e., a master key that encrypts all other keys). Since the keys will not reside in the memory unencrypted at any time, an attacker cannot learn the keys by taking the snapshot of the system. Also, any attempt by the attacker to take control of (or tamper with) the coprocessor, either through software or physically, will clear the coprocessor, thus eliminating a way to decrypt any sensitive information. This framework will facilitate (a) secure data storage and (b) assured information sharing. For example, SCPs can be used for privacy-preserving information integration that is important for assured information sharing [AGRA06].

32.2.4 Software Component of the Infrastructure

32.2.4.1 Component Part to Store, Query, and Mine Semantic Web Data

This part of the software component consists of the following:

Jena: This is a framework that is widely used for solving SPARQL queries over RDF data [JENA]. But the main problem with Jena is scalability. It scales in proportion to the size of the main memory. It does not have distributed processing. However, we are using Jena in the initial stages of our preprocessing steps.

Pellet: We use Pellet to reason at various stages. We do real-time query reasoning using Pellet libraries [PELL] coupled with Hadoop's Map/Reduce functionalities.

Pig Latin: Pig Latin is a scripting language that runs on top of Hadoop [GATE09]. Pig is a platform for analyzing large data sets. Pig's language, Pig Latin, facilitates the sequence of data transformations such as merging data sets, filtering them, and applying functions to records or groups of records. It comes with many built-in functions but we can also create our own user-defined functions to do special-purpose processing. Using this scripting language, we avoid writing our own Map/Reduce code; we rely on Pig Latin's scripting power that automatically generates the script code to Map/Reduce code.

Mahout, Hama: These are open-source data mining and machine-learning packages that already augment Hadoop [MAHO, HAMA, MORE08].

SPARQL query over Hadoop and its optimization: SPARQL is a query language used to query RDF data. The software part we are developing is a framework to query RDF data distributed over Hadoop [NEWM08, MCNA07, ROHL07]. There are a number of steps to preprocess and query RDF data (see Figure 32.5). With this part, researchers can obtain results to optimize query processing of massive amounts of data. Below, we discuss the steps involved in the development of this part.

Preprocessing: Generally, RDF data is in XML format (see LUBM, RDF data). To execute an SPARQL query, we carry out data preprocessing steps and store the preprocessed data into HDFS. We have an *N*-triple convertor module that converts RDF/XML format of data into *N*-triple format as this format is more understandable. We use the Jena framework for this conversion purpose. In predicate-based file splitter module, we split all *N*-triple format files based on the predicates. Therefore, the total number of files for a dataset is equal to the number of predicates in the ontology/taxonomy. In the last module of the preprocessing step, we further divide predicate files on the basis of the type of object it contains. So, now, each predicate file has specific types of objects in it. This is done with the help of the Pellet library. These preprocessed data are stored in Hadoop.

Query execution and optimization: We have developed an SPARQL query execution and optimization module for Hadoop (discussed in Chapter 13). As our storage strategy is based on predicate splits, first, we look at the predicates present in the query. Second, rather than looking at all the input files, we look at a subset of the input files that are matched with predicates. Third, SPARQL queries generally have many joins in them and all these joins may not be possible to perform in a single Hadoop job. Therefore, we devise an algorithm that decides the number of jobs required for each kind of query. As part of the optimization, we apply a greedy strategy and cost-based optimization to reduce query processing time. An example of greedy strategy is to cover the maximum number of possible joins in a single job. For the cost model,

the join to be performed first is based on summary statistics (e.g., selectivity factor of a bounded variable, join triple selectivity factor for three triple patterns). For example, consider a query for LUBM dataset:
"List all persons who are alumni of a particular university."

In SPARQL, this query is specified as follows:

PREFIX rdf: <http://www.w3.org/1999/02/32-rdf-syntax-ns#>
PREFIX ub: <http://www.lehigh.edu/~zhp2/2004/0401/univ-bench.owl#>
SELECT ?X WHERE {
?X rdf:type ub:Person.
<http://www.University0.edu> ub:hasAlumnus ?X}

The query optimizer takes this query input and decides a subset of input files to look at based on the predicate appearing in the query. Ontology and Pellet Reasoner identify three input files (underGraduateDegreeFrom, masterDegreeFrom, and DoctoraldegreeFrom) related to the predicate, "hasAlumns." Next, from the type of file, we filter all the records whose objects are a subclass of person using the Pellet library. From these three input files (underGraduateDegreeFrom, masterDegreeFrom, and DoctoraldegreeFrom), the optimizer filters out triples on the basis of <http://www.University0.edu> as required in the query. Finally, the optimizer determines the requirement for a single job for this type of query and then the join is carried out on the variable *X* in that job.

32.2.4.2 Integrating SUN XACML Implementation into HDFS with IRMs

The current Hadoop implementations enforce a very coarse-grained access control policy that permits or denies a principal access to essentially all system resources as a group without distinguishing among resources. For example, users who are granted access to the Namenode may execute any program on any client machine, and all client machines have read-and-write access to all files stored on all clients. Such coarse-grained security is clearly unacceptable when data, queries, and the system resources that implement them are security relevant, and when not all users and processes are fully trusted. The current work [ZHAN09] addresses this by implementing standard access control lists for Hadoop to constrain access to certain system resources, such as files; however, this approach has the limitation that the enforced security policy is baked into the OS and therefore cannot be easily changed without modifying the OS. We are enforcing a more flexible and fine-grained access control policy on Hadoop by designing an IRM implementation of Sun XACML. XACML [MOSE05] is an OASIS standard for expressing a rich language of access control policies in XML. Subjects, objects, relations, and contexts are all generic and extensible in XACML, making it well suited for a distributed environment where

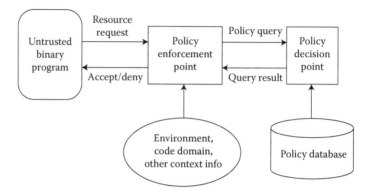

Figure 32.6 XACML enforcement mechanism. (From Hamlen, K.W., Kantarcioglu, M., and Khan, L. Security Issues for Cloud Computing, *This paper appears in the International Journal of Information Security and Privacy,* **Namati, H. (ed.), 4(2), 36–48. © 2010, IGI Global. With permission.)**

many different subpolicies may interact to form larger, composite, and system-level policies. An abstract XACML enforcement mechanism is depicted in Figure 32.6. Untrusted processes in the framework access security-relevant resources by submitting a request to the resource's PEP. The PEP reformulates the request as a policy query and submits it to a PDP. The PDP consults any policies related to the request to answer the query. The PEP either grants or denies the resource request based on the answer it receives. While the PEP and PDP components of the enforcement mechanism are traditionally implemented at the level of the OS or as trusted system libraries, we achieve greater flexibility by implementing them in our infrastructure as IRMs. IRMs implement runtime security checks by in-lining those checks directly into the binary code of untrusted processes. This has the advantage that the policy can be enforced without modifying the OS or system libraries. IRM policies can additionally constrain program operations that might be difficult or impossible to intercept at the OS level. For example, memory allocations in Java are implemented as Java bytecode instructions that do not call any external program or library. Enforcing a fine-grained memory-bound policy as a traditional reference monitor in Java therefore requires modifying the Java virtual machine or JIT compiler. In contrast, an IRM can identify these security-relevant instructions and inject the appropriate guards directly into the untrusted code to enforce the policy.

Finally, IRMs can efficiently enforce history-based security policies, rather than merely policies that constrain individual security-relevant events. For example, our past work [JONE09] has used IRMs to enforce fairness policies that require untrusted applications to share as much data as they request. This prevents processes from affecting denial of service attacks based on freeloading behavior. The code injected into the untrusted binary by the IRM constrains each program operation based on the past history of program operations rather than in isolation. This involves injecting security state variables and counters into the untrusted code, which is difficult to accomplish efficiently at the OS level.

The core of an IRM framework consists of a *binary-rewriter*, which statically modifies the binary code of each untrusted process before it is executed to insert security guards around potentially dangerous operations. Our binary-rewriter implementation is based on SPoX (security policy XML) [HAML08], which we developed to enforce declarative, XML-based, IRM policies for Java bytecode programs. To provide strong security guarantees for our system, we apply automated software verification technologies, including type and model checking, which we have previously used to certify the output of binary-rewriters [HAML06, DEVR09]. Such certification allows a small, trusted verifier to independently prove that the rewritten binary code satisfies the original security policy, thereby shifting the comparatively larger binary-rewriter out of the trusted computing base of the system.

Once we have the basic framework implemented, in the future, we can extend this by incorporating context and temporal policies as well as policies for data provenance, roles, and usage.

32.2.4.3 Component Part for Strong Authentication

Currently, Hadoop does not authenticate users. This makes it hard to enforce access control for security-sensitive applications and makes it easier for malicious users to circumvent file permission checking done by HDFS. To address these issues, the open-source community is actively working to integrate Kerberos protocols with Hadoop [ZHAN09]. On top of the Kerboros protocol, for some assured information-sharing tasks, there may be a need for adding simple authentication protocols to authenticate with secure coprocessors. For this reason, we add a simple PKI to our infrastructure so that users can independently authenticate with secure coprocessors to retrieve the secret keys used for encrypting sensitive data. We plan to use open-source PKI such as the OpenCA PKI implementation for our infrastructure [OPEN].

32.2.5 Data Component of the Infrastructure

This component consists of the semantic web data repository. We use the Lehigh University Benchmark [LUBM] and the Barton dataset [HURT06]. The LUBM dataset is a synthetic dataset representing a university domain. This allows us to vary the number of triples in the dataset to test scalability. The Barton dataset is not a synthetic dataset; instead, it is an RDF representation of the MIT library catalog. We have chosen it primarily as a common denominator for the evaluation of prior research in semantic web. The Barton dataset is used for evaluation in [WEIS08].

The Barton dataset includes a high number of unique URIs: 18.5 million in a dataset of 50 million triples. The repository can be built on either our current clusters or on the new infrastructure for any of the datasets we use depending on the size of the data. We are building a repository into our infrastructure that can store up to 800 TB of data that are much more than 100 billion RDF triples. In addition, this new infrastructure can process larger amounts of data because of larger disk space (24 TB) and main memory (24 GB) in each individual machine.

32.3 Integrating the Cloud with Existing Infrastructures

We are also integrating the infrastructure with clusters operating at SAIAL at UTD as well as with the infrastructure set up at each of the research labs. We also have an additional lab (currently not in use) to store some of the hardware parts. We are exploring two approaches for the integration:

Separate the current infrastructure and the new infrastructure: Here, we have data in normalized form with the current clusters that can then be loaded into the new infrastructure. Later on, different Map Reduce algorithms are executed and tested on the normalized data present on the infrastructure. The advantage is that we separate the old hardware with the new hardware. The main drawback is when we have to generate and process very large amounts of data. Consider the SPARQL query optimization module using LUBM dataset. Our current infrastructure can handle about 5.5 billion triples with the total size of 414 GB. To generate large data for 100 billion triples using our current clusters, we need to do the data generation in steps and transfer it to the new infrastructure periodically.

Integrate the new infrastructure with the current infrastructure: Here, we can merge both the current infrastructure with the new infrastructure and use the combined power for data generation, data preprocessing, and for executing and testing Map Reduce algorithms. Hadoop gives us the flexibility to add or remove nodes from the cluster at any point in time. To merge them, we have to set up all the machines on the same internal network and this can be achieved by using switches. The drawback is that with the mixture of different hardware, performance may suffer without performance-oriented variable settings. Our entire cluster is a mixture of a few nodes (old machines) having 2–4 GB of main memory and about 200 GB of hard disk space whereas other nodes (new infrastructure) have 24 GB of main memory with 8 TB of disk space. However, performance can be improved by tuning a few performance-oriented variables available in Hadoop. Therefore, based on the above discussions, we are inclined to integrate our infrastructure with the current training and research infrastructures.

Integrating with external infrastructures: The UTD team is conducting experiments with HP Lab's Open Cirrus test bed. This test bed will be greatly enhanced by our infrastructure. In addition, we are planning to work with the NSF/DOE (Department of Energy) open-science researchers as well as DOD researchers to integrate our infrastructure.

32.4 Sample Projects Utilizing the Cloud Infrastructure

1. *An integrated approach for efficient privacy-preserving distributed data analytics:* Currently, we are developing efficient privacy-preserving data analysis tools for large distributed data sets. The infrastructure is an excellent vehicle for building several experiments to simulate mining large amounts of privacy-sensitive electronic medical records using our novel techniques. In addition, the infrastructure enables us to explore the possible usage of the modern security hardware such as SCPs in large-scale privacy-preserving data analysis applications.

2. *A semantic framework for policy specification and enforcement in a need to share environment:* As a part of this project, we have developed a policy framework that leverages the semantic web tools for ontology management and reasoning. One of the problems with the current semantic web tools is that they do not scale well with respect to storage as well as reasoning. We believe that the infrastructure's storage, query, and reasoning capabilities could be used to enable efficient storage, query, and reasoning.

3. *A framework for assured information sharing life cycle:* To test the solutions that we are developing, we need a scalable platform that supports complex policy management. We believe that the infrastructure provides such a platform. For example, the scalable implementation of XACML policies could be used for information sharing across organizations. The SCP part could be augmented with the assured information-sharing infrastructure to store and query encrypted data. This project gives us the opportunity to distribute our cloud across multiple sites and test our infrastructure.

4. *Certified in-lined reference monitoring:* We are developing a suite of tools for parsing, analyzing, and enforcing declaratively specified IRM security policies through automatic rewriting of Java bytecode binaries. An important facet of this endeavor is to apply and test the technology on large-scale applications and in real-world, security-sensitive architectures. The infrastructure is an excellent platform for investigating our research questions and for developing practical solutions to some of the challenges related to efficient IRM implementations for concurrent, highly distributed architectures.

5. *Relational transformation of RDF data:* Our current implementation of relational transformation of RDF data does not scale well [RAMA09a, RAMA09b]. It can handle a limited number of RDF triples (millions) to handle SPARQL queries. However, using our infrastructure's SPARQL query over Hadoop and its optimization, we will be able to handle billions of triples. Hence, by utilizing the infrastructure, the R2D wrapper will provide a scalable solution for the semantic web community.

6. *Schema/ontology matching:* To facilitate ontology/schema matching [PART09], [PART08], [SUBB07], and [ALIP11], we need to extract a high-dimensional feature set and determine its corresponding weights. This feature-extraction process is time consuming with the current state of the art due to its serial

nature. Our infrastructure will be able to extract large feature sets rapidly. Therefore, we will exploit our infrastructure's parallel and distributed processing capability to enhance our research.

7. *Event cube: An organized approach for mining and understanding anomalous aviation events*—Our microcluster/summary strategies may adversely affect classification accuracy due to the imprecise nature of the summary data. It would be better if we keep raw data along with the summary data. Owing to the main memory limitations, currently, we need to discard raw data from each chunk immediately [MASU08], [MASU09]. However, using HDFS along with Pig Latin [GATE09], we will be able to handle massive volumes of data rapidly. This way, we can accommodate raw data along with summary data in high-speed memory. Furthermore, SSD will facilitate high-speed retrieval of data thereby dramatically increasing the speed of classification training and testing.

8. *Secure cloud computing:* We have developed several secure cloud computing technologies including secure cloud data and information management (see Chapters 13, 14, 15, 22, 23, 24, 25, 26, 27, 28 in Parts IV, VI, and VII). In addition, we have also developed security models for the cloud. We can test out techniques and tools using the infrastructure. We will discuss some of the details of this research in Chapter 34 and will also provide several references.

32.5 Education and Performance

32.5.1 Education Enhancement

We offer several courses on information security and information management including courses in data and applications, security, privacy, cryptography, digital forensics, software and language security, trustworthy semantic web, data mining, multimedia information systems, and web services. These courses are benefitting from the infrastructure. We are also developing new courses on secure cloud computing as part of an NSF grant and will be discussed in Chapter 33. Furthermore, as part of the programming projects for the data and applications security as well as for the trustworthy semantic web courses, we have devised class projects that the students carry out to support the development of the infrastructure. One such project is to enhance XACML implementation and to provide access based on context, time, and usage. Therefore, not only are the courses benefitting from the infrastructure, the infrastructure is also benefitting from the courses.

32.5.2 Performance

The SPARQL query processing part of the software component is an ideal candidate for evaluating performance. We are implementing and evaluating experiments with the two benchmarks, the Lehigh University Benchmark [LUBM] and the Barton dataset [HURT06]. We have experimented with datasets ranging from 1 million to 5.5 billion triples with LUBM. This dataset provides a well-defined OWL ontology and includes rules for inference. Many research projects including Hexastore [WEIS08] have used LUBM for evaluation. We have created a database with 5.5 billion triples/tuples with a storage size of 1.2 TB (for intermediate file-n3 format)/414 GB (normalized data). As a part of the evaluation, we are conducting more experiments with larger datasets.

32.6 Summary and Directions

In this chapter, we have described the infrastructure we are developing for a secure cloud to support our projects. Our cloud consists of a hardware component, a software component, and a data component. We are integrating the cloud with our current infrastructures and have developed a number of tools that utilize our infrastructure. Some of these tools were discussed in the Chapters 13, 14, 15, 22, 23, 24, 25, 26, 27, 28 in Parts IV, VI, and VII of this book. These include secure query processing in the cloud, social networking in the cloud, and malware detection in the cloud. We utilize the Hadoop/MapReduce technologies to provide the data storage for the cloud.

We will continue to enhance our infrastructure to meet our needs for both research and education. Furthermore, as the technologies advance, we will upgrade the cloud. One challenge we have is whether to build our own cloud or utilize clouds such as Amazon's EC2. We will be utilizing both our cloud and clouds offered by third-party vendors. We believe that for some of our research and education efforts, we need to have our own cloud. However, for carrying out massive amounts of data processing, we may benefit by the use of clouds such as Amazon EC2.

References

[AGRA06] Agrawal, R., D. Asonov, M. Kantarcioglu, and Y. Li, Sovereign joins. *Proceedings of International Conference on Data Engineering (ICDE)*, 2006.

[ALIP11] Alipanah, N., L., Khan, and B., Thuraisingham, Ontology-driven query expansion methods to facilitate federated queries, Technical report, UTDCS-30-11, The University of Texas at Dallas, 2011.

[CHU07] Chu, C.-T., S. K. Kim, Y.-A. Lin, Y. Yu, G. Bradski, A. Y. Ng, and K. Olukotun, Map-Reduce for machine learning on multicore. *Proceedings of Conference on Neural Information Processing Systems (NIPS)*, 2006.

[DEAN04] Dean, J. and S. Ghemawat, Map Reduce: Simplified data processing on large clusters Osdi'04. *Proceedings of the 6th Conference on Symposium on Operating Systems Design and Implementation*, 10 pp., 2004, p. 137–150, San Francisco, CA.

[DEVR09] DeVries, B. W., G. Gupta, K. W. Hamlen, S. Moore, and M. Sridhar, Action script bytecode verification with co-logic programming. In *Proceedings of the ACM*

SIGPLAN Workshop on Programming Languages and Analysis for Security (PLAS), June 2009, Dublin, Ireland.

[GATE09] Gates, F., O. Natkovich, S. Chopra, P. Kamath, S. M. Narayanamurthy, C. Olston, B. Reed, S. Srinivasan, and U. Srivastava, Building a high-level data flow system on top of Map-Reduce: The Pig experience. *Proceedings of VLDB Endowment*, 2(2), August 2009.

[HADO] HADOOP: http://hadoop.apache.org; http://hadoop.apache.org/core/docs/r0.18.3/hdfsdesign.html

[HAMA] HAMA: http://cwiki.apache.org/labs/cloudsglossary.html

[HAML06] Hamlen, K. W., G. Morrisett, and F. B. Schneider, Certified in-lined reference monitoring on .NET. In *Proceedings of the ACM SIGPLAN Workshop on Programming Languages and Analysis for Security (PLAS)*, June 2006, Ottawa, Canada.

[HAML08] Hamlen, K. W. and M. Jones, Aspect-oriented in-lined reference monitors. In *Proceedings of the ACM SIGPLAN Workshop on Programming Languages and Analysis for Security (PLAS)*, June 2008, Tucson, AZ.

[HAML10] Hamlen, K.W., Kantarcioglu, M., and Khan, L. Security Issues for Cloud Computing, *This paper appears in the International Journal of Information Security and Privacy*, Namati, H. (ed.), 4(2), 2010, p. 36–48.

[HURT06] Hurtado, C.A., A. Poulovassilis, and P. T. Wood, A relaxed approach to RDF querying. *In Proceedings of International Semantic Web Conference*, pp. 314–328, 2006, Athens, GA.

[IBM04] IBM. IBM PCI cryptographic coprocessor, 2004. http://www.ibm.com/security/cryptocards.

[JENA] Jena: http://jena.sourceforge.net

[JONE09] Jones M. and K. W. Hamlen, Enforcing IRM security policies: Two case studies. In *Proceedings of the IEEE Intelligence and Security Informatics Conference (ISI)*, June 2009, Dallas, TX.

[LUBM] Lehigh University Benchmark (LUBM). http://swat.cse.lehigh.edu/projects/lubm.

[MAHO] Mahout: http://lucene.apache.org/mahout/

[MASU08] Masud, M., J. Gao, L. Khan, J. Han, and B. M. Thuraisingham, A practical approach to classify evolving data streams: Training with limited amount of labeled data, In *Proceedings of IEEE International Conference on Data Mining (ICDM 2008)*, Pisa, Italy, pp. 929–934, December 2008.

[MASU09] Masud, M., J. Gao, L. Khan, J. Han, and B. M. Thuraisingham, Integrating novel class detection with classification for concept-drifting data streams, *Proceedings of the European Conference on Machine Learning and Principles and Practice of Knowledge Discovery in Databases (ECML/PKDD)*, Bled, Slovenia, September 7–11, 2009, 79–94, Part II.

[MCNA07] McNabb, A. W. Monson, K. Christopher, and K. D. Seppi, MRPSO: MapReduce particle swarm optimization GECCO '07: *Proceedings of the 9th Annual Conference on Genetic and Evolutionary Computation*, 177 ACM Press, 2007, London, UK.

[MORE08] Moretti, C., K. Steinhaeuser, D. Thain, and N. V. Chawla, Scaling up classifiers to cloud computers, *IEEE International Conference on Data Mining (ICDM)*, 2008, Pisa, Italy.

[MOSE05] Moses, T., ed. *eXtensible Access Control Markup Language (XACML) Version 2.0*, OASIS Standard, February 2005. http://docs.oasis-open.org/xacml/2.0/access_control-xacml-2.0-core-spec-os.pdf

[MUYS06] Muys, A., Building an enterprise-scale database for RDF data, 2006, Netymon Technical Paper.

[NEWM08] Newman, A., J. Hunter, Y. F. Li, C. Bouton, and M. Davis, A scale-out RDF molecule store for distributed processing of biomedical data WWW '08: *Proceedings of the 17th International Conference on World Wide Web*, pp. 595–604, 2008, Beijing, China.

[OPEN] OpenCA implementation, http://www.openca.org/projects/openca/

[PART08] Partyka, J., N. Alipanah, L. Khan, B. M. Thuraisingham, and S. Shekhar, Content-based ontology matching for GIS datasets, *ACM International Symposium on Geographic Information Systems, ACM-GIS 2007*, November 7–9, 2008, Seattle, Washington, USA, pp. 407–410.

[PART09] Partyka, J., L. Khan, and B. Thuraisingham, Semantic schema matching without shared instances, *Third IEEE International Conference on Semantic Computing*, Berkeley, CA, USA, September 14–16, 2009, 297–302.

[PELL] Pellet: http://clarkparsia.com/pellet

[RAMA09a] Ramanujam, S., A. Gupta, L. Khan, S. Seida, and B. Thuraisingham, R2D: A bridge between the semantic web and relational visualization tools, to appear in *Third IEEE International Conference on Semantic Computing*, Berkeley, CA, USA, September 14–16, 2009, 303–311.

[RAMA09b] Ramanujam, S., A. Gupta, L. Khan, S. Seida, and B. M. Thuraisingham, Relationalizing RDF stores for tools reusability. *18th International Conference on World Wide Web, WWW 2009*, Madrid, Spain, April 20–24, 2009, pp. 1059–1060.

[RAMA09c] Ramanujam, S., A. Gupta, L. Khan, and S. Seida, R2D: Extracting relational structure from RDF stores, *ACM/IEEE International Conference on Web Intelligence*, September, 2009, Milan, Italy.

[ROHL07] Rohloff, K., M. Dean, I. Emmons, D. Ryder, and J. Sumner, *An Evaluation of Triple-Store Technologies for Large Data Stores on the Move to Meaningful Internet Systems 2007*. OTM 2007 Workshops, pp. 1105–1114, 2007, Part II, Vilamoura, Portugal.

[SMIT99] Smith, S.W. and S.H. Weingart, Building a high-performance, programmable secure coprocessor. *Computer Networks (Special Issue on Computer Network Security)*, (31): 831–860, 1999.

[SUBB07] Subbiah, G., A. Alam, L. Khan, and B. M. Thuraisingham, Geospatial data qualities as web services performance metrics, in *Proceedings of ACM International Symposium on Geographic Information Systems, ACM-GIS 2007*, November 7–9, 2007, Seattle, Washington, USA.

[TESW07] Teswanich, W. and S. Chittayasothorn, A transformation of RDF documents and schemas to relational databases, *IEEE Pacific Rim Conferences on Communications, Computers, and Signal Processing, 2007*, pp. 38–41, Victoria, B. C., Canada.

[WEIS08] Weiss, C., P. Karras, and A. H. Bernstein, : Sextuple indexing for semantic web data management. *In Proceedings of Very Large Data Bases (VLDB 2008)*, Auckland, New Zealand.

[ZHAN09] Zhang, K., Adding user and service-to-service authentication to Hadoop, https://issues.apache.org/jira/browse/HADOOP-4343.

Chapter 33

An Education Program for a Secure Cloud

33.1 Overview

As stated in Chapter 32, to address the limitations of current cloud computing platforms, at UTD, we have utilized state-of-the-art hardware, software, and data components based on Hadoop and MapReduce technologies and are developing a secure cloud computing infrastructure for the AFRL since 2008 [AFRL]. In particular, we have used modern hardware parts (e.g., secure coprocessors) to improve the performance due to incorporating additional security functionalities, integrated open source software parts, as well as custom-developed software parts to support secure cloud query operations on complex data, provide fine-grained access control and reference monitor support as well as provide strong authentication mechanisms.

To build effective secure cloud computing systems, we also need to build a strong education program on this topic so that we get students to work on the projects. Therefore, in addition to developing our cloud infrastructure discussed in Chapter 32, we are also establishing a strong education program with several courses in assured cloud computing with funding from NSF received in 2011. These courses form a comprehensive set that will provide an example for secure cloud computing capacity building and education in other institutions. Our capacity building project leverages the extensive investments we have made in assured cloud computing research and IA education at UTD to develop courses in assured cloud computing. In particular, we are developing new courses related to building and assuring the cloud as well as enhancing our existing courses on network

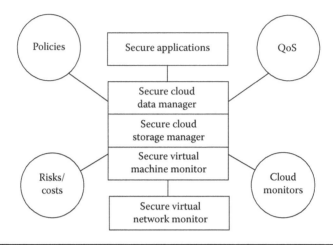

Figure 33.1   Cloud computing framework.

security, data and applications security, data mining for security applications, and digital forensics by introducing a major component in secure cloud computing for each of these courses. We are also enhancing the current cloud computing framework that we have developed so that students can (i) utilize this framework for their course projects and (ii) build features to this framework as a part of their class programming projects. Our courses are being made available to a number of partners we are collaborating with in cloud computing research. Our cloud computing framework is illustrated in Figure 33.1.

Our education program in assured cloud computing is built on our strong education program in Information Assurance (IA) since 2000 at UTD. We were designated an NSA/DHS (National Security Agency/Department of Homeland Security) Center for Excellence in Education in 2004 and for Research in 2008. We received the NSF SFS (Scholarship for Service) award in 2010 and are training students to obtain master's degrees in IA. Our course offerings include systems secure and privacy, network security, data/applications security, trustworthy web services/semantic web, cryptography, data mining for security and digital forensics. As illustrated in Figure 33.2, our research in assured cloud computing as well as our education program in IA will be integrated to build a strong capacity for assured cloud computing education at UTD.

The organization of this chapter is as follows. In Section 33.2, we will describe our current IA program including course offerings, degrees, and certificates. Our education program will be described in Section 33.3. Our evaluation plan will be discussed in Section 33.4. This chapter is summarized in Section 33.5. It should be noted that our project is in progress and is expected to be completed by 2014. The contents of this chapter are illustrated in Figure 33.3. An overview of our approach to cloud computing is discussed in [HAML10].

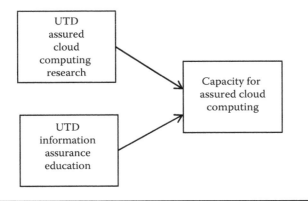

Figure 33.2 Assured cloud computing.

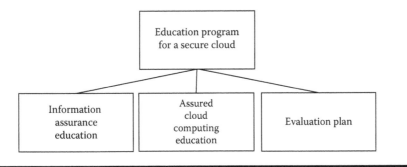

Figure 33.3 An education program for a secure cloud.

33.2 IA Education at UTD

33.2.1 Overview of UTD CS

UTD is located in an area that is only second to Silicon Valley in terms of the number of high-tech companies that are housed there. UTD Computer Science plays a vital role for this high-tech industry by supplying graduates and interns as well as collaborative industrial research. UTD CS ranked fifth in the nation last year in terms of total number of graduates produced. UTD CS has made significant investments in developing the infrastructure for IA education and research and identified "make the nation secure" as one of its six strategic goals.

The CS Department made significant investment in developing the research and teaching infrastructure for cyber security. These include: (i) establishment of multiple faculty lines to hire faculty members in the area of computer security and

IA; (ii) efforts to become an NSA Center of Excellence in Information Assurance Education (2004) and Research (2008); (iii) establishing the Cyber Security and Emergency Preparedness Institute, which houses the Cyber Security Research and Education Center; (iv) making significant investment to build the *Security Analysis and Information Assurance Laboratory* (SAIAL) to meet MIL-STD-285 standards; (v) offering several courses in the area of Cyber Security and Information Assurance; and (vi) offering graduate and undergraduate certificates in Information Assurance (since 2004), a minor in Information Assurance (since 2006) and an MS track in IA (since 2010).

33.2.2 Course Offerings in IA

CS department offers a strong curriculum at both the graduate and the undergraduate levels. Our course offerings can be found in [CS]. With the hiring of the new faculty, there has been a significant increase in the number of new course offerings in IA. The current IA courses in CS department include:

Undergraduate Level

1. Computer and network security
2. Data and application security
3. Digital forensics

Graduate Level

4. Cyber security essentials (covers the 10 CISSP modules)
5. Information security
6. Cryptography (both introductory and advanced levels)
7. Network security
8. Data and application security
9. Data privacy
10. Language-based security
11. Building trustworthy semantic web and web services
12. Data mining for security applications
13. Systems security and forensics
14. Reverse engineering and malware analysis
15. Biometrics
16. Critical infrastructure protection
17. Secure social networks
18. Secure cloud computing

As a part of our cloud computing initiative, we have introduced a number or courses including secure cloud data security and secure WS and cloud computing. These courses will be discussed in Section 33.3. Education and research in IA

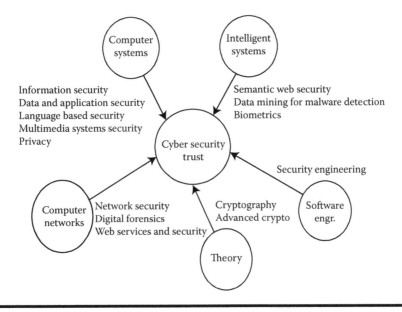

Figure 33.4 Computer science program.

currently cuts across the five concentration areas in the CS department as illustrated in Figure 33.4. For example, the computer systems track offers courses in information/systems security while the theory track offers courses in cryptography. Our students have exposure to activities in IA in government labs as well as in commercial industry and with defense contractors. For example, our students in the digital forensics class are taken on field trips to tour the North Texas FBI Lab and receive guest lectures from the Richardson Police department. In addition to the above CS courses, the School of Management (SoM) and the School of Economics, Policy, and Political Sciences (EPPS) at UTD offer courses that are related to management, and policy aspects of IA including risk analysis. We are collaborating with these schools on interdisciplinary research and proposing an interdisciplinary graduate program in cyber security.

33.2.3 Our Educational Programs in IA

The CS department at UTD has several programs in IA including a minor in IA for non-CS students, certification programs both at the undergraduate and graduate levels, and a recently instituted masters concentration track at the graduate level. The department also offers security-related courses under the professional education program that is open to professionals in the DFW (Dallas-Fort Worth) Metroplex. The undergraduate minor requires students to complete three undergraduate level IA courses including data and applications security, computer and network security, and digital forensics along with the pre-requisites. The undergraduate certificate program is open to CS students and requires students to complete the above mentioned three IA courses. At the graduate level, the certification has multiple options. Since the program's inception in 2003, over 250 students have received IA certifications. The CS department offers a concentration track in IA at the graduate level. The IA track started in Fall 2010 semester and requires students to complete a set of five or more IA-specific courses. More details about the concentration track in IA can be found at the department web site (http:// cs.utdallas.edu/about/degreesoffered.html).

33.2.4 Equipment and Facilities for IA Education and Research

The CS department houses several laboratory facilities that are actively used for IA education and research. SAIAL, a state-of-the-art laboratory, was founded in 2004 and is a major facility that faculty use for research and education. The lab consists of three separate rooms each individually tested to meet MIL-STD-285 TEMPEST standard. Figure 33.5 gives an outline of the facility and its equipment. Some of the research uses of the lab include: (i) simulations and testing to identify security vulnerabilities of multi-vendor systems and networks; (ii) benchmarking and quantifying security vulnerabilities utilizing customized and commercial-off-the-shelf (COTS) tools, "white hat" hacking techniques to advance the use of customized and COTS software analysis tools, and repository of known and suspected vulnerabilities and analysis techniques for vulnerability assessment, including viruses, worms; (iii) development and testing of advanced digital forensic techniques as well as conducting forensics, and (iv) conducting lab exercises in network security courses and experimenting with intrusion detection and intruder tracking.

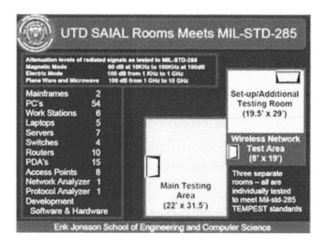

Figure 33.5 SAIAL at UTD.

In addition to the SAIAL, the department has a Computer Networks Instructional Lab (CNIL) that is used in our Networks Laboratory course and our hands-on lab experiments in the network security course. This lab initially was funded by the Jonsson School with funds from the State of Texas and included networking equipment. Recently, with the help of a capacity building grant from the DoD IASP (Information Assurance Scholarship Program), we acquired equipment for practical hands-on network security education purposes. The equipment includes three high-end Dell R805 servers with multi-core Opteron processors and 64 GB memory. Using VMware virtualization software system, this equipment is capable of supporting 100-node network environments to perform a diverse set of network security lab exercise activities. There are also additional labs managed by the IA professors (e.g., Data Security and Privacy Lab, Data Mining Lab, Information Assurance Lab, and Software Security Lab). In addition, UTD is building a secure cloud computing infrastructure discussed in Chapter 32 as part of our secure cloud project funded by AFOSR and NSF.

33.3 Assured Cloud Computing Education Program

33.3.1 Organization of the Capacity-Building Activities

Our capacity-building project consists of two major components: (i) curriculum development and (ii) laboratory development. A capstone project course around cloud security is one of the major outcomes of this effort. Cloud systems are comprehensive systems including different layers making up a fairly complex and critical computing resource. Securing a cloud system involves different aspects of security all the way from data security to access control to defense against social engineering attacks from system-level security to network security to the use of various security technologies (firewall systems, intrusion detection systems, etc.). Our course emphasizes how the principles of distributed computing come together to build a secure cloud. In particular, we use knowledge in known security vulnerabilities of distributed systems and known and new ways to address those vulnerabilities in the context of securing a cloud computing system.

Our current secure cloud computing framework includes secure cloud VM, secure cloud data management, secure cloud storage, and secure cloud monitoring. In addition, we are utilizing our extensive interdisciplinary research on integrating risk and cost analysis for secure systems to teach aspects of risk-based secure cloud management. We are closely examining the additional considerations for cloud forensics and incorporating these aspects into our course. The second part of the capacity project is to build a realistic instructional cloud system with all the necessary components and develop necessary curriculum around it to teach various aspects of information assurance and computer security as it relates to securing such large-scale cloud systems. Our system will be open to other institutions for similar educational purposes and we will share the curriculum material and the use of our instructional cloud system in their curriculum in accordance with the NSF and UTD policies and procedures. Our curriculum will be discussed in Section 33.3.2. Our programming projects for students will be discussed in Section 33.3.3. Instructional cloud computing facility will be discussed in Section 33.3.4.

33.3.2 Curriculum Development Activities

We are taking a two-pronged approach to curriculum development: the first is a capstone course on assured cloud computing and the second is to introduce components into several of our key courses in IA. We will discuss details of both approaches below. Our approach is illustrated in Figure 33.6.

33.3.2.1 Capstone Course

Our capstone course is motivated by (a) research and development in cloud computing, (b) emerging assured cloud computing research, prototypes, products, and standards, and (c) the research and experimentation UTD is conducting for

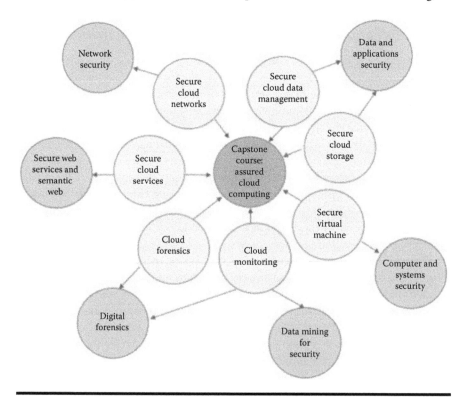

Figure 33.6 Course offerings in assured cloud computing.

AFOSR on (i) secure storage management with virtualization and secure query processing in clouds, (ii) in-line reference monitors for policy management ,and (iii) risk/incentive-based assured information sharing. The capstone course on assured cloud computing includes components in (1) secure hypervisors using hardware/software codesign, (2) secure cloud storage algorithms with VMs, (3) secure cloud query processing algorithms and risk aware access control, (4) secure virtual network monitor implementation, (5) cloud forensics, and (6) tools for monitoring clouds.

Our assured cloud computing course is based on the framework of Figure 33.1. This framework is based on layered SOA consisting of a secure VM, the secure cloud storage, the secure cloud data, and the secure virtual network monitor layers. Cross-cutting services are provided by the policy layer, the cloud monitoring layer, the risk analysis layer, and the QoS (quality of service) layer. The first part of the capstone course focuses on general cloud computing principles and components, including hypervisors, storage, and data management and networking components. In addition, various standards as well as products from IBM, Microsoft, Oracle, and Salesforce.com are presented. The second part of the course includes the developments in assured cloud computing as well as results from our research in this field. In particular, our course includes the following components.

i. *Secure Hypervisors:* VM technology is widely adopted as an enabler of cloud computing and provided through hypervisors. Ensuring the security of hypervisors is essential for assured cloud computing. Our course includes the developments in secure hypervisors including secure VMware and Secure XEN platforms. In addition, we are incorporating results from our research. For example, our research has found that the combination of hardware/software approach is effective for system assurance. We are designing and prototyping components in hypervisors, in addition to the traditional execution platforms. In particular, our course includes descriptions of hardware/software-combined solutions in VMs to defend against security threats, such as key logger, buffer overflow, and intrusions.

ii. *Secure Cloud Storage Management:* Our course includes various security issues related to cloud storage systems including security for the Hadoop framework. In addition, we are incorporating results from our research into the course. For example, we are developing a storage infrastructure which integrates resources from multiple providers to form a massive virtual storage system. When a storage node hosts the data from multiple domains, a VM is created for each domain to isolate the information and corresponding data processing. Since data may be dynamically created and allocated to storage nodes, it is necessary to support secure VM management services such as pool management. The VM is created dynamically to host data and support processing for each domain. We leverage the thread pool concept and create the technique of VM pools. The VM pool grows and shrinks according to the demands and resource constraints. We are implementing the virtual global cloud storage infrastructure on top of XEN and VMware.

iii. *Secure Cloud Data Management:* Our course includes various security issues related to cloud data management such as cloud query optimization and query rewriting. In addition, we are also introducing results from our research. For example, we have developed secure query processing algorithms for RDF data in clouds with an XACML-based policy manager utilizing the Hadoop/MapReduce Framework (see Chapter 23). We have also designed algorithms for secure query processing based on the HIVE framework (see Chapter 24). These results as well as our experiences are being incorporated into our course. We are also including results based on our research on risk-aware access control and query processing for cloud computing as well as QoS for clouds. For example, this module discusses how different choices for cloud data processing can affect the security risks. In addition, basic risk management and analysis tools are also covered in the context of cloud.

iv. *Secure Cloud Services:* Our course includes various security issues related to cloud services. In particular, we investigate security aspects of platform as a service, software as a service, and infrastructure as a service. Various security standards, products, and prototypes are discussed.

v. *Secure Cloud Network Management:* Our course includes various issues related to virtual network security and management. The potential impact of network-based security threats on cloud computing systems and their hosted applications makes cloud computing systems prime targets for adversaries. Securing such systems requires a multi-level approach as potential security threats may come from various entities both internal as well as external to the system. In addition, a potential security attack on a hosted service application may also have a negative impact on other colocated services or applications. Our course includes discussions of such network-based security threats on cloud computing systems and available detection and mitigation techniques in cloud network management.

vi. *Security Policy Management for Cloud Computing*: We are incorporating various types of policy management in cloud systems into our course. In addition, we are incorporating results from our research on the in-line reference monitor concept as applied to clouds. For example, cloud frameworks often demand more sophisticated policy languages for fine-grained data confidentiality policies, accountability policies, and identity management policies. To support such policies, customized OS usually become necessary. Such OS's incur computational overhead, both in terms of resource consumption and process load times. The need to customize the OS to support new policies introduces inflexibility to the policy language and can lead to large additions to the trusted computing base of the system. To achieve more flexible, lighter-weight, yet high-assurance protection for process-level cloud security, we are extending the traditional hypervisor architecture with an extra level of security based on certified in-lined reference monitors (IRMs).

vii. *Cloud Monitoring:* We are developing two sets of cloud monitoring tools. The first set of tools extends the data mining algorithms we have developed for malicious code detection and network traffic analysis for clouds. Our algorithms mine data streams and detect novel classes of malicious code. The second set of tools is developed solely to monitor clouds. For example, for IaaS type of cloud computing applications, we are developing tools to monitor the utilization and load distribution in the underlying physical resources. These tools are being incorporated into our course.

viii. *Cloud Forensics:* We include topics in cloud forensics such as using the cloud to conduct forensics analysis and determining the sources of attacks in clouds. In particular, we include information on how current forensics tools can be extended for use in clouds as well as developing auditing and accountability tools for clouds. Data extraction and analysis techniques are also discussed. While our current research on assured clouds does not include cloud forensics, we are conducting joint research with Purdue University on accountability in clouds. For example, we are collecting accountability data per job in a cloud and per node in a cloud and conducting analysis. These results are also being incorporated into our course.

33.3.2.2 Component Insertion into Existing Courses

As illustrated in Figure 33.6, several of the components that we introduce into our capstone course fit nicely into our current courses in IA. We describe the enhancements to our current courses. Figure 33.6 also illustrates how the new components will enhance our current IA courses as well as contribute toward our capstone course.

33.3.2.2.1 Computer Security

In this course students are introduced to advanced concepts in information security with a special emphasis on OSs security. In particular, secure memory management, file system management, and interprocess communication are discussed. Students also program viruses and worms. We introduce an additional module on cloud systems security and provide an overview of secure VMWare and other hypervisors. In addition, results of our research on secure hypervisors are included. In particular, we include descriptions of hardware/software-combined solutions in VMs to defend against security threats, such as key logger, buffer overflow, and intrusions.

33.3.2.2.2 Data and Applications Security

In this course we introduce policy management in databases, multilevel secure data management, inference problem, secure objects and multimedia systems, assured information sharing, secure information integration, secure data warehousing, privacy-preserving data mining, secure social networks, secure knowledge management, and attacks to databases. We are incorporating additional modules into this course that are based on secure cloud data management such as secure query optimization and query rewriting and secure indexing. In addition, we introduce modules based on secure cloud storage management such as encrypted data storage and risk-based access control.

33.3.2.2.3 Network Security

This course covers both traditional topics in network security and more practical topics related to the security of the Internet and its applications. The course also includes an important hands-on exercise component where students do exercises on several practical Internet security topics, including password cracking, vulnerability scanning, and exploitation. We are incorporating additional topics into this course related to security challenges in clouds and available solutions to address them.

33.3.2.2.4 Digital Forensics

At present this is an undergraduate course and we have plans to introduce a graduate course in the near future. For the senior undergraduate course, students learn about forensic data recovery, forensic data analysis, event reconstruction, and file system forensics. Students also conduct forensic analysis using Encase tool. We introduce a new module on cloud forensics. In particular, we discuss how the cloud can be used to conduct forensics analysis. We also discuss the new attacks that can occur due to the cloud and explore ways of extending the current forensics tools to operate in a cloud.

33.3.2.2.5 Data Mining for Security Applications

This is a doctoral level course. Students are introduced to a variety of data mining techniques and then explore applications in cyber security such as intrusion detection, malicious code detection, buffer overflow detection, and botnet detection. Students build data mining tools for security applications. We introduce a new module that discusses how cloud computing can be used for scalable data mining. In addition, we also examine how data mining may be used for security problems in cloud computing such as auditing and accountability. Recently, we have introduced a new course on big data analytics that overlaps with the course data mining for security applications.

33.3.2.2.6 Building Secure Semantic Web Services

This is a PhD level course where students are introduced to semantic web and WS technologies as well as security issues for these technologies. In particular, semantic web for policy representation as well as securing semantic web technologies are discussed. Various security standards for WS are also provided. We introduce a new module to this course to discuss security resulting from Platform as a service and Infrastructure as a service among others. In addition, our research results on secure processing of semantic web data in a cloud (e.g., RDF data) is discussed. Various secure cloud services being implemented by corporations such as IBM, Microsoft, and Oracle are also discussed.

33.3.2.2.7 Cryptography

In this course students are introduced to a variety of cryptographic protocols and techniques. In addition, topics such as SMC are included. We are adding modules on using the cloud for computational-intensive cryptographic algorithms. In addition, secure data storage issues are also discussed.

33.3.2.2.8 Language Security

In this course students are introduced to language security concepts including program verification methods. Our module on policy management and in-line reference monitor techniques for clouds will be incorporated into this course.

33.3.3 Course Programming Projects

As part of the courses that we have described in Section 4.2, students can carry out a number of programming projects that will enhance their skills in assured cloud computing as well as contribute to our cloud computing platform. On the basis of the research we are carrying out, the following are some sample programming projects for our students.

33.3.3.1 Fine-Grained Access Control for Secure Storage

Current Hadoop implementations enforce a coarse-grained access control policy that permits or denies principal access to essentially all system resources as a group without distinguishing among resources. Such coarse-grained security is not sufficient when data, queries, and the system resources that implement them are security-relevant, and when not all users and processes are fully trusted. Current work addresses this by implementing standard access control lists for Hadoop to constrain access to certain system resources, such as files; however, this approach has the limitation that the enforced security policy is baked into the OS and therefore cannot be easily changed without modifying the OS. A course project for students will be to build flexible and fine-grained access control policies on Hadoop such as RBAC (Role Based Access Control), UCON (Usage Control), and ABAC (Attribute Based Access Control).

33.3.3.2 Flexible Authentication

The current beta version of Hadoop supports authentication with Kerberos and tokens. On top of the Kerberos protocol, for assured information tasks, there may be a need for adding simple authentication protocols to authenticate with secure co-processors. A second programming project is for students to add a simple public key implementation so that users can independently authenticate with secure coprocessors to retrieve secret keys used for encrypting sensitive data.

33.3.3.3 Secure Virtual Machine Management

We have examined VMware and other VMs and have selected XEN for our cloud implementation as it is available as open source and has excellent documentation and user manuals. XEN also supports non-Linux systems. Furthermore, XEN has certain security features that we can use to build additional security. A third programming project is for students to build access control features into XEN.

33.3.3.4 Secure Co-Processor for Cloud

Basically, SCP is a tamper-resistant hardware capable of limited general-purpose computation. When installed on the server, it is capable of performing local computations that are completely hidden from the server. If tampering is detected, then the SCP clears the internal memory. Since the SCP is tamper-resistant, one could be tempted to run the entire sensitive data storage server on the SCP. Pushing the entire data storage functionality into a SCP is not feasible due to the following: (i) the tamper-resistant shell. SCPs have usually limited memory (only a few megabytes of RAM—random access memory—and a few kilobytes of nonvolatile memory) and computational power. Performance will improve over time, but problems such as heat dissipation/power use (which must be controlled to avoid disclosing processing) will force a gap between general purposes and secure computing. (ii) Another issue is that the software running on the SCP must be totally trusted and verified. This security requirement implies that the software running on the SCP should be kept as simple as possible. Therefore, a fourth programming project for the students is to build secure storage for cloud using SCP.

33.3.3.5 Scalable Techniques for Malicious Code Detection

We are developing efficient and scalable feature extraction techniques, and applying these techniques on a large corpus of real benign and malicious executables. This feature extraction and selection process is both computational and storage-intensive. For example, in our previous work we extracted roughly a quarter billion n-grams (n contiguous hexadecimal digit) from a corpus of only 3500 executables.

The feature extraction process required disk I/O as all the features could not be stored in main memory. It took around 2 h and Gigabytes of disk space for a machine with Quad processor and 12 GB memory. Note that this was the resource requirement for a static dataset. If the dataset is dynamic, like a data stream where new data are continuously arriving, and this feature extraction and selection is to be executed repeatedly to discover newer features, this process would be a main bottleneck. For example, we consider all together 105,388 executables. Hence, for this huge dataset, our previous approach may not scale well in terms of limited storage and timing. Therefore, we are developing scalable solutions by using our cloud computing framework. We can devise programming projects for students to examine scalability of our algorithms.

33.3.4 *Instructional Cloud Computing Facility*

We use various open source tools to get students familiar with the basic cloud computing concepts. For large-scale data analysis in the cloud, we dedicate part of our research cloud infrastructure consisting of a Hadoop cluster. Students conduct programming projects using this cluster. In addition, students have hands-on experience using Hadoop for the various activities we have described in the previous section. For example, for the data and applications security class, the students can use this infrastructure to carry our programming assignments for assured information sharing. Students are divided into groups. Each group acts as a coalition partner and designs their policies for the other groups and stores the policies with the data in the cloud. For example, Group A devises a set for policies for Group B and a different set of policies for Group C. Appropriate policies will be executed against the data when a group (e.g., B or C) wants to access the data placed by Group A. In addition to structured data, the students also experiment with unstructured data (e.g., text, image).

In addition to the cloud described above, we plan to install Apache VCL (Virtual Computing Lab) as a part of our lab environment. Information on VCL can be found in [VCL]. Basically, the VCL is an open source system used to dynamically provision and broker remote access to a dedicated computer environment for an end-user. Such a system will be useful for introducing students to infrastructure as a service type of cloud applications. Using this instructional cloud computing facility, we will devise various hands-on lab exercises and assignments where students can apply their knowledge to practical problems. We are creating a second cloud cluster to be used entirely for educational purposes. With this cluster we will conduct cloud penetration and cloud forensics exercises as part of the capstone course as well as the digital forensics, network, systems, and data security courses. This cloud will be used solely for educational purposes. During the course of the project, we will develop detailed instructional material that will include lecture notes as well as lab exercises that we will design and place on the project web site. In addition, user manuals will be developed.

33.4 Evaluation Plan

The best evaluators of our courses and experiments are our students. We are obtaining detailed evaluations from our students and discussing with them how we can enhance the courses. We also get inputs from our partners and use these inputs to improve our courses. Our evaluations will be included in the interim and final reports we will prepare for the NSF. On the basis of the inputs we get, we will also produce user manuals for our cloud so that students from around the country can log into our system and learn how to use our cloud for their education and experiments.

We propose three broad stages of program evaluations: (1) effectiveness of the project implementation; (2) meeting our goals and objectives; and (3) the overall impact of the program. Second, the processes to evaluate are made of two major parts. Formative evaluation will be conducted to monitor activities that involve project implementation for further refinements and continual improvement. The purpose of this stage of evaluation is to document successes and challenges as well as lessons learned from the implementation stages and to monitor status of project activities. Second, summative evaluation will be conducted for meeting our program goals and objectives, impact of our program on student learning, and improvement of cloud computing education.

33.5 Summary and Directions

In this chapter, we have built the secure cloud infrastructure discussed in Chapter 32 and presented our strategy for education in cloud computing. Some of the courses we have discussed have already been offered while some others are in progress. We are utilizing the infrastructure discussed in Chapter 32 for our course programming projects. Many of our students have become experts on programming with the Hadoop/MapReduce framework. At present, we are offering a new course on big data analytics in the cloud and will involve the implementation of various data mining algorithm in the cloud. There is some overlap between our courses in secure cloud computing and big data analytics. Our research and education on secure cloud computing is presented in [CLOUD].

We will continue to enhance both our cloud computing framework as well as the courses we offer. For example, during the Spring Semester of 2013 (January–May 2013) we are offering a new course on analyzing and securing social networks. This course will also utilize our cloud infrastructure for the programming projects. Specifically we will expand on the work on SNODOC discussed in Chapter 14 with security features as part of the class projects. That is, we will develop techniques to mine various social network data (e.g., Twitter, YouTube, etc.), enforce security and privacy policies, and implement the techniques in the cloud (e.g., use of Storm). We believe that as the need for big data analytics increases the need for better cloud infrastructures as well as more courses on assured cloud computing will also increase. Security will be a major aspect with respect to the infrastructures developed as well as the courses offered about the cloud.

References

[AFRL] AFOSR-Funded Initiative Creates More Secure Environment for Cloud Computing, http://www.wpafb.af.mil/news/story.asp?id=123209377

[CLOUD] Assured Cloud Computing Education, http://csrc.utdallas.edu/Education/Assured-Cloud-Computing/Home.html

[CS] Computer Science Department, the University of Texas at Dallas, http://cs.utdallas.edu/

[HAML10] Hamlen, K. W.,M. Kantarcioglu, L. Khan, B. M. Thuraisingham, Security issues for cloud computing. *IJISP*, 4(2): 36–48, 2010.

[VCL] Virtual Computing Lab, https://cwiki.apache.org/VCL/

Chapter 34

A Research Initiative for a Secure Cloud

34.1 Overview

As we have discussed throughout this book, while cloud computing has received a great deal of attention, there is a lot of work to be done on securing the cloud. Therefore, we started a collaborative research project funded by the AFOSR between 2008 and 2014 that included an investigation of security issues for the cloud. While our initial investigation was on securing the grid, we migrated to securing the cloud. Initially the two universities that collaborated on this effort were UTD and Purdue University. Subsequently, we collaborated with other universities such as the University of California Irvine, King's College, University of London, and the University of Insubria, Italy. We also collaborated with ADB Consulting in areas such as entity extraction with the ultimate goal toward implementing the algorithms in the cloud. This project represented one of the first comprehensive multi-organizational collaborative efforts in investigating security issues for the cloud, including storage, information management, and collaboration tools for sensitive data. This project also focused on the needs of the DoD community and the National Security Agency which have been working extensively on the GIG (Global Information Grid), where many challenging security concerns emerged. In this chapter, we will describe some of the developments we have made on this project with respect to securing the cloud and our future plans.

It should be noted that many of the experimental systems that we discussed in this book are due to the developments made under this project. In this section, not only do we discuss our research contributions at UTD, some of which have been discussed in earlier chapters, but we also discuss the contributions made by our university partners. The organization of this chapter is as follows. The research contributions including the development of secure query processors, hybrid data storage schemes, privacy for the cloud, and using the cloud for malware analysis are discussed in Section 34.2. Our future plans are discussed in Section 34.3.

34.2 Research Contributions

34.2.1 Overview

Much of our research contributions on secure cloud have been discussed in Parts VI and VII of this book. We summarize some of this research as well as discuss some of our additional research in this chapter. We also discuss the research carried out by Purdue University under the collaborative research project that we have led at UTD.

We have discussed the research in three sections. In Section 34.2.2, we discuss the research on secure cloud data and information management. Specifically our research prototypes discussed in Part VI will be listed in this section. In Section 34.2.3, we discuss the research on the use of cloud for security applications. That is, the systems discussed here illustrate the cloud providing security as a service. These systems are also discussed in Part VII. In Section 34.2.4, we discuss various security models for the cloud. These models include information flow models, access control models, and accountability models. In Section 34.2.5, we discuss some of the research we are conducting toward developing secure social networks with the ultimate goal of implementing the techniques in the cloud.

While much of the research study discussed in Sections 34.2.2 and 34.2.3 was carried out at UTD, the study mentioned in Section 34.2.4 was carried out at Purdue University and the study discussed in Section 34.2.5 was carried out by ADB Consulting as part of the collaborative research project led by UTD. Sample references for the research are provided throughout the section. Figure 34.1 illustrates the research.

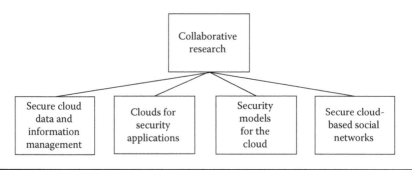

Figure 34.1   Collaborative research.

34.2.2 Secure Cloud Data and Information Management

34.2.2.1 Data Intensive Secure Query Processing in the Cloud

Semantic web is an emerging area to augment human reasoning for which various technologies are being developed. These technologies have been standardized by the W3C. One such standard is the RDF. With the explosion of semantic web technologies, large RDF graphs are common place. This poses significant challenges for the storage and retrieval of RDF graphs. Current frameworks do not scale for large RDF graphs and as a result do not address these challenges. Here, we describe a framework that we built using Hadoop to store and retrieve large numbers of RDF triples by exploiting the cloud computing paradigm. We describe a scheme to store RDF data in a Hadoop DFS. More than one Hadoop job may be needed to answer a query because a triple pattern in a query cannot take part in more than one join in a Hadoop job. To determine the jobs, we present an algorithm to generate near optimal query plan based on a greedy approach to answer a SPARQL Protocol and RDF Query Language (SPARQL) query. We use Hadoop's MapReduce framework to answer the queries. Our results show that we can store large RDF graphs in Hadoop clusters built with cheap commodity class hardware. Furthermore, we show that our framework is scalable and efficient and can handle large amounts of RDF data, unlike traditional approaches. We are implementing XACML-based policy management and integrating it with our query processing strategies. We discussed the system in Chapter 22. Details are given in [KHAL10].

In addition to secure query processing with semantic web data, we also developed prototype systems for secure query processing for relational data. In this system, the policies were specified in XACML. The relational data was managed by HIVE. We discussed this system in Chapter 22. Details are given in [THUR10].

34.2.2.2 Secure Data Processing in a Hybrid Cloud

Cloud computing has made it possible for a user to be able to select a computing service precisely when needed. However, a user needs to make an informed decision as to whether or not to use cloud services based on factors such as the level of information privacy desired, regulatory issues and local computing capacity. Given these issues, for certain users it may be a better choice to adopt a hybrid cloud (public and private) approach rather than relying solely on a CSP. Such a hybrid solution enables certain mission- or organization-critical tasks to be executed locally at a user's site while allowing less important tasks to be outsourced to a public cloud. Moreover, this increases throughput while reducing operational costs with a high-level of data security. We foresee three challenges that must be overcome before the adoption of a hybrid cloud approach:

1. *Data design:* How to partition relations in a hybrid cloud? A solution to this problem must account for the sensitivity of attributes in a relation as well as the workload of a user. Further, a solution must take into consideration the monetary cost of storing relations over a hybrid cloud and the risk associated with releasing sensitive information to a public CSP. Additionally, a solution must also be able to adapt to a user's changing data and workload requirements.

   In our approach, the data design problem is formulated as a multi-objective optimization problem where each objective captures one of the above sub-problems. Further, we have shown that this problem is NP-Complete, and therefore we have provided dynamic programming and hill-climbing solutions to the problem.

2. *Data security:* How to protect a user's data in a public cloud with encryption while enabling query processing over this encrypted data? A solution to this problem must ensure that neither a service provider nor a hacker who hacks into a service provider can learn any meaningful information from the stored data. Data security can be achieved by encrypting the stored data. However, encryption presents a new set of challenges such as granularity of encryption and query processing over encrypted data.

   In our approach, we use the "bucketization" technique to provide data security. This technique does not leak any data to a service provider or a hacker. Furthermore, this technique allows us to efficiently query the encrypted data. This allows us to push a significant amount of query processing work to a public CSP.

3. *Query processing:* How can a user issue queries transparently to a hybrid cloud? How to execute queries efficiently over both, encrypted and unencrypted data? A solution to these problems must first be able to estimate the cost of executing queries over both, unencrypted and encrypted data. This cost estimation can then be used to optimize query execution over a hybrid cloud.

   In our approach, we develop a set of query rewriting rules that is used to split a given query into its constituent sub-queries that can then be executed over public and private clouds. We use a linear cost estimation model to approximate the cost of a given query. The goal of our model is to compute the total response time for a query. This model takes into account the actual processing time as well as the time to transfer results from a public cloud to a private cloud. This model makes use of the query rewriting rules to split a query into sub-queries over public and private clouds. Query optimization in our approach is done by estimating the cost of several alternate plans and then selecting a plan with the lowest response time.

We have incorporated the above solutions into an add-on tool for a Hadoop and Hive-based cloud computing infrastructure. This is a project we carried out jointly with the University of California at Irvine. Details of our research are discussed in [OKTA12].

34.2.2.3 Secure Information Integration in the Cloud

Cloud computing services like Amazon S3 are gaining a lot of popularity because of factors like cost efficiency and ease of maintenance. We have evaluated the feasibility of using S3 storage services for storing semantic web data. The Intelligence Community's Blackbook uses several semantic data sources to produce search results. In our approach, we stored one of the Blackbook data sources on Amazon S3 in a secure manner, thus leveraging cloud computing services within a semantic web-based framework. We encrypted the data source using Advanced Encryption Standard (AES) before storing it on Amazon S3. Also, we do not store the original key anywhere in our system. Instead, the key is generated by two separate components; each called a "Key Server." Then, the generated key is used to encrypt data. We essentially showed how information may be securely integrated with Amazon WSs. Details of this work were provided in Chapter 24. More information can also be found in [PARI12].

34.2.2.4 Secure Social Networking in the Cloud

We developed a social intelligence application to identify the location of the user on social networking sites by mining information from his social graph and the messages posted by him. Our system not only identifies the city level home location of a user, but goes one step further to pinpoint specific venues or point of interests that the user may have visited or has talked about in his messages. We have performed extensive experiments to prove the efficacy of the algorithm in terms of accuracy and running time. The algorithm outperforms all existing location extraction approaches. To show the applicability of the algorithm in security analytics, we developed a powerful tool that allows analysts to identify the location of any Twitter user and his friends, tie in text to reveal what different users are talking about around the world in real time. The tool provides an intuitive graphical interface which an analyst can use to visualize the places visited by a user and his friends (determined by the algorithm) to identify and monitor potential security threats. In the current world scenario where uprisings, political meetings such as the Arab spring or London riots are organized on social networking sites like Twitter, our system proves to be a great tool for detecting, recognizing, and tracking users with mal-intent.

Much of the focus has been on developing information integration as well as the reasoning components for our system. In particular, information from multiple social networks was integrated securely and analyzed and reasoned to detect future events. We are currently investing security and privacy for the system as well as implementing the system in a cloud. Details of our work are given in [ABRO09].

34.2.3 *Cloud-Based Security Applications*

34.2.3.1 *Cloud-Based Malware Detection for Evolving Data Streams*

Data stream classification for intrusion detection poses at least three major challenges. First, these data streams are typically infinite-length, making traditional multi-pass learning algorithms inapplicable. Second, they exhibit significant concept-drift as attackers react and adapt to defenses. Third, for data streams that do not have any fixed feature set, such as text streams, an additional feature extraction and selection task must be performed. If the number of candidate features is too large, then traditional feature extraction techniques fail.

To address the first two challenges, we developed a multi-partition, multi-chunk ensemble classifier in which a collection of v classifiers is trained from r consecutive data chunks using v-fold partitioning of the data, yielding an ensemble of such classifiers. This multi-partition, multi-chunk ensemble technique significantly reduces classification error compared to the existing single-partition, single-chunk ensemble approaches, wherein a single data chunk is used to train each classifier.

To address the third challenge, a feature extraction and selection technique is developed for data streams that do not have any fixed feature set. The technique's scalability is demonstrated through an implementation for the Hadoop MapReduce cloud computing architecture. If the feature space of the data points is not fixed, a subproblem of the classification problem is the extraction and selection of features that describe each data point. As in prior work by Kolter and Maloof, we use binary n-grams as features for malware detection. However, since the total number of possible n-grams is prohibitively large, we judiciously select n-grams that have the greatest discriminatory power. This selection process is ongoing; as the stream progresses, newer n-grams appear that dominate the older n-grams. These newer n-grams replace the old in our model in order to identify the best features for a particular period.

Naive implementation of the feature extraction and selection process can be both time and storage-intensive for large datasets. For example, our previous work extracted roughly a quarter billion n-grams from a corpus of only 3500 executables. This feature extraction process required extensive virtual memory (with associated performance overhead), since not all of these features could be stored in main memory. Extraction and selection required about 2 hours of computation and many gigabytes of disk space for a machine with a quad-core processor and 12 GB of memory. This is despite the use of a purely static dataset; when the dataset is a dynamic stream, extraction and selection must recur, resulting in a major bottleneck. In this current approach, we consider a much larger dataset of 105 thousand executables for which our previous approach is insufficient.

We therefore design a scalable feature selection and extraction solution that leverages a cloud computing framework by Dean and Ghemawat. We show that depending on the availability of cluster nodes, the running time for feature extraction and selection can be reduced by a factor of m, where m is the number of nodes in the cloud cluster. The nodes are machines with cheap commodity hardware. Therefore, the solution is also cost-effective as high-end computing machines are not required.

Both theoretical and empirical evidence demonstrates its effectiveness over other state-of-the-art stream classification techniques on synthetic data, real botnet traffic, and malicious executables. Details of this were presented in Chapter 25. More details can also be found in [MASU11].

34.2.3.2 Cloud-Based Insider Threat Detection

Evidence of malicious insider activity is often buried within large data streams, such as system logs accumulated over months or years. Ensemble-based stream mining leverages multiple classification models to achieve highly accurate anomaly detection in such streams even when the stream is unbounded, evolving, and unlabeled. This makes the approach effective for identifying insider threats who attempt to conceal their activities by varying their behaviors over time. Our approach applies ensemble-based stream mining, unsupervised learning, supervised learning, and graph-based anomaly detection to the problem of insider threat detection, demonstrating that the ensemble-based approach is significantly more effective than traditional single-model methods. We further investigate suitability of various learning strategies for evolving insider threat data. We also developed unsupervised machine learning algorithms for insider threat detection. Our implementation is being hosted on the cloud. Some of the details were discussed in Chapter 26. More information can also be found in [PARV12].

34.2.3.3 Cloud-Based Assured Information Sharing

Daniel Wolfe (formerly of the National Security Agency) defined assured information sharing (AIS) as one that "provides the ability to dynamically and securely share information at multiple classification levels among U.S., allied and coalition forces." The DoD's vision for AIS is to "deliver the power of information to ensure mission success through an agile enterprise with freedom of maneuverability across the information environment." More recently National Security Agency CIO Lonny Anderson has stated that the agency is focusing on a "cloud-centric" approach to information sharing with other agencies. To address the needs of the DoD, our project is developing technologies and tools for cloud-centric assured information sharing funded by the AFOSR. In our approach the organizations place their policies and data in the cloud. The data are shared among the organizations according to the policies.

We have developed demonstration systems with our European partners: King's College, University of London, and the University of Insubria, Italy who are funded by EOARD (The European Office of Aerospace Research and Development). The first demonstration illustrates how information may be shared in our cloud, based on policies specified in XACML. In the second demonstration, we are implementing a semantic web-based policy engine and will show how multiple social networks may share information on our cloud based on semantic web-based policies. For both demonstrations, we will use the secure cloud data managers we have implemented. These demonstration systems were described in Chapters 27 and 28. Details can also be found in [CADE12], [THUR12].

34.2.4 Security Models for the Cloud

34.2.4.1 A Fine-Grained Model for Information Flow Control in Service Cloud

With increasing advances in SOA and the push for powerful service clouds, rapid prototyping and deployment of applications by integrating services from various providers is becoming a reality. While service clouds have many benefits, security is still a major concern. Access and information flow control are major issues in service cloud security. We summarize our research results in the following paragraph. Details are given in [TU10] and [SHE12].

We have developed a novel model to support the fine-grained information flow control in WS compositions, namely, the Service Chain Information Flow Control (SCIFC) model. As the data exchanged between services in a service chain are potentially correlated, to avoid undesired information leakage, each service in the chain should consider all the services that may receive its data in either the raw or transformed form. In the response flow, the service chain has already been established and each service knows who may directly or indirectly access the information in its response. In this case, service s_i determines whether to allow the data contained in its response to be released directly or indirectly to $s_{i-1}, \ldots, s_1$. In the request flow, the service chain is to be established and the concrete services in the chain cannot be predetermined. Service s_i, upon composing the next service s_{i+1}, needs to figure out whether the data originators are willing to reveal their sensitive data, potentially derivable from s_{i-1}'s request, to s_{i+1}. Thus, it is necessary to support a back-check protocol to let s_i check with s_1 through s_{i-1} to decide whether s_{i+1} can be composed into the chain.

Performing back-checks allows the services in a chain to control the flow of their sensitive information via cooperation. However, this mechanism may incur a high communication overhead. To reduce the protocol complexity, we allow a service to carry along and enforce other services' security policies. That is, s_1 can send its security policies to s_2 to allow s_2 to make the composition decision based on the policies of both s_1 and s_2.

The mechanisms provided above are somewhat "blind." That is, whether performing back-check or enforcing security policies remotely, each service s_i must consider all its prior services, from s_1 to s_{i-1}, for sending out the data Q_i in s_i's request.

However, if it is impossible to derive s_j's sensitive data ($1 \leq j < i$) from Q_i, then s_i can disregard s_j when composing s_{i+1}. We define the concepts of transformation factor to model the transformation effect of the service functions upon the data contained in the requests/responses. Based on the transformation factor, unnecessary back-checks and/or policy enforcements in the information flow control protocols can be eliminated.

With the SCIFC protocols, the WSs in a service chain are empowered to specify how to protect their sensitive information without the risk of leaking critical information to the services they do not trust. Also, the protocols do not prevent any composition from forming unless there is a potential of undesired information leakage. The SCIFC protocol is carefully designed to minimize the potential overhead and, hence, making the fine-grained information flow control feasible. Experiments have been conducted to study the performance of the SCIFC protocol. The results show that the overhead of the SCIFC protocol is approximately 16% on average for a length-20 service chain, which is reasonable considering its benefit of enabling fine-grained security control.

34.2.4.2 CloudMask: Fine-Grained Attribute-Based Access Control

DaaS is an emerging cloud service where organizations can seamlessly store in the cloud and retrieve based on the access control policies that cover the legal requirements and organizational policies. Amazon S3 and Microsoft Azure storage service are two such popular services currently available. An important requirement in this context is represented by fine-grained access control to data stored in a cloud; access control should be performed according to policies expressed in terms of the properties of subjects, referred to as identity attributes. The email address, the role a user plays in her organization, the age and the location a user accesses from are a few examples of such identity attributes. The identity attributes that subjects should possess in order to access protected objects are referred to as conditions. A crucial issue that has not been addressed by previous research is that the identity attributes in the conditions often encode privacy-sensitive information.

Many existing cloud data services do provide some access control models. However, the privacy of the users is not protected in such models. Privacy, both individual as well as organizational, is considered a key requirement in all solutions, including cloud services, for digital identity management. Further, insider threats are considered one of the major sources of data theft and privacy breaches. With cloud computing initiatives, the scope of insider threats is no longer limited to the organizational perimeter.

In this work, we have developed CloudMask, an approach that supports fine-grained attribute-based access control based on encryption while at the same time assuring the privacy of the identity attributes of the users accessing the data. The CloudMask approach is based on fine-grained encryption of data according to different symmetric encryption keys. Such are selectively made available to users according to the access control policies specified by users. To assure scalability and privacy of the identity attributes, in the CloudMask approach, users are not given the symmetric keys directly. Instead, users are given one or more secrets that they can use to derive the key on the fly in conjunction with some variable public information, which is stored on the cloud along with the data. CloudMask provides forward and backward secrecy without affecting the secrets given to existing users. In other words, CloudMask handles rekey operations efficiently since it does not directly share the same key with multiple users. Secrets are distributed to users by the oblivious commitment-based envelope (OCBE) technique. According to this technique, users are able to decrypt the encrypted secrets (i.e., to open the envelope) only if their identity attributes, hidden in cryptographic commitments to assure privacy, verify the policy conditions associated with the data. An implementation of these protocols has been carried out. Results of this research are published in [NABE10], [DAMI10].

34.2.4.3 Delegated Access Control in the Storage as a Service Model

This work develops a novel approach that enhances the performance of CloudMask by delegating to the cloud the re-encryption of data when the access control policies change. Unlike the basic approach of CloudMask requiring the data owner to perform a new data encryption with different keys when the access control policies changes, the enhanced schema does not require the owner to do the encryption. Under the enhanced schema, the cloud hosting the data is delegated to the re-encryption operations; however, the cloud does not learn anything about the data.

One's approach is based on the use of two-layer encryption and incremental encryption. Under the two-layer encryption, a first "coarse" encryption step is performed by the data owner; this first step encrypts all data (or large chunks of data) with the same key. The cloud performs the second encryption step in order to implement fine-grained access control. Experimental results show that this approach greatly reduces the overhead at the data owner. This research is reported in [NABE12].

34.2.4.4 Attribute-Based Group Key Management Scheme

Attribute-based systems enable fine-grained access control among a group of users each identified by a set of attributes. Secure collaborative applications, like the ones enabled by the cloud, need such flexible attribute-based systems for managing and distributing group keys. However, current group key management schemes are not well designed to manage group keys based on the attributes of the group members.

In this work, we have defined and implemented novel key management schemes that allow users whose attributes satisfy a certain access control policy to derive the group key. Our schemes efficiently support rekeying operations when the group changes due to joins or leaves of group members. During a rekey operation, the private information issued to existing members remains unaffected and only the public information is updated to change the group key. Our schemes are expressive; they are able to support any monotonic access control policy over a set of attributes. Our schemes are resistant to collusion attacks; group members are unable to pool their attributes and derive the group key which they cannot derive individually. Experimental results show that our underlying constructs are efficient and practical, and that are much more efficient than the scheme based on attribute-based encryption (ABE). This research is reported in [NABE11].

34.2.4.5 Privacy-Preserving Access Control in the Cloud

Data stored in the cloud often encode sensitive information and should be protected as mandated by various organizational policies and legal regulations. A commonly adopted approach to address security and privacy is to encrypt the data before uploading them to the cloud. Encryption alone however is not sufficient as often organizations have to enforce fine-grained access control on the data. Such control is often based on information such as role of data users in the organization, projects on which users are working, and so forth. Therefore, an important requirement is to support fine-grained access control, based on policies specified in an expressive access control language, over encrypted data hosted in the cloud. In particular, an expressive access control model, such as XACML, allows one to specify access control policies on protected objects in terms of the properties of subjects, referred to as identity attributes. The email address, the role a user plays in one's organization; the age and the location a user accesses from are a few examples of such identity attributes. The identity attributes that subjects should possess to access protected objects are referred to as conditions. Such an attribute-based access control model is crucial to support fine-grained access control policies to data.

A crucial issue in this context is that the identity attributes in the access control policy conditions often encode privacy-sensitive information. The privacy of the users is thus not protected if their identity attributes are not protected. Privacy, both individual as well as organizational, is considered a key requirement in all solutions, including cloud services, for digital identity management. Further, as insider threats are one of the major sources of data theft and privacy breaches, identity attributes must be strongly protected even from accesses within the organization. With cloud computing initiatives the scope of insider threats is no longer limited to the organizational perimeter. Therefore, protecting the identity attributes of the users while enforcing attribute-based access control both within the organization and in the cloud is an important requirement. The results of this research are reported in [BERT09], [NABE12].

34.2.4.5.1 Accountability in Grid

Grid computing systems provide vast amounts of computing resources such as computing power, data storage, and network bandwidth. Accountability in grids makes it possible to audit activities of users and resource providers, and to investigate security breaches through the collection and analysis of accountability data. However, accountability data are difficult to obtain because of the complex and heterogeneous nature of the grids and the lack of suitable accountability systems. Our previous work has developed an approach to address accountability based on some special purpose agents, referred to as accountability agents. These agents are placed at strategic locations across the grids, and collect accountability data according to some policies, referred to as accountability policies. The accountability policies specify which data to collect and when to collect them, and more importantly, how to coordinate data collection among different administrative domains.

A major problem in this context is represented by conflicts among the various grid nodes as not all nodes may be able (or willing) to collect the required accountability data. To address such problem and yet achieve a flexible accountability system, we have developed a profile-based policy selection mechanism. Under this approach, the best accountability policy is chosen based on the attributes of jobs and grid nodes, and the capability of each node to collect accountability data. The selected policy preserves the minimum level of accountability and approximates the requirements of the shared policy. The results of this research are given in [LEE11a] and [LEE11b].

34.2.5 Toward Building Secure Social Networks in the Cloud

34.2.5.1 Secure Social Networking

Since its inception in the mid-1990s, social networks have provided a way for users to interact, reflecting social networks or social relations among people, for example, who share interests and/or activities. At the forefront of emerging trends in social networking sites is the concept of "real time" and "location based." So what makes location-based social media services so important?

Privacy and Safety: Posting updates on location-based social networking websites and publishing your current location to the user, can result in problems like personalized attacks by spammers, posing threat to your safety.

Trustworthiness of User Location: In certain scenarios, such as the political scenario of the Iran elections of 2009, it becomes important for organizations monitoring the data to be able to verify the location of a user.

Advertising and Marketing: Social networks connect people at low cost and can be beneficial for entrepreneurs and small businesses looking to expand their contact bases. These networks often act as a customer relationship management tool for companies selling products and services.

Having highlighted the importance of location of the user in social media, it is important to understand that it is not provided explicitly by the users for a number of reasons. Some of the users are concerned about their privacy and security; others do not find any incentive in sharing the location. Apart from this class of users who do not disclose their location, there are others who provide locations which are either incorrect or not machine readable or reveal just the state/country. The unstructured and free form of the text consisting of Internet slang and incomplete sentences makes use of traditional Natural Language Processing and gazetteer-based data mining approaches produce inaccurate results.

We have developed a social intelligence system that integrates multiple social networks, determines the locations and many other attributes of the users, and also analyzes the integrated information and predicts threats. Our research has also influenced system such as SNODSOC. Some of the details can be found at [ABRO09], [ABRO10], [ABRO12a], [ABRO12b].

34.2.5.2 Trustworthiness of Data

Purdue University has collaborated with us and addressed the problem of data trustworthiness for social networks. The work has investigated the problem of data trustworthiness in social networks when repositories of anonymized social networks exist and has designed and validated approaches by which one can assign a *trust score* to user profiles (or specific information within user profiles) in a social network. The trust score is a numeric indicator ranging from 0 to 1 that conveys the confidence that the associated information is truthful; a value close to 0 indicates a low confidence whereas a value closer to 1 indicates high confidence.

Notice that this trust score is just an indicator and final decisions about whether a certain piece of information can be trusted or not may require additional analysis steps. The approach that we have developed is based on comparing the information in the social network of interest with anonymized data from other social networks (called reference social networks). Details can be found at [LIM12].

34.2.5.3 Text Mining and Analysis

Under the leadership of the late Dr. James R. Johnson and Ms. Anita Miller, ADB Consulting has collaborated with us on exploring semantic processing approaches for determining related information of interest between documents on a sub-sentence level. As the research progressed it was discovered that semantic graph matching methods yield both related information of interest as well as new augmented information linked to the graph being matched to a reference graph. It was also found that relatedness and augmented information measures could be used to sort relevant information. It became clear that the developed approach is applicable to other domains such as intelligence, monitoring of news reports, identifying cyber threats and attacks, as well as information of interest-driven Internet searches.

The approach was tested with encouraging results against cyber threat messages exchanged by the Anonymous activists and against published FBI reports.

This research significantly expanded semantic analysis of free text by (1) quantifying semantic content and semantic context, (2) incorporating DLSafe Rules and abductive hypotheses that model processes and generate inferences for increased likelihood of matching related content and discovering new knowledge, and (3) creating a rigorous definition of a new expanded semantic graph structure with semantic relatedness measures for quantifying identified information on a level not previously achieved. These new techniques lay the foundation for cross-domain applications including the support of national intelligence analysts who need to identify focused information from large volumes of free text. Some of the details of the research can be found in [JOHN12a], [JOHN12b], and [JOHN12c].

34.3 Summary and Directions

In this chapter, we have provided an overview of our research on securing the cloud. This is part of a larger initiative on Data and Applications Security that also includes topics such as secure data provenance and semantic web technologies for security applications. This chapter focused on four aspects of our contributions. They are secure cloud data and information management, using the cloud for secure applications, developing security models for the cloud and technologies, and developing secure social networks in the cloud.

The technologies we have developed are relevant to the various layers of the secure cloud framework that we have defined. We believe that there is no one way to develop a secure cloud. That is, we need to mix and match a collection of technologies to meet the needs of our applications. The challenge is to integrate multiple secure technologies in a secure manner to develop a secure cloud. As we have stated earlier, it is almost impossible to provide 100% security. Therefore, we need to design secure clouds that will provide as much security as possible to carry out the mission. That is, the challenge is to develop a secure cloud from the components that may be compromised. Some of the challenges in developing secure systems from untrusted components are given in [UTD10]. We need to develop similar solutions for securing the cloud.

References

[ABRO09] Abrol, S. and L. Khan, Tweethood: Agglomerative clustering on fuzzy k-closest friends with variable depth for location mining. *SocialCom/PASSAT*153–160, 2010, Minneapolis, MN.

[ABRO10] Abrol, S. and L. Khan, TWinner: Understanding news queries with geo-content using Twitter. *Geographic Information Retrieval (GIR)*, 2010, Zurich, Switzerland.

[ABRO12a] Abrol, S., L. Khan, V. Khadilkar B. M. Thuraisingham, and T. Cadenhead, Design and implementation of SNODSOC: Novel class detection for social network analysis. *Intelligence and Security Informatics (ISI)*, 215–220, 2012, Washington, DC.

[ABRO12b] Abrol, S., L. Khan, and B. M. Thuraisingham, Tweecalization: Efficient and intelligent location mining in Twitter using semi-supervised learning. *Collaborate Com* 2012:514–523.

[BERT09] Bertino, E., F. Paci, and R. Ferrini, N. Shang Privacy-preserving digital identity management for cloud computing. *IEEE Data Eng. Bull.* 32(1):21–27, 2009.

[CADE12] Cadenhead, T., M. Kantarcioglu, V. Khadilkar, and B. M. Thuraisingham, Design and implementation of a cloud-based assured information sharing system. *MMM-ACNS* 2012:36–50, St. Petersburg, Russia.

[DAMI10] Damiani, M. L., C. Silvestri, and E. Bertino, Analyzing semantic locations cloaking techniques in a probabilistic grid-based map, *Geographic Information Systems (GIS)*, 522–523, 2010, San Jose, CA.

[JOHN12a] Johnson, J., A. Miller, L. Khan, and B. Thuraisingham, Extracting semantic information structures from free text law enforcement data. *IEEE Intelligence and Security Informatics (ISI)*, Washington, DC, July 11–14, 2012.

[JOHN12b] Johnson, J., A. Miller, L. Khan, and B. Thuraisingham, Measuring relatedness and augmentation of information of interest within free text law enforcement documents. *2012 IEEE European International Security and Informatics, (EISI)*, Odense, Denmark, Aug 22–24, 2012.

[JOHN12c] Johnson, J., A. Miller, L. Khan, and B. Thuraisingham, Graphical representation of semantic information, *International Conference on Semantic Computing (ICSC)*, Palermo, September 19–21, 2012.

[KHAL10] Khaled, A., M. Husain, L. R. Khan, K. Hamlen, and B. M. Thuraisingham, A token-based access control system for RDF data in the clouds, In *Proceedings of 2nd IEEE International Conference on Cloud Computing Technology and Science (CloudCom 2010)*, Indianapolis December 2010.

[LEE11a] Lee, W., A. Squicciarini, and E. Bertino, Profile-based accountability policies in grid computing systems. *Proceedings of IEEE International Symposium on Policies for Distributed Systems and Networks (POLICY)*, June 2011, Pisa, Italy.

[LEE11b] Lee, W., A. Squicciarini, and E. Bertino, Detection and protection against distributed denial of services in accountable grid systems. *Proceedings of 11th IEEE/ACM International Symposium on Cluster, Cloud and Grid Computing (CCGrid)*, May 2011, Newport Beach, CA.

[LIM12] Lim, H.-S., G. Ghinita, E. Bertino, and M. Kantarcioglu, A game-theoretic approach for high-assurance of data trustworthiness in sensor networks. *International Conference on Data Engineering (ICDE)*, 2012:1192–1203, Arlington, VA.

[MASU11] Masud, M. M., T. Al-Khateeb, K. W. Hamlen, J. Gao, L. Khan, J. Han, and B. M. Thuraisingham, Cloud-based malware detection for evolving data streams. *ACM Trans. Manage. Inf. Syst.* 2(3):16, 2011.

[NABE10] Nabeel, M., N. Shang, J. Zage, and E. Bertino, Mask: A system for privacy-preserving policy-based access to published content. *SIGMOD Conference*:1239–1242, 2010, Indianapolis, IN.

[NABE11] Nabeel M. and E. Bertino, POSTER: Towards attribute based group key management. *ACM Conference on Computer and Communications Security:* 821–824, 2011, Chicago, IL.

[NABE12] Nabeel, M. and E. Bertino, Privacy-preserving fine-grained access control in public clouds. *IEEE Data Eng. Bull.* 35(4):21–30, 2012.

[OKTA12] Oktay, K. Y., V. Khadilkar, B. Hore, M. Kantarcioglu, S. Mehrotra, and B. M. Thuraisingham, Risk-aware workload distribution in hybrid clouds. *IEEE CLOUD*:229–236, 2012, Honolulu, HI.

[PARV12] Parveen, P., N. McDaniel, V. S. Hariharan, B. M. Thuraisingham, and L. Khan, Unsupervised ensemble based learning for insider threat detection. *SocialCom/PASSAT*:718–727, 2012, Amsterdam, The Netherlands.

[PARI12] Parikh, P., M. Kantarcioglu, V. Khadilkar B. M. Thuraisingham, and L. Khan, Secure information integration with a semantic web-based framework. *IRI*:659–663, 2012, Las Vegas, NV.

[SHE12] She, W., I. Yen, B. Thuraisingham, and E. Bertino, Security-aware service composition with fine-grained information flow control to appear. *IEEE Transactions on Services Computing.*

[THUR10] Thuraisingham, B. M., V. Khadilkar, A. Gupta, M. Kantarcioglu, and L. Khan, Secure data storage and retrieval in the cloud. *Collaborate Com:* 1–8, 2010, Chicago, IL.

[THUR12] Thuraisingham, B. M., V. Khadilkar, J. Rachapalli, T. Cadenhead, M. Kantarcioglu, K. W. Hamlen, L. Khan, and M. F. Husain, Cloud-centric assured information sharing. *PAISI*:1–26, 2012, Kuala Lumpur, Malaysia.

[TU10] Tu, M., P. Li, I.-L. Yen, B. Thuraisingham, and L. Khan, Secure data objects replication in data grids. *IEEE Transactions on Dependable and Secure Computing* , 7(1): 50–64, January–March 2010.

[UTD10] Securing the Execution Environment Applications and Data from Multi-Trusted Components, Technical Report, UTDCS 3–10, The University of Texas at Dallas, 2010.

Chapter 35

Summary and Directions

35.1 About This Chapter

This chapter brings us to a close of *Building and Securing the Cloud*. We discussed several aspects including secure services technologies, secure semantic web technologies, cloud computing technologies, secure cloud computing technologies, experimental cloud computing systems, experimental secure cloud computing systems, cloud computing systems for security applications, building trustworthy clouds, and developing an infrastructure, education initiative and research program for a secure cloud. The topics discussed included cloud virtualization, cloud data management, cloud storage, and the security issues for cloud functions. In addition, we also discussed the emerging commercial products. The experimental systems are the ones that we have developed at UTD and include secure cloud query processing systems as well as cloud-based assured information-sharing systems.

The organization of this chapter is as follows. In Section 35.2, we summarize the book. This summary has been taken from the summaries of each chapter. In Section 35.3, we discuss directions for secure cloud computing. In Section 35.4, we discuss our goals in secure cloud computing. In Section 35.5, we give suggestions as to where to go from here.

35.2 Summary of This Book

We summarize the contents of each chapter essentially taken from the summary and directions section of each chapter. Chapter 1 provided an introduction to the book. We first provided a brief overview of the supporting technologies for cloud computing which included information security, as well as data, information and knowledge management. Then, we discussed various topics addressed in the book, including secure web services and secure semantic web which are at the heart of secure cloud computing. We also discussed cloud computing and secure cloud computing. Our framework is a nine-layer framework and each layer was addressed in one part of this book. This framework was illustrated in Figure 1.11. We replicate this framework in Figure 35.1.

The book was divided into nine parts. Part I, which described security and data management technologies, consisted of three chapters: 2, 3, and 4. Chapter 2

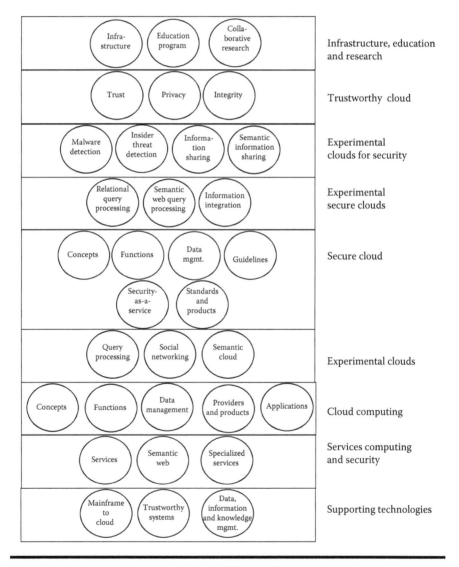

Figure 35.1   Layered framework for building and secure the cloud.

provided an overview of the evolution of computing. Chapter 3 provided an overview of secure systems. Data, information and knowledge management was discussed in Chapter 4.

Part II, which described secure services, consisted of three chapters: 5, 6, and 7. Chapter 5 discussed web services and secure web services. In particular, we first discussed what is meant by services. Next, we discussed high-level concepts in service-oriented computing. Realizing service-oriented information systems through service-oriented archive turns and web services was discussed next. We also discussed security issues for services. Chapter 6 discussed semantic web services since several of our prototypes for the cloud utilize semantic web technologies. Specialized secure web services and security were the subject of Chapter 7.

Part III, which described cloud computing, consisted of five chapters: 8, 9, 10, 11, and 12. We provided an overview of cloud computing in Chapter 8. Cloud computing functions were discussed in Chapter 9. Cloud data management, which is a main focus of our research and development, was discussed in Chapter 10. Cloud computing products and standards was the subject of Chapter 11. Finally some specialized cloud services such as mobile clouds were discussed in Chapter 12.

Part IV, which described experimental cloud computing systems, consisted of three chapters: 13, 14, and 15. Chapter 13 discussed our prototype system on semantic web-based cloud query processing. Chapter 14 discussed our work on hosting social networks on the cloud. Chapter 15 discussed multiple prototypes that we have developed, including cloud computing for social networks, cloud computing for semantic web data storage and cloud computing for ontology-based query processing.

Part V, which described secure cloud computing, consisted of six chapters: 16, 17, 18, 19, 20, and 21. Chapter 16 provided an overview of secure cloud computing concepts. Secure cloud computing functions were discussed in Chapter 17. Secure cloud data management was the subject of Chapter 18. Secure cloud computing guidelines were discussed in Chapter 19. The notion of security-as-a-service was discussed in Chapter 20. Secure cloud computing products were discussed in Chapter 21.

Part VI, which described experimental secure cloud computing systems, consisted of three chapters: 22, 23, and 24. Our secure relational data query processor in the cloud was discussed in Chapter 22. Our secure semantic web data query processor in the cloud was discussed in Chapter 23. Our work on secure information integration in the cloud was discussed in Chapter 24.

Part VII, which described the use of cloud for security applications, consisted of four chapters: 25, 26, 27, and 28. Our cloud-based malware detection system was discussed in Chapter 25. Our insider threat detection in the cloud was discussed in Chapter 26. Our assured information-sharing system in the cloud was discussed in Chapter 27. Our approach to assured information sharing in the semantic cloud was discussed in Chapter 28.

Part VIII consisted of three chapters: 29, 30, and 31. It discussed our ideas on developing trustworthy clouds. In Chapter 29, we discussed trust management for cloud services. In Chapter 30, we discussed privacy issues for cloud services. In Chapter 31, we discussed integrity and data quality for cloud services.

Part IX consisted of three chapters: 32, 33, and 34. It discussed our approach to building an infrastructure, an education initiative, and a research program for secure cloud computing. Chapter 32 discussed the secure cloud computing infrastructure we have developed. Our educational program in secure cloud computing was discussed in Chapter 33. Finally, in Chapter 34, we discussed our multi-organizational collaborative research program on secure cloud computing. The contents in Chapters 32, 33, and 34 form the foundations for our experimental work in secure cloud computing.

This book has four appendices. In Appendix A, we provide the broad picture how all the books we have written are related to one another. In Appendix B, we discuss data mining techniques. Our research in secure cloud computing has utilized many of these techniques. In Appendix C, we discuss secure data management. Our work on secure cloud data management is built on the concepts discussed in Appendix C. Finally in Appendix D, we discuss our collaborative research on assured information sharing which provided the main motivation for our work on cloud-based assured information sharing.

As we have stressed, there are many developments in the field and it is impossible for us to list all of them. We have provided a broad but fairly comprehensive overview of the field. The book is intended for technical managers as well as technologists who want to get a broad understanding of the field. It is also intended for students who wish to pursue research in data and applications security, in general, and secure cloud computing, in particular.

35.3 Directions for Cloud Computing and Secure Cloud Computing

There are many directions for cloud computing and secure cloud computing. We discuss some of them for each topic addressed in this book. Figure 35.2 illustrates the directions and challenges.

35.3.1 Secure Services

Web services and SOAs are at the heart of the cloud. While there are numerous developments on web services, much research is needed on secure web services. Furthermore, major initiatives such as the global information grid and the network centric enterprise services are based on web services and SOAs. Therefore, securing these technologies as well as making web services more intelligent by using the semantic web will be critical for the next-generation cloud.

Figure 35.2 **Directions and challenges in cloud computing and secure cloud computing.**

35.3.2 Cloud Computing

There has been a lot of recent work on cloud computing including virtualization, cloud data storage, and cloud data management. The major challenge for cloud computing is handling massive amounts of data and processing. That is, solving the big data problem using the cloud is a challenge. Furthermore, cloud computing should also be examined for security applications such as malware detection and email spam filtering.

35.3.3 Secure Cloud Computing

We need to examine security for virtualization, storage, data management, and networking in the cloud. With respect to identity management and access control in the cloud, a lot of work remains to be done. We need appropriate security models for the clouds. For example, models such as ABAC need to be examined for the cloud. We need to develop standards similar to SAML and XACML to include more sophisticated forms of fine-grained access control. As web services explode and we carry out more and more transactions on the cloud as well as get involved in social networks, it is critical that we protect the identity of individuals as well as ensure authorized access. Secure virtualization and cloud forensics and auditing are also areas that need a lot of work. Finally, we need to determine aspects such as governance, business continuity planning, legal aspects as well as operations management for the cloud.

35.4 Our Goals on Securing the Cloud

While we have discussed many concepts on cloud computing and secure cloud computing such as virtualization, cloud forensics, and governance aspects, much of our research has focused on secure cloud data management. Therefore, one of the major

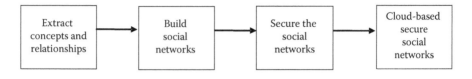

Figure 35.3   Our goals on securing the cloud.

goals for us is to continue to develop systems in secure cloud data storage, secure cloud data management as well as in implementing applications such as malware detection, insider threat detection, and assured information sharing in the cloud.

A major aspect of our research is to (i) extract entities and relationships between the entities from the numerous data sources both structured and unstructured, (ii) build networks from the extracted entities and relationships between the entities, and (iii) analyze the networks and extract the nuggets from the networks that will be useful for the analyst. Our goal is to implement the social networking systems that we are developing in the cloud. Furthermore, as we make progress with security and privacy for social networks, we will also implement the secure social networks in the cloud.

Our team at UTD is also conducting extensive research on secure cloud virtualization, cloud forensics, and formal policy analysis for the cloud. Therefore, we will continue to explore the fundamental issues surrounding the cloud. Figure 35.3 illustrates our goals on securing the cloud.

35.5 Where Do We Go from Here?

This book has focused on secure services, cloud computing, and secure cloud computing. We have stated many challenges in this field in Section 35.3. We need to continue with research and development efforts if we are to make progress in this very important area.

The question is where do we go from here? First of all, those who wish to work in this area must have a good knowledge of the supporting technologies, including services, semantic web, information security and data, information and knowledge management. For example, it is important to understand the technologies that comprise the web services and how they are used for the cloud. Furthermore, one also needs to understand the numerous standards that are being developed and be able to identify the standards that are most appropriate for their organizations.

Next, since the field is expanding rapidly and there are many developments in the field, the reader has to keep up with the developments including reading about the commercial products and prototypes. Finally, we encourage the reader to experiment with the products and also develop security tools. This is the best way to get familiar with a particular field. That is, work on hands-on problems and provide solutions to get a better understanding. The developers should be familiar with technologies such as Hadoop, MapReduce, HBase, and Storm. The cloud will continue to have a major impact on handling massive amounts of data and processing and therefore security for the cloud will be crucial. This way, organizations will be more comfortable with storing their data in the cloud.

We need research and development support from the federal and local government funding agencies. Agencies such as the NSF, National Security Agency, the US Army, Navy, Air Force, the Defense Advanced Research Projects Agency, the Intelligence Advanced Research Projects Activity, and the Department of Homeland Security are funding research in security. The Air Force is focusing a great deal on securing the cloud. We also need commercial corporations to invest research and development funds so that progress can be made in industrial research as well as be able to transfer the research to commercial products. We also need to collaborate with the international research community to solve problems and promote standards that are not only of national interest but also of international interest. In summary, we need public/private/academic partnerships to develop breakthrough technologies in the very important area of securing the cloud.

Conclusion to Part IX

The chapters in Part IX described the infrastructure, education initiative, and research program we are developing at the UTD. This work has been instrumental in the prototypes that we have discussed in the previous parts.

In Chapter 32, we described the infrastructure we are developing for a secure cloud to support our projects. Our cloud consists of a hardware component, a software component, and a data component. We are integrating the cloud with our current infrastructures and have developed a number of tools that utilize our infrastructure. These tools have been discussed in several chapters of this book and include secure query processing in the cloud, social networking in the cloud, and malware detection in the cloud. We utilized the Hadoop/MapReduce technologies to provide the data storage for the cloud.

In Chapter 33, we discussed our education program for assured cloud computing. In particular, we have developed a number of units in secure cloud computing, including secure cloud data management, secure cloud data storage, and secure cloud forensics. In addition, we have also developed a flagship course in secure cloud computing.

In Chapter 34, we discussed the various research projects led by the UTD that are ongoing on secure cloud computing. In particular, we discussed secure cloud query processing, security models for the cloud, and the work toward building secure social networks in the cloud.

Appendix A: Data Management Systems— Developments and Trends

A.1 Overview

The main purpose of this appendix is to set the context of the series of books we have written in data management, data mining, and data security. Our series started way back in 1997 with our book on *Data Management Systems Evolution and Interoperation* [THUR97]. Our subsequent books have evolved from this first book. We have essentially repeated Chapter 1 of our first book in Appendix A of our subsequent books. The purpose of this appendix is to provide an overview of data management systems. We will then discuss the relationships between the books we have written.

As stated in our series of books, the developments in information systems technologies have resulted in computerizing many applications in various business areas. Data have become a critical resource in many organizations and therefore, efficient access to data, sharing the data, extracting information from the data, and making use of the information, have become urgent needs. As a result, there have been several efforts on integrating the various data sources scattered across several sites. These data sources may be databases managed by database management systems or they could simply be files. To provide the interoperability between the multiple data sources and systems, various tools are being developed. These tools enable users of one system to access other systems in an efficient and transparent manner.

We define data management systems to be systems that manage the data, extract meaningful information from the data, and make use of the information extracted. Therefore, data management systems include database systems, data warehouses, and data mining systems. Data could be structured data such as that found in relational databases or it could be unstructured such as text, voice, imagery, and video. There have been numerous discussions in the past to distinguish between data, information, and knowledge. We do not attempt to clarify these terms. For our purposes, data could be just bits and bytes or it could convey some meaningful information to the user. We will, however, distinguish between database systems and database management systems. A database management system is that component which manages the database containing persistent data. A database system consists of both the database and the database management system.

A key component to the evolution and interoperation of data management systems is the interoperability of heterogeneous database systems. Efforts on the interoperability between database systems have been reported since the late 1970s. However, it is only recently that we are seeing commercial developments in heterogeneous database systems. Major database system vendors are now providing interoperability between their products and other systems. Furthermore, many of the database system vendors are migrating toward an architecture called the client–server architecture, which facilitates distributed data management capabilities. In addition to efforts on the interoperability between different database systems and client–server environments, work is also directed toward handling autonomous and federated environments.

The organization of this appendix is as follows. Since database systems are a key component of data management systems, we first provide an overview of the developments in database systems. These developments are discussed in Section A.2. Then we provide a vision for data management systems in Section A.3. Our framework for data management systems is discussed in Section A.4. Note that data mining, warehousing as well as web data management are components of this framework. Building information systems from our framework with special instantiations is discussed in Section A.5. The relationship between the various texts that we have written (or are writing) for CRC Press is discussed in Section A.6. This appendix is summarized in Section A.7.

A.2 Developments in Database Systems

Figure A.1 provides an overview of the developments in database systems technology. While the early work in the 1960s focused on developing products based on the network and hierarchical data models, much of the developments in database systems took place after the seminal paper by Codd describing the relational model [CODD70] (see also [DATE90]). Research and development work on relational database systems was carried out during the early 1970s and several prototypes were developed throughout the 1970s. Notable efforts include IBM's (International Business Machine Corporation's) System R and University of California at Berkeley's INGRES. During the 1980s, many relational database system products were being marketed (notable among these products are those of Oracle Corporation, Sybase Inc., Informix Corporation, INGRES Corporation, IBM, Digital Equipment Corporation, and Hewlett Packard Company). During the 1990s, products from

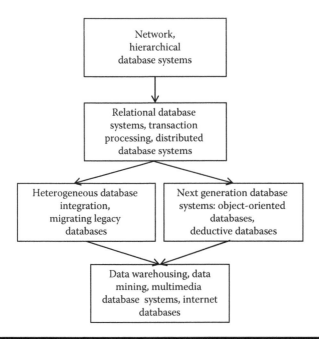

Figure A.1   Developments in database systems technology.

other vendors emerged (e.g., Microsoft Corporation). In fact, to date numerous relational database system products have been marketed. However, Codd has stated that many of the systems that are being marketed as relational systems are not really relational (see, e.g., the discussion in [DATE90]). He then discussed various criteria that a system must satisfy to be qualified as a relational database system. While the early work focused on issues such as data model, normalization theory, query processing and optimization strategies, query languages, and access strategies and indexes, the focus later shifted toward supporting a multi-user environment. In particular, concurrency control and recovery techniques were developed. Support for transaction processing was also provided.

Research on relational database systems as well as on transaction management was followed by research on distributed database systems around the mid-1970s. Several distributed database system prototype development efforts also began around the late 1970s. Notable among these efforts include IBM's System R*, DDTS (Distributed Database Testbed System) by Honeywell Inc., SDD-I Multibase by CCA (Computer Corporation of America), and Mermaid by SDC (System Development Corporation). Furthermore, many of these systems (e.g., DDTS, Multibase, Mermaid) function in a heterogeneous environment. During the early 1990s, several database system vendors (such as Oracle Corporation, Sybase Inc., Informix Corporation) provided data distribution capabilities for their systems. Most of the distributed relational database system products are based on client–server architectures. The idea is to have the client of vendor A communicate with the server database system of vendor B. In other words, the client–server computing paradigm facilitates a heterogeneous computing environment. Interoperability between relational and nonrelational commercial database systems is also possible. The database systems community is also involved in standardization efforts. Notable among the standardization efforts are the ANSI/SPARC 3-level schema architecture, the IRDS (Information Resource Dictionary System) standard for Data Dictionary Systems, the relational query language SQL (Structured Query Language), and the RDA (Remote Database Access) protocol for remote database access.

Another significant development in database technology is the advent of object-oriented database management systems. Active work on developing such systems began in the mid-1980s and they are now commercially available (notable among them include the products of Object Design Inc., Ontos Inc., Gemstone Systems Inc., Versant Object Technology). It was felt that new-generation applications such as multimedia, office information systems, CAD/CAM, process control, and software engineering have different requirements. Such applications utilize complex data structures. Tighter integration between the programming language and the data model is also desired. Object-oriented database systems satisfy most of the requirements of these new-generation applications [CATT91].

According to the Lagunita report published as a result of an NSF workshop in 1990 (see [SILB90] and [KIM90]), relational database systems, transaction processing, and distributed (relational) database systems are stated as mature technologies. Furthermore, vendors are marketing object-oriented database systems and demonstrating the interoperability between different database systems. The report goes on to state that as applications are getting increasingly complex, more sophisticated database systems are needed. Furthermore, since many organizations now use database systems, in many cases of different types, the database systems need to be integrated. Although work has begun to address these issues and commercial products are available, several issues still need to be resolved. Therefore, challenges faced by the database systems researchers in the early 1990s were in two areas. One was next-generation database systems and the other was heterogeneous database systems.

Next-generation database systems include object-oriented database systems, functional database systems, special parallel architectures to enhance the performance of database system functions, high-performance database systems, real-time database systems, scientific database systems, temporal database systems, database systems that handle incomplete and uncertain information, and intelligent database systems (also sometimes called logic or deductive database systems). Ideally, a database system should provide the support for high-performance transaction processing, model complex applications, represent new kinds of data, and make intelligent deductions. While significant progress has been made during the late 1980s and early 1990s, there is much to be done before such a database system can be developed.

Heterogeneous database systems have been receiving considerable attention during the past decade [MARC90]. The major issues include handling different data models, different query processing strategies, different transaction processing algorithms, and different query languages. Should a uniform view be provided to the entire system or should the users of the individual systems maintain their own views of the entire system? These are questions that have yet to be answered satisfactorily. It is also envisaged that a complete solution to heterogeneous database management systems is a generation away. While research should be directed toward finding such a solution, work should also be carried out to handle limited forms of heterogeneity to satisfy the customer needs. Another type of database system that has received some attention lately is a federated database system. Note that some have used the terms heterogeneous database system and federated database system interchangeably. While heterogeneous database systems can be part of a federation, a federation can also include homogeneous database systems.

The explosion of users on the web as well as developments in interface technologies has resulted in even more challenges for data management researchers. A second workshop was sponsored by NSF in 1995, and several emerging technologies have been identified to be important as we enter the twenty-first century [WIDO96]. These include digital libraries, managing very large databases, data administration issues, multimedia databases, data warehousing, data mining, data management for collaborative computing environments, and security and privacy. Another significant development in the 1990s is the development of object-relational systems. Such systems combine the advantages of both object-oriented database systems and relational database systems. Also, many corporations are now focusing on integrating their data management products with web technologies. Finally, for many organizations there is an increasing need to migrate some of the legacy databases and applications to newer architectures and systems such as client–server architectures and relational database systems. We believe there is no end to data management systems. As new technologies are developed, there are new opportunities for data management research and development.

A comprehensive view of all data management technologies is illustrated in Figure A.2. As shown, traditional technologies include database design, transaction processing, and benchmarking. Then there are database systems based on data models such as relational and object oriented. Database systems may depend on features that they provide such as security and real time. These database systems may be relational or object-oriented. There are also database systems based on multiple sites or processors such as distributed and heterogeneous database systems, parallel systems, and systems being migrated. Finally, there are the emerging technologies such as data warehousing and mining, collaboration, and the web. Any comprehensive text on data management systems should address all of these technologies. We have selected some of the relevant technologies and put them in a framework. This framework is described in Section A.5.

Traditional technologies:	Database systems based on data models:	Database systems based on features:
• Data modeling and database design • Enterprise/business modeling and application design • DBMS design • Query, metadata, transactions • Integrity and data quality • Benchmarking and performance • Data administration, auditing, database administration • Standards	• Hierarchical • Network • Relational • Functional • Object-oriented • Deductive (logic-based) • Object-relational	• Secure database • Real-time database • Fault-tolerance database • Multimedia database • Active database • Temporal database • Fuzzy database
	Multi-site/processor-based systems:	**Emerging technologies:**
	• Distribution • Interoperability • Federated • Client-server • Migration • Parallel/high performance	• Data warehousing • Data mining • Internet • Collaboration • Mobile computing

Figure A.2   Comprehensive view of data management systems.

A.3 Status, Vision, and Issues

Significant progress has been made on data management systems. However, many of the technologies are still standalone technologies as illustrated in Figure A.3. For example, multimedia systems are yet to be successfully integrated with warehousing and mining technologies. The ultimate goal is to integrate multiple technologies so that accurate data, as well as information, are produced at the right time and distributed to the user in a timely manner. Our vision for data and information management is illustrated in Figure A.4.

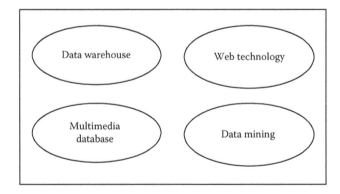

Figure A.3   Standalone systems.

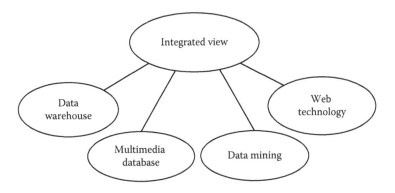

Figure A.4   Vision.

The work discussed in [THUR97] addressed many of the challenges necessary to accomplish this vision. In particular, integration of heterogeneous databases, as well as the use of distributed object technology for interoperability, was discussed. While much progress has been made on the system aspects of interoperability, semantic issues still remain a challenge. Different databases have different representations. Furthermore, the same data entity may be interpreted differently at different sites. Addressing these semantic differences and extracting useful information from the heterogeneous and possibly multimedia data sources are major challenges. This book has attempted to address some of the challenges through the use of data mining.

A.4 Data Management Systems Framework

For the successful development of evolvable interoperable data management systems, heterogeneous database systems integration is a major component. However, there are other technologies that have to be successfully integrated with each other to develop techniques for efficient access and sharing of data as well as for the extraction of information from the data. To facilitate the development of data management systems to meet the requirements of various applications in fields such as medical, financial, manufacturing, and military, we have proposed a framework, which can be regarded as a reference model, for data management systems. Various components from this framework have to be integrated to develop data management systems to support the various applications.

Figure A.5 illustrates our framework, which can be regarded as a model, for data management systems. This framework consists of three layers. One can think of the component technologies, which we will also refer to as components, belonging to a particular layer to be more or less built upon the technologies provided by the lower layer. Layer I is the Database Technology and Distribution Layer. This layer

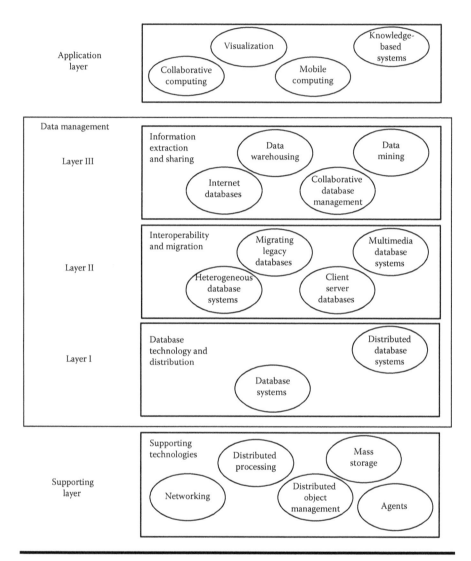

Figure A.5 Data management systems framework.

consists of database systems and distributed database systems technologies. Layer II is the Interoperability and Migration Layer. This layer consists of technologies such as heterogeneous database integration, client-server databases, and multimedia database systems to handle heterogeneous data types, and migrating legacy databases. Layer III is the Information Extraction and Sharing Layer. This layer essentially consists of technologies for some of the newer services supported by data management systems. These include data warehousing, data mining [THUR98], web databases, and database support for collaborative applications. Data management systems may utilize lower-level technologies such as networking, distributed processing, and mass storage. We have grouped these technologies into a layer called the Supporting Technologies Layer. This supporting layer does not belong to the data management systems framework. This supporting layer also consists of some higher-level technologies such as distributed object management and agents. Also, shown in Figure A.5 is the Application Technologies Layer. Systems such as collaborative computing systems and knowledge-based systems which belong to the Application Technologies Layer may utilize data management systems. Note that the Application Technologies Layer is also outside of the data management systems framework.

The technologies that constitute the data management systems framework can be regarded to be some of the core technologies in data management. However, features like security, integrity, real-time processing, fault tolerance, and high-performance computing are needed for many applications utilizing data management technologies. Applications utilizing data management technologies may be medical, financial, or military, among others. We illustrate this in Figure A.6, where a three-dimensional view relating data management technologies with features and applications is given. For example, one could develop a secure distributed database management system for medical applications or a fault-tolerant multimedia database management system for financial applications.

Integrating the components belonging to the various layers is important to developing efficient data management systems. In addition, data management technologies have to be integrated with the application technologies to develop successful information systems. However, at present, there is limited integration

Figure A.6   A three-dimensional view of data management.

between these various components. Our previous book *Data Management Systems Evolution and Interoperation* [THUR97] focused mainly on the concepts, developments, and trends belonging to each of the components shown in the framework. Furthermore, our current book on web data management, which we also refer to as web data management, focuses on the web database component of Layer 3 of the framework in Figure A.5.

Note that security cuts across all the layers. Security is needed for the supporting layers such as agents and distributed systems. Security is needed for all of the layers in the framework, including database security, distributed database security, warehousing security, web database security, and collaborative data management security. This is the topic of this book. That is, we have covered all aspects of data and applications security including database security and information management security.

A.5 Building Information Systems from the Framework

Figure A.5 illustrated a framework for data management systems. As shown in that figure, the technologies for data management include database systems, distributed database systems, heterogeneous database systems, migrating legacy databases, multimedia database systems, data warehousing, data mining, web databases, and database support for collaboration. Furthermore, data management systems take advantage of supporting technologies such as distributed processing and agents. Similarly, application technologies such as collaborative computing, visualization, expert systems, and mobile computing take advantage of data management systems.

Many of us have heard of the term information systems on numerous occasions. These systems have sometimes been used interchangeably with data management systems. In our terminology, information systems are much broader than data management systems, but they do include data management systems. In fact, a framework for information systems will include not only the data management system layers, but also the supporting technologies layer as well as the application technologies layer. That is, information systems encompass all kinds of computing systems. It can be regarded as the finished product that can be used for various applications. That is, while hardware is at the lowest end of the spectrum, applications are at the highest end.

We can combine the technologies of Figure A.5 to put together information systems. For example, at the application technology level, one may need collaboration and visualization technologies so that analysts can collaboratively carry out some tasks. At the data management level, one may need both multimedia and distributed database technologies. At the supporting level, one may need mass storage as well as some distributed processing capability. This special framework is illustrated in Figure A.7. Another example is a special framework

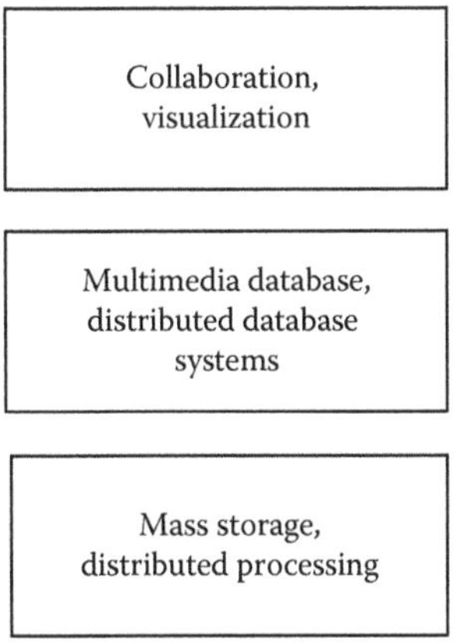

| Collaboration, visualization |
| Multimedia database, distributed database systems |
| Mass storage, distributed processing |

Figure A.7   Framework for multimedia data management for collaboration.

for interoperability. One may need some visualization technology to display the integrated information from the heterogeneous databases. At the data management level, we have heterogeneous database systems technology. At the supporting technology level, one may use distributed object management technology to encapsulate the heterogeneous databases. This special framework is illustrated in Figure A.8.

Finally, let us illustrate the concepts that we have described above by using a specific example. Suppose a group of physicians/surgeons want a system where they can collaborate and make decisions about various patients. This could be a medical

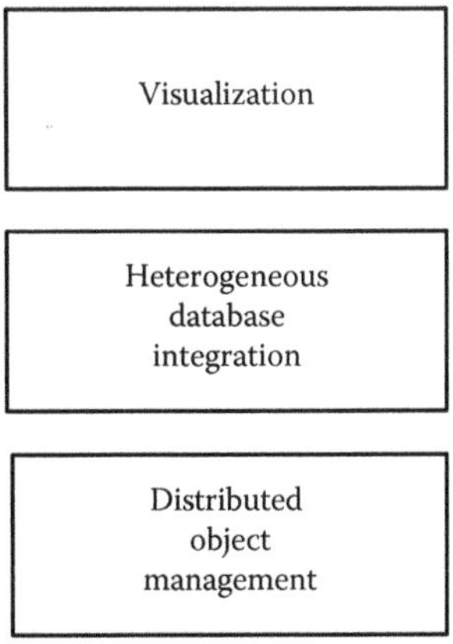

| Visualization |
| Heterogeneous database integration |
| Distributed object management |

Figure A.8   Framework for heterogeneous database interoperability.

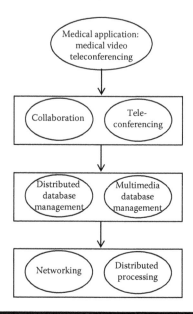

Figure A.9   Specific example.

video teleconferencing application. That is, at the highest level, the application is a medical application and, more specifically, a medical video teleconferencing application. At the application technology level, one needs a variety of technologies including collaboration and teleconferencing. These application technologies will make use of data management technologies such as distributed database systems and multimedia database systems. That is, one may need to support multimedia data such as audio and video. The data management technologies in turn draw upon lower-level technologies such as distributed processing and networking. We illustrate this in Figure A.9.

In summary, information systems include data management systems as well as application-layer systems such as collaborative computing systems and supporting-layer systems such as distributed object management systems.

While application technologies make use of data management technologies and data management technologies make use of supporting technologies, the ultimate user of the information system is the application itself. Today numerous applications make use of information systems. These applications are from multiple domains such as medical, financial, manufacturing, telecommunications, and defense. Specific applications include signal processing, electronic commerce, patient monitoring, and situation assessment. Figure A.10 illustrates the relationship between the application and the information system.

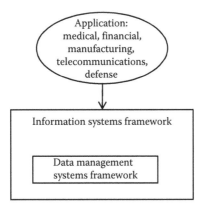

Figure A.10   Application–framework relationship.

A.6 Relationship between the Texts

We have published two book series. The first series is mainly for technical managers, while the second series is for researchers and developers. This book is the tenth in the first series. Our previous nine books are *Data Management Systems: Evolution and Interoperation* [THUR97], *Data Mining: Technologies, Techniques, Tools and Trends* [THUR98], *Web Data Management and Electronic Commerce* [THUR00], *Managing and Mining Multimedia Databases for the Electronic Enterprise* [THUR01], *XML, Databases and The Semantic Web* [THUR02], *Web Data Mining and Applications in Business Intelligence and Counter-terrorism* [THUR03], *Database and Applications Security: Integrating Data Management and Information Security* [THUR05]. *Building Trustworthy Semantic Web* [THUR07], and *Secure Semantic Service-Oriented Systems* [THUR10]. Our current book [THUR13] has evolved from our previous book on *Secure Semantic Service-Oriented Systems*. All of these books have evolved from the framework that we illustrated in this appendix and address different parts of the framework. The connection between these texts is illustrated in Figure A.11.

We have published two books on the second series. The first is titled *Design and Implementation of Data Mining Tools* [AWAD09] and second is titled *Data Mining Tools for Malware Detection* [MASU11]. This is illustrated in Figure A.12.

A.7 Summary and Directions

In this appendix, we have provided an overview of data management. We first discussed the developments in data management and then provided a vision for data management. Then we illustrated a framework for data management. This framework consists of three layers: database systems layer, interoperability layer, and information

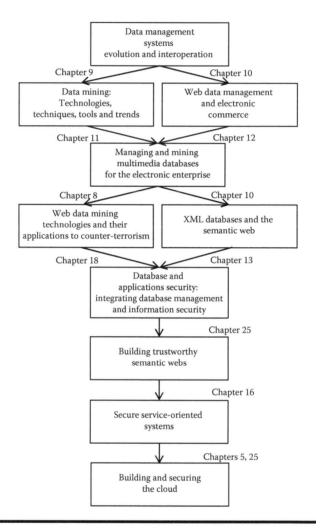

Figure A.11   Relationship between texts—series I.

extraction layer. Web data management belongs to layer 3. Finally, we showed how information systems could be built from the technologies of the framework.

We believe that data management is essential to many information technologies including data mining, multimedia information processing, interoperability, and collaboration and knowledge management. This appendix stresses on data management. Security is critical for all data management technologies and we rely on these technologies for our work on cloud computing. We will provide background information on data mining in Appendix B. Background on access control in data management will be provided in Appendix C. Our approach to assured information sharing will be discussed in Appendix D.

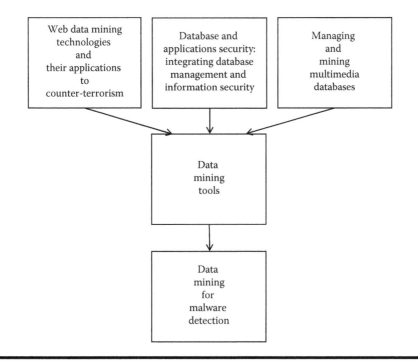

Figure A.12   Relationship between texts—series II.

References

[AWAD09] Awad, M., L. Khan, B. Thuraisingham, and L. Wang, *Design and Implementation of Data Mining Tools*, CRC Press, Boca Raton, FL, 2009.

[CATT91] Cattell, R., *Object Data Management Systems*, Addison- Wesley, MA, 1991.

[CODD70] Codd, E. F., A relational model of data for large shared data banks. *Communications of the ACM*, 13(6): 377–387, June 1970.

[DATE90] Date, C. J., *An Introduction to Database Management Systems*. Addison-Wesley, MA, 1990 (8th edition, 2003, MA).

[KIM90] Kim, W. (Ed.), *Directions for Future Database Research & Development*. ACM SIGMOD Record, December 1990, 19(4).

[MARC90] March, S. T. (Ed.), *Special Issue on Heterogeneous Database Systems*, ACM Computing Surveys, September 1990, 22(3).

[MASU11] Masud, M., B. Thuraisingham, and L. Khan, *Data Mining Tools for Malware Detection*, CRC Press, Boca Raton, FL, 2011.

[SILB90] Silberschatz, A., Stonebraker, M., and Ullman, J.D. (Eds) (1990), *Database Systems: Achievements and Opportunities, The Lagunita Report of the NSF Invitational Workshop on the Future of Database Systems Research,* February 22–23, Palo Alto, CA (TR-90-22), Department of Computer Sciences, University of Texas at Austin, Austin, TX (also in *Communications of the ACM*, 34(10), October 1991, 110–120).

[THUR97] Thuraisingham, B., *Data Management Systems: Evolution and Interoperation*, CRC Press, Boca Raton, FL, 1997.

[THUR98] Thuraisingham, B., *Data Mining: Technologies, Techniques, Tools and Trends*, CRC Press, Boca Raton, FL, 1998.

[THUR00] Thuraisingham, B., *Web Data Management and Electronic Commerce*, CRC Press, Boca Raton, FL, 2000.

[THUR01] Thuraisingham, B., *Managing and Mining Multimedia Databases for the Electronic Enterprise*, CRC Press, Boca Raton, FL, 2001.

[THUR02] Thuraisingham, B., *XML, Databases and the Semantic Web*, CRC Press, Boca Raton, FL, 2002.

[THUR03] Thuraisingham, B., *Web Data Mining Applications in Business Intelligence and Counter-terrorism*, CRC Press, Boca Raton, FL, 2003.

[THUR05] Thuraisingham, B., *Database and Applications Security: Integrating Data Management and Information Security*, CRC Press, Boca Raton, FL, 2005.

[THUR07] Thuraisingham, B., *Building Trustworthy Semantic Webs*, CRC Press, Boca Raton, FL, 2007.

[THUR10] Thuraisingham, B., *Secure Semantic Service-Oriented Systems*, CRC Press, Boca Raton, FL, 2010.

[THUR13] Thuraisingham, B., *Building and Securing the Cloud*, CRC Press, Boca Raton, FL, 2013.

[WIDO96] Widom, J., (Ed.), Database research: Achievements and opportunities into the 21st century. *Proceedings of the Database Systems Workshop, Report Published by the National Science Foundation, 1995*, 25(1), (also in ACM SIGMOD Record, March 1996).

Appendix B: Data Mining Techniques

B.1 Overview

Data mining outcomes (also called tasks) include classification, clustering, forming associations as well as detecting anomalies. Our tools have mainly focused on classification as the outcome and we have developed classification tools. The classification problem is also referred to as supervised learning, in which a set of labeled examples is learned by a model, and then a new example with unknown label is presented to the model for prediction.

There are many prediction models that have been used such as Markov model, decision trees, artificial neural networks (ANN), support vector machines (SVM), association rule mining (ARM), and many others. Each of these models has its own strengths and weaknesses. However, there is a common weakness among all of these techniques which is the inability to suit all applications. The reason that there is no such ideal or perfect classifier is that each of these techniques is initially designed to solve specific problems under certain assumptions.

In this chapter, we discuss the data mining techniques we have utilized in our tools. Specifically, we present the Markov model, SVM, ANN, ARM, the problem of multi-classification as well as image classification which is an aspect of image mining. In our research and development, we develop hybrid models to improve the prediction accuracy of data mining for various applications, namely, intrusion detection, web page prediction and image classification. Some of these applications hosted on clouds were discussed in this book.

The organization of this chapter is as follows. In Section B.2, we provide an overview of various data mining tasks and techniques. The techniques that are relevant to the contents of this book are discussed in Sections B.2 through B.6. In particular, neural networks, SVM, Markov models, and ARM as well as some other classification techniques will be described. This chapter is summarized in Section B.7.

B.2 Overview of Data Mining Tasks and Techniques

Before we discuss data mining techniques we provide an overview of some of the data mining tasks (also known as data mining outcomes). Then we will discuss the techniques. In general data mining tasks can be grouped into two categories; predictive and descriptive. Predictive tasks essentially predict whether an item belongs to a class or not. Descriptive tasks in general extract patterns from the examples. One of the most prominent predictive tasks is classification. In some cases other tasks such as anomaly detection can be reduced to a predictive task such as whether a particular situation is an anomaly or not. Descriptive tasks in general include making associations and forming clusters. Therefore, classification, anomaly detection, making associations, and forming clusters are also thought to be data mining tasks.

Next, the data mining techniques can either be predictive, descriptive, or both. For example, neural networks can perform classification as well as clustering. Classification techniques include decision trees, SVM as well as memory-based reasoning. ARM techniques are used in general to make associations. Link analysis that analyzes links can also make associations between links and predict new links. Clustering techniques include K-means clustering. An overview of the data mining tasks (i.e., the outcomes of data mining) are illustrated in Figure B.1. The techniques to be discussed in this book (e.g., neural networks, SVM) are illustrated in Figure B.2.

B.3 Artificial Neural Networks

ANN is a very well-known, powerful, and robust classification technique that has been used to approximate real-valued, discrete-valued, and vector-valued functions. From examples [MITC97] ANNs have been used in many areas such as interpreting visual scenes, speech recognition, and learning robot control strategies. An ANN simulates the biological nervous system in the human brain. Such

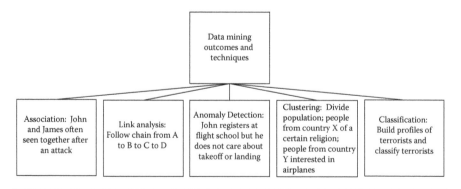

Figure B.1 Data mining tasks.

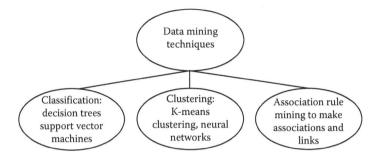

Figure B.2 Data mining techniques utilized in the tools.

nervous system is composed of large number of highly interconnected processing units (neurons) working together to produce our feelings and reactions. ANNs, like people, learn by example. The learning process in human brain involves adjustments to the synaptic connections between neurons. Similarly, the learning process of ANN involves adjustments to the node weights. Figure B.3 presents a simple neuron unit, which is called perceptron. The perceptron input, x, is a vector or real-valued inputs. w is the weight vector, in which its value is determined after training. The perceptron computes a linear combination of an input vector x as follows (Equation 2.1).

$$o(x_1,...,x_n) = \begin{cases} 1 & \text{if } w_0 + w_1 x_1 + \cdots + w_n x_n > 0 \\ -1 & \text{otherwise} \end{cases} \tag{B.1}$$

Notice that w_i corresponds to the contribution of the input vector component x_i of the perceptron output. Also, in order for the perceptron to output a 1, the weighted combination of the inputs ($\sum_{i=1}^{n} w_i x_i$) must be greater than the threshold w_0.

Learning the perceptron involves choosing values for the weights $w_0 + w_1 x_1 + \cdots + w_n x_n$. Initially, random weight values are given to the perceptron.

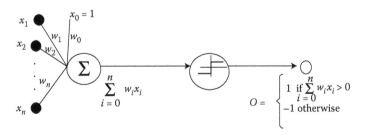

Figure B.3 The perceptron.

Then the perceptron is applied to each training example updating the weights of the perceptron whenever an example is misclassified. This process is repeated many times until all training examples are correctly classified. The weights are updated according to the following rule (Equation B.2):

$$\begin{cases} w_i = w_i + \delta w_i \\ \delta w_i = \eta(t - o)x_i \end{cases} \tag{B.2}$$

where η is a learning constant, o is the output computed by the perceptron, and t is the target output for the current training example.

The computation power of a single perceptron is limited to linear decisions. However, the perceptron can be used as a building block to compose powerful multi-layer networks. In this case, more complicated updating rule is needed to train the network weights. In this work, we employ an ANN of two layers and each layer is composed of three building blocks (see Figure B.4). We use the back propagation algorithm for learning the weights. The back propagation algorithm attempts to minimize the squared error function.

A typical training example in WWW prediction is $<[k_{t-\tau+1},...,k_{t-1},k_t]^T,d>$, where $[k_{t-\tau+1},...,k_{t-1},k_t]^T$ is the input to the ANN and d is the target web page. Notice that the input units of the ANN in Figure B.5 are τ previous pages that the user has recently visited, where k is a web page id. The output of the network is a boolean value, not a probability. We will see later how to approximate the probability of the output by fitting a sigmoid function after ANN output. The approximated probabilistic output becomes $o' = f(o(I)) = p_{t+1}$, where I is an input session and $p_{t+1} = p(d|k_{t-\tau+1},...,k_t)$. We choose the sigmoid function (Equation B.3), as a transfer function so as the ANN can handle nonlinearly separable data set [MITC97]. Notice that in our ANN design (Figure B.5), we use a sigmoid transfer function, Equation B.3, in each building block. In Equation B.3, I is the input to the network, O is the output of the network, W is the matrix of weights, and σ is the sigmoid function.

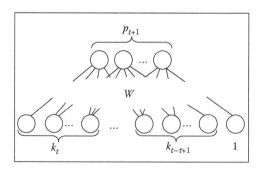

Figure B.4 Artificial neural network.

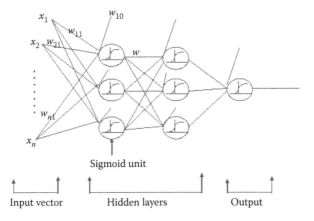

Figure B.5 The design of ANN used in our implementation.

$$\begin{cases} o = \sigma(w \cdot I) \\ \sigma(y) = \dfrac{1}{1 + e^{-y}} \end{cases} \tag{B.3}$$

$$E(W) = \frac{1}{2} \sum_{k \in D} \sum_{i \in ouputs} (t_{ik} - o_{ik})^2 \tag{B.4}$$

$$\begin{cases} w_{ji} = w_{ji} + \delta w_{ji} \\ \delta w_{ji} = -\eta \dfrac{\partial E_d}{\partial w_{ji}} \end{cases} \tag{B.5}$$

$$\delta w_{ji}(n) = -\eta \frac{\partial E_d}{\partial w_{ji}} + \alpha \delta w_{ji}(n-1) \tag{B.6}$$

We implement the back propagation algorithm for training the weights. The back propagation algorithm employs gradient descent to attempt to minimize the squared error between the network output values and the target values of these outputs. The sum of the error over all of the network output units is defined in Equation B.4. In Equation B.4, the *outputs* is the set of output units in the network, D is the training set, and t_{ik} and o_{ik} are the target and the output values associated with the ith output unit and training example k. For a specific weight w_{ji} in the network, it is updated for each training example as in Equation B.5, where η is the learning rate and w_{ji} is the weight associated with the ith input to the network unit j (for details see [MITC97]). As we can see from Equation B.5, the search direction δw is computed using the gradient descent which guarantees convergence toward a local minimum. To mitigate that, we add a momentum to the weight update rule such that the weight update direction $\delta w_{ji}(n)$ depends partially on the update direction in the previous iteration $\delta w_{ji}(n-1)$. The new weight update direction is shown in Equation B.6, where n is the current iteration, and α is the momentum constant. Notice that in Equation B.6, the step size is slightly larger than in Equation B.5. This contributes to a smooth convergence of the search in regions where the gradient is unchanging [MITC97].

In our implementation, we set the step size η dynamically based on the distribution of the classes in the dataset. Specifically, we set the step size to large values when updating the training examples that belong to low distribution classes and vice versa. This is because when the distribution of the classes in the dataset varies widely (e.g., a data set might have 5% positive examples and 95% negative examples), the network weights converge toward the examples from the class of larger distribution, which causes a slow convergence. Furthermore, we adjust the learning rates slightly by applying the momentum constant, Equation B.6, to speed up the convergence of the network [MITC97].

B.4 Support Vector Machines

SVM are learning systems that use a hypothesis space of linear functions in a high-dimensional feature space, trained with a learning algorithm from optimization theory. This learning strategy, introduced by Vapnik et al. [CRIS00], is a very powerful method that has been applied in a wide variety of applications. The basic concept in SVM is the hyper-plane classifier, or linear separability. To achieve linear separability, SVM applies two basic ideas—margin maximization and kernels, that is, mapping input space to a higher dimension space, feature space.

For binary classification, SVM problem can be formalized as in Equation B.7. Suppose we have N training data points $\{(x_1, y_1), (x_2, y_2), \ldots, (x_N, y_N)\}$, where $x_i \in R^d$ and $y_i \in \{+1, -1\}$. We would like to find a linear separating hyper-plane classifier as in Equation B.8. Furthermore, we want this hyper-plane to have the maximum separating margin with respect to the two classes (see Figure B.6). The functional margin, or the margin for short, is defined geometrically as the Euclidean distance of the closest point from the decision boundary to the input space. Figure B.7 gives an intuitive explanation of why margin maximization gives the best solution of separation. In part A of Figure B.7, we can find infinite number of separators for a specific data set. There is no specific or clear reason to favor one separator over another. In part B, we see that maximizing the margin provides only one thick separator. Such a solution proves to achieve the best generalization accuracy, that is, prediction for the unseen [VAPN95], [VAPN98], and [VAPN99].

$$\begin{cases} \text{minimize}_{(w,b)} \dfrac{1}{2} w^T w \\ \text{subject to } y_i(w \cdot x_i - b) \geq 1 \end{cases} \qquad (B.7)$$

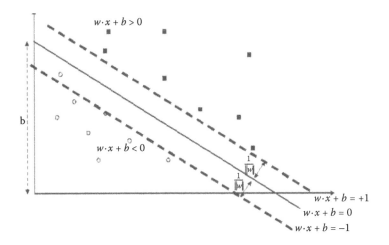

Figure B.6 Linear separation in SVM.

$$f(x) = \text{sign}(w \cdot x - b) \tag{B.8}$$

$$\text{maximize } L(w,b,\alpha) = \frac{1}{2}w^T w - \sum_{i=1}^{N} \alpha_i y_i (w \cdot x_i - b) + \sum_{i=1}^{N} \alpha_i \tag{B.9}$$

$$f(x) = \text{sign}(wx - b) = \text{sign}\left(\sum_{i=1}^{N} \alpha_i y_i (x \cdot x_i - b) \right) \tag{B.10}$$

Note that Equation B.8 computes the sign of the functional margin of point x in addition to the prediction label of x, that is, functional margin of x equals $wx - b$.

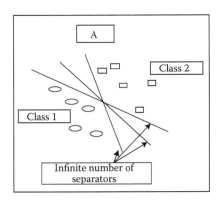 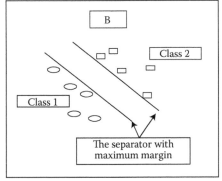

Figure B.7 The SVM separator that causes the maximum margin.

SVM optimization problem is a convex quadratic programming problem (in w, b) in a convex set Equation B.7. We can solve the Wolfe dual instead as in Equation B.9 with respect to α, subject to the constraints that the gradient of $L(w, b, \alpha)$ with respect to the primal variables w and b vanish and $\alpha_i \geq 0$. The primal variables are eliminated from $L(w, b, \alpha)$ (see [CRIS00] for more details). When we solve α_i we can get $w = \sum_{i=1}^{N} \alpha_i y_i x_i$ and we can classify a new object x using Equation B.10. Note that the training vectors occur only in the form of dot product; and that there is a Lagrangian multiplier α_i for each training point, which reflects the importance of the data point. When the maximal margin hyper-plane is found, only points that lie closest to the hyper-plane will have $\alpha_i 0$ and these points are called *support vectors*. All other points will have $\alpha_i = 0$ (see Figure B.8a). This means that only those points that lie closest to the hyper-plane give the representation of the hypothesis/classifier. These most important data points serve as support vectors. Their values can also be used to give an independent boundary with regard to the reliability of the hypothesis/classifier [BART99].

Figure B.8a shows two classes and their boundaries, that is, margins. The support vectors are represented by solid objects, while the empty objects are nonsupport vectors. Notice that the margins are only affected by the support vectors, that is, if we remove or add empty objects, the margins will not change. Meanwhile any change in the solid objects, either adding or removing objects, could change the margins. Figure B.8b shows the effects of adding objects in the margin area. As we can see, adding or removing objects far from the margins, for example, data point 1 or −2, does not change the margins. However, adding and/or removing objects near the margins, for example, data point 2 and/or −1, has created new margins.

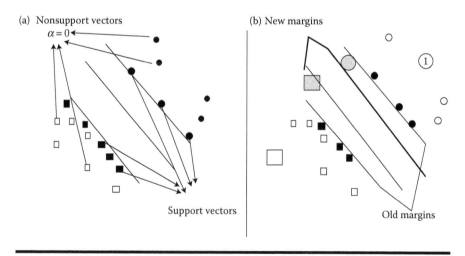

(a) Nonsupport vectors

$\alpha = 0$

Support vectors

(b) New margins

1

Old margins

Figure B.8 (a) The values of for support vectors and nonsupport vectors. (b) The effect of adding new data points on the margins.

B.5 Markov Model

Some recent and advanced predictive methods for web surfing are developed using Markov models [YANG01], [PIRO96]. For these predictive models, the sequences of web pages visited by surfers are typically considered as Markov chains which are then fed as input. The basic concept of Markov model is that it predicts the next action depending on the result of previous action or actions. Actions can mean different things for different applications. For the purpose of illustration, we will consider actions specific for the WWW prediction application. In WWW prediction, the next action corresponds to prediction of the next page to be traversed. The previous actions correspond to the previous web pages to be considered. On the basis of the number of previous actions considered, Markov model can have different orders.

$$pr(P_k) = pr(S_k) \tag{B.11}$$

$$pr(P_2 \mid P_1) = pr(S_2 = P_2 \mid S_1 = P_1) \tag{B.12}$$

$$pr(P_N \mid P_{N-1}, ..., P_{N-k}) = pr(S_N = P_N \mid S_{N-1} = P_{N-1}, ..., S_{N-k} = P_{N-k}) \tag{B.13}$$

The zeroth-order Markov model is the unconditional probability of the state (or webpage) (Equation B.11). In Equation B.11, P_k is a web page and S_k is the corresponding state. The first-order Markov model, Equation B.12, can be computed by taking page-to-page transitional probabilities or the n-gram probabilities of $\{P_1, P_2\}, \{P_2, P_3\}, ..., \{P_{k-1}, P_k\}$.

In the following, we present an illustrative example of different orders of Markov model and how it can predict.

EXAMPLE

Imagine a web site of six web pages: P1, P2, P3, P4, P5, and P6. Suppose we have user sessions as in Table B.1. Table B.1 depicts the navigation of many users of that web site. Figure B.9 shows the *first-order Markov model*, where the next action

Table B.1 Collection of User Sessions and Their Frequencies

Session	Frequency
P1, P2, P4	5
P1, P2, P6	1
P5, P2, P6	6
P5, P2, P3	3

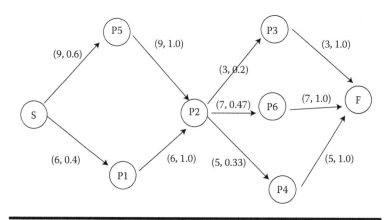

Figure B.9 First-order Markov model.

is predicted based on only the last action performed, that is, last page traversed, by the user. States S and F correspond to the initial and final states, respectively. The probability of each transition is estimated by the ratio of the number of times the sequence of states was traversed and the number of times the anchor state was visited. Next to each arch in Figure B.8, the first number is the frequency of that transition, and the second number is the transition probability. For example, the transition probability of the transition (P2–P3) is 0.2 because the number of times the users traverse from page 2 to page 3 is 3 and the number of times page 2 is visited is 15 (i.e., 0.2 = 3/15).

Notice that the transition probability is used to resolve prediction. For example, given that a user has already visited P2, the most probable page she visits next is P6. That is because the transition probability from P2 to P6 is the highest.

Notice that transition probability might not be available for some pages. For example, the transition probability from P2 to P5 is not available because no user has visited P5 after P2. Hence, these transition probabilities are set to zeros. Similarly, the Kth-order Markov model is where the prediction is computed after considering the last Kth action performed by the users, Equation B.13. In WWW prediction, the Kth-order Markov model is the probability of the user visit to P_kth page given its previous $k-1$ page visits.

Figure B.10 shows the second-order Markov model that corresponds to Table B.1. In the second-order model we consider the last 2 pages. The transition probability is computed in a similar fashion. For example, the transition probability of the transition (P1, P2) to (P2, P6) is 0.16 = 1 × 1/6 because the number of times the users traverse from state (P1, P2) to state (P2, P6) is 1 and the number of times pages (P1, P2) is visited is 6 (i.e., 0.16 = 1/6). The transition probability is used for prediction. For example, given that a user has visited P1 and P2, she most probably visits P4 because the transition probability from state (P1, P2) to state (P2, P4) is greater than the transition probability from state (P1, P2) to state (P2, P6).

The order of Markov model is related to the sliding window. The Kth-order Markov model corresponds to a sliding window of size $K-1$.

Notice that there is another concept that is similar to the sliding window concept, which is *number of hops*. In this thesis, we use *number of hops* and sliding window interchangeably.

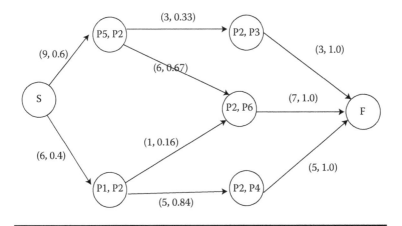

Figure B.10 Second-order Markov model.

In WWW prediction, Markov models are built based on the concept of *n*-gram. The *n*-gram can be represented as a tuple of the form $<x_1, x_2, \ldots, x_n>$ to depict sequences of page clicks by a population of users surfing a website. Each component of the *n*-gram takes a specific page id value that reflects the surfing path of a specific user surfing a webpage. For example, the *n*-gram $<P_{10}, P_{21}, P_4, P_{12}>$ for some user U states that the user U has visited the pages 10, 21, 4, and finally page 12 in a sequence.

B.6 Association Rule Mining

Association rules is a data mining technique that has been applied successfully to discover related transactions. Association rules technique finds the relationships among item sets based on their co-occurrence in the transactions. Specifically, ARM discovers the frequent patterns (regularities) among those items sets. For example, what are the items purchased together in a super store. In the following, we briefly introduce ARM. For more details, see [AGRA 1993][AGRA 1994].

Assume we have *m* items in our database; define $I = \{i_1, i_2, \ldots, i_m\}$ as the set of all items. A transaction T is a set of items such that $T \subseteq I$. Let D be the set of all transactions in the database. A transaction T contains X if $X \subseteq T$ and $X \subseteq I$. An association rule is an implication of the form $X \rightarrow Y$, where, $X \subset I$, $Y \subset I$, and $X \cap Y = \phi$. There are two parameters to consider a rule: Confidence and support. A rule $R = X \rightarrow Y$ holds with confidence *c* if *c*% of the transactions of D that contain X also contain Y (i.e., $c = pr(Y|X)$). The rule R holds with support *s* if *s*% of the transactions in D contain X and Y (i.e., $s = pr(X,Y)$). The problem of mining association rules is defined as: Given a set of transactions D, we would like to generate all rules that satisfy a confidence and a support greater than a minimum confidence (σ), *minconf*, and minimum support (ϑ), *minsup*. There are several efficient algorithms to find association rules such as AIS algorithm [AGRA93][AGRA94], SETM algorithm [HOUT95], and AprioriTid [AGRA94].

In the case of Web transactions, we use association rules to discover navigational patterns among users. This would help to cache a page in advance and reduce the loading time of a page. Also, discovering a pattern of navigation helps in personalization. Transactions are captured from the clickstream data captured in Web server logs.

In many applications, there is one main problem in using ARM. First, a problem with using global minimum support (*minsup*), because rare hits, that is, web pages that are rarely visited, will not be included in the frequent sets because it will not achieve enough support. One solution is to have a very small support threshold; however, we will end up with a very large frequent itemsets, which is computationally hard to handle. Liu et al. [LIU99] discuss a mining technique that uses different support thresholds for different items. Specifying multiple thresholds allow rare transactions, which might be very important, to be included in the frequent itemsets. Other issues might raise depending on the application itself. For example, in case of WWW prediction, a session is recorded for each user. The session might have tens of clickstreams (and sometimes hundreds depending on the duration of the session). Using each session as a transaction will not work because it is rare to find two sessions that are frequently repeated (i.e., identical); hence it will not achieve even a very high support threshold, *minsup*}. There is a need to break each session into many subsequences. One common method is to use a sliding window of size w. For example, suppose we use a sliding window $w = 3$ to break the session $S = <A, B, C, D, E, E, F>$, then we will end up with the subsequences $S' = \{<A,B,C>, <B,C,D>, <C,D,E>, <D,E,F>\}$. The total number of subsequences of a session S using window w is *length(S)-w*. To predict the next page in an active user session, we use a sliding window of the active session and ignore the previous pages. For example, if the current session is $<A,B,C>$, and the user references page D, then the new active session becomes $<B,C,D>$, using a sliding window 3. Notice that page A is dropped, and $<B,C,D>$ will be used for prediction. The rationale behind this is because most users go back and forth while surfing the Web trying to find the desired information, and it may be most appropriate to use the recent portions of the user history to generate recommendations/predictions [MOBA01].

Mobasher et al. [MOBA01] discuss a recommendation engine that matches an active user session with the frequent itemsets in the database, and predicts the next page the user most probably visits. The engine works as follows. Given an active session of size w, the engine finds all the frequent itemsets of length $w + 1$ satisfying some minimum support *minsup* and containing the current active session. Prediction for the active session A is based on the confidence (ψ) of the corresponding association rule. The confidence (ψ) of an association rule $X \rightarrow z$ is defined as $\psi(X \rightarrow z) = \sigma(X \cup z)/\sigma(X)$, where the length of z is 1. Page p is recommended/predicted for an active session A, iff

$\forall V, R$ in the frequent itemsets,
$length(R) = length(V) = length(A) + 1 \wedge$
$R = A \cup \{p\} \wedge$
$V = A \cup \{q\} \wedge$
$\psi(A \rightarrow p) > \psi(A \rightarrow q)$

The engine uses a cyclic graph called Frequent Itemset Graph. The graph is an extension of the lexicographic tree used in the tree projection algorithm of [AGRA01]. The graph is organized in levels. The nodes in level l has itemsets of size of l. For example, the sizes of the nodes (i.e., the size of the itemsets corresponding to these nodes) in levels 1 and 2 are 1 and 2, respectively. The root of the graph, level 0, is an empty node corresponding to an empty itemset. A node X in level l is linked to a node Y in level $l + 1$ if $X \subset Y$. To further explain the process, suppose we have the following sample Web transactions involving pages 1, 2, 3, 4, and 5 as in Table B.2. The a priori algorithm produces the itemsets as in Table B.3 using a *minsup* = 0.49. The frequent itemset graph is shown in Figure B.11.

Suppose we are using a sliding window of size 2, and the current active session $A = <2, 3>$. To predict/recommend the next page, we first start at level 2 in the Frequent Itemset Graph, and extract all the itemsets in level 3 linked to A. From Figure B.11, the node {2, 3} is linked to {1, 2, 3} and {2, 3, 5} nodes with confidence:

$$\psi(\{2,3\} \rightarrow 1) = \sigma(\{1,2,3\}/\sigma(\{2,3\}) = 5/5 = 1.0$$
$$\psi(\{2,3\} \rightarrow 5) = \sigma(\{2,3,5\}/\sigma(\{2,3\}) = 4/5 = 0.8$$

Table B.2   Sample Web Transaction

Transaction Id	Items
T1	1, 2, 4, 5
T2	1, 2, 5, 3, 4
T3	1, 2, 5, 3
T4	2, 5, 2, 1, 3
T5	4, 1, 2, 5, 3
T6	1, 2, 3, 4
T7	4, 5
T8	4, 5, 3, 1

Table B.3 Frequent Itemsets Generated by the A Priori Algorithm

Size 1	Size 2	Size 3	Size 4
{2}(6)	{2, 3}(5)	{2, 3, 1}(5)	{2, 3, 1, 5}(4)
{3}(6)	{2, 4}(4)	{2, 3, 5}(4)	
{4}(6)	{2, 1}(6)	{2, 4, 1}(4)	
{1}(7)	{2, 5}(5)	{2, 1, 5}(5)	
{5}(7)	{3, 4}(4)	{3, 4, 1}(4)	
	{3, 1}(6)	{3, 1, 5}(5)	
	{3, 5}(5)	{4, 1, 5}(4)	
	{4, 1}(5)		
	{4, 5}(5)		
	{1, 5}(6)		

and the recommended page is 1 because its confidence is larger. Notice that, in Recommendation Engines, the order of the clickstream is not considered, that is, there is no distinction between a session <1, 2, 4> and <1, 4, 2>. This is a disadvantage of such systems because the order of pages visited might bear important information about the navigation patterns of users.

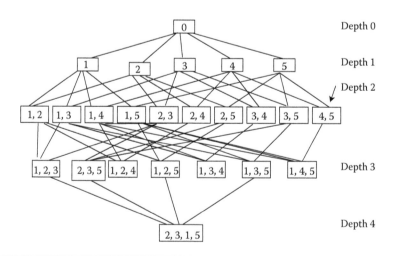

Figure B.11 Frequent itemsets graph.

B.7 Multi-Class Problem

Most classification techniques solve the binary classification problem. Binary classifiers are accumulated to generalize for the multi-class problem. There are two basic schemes for this generalization, namely, one-vs-one, and one-vs-all. To avoid redundancy, we will present this generalization only for SVM.

B.7.1 One-vs-One

The one-vs-one approach creates a classifier for each pair of classes. The training set for each pair of classifier (i, j) includes only those instances that belong to either class i or j. A new instance x belongs to the class upon which most pair classifiers agree. The prediction decision is quoted from the majority vote technique. There are $n(n - 1)/2$ classifiers to be computed, where n is the number of classes in the data set. It is evident that the disadvantage of this scheme is that we need to generate a large number of classifiers, especially if there are a large number of classes in the training set. For example, if we have a training set of 1000 classes, we need 499,500 classifiers. On the other hand, the size of training set for each classifier is small because we exclude all instances that do not belong to that pair of classes.

B.7.2 One-vs-All

One-vs-all creates a classifier for each class in the data set. The training set is preprocessed such that for a classifier j instances that belong to class j are marked as class (+1) and instances that do not belong to class j are marked as class (–1). In the one-vs-all scheme, we compute n classifiers, where n is the number of pages that users have visited (at the end of each session). A new instance x is predicted by assigning it to the class that its classifier outputs the largest positive value (i.e., maximal marginal) as in Equation B.15. We can compute the margin of point x as in Equation B.14. Notice that the recommended/predicted page is the sign of the margin value of that page (see Equation B.10).

$$f(x) = wx - b = \sum_{i}^{N} \alpha_i y_i (x \cdot x_i - b) \tag{B.14}$$

$$\text{prediction}(x) = \arg\max_{1 \le c \le M} f_c(x) \tag{B.15}$$

In Equation B.15, M is the number of classes, $x = \langle x_1, x_2, \ldots, x_n \rangle$ is the user session, and f_i is the classifier that separates class i from the rest of the classes. The prediction decision in Equation B.15 resolves to the classifier f_c that is the most distant from the testing example x. This might be explained as f_c has the most separating power, among all other classifiers, of separating x from the rest of the classes.

The advantage of this scheme (one-vs-all), compared to the one-vs-one scheme, is that it has fewer classifiers. On the other hand, the size of the training set is larger for one-vs-all than for a one-vs-one scheme because we use the whole original training set to compute each classifier.

B.8 Image Mining

Along with the development of digital images and computer storage technologies, huge amounts of digital images are generated and saved everyday. Applications of digital image have rapidly penetrated many domains and markets, including commercial and news media photo libraries, scientific and nonphotographic image databases, and medical image databases. As a consequence, we face a daunting problem of organizing and accessing these huge amounts of available images. An efficient image retrieval system is highly desired to find images of specific entities from a database. The system expected can manage a huge collection of images efficiently, respond to users' queries with high speed and deliver a minimum of irrelevant information (high precision), as well as ensuring that relevant information is not overlooked (high recall).

To generate such kind of systems, people have tried many different approaches. In the early 1990s, because of the emergence of large image collections, Content-Based Image Retrieval (CBIR) was discussed. CBIR computes relevance based on the similarity of visual content/low-level image features such as color histograms, textures, shapes, and spatial layout. However, the problem is that visual similarity is not semantic similarity. There is a gap between low-level visual features and semantic meanings. The so-called semantic gap is the major problem that needs to be solved for most CBIR approaches. For example, a CBIR system may answer a query request for a "red ball" with an image of a "red rose." If we undertake the annotation of images with keywords, a typical way to publish an image data repository is to create a keyword-based query interface addressed to an image database. If all images came with a detailed and accurate description, image retrieval would be convenient based on current powerful pure text search techniques. These search techniques would retrieve the images if their descriptions/annotations contained some combination of the keywords specified by the user. However, the major problem is that most of images are not annotated. It is a laborious, error-prone, and subjective process to manually annotate a large collection of images. Many images contain the desired semantic information, even though they do not contain the user specified keywords. Furthermore, keyword-based search is useful especially to a user who knows what keywords are used to index the images and who can therefore easily formulate queries. This approach is problematic, however, when the user does not have a clear goal in mind, does not know what is in the database, and does not know what kind of semantic concepts are involved in the domain.

Image mining is a more challenging research problem than retrieving relevant images in CBIR systems. The goal of image mining is to find an image pattern which is significant for a given set of images and helpful to understand the relationships between high-level semantic concepts/descriptions and low-level visual features. Our focus is on aspects such as feature selection and image classification.

B.8.1 Feature Selection

Usually, data saved in databases is with well-defined semantics such as numbers or structured data entries. In comparison, data with ill-defined semantics is unstructured data. For example, images, audio, and video are data with ill-defined semantics. In the domain of image processing, images are represented by derived data or features such as color, texture, and shape. Many of these features have multi values (e.g., color histogram, moment description.) When people generate these derived data or features, they generally generate as many features as possible, since they are not aware which feature is more relevant. Therefore, the dimensionality of derived image data is usually very high. Actually, some of the selected features might be duplicated or may not even be relevant to the problem. Including irrelevant or duplicated information is referred to as noise. Such problems are referred to as the "curse of dimensionality." Feature selection is the research topic for finding an optimal subset of features. In this dissertation, we will discuss this curse and feature selection in detail.

We developed a wrapper-based simultaneous feature weighing and clustering algorithm. Clustering algorithm will bundle similar image segments together and generate a finite set of visual symbols (i.e., blob-token). On the basis of histogram analysis and chi-square value, we assign features of image segments of different weights instead of removing some of them. Feature weight evaluation is wrapped in a clustering algorithm. In each iteration of the algorithm, feature weights of image segments are re-evaluated based on the clustering result. The re-evaluated feature weights will affect the clustering results in the next iteration.

B.8.2 Automatics Image Annotation

Automatic image annotation is research concerned with object recognition, where the effort is concerned with trying to recognize objects in an image and generate descriptions for the image according to semantics of the objects. If it is possible to produce accurate and complete semantic descriptions for an image, we can store descriptions in an image database. On the basis of a textual description, more functionality (e.g., browse, search, and query) of an Image DBMS could be implemented easily and efficiently by applying many existing text-based search techniques. Unfortunately, the automatic image annotation problem has not been solved in general and perhaps this problem is impossible to solve.

However, in certain sub-domains, it is still possible to obtain some interesting results. Many statistical models have been published for image annotation. Some of these models took feature dimensionality into account and applied singular-value decomposition (SVD) or principle component analysis (PCA) to reduce dimension. But none of them considered feature selection or feature weight. We developed a new framework for image annotation based on a translation model (TM). In our approach, we applied our weighted feature selection algorithm and embedded it in image annotation framework. Our weighted feature selection algorithm improves the quality of visual tokens and generates better image annotations.

B.8.3 Image Classification

Image classification is an important area, especially in the medical domain because it helps managing large medical image databases and has great potential on diagnostic aid in a real-world clinical setting. We describe our experiments for the image CLEF medical image retrieval task. Sizes of classes of CLEF medical image dataset are not balanced which is a really serious problem for all classification algorithms. To solve this problem, we resample data by generating sub windows. K Nearest Neighbor (KNN) algorithm, distance weighted KNN, fuzzy KNN, nearest prototype classifier, and evidence theory-based KNN are implemented and studied. The results show that evidence-based KNN has the best performance based on classification accuracy.

B.9 Summary and Directions

In this chapter, we first provided an overview of the various data mining tasks and techniques and then discussed some of the techniques that we will utilize in this book. These include neural networks, SVMs and ARM.

Numerous data mining techniques have been designed and developed and many of them are being utilized in commercial tools. Several of these techniques are variations of some of the basic classification, clustering, and ARM techniques. One of the major challenges today is to determine the appropriate techniques for various applications. We still need more benchmarks and performance studies. In addition, the techniques should result in fewer false positives and negatives. While there is still much to be done, the progress over the last decade is extremely promising.

References

[AGRA93] Agrawal, R., T. Imielinski, and A. Swami, Mining association rules between sets of items in large database. In *Proceedings of the ACM SIGMOD Conference on Management of Data*, Washington, DC, May 1993, pp. 207–216.

[AGRA94] Agrawal, R. and R. Srikant, Fast algorithms for mining association rules in large database. In *Proceedings of the 20th International Conference on Very Large Data Bases*, San Francisco, CA, 1994, pp. 487–499.

[AGRA01] Agrawal, R., C. Aggarawal, and V. Prasad, A tree projection algorithm for generation of frequent item sets. *Journal of Parallel and Distributed Computing Archive*, 61(3): 350–371, 2001, Orlando, FL.

[BART99] Bartlett, P. and J. Shawe-Taylor, Generalization performance of support vector machines and other pattern classifiers. In: (B. Schölkopf, C. Burges, A. Smola, Eds.) *Advances in Kernel Methods – Support Vector Learning*, MIT Press, Cambridge, UK, 1999, pp. 43–54.

[CRIS00] Cristianini, N. and J. Shawe-Taylor, *Introduction to Support Vector Machines*, 1st ed., Cambridge University Press, 2000, pp. 93–122, Cambridge, UK.

[HOUT95] Houtsma, M. and A. Swanu, Set-oriented mining of association rules in relational databases. In *Proceedings of the Eleventh International Conference on Data Engineering*, Washington, DC, 1995, pp. 25–33.

[LIU99] Liu, B., W. Hsu, and Y. Ma, Association rules with multiple minimum supports. in *Proceedings of the Fifth ACM SIGKDD International Conference on Knowledge discovery and Data Mining*, San Diego, CA, 1999, pp. 337–341.

[MITC97] Mitchell, T.M, *Machine Learning*, McGraw-Hill, 1997, chap. 4.

[MOBA01] Mobasher, B., H. Dai, T. Luo, and M. Nakagawa, Effective personalization based on association rule discovery from web usage data. In *Proceedings of the ACM Workshop on Web Information and Data Management (WIDM01)*, Atlanda, GA, 2001, pp. 9–15.

[PIRO96] Pirolli, P., J. Pitkow, and R. Rao, Silk from a sow's ear: Extracting usable structures from the web. In *Proceedings of 1996 Conference on Human Factors in Computing Systems (CHI-96)*, Vancouver, British Columbia, Canada, 1996, pp. 118–125.

[VAPN95] Vapnik, V.N., *The Nature of Statistical Learning Theory*, Springer, New York, NY, 1995.

[VAPN98] Vapnik, V.N., *Statistical Learning Theory*, Wiley, New York, 1998.

[VAPN99] Vapnik, V.N., *The Nature of Statistical Learning Theory*, Springer-Verlag, New York, NY, 1999.

[YANG01] Yang, Q., H. Zhang, and T. Li, Mining web logs for prediction models in WWW caching and prefetching. In *The 7th ACM SIGKDD International Conference on Knowledge Discovery and Data Mining KDD*, San Francisco, CA, August 26–29, 2001, pp. 473–478.

Appendix C: Access Control in Database Systems

C.1 Overview

Since much of the discussion in this book is on cloud data management and secure cloud data management, we will provide a fairly comprehensive overview on access control for data management systems. In particular, we will discuss security policies as well as enforcing the policies in database systems. Our focus will be on discretionary security policies. More details on secure data management can be found in [FERR00] and [THUR05].

The most popular discretionary security policy is the access control policy. Access control policies were studied for operating systems back in the 1960s and then for database systems in the 1970s. The two prominent database systems System R and INGRES were one of the first to investigate access control for database systems (see [GRIF76] and [STON74]). Since then several variations of access control policies have been reported. Other discretionary policies include administration policies. We also discuss identification and authentication under discretionary policies. Note that much of the discussion in this appendix will focus on discretionary security in relational database systems. Many of the principles are applicable to other systems such as object database systems, distributed database systems and cloud data management systems.

Before one designs a secure system, the first question that must be answered is what is the security policy to be enforced by the system? Security policy is essentially a set of rules that enforce security. Security policies include mandatory security policies and discretionary security policies. Mandatory security policies are the policies that are "mandatory" in nature and should not be bypassed. Discretionary security policies are policies that are specified by the administrator or anyone who is responsible for the environment in which the system will operate.

By policy enforcement, we mean the mechanisms to enforce the policies. For example, back in the 1970s, the relational database system products such as System R and INGRES developed techniques such as the query modification mechanisms for policy enforcement (see, e.g., [GRIF76] and [STON74]). The query language SQL has been extended to specify security policies and access control rules. More recently, languages such as XML and RDF have been extended to specify security policies (see, e.g., [BERT02] and [CARM04]).

In Section C.2, we introduce discretionary security including access control and authorization models for database systems. We also discuss role-based access control systems. In Section C.3, we discuss ways of enforcing discretionary security including a discussion on query modification. We also provide an overview of the various commercial products. The appendix is summarized in Section C.4. The discussion in this appendix will provide an overview of essentially the basics of discretionary security focusing primarily on relational database systems.

C.2 Security Policies

The organization of this section is as follows. In Section C.2.1, we will provide an overview of access control policies. Administration policies will be discussed in Section C.2.2. Issues on identification and authentication will be discussed in action C.2.3. Auditing a database management system will be discussed in Section C.2.4. Views as security objects will be discussed in Section C.2.5. Figure C.1 illustrates various components of discretionary security policies.

C.2.1 Access Control Policies

Access control policies were first examined for operating systems. The essential point here is that can a process be granted access to a file? Access could be read access or write access. Write access could include access to modify, append, or delete. These principles were transferred to database systems such as Ingres and System R. Since

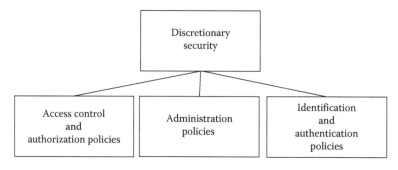

Figure C.1   Discretionary security policies.

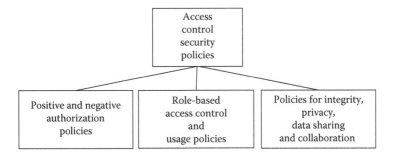

Figure C.2   Access control security policies.

then various forms of access control policies have been studied. Notable among those are the role-based access control policies which are now implemented in several commercial systems. Note that access control policies also include mandatory policies. Figure C.2 illustrates the various access control policies.

C.2.1.1 Authorization-Based Access Control Policies

Many of the access control policies are based on authorization policies. Essentially what this means is that users are granted access to data based on authorization rules. In this section, we will discuss various types of authorization rules. Note that authorization policies are discussed in detail in the book chapter by Ferrari and Thuraisingham [FERR00].

Positive authorizations: Early systems focused on what is now called positive authorization rules. Here, user John is granted access to relation EMP or user Jane is granted access to relation DEPT. These are access control rules on relations. One can also grant access to other entities such as attributes and tuples. For example, John has read access to attribute Salary and Write access to attribute Name in relation EMP. Write access could include append, modify, or delete access.

Negative authorization: The question is if John's access to an object is not specified, does this mean John does not have access to that object? In some systems any authorization rule that is not specified is implicitly taken to be a negative authorization while in other systems negative authorizations are explicitly specified. For example, we could enforce rules such as John does not have access to relation EMP or Jane does not have access to relation DEPT.

Conflict resolutions: When we have rules that are conflicting then how do we resolve the conflicts? For example, we could have a rule that grants John read access to relation EMP. However we can also have a rule that does not grant John read access to the salary attribute in EMP. This is a conflict. Usually a system enforces the least privilege rule in which case John has access to EMP except for the salary values.

Strong and weak authorization: Systems also enforce strong and weak authorizations. In the case of strong authorization the rule holds regardless of conflicts.

In the case of weak authorizations, the rule does not hold in case of conflict. For example, if John is granted access to EMP and it is a strong authorization rule and the rule where John is not granted access to salary attribute is a weak authorization, there is a conflict. This means the strong authorization will hold.

Propagation of authorization rules: The question here is how do the rules get propagated? For example, if John has read access to relation EMP then does it automatically mean that John has read access to every element in EMP? Usually this is the case unless we have a rule that prohibits automatic propagation of an authorization rule. If we have a rule prohibiting the automatic propagation of a rule then we must explicitly enforce authorization rules that specify the objects that John has access to.

Special rules: In our work on mandatory policies, we have explored extensively the enforcement of content and context-based constraints. Note that security constraints are essentially the security rules. Content and context-based rule are rules where access is granted depending on the content of the data or the context in which the data are displayed. Such rules can be enforced for discretionary security also. For example, in the case of content-based constraints, John has read access to tuples only in DEPT D100. In the case of context or association-based constraints, John does not have read access to names and salaries taken together, however, he can have access to individual names and salaries. In the case of event-based constraints, after the election, John has access to all elements in relation EMP.

Consistency and completeness of rules: One of the challenges here is ensuring the consistency and completeness of constraints. That is, if the constraints or rules are inconsistent then do we have conflict resolution rules that will resolve the conflicts? How can we ensure that all of the entities (such as attributes, relations, elements, etc.) are specified in access control rules for a user? Essentially what this means is, are the rules complete? If not what assumptions do we make about entities that do not have either positive or negative authorizations specified on them for a particular user or a class of users?

We have discussed some essential points with respect to authorization rules. Some examples are given in Figure C.3. In the next section, we will discuss a very

---

Authorization rules

- John has read access to employee relation
- John does not have write access to department relation
- Jane has read access to name values in employee relation
- Jane does not have read access to department relation

Figure C.3   Authorization rules.

popular access control policy and that is role-based access control, which is now implemented in commercial systems.

C.2.1.2 Role-Based Access Control

Role-based access control has become one of the most popular access control methods (see [SAND96]). This method has been implemented in commercial systems including Trusted Oracle. The idea here is to grant access to users depending on their roles and functions.

The essential idea behind role-based access control also known as RBAC is as follows. The users need access to data depending on their roles. For example, a president may have access to information about his/her vice presidents and the members of the board while the chief financial officer may have access to the financial information and information on those who report to him. A director may have access to information about those working in his division while the human resources director will have information on personal data about the employees of the corporation. Essentially role-based access control is a type of authorization policy, which depends on the user role and the activities that go with the role.

Various research efforts on role hierarchies have been discussed in the literature. There is also a conference series called SACMAT (*Symposium on Access Control Models and Technologies*) that evolved from role-based access control research efforts. For example, how does access get propagated? Can one role subsume another? Consider the role hierarchy illustrated in Figure C.4. This means if we grant access to a node in the hierarchy does the access propagate upwards? That is, if a department manager has access to certain project information does that access get propagated to the parent node, which is a director node? If a section leader has access to employee information in his/her section does the access propagate to the department manager who is the parent in the role hierarchy? What happens to the child nodes? That is, does access propagate downwards? For example, if a department manager has access to certain information, then do his subordinates have access to that information? Are there cases where the subordinates have access to data that the department manager does not have? What happens if an employee has to report to two supervisors, one his department manager and the other his project manager? What happens when the department manager is working on a project and has to report to his project leader who also works for him?

Role-based access control has been examined for relational systems, object systems, distributed systems, and now some of the emerging technologies such as data warehouses, knowledge management systems, semantic web, e-commerce systems, and digital libraries. Furthermore, object models have been used to represent roles and activities (see, e.g., *Proceedings of the IFIP Database Security Conference Series*). This is an area that will continue to be discussed and the ACM SACMAT (*Symposium on Access Control Models and Technologies*) is a venue for publishing high-quality papers on this topic.

Figure C.4   Role hierarchy.

More recently, Sandhu et al. have developed yet another access control-like model and that is the usage control model, which he refers to as UCON (see, e.g., the work reported in [PARK04]). UCON model attempts to integrate three policies and they are trust management, access control, and rights management. The idea is to provide control on the usage of objects. While the ideas are somewhat preliminary, this model shows a lot of promise.

C.2.2 Administration Policies

While access control policies specify access that specific users have to the data, administration policies specify who is to administer the data. Administration duties would include keeping the data current; making sure the metadata is updated whenever the data is updated, and ensuring recovery from failures and related activities.

Typically, the database administer (DBA) is responsible for updating say the metadata, the index, and access methods and also ensuring that the access control rules are properly enforced. The system security officer (SSO) may also have a role. That is, the DBA and SSO may share the duties between them. The security-related issues might be the responsibility of the SSO while the data-related issues might be the responsibility of the DBA. Some other administration policies being considered include assigning caretakers. Usually owners have control of the data that they

Figure C.5   Administration policies.

create and may manage the data for its duration. In some cases owners may not be available to manage the data in which case they may assign caretakers.

Administration policies get more complicated in distributed environments especially in a web environment. For example, in web environments, there may be multiple parties involved in distributing documents including the owner, the publisher, and the users requesting the data. Who owns the data? Is it the owner or the publisher? Once the data has left the owner and arrived at the publisher, does the publisher take control of the data?

There are many interesting questions that need to be answered as we migrate from a relational database environment to a distributed and perhaps a web environment. These also include managing copyright issues, data quality, data provenance, and governance. Many interesting papers have appeared in recent conferences on administration policies. Figure C.5 illustrates various administration policies.

C.2.3 Identification and Authentication

For the sake of completion, we discuss identification and authentication as part of our discussion on discretionary security. By identification we mean users must identify themselves with their user ID and password. Authentication means the system must then match the user ID with the password to ensure that this is indeed the person he is purporting to be. A user may also have multiple identities depending on his roles. Identity management is receiving a lot of attention lately (see [BERT02]).

Numerous problems have been reported with the password-based scheme. One is that hackers can break into the system and get the passwords of users and then masquerade as the user. In a centralized system, the problems are not as complicated as in a distributed environment. Now, with the WWW and e-commerce applications, financial organizations are losing billions of dollars when hackers masquerade as legitimate users.

More recently, biometrics techniques are being applied. These include face recognition and voice recognition techniques to authenticate the user. These techniques are showing a lot of promise and are already being used. We can expect widespread use of biometric techniques as face recognition technologies advance.

C.2.4 Auditing a Database System

Databases are audited for multiple purposes. For example, they may be audited to keep track of the number of queries posed, the number of updates made, the number of transactions executed and the number of times the secondary storage is accessed so that the system can be designed more efficiently. Databases can also be audited for security purposes. For example, have any of the access control rules been bypassed by releasing information to the users? Has the inference problem occurred? Has privacy been violated? Have there been unauthorized intrusions?

Audits create a trail and the audit data may be stored in a database. This database may be mined to detect any abnormal patterns or behaviors. There has been a lot of work in using data mining for auditing and intrusion detection. Audit trail analysis is especially important these days with e-commerce transactions on the web. An organization should have the capability to conduct an analysis and determine problems like credit card fraud and identity theft.

C.2.5 Views for Security

Views as a mechanism for security has been studied a great deal both for discretionary security and mandatory security. For example, one may not want to grant access

EMP

SS#	Ename	Salary	D#
1	John	20 K	10
2	Paul	30 K	20
3	Mary	40 K	20
4	Jane	20 K	20
5	Bill	20 K	10
6	Larry	20 K	10
1	Michelle	30 K	20

Rules:
John has Read access to V1
John has Write access to V2

V1. VIEW EMP (D# = 20)

SS#	Ename	Salary
2	Paul	30 K
3	Mary	40 K
4	Jane	20 K
1	Michelle	30 K

V2. VIEW EMP (D# = 10)

SS#	Ename	Salary
1	John	20 K
5	Bill	20 K
6	Larry	20 K

Figure C.6   Views for security.

to an entire relation especially if it has say 25 attributes such as healthcare records, salary, travel information, personal data, and so on. Therefore, the DBA could form views and grant access to the views. Similarly in the case of mandatory security, views could be assigned security levels and we will discuss this in Part IV.

Views have problems associated with them including the view update problem (see [DATE90]). That is, if the view is updated then we need to ensure that the base relations are updated. Therefore, if a view is updated by John and John does not have access to the base relation, then can the base relation still be updated? That is, do we create different views for different users and then does the DBA merge the updates on views as updates on base relations? Figure C.6 illustrates views for security.

C.3 Policy Enforcement and Related Issues

The organization of this section is as follows. SQL extensions for security are discussed in Section C.3.1. In Section C.3.2, we discuss query modification. Impact of discretionary security on other database functions will be discussed in Section C.3.3. Visualization of security policies is discussed in Section C.3.4. Discussion of prototypes and products that implement discretionary security policies will be given in Section C.3.5. Note that we will focus on relational database systems. Figure C.7 illustrates the various aspects involved on enforcing security policies. These include specification, implementation, and visualization.

C.3.1 SQL Extensions for Security

This section discusses policy specification. While much of the focus will be on SQL extensions for security policy specification we will also briefly discuss some of the

```
Policy enforcement

Query modification algorithm

Rule processing to enforce the access control
rules

Theorem proving techniques to determine if
policies are violated

Consistency and completeness checking of
policies
```

Figure C.7   Policy enforcement.

emerging languages. Note that SQL was developed for data definition and data manipulation for relational systems. Various versions of SQL have been developed including SQL for objects, SQL for multimedia, and SQL for the web. That is, SQL has influenced data manipulation and data definition a great deal over the past 20 years (see [SQL3]).

As we have stated, SQL is a data definition and data manipulation language. Security policies could be specified during data definition. SQL has GRANT and REVOKE constructs for specifying grant and revoke access to users. That is, if a user John has read access to relation EMP, then one could use SQL and specify something like "GRANT JOHN EMP READ" and if the access is to be revoked, and then we need something like "REVOKE JOHN EMP READ." SQL has also been extended with more complex constraints such as granting John read access to a tuple in a relation and granting Jane write access to an element in a relation.

In [THUR89], we specified SQL extensions for security assertions. These assertions were for multilevel security. We could use similar reasoning for specifying discretionary security policies. For example, consider the situation where John does not have read access to names and salaries in EMP taken together, but he can read names and salaries separately. One could specify this in SQL-like language as follows.

> *GRANT JOHN READ*
> *EMP.SALARY*
> *GRANT JOHN READ*
> *EMP.NAME*
> *NOT GRANT JOHN READ*
> *Together (EMP.NAME, EMP.SALARY).*

If we are to grant John read access to the employees who earn less than 30 K, then this assertion is specified as follows.

> *GRANT JOHN READ*
> *EMP*
> *Where EMP.SALARY < 30 K*

Note that the assertions we have specified are not standard assertions. These are some of our ideas. We need to explore ways of incorporating these assertions into the standards. SQL extensions have also been proposed for role-based access control. In fact, products such as Oracle's Trusted database product enforce role-based access control. The access control rules are specified in an SQL-like language. Note that there are many other specification languages that have been developed. These include XML, RDF, and related languages for the web and the semantic web. Figure C.8 illustrates specification aspects for security policies.

Policy specification

SQL extensions to specify security policies

Rule-based languages to specify policies

Logic programming languages such as prolog to specify policies

Figure C.8   Policy specification.

C.3.2 Query Modification

Query modification was first proposed in the INGRES project at the University of California at Berkeley (see [STON74]). The idea is to modify the query based on the constraints. We have successfully designed and implemented query modification for mandatory security (see [DWYE87], [THUR87], [THUR93]). However, much of the discussion in this section will be on query modification based on discretionary security constraints. We illustrate the essential points with some examples.

Consider a query by John to retrieve all tuples from EMP. Suppose that John only has read access to all the tuples where the salary is less than 30 K and the employee is not in the Security department. Then the query

*Select * from EMP*
Will be modified to
*Select * from EMP*
Where salary < 30 K
And Dept is not Security

Where we assume that the attributes of EMP are say Name, Salary, Age, and Department.

Essentially what happens is that the "where" clause of the query has all the constraints associated with the relation. We can also have constraints that span across multiple relations. For example, we could have two relations EMP and DEPT joined by Dept #. Then the query is modified as follows:

*Select * from EMP*
Where EMP.Salary < 30 K
And EMP.D# = DEPT.D#
And DEPT.Name is not Security

We have used some simple examples for query modification. The detailed algorithms can be found in [DWYE87] and [STON74]. The high-level algorithm is illustrated in Figure C.9.

Query modification algorithm

Input: Query, security constraints
Output: Modified query

For constraints that are relevant to the query, modify the where clause of the query via a negation

For example: If salary should not be released to Jane and if Jane requests information from employee, then modify the query to retrieve information from employee where attribute is not salary

Repeat the process until all relevant constraints are processed

The end result is the modified query

Figure C.9   Query modification algorithm.

C.3.3 Discretionary Security and Database Functions

In Section C.3.2, we discussed query modification which is essentially processing security constraints during the query operation. Query optimization will also be impacted by security constraints. That is, once the query is modified, then the query tree has to be built. The idea is to push selections and projection down in the query tree and carry out the join operation later.

Other functions are also impacted by security constraints. Let us consider transaction management. Bertino et al. have developed algorithms for integrity constraint processing for transactions management (see [BERT89]). We have examined their techniques for mandatory security constraint processing during transaction management. The techniques may be adapted for discretionary security constraints. The idea is to ensure that the constraints are not violated during transaction execution.

Constraints may be enforced on the metadata. For example, one could grant and revoke access to users to the metadata relations. Discretionary security constraints for metadata could be handled in the same way as they are handled for data.

Other database functions include storage management. The issues in storage management include developing appropriate access methods and index strategies. One needs to examine the impact of the security constraints on the storage management functions. That is, can one partition the relations based on the constraints and store them in such a way so that the relations can be accessed efficiently? We need to develop secure indexing technologies for database systems.

> **Secure database functions**
>
> Query processing: Enforce access control rules during query processing; inference control; consider security constraints for query optimization
>
> Transaction management: Check whether security constraints are satisfied during transaction execution
>
> Storage management: Develop special access methods and index strategies that take into consideration the security constraints
>
> Metadata management: Enforce access control on metadata; Ensure that data is not released to unauthorized individuals by releasing the metadata
>
> Integrity management: Ensure that integrity of the data is maintained while enforcing security

Figure C.10   Security impact on database functions.

Databases are audited to determine whether any security violation has occurred. Furthermore, views have been used to grant access to individuals for security purposes. We need efficient techniques for auditing as well as for view management.

In this section, we have examined the impact of security on some of the major database functions including query management, transaction processing, metadata management, and storage management. We also need to investigate the impact of security on other functions such as integrity constraint processing and fault-tolerance computing. Figure C.10 illustrates the impact of security on the database functions.

C.3.4 Visualization of Policies

There are three aspects to policy enforcement. One is policy specification, the other is policy implementation, and the third is policy visualization. Policy visualization is especially useful for complex security policies.

Visualization tools are needed for many applications including geospatial applications as well as web-based applications so that the users can better understand the data in the databases. Visualization is also useful for integrating security policies. For example, if multiple systems from multiple organizations are to be merged then their policies have to be visualized and merged so that the

---

Visualization for policy integration

Semantic data models to represent the application, security constraints and detect security violations via inference

Apply visualization tools to check for the consistency of policies

Example: Jane has access to salary values in relation EMP and at the same time Jane does not have read access to EMP. Use colors to represent data that Jane does and does not have access to. If a data element has two colors associated with it, then there is a conflict

Use hyper media systems to browse security policies

Figure C.11   Visualization for policy integration.

administrator can have some idea of the integrated policy. Figure C.11 illustrates visualization for policy integration.

Policy visualization is also helpful for dynamic policies. That is, when policies change often, visualizing the effects would be quite useful in designing secure systems. In some of our work, we have used graph structures to specify constraints instead of simple rules. This is because graphs enable us to visualize what the rules look like. Furthermore, policies may be linked to one another and with graph structures one can analyze the various links to obtain the relationships between the policies.

The area of policy visualization is a relatively new research area. There are some research programs at DARPA on policy visualization. This is an area that needs work especially in a web environment where organizations collaborate with each other and carry out e-business. Policy visualization is also important for homeland security applications where various agencies have to work together and share information and yet maintain their autonomy.

C.3.5 Prototypes and Products

We now discuss discretionary security as implemented in System R and Oracle. Note that System R is a prototype and Oracle is a product. Both are based on the relational model. Several prototypes and products have implemented discretionary access control and some of them are listed in Figure C.12.

Note that information on prototypes and products will be changing continually as technology progresses. Therefore, in many cases information about the prototypes and products may be soon outdated. Our purpose in discussing prototypes

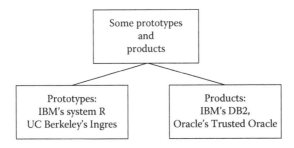

Figure C.12   Prototypes and products.

and products is to explain the concepts. Up-to-date information on prototypes and products can be obtained from the vendor and possibly from the web.

System R was one of the first systems to introduce various discretionary security concepts (see [GRIFF76]). In this system objects to be protected are represented by tables and views. Subjects can enforce several privileges on the security objects. Privileges supported by the model include select (select tuples), update (modify tuples), insert (add tuples), delete (delete tuples), and drop (delete table). The model also supports decentralized administration facilities. A subject can grant privileges it has to other subjects. The model also enforces recursive revocation. That is, when a subject A revokes an authorization on a table to subject B, then B in turn revokes authorization of the table to C that it had previously granted access to.

System R model has been extended in many directions. These include group management where access is granted and revoked to groups of users, distributed database management where authorization is extended for System R* which is the distributed version of System R, and negative authorizations. Note that much of the research carried out for System R on security has been transferred to the DB2 commercial product. A detailed discussion of System R authorization model and its extensions can be found in [FERR00].

In the Oracle Databases Server, privileges can be granted to either users or roles. Roles are hierarchically organized. A role acquires all the privileges that are in lower positions of the hierarchy. A user can be authorized to take on several roles, while there is a limit. A role can be enabled or disabled at a given time. With each role, a password may be assigned to ensure only authorized use of privileges are granted to the role.

The privileges can be divided into two categories: system and object privileges. System privileges allow subjects to perform system-wide action on a particular type of object. Examples of system privileges are the privileges to delete the tuples of any table in a database or create a cluster. Object privileges allow subjects to perform a particular action on a particular object. Examples include insert or delete tuples from a particular table. Other issues such as cascading privileges and revocation of privileges are discussed in detail in [FERR00].

C.4 Summary and Directions

In this appendix, we have provided an overview of discretionary security policies in database systems. We started with a discussion of access control policies including authorization policies and role-based access control. Then we discussed administration policies. We briefly discussed identification and authentication. Finally, we discussed auditing issues as well as views for security. Next, we discussed policy enforcement. The major issues in policy enforcement are policy specification, policy implementation, and policy visualization. We discussed SQL extensions for specifying policies and as well provided an overview of query modification. We also briefly discussed how policy visualization might be used to integrate multiple policies. Finally, we discussed some prototypes and products that implement discretionary security. We focused mainly on relational databases systems.

There is still a lot of work to be done. For example, much work is still needed on role-based access control for emerging technologies such as digital libraries and the semantic web. We need administration policies to manage multi-party transactions in a web environment. We also need biometric technologies for authenticating users. Digital identity is becoming an important research area especially with cloud systems.

Security policy enforcement is a topic that will continue to evolve as new technologies emerge. We have advanced from relational to object to multimedia to web-based to cloud data management systems. Each system has some unique features that are incorporated into the security policies. Enforcing policies for the various systems will continue to be a major research focus. We also need to carry out research on the consistency and completeness of policies. Policy visualization may help toward this.

Policy management in the cloud is an active area of research. Our work includes access control as well as policy-based information sharing in the cloud. The experimental systems we have developed on security policy enforcement in the cloud are discussed throughout this book.

References

[BERT89] Bertino, E. and D. Musto, Integrity constraint processing during transaction processing. *Acta Informatica*, 1988, 26(1-2), 25–57.

[BERT02] Bertino, E. et al., Access control for XML documents. *Data and Knowledge Engineering*, 34(3): 2002.

[CARM04] Carminati, B. et al., Security for RDF. *Proceedings of the DEXA Conference Workshop on Web Semantics*, Zaragoza, Spain, August, 2004.

[DATE90] Date, C., *An Introduction to Database Systems.* Addison-Wesley, Reading, MA, 1990.

[DWYE87] Dwyer, P. et al., Multilevel security for relational database systems. *Computers and Security*, 6(3): 1987, 252–260.

[FERR00] Ferrari, E. and B. Thuraisingham, Secure database systems. In *Advances in Database Management* (Eds. M. Piatini and O. Diaz), Artech House, UK, 2000.

[GRIF76] Griffiths, P. and B. Wade, An authorization mechanism for a relational database system. *ACM Transactions on Database Systems*, 1(3): 1976, 242–255.

[PARK04] Park, J. and R. Sandhu, The UCON usage control model. *ACM Transactions on Information and Systems Security*, 7(1): 2004, 128–174.

[SAND96] Sandhu, R. et al., Role-based access control models. *IEEE Computer*, 29(2): 1996, 38–47.

[SQL3] en.wikipedia.org/wiki/SQL, *American National Standards Institute*, Draft, Maynard, MN,1992.

[STON74] Stonebraker, M. and E. Wong, Access control in a relational data base management system by query modification. *Proceedings of the ACM Annual Conference*, ACM Press, NY, 1974.

[THUR87] Thuraisingham, B., Security checking in relational database management systems augmented with inference Engines, *Computers and Security*, 6(6): 1987, 479–492.

[THUR89] Thuraisingham, B. and P. Stachour, SQL extensions for security assertions. *Computer Standards and Interface Journal*, 11(1): 1989.

[THUR93] Thuraisingham, B., W. Ford, and M. Collins, Design and implementation of a database inference controller, *Data and Knowledge Engineering Journal*, 11(3): 1993, 5–14.

[THUR05] Thuraisingham, B., *Database Security*. Integrating Database Systems and Information Security, CRC Press, 2005.

Appendix D: Assured Information Sharing Life Cycle

D.1 Overview

This chapter describes our approach to Assured Information Sharing (AIS). The research is being carried out under a MURI (Multi-university Research Initiative) project funded by the Air Force Office of Scientific Research (AFOSR). The main objective of our project is *define*, *design*, and *develop* an assured information-sharing life cycle (AISL) that realizes the DoD's information-sharing value chain. In this chapter we describe the problem faced by the Department of Defense and our solution to developing an AISL system.

Daniel Wolfe (formerly of the NSA) defined AIS as a framework that "provides the ability to dynamically and securely share information at multiple classification levels among U.S., allied and coalition forces." The DoD's vision for AIS is to "deliver the power of information to ensure mission success through an agile enterprise with freedom of maneuverability across the information environment." In our current project on AIS, our objective is to help achieve this vision by defining an AIS life cycle and developing a framework to realize it.

The main objectives of our project are *define*, *design*, and *develop* an AISL that realizes the DoD's information sharing value chain. To achieve this objective, we are developing tools and techniques that include following: (i) a comprehensive policy framework that provides support to specify and reason with a variety of policies including confidentiality, accountability, and trust, (ii) an event-based secure SOA that will support the services for AIS, (iii) a security infrastructure that will provide the services needed to enforce the policies for life cycle-oriented applications and management, (iv) techniques to exploit social networks to forge information mobility, (v) approaches for assured information integration, analysis, and quality; and (vi) tools for assured behavior-based incentivized information sharing.

The organization of this appendix is as follows. In Section D.2, we discuss the problem. In Section D.3, we discuss the AISL framework. Incentives for information sharing are discussed in Section D.4. The appendix is summarized in Section D.5. Six universities are participating in this project. They are the University of Maryland, Baltimore Count, Purdue University, UTD, the University of Illinois at Urbana Champaign, the University of Michigan, and the University of Texas at San Antonio.

D.2 The Problem

To fight the global war on terror the DoD, federal agencies, coalition partners, and first responders, among others have to proactively share information and make effective decisions. Yet in doing so, one must protect the confidentiality of sensitive information and appropriately respect the privacy of individuals. Traditional security policies are often based on the concept of "need to know" and are typified by predefined and often rigid specifications of which principals and roles are pre-authorized to access what information. One of the recommendations of the 9/11 commission (MARK03) was to find ways to move from this traditional perspective toward one that emphasizes the "need to share." Our research to address the above problem will be guided by (i) DoD's information-sharing strategy and (ii) scenarios that are relevant to information sharing needs of the DoD and other Government agencies. Information includes contextual data, metadata, and descriptions of architectures, resources, policies, processes, and strategies.

In May 2007, the DoD CIO published a document (DoD 2007) that articulated DoD's information-sharing strategy. The vision for information sharing is to "develop the power of information to ensure mission success through an agile enterprise with freedom of maneuverability across the information environment." To achieve this vision, the DoD has formulated the following four goals: (i) "Promote, encourage and incentivize sharing," (ii) "Achieve an extended enterprise," (iii) "Strengthen the agility in order to accommodate unanticipated partners and events," and (iv) "Ensure trust across organizations." DoD has stated that the four information-sharing goals will be realized through five implementation strategies that we address in our work.

Our initial scenario pertains to the Distributed Common Ground System (DCGS). To ensure the horizontal integration of joint Intelligence, Surveillance, and Reconnaissance (ISR), sensor platforms for improving time critical targeting, the DoD is developing DCGS as a global intelligence-sharing network, based on network centric enterprise SOA. While the Air Force is developing DCGS (with Raytheon Corporation as the prime contractor), the Navy is developing its version called DCGS-N and the Army is developing its version called DCGS-A. The three organizations must share information for combat operations via DCGS as well as with foreign intelligence services (NRC 2006). We will show how our research can enable and enhance this system, and also explore other scenarios with our collaborators. Details of our work are given in [ISI09].

D.3 Assured Information Sharing Life Cycle

AISL consists of three major phases shown in Figure D.1: (1) information discovery and advertising, (2) information acquisition, release, and integration, and (3) information usage and control. These phases will realize the information-sharing value chain of (DoD 2007). During the *discovery phase* parties advertise the information they own and search for relevant information. Each party in the *information landscape* may thus play two main roles: information provider and information consumer. Information discovery and advertising entail several issues: determining what and to whom to advertise, supporting selective advertising, ensuring confidentiality and verifying integrity, and determining incentives for information sharing. Information *acquisition, release, and integration* entails several issues: determining what information to release and to whom, verifying the need for the information, evaluating the risk and benefits in acquiring/releasing the information, and stating and evaluating obligations derived from information acquisition and release. In the *usage and control* phase, a key requirement is that information providers maintain "an awareness of where and how this information is used" (DoD 2007). This entails addressing several issues: controlling how information is used once it is released, joint administration, access control and accountability, investigating confidentiality and integrity breaches, and assessing the benefits derived from its use.

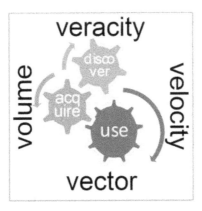

Figure D.1   The AISL. (T. Finin et al., Assured information sharing life cycle, *Proceedings of the IEEE Intelligence and Security Informatics Conference,* **Dallas, TX. © (2009) IEEE.)**

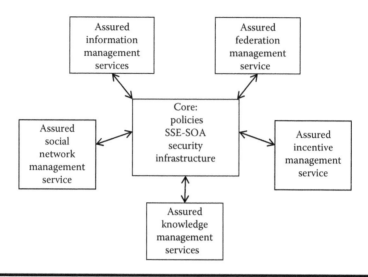

Figure D.2   Secure services. (T. Finin et al., Assured information sharing life cycle, *Proceedings of the IEEE Intelligence and Security Informatics Conference,* **Dallas, TX. © (2009) IEEE.)**

The AISL is a concrete embodiment of *the notion of assured information sharing value chain* in that it provides a set of services, tools, and processes collectively able to *securely* assemble the right combination of information sources and instantly being able to *securely* communicate, coordinate, and respond appropriately to the situation at hand. As such the AISL is highly dynamic and can rapidly react to situations but at the same time provides security guarantees. The above three phases are executed multiple times by several processes and for different classes of information. Figure D.2 illustrates the various modules that will implement AISL. The glue consists of policies, secure semantic event-based service-oriented architecture (SSE-SOA) that supports web services, and a security infrastructure that supports the enforcement of the policies. The high-level web services include assured information management, assured knowledge management, assured social networking, assured incentive management, and assured federation management.

Our goal is to *get the right information to the decision maker so that he/she can make decisions in the midst of uncertain and unanticipated situations.* We are developing tools and techniques to assess and/or quickly revalidate the information to be used for decision making, as well as to enhance the information about *origin,* through the use of accountability processes. By using our tools, the decision maker can determine the origin of the information. Such awareness may prompt for additional fast validation of information, leading to rapid search for other information that can confirm or invalidate the initial information. The AISL is dynamic and supported by information quality and provenance techniques in all its phases.

D.4 Incentives and Information Sharing

The AISL project has made many contributions to developing policies, models, and technologies for information sharing. One of the unique contributions that we at the UTD have made to this project is on incentive-based information sharing.

We have built mechanisms to give incentives to individuals/organizations for information sharing. Once such mechanisms are built, we can use concepts from the *theory of contracts* to determine appropriate rewards such as ranking or, in the case of certain foreign partners, monetary benefits. First, we explored how to leverage secure distributed audit logs to rank individual organizations between trustworthy partners. To handle situations where it is not possible to carry out auditing, we developed game theoretic strategies for extracting information from the partners. We conducted studies based on economic theories and integrate relevant results into incentivized AIS.

A risk in modeling complex issues of information sharing in the real world to formal analysis is making unrealistic assumptions. By drawing on insights from psychology and related complementary decision sciences, we considered a wider range of behavioral hypotheses, aimed at improving the interface between the system and its intended users. The system built seeks to integrate numerous sources of information and provide a variety of quantitative output to help monitor the system's performance, most importantly, sending negative alerts when the probability that information is being misused rises above preset thresholds. The quality of the system's overall performance will ultimately depend on how human beings wind up using it. The field of behavioral economics emerged in recent decades, borrowing from psychology to build models with more empirical realism underlying fundamental assumptions about the way in which decision makers arrive at inferences and take actions. We augmented the formal analysis of the incentivized information-sharing component of the system with a wider consideration of motivations, including interpersonal comparisons, as factors that systematically shape behavioral outcomes and, consequently, the performance of information-sharing systems. Our results are reported in [NIX12].

D.5 Summary and Directions

The project has made several novel contributions and they have been reported in [AISL]. These include security models, frameworks, architectures, information management, social networks, and incentives for information sharing.

In our work, we integrated the research results with the cloud to develop cloud-based AIS systems. These systems were reported in Part VII. In addition to enhancing our systems, we plan to discuss our project with DARPA (Defense Advanced Research projects Organization) or IARPA (Intelligence Advanced Research Projects Activity) to develop real-world operational systems for AIS. The executive directive signed by the president of the United States in February 2013 makes Cyber Security and AIS among agencies, companies, and universities even more critical.

References

[AISL] Assured Information Sharing Lifecycle: http://aisl.umbc.edu/

[CYBER] The White House National Security Council: http://www.whitehouse.gov/cyber security

[DoD07] DoD (Department of Defense) Information sharing strategy. May 2007, http://www.defenselink.mil/cio-nii/docs/InfoSharingStrategy.pdf

[ISI09] T. Finin A. Joshi, H. Kargupta, Y. Yesha, J. Sachs, E. Bertino, L. Ninghui, C. Clifton et al., Assured information sharing life cycle, *Proceedings of the IEEE Intelligence and Security Informatics Conference*, Dallas, TX, June 2009.

[MARK03] Creating a Trusted Information Network for Homeland Security. The Markle Foundation, 2003.

[NIX12] R. Nix, M. Kantarcioglu, Incentive compatible privacy-preserving distributed classification. *IEEE Trans. Dependable Sec. Comput.* 9(4): 451–462, 2012.

Index